Cognition in Action
Second Edition

Mary M. Smyth
Alan F. Collins
Peter E. Morris
Philip Levy

Department of Psychology
Lancaster University
UK

[LEA] LAWRENCE ERLBAUM ASSOCIATES, PUBLISHERS [LEA]
Hove (UK)   Hillsdale (USA)

Lawrence Erlbaum Associates Ltd., Publishers
27 Palmeira Mansions
Church Road
Hove
East Sussex, BN3 2FA
UK

British Library Cataloguing in Publication Data

A catalogue record for this book is available from the British Library

  ISBN 0–86377–347–8 (Hbk)
  ISBN 0–86377–348–6 (Pbk)

Typeset by J&L Composition Ltd., Filey, North Yorkshire
Printed and bound in the United Kingdom by BPC Wheatons Ltd., Exeter

Contents

Introduction

In this book, we approach cognitive psychology by asking what it has to tell us about how people carry out everyday activities. In other words, we ask how do people organise and use their knowledge in order to behave appropriately in the world in which they live. Each chapter in the book starts with an example (which makes up the first part of the chapter title), and then uses the example to introduce some aspects of the overall cognitive system. In this way, the more general psychological functions described in the second part of each chapter title are introduced and explained.

Some of the examples we use are serious ones, like making a medical decision, and others are fairly trivial, like tapping your head and rubbing your stomach at the same time. Some of the examples, like doing mental arithmetic, are simply used to introduce problems and questions about an aspect of cognitive functioning, and are not the topic of the chapter itself. Other examples, like reading a word, do provide the topic for the whole chapter. This is partly because language processing is something we do every day, as well as a central research area for many psychologists. Other everyday activities may not themselves be studied directly by psychologists, or may only be studied as part of a wider enquiry.

Cognition is concerned with knowledge, and cognitive psychology is concerned with the acquisition and use of knowledge, and with the structures and processes which serve this. The cognitive system, although it is complex, normally operates as a whole, and it can be misleading to separate out parts of the system for special attention without emphasising that each part can only be understood properly in its place in the functioning of the whole. Traditionally, textbooks on cognitive psychology have taken topics such as perception, memory and language as major themes, and in doing so have sometimes emphasised the component parts of the system while obscuring its purposes and functions. These divisions also suggest to the reader that cognition presents itself in neat sub-compartments which we can study, rather than that we create the components as we investigate cognition.

Of course, to study any complex system it is necessary to introduce some subdivisions, and the problem is to present these without leading readers to believe that a topic such as memory can be completely understood in isolation. Our solution has been to identify important components in the cognitive system, and to illustrate them through examples of cognition in action. So, for example, all cognition depends on our initial perceptions of the world, and perceptual processing is referred to over and over again throughout the book. However, perception plays an especially important part in reading and in recognising faces, and by starting with these examples in the first two chapters we are able to highlight the major aspects of the initial perception components of the system.

Unlike other texts, we do not make a rigorous division into "stages" of cognitive processing; rather, we emphasise different aspects of the system in different ways. For example, new information entering the system must be appropriately organised and classified, relevant old information must be retrieved to aid construction and interpretation, the elements of the old and new must be held in a temporary form while the new construction is assembled and decisions made, and a record of what has occurred becomes part of the store of information that is held for future use. Each of these aspects, and many others, can be emphasised in the context of a particular task, so we do not have chapters which treat cognitive processes or stages in isolation from tasks. Thus, while the book moves from what are traditionally "lower" aspects of cognition, such as perceiving faces and producing actions, to "higher" aspects, such as comprehension and problem solving, these are not seen as stages but as important parts of normal human functioning which cognitive psychology has approached in different ways.

Cognitive psychologists have in the past concentrated on experimental laboratory studies. Their research has sometimes moved a long way from the original questions they asked, and a very long way from cognition in action. This can make the topics seem both difficult and irrelevant to the student. Indeed, one of the original reasons for writing a book like this was that our own students found it very difficult to understand why the topics they were studying mattered and how they related to real questions about the mind. Nevertheless, in many cases, we do need to move into the laboratory to control some aspects of normal functioning in order to get a better understanding of how cognitive processes operate. What is important is that such research should give results which can be used to help us answer the original questions, or even to show us that they are not the best questions to ask. We have tried to select such research for this book.

More recently, cognitive psychologists have drawn upon a wider range of sources of evidence. One important source for evidence about the structure of cognition comes from neuropsychology, the study of people who have suffered brain damage. Cognitive models have to be able to account for the patterns of disability which are found following brain damage, and we use this sort of evidence throughout the book. A second major influence on how cognitive psychologists develop and test their theories is the development of computer models, and in particular the development of network models, which have some plausible similarities to the way the nervous system works. These models have changed some aspects of the ways in which cognitive psychologists think about how information is represented, and they also provide a way of testing hypotheses by developing models and comparing the behaviour they produce with the behaviour produced by people in situations similar to those being modelled. Network models appear in the very first chapter of this book, but explaining them and how they are relevant fits into some of the questions raised in Chapter 2, so that is where we have located an introduction to this style of thinking. We also discuss these sorts of models in many of the other chapters.

In writing this book, we have been selective about the research we have used. This means that some topics which are found in other cognition texts do not appear here, and we may have chosen to omit studies which other people feel are important. Our selection depends on the line of argument being made from the examples and questions in real life to the issues which arise in cognitive research. In some chapters, where there is a long tradition of research that seems to us to have approached problems in intuitively sensible ways, we have reported the work, even if it does not provide complete answers to our questions. This is the second edition of the book, and some chapters and sections of chapters have been extensively rewritten. We have, however, kept to our original intention to discuss relevant work whether it was recent or not, and not to include studies simply because they have been done. Experiments and research programmes have little value by themselves; they only matter when they help us to understand something of how the cognitive system does or doesn't work.

It is easy to take for granted activities such as reading words, recognising people we know and telling tables from chairs. Sometimes it is only when we have had problems with these activities or when we realise that other people have problems with them that we realise that there is something to be explained. In this book, we take the view that there is something to be explained every time anyone reads or fails to read a word, recognises or fails to recognise a face, remembers or fails to remember an intention. We have to ask the question "How did I do that?" when we succeed at these activities in order to understand what it is that cognitive psychologists study. This book does not present the argument that everyday cognition can only be studied in the everyday world, but rather that everyday cognition gives us our problems and our questions. Our answers — however we obtain them — must always relate back to cognition in action.

In writing the second edition, we were unable to call on Andy Ellis who was one of the authors of the first edition. His ideas, his examples and even some of his very words remain in this version. It wouldn't be the same without him. The errors, as always, remain our own.

1 Recognising Faces: Perceiving and Identifying Objects

It is a busy Saturday afternoon in your town. The streets are swarming with shoppers pushing and shoving. You are trying to find a pair of shoes you like and wondering why on earth you didn't do your shopping midweek when things were quieter. In the distance, you notice two people walking towards you. The one on the left you recognise immediately as your grandmother; the one on the right you do not recognise.

What could be a more commonplace and everyday occurrence than recognising the face of someone you know? We do it all the time — at home, at work, watching television, in town. "But", asks the cognitive psychologist, "*How* do we do it? *How* do we recognise the lady approaching us as granny? What processes go on in our minds that allow us to identify the lady on the left as familiar while rejecting the person on the right as unfamiliar?" Person and face recognition must be a matter of achieving a match between a perceived stimulus pattern and a stored representation. When you get to know someone, you must establish in memory some form of representation or description of his or her appearance. Recognising the person on subsequent occasions requires the perceived face to make contact with the stored information, otherwise the face will seem unfamiliar.

As cognitive psychologists try to develop a more specific account of recognising a person, problems start to arise. What form does the internal representation of a familiar face take? How are seen faces matched against stored representations? How does seeing a familiar face trigger the wider knowledge you have about that person, including his or her name? When you see a familiar person, he or she is often moving against a complex visual background: How does your visual system isolate elements of the whole visual scene as constituting one object (a person) moving in a particular way at a particular speed? These are some of the questions a complete theory of visual processing should be able to answer, and some of the questions that are addressed in this chapter. We use face recognition in this chapter to introduce some of the important questions about how we perceive and recognise objects in general, not just faces. We will consider both the general issue of how we recognise objects, including people, and the more specific questions concerning how we recognise people we know.

RECOGNISING FAMILIAR PATTERNS

There are lots of faces visible in the shopping crowd in our example, but you recognise only one of them. How? A ploy commonly adopted by cognitive psychologists when trying to understand how the mind performs a particular task is to ask how we could create an artificial device capable of performing the same task. How could we, for example, program a computer to recognise a set of faces and reject others?

First of all, the computer would need to somehow memorise the set of faces it had to recognise. It would then need to compare each face it saw (through a camera input, for example) with the set stored in memory to see if there was a match. If a satisfactory match was achieved, the face would be "recognised"; if not, it would be rejected as unfamiliar.

Now, within those broad outlines, there are a number of options available regarding the possible nature of the representation of each face to be stored in memory and the manner in which the perceived face could be compared against the stored set. The stored set of faces could form a set of templates, with the new face being matched to each template and recognition occurring when a complete or nearly complete match of template and pattern took place. Perhaps recognising a particular face would require the stimulation of a particular pattern of cells within the retina of the eye. Different patterns of stimulation would be stored for each known face. Pattern recognition systems along these lines have been used for many years in, for example, the mechanical reading of the numbers upon bank cheques.

Template mechanisms of pattern recognition are relatively simple to set up. However, they have serious limitations which suggest that they are not the mechanism used by the human perceptual system when recognising familiar objects. Problems arise as soon as there is any change in the original stimulus. For example, if you see your grandmother from a different distance to that for which the template was set up, then a smaller or larger image will be projected onto the retina of your eye and will stimulate a different set of cells. Similar problems arise if you see your grandmother from an angle different to that for which the template was created. Also, people change in their appearance — their hairstyles, their spectacles, their faces age, and so on. While such changes can cause us problems in recognition, we do normally still identify our acquaintances. However, the mismatch with any template would be sufficient for it to fail to be selected.

Template-based systems of pattern recognition can be elaborated. They can, for example, include more than one template, so that common views of the same object can be recognised. Face recognition might include templates for views of the full face, three-quarter (portrait) and profile angles. There is evidence that cells in the brains of monkeys are differentially sensitive to such alternative views (Perrett et al., 1984). It is possible to "normalise" a new pattern until it is a standard size and orientation before it is matched to the templates. Some theorists of face recognition have considered template accounts (e.g. Ellis, 1975). However, most researchers have looked to more sophisticated ways in which the information about known objects and people might be matched to a newly experienced pattern.

One alternative might be the storing of the description of a person's face in terms of a list of *features* (a feature being a property of an object that helps discriminate it from other objects). Granny's face might then be held in memory as a feature list something like:

+ white hair
+ curly hair
+ round face
+ hooked nose
+ thin lips
+ blue eyes
+ round gold-rimmed spectacles
+ wrinkles

and so on. The features of each face to appear before the camera could then be compared against the stored list. If all features agreed, then the face would be recognised as granny's, but if the person before the camera had, say, a long, thin face rather than a round one, it would be rejected as unfamiliar. This would be a *feature-based* model of recognition. One of the advantages of such models is that they do not tightly specify how the features go together as is the case with template models. For example, the same set of features can be recognised from many different views of the same face.

There is no denying that features play a role in face recognition, or that some features are more important than others. In free descriptions of unfamiliar faces, subjects utilise features, mentioning the hair most often, followed by eyes, nose, mouth, eyebrows, chin, and forehead in that order (Shepherd, Davies, & Ellis, 1981). As faces become familiar, there is evidence of a decreasing reliance on external features such as hairstyle, colour and face shape towards a reliance on the internal features of eyes, nose and mouth (Ellis, Shepherd, & Davies, 1979). This may be because hairstyle in particular can change, and so is a relatively unreliable cue to recognition, whereas internal features are comparatively stable and reliable.

The problem with any simple feature-based model is illustrated by Fig. 1.1. A "scrambled" face contains the same features as a normal face, but their *configuration* has been altered. Although it may be possible to

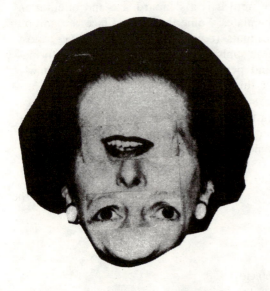

FIG. 1.1 The scrambled face of a well-known person illustrates the importance of configuration in pattern recognition. Reproduced with permission from Bruce and Valentine (1985).

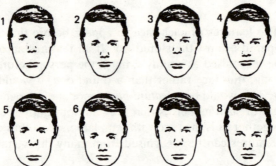

FIG. 1.2 Each pair of faces (1 and 2; 3 and 4; 5 and 6; 7 and 8) differ only in the configuration of their internal features. Adapted with permission from Sergent (1984).

recognise the scrambled face of a well-known person, it is much harder than recognising a normal face. Also, as Fig. 1.2 shows, varying the configuration of a fixed set of features can substantially alter the appearance of the face. So, while template models may be too specific about the details of each face, a simple feature list model would not be specific enough. A satisfactory model of face recognition will take into account the configuration of the features but will be sufficiently flexible that it can recognise the same face despite the patterns actually experienced varying considerably, because the person is being seen from one of many possible angles or distances.

You will be beginning to appreciate the challenge faced by object and person recognition systems, whether our own or those that might be created, for example, to allow robots to behave like humans as they do in science fiction stories. Such recognition in a world of moving, changing objects is very difficult. However, the challenge is greater still than we have discussed so far. How do we even manage to perceive an object as an object? We will consider this even more basic question in the next section.

SEEING OBJECTS

Your grandmother is moving through a crowd of shoppers carrying a couple of bags. Parts of her periodically disappear from view when she passes behind a bench seat, or when another shopper passes in front of her. Your visual system is confronted with a kaleidoscope of patches of light of different colours, reflecting off surfaces of objects at varying distances, moving in varying directions at varying speeds. What you *perceive*, however, is a coherent scene composed of distinct objects set against a stable background. This unified impression is the *end-product* of processes of visual perception which psychologists have sought to understand.

Some of the first psychologists to be interested in how we perceive one part of a visual display as belonging with another were the German Gestalt psychologists. From 1912 onwards, Gestalt psychologists, led by Wertheimer and his students Kohler and Koffka, concentrated upon the way in which the world we perceive is almost always organised as whole objects set against a fixed background. Even three dots on a page (see Fig. 1.3) will cohere as a triangle. Our perceptual systems are organised to derive forms and relationships from even the simplest of inputs. The Gestalt psychologists argued that our perceptual systems have evolved to make object perception possible. They set out to describe the principles that the perceptual system uses to group together the elements in the perceptual field. Subsequently, those attempting to model object perception (e.g. Marr, 1982) have incorporated these principles into their models, as we describe later in the chapter.

FIG. 1.3. Three simple dots on a page cannot but be seen as a triangle.

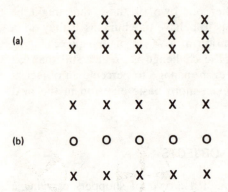

(a)

(b)

(c)

(d) **HELLO**

FIG. 1.4 Examples of Gestalt principles in action. (a) *Proximity*: the arrangement of the crosses causes them to be perceived as being in columns rather than rows. (b) *Similarity*: the similarity of the elements causes them to be perceived as being in rows rather than columns. (c) *Good continuity*: causes you to interpret this as two continuous intersecting lines. (d) *Closure*: the gap in the "O" is perceptually completed.

The Gestalt psychologists formulated several principles to describe the way in which parts of a given display will be grouped together (see Fig. 1.4a). However, grouping is modified by the similarity of components. So, in Fig. 1.4b, the noughts and crosses tend to be seen in lines because they are similar. In Fig. 1.4c, the lines of dashes are seen as crossing one another, rather than meeting at a point turning at an angle and moving away. This illustrates the Gestalt principle of *good continuation*, which maintains that elements will be perceived together where they maintain a smooth flow rather than changing abruptly. In a similar way, the perceptual system will opt for an interpretation that produces a closed, complete figure rather than one with missing elements. Sometimes this can lead to the overlooking of missing parts in a familiar object. If you had not been primed to look for it by the text, it would be easy to conceptually complete the word and overlook the gap in one of the letters in Fig. 1.4d. Other perceptual preferences highlighted by the Gestalt psychologists were for bilaterally symmetrical shapes (e.g. Fig. 1.5a). Other things being equal,

FIG. 1.5 (a) Organisation by lateral symmetry. The symmetrical form on the right is much more easily perceived as a coherent whole than the asymmetrical form on the left. (b) The preference here is to perceive the smaller area as the figure and the larger area as the ground, i.e. as a black cross on a white background. (c) If the larger areas is to be perceived as the figure (i.e. a white cross on a black background), then orienting the white area around the horizontal and vertical axes makes this easier.

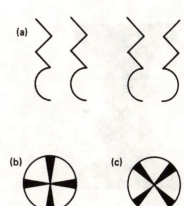

the smaller of two areas will be seen in the background, and this is enhanced by them being in a vertical or horizontal arrangement (see the black and white crosses in Figs 1.5b and c).

To summarise their principles, Wertheimer proposed the Law of Pragnanz. This states that, of the many geometrically possible organisations that might be perceived from a given pattern of optic stimulation, the one that will be perceived is that possessing the best, simplest and most stable shape. Sometimes, the input can be interpreted in more than one way and the result is a dramatic alternating in our perception. The face–vase illusion (Fig. 1.6) devised by the Gestalt psychologist Rubin is a well-known example. The information in the picture allows it to be interpreted either as a vase or as two faces. When the interpretation shifts, the part that had been the figure becomes the background, and vice versa.

Although we have illustrated the Gestalt principles using very simple examples and illustrations, their application to normal, intricate visual processing is in the way they assist the visual system to unite those components of the visual array that constitute single objects. There are other cues that assist in this unification. All the cues discussed so far apply to stationary objects, but additional cues arise when an object moves. If an object is moving, it will cover progressively more of the visual field if it is approaching, less if it is going away, and will successively obscure and reveal the background over which it passes. This movement is a major source of object perception. Elements that move together are usually perceived as being part of the same object, a principle known to the Gestalt psychologists as *common fate*.

How do all these principles apply to our example of recognising our grandmother? To see her as an object at all we must perceive which parts of our current visual array are a part of her body and which are not. Granny's good continuation, the common fate of her parts and so on, will

FIG. 1.6 Rubin's well-known ambiguous figure, which can be seen as either a black vase against a white background, or as two white faces against a black background (but not both at once).

all help you to unify those components of your current perceptual field which belong together as the parts of the single object that is your grandmother. It is convenient for the purpose of the illustration, earlier, to isolate each cue and demonstrate it in simplified form, but in the real world these cues are all operating together, and their function is to assist the visual system in identifying objects in the visual scene with a view to recognising them for what they are. So far, we have been considering how aspects of the visual array can be used, as summarised in the Gestalt principles, to identify objects from their backgrounds. Such identification is often not in the interest of a carnivorous animal seeking its prey, or of the prey itself. The evolution of camouflage in the natural world can be analysed as a variety of attempts to disrupt and confound the Gestalt principles, making an animal hard to distinguish from the background scene.

DISTANCE AND MOVEMENT

We have considered some of the ways in which an object may be separated from its background, but much more needs to be perceived than that about the behaviour of animate or inanimate objects if the perceiver is to survive long! Two very important properties of the object are its distance and the way it is moving. As soon as you become aware of granny's presence in the crowd, you also have an impression of how far away she is. Judgement of the relative distances of visible objects is an important aspect of perception.

Binocular Depth Cues

One source of distance information is the stereoscopic information provided by the two slightly different views of the same scene obtained by our

FIG. 1.7 Julesz dot patterns (see text for explanation). Reproduced with permission from Julesz (1964).

two eyes. Given the disparity between the images to the two eyes, it is possible to calculate the distance of an object, because the closer an object is, the greater is the disparity between the two different views of it.

Stereoscopes were invented in the 1830s by Wheatstone and have been popular at various times since for the vivid three-dimensional experience they produce. A different picture is presented to each eye, each picture representing what would be seen if the actual objects were present in three dimensions. So, if the pictures are photographs, the two photos are taken from positions a few inches apart, thus reproducing the views from our two eyes.

How exactly is the discrepant information from the two eyes combined to allow depth to be computed? The traditional view was that the images from each eye were separately processed, identifying the objects in the scene, and only then fused together (e.g. Sherrington, 1906). However, the work of Julesz (1971) has suggested that this is not so. Julesz developed the *random-dot stereogram* (see Fig. 1.7). This consists of patterns of black and white dots. Viewed without a stereoscope, the two patterns shown in Fig. 1.7 look similar. If, however, the patterns are projected one to each eye, a central square of dots will be seen floating closer to the observer. The reason is that the two random-dot stereograms are not identical. The right-hand one has a square part of the left-hand pattern shifted to the right and the space remaining filled with random dots. To the retina of each eye, this provides the same information that would be seen if that square was actually in front of the rest of the main square, and it is seen in that way when the stereoscopic information is combined. In fact, it is only possible to see the square stereoscopically. What Julesz random-dot stereograms demonstrate is that one can see stereoptically without having

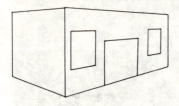

FIG. 1.8 Converging lines give a strong impression of depth.

to first recognise and fuse an object separately for each eye. When seen separately we cannot see the object, the square, which only appears when the images are combined.

Monocular Depth Cues

We have discussed depth perception using two eyes, but even with one eye closed we can normally judge how far away an object is. With one eye closed we could still shake hands with our grandmother's friend! There are many cues to distance in most static visual scenes. First, there is the relative size of known objects — the farther away your grandmother is, the smaller the area of the retina upon which her image is projected. Second, things that are closer will often be superimposed upon and obscure parts of the view of things farther away. Shadows give impressions of solidity and depth to individual objects. The texture of the things we perceive becomes less obvious and finer at greater distances. For example, in a field, we can see the details of the blades of grass near our feet, but such detail is lost as we look farther away. This texture gradient is a strong cue to distance. Especially in a world of rooms and buildings with their straight lines, right angles and flat planes, perspective is another strong depth cue. As they recede into the distance, parallel lines converge, and line drawings that incorporate such features give a convincing impression of depth (see Fig. 1.8). Furthermore, the intersection of edges and the obscuring of parts of objects provide further cues to depth. Where one edge meets another in a T-junction, one object is normally in front of another. As we discuss later, this is a feature that has been used in scene analyses.

By careful building, it is possible to construct visual displays that set monocular cues against one another and produce visual illusions. A famous one is Ames' room (Ittelson, 1952). In Fig. 1.9, photographed inside the room, it appears as if the person on the right is very much bigger than the one on the left, yet both are actually normal-sized adults. In Ames' room, the normal depth cue of our knowledge of relative sizes is overwhelmed by the manipulation of the perspective provided by the decorations on the walls. To the viewer, the room looks rectangular because the decorations resemble doors and windows as they would appear in a normal rectangular

FIG.1.9 Ames' room (see text for explanation). Reproduced with the permission of Eastern Counties Newspapers Limited.

room. In fact, the room increases in distance and height away to the left and the decorations are trapezoidal, not rectangular. The person who appears smaller is much farther away than the other one. Ames' room illustrates how, when depth cues conflict, our perceptual system will sacrifice and re-scale familiar features to produce a consistent representation.

A moving person or object supplies additional information to help in the judgement of distance. The farther away a moving object is, the slower it will move through the visual field. When we are ourselves moving, then the world that we see seems to flow past us. The speed and direction of the optic flow provide excellent information about the direction and speed of our travel. This optic flow is illustrated in Fig. 1.10. Gibson (1966; 1979) has argued strongly that too much emphasis in psychology has, in the past, been placed on the perception of static, very simple displays by static observers in a highly uniform, often visually degraded environment. Our perceptual systems have actually evolved to cope with a visually extremely rich world in which we are constantly moving and experiencing changes in the visual array, and the cues afforded by movement and change are important in determining the interpretation we place upon a visual scene.

When it comes to grouping elements of an array together as components of a single object, or judging how far away that object is, then the

FIG. 1.10 The optic flow field for a pilot landing an aeroplane. Reproduced with permission from Gibson (1950).

processes involved are likely to be the same whether or not you recognise the individual object concerned (they will treat granny and the unfamiliar lady walking alongside her alike). For the remainder of this chapter, we return to the processing of familiar objects, concerning ourselves with such things as how, having recognised an object, you retrieve the relevant information about it that you have stored in memory (including its name), and what role context plays in the recognition of familiar objects.

IDENTIFYING OBJECTS

Scene Analysis Programs

In the 1960s and 1970s, researchers in artificial intelligence tried to write computer programs that would be capable of identifying objects. Such attempts at the computer simulation of human skills are often stimulated by both practical and theoretical motives. The practical one is the need for any mechanical device that moves around and handles newly encountered objects to be able to perceive those objects. The theoretical aspect is that the need to produce a working computer simulation forces researchers to consider all the elements of the problem, including some which will not have occurred to the armchair speculator on the problem. To simplify this problem, they concentrated upon recognising evenly lit, smooth-sided blocks and prisms. Guzman (1968), Clowes (1971) and Waltz (1975) developed programs which analysed the lines that were present in, for example, the display in Fig. 1.11.

The analyses concentrated upon line junctions, with different types of junctions being classified as indicating different relationships between the blocks. So, an arrow junction (A in Fig. 1.11) generally involves planes from the same body, whereas T-junctions (B in Fig. 1.11) normally occur where the crossbar and shaft of the T are part of different bodies. Edges were labelled as *lower* (pointing outwards), *concave* (pointing inwards) and

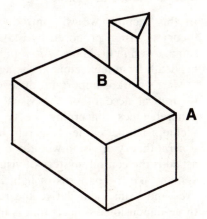

FIG. 1.11 A block and prism suitable for analysis by scene analysis programs. A is an arrow junction and B is a T junction.

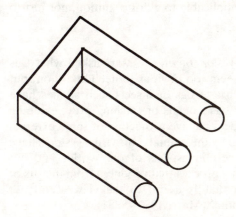

FIG. 1.12 An impossible figure that would be rejected by scene analysis programs.

occluding (i.e. occluding other bodies by being the outer edge of the solid as seen by the observer). In this way, impossible figures such as that in Fig. 1.12 could be rejected by the programs.

While interesting for their analysis of the relationship between edges in solid bodies, these programs were limited by their artificial world. Real scenes rarely have straight lines with angular junctions and are much more misleading with their textures, shadings and internal details of objects. There will always be limitations on artificial worlds, and to cope with the complexity, variability and richness of the real perceptual world a more sophisticated analysis was required. One such analysis was provided by Marr and his associates (Marr, 1982).

Marr's Theory of Vision

In this section, we will introduce the very influential computational theory of vision proposed by Marr and his colleagues. Marr's work was summarised in his book *Vision*, published posthumously in 1982 following his death from leukaemia at the age of 35.

Marr's work is important for several reasons. Not only did he provide a theoretical account of the visual processes, he also highlighted more general issues concerning the types of explanation that we should be seeking. Unlike earlier research, he started from the question of what a *general* theory of vision would require. The fundamental question that he asked is the central mystery of visual perception. How can our processing system take the patterns of light intensity stimulating the retinas of our eyes and from them derive the representations of a world made up of three-dimensional objects that is the form of our conscious perception of the world? Much of Marr's work was directed towards answering this question. However, he realised that the form that an answer must take depends upon asking the right questions and seeking an appropriate level of explanation. This is an insight applicable to all of cognition, not just to vision.

What Does an Explanation of Vision Involve?   Marr asked what was the purpose of vision? This may seem too obvious to need attention, but the visual systems of animals such as frogs or insects such as flies have evolved to be integrated into the basic needs of catching prey, escaping danger, etc., rather than to provide a passive projection of some external world to be contemplated in repose by the animal. Our visual systems have evolved to selectively represent certain aspects of our worlds and not others. In Marr's words, "vision is a process that produces from images of the external world a description that is useful to the viewer and not cluttered with irrelevant information" (Marr, 1982, p. 31).

But what would constitute a description of the visual process? Would it be a description of the interconnections of the neurons of the brain that are involved in vision? That would certainly form part of a complete understanding of the visual system. But would it be sufficient? Marr asked, suppose that one actually found the apocryphal grandmother cell, a cell that fires only when one's grandmother comes into view, would that really tell us anything much at all? It would not tell us *why* such a cell existed in the system, nor how it used the outputs of other cells to create its unique property of recognising grandmother. There is, therefore, much more to understanding vision than this. Marr commented that trying to understand perception by studying only neurons was like trying to understand bird flight by studying only feathers. The structure of feathers and birds' wings make sense only if we understand aerodynamics. Similarly, we will understand the interconnections and firing of the cells of the nervous system only if we can place it in the context of the functions that it is serving. So, an understanding of vision or any cognitive process will require an understanding of the functions served with the life of the individual.

Levels of Explanation. When we come to analyse any information-processing system, Marr argued that we need to recognise that there are at least three levels of explanation that need to be considered. One is the physical mechanism itself, what Marr, as a computer scientist, called the *hardware implementation*. For the visual system, this is the eye and the cells of the brain that process the output from the eye. However, the activities of these cells can only be understood if we know what is the *goal* of the processing — what has the system evolved or been designed to achieve? For visual processing, Marr identified the underlying task as to reliably derive properties of the world from images of it. When fully specified, this is what Marr called the *computational theory* of vision, and much of his book entitled *Vision* (1982) was directed towards specifying this theory. Marr identified a third level at which an information-processing device needs to be understood. This is the way in which the input and output of the system are represented and the *algorithm* that accomplishes the transformation.

We can take Marr's example of a cash register in a supermarket to help to explain these three levels. The hardware implementation of a cash register has changed over the years. Mechanical machines have been replaced by increasingly sophisticated electrical machines. So, the hardware implementation of a cash register can take many forms, and its implementation in a modern supermarket is different from that in a store 20 years ago. However, the reasons for the cash register's processing and the computational theory underlying its design remain the same. The register carries out addition — that is its computational theory. However, the way in which it actually calculates the addition may vary from machine to machine, because there are several ways to represent the values — for example, all calculations could take place in the decimal system. That is the form in which the customer understands the prices and will expect to be told the total. However, decimal codes may be converted to binary codes to suit the computing hardware. Bar codes provide another alternative input requiring conversion to a price. What about the computing algorithm? A common algorithm for addition is to combine the least significant figures first, then the next, working from right to left and "carrying" if the sum exceeds 9 in decimal, or 1 in binary. This same algorithm will be used by many very different processing systems — a person carrying out mental arithmetic, an old mechanical calculator or a modern electronic calculator. On the other hand, different algorithms might be used to reach the same result — so long as they implement the theory of arithmetical addition.

To summarise, there are the three levels of (1) computational theory, (2) realisation through representation and algorithm and (3) the hardware implementation. They are interconnected, since the computational theory restricts the means of realisation, while the algorithms and representations restrict the possible hardware implementations. But all three levels need investigation. Cognitive psychologists concern themselves with the first and second levels, while physiologists and neuroanatomists try to map out the biological hardware of cognition.

The Computational Theory Underlying Vision. Marr argued that we should ask what is the computational theory underlying the visual system? How are the computations carried out and what physiological and biochemical processes allow this to happen? Marr recognised that perceiving objects was a major purpose of the system. This might seem devious, but it is not necessarily so. The visual systems of some more primitive animals seem to be particularly sensitive to movement, as if that was their main purpose. As we showed earlier, the human visual system, as the Gestalt psychologists pointed out, seems to seek for objects within the visual array. Marr argued that what was required was "a theory in which the main job of vision was to derive a representation of shape". Other aspects of vision (colour, texture, etc.) he saw as secondary. Marr suggested that the processing would be *modular*, with parts functioning as independently as possible to minimise the problems with failures in any module.

Marr now faced the problem of how stimulation of the cells of the retina by light leads to the perception of objects. At the retina, cells called *rods* and *cones* fire if stimulated by light. These cells interconnect with others, still within the retina, which they excite or inhibit depending upon the pattern of the light stimulation. These cells, in turn, interconnect, exciting and inhibiting cells further back in the visual pathway to the visual cortex.

How could all this lead to our conscious perception of objects? Not simply! However, Marr proposed that there are several stages in this processing. At each stage, a representation is constructed as the result of that stage's processing. Algorithms operate upon the representation derived from the previous stage to produce a new representation. These successive processes gradually transform the information from the pattern of intensity of light stimulating the retina into three-dimensional representations of objects. At each stage, the processing makes use of properties of the representation and consistencies in the world.

The starting point is the retinal image. It gives the distribution of the intensity of stimulation across the retina. From the retinal image, information about the organisation and relationships of *changes* in intensity are, according to Marr, explicitly extracted. This leads to the first stage, which Marr called the *primal sketch*. The type of information that it contains makes possible the detecting of surfaces, as we will describe shortly. The next stage in Marr's theory he called *the 2½ dimensional (2½-D) sketch*. In this, the orientation and rough depth of visible surfaces emerges — a "picture" of the world, but only from the perceiver's viewpoint. In the final stage, the *three-dimensional model* representation of the shapes and their relationships form a model of the external world. This model is independent of the particular orientation of the original stimulation of the retina so that, for example, familiar objects will be recognised irrespective of the particular angle from which they are seen.

The Primal Sketch

The primal sketch is made up of a very large number of what Marr called *primatives*. These are derived from the retinal image through computational transformations. These primatives indicate edges, bars, terminations of those edges, blobs, etc. Then, further processing can be carried out on these primatives. For example, where adjacent primatives have a common property (e.g. the same orientation), they are replaced by *tokens* to represent this common property. These then form boundaries between the parts of the *full primal sketch*.

To illustrate the extraction of primatives, we will consider how the system locates what Marr called *zero crossings*, which are of particular importance in his theory, since they are the basis of the *raw primal sketch* prior to the assignment of *tokens* in deriving the full primal sketch.

Zero crossings indicate the sudden change in the intensity of stimulation of the retina. They are used in Marr's model in the identification of edges. When identifying objects, locating their edges is, clearly, especially important. It is common for the intensity of stimulation to change suddenly at an edge, rather than gradually as it does across a continuous surface. Figure

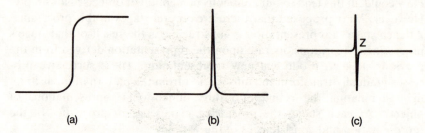

FIG. 1.13 (a) Change in intensity of stimulation at an edge. (b) The rate of change of that stimulation. (c) Rate of change of (b), with a zero crossing at z.

1.13a represents how the intensity of stimulation on a line from A to B across a small part of the retina might change from low stimulation to high stimulation where there is the edge of an object. It is possible to examine this change in stimulation in a number of ways. If, instead of plotting the intensity of stimulation from A to B, we plotted the *rate of change* in intensity — that is, how quickly it was increasing or decreasing — that would show a sharp rise where the intensity began to increase and a sharp fall when it levelled off. This is shown in Fig. 1.13b. If we now consider further the rate of change shown in Fig. 1.13b, it rapidly increases to a positive peak, then rapidly decreases to a negative peak and then returns to level. This is illustrated in Fig. 1.13c. In moving from its positive to its negative peaks, the graph displays a *zero crossing*, i.e. its value goes through zero. This is what Marr means by zero crossing. Essentially, it is a place where the intensity of stimulation of the retina changes abruptly. It is these crossings that are identified and their position recorded in the primal sketch. By so doing, Marr showed that the outline of shapes can be abstracted from the retinal image.

The identification of zero crossings may sound complicated, but it is easy to calculate mathematically. More importantly, it is possible to use actual filters operating in this way to analyse real photographs and identify lines, edges, etc., from them, so demonstrating that the theory is practicable. It is also possible to propose ways in which the cells that receive signals from the retina may identify zero crossings.

Marr (1982; see also Marr & Hildreth, 1980) analysed images with a range of spatial filters, sensitive to differing spatial frequencies. Figure 1.14 illustrates the result of applying two spatial filters to the same image. In Marr's approach, several spatial frequencies were compared and used to confirm the existence of edge features. If zero crossings were found in the same position for the outputs from a number of spatial frequencies, this was evidence that the zero crossings were the result of edges in the external world.

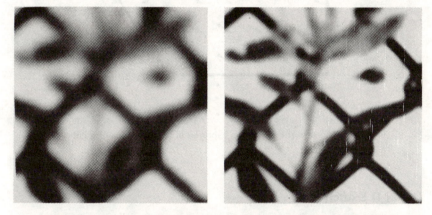

FIG. 1.14 An image (above) blurred by Gaussian filters of two different widths (below). The more blurred picture is produced by the wider filter. Reproduced with permission from Marr and Hildreth (1980).

Much remains to be clarified and elaborated in the underlying procedures that lead to Marr's primal sketch. Georgeson and Shackleton (1989), for example, have shown that the spatial filters need to be more sophisticated than earlier workers assumed. However, the approach has proved very promising. For example, Marr and Poggio (1976) were able to propose a solution to the problem of how stereoscopic depth could be seen using Julesz random-dot patterns. Their algorithm has been implemented as a connectionist program that successfully identifies the stereoscopic pattern (see Chapter 2 for an account of connectionist models).

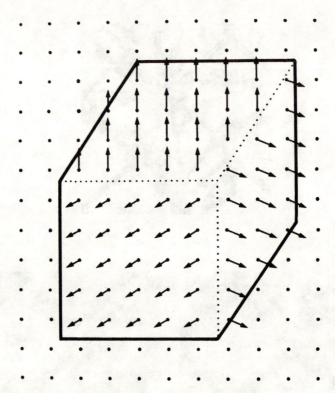

FIG. 1.15 The sort of information captured in a 2½-D sketch of a cube.

The 2½-D Sketch

From the representation provided by the full primal sketch, Marr hypothe-sised that a description of the visible surfaces in the environment, from the viewpoint of the observer, could be produced. This takes place by applying further algorithms to analyse the patterns of tokens in the primal sketch. The resulting representation, which he called the 2½-D sketch, captures details of orientation and relative depths, but only local changes in depth are represented accurately. Figure 1.15 illustrates the sort of information captured in the 2½-D sketch.

The representation in the 2½-D sketch has new primitives representing orientation that Marr depicts as "needles" with their length and angle representing the degree of tilt and the direction in which the surface slants, respectively. The sketch is called 2½-D because it contains some, but not all, depth information. Marr still called it a "sketch" because it was from the observer's viewpoint.

AXIS

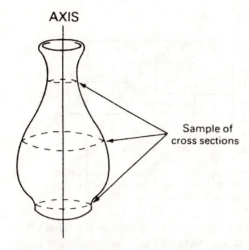

Sample of
cross sections

FIG. 1.16 One example of a generalised cone. The shape is created by moving a cross-section of constant shape but variable size along an axis.

Marr and Nishihara's Object Recognition Theory

So far, the analysis from the retinal image to the 2½-D sketch is one of the perception of a scene. Within that scene, however, there are objects that we can recognise despite considerable variation in their orientation. You recognise your grandmother whichever way she is facing, or if we meet her on a staircase and are looking down or up at her.

Marr and Nishihara (1978) based their theory of object recognition upon the assumption that many shapes can be described as *generalised cones*. A generalised cone has an axis along which a shape is moved to map out the contours of the object. The shape must remain the same (e.g. a circle), but its size can vary; so, for example, the base in Fig. 1.16 is a generalised cone. Marr and Nishihara assume that more complex shapes can be accommodated as a hierarchy of 3-D models, each with its own generalised cone around a specific axis. The analysis for a human shape is shown in Fig. 1.17. These hierarchies, called 3-D model descriptions, allow general distinctions between, for example, types of animals to be made.

Marr suggested that the contours of shapes can be derived from the 2½-D sketch and that these can be analysed into generalised cones. This could be used to access stored information about 3-D model descriptions of different types of objects, and these, in turn, can guide the clarification of the analysis of the object being perceived.

Despite progress in understanding the nature of the objects we perceive, there is very much more to be discovered about how objects as complex as those with which we habitually and effortlessly live are identified by our perceptual systems. The theories of Marr deal with only the most general

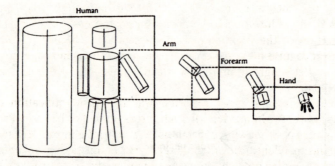

FIG. 1.17 A hierarchy of 3-D models. Each box shows the major axis for the figure of interest on the left, and its component axes on the right. Reproduced with permission from Marr and Nishihara (1978).

classification of objects, while as we know we can recognise the most subtle differences between objects or faces. Nevertheless, as we discuss in the next section, Marr's accounts of the stages of representations have influenced some theories of face recognition.

RECOGNISING AND NAMING FAMILIAR FACES

We have spent some time considering how the visual system may identify objects. Now we want to turn to research that has taken the specific task of recognising that a special sort of object, a human face, is a face that has been seen before. Accompanying this recognition is often the recall of much that you know about the person. When you see granny walking towards you, the act of recognition is typically accompanied by more than just a feeling of familiarity. Something of what you know about her also springs to mind. You may remember that she is a little hard-of-hearing and resolve to speak clearly; you may remember that she is critical of what she considers untidy appearance and surreptitiously try to spruce yourself up; you may remember that she holds strong political opinions somewhat different from your own and make a mental note to steer clear of contentious topics. You will also be able to remember her name.

Errors in Person Recognition

This is what *normally* happens, and what *should* happen, but we all know that our cognitive processes sometimes let us down. Young, Hay and Ellis (1985) persuaded 22 volunteers to keep diaries of their everyday errors and problems in person recognition. A total of 1008 incidents were recorded. They fell into several different categories, four of which we will consider.

The first type of error was the simple failure to recognise a familiar person: 114 such incidents were recorded. The explanation for such errors is presumably the failure of the perceived face to access the internal stored representation of the familiar person's appearance. Someone you know but fail to recognise may, for example, have cut their hair and shaved off a beard, or lost weight dramatically, or may have aged 15 years since you last saw them.

The second type of error reported was the misidentification of one person as another (314 incidents). Such errors tended to be short-lived and to occur under poor viewing conditions (e.g. a brief glimpse of someone). Usually, the misidentification took the form of mistaking an unfamiliar person for a familiar one (thinking the person walking towards you is your granny then realising she is a stranger). The similarity is sufficient to momentarily activate the stored representation of the familiar face, though a second and better look reveals the discrepancies.

Young et al. (1985) collected 233 reports of a third type of error. This involved seeing a person, knowing she is familiar (i.e. that you have seen her somewhere before), but being quite unable to think who she is, where you know her from, or what her name is. Typically this happened with slight acquaintances (rather than close friends or relatives) encountered out of their usual context — for example, seeing a clerk from your bank out shopping in the street.

The fourth and final type of error is the inability to remember someone's name (190 incidents). In over 90% of these instances, the diarists reported being fully aware of who the person was in the sense of what her occupation was (99%) and where she was usually seen (92%), but the name remained elusive. There seems to be something different, and something difficult, about names.

Young et al. (1985) interpret the fact that you may be able to recall all you know about someone except their name as suggesting that names may somehow be stored apart from the other information you possess about familiar people. They argue that satisfactory face recognition requires the involvement of at least three separate mental systems. The first is the *face recognition system*, in which the stored representations of familiar faces are held. The second is a *semantic system*, in which is located all the general knowledge you possess about people you know. Third and last is a system from which the spoken forms of words, including names, are retrieved.

Drawing upon the findings of Young et al. (1985), and much other research on face recognition, Bruce and Young (1986) proposed the model of face recognition illustrated in Fig. 1.18. We will concentrate initially upon the right-hand side of the model. Each box represents a separate processing module or store and the arrows indicate transmission of information between these modules.

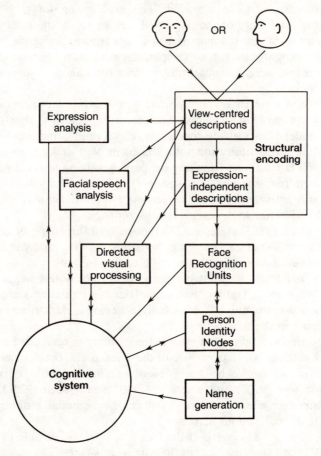

FIG. 1.18 Bruce and Young's (1986) model of face recognition (redrawn from the original).

The model begins by postulating that structural descriptions of the face are derived, first view centred, as in Marr's $2\frac{1}{2}$-D sketch, then as 3-D representations that are *independent* of facial expression. The independence is introduced partly because we recognise faces of familiar people independently of whether they are smiling or frowning, but also because there is neuropsychological evidence, reviewed by Bruce and Young (1986), that expressions are processed separately. So, some patients with neurological damage can correctly identify faces but not their emotional expression, while other patients show the reverse effect. Therefore, Bruce and Young included a separate *expression analysis* module in their model.

The structural encoding stimulates the *face recognition units*. Each of these units contains stored details of the face of a known person. The closer the newly seen face is to the stored details in any face recognition unit, the higher the activation in that unit will be. The face recognition units are linked both to the *cognitive system* and to *person identity nodes*. The cognitive system is the store of information about the individual and is therefore a part of semantic memory (see Chapter 9). So, when the face recognition unit for a familiar face is activated, for example by seeing Marilyn Monroe, that makes available from the cognitive system semantic information about Ms Monroe, such as the fact that she was a famous film star. The *person identity nodes* are the point at which person recognition is achieved. They receive input not only from face recognition units but also from an analysis of voices, names, posture, clothing, etc. Such a level is included in the model because recognising a person does not require seeing his or her face. It might come about through hearing his or her name, or his or her voice, etc. Only when the person identity node has been sufficiently stimulated by input from one or more of its sources is the person recognised. Only after such recognition can the name of the person be generated, hence the final *name generation* box.

The structure of this model captures the data reported by Young et al. (1985). Where errors were found in that study, it is possible to locate them in the failure of processing within the Bruce and Young model. So, for example, recognising that a face is familiar but not knowing any more about the person implies that a face recognition unit has been activated but that, for some reason, this has not stimulated the cognitive system or the person identity node sufficiently to retrieve more information about the person. A failure to recall a name for someone about whom one can recall many other details implies problems at the final stage between the person identity node and the name generation system.

Two remaining modules require a brief explanation. Bruce and Young included a *directed visual processing* module because they point out that we can, strategically, actively direct our attention to process certain aspects of a face. We may look for particular features; for example, if we know that the friend that we are to meet at the station has long blonde hair we may look specifically for such hair, among the distant alighting passengers. The *facial speech analysis* module is included because lip-reading has been shown to be a separate cognitive ability, independent of face recognition (Campbell, Landis, & Regard, 1986). Some individuals who have suffered brain damage can recognise faces but not lip-read, while others may lip-read but be unable to identify familiar faces. So facial speech analysis seems to be a separate system.

AN INTERACTIVE ACTIVATION MODEL OF FACE RECOGNITION

While models such as those of Bruce and Young (1986) are important in clarifying theoretical ideas, even greater power comes from models that can be formally simulated by computer programs. Such simulations usually highlight any lack of specificity in the modelling and can reveal properties

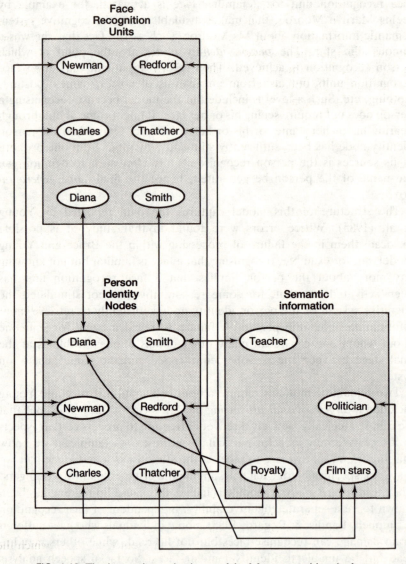

FIG. 1.19 The interactive activation model of face recognition (redrawn from Burton et al., 1990).

of the model that were not obvious even to the authors of the model. Burton, Bruce and Johnston (1990), therefore, developed a computational model based upon the Bruce and Young (1986) framework.

Burton et al.'s (1990) model has three separate "pools" of units, as has Bruce and Young's model. These contain, respectively, units for face recognition (FRUs) for each individual's face, person identity nodes (PINs) for each person "known" to the model, and semantic information known about the individuals. These units are linked in appropriate ways (see Fig. 1.19). There are FRUs and PINs for each person represented in the model, and these are connected to appropriate semantic information. So, for example, there would be a FRU for Ms Monroe's face, a PIN for her and links from the PIN to semantic information about her, such as her being dead, having been a film star, etc. Unlike Bruce and Young's model, semantic information is linked to PINs but not to FRUs. One result of the formalising of the model was to demonstrate that the FRU → semantics link was inappropriate.

In the model, recognition occurs if the activation in the relevant PIN reaches a given threshold. Where units are linked they will transmit excitation to other units to which they are linked if they themselves are excited. As with all such models (see Chapter 2), there are inhibitory links between units to counterbalance this excitation. So, whenever one PIN increases in excitation, this is transmitted through *inhibitory* links with all other PINs and will *reduce* their activation.

Burton and et al.'s model has been very successful in simulating a wide range of experimental findings about face recognition. We will take two examples, first explaining the research findings that must be simulated by an adequate model. One example is semantic priming. When the face to be identified is preceded by the face of someone with whom the person is associated (e.g. a picture of Stan Laurel preceded by one of Oliver Hardy), the recognition of the face as familiar is quicker than if the preceding face is of an unrelated but familiar person (e.g. Bruce & Valentine, 1986). Burton and co-workers' model simulates this priming by producing easier recognition when an associated face follows seeing a given face than when the second face is unconnected with the first.

Burton et al.'s model also simulates the *distinctiveness effect*. It is well established that distinctive familiar faces are more quickly recognised than more typical faces (e.g. Valentine & Ferrara, 1991). It is also frequently reported that recognition of faces from one's own race is easier than for other races. Why should this be so? Valentine and his associates (e.g. Valentine, 1991; Valentine & Endo, 1992) have developed a theoretical framework which proposes that faces are encoded as points in a multi-dimensional space, where the dimensions represent those upon which the faces are encoded. Decisions on whether a face is familiar, in Valentine's model, are based upon analysing the new face on the multiple dimensions, determining the distance of this new face from its nearest neighbour. Distinctive faces are more dissimilar to other faces across these multiple dimensions. Valentine and Endo (1992) are able to explain the finding that it is easier to recognise faces from one's own race than those of other races by assuming that the dimensions upon which faces are encoded are refined over a lifetime's experience, but that the important dimensions for recognising, say, an Afro-Caribbean face, may not be those which best discriminate between Chinese faces.

These distinctiveness effects are simulated by Burton and et al.'s model. It assumes that distinctive faces share less features than do typical faces. Typical and distinctive faces were modelled with typical FRUs receiving inputs from features shared with several other faces, while distinctive FRUs had features shared with few other faces. When the model was run, the PINs for distinctive FRUs were more quickly and strongly activated than those for typical faces.

We have illustrated how the model of Burton et al. is able to simulate two important features of face recognition. One unexpected outcome from developing the simulation was that an explanation for the poor recall of names emerged that did not require the assumption of a separate name store, as in Bruce and Young's model, somewhere at the very end of the processing. The "name effect" is a robust finding, and it occurs not just within the diary data of Young et al. (1985). For example, McWeeny, Young, Hay and Ellis (1987) showed that people take longer to put names to faces than occupations to faces, even when the names are actually occupations and the *same* words are used as occupations or names, for example "Mr Baker" or "is a baker".

Burton and Bruce (1992) pointed out that, unlike most semantic properties associated with an individual, a person's name is connected to only one PIN. So, while the semantic information that X is a doctor, a parent, lives in Blackpool and so on is likely to be shared with other known individuals, the fact that her name is Marigold Beckett is likely to be a unique link between the name and the person node. When this was represented in simulation runs of Burton et al.'s model, it was always found that names received the least activation and were slowest in reaching their maximum activation of *all* the semantic information units. All the semantic information was activated before the name was retrieved. Thus, the simple interactive simulation model was able to show that what had for so long seemed a puzzling feature of recognising a person, and had led to specific boxes being added to the model, was really a natural consequence of the nature of the associative network linking the information about any individual. Names are special only in so far as they are special and distinctive for an individual. It is not necessary to assume that they are treated in a different manner to other information about an individual within the cognitive system.

THE ROLE OF CONTEXT IN OBJECT RECOGNITION

If you met your grandmother outside her house, you would almost certainly immediately recognise her. However, if you passed her in the street in a different town that you did not expect her to be visiting, you might miss her, or doubt that the person really was her. Object recognition is clearly determined in large measure by the visual description of an object, but objects are also normally perceived in contexts. Does the context in which an object appears affect the speed or accuracy with which it can be recognised for what it is?

The subjects in Palmer's (1975) experiment were asked to identify briefly presented line drawings of objects. On some trials, they were first given a picture of a scene (e.g. of a kitchen scene) to inspect. The briefly presented drawing which followed could then be either appropriate to the preceding scene (e.g. a loaf of bread) or inappropriate (e.g. a drum). Accuracy of object identification was highest when the object picture followed an appropriate scene, and lowest when it followed an inappropriate one. With no preceding scene, accuracy was intermediate. We may say, then, that the context provided by an appropriate scene *facilitates* the subsequent recognition of a briefly seen object, whereas that provided by an inappropriate scene *inhibits* subsequent recognition.

As described in the previous section, experimenters have asked whether one person's face is more easily recognised if it is seen immediately after the face of a second person with whom the first is associated than if it is seen after the face of an unassociated person. "Association" here means pairs of people who share a common occupation and/or tend to be seen together. Bruce and Valentine (1986) showed that where two famous faces occurred together in the sequence, the time taken to respond to the second face was less if the first face was associated than if the first face was unrelated.

It would appear, then, that the recognition of an object can be facilitated by the context in which it is seen — either the general background context as in Palmer's (1975) object recognition experiment, or the other objects recently recognised as in Bruce and Valentine's (1986) face-priming experiment. But *how* can context influence recognition? We have already argued that recognition occurs when an analysed pattern accesses and activates a stored representation. One possibility proposed by Seymour (1973) and Warren and Morton (1982) for objects, and by Hay and Young (1982) and Bruce (1983) for faces, is that context works by contributing some activation to the representations for patterns that the context suggests are likely to be perceived. Representations that are already partially activated from within by the context will then require less input from the stimulus pattern to be fully activated and to trigger recognition. Inspecting a kitchen scene will, on this account, cause partial activation of the stored representations of the appearance of objects likely to be encountered in a kitchen (loaves of bread, forks, casseroles, cookers, etc.). Each of these visual patterns will be recognised more easily as a result of this priming than if it suddenly intruded into, say, a jungle scene. Similarly, if Nancy Reagan's face appears on the television, you will recognise her more easily if you have recently recognised Oliver Hardy.

SUMMARY

Recognising a familiar face must involve comparing a perceived stimulus pattern against a set of stored representations. Simple template and feature models have problems coping with the variability of natural patterns (e.g. familiar faces in different orientations, with changing hairstyles, etc.). Where faces are concerned, the visual system appears to try to counteract the variability of external features like hairstyle by an increasing reliance on internal features as the basis of the recognition of familiar faces.

Faces and objects are normally encountered against a complex, changing visual background. Psychologists have made some progress in identifying the cues that enable elements of a visual array to be grouped together as parts of the same object. Such grouping is a necessary preliminary to recognition. In particular, the work of Marr (1982) not only suggests possible stages through which object recognition may be accomplished, but also clarifies the types of explanation that need to be sought when attempting to understand any part of the cognitive system. The cues underlying distance and movement perception have also been analysed in some detail.

It is commonly assumed that word, face and object recognition converge on a common "semantic" stage at which is held knowledge of the meanings and uses of words, the uses and properties of objects, and the characteristics and personalities of people. A model was presented to account for the interconnection between the cognitive processors responsible for different types of recognition, for comprehension and for naming, using as sources of relevant evidence the recognition problems experienced by both normal and brain-injured individuals.

Fuller accounts of visual perception will be found in V. Bruce and P. Green (1990), *Visual perception: Physiology, psychology and ecology*, 2nd edn, and in G.W. Humphreys and V. Bruce (1989), *Visual cognition: Computational, experimental and neuropsychological perspectives*.

2 Reading Words: Sight and Sound in Recognising Patterns

Imagine that one evening you arrive home late with a friend and on the kitchen table you spot a note addressed to you. You pick the note up and read: *Please wash the potatoes and put the casserole in the oven.* Now you might object to this request, but you do not find it difficult to decide what "potatoes" means. A 7-year-old child, on the other hand, might have considerable difficulty in deciding what to wash and what to put in the oven. Anyway, having read the note, you both decide to have a drink and put your feet up for a while before starting to prepare the meal. This is a simple scenario and ones like it must happen thousands of times each day, yet the processes that allow us to read the note, to remember its content, to develop intentions about future actions, to remember those intentions and so on are taken for granted. Much of this book is aimed at showing that although these actions seem easy to perform and to require little conscious effort, that does not make them easy to explain. Likewise, at a number of points we will see how simply reflecting on our subjective experiences of reading is not always a reliable guide to how we actually do it.

Reading has been extensively studied by psychologists, partly because it is a skill that requires some effort to acquire (even if the effort is then soon forgotten), and partly because it is a specifically human, culturally transmitted cognitive activity. When Huey (1908) reviewed the first 10–15 years of experimental research on reading, he remarked that: "to completely analyse what we do when we read would almost be the acme of a psychologist's achievement, for it would be to describe very many of the most intricate workings of the human mind, as well as to unravel the tangled story of the most remarkable specific performance that civilisation has learned in all its history". Psychologists have not yet finished unravelling the complexities of that remarkable performance, but they have made a start.

Where should the study of reading begin? One obvious place might be the recognition of letter shapes, since letters are the building blocks of written words. But there is an even earlier stage in reading. Before you can begin to recognise a letter or the word in which it belongs, your eyes must first alight on the word. The eye movements made during reading are quite subtle and we begin with a discussion of them. Later in the chapter, we consider the processes by which a written word evokes its meaning and sound in the reader's mind.

SCANNING THE NOTE: EYE MOVEMENTS AND TAKING IN INFORMATION

As you read the note about the potatoes and the casserole, you were probably unaware of your eye movements. Even if you had been attending to them — perhaps having read a chapter like this earlier in the day — you may not have had an accurate feeling for what was going on. However, had your companion observed you while you were reading the note, he or she might have noticed that your eyes did not move smoothly along the line of print but progressed by a succession of quick flicks interspersed by moments when your eyes were quite still.

The stationary moments are called *fixations* and the flicks are referred to as *saccades* (the term used by the French ophthalmologist Javal who first reported them in 1887). Saccades and fixations are not unique to reading; they happen whenever we inspect a static scene. In fact, the only time we can move our eyes smoothly is when we are tracking a moving target. You can easily verify this by asking a friend first to fixate the tip of a pencil while you move it in a straight line, and then to move his or her eyes in a straight line without a target to follow. In the first condition, you will observe smooth, continuous eye movements; in the second, you will see saccades and fixations.

Figure 2.1 shows a passage of text and superimposed upon it a somewhat idealised representation of the eye movements that a skilled reader would be expected to make. The circles above the words represent fixations, with the diameter of the circle indicating their likely durations (larger circles for longer fixations). The arrows show the saccades. Note that most saccades are forwards, but in reality some 10–20% of eye movements (excluding those from the end of one line to the beginning of the next) go backwards to re-fixate words which have been fixated once already. These are called *regressions*.

The average fixation of a skilled reader lasts 200–250 msec (that is, between one-fifth and one-quarter of a second). The average saccade takes only 25–30 msec (a mere one-fortieth of a second). Compare these two figures and you will realise that a reader's eyes are in fact still — that is, fixating — for about 90% of the time during reading. It may *feel* as if your eyes are constantly moving when you read, but they are stationary for most of the time, which illustrates how misleading one's subjective impressions can be.

All of the uptake of useful information in reading occurs during

Once upon a time there were three bears who lived

in a house on the edge of a wood. Every day a

little girl called Goldilocks walked through the wood

on her way to her Grandmother's house in the

nearby village of Gorehampton.

FIG. 2.1 The pattern of eye movements that a skilled reader might make in reading a passage of text. Circles represent fixations, with larger circles indicating longer fixations, and arrows represent saccades. (For simplification, we have omitted the 10% or so of backward, "regressive" eye movements that occur in natural reading.)

fixations. We have known since the work of Dodge (1900) and Holt (1903) that little or nothing is perceived during a saccade (a phenomenon known as "saccadic suppression"). Even a strong flash of light is unlikely to be perceived if it occurs entirely within a saccade (Latour, 1962). Suppression also extends into the first 60–80 msec of a fixation: both in reading and viewing a scene, it takes that long after a saccade before information begins to be utilised (McConkie, 1983).

But why is it necessary to make these eye movements at all when reading? Why is it not possible to read a whole page of a book or a whole notice by giving it one long fixation in the middle? One of the main reasons is that the quality of visual information picked up declines rapidly with distance from the point of fixation. Detailed vision is made possible by light-sensitive cells called *cones*, which are located in the retina at the back of the eye. The cones are most densely packed at the central region of the retina, the *fovea*, and this allows greatest visual acuity. When one fixates on a point, light from that point impinges on the fovea. Moving away from the fovea, the density of cones decreases, bringing with it a corresponding decrease in visual acuity away from the fixation point. Reading requires reasonably high visual acuity. If letters or words are briefly displayed at various positions in the visual field, then the likelihood of being able to identify them correctly declines rapidly with distance away from the fixation point.

Although acuity declines more or less symmetrically around the fixation point, information uptake in reading is not symmetrical. One of the most important findings showing this lack of symmetry refers to something called the "perceptual span". The perceptual span is the area of text around the fixation point from which useful information is picked up. When reading normal English text, this area extends further to the right than it does to the left. Rayner, Well and Pollatsek (1980) suggest that the span is up to 15 characters to the right but only 3–4 characters to the left (see Fig. 2.2). One obvious reason for this asymmetry in English might be that information to the left of fixation has already been processed (equally obvious is that information to the right of fixation has not been processed — both factors probably contribute to the asymmetry). Unlike visual acuity, the asymmetry of the perceptual span is constrained by our learning experiences rather than by anatomy. Pollatsek, Bolozky, Well and Rayner (1981) showed that for readers of Hebrew, which runs from right to left, the perceptual span is biased to the left of the fixation point. Inhoff, Pollatsek, Posner and Rayner (1989) asked readers of English to read English texts that were printed from right to left rather than the usual left to right. After a short amount of practice on these reversed texts, Inhoff et al. showed that the asymmetry of the readers' perceptual span reversed, so that more letters were picked up to the left of the fixation point than to the right. This suggests that the form of the perceptual span is guided by our reading experiences but remains very flexible.

Readers tend to fixate on a point somewhere between the beginning and middle of a word (Rayner, 1979). This point is referred to as the preferred viewing location. However, this point is not always the optimal viewing location, which is the point in the word from which viewers can obtain most information about the word. In English, this optimal point is usually slightly to the left of the centre of the word. O'Regan and Jacobs (1992)

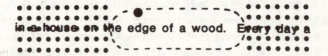

FIG. 2.2 The "perceptual span" in reading typically extends further to the right of the fixation pont than to the left.

showed that deviation from the optimal viewing position, as measured in number of letters away from the optimal point, slows down reading of a single word to the extent of 20 msec per letter.

The discrepancy between the preferred and optimal viewing positions is attributed to two factors: inaccuracy in the eye movements themselves and something called preview benefit (Rayner & Morris, 1992). The region of text which is in view but which does not fall on the fovea falls on an area known as the parafovea. For example, in Fig. 2.2, if you fixate on the **d** in **edge** at a normal reading distance, then the word **wood** falls in the parafovea. Experiments have shown that if a word has been "previewed" in the parafovea, then when it is fixated upon the duration of that fixation is shorter than if the word had not been "previewed". The argument is that the preview gives some information in advance and so the point to which the eyes then move need not correspond to the optimal point. Exactly what information is gleaned from preview is a matter of some debate, but whatever it is it clearly has an influence on the pattern of fixations.

Fixating on a word is only the first step in reading it. If you fixate a word in a foreign language, particularly one in an unfamiliar alphabet like Russian or Arabic, then you are unlikely to make much sense of it. If the word is from your own language, however, the word will activate its meaning and its sound without apparent effort. How is this achieved? What happens inside your head that distinguishes between fixating a word that is written in your own language and fixating on a word that is part of a language that you cannot read? If we could answer that question completely, we would have reached Huey's "acme". We haven't yet succeeded in doing so, but we can at least sketch the outlines of a plausible answer.

A PRELIMINARY ACCOUNT OF THE RECOGNITION OF FAMILIAR WRITTEN WORDS

Recognising Letters

Many theories of visual word recognition assume that at least some of the component letters of a written word must be identified before the word itself can be recognised. By "identify a letter" we do not mean name it. Here, identification refers to the visual categorisation of a stimulus pattern such as a letter as an exemplar of a known type, in this case as a particular letter of the alphabet. Coltheart (1981) reported the case of a man who, following brain injury, could understand most written words, but could pronounce very few, and was rarely able to read aloud invented nonwords like ANER. His letter naming was also poor, yet he could reliably respond "same" to pairs of nonwords like ANER/aner and "different" to pairs like ANER/aneg. These decisions were possible because the man could still identify and compare the component letters of words or nonwords visually, though he could no longer pronounce or name them.

Letter recognition is commonly assumed to be a necessary part of word recognition, but we have as yet only an ill-defined notion of how exactly it might be achieved. An early theory proposed that we might possess internal letter *templates* against which stimuli could be compared. You can think of these templates as stencils, which you could place over a letter to check for a match. The problem with this theory is evident from the limitations of machine systems that employ this mode of letter recognition. An example is the computer reading of the lettering on cheques. Those rather odd letter shapes are designed to be minimally confusable (at least to the computer), and the systems that recognise them are very intolerant of even slight changes in letter shape. Yet as Fig. 2.3 illustrates, even within upper or lower case, the same letter can take a variety of different, if related, forms. Recently, Loomis (1990) has produced a complex model of character recognition, implemented on a computer, that makes use of templates. In a series of experiments on visual and tactile stimuli, he compared the performance of his model to that of people. The task of the subjects in his experiments was to learn sets of characters, many of which were entirely novel. Not surprisingly, people found it harder to learn the characters in some sets than in others. When tested on the same series of character sets, Loomis' computer model had most difficulty distinguishing characters within those sets which people also found most difficult, while having least difficulty with those that people also found least difficult. Loomis is careful to point out that this does not mean that his model would also mimic people's performance on letter recognition tasks involving other measures of performance, such as reaction times, but the model's success on discrimination tasks at least suggests that there could be some role for templates in letter recognition. However, it is fair to say that the model came nowhere near dealing with the type of variation of the same character that is found in the vast array of different scripts and handwritings that we encounter as readers.

As an alternative to templates, some theorists propose that letters are recognised in terms of sets of *distinctive features* (Oden, 1979). A distinctive feature is a property or aspect of an object that helps to distinguish it from other objects. The distinctive features of letters might include lines and curves in varying orientations. Thus, the features for the letter A might be [right-sloping oblique], [left-sloping oblique], [horizontal line]. That would not be enough, however, since there are many ways you could combine two sloping and one horizontal line without forming a letter A (see Fig. 2.4). The "features" therefore would need to include specifications of the *configuration* that the elements must adopt in order to be an

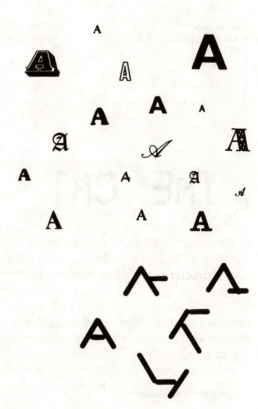

FIG. 2.3 Any template-based model of letter recognition would have great difficulty coping with variations in letter shape and size.

FIG. 2.4 All these shapes contain two sloping and one horizontal line, yet only one is a letter "A". Distinctive features would need to incorporate essential configurational information.

acceptable letter. Some theorists have suggested that there are separate stages for locating and integrating features of objects such as letters: the first stage happens in parallel and the parts or features are located in the visual array, and it is not until the second stage, where the processes are serial, that features are related to one another in a way that forms structured wholes (Treisman & Gelade, 1980).

As with templates, computer systems have been created which recognise letters using distinctive features (the system of McClelland and Rumelhart which we discuss later in this chapter is an example). But again, as with templates, feature systems have their problems, as illustrated in Fig. 2.5. Particularly when one moves from print to handwriting, the variability of letter shapes becomes enormous, and it has yet to be proven that feature-based systems can cope with that variability any better than template systems. Additionally, as Fig. 2.6 shows, the same physical shape can be classified differently depending on the word-context in which it occurs. Such demonstrations undermine the assumption that letter recognition must occur prior to, and independently of, word recognition. As we

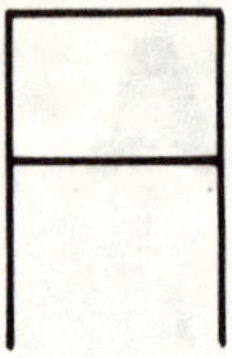

FIG. 2.5 A feature system set up to utilise the two sloping lines of the letter "A" as crucial would fail to identify this symbol.

(a) **THE CAT**

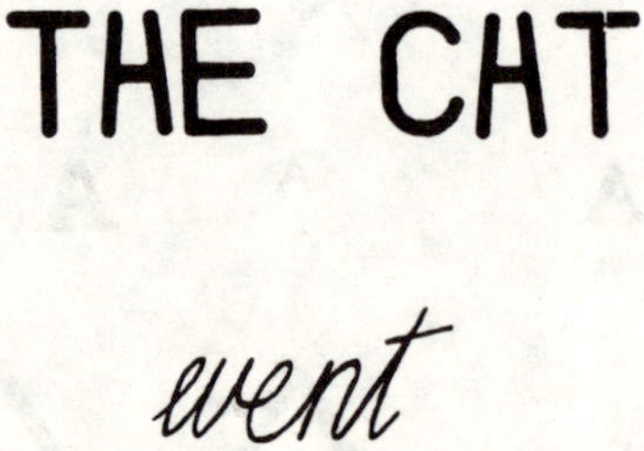

(b) *went*

FIG. 2.6 The same physical shape can be identified as two different letters depending on the context in which it occurs. In (a) the same shape is identified as an "H" in the first word and as an "A" in the second word; (b) will be read as either "went" or "event" depending on the surrounding context.

shall see shortly, there is other evidence which points to the conclusion that letter and word recognition are interacting rather than independent operations.

Recognising Words

When psychologists have turned their attention from letters to words, they have tended to adopt the same sort of approach and to utilise the same sorts of explanatory concepts. It has often been proposed that there exists a separate "word recognition unit" for each familiar written word (McClelland & Rumelhart, 1981; Morton, 1979). The idea is that each word familiar to a reader is represented by a separate recognition unit in his or her mental lexicon (the lexicon is our store of knowledge about words). The word *farm*, for example, would be represented by a single unit that would be activated when the letters f, a, r and m are recognised in the correct arrangement.

The alert reader may already have spotted one or two problems with this account. For a start, words, like letters, come in various forms. It would be inefficient to have separate word recognition units for *FARM*, FARM, *farm* and farm, so we should perhaps prefer there to be just one unit capable of identifying these different instantiations of the same word. There are a number of ways this goal could be achieved. One possibility, shown in Fig. 2.7, would be to have the recognisers for each form of a letter feed directly into the word-recognition unit. Another possibility,

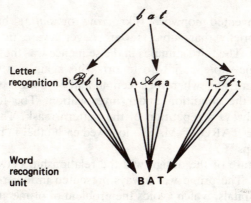

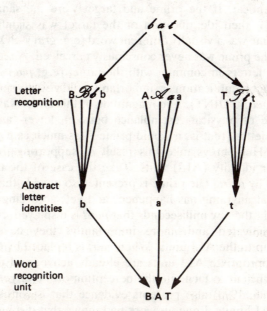

FIG. 2.7 Two possible ways that
letter and word recognition
processes might interrelate.

favoured by Coltheart (1981) and illustrated in Fig. 2.7, has letter forms
feeding first into an "abstract letter identity unit" for that letter. The
abstract letter identity units would then pass activation up to the word
level.

Evidence for a stage of abstract letter identities has been claimed by
Evett and Humphreys (1981). Their experiments involved the rapid
presentation of a sequence of four stimuli. The first was always a random
jumble of letter fragments known as a "pattern mask". The second
stimulus was a letter string called the "prime". The prime could be a real

word or an invented nonword (like *crove* or *smife*), but was always displayed so briefly that subjects were never aware that it had been presented at all. The third stimulus in the sequence was the "target" word, which it was the subject's job to report. This again was brief, but long enough to ensure somewhere between 40 and 80% correct identification depending on the condition under investigation. The fourth and last stimulus was always a repetition of the pattern mask. The four stimuli, MASK–PRIME–TARGET–MASK, followed each other in rapid succession without any gaps.

The key feature of the design was the relationship between the prime and the target. The prime was always presented in lower-case print and the target in capitals, which avoids the problem of prime and target being physically identical. If the prime and target were the same word (e.g. *point*–POINT), then identification of the target was significantly better than if the prime was a visually different word (e.g. *gravy*–POINT), despite the fact that the prime was never consciously perceived. A real-word prime which shared letters in common with the target (e.g. *paint*–POINT) also improved target identification as, importantly, did visually similar nonword primes (e.g. *pairt*–POINT). The magnitude of this effect was independent of the degree of physical resemblance between lower- and upper-case versions of a letter (that is, a would prime A as much as p primed P).

Evett and Humphreys take this result as supporting the concept of abstract letter identity (ALI) units. Take the case of the target POINT being primed by *pairt*. The prime is presented so quickly that subjects are not aware that anything has happened, and yet, according to Evett and Humphreys, in the few milliseconds that *pairt* is displayed, the letter units have been activated and, more importantly, they have transmitted information up to the ALI units. When *pairt* is replaced by POINT, three of the five appropriate ALI units are already active, and that degree of priming is sufficient to facilitate the perception of the target.

Bigsby (1988; 1990) also presents evidence that is consistent with the existence of ALI units. Previous work had shown that if subjects are asked to say whether two letters match, they are quicker to respond "yes" when both are in the same case, BB, than if they are in different cases, Bb (Posner & Mitchell, 1967). On the ALI account, this difference arises because the processes prior to accessing the ALIs are not the same when the pair is of mixed case; that is, although the same ALI is accessed for all the different instances of B, this access is facilitated when both instances of a pair are processed in precisely the same way *prior* to the ALI. Now consider the letter pairs: *ℬ*b and *ℬ*B. Here, although the same ALI is accessed for all four instances of B, there is no physical identity between members of a pair (Bigsby chose an unfamiliar typeface to try and ensure that overlap was minimal even when letters were the same case). The consequence of this is that the processes preceding access to the ALI are not identical for either pair. Therefore, when doing a matching task, the members of pairs such as *ℬ*B should not be easier to match than members of pairs such as *ℬ* b, and so, on the ALI account, there should be no difference in times to match them. Bigsby (1988) found exactly this lack of difference for such pairs while still finding that when members of a pair were physically identical (BB), they were processed more quickly than non-identical pairs (Bb).

We have talked so far as if there was only one abstract letter identity unit for each letter, which recognised its letter wherever it occurred. The problem here is that the word pairs *was — saw, lose — sole and orchestra — carthorse* contain the same letters in different positions. Word recognition units must be informed not only of the occurrence of particular letters, but also of the positions those letters occupy (Boston Philharmonic Carthorse really doesn't look right, does it?)

One solution to this problem might be to propose a separate letter unit for each position that a letter can occupy. That way, the component letters of *orches*tra and *carthorse* would activate completely different sets of letter units. Position-specific letter recognisers were favoured by McClelland and Rumelhart (1981) in an influential computer simulation of visual word recognition that we shall discuss shortly. Their system was, however, limited to a vocabulary of exclusive four-letter words, so that there were just four position-specific units for each letter. No-one has yet shown that a system working on this principle could cope successfully with natural variations in word length from hip to hippopotamus. More recently, Humphreys, Evett and Quinlan (1990) have used the priming technique described earlier to suggest that it is the relative position of letters in a word that is important and not their specific position. For example, Humphreys et al. showed that when asked to identify the target word BLACK, subjects' performance was improved when this had been preceded by the prime *blck*. Note that this prime is only four letters long, so specific positions cannot be used but relative positions remain the same. Humphreys et al. went on to show that the degree to which relative positions were preserved was a good predictor of the size of the benefit gained from the prime, so that, for example, *blck* was a more effective prime than *bclk*.

INTERACTIONS BETWEEN THE WORD LEVEL AND THE LETTER LEVEL

Our preliminary account of word recognition had two stages: first, the identification of letters, and, second, the identification of words. Many traditional cognitive theories might have assumed that the first stage must be completed before the second could begin; that is, the identification of lines and curves as letters must be finished before the letter information could start to trigger word recognition units. However, McClelland and Rumelhart (1981) deliberately violate this assumption in their computer simulation of word recognition. In that simulation, as soon as a letter unit begins to be activated by featural information, it starts to transmit activation up to the word units to which it is connected. What is more, the word units feed activation back down to the letter units which supply them.

What is the purpose of having letter units activated both from above (the word units) and below (the external stimulus)? The purpose in one sense is to explain a phenomenon known as the "word superiority effect". This effect was discovered by Reicher (1969) and Wheeler (1970), and has been the subject of much experimentation since (Henderson, 1982b). In a typical experiment, a subject is shown very briefly a letter string which could be a word (e.g. MADE) or a pronounceable nonword (e.g. MIDE) or a string of consonants (e.g. MTDG). The brief string is followed by a pattern mask of jumbled letter fragments which cuts out any short-term visual image of the stimulus (the so-called "iconic image"). The subject is then quizzed on what the letter in a particular position was (for example, following MADE the subject might be asked whether the third letter was D or L). In such circumstances, accuracy is greater for letters in words than for letters in nonwords or consonant strings. That is, although the subject is only ever being asked which of two letters occurred at a particular position, performance is enhanced if the target letter happens to be contained within a familiar word.

McClelland and Rumelhart (1981) successfully mimicked this effect in their computer simulation of word recognition, a simplified diagrammatic representation of which is shown in Fig. 2.8. The model has recognition units at three levels — a feature level, a letter level and a word level. Because the model only recognises words written in capital (upper-case) letters in a particular typeface, the problems mentioned earlier about multiple and variable forms of letters are avoided. As was also mentioned earlier, the model only deals with four-letter words, making it feasible to have a unit for each letter at each of the four positions.

Units at each level send two sorts of connection to units at levels further down the line. The first are activating connections which seek to increase the level of activity in relevant higher level units, and the second are inhibitory and seek to suppress activity in inappropriate higher level units. Thus there will be at the feature level a unit activated by a vertical line at the left-hand side of a letter. It will send activation up to appropriate letter units (B, D, E, F, H, K, L, M, N, P and R) and inhibition up to all other letter units. Suppose the word being recognised begins with an M. The letter unit for M (in initial position) will be achieved by the left-vertical feature detector, and also by feature units responding to the central oblique lines and the vertical line on the right. Letter units for letters

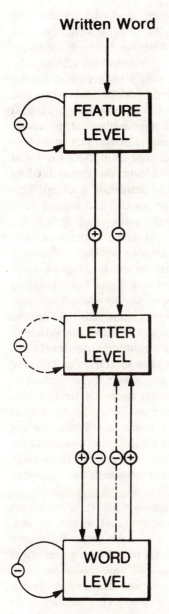

Written Word

FEATURE LEVEL

Features identified in individual letters. Feature detectors inhibit one another.

Feature detectors activate position-specific letter detectors containing their feature and inhibit all other letter detectors.

LETTER LEVEL

Individual letters identified. Letter detectors receive activatory and inhibitory inputs from feature detectors, and activatory inputs from word level units. Inhibition between letter detectors is permitted in the R & M model but not used in the simulations.

Letter detectors activate word recognition units containing their letter and inhibit all other units. Letter detectors are, in turn, activated by feedback from the word level. Word-to-letter level inhibition is permitted in the model but not always used in the simulations.

WORD LEVEL

Word recognition units respond to activatory and inhibitory inputs from the letter level and also mutually inhibit each other. The word recognized is the one whose activation level remains high while the others are suppressed.

FIG. 2.8 A simplified representation of McClelland and Rumelhart's (1981) computer model of visual word recognition. Reproduced with permission from Ellis (1984).

sharing the left-vertical feature will, in contrast, be inhibited by these other features, so the M detector at the letter level will emerge as the one most highly activated.

The initial detector will send activation in turn to word-level units for all words beginning with M (MORE, MILL, MOAT, MADE, MALE, etc.), and inhibit units for words not beginning with that letter. If the target word to be recognised happened to be MADE, it would be activated by the four appropriate letter detectors. MILL would be activated by the initial M but would be inhibited by the A, D and E. MALE would receive three excitatory inputs (M, A and E) and only one inhibitory input (D) and so would take longer to be rejected. That rejection would, however, be hastened in McClelland and Rumelhart's model by the fact that there are additional inhibitory connections within the word level. As a word unit gains activation it seeks to suppress other units, and the strength of its inhibitory influence increases as its own level of activation goes up. This within-level inhibition, which also occurs at the feature and letter levels, causes the total system to settle down more rapidly, and speeds the identification of the letter string which has been presented to the computer.

We have now accounted for all the connections in Fig. 2.8 except those introduced to permit the model to simulate the findings on word superiority effects with which we began this section. Letters presented in familiar words, it will be remembered, seem to be identified more accurately at brief, masked exposures than letters in nonwords. McClelland and Rumelhart simulate this finding in the model by allowing activated word units to contribute to the current level of activity in letter-level units for the word's component letters. Consider the D in MADE. The first step towards its eventual identification as a D will begin with the activation of the appropriate feature detectors. They will begin to feed activation into the letter unit for a D in a third position. At the same time, the letter units for an initial M, second A and final E will be warming up. While still less than fully activated, they will be passing activation up to the word unit for MADE. And as it begins to warm up, it will feed activation back down to those letter units, thus hastening the moment at which they achieve maximal activation.

Now suppose the D had formed part of the nonword MIDE. Letter units would begin to be activated by the feature detectors and would, in turn, send activation up to the word level. But there is no word unit which would receive wholly excitatory inputs — even units for similar looking real words like MILE, SIDE or MADE will all receive at least one inhibitory input from MIDE. The word level will accordingly warm up much less than it did with MADE. The important consequence of this is that the top-down contribution of the word level to the activation of the letter units, and hence to the perception of component letters, will be less for nonwords than words. So when the presentation of a letter string is brief and curtailed by a pattern mask, the letter level will have made less progress in resolving the identity of the letters if they had formed a nonword than if they formed a familiar word. Consonant strings like MTDG will cause even less activity

FIG. 2.9 A dramatic illustration of the capacity of context to induce illusory letter perception. Reproduced with permission from Frisby (1979).

at the word level, so their perception will be even more heavily data-driven and slower as a consequence. In McClelland and Rumelhart's simulation such strings are the slowest to be identified, and in experiments on letter identification using human subjects they fare worst of all.

It is not only the word superiority effect that can be explained by allowing the word level to influence the letter level. Under certain conditions, the effect of word-context may be so strong that it induces the illusory perception of a letter that is not in fact there. The classic demonstration of this phenomenon we owe to Pillsbury (1897). He deliberately smudged some letters in words or replaced them with others, then displayed the words briefly (though no briefer than an average fixation duration) to skilled readers. The readers were asked to indicate, with some estimate of their degree of confidence, exactly what they had seen. Pillsbury discovered that people would report with confidence having seen letters which had, in fact, been replaced by a smudge or by another letter.

Figure 2.9 (from Frisby, 1979) illustrates the power of context to induce letter restoration. Have a look at it. Now have another look — there is no P in SPRING!

In terms of the interactive activation model, what appears to be happening is this: You often do not need all of the letters in a word to activate its word recognition unit (e.g. *elxphxnt*; *gxrxffe*) particularly in the light of other contextual information. If a letter has been omitted from a word, either through a printer's error or an experimenter's deviousness, the remaining letters may be sufficient to activate the word unit. It will then feed activation back down to the letter units for all its component letters, including the missing one. It will be "seen" because it has been activated from within, not from without. The broader context in which a misprinted word appears is also known to affect the probability of illusory letter restoration, a fact we shall discuss later. Interactions between letter and word levels also help account for the effects of context on letter identification illustrated in Fig. 2.6.

A further important aspect of interactive models should be noted. Although the three stages of the McClelland and Rumelhart model are distinct and occur in sequence, processing of information at one level does not have to be completed before processing at the next level begins. Instead, as soon as activation starts to build up at one level, it is transmitted to the next. Because of the additional feature of reverse, "top-down" flow of activation, higher levels can interact with and influence lower levels. The simulation thus avoids many of the unwanted features of earlier linear-stage models in cognitive psychology, at the same time providing a model of the way in which stored knowledge of the world (in this case, knowledge of the spellings of familiar words) can interact with incoming stimulus information to determine what is actually perceived.

The interactive activation model has been the subject of considerable debate. One of the main criticisms was of its reliance on position-specific letter codes which we discussed earlier in the chapter. However, there have been other criticisms. For example, one of the rationales for feedback of activation from higher to lower levels was that it helped give a detailed account of the word superiority effect. However, Massaro (1988) has argued that the assumption of top-down feedback leads to predictions that are not supported by other data from experiments on word recognition. Brown (1987) also questions the need for top-down feedback and he describes a model which reproduces a number of established effects on word identification and naming without recourse to feedback. Whether feedback is required in the model will depend upon whether or not effects can be found which cannot be explained in any other way.

ROUTES FROM PRINT TO MEANING AND SOUND

If we return for a moment to the scenario with which we opened this chapter, it is easy to imagine that as you read the note, you are aware that you can hear its words in your head. Indeed, you may have the experience of hearing in your head the words of the present sentences as you read them. Since research on reading began, there has been considerable speculation about the role of the sounds of words in both learning to read and reading fluently. While reading silently to ourselves, many of us feel that we "hear" the sounds of the words in our heads and the obvious assumption is that these sounds are somehow necessary or at least helpful to us as a reader. In part, this led to the view that reading was parasitic upon speech — that is, reading made use of existing linguistic abilities such as those involved in speech perception and recognition. However, this still leaves unspecified the precise role of sound in fluent reading. One possibility would be that we can only access the meanings of words via their sounds. Another view might be that sound is not needed to access meanings at all, but it is needed to maintain some record of what has already been read (Baddeley, 1979). However, how we access word meanings and when we convert written forms to sound forms cannot be reliably determined by our introspections and so has given rise to a large number of experiments aimed at answering these deceptively simple questions.

The Direct Access Route to Meaning

In direct access to meaning, the output of abstract letter identity (ALI) units feeds into units for recognising words. For example, activation in the units for y a c h t would feed into the word recognition unit for *yacht*. One detailed proposal for such a scheme was McClelland and Rumelhart's (1981) model discussed earlier. The activity in the word units is then thought to activate the word's meaning. The direct route can be represented as follows:

Written	IDENTIFY	IDENTIFY	ACCESS	ACCESS
word →	LETTERS →	WORD →	MEANING →	PRONUNCIATION

The Phonic Mediation Route to Meaning

The process of converting letters or letter clusters to sounds and then using these sounds to access meaning is often referred to as *phonic mediation*. We may represent the phonic mediation route as follows:

Written	IDENTIFY	CONVERT	IDENTIFY	ACCESS
word →	LETTERS →	LETTER →	SPOKEN FORM →	MEANING
		STRINGS TO		
		SOUNDS		

Few people have doubted that people can convert letter strings to sound in order to understand them. For, example take the sentence: *Wunss uppon a tyme thear wur thrie beirs hoo livd inn a hows onn the ej ov a phorrest*. To be able to read and understand this requires the reader to convert an unfamiliar visual form to a sound-based representation. If the sound-based representation then matches a word whose sound-form we can recognise, we can use this new code to access the word's meaning. Quite often a word whose written form is unfamiliar will be one that the reader has heard before and of which he or she knows the meaning. Consequently, the phonic route may be used for words unfamiliar in their written form. The main point then is not whether we can convert letters to a sound form to recognise words, but whether we typically do so when reading familiar words.

Suppose that phonic mediation were necessary for accessing the meaning of words, what might this imply for readers of English? English is a language with a large number of words whose pronunciation cannot be derived from their spelling in a straightforward way and these are known as irregular or exception words (examples are YACHT, CHOIR, COLONEL). Conversely, there are many more words whose pronunciation is regular (CRAFT, CHEEK). Several theories of how written forms are converted to sound forms have proposed that for regular words rules are used to produce the sound form. However, for many irregular words it is hard to see what the rule might be. For example, what rule could capture the relationship between OLO and its pronunciation as "er" in COLONEL while not conflicting with other rules about how to pronounce OLO (as in POLO, COLON)? Furthermore, how can a rule-based system ensure that words which are spelled differently but pronounced the same (known as homophones), such as PIECE and PEACE, receive the correct interpretation? These kinds of difficulties have often been cited as arguments that one could not read English using only a phonic route, and that such a route would need to exist alongside the direct semantic route described above.

Other evidence on how we read words comes from people who have unfortunately suffered brain damage and have subsequently developed difficulties with reading where prior to the injury there was no indication of them having had such a difficulty, something known as *acquired dyslexia*. Acquired dyslexia takes many different forms and one of these is known as *acquired phonological dyslexia* (Funnell, 1983). Funnell describes a patient, known as W.B., who was able to read aloud correctly only 1 of 30 nonwords, all of which were either four or five letters long (examples are *cobe, nust, bleam, tode*). However, when asked to read words, W.B. was able to read aloud correctly 75 of the first 80 words on a graded reading test. Funnell (1983) argues that this pattern of reading performance is consistent with the idea that W.B. has lost the ability to assemble the pronunciation of new or unfamiliar words via a phonic mediation route but could still read words he knew before suffering brain damage by using the direct route to meaning described above.

The contrasting pattern to phonological dyslexia is loss of the direct semantic route with preservation of phonic mediation, something which is known as *surface dyslexia* (Patterson, Marshall, & Coltheart, 1985). Although such patients often retain a limited "sight vocabulary", many words that were formerly recognised directly from their visual appearance now appear unfamiliar. On the two-route model proposed so far, such people are then forced to attempt to read words by phonic mediation. As has already been argued, this can be successful if the word they are attempting to read has a regular spelling–sound correspondence (e.g. *pistol* or *boat*), but words with irregular correspondences are likely to be mispronounced and hence not understood. Although the pattern of evidence on surface dyslexia is not always clear-cut, there is a recurrent tendency to find irregular words far more difficult to read and understand which is consistent with someone who has to rely on the phonic mediation route.

Despite the objections to relying solely on phonic mediation to access word meanings, some recent work has suggested that normally as we read words we may, in fact, be using their sounds in accessing meanings. Van Orden (1987) gave people a categorisation task in which they had to decide whether a particular instance was a member of a category. For example, one might see the category label FLOWER and then a word that could either be a category member (ROSE) or not (ROCK). On some trials, subjects saw a word which was not a category member but which sounded like one, (e.g. ROWS), something which we will call the *pseudomember* condition. What van Orden found was that in the pseudomember condition, subjects incorrectly responded "yes" 25% of the time. However, non-members such as ROBS resulted in such errors on only 8% of occasions. One could argue that this different error rate arose because although the meaning of ROWS was accessed directly, this meaning then automatically accessed the sound form and so resulted in confusion making errors more likely (Pollatsek & Rayner, 1989). However, in a further experiment, van Orden, Johnston and Hale (1988) found similar results when using nonwords — that is, people were particularly prone to respond YES when asked if SUTE was an instance of the category CLOTHING. According to van Orden et al., such a finding cannot be explained by a model where the direct semantic route is the normal route because nonwords such as SUTE do not have word recognition units and so cannot be read for meaning via the visual word recognition units that are an essential part of the direct route.

Van Orden, Pennington and Stone (1990) also argue that while there is good evidence for phonic mediation, the evidence for a direct semantic route is weak. For example, while the homophones PIECE and PEACE cannot be distinguished by sound alone, this does not mean that sound is not involved in accessing their meanings but just that a phonic mediation procedure must be supplemented by some kind of spelling check or verification procedure. When it comes to phonological dyslexia, van Orden et al. point out that there have been very few cases as pure as that of W.B. described above. They suggest that what one might be seeing in such cases of acquired phonological dyslexia are adult developmental phonological dyslexics: in effect, people who had had a mild reading problem prior to the brain injury but the deficit was only noticed subsequently. Such a form of developmental dyslexia is very rare and so one would not expect many such cases among brain-damaged patients.

We are now in a position where there are conflicting claims over whether phonic mediation is a form of processing upon which readers of English normally rely in their everyday reading. One possible resolution of this conflict is that both direct and phonically mediated routes are available, but the reliance placed on the output from the two routes is highly sensitive to context. Apart from the demonstration above which used a rewritten opening to a children's story (*Wunss uppon a tyme* . . .), there is experimental evidence for this ability to place different reliance on the two routes. Monsell et al. (1992) compared times to read aloud irregular words when presented in lists which contained only irregular words (pure lists) with times to read them when presented in lists containing both nonwords and irregular words (mixed lists). They found that reading times were much faster in the pure lists than in the mixed lists. Monsell et al. concluded that this was because the readers could reduce the reliance placed on output from the phonic route when only exception words were expected. On such an account, in the experiments described by van Orden et al. (1988), a crucial factor may be the proportion of nonwords that when converted to sound form a real word. Baluch and Besner (1991) also showed that when reading Persian, the presence or absence of nonwords in a reading task affected whether reading is primarily via a phonic route or primarily direct. It may be that in everyday reading, different emphasis on the different routes is largely a matter of reading skill: skilled readers usually rely upon the direct semantic route, but when unfamiliar words or nonwords are encountered readers switch to the phonic route (Ellis, 1984). It is probably fair to say that currently most researchers support the idea of at least two routes to meaning — a direct route and a phonic route — but the work of van Orden and others suggests that the phonic mediation debate is far from over (Coltheart, Avons, Masterson, & Laxon, 1991).

Reading Aloud

On balance, it would appear that we have two routes for accessing the meaning of a written word: a direct visual route via meaning and a phonically mediated one. Obviously, these two routes can also be used as routes to reading aloud provided that the processes linking word meanings to the speech production system are intact. However, there is evidence, again from acquired dyslexia, suggesting that there may be a third means of reading words aloud.

Coslett (1991) describes the case of a woman, W.T., who had suffered damage to the left temporal lobe of her brain. Following this damage, W.T. read aloud regular and irregular words with a good degree of accuracy. However, when asked to read nonwords, W.T. read only 25% correctly. This pattern of performance is very similar to that of W.B. described by Funnell (1983) and discussed above. The implication is again that W.T. cannot read using the phonic route. On the model discussed so far, then, W.T. should have to read words aloud by going through semantics. However, unlike W.B., when W.T.'s understanding of words was tested, it was found to be impaired.

W.T.'s ability to understand written words was tested by presenting her with a pair of words such as REFRIGERATOR and OVEN followed by a card on which a third word, STOVE, was printed. W.T.'s task was to point to the word from the first pair which was closest in meaning to the third word. W.T. was able to do this task if the words were of high imageability, but performed at chance when they were of low imageability (imageability refers to the ease with which people can conjure up a mental picture, sound or some form of sensory experience when given the word, Paivio, 1971). The implication of this is that W.T. is no longer able to access the meanings of low imageability words. However, when asked to read words aloud, W.T. was just as good at reading low imageability words as high imageability ones. If W.T. is unable to access the meaning of low imageability words yet can read them aloud, how could she be using the direct semantic route?

W.T. seems largely unable to use the phonic route to read aloud. She also seems unable to access semantics for low imageability words and so should not be able to read them aloud via the direct semantic route. Consequently, on the model as presented so far, one would predict that W.T. should not be able to read aloud low imageability words at all, but when asked to do this she can. W.T. is not the only person to have shown this pattern of preserved reading aloud of words with impaired understanding and an inability to read nonwords (Lytton & Brust, 1989; Schwartz, Saffran & Marin, 1980).

The proposed solution to the conundrum presented by dyslexics with this pattern of abilities is that there is a third route in reading where the units for recognising a word are linked directly to their corresponding pronunciations. According to this idea, one does not assemble the sound of a word by taking letters and converting them to sound by rules, nor does one read aloud via meaning. It is more as though there is a pointer from the unit for recognising a word to its pronunciation — a one-to-one linking of word recognition units and their pronunciations. This whole word route to reading aloud can be represented as below:

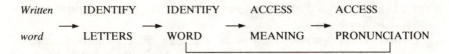

Written	IDENTIFY	IDENTIFY	ACCESS	ACCESS
word	LETTERS	WORD	MEANING	PRONUNCIATION

The Process of Converting Written Forms to Sound Forms

We have already discussed some evidence that is consistent with a distinction between two routes to pronunciation, both of which do not require going through meaning: a phonic mediation route operating on grapheme–phoneme conversion rules and a route with direct, one-to-one links from visual word recognition units to pronunciations. These in turn imply two different ways of converting written forms to sound forms. On the phonic route, the conversion process is typically envisaged as a set of rules that operate on letters or letter clusters, whereas the direct, one-to-one route does not require this kind of conversion rule. However, a moment's thought reveals that these routes are not so different. For both routes, one could express the conversion process as something like "If X is activated pronounce it as Y", the only difference between the routes being what counts as X (letters or a whole word) and what counts as Y (phonemes or a whole word). Perhaps what the two "routes" represent are two ends of a continuum, with at one end the most minute of conversions, a single letter to a single phoneme, and at the other a more gross conversion of a whole word to its pronunciation. In between these two extremes, there may be other conversion processes operating on letter clusters and various forms of syllable. Note that, for English, the idea of explicit rules converting letters or letter clusters to a sound does run into problems, as so few letters are pronounced in the same way on all occasions. Nevertheless, there are schemes that propose that most letter sequences have a regular pronunciation which can be described by rule. For example, take GAVE and HAVE. Of this pair, GAVE is considered regular because the vowel sound has been lengthened by the final E, which is the typical pattern in such words (as further illustration of this, try removing the E from GAVE and from HAVE to produce the two nonwords GAV and HAV — for the former the pronunciation has changed, whereas for the latter it is unaltered).

One source of evidence which is compatible with the idea of multiple levels of conversion of written forms to sound forms is studies of the effects of consistency on reading time. Several experiments have shown that the time to read a nonword is influenced by how consistent the pronunciation is of visually similar words (Glushko, 1979). As we have already illustrated, the letter sequence -AVE is inconsistently pronounced in English (HAVE, RAVE, GAVE). However, other letter sequences, such as -INK, are pronounced in a consistent way (BLINK, STINK, MINK, RINK, WINK). Consistency is not the same as regularity, so that there are words whose pronunciation is regular but inconsistent (for example, PINK is regular and consistent but WAVE is regular and inconsistent). Glushko (1979) found that nonwords with consistent neighbouring words, such as BINK, were named more quickly than nonwords with inconsistent neighbours, such as MAVE. A similar effect has been found when comparing regular consistent words, PINK, with regular inconsistent words, MINT (though the strength of this effect varies according to a number of factors; Stanhope & Parkin, 1987). If phonic mediation is achieved by rules that reflect regularity and so assign the most regular pronunciation to a string, it is hard to see why consistency should have any effect.

An alternative to the rule-based explanation that does take account of consistency proposes that when using the phonic route for novel items, a pronunciation can be assembled by using analogies: there is a comparison of the visual form of the incoming sequence to existing sequences. The degree of visual similarity between the input and the stored information determines what pronunciation is selected; where similar items are consistently pronounced, there is no conflict, but inconsistency requires more time for the pronunciation to be derived. The process of analogy suggests that rules are not involved in producing sound forms and that all the phonic conversion processes could occur via one route — a route that relies on deriving a sound form through analogy between the input sequence and existing knowledge of the pronunciation of written forms. In the next section, we look at a computer model that does just this. It derives the pronunciations of words on the basis of similarities to other words rather than by using some abstract rule. We describe the model in detail because, besides addressing an important issue in cognitive models of reading, it also exemplifies an increasingly influential approach to modelling cognition known as *connectionism*.

COMPUTER MODELS, CONNECTIONISM AND A MODEL OF READING ALOUD

The growing importance of connectionism in cognitive psychology means that before we get on to the connectionist model of word recognition and naming, it is worth spending a little time outlining some of the attractions of computer models and connectionism (connectionism is very closely related to parallel distributed processing and neural network modelling and sometimes the terms are used interchangeably).

Computer Modelling and Cognitive Psychology

In Chapter 1, we described models that were implemented on computers, such as Marr's work on vision. We also touched on some of the reasons why a cognitive psychologist might be interested in developing computational models, but it is worth spending a little more time reflecting on why computers might help us in our understanding of cognition. An extreme position on this issue would be that the essence of the intelligent behaviour exhibited by people and (more controversially) by computers has the same source — that is, computers and people are in some important sense the same kind of thing (Newell, Shaw, & Simon, 1958; Pylyshyn, 1984). However, one need not go this far to see considerable advantages in using computers to model cognition.

Building a computer program can be a means of expressing a theory about how people perform a particular task. Creating a model in this way forces the researcher to specify his or her theory in sufficient detail for a program to work. Frequently, this requirement reveals gaps in the existing theory. There is a danger that such gaps are covered over using assumptions about cognitive processes that are not justified. Equally, however, in this way one may become aware of previously unseen deficiencies in a theory. A second point is that if one can get a computer to behave in the same way as people do on a task, then one has achieved something which a paper and pencil model simply cannot do. In this sense, producing a computer model is one way of testing the plausibility of a theory. If the model is to be a credible one, it should be able to reproduce a number of existing findings and, in doing so, help us understand them more fully. One example of this described earlier in the chapter was the way in which McClelland and Rumelhart's model of word recognition mimicked the word superiority effect. Of course, showing that a model can work in a certain way is not the same thing as showing that the same processes are operating in people's heads, but such models do at least provide a starting point for debate and experimentation. A third advantage is that many theories of cognitive processes are so complex that it is hard to know exactly what predictions they make in certain circumstances. By building a computer model of the process, one can see how the model behaves in such circumstances and the outcome is then a prediction about how people should behave in similar circumstances. McClelland and Rumelhart's word recognition model described earlier made several such predictions which were then confirmed by experiment (Rumelhart & McClelland, 1982). Once implemented, computer models can sometimes offer explanations of effects which had previously remained inexplicable.

Recently, a form of computer modelling known as connectionism has become particularly influential in cognitive psychology. It has been greeted with such a wave of enthusiasm and has stimulated so much work that some have referred to it as creating a revolution in cognitive science. In the next section, we give a brief description of the essential characteristics of connectionism before describing how it has been applied to modelling the conversion of letter strings to sounds.

The Basics of Connectionism

Unlike many approaches to cognition, connectionist approaches take the nature of the brain to be an important factor when constructing cognitive models. This leads to a style of modelling called brain style computation (Rumelhart, 1989). The idea is most clearly reflected in the two main components of a connectionist system: *units* and *links*. Units are very simple processing elements: all they do is take on a certain level of activation. Links or connections are rather like wires running between units: they offer a means of transmitting activation between units. Links can differ in the efficiency with which they transmit activation and this efficiency is referred to as the *weight* of a connection. For example, if two units are connected by a link with a large weight, this means that the activation level of one unit has a big effect on the activation level of the other. However, if the same two units were connected by a link with a small weight, then the effect of one unit's activation on the other would be much smaller. Links are often bidirectional, so that activation can be passed in either direction. Links may be *excitatory* or *inhibitory* and, depending on which type of link connects them, the activation of one unit might tend to increase or decrease the activation of another unit. One can see how the ideas of units, levels of activation and the transmission of activation have some parallels with the behaviour of neurons in the brain. Although this analogy should not be taken too literally, it is clear that the spirit of connectionist models owes much to what we know of how the brain works.

In many connectionist models, it is useful to distinguish three types of unit: *input units*, *hidden units* and *output units*. The terms really refer to the function of units in the system and not to differences in performance characteristics. Consequently, activation over the input units corresponds to the input to the system and this might be analogous to a stimulus from the external world or, more likely, activation passed to this part of the brain from other networks. Activation over the output units is the network's response to the input — its answer if you like. So, for example, the input might represent a string of letters forming a word and the output might represent a spoken version of that word. In between these two sets of units it is often necessary to have a layer of hidden units. This term is a little confusing because in some sense all of the units are "hidden" (as they correspond to processes within the brain), yet in another sense they are not "hidden" at all (as the modeller can observe the changes in activation levels of all the units). What distinguishes them from input and output units is not their visibility but the fact that their role in the system is to mediate between the input and output patterns with which the model is most concerned. This is not to say that hidden units are not important. On the contrary, such units are vital if many processes are to be modelled at all by connectionism (Rumelhart, Hinton, & Williams, 1986).

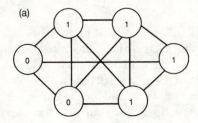

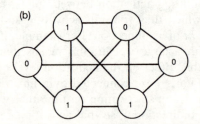

FIG. 2.10 A set of units showing how different patterns of activation and thus different representations can be distributed across the same set of units. (a) A set of units showing connections between units and levels of activation of each unit. This pattern of activation could represent "item x". (b) The same set of units as in (a), but with a different pattern of activation. This pattern could represent "item y".

The above description of the basic components of a connectionist model may remind you of the McClelland and Rumelhart's (1981) interactive activation model of word recognition described earlier in the chapter. The interactive activation model is a form of connectionist model in which each unit in the network of units is ascribed a role so that, for example, there is a unit which represents the letter P and one which represents the word form of POST. Such a model is called a localist model: there is a clear relationship between the activation of a particular unit and some concept in the theory behind the model. In other connectionist models, a particular theoretical concept corresponds to the pattern of activity of a number of units, that is, no single unit would correspond to the letter P. These kinds of connectionist models are called *distributed models* (Hinton, McClelland, & Rumelhart, 1986). Figure 2.10 shows how in a distributed model different patterns of activity over the same set of units could encode different entities.

Connectionist models have many strengths, but one of the most appealing is that they are able to learn. An important question for any cognitive model is how the representations and processes it contains were acquired — in the absence of a plausible answer, then, the model provides a less persuasive account. Despite this, learning has received relatively little attention in cognitive psychology and connectionism has been of considerable help in redressing this imbalance. In a connectionist model, learning occurs by adjusting the weights of connections. The result of this is that the effect of one unit upon another has been changed so that the same input will produce a different output. If one imagines this scaled up to networks where there are hundreds of interconnected units, one can see that there is potential for the behaviour of units in a net to alter dramatically depending on the extent of changes to the weights of the connections. This also highlights why it is often said that the knowledge in a connectionist model is in the connections, something which is also said of the brain itself (Rumelhart & McClelland, 1986).

If changes in connection weights are a central feature of connectionist models, how are such changes in weights achieved? There are two basic ways of training a connectionist model: *supervised learning* and *unsupervised learning*. Supervised learning approximates to the following kind of situation. Suppose you are learning a new language and you encounter a new written word: *kluncl*. You attempt to pronounce it aloud but your attempt is imperfect, and a person who is fluent in the language provides an example of how it should be pronounced. In this situation, you are producing a response which is then compared to what the correct response should have been, so that you are being guided in your learning. Supervised learning in a network takes a similar form. A pattern of activation is invoked over the input units and spreads via links and any hidden units to the output units. This output is the system's response and in the early stages of learning it is likely to be incorrect. One way to measure the amount of error in this response is to compare it to what that response should have been. How can the model know what the response should have been? In most cases, the researcher specifies what the response should be. While this may sound like a bit of a cheat, it is supposed to be akin to those many occasions where when learning to speak or read, for example, a second person provides the learner with the correct response against which the learner's effort can be compared. The discrepancy between the actual response and the desired response is calculated and is used to alter the weight of the various connections so that next time the same input is presented, the system is more likely to produce the correct output. For example, the output of one unit might be 0 when it should be 1. To correct this error, all the excitatory inputs to that unit which are connected to units earlier in this system could be more heavily weighted.

This is a very crude example of supervised learning and the numerical equations (called *learning algorithms*) that calculate which weights need to be changed and by how much are extremely sophisticated. Even more sophisticated are networks which learn without supervision. Here the network learns ways of organising the inputs together, but the mechanisms which allow nets to do this involve procedures beyond the scope of the present account (Kohonen, 1984).

We have briefly introduced some of the key notions of connectionism and we are now in a position to see how such ideas have been applied to one of the key issues in reading — how does one derive the sound form of a word from its written form?

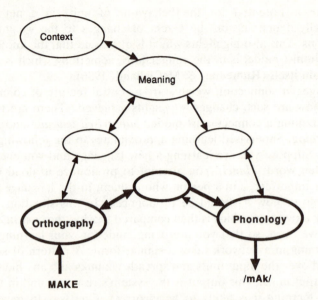

FIG. 2.11 Seidenberg and McClelland's (1989) model of word recognition and naming with implemented pools and connections shown in **bold** type. The ovals represent pools of units, and the arrows show connections between pools of units. Reproduced with permission.

A Connectionist Model of Word Recognition and Reading Aloud

Seidenberg and McClelland (1989) have produced a connectionist model of word recognition and naming which can reproduce a wide range of findings both from experiments on skilled readers and studies of people with acquired dyslexia (Patterson, Seidenberg, & McClelland, 1989). The basic structure of the model is shown in Fig. 2.11. Note that the parts in **bold** represent the implemented model. As it stands, this model is a dual-route model with access to word meanings being possible through a direct route and via phonology. However, the implemented part of the model is primarily concerned with how to produce a phonological form of a written word and our discussion will focus on this aspect.

In the implemented model, there are three pools of units: a set of inputs for coding the written (orthographic) form of the words, a set of hidden units, and a set of output units for coding the sound (phonological) forms of the words. The orthographic and hidden units are connected by bidirectional links (so that the activation patterns in each set of units influences activation patterns in the other set). However, in the implemented version, the links between the hidden units and the phonological units are unidirectional, with activation going only from the hidden units to the phonological units but not vice versa (though the model described by Seidenberg and McClelland allows for such links, they are not present in the implemented version of it; see Fig. 2.11).

The written form of a single word is represented by a pattern of activity distributed over a number of input units. Likewise, the sound form of a word is represented by a pattern of activity distributed over the phonological units. Initially, the weights between sets of units are given a random value between +0.5 and −0.5. This means that initially any written input will produce an unrelated sound form: the system knows nothing about the relationship between written and spoken forms. Learning then occurs by presenting an input pattern distributed over the orthographic units. Activation then spreads forward to the hidden units. From the hidden units, activation passes back to the orthographic units and forward to the phonological output units. The level of activation across the output units is then compared with what the pattern of activity should be if the network had produced the correct pronunciation for that input. The difference between the two is calculated and the resulting discrepancy is used to adjust the weights of all the links in the network using a procedure known as *back-propagation* (Rumelhart et al., 1986). In effect, this learning algorithm is trying to find a set of weights which will allow the network to pronounce all the words correctly. Such a process is gradual and requires a large number of learning trials when there are a large number of words.

The model was trained on 2897 words three or more letters long. All of the words were monosyllabic and appeared in an existing corpus of word frequencies in American English. To make their testing of the model more comprehensive, Seidenberg and McClelland also tested it on some words which did not appear in the corpus, such as DOTS. The number of times a word was presented to the network for learning was a probabilistic function of that word's frequency in the written language, so common words like THE, AND and TIME were frequently presented, whereas less common words such as BIN, LIP and CODE were presented relatively infrequently. In total, the network experienced 150,000 learning trials.

After training, Seidenberg and McClelland were in a position to test the model's performance to see if it could reproduce some existing effects in the word recognition literature. There is not room here to review all of the tests of the model, so we will focus on two that relate to issues raised earlier in the chapter — the effect of a word's regularity and the network's performance after being damaged.

A number of studies have shown that fluent readers are slower to name low-frequency irregular words than low-frequency regular words, but that for high-frequency words regularity has little or no effect (Taraban & McClelland, 1987). To test whether or not the model behaved in the same way, Seidenberg and McClelland took the same words used by Taraban and McClelland (1987, experiment 1) and used these as inputs to the trained network. The measure of the network's performance was the

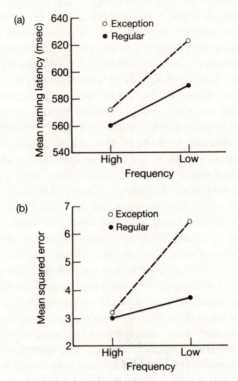

FIG. 2.12 The results of Taraban and McClelland's word naming study (a) compared with the performance of Seidenberg and McClelland's computer model (b) on exception (□) vs regular (●) words. Based on Taraban and McClelland (1987) and Seidenberg and McClelland (1989).

accuracy of the phonological form produced (the assumption being that the more accurate this representation, the more efficient the remaining cognitive processes in speech production would be). The pattern of results for the model and the observed data from the experiment were remarkably similar (see Fig. 2.12).

Why is there only a regularity effect with low-frequency words but little or no effect with high-frequency words? Looking at the performance of the model, Seidenberg and McClelland (1989) concluded that the model had reached the best level of performance it could on the high-frequency words, whether they were regular or irregular. However, for low-frequency words, there were insufficient learning trials for the model to reach its best level of performance. Once matched for frequency, one would expect better performance on regular words, as typically these have a lot of similar neighbours and so the same connections are reinforced over and over again. For example, the regular word HINT has several words with the same spelling and pronunciation pattern (MINT, TINT, LINT), so the correct pronunciation of HINT benefits from learning trials involving these neighbours. The irregular word PINT, despite its popularity in student conversations, is a low-frequency written word which has few words sharing the same letter-to-sound correspondences and so does not benefit from the influence of neighbours on the pattern of the weights.

You may have noticed that the explanation in the above paragraph suggests that with enough practice the model should reach a level of performance where even for low-frequency words there is no difference between regular and irregular forms. In a sense, the model is really like a single skilled reader (albeit an idealised "average" one) whose performance is being compared with results obtained from groups of people doing an experiment. It may be that if one subdivides the group of readers, one would find readers who do not show a regularity effect. Seidenberg (1985) did just this and found that for the most skilled readers in his experiment (as measured by reading speed), there was no regularity effect even on low-frequency words. In the model, the suggestion is that it too could show no regularity effect if it received sufficient training on the low-frequency items. One snag with such an explanation is that differences in skill are being explained by frequency of exposure alone, and this is unlikely to be a sufficient account of variation in people's reading skill.

So far, we have seen that the model behaves like a skilled reader. As we have discussed earlier in this chapter, another source of evidence about how we read comes from people who have suffered brain damage and found that their ability to read is impaired, something known as acquired dyslexia (Coltheart, Patterson, & Marshall, 1980). In a similar way, if the present model is a plausible one, then it should be possible to see how its reading abilities are altered by damaging it.

In a number of simulations, Patterson et al. (1989) showed that after training the model, if units and connections were made inoperative, they could get the model to behave rather like an acquired dyslexic. Patterson et al. were most interested in showing that the computer model showed some of the characteristics of surface dyslexia. One of the key features of surface dyslexia is that the dyslexic is able to read aloud regular words and nonwords with far greater accuracy than irregular words (Bub, Cancelliere, & Kertesz, 1985; Marshall & Newcombe, 1973). Also, many of the surface dyslexic's errors on irregular words are regularisations such as reading ISLAND as *izland*.

Patterson et al. inflicted damage on the model at various points and to varying degrees. Some of the most interesting data came when 60% of the hidden units were made inoperative (exactly which of the hidden units were damaged was determined by chance). When this happened, the model behaved very much like a surface dyslexic: for 24% of irregular words it produced a regularisation error, whereas for regular words it only preferred an alternative pronunciation on 7.5% of occasions. One should not take these figures too literally because, as we noted earlier, the model is rather like an idealised individual reader and so one should not expect its performance to mimic perfectly the performance of any one surface dyslexic because of differences in reading experiences. However, the general bias towards regularisation of irregular words, which is the key feature of surface dyslexia, is impressive.

Although performance did decline as a consequence of damage, even when 60% of hidden units were removed the model still produced relatively few errors. This is one of the great advantages of distributed representations: if knowledge about how to pronounce a word is not located in a single unit or a single link, then the system is far less vulnerable to damage. When damage does occur, the system is often still able to perform a task albeit at a lower level of accuracy — something known as *graceful degradation*. It is frequently argued that a similar style of impairment is the norm when brain damage occurs (though this does not go so far as to say that in very severe brain damage there will not be complete loss of some abilities).

In conclusion, Seidenberg and McClelland's model has provided an impressive series of simulations of results from experiments on skilled adult readers and studies of acquired surface dyslexics. To the extent that it is consistent with the existing data, the model can be viewed as a plausible candidate explanation. However, you might object that the model offers nothing new, that we already had theories and models of word recognition which could explain the data. This is a fair point, but it overlooks a number of things. First, connectionism brings with it a number of general advantages that models of that style "inherit". For example, it offers accounts of learning and graceful degradation which were not present in most earlier accounts. Second, the model does propose something new: there is no need for discrete word recognition units in reading aloud. That is, unlike the models proposed earlier in this chapter, there is no suggestion that for each word we know there is a single, separate recognition unit whose "job" is to recognise a particular word and only that word. This is clearly different from previous accounts, and while controversial (Besner, Twilley, McCann, & Seergobin, 1990) it shows how implementing a model can alter one's conception of how something works. Third, the model shows that it is not necessary to have a phonic mediation procedure based on rules to account for surface dyslexia. Seidenberg and McClelland's model is proposing that instead of two routes for retrieving the sound of a written word (the phonic route and one-to-one links from word recognition units to sound forms), there is just one conversion mechanism, a possibility discussed earlier in this chapter.

SUMMARY

Reading is an acquired skill which involves perceptual, linguistic and general cognitive processes. As such, it is an obvious target for psychological investigation. The reading of text requires a well coordinated pattern of eye movements containing fixations (moments when the eyes are stationary and during which visual information is taken in) and saccades (rapid eye movements between fixations). At each fixation, visual information is registered from within an area known as the "perceptual span". In English readers, this span is biased to the right of the fixation point, though this bias can be changed according to one's reading experiences. Words that are not being fixated upon but which fall within the perceptual span are read more quickly when eventually fixated upon than if they did not appear within the span.

Letter recognition has been much studied as an example of skilled pattern recognition. "Template"- and "feature"-based models have been proposed, but it has not yet been established that either of these can cope adequately with the variability of letter shapes or with the influence of context on letter identification.

There is evidence that the different forms a letter may take converge upon "abstract letter identities" prior to actual word recognition. McClelland and Rumelhart (1981) have developed a computer simulation of word recognition which proposes that letter and word recognition processes interact, and show that their model provides an explanation of various phenomena, including letter, word and nonword recognition.

Cognitive psychologists have proposed several routines for accessing word meanings from print. According to the dual-route hypothesis, familiar words are typically identified directly from their visual form. On this hypothesis, unfamiliar words may be understood by converting the written form to a sound form and that sound form recognised if familiar. However, there is now some evidence to suggest that all words may be converted to a sound form before their meaning is accessed. Studies of acquired dyslexics suggest a third route to reading aloud, whereby recognition of a word's written form links directly to its spoken form. An alternative view is that instead of two routes to sound that bypass meaning, there is in fact a whole set of processes for conversion, and that what one is seeing in evidence for the two routes is just the opposite extreme of these different types of process.

A class of computer models known as connectionist models has re-emerged in recent years. The workings of these models are intended to be analogous to the workings of the brain and knowledge is distributed. From apparently simple basic components, models of complex cognitive processes can be built. Seidenberg and McClelland (1989) have developed a connectionist model of word recognition and naming. The model is able to learn pronunciations and to mimic a range of experimental phenomena. When damaged, the model behaves in a way akin to surface dyslexics. The model presents a new account of word recognition which does not rely on word recognition units and gives an account of converting words to sound which involves just a single route. The model illustrates the potential of the connectionist approach for those interested in understanding the processes of word recognition in reading.

In this chapter, we have covered a lot of ground. In part, this is due to the richness of the problems posed when one asks: "How do we read?" The question allows for many different approaches: experimentation on skilled readers, studies of people with reading difficulties and the development of computer models. We have also introduced a highly influential way of constructing computer models of cognitive processes — that is, connectionism — which will recur in many other chapters. Despite this, we have focused almost exclusively on recognition of single words: even the simplest of questions about cognitive processes turn out to be rather complicated. In Chapter 8, we go on to consider how sentences are processed and some of the processes necessary in understanding and comprehending larger chunks of language.

Aitchison (1987) gives an overview of issues around lexical access, while Quinlan (1991), *Connectionism and psychology*, gives a difficult but thorough account of how various aspects of cognition have been modelled using connectionism. Ellis (1993), *Reading, writing and dyslexia* (2nd edn), provides an excellent, clear introduction to the acquired dyslexias and their implications for models of reading.

3 Telling Sheep from Goats: Categorising Objects

Has the origin of the phrase "telling the sheep from the goats" ever puzzled you? It has a biblical flavour and it means something like "telling the believers from the unbelievers", but why sheep and goats? After all, believers and unbelievers may not look very different but sheep and goats definitely do. A sheep is covered with curly fleece, has a weak-looking face, skinny ankles, is rather plump, and may or may not have horns. A goat is thin, with straight hair, a strong face, long legs, and may or may not have horns. Both kinds of animals have legs, heads, eyes, and so on, but they share these with a great many other animals, so they are not very useful in discriminating one animal from another. The description given above relates to sheep and goats in England and in other parts of northern Europe. Yet in countries around the Mediterranean, animals grazing on a hillside cannot be classified so easily by a northern visitor. They have not got a lot of fleece, but they are not as thin as goats. Their faces don't fit either the strong goat or the weak sheep. There are flocks of them, which seems more sheep-like than goat-like. Altogether, it is not very easy to tell sheep from goats.

The tourist's classification of sheep and goats breaks down in the Mediterranean, but for the local farmer the distinction will be an important one. It may not be an easy distinction to make at a distance, so it becomes important to bring the flock together in order to distinguish sheep from goats. The example is important because it shows us that we take our systems of categorisation very much for granted; and that they depend on the situations in which they were learned, and the purposes which make them necessary. After all, if no-one made a distinction between sheep's milk and goat's milk, or sheep's meat and goat's meat, there might not be much need to tell sheep from goats. It is also important because it directs us to ways in which we might extend our classification in order to apply it to things we have not met before. Telling sheep from goats is an example of categorisation. However, this chapter is more generally about how we organise our knowledge.

Putting things into groups is one of the most basic ways to organise what you know. If you cannot categorise, you have to meet each object or event in the environment as a new thing, so you would have to keep on learning how to deal with it. If you learn that a berry of one particular shade of red makes you sick when you eat it, you could subsequently avoid all berries, but that means that you can generalise to small round things regardless of their colour. To avoid all red berries means that you have to lump together the many hundreds of shades of red which the human eye is capable of discriminating. So either you create a category of small round things, or you create a category of small round red things, or you go further and add other features of the bush, the situation, and so on. Our experience of relevant instances is necessarily limited and so, usually, is our ability to analyse all the factors involved. When we categorise we are making up our minds about the meaning of things or how to behave towards them. In general, "categorising serves to cut down the diversity of objects and events that must be dealt with uniquely by an organism of limited capacities" (Bruner, Goodnow, & Austin, 1956, p. 235).

The range of things that we can classify is not limited to physical objects with some similar perceptual characteristics. When we try to identify a famous face we often attach a label like "politician" or "TV actor" to it before we can retrieve the name; these are groups of people whose *behaviour* provides the basis for the classification, although their appearance may help a little. We can also make more abstract classifications like "believer" and "unbeliever" which make appearance a poor indicator, and even cast doubts on behaviour as the basis for identification. We classify and categorise everything, from animals to emotions and from the concrete to the abstract. Indeed, we have to think of our knowledge of the world and our abilities to form categories as being tightly bound together.

The process of abstraction is, however, the key activity underlying a concept. "Abstraction" can imply many things. The isolation of a subset of features most relevant to the concept is one aspect of abstraction, as in our attempts to say in what ways sheep and goats are alike and different. The tolerance of a certain amount of variability in the way features are expressed is another aspect. In Chapters 1 and 2, we saw examples of our ability to tolerate variability in stimuli in the recognition of objects and words. In general, the process of abstraction identifies something beyond the immediate and the particular, allowing us to match up things and to retrieve things previously experienced that may bear upon the current experience. So the study of concepts is but one way of probing into the structure of our knowledge. In this chapter, we look at categorising and concepts as one way of studying the question, "How are all the things we know organised in our heads?" Later chapters will develop further answers to the same question.

EARLY STUDIES IN CONCEPT IDENTIFICATION

Categorising results in concepts, that is, in abstract knowledge that is not related to individual instances. To know something about "chair" or "fear" does not necessarily mean remembering a particular chair or a particular fear. Early studies of how such abstract concepts developed tended to involve requiring children or adults to learn which objects went into which category in situations in which there was no previous experience of the links between the features which the experimenter was using to define category membership.

The Russian psychologist Vygotsky (1934/1962), who was interested in the relationship between thought and language, used a set of 22 blocks which differed in colour, shape, height and area. They were divided into four groups on the basis of height and area, and given nonsense names, so that *lag* meant tall and large, *bik* meant tall and small, *mur* meant short and large, and *cev* meant short and small. When young children are shown one block and given its name and then asked to pick others which have the same name, they first produce unorganised heaps or select the ones closest in space to the one they were shown. They then move to what Vygotsky called "complexes" — they put all the red things together, or they chain items so that when given a big red circle they next choose more red things, but follow a red triangle with a blue triangle, and so on. The complex is not a concept because it is tied to the single elements of the items, and rising above the elements requires subjects to recognise that just two of the features must be summed while the others must be ignored. This understanding, that some features are relevant and some are not, is an important step in developing abstractions which form concepts.

Associationism

The early American research on concept learning grew out of association models for stimulus–response learning. These models suggested that each time an example of a category was encountered, the links between the category and all the features of that example were strengthened. The first experimental study of this process was carried out by Hull (1920). He asked his subjects to learn to say distinct sounds, such as "li" and "ta" to each of a set of 12 Chinese characters. He then switched to a second set of characters and taught them to say the same sounds to them. Within both sets were features common to both of the characters which went with the same sound, although the subjects were never told this. The subjects were trained to produce the sound to more and more sets of 12, each containing the same crucial feature, and eventually they were often able to guess the correct response to a new Chinese character without being taught it (see Fig. 3.1). Hull interpreted this to mean that there was a steady strengthening between a sound (or name) and the features which were common to each character which went with it, and this led to production of the correct name when a new character was presented. Although the subjects could

FIG. 3.1 Stimuli used by Hull (1920). Six of the Chinese radicals that Hull used are shown here. First, the subject was shown a Chinese character and asked to guess its "name" (e.g. "oo"); then the experimenter gave the correct name, and so on. Characters with the same radicals were always given the same name, so that after going through several packs of characters, the subjects improved their performances and were eventually able to name correctly characters they had never seen before.

respond correctly, they often did not know what it was that was crucial in linking a character to the sound which went with it.

Hypothesis Testing

The view that concepts are learned slowly through association of features without people really knowing what is going on, was opposed by psychologists who argued that people often make an effort to look for patterns in their experiences. This appears most readily in cases when features can be easily detected and then combined in various ways to make hypotheses about concepts. The most widely quoted research in this area was carried out by Bruner et al. (1956). They used 81 cards, each of which had a pattern made up of four dimensions (shape, colour, number of borders, number of objects), with each dimension having one of three values. So one card could have three red circles with two borders, while another had one green square with three borders, and so on. The experimenters defined concepts in three ways: concepts with single values on one dimension (e.g. red), concepts requiring single values on two dimensions (e.g. circles and two borders), and concepts which had either one value on one dimension or one value on another dimension (e.g. green or square). Subjects showed different strategies in trying to work out what the concepts were, sometimes trying to remember all the attributes of the examples of a concept or trying to form one hypothesis at a time and see if further instances fitted it, and so on. All the tasks used made a considerable demand on memory, and did seem to show different strategies for testing hypotheses about the relationships between features and concepts.

Levine (1966) used simpler materials to investigate both hypothesis testing and memory. Levine showed his subjects pairs of letters on a card. The letters differed in four ways: the letter itself (T or X), its colour (black or white), its size (large or small) and its position (left or right). The experimenter picked one of these eight possible characteristics to be the concept on a particular trial. The subjects were shown four cards, one after the other. For each card, they indicated which of the two items — the one on the left or the one on the right — was the member of the target class, and they were told whether they were correct or not. The order of one possible set of four cards is shown in Fig. 3.2. As you can see from the figure, the first card allows the subject to cut the number of hypotheses from 8 to 4. If "right–large–black–T" includes the relevant characteristic, then "left", "small," "white" and "X" are no longer possible hypotheses. After a second trial the number of possible hypotheses is cut to two and after the third trial it drops to one. If subjects could remember all the things they had rejected on each trial, then they should be able to make the correct judgement by the fourth trial. Levine then allowed subjects to continue with four more trials in which they were shown the same sort of cards, and asked to pick the items which had the relevant attribute, but

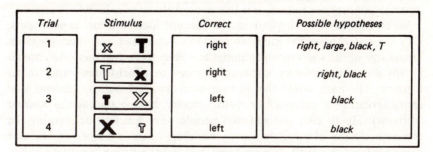

Trial	Stimulus	Correct	Possible hypotheses
1	✗ T	right	right, large, black, T
2	T ✗	right	right, black
3	T ✗	left	black
4	✗ T	left	black

FIG. 3.2 A sequence of trials using Levine's task, showing how a subject could in principle select the correct hypotheses after three trials with feedback of the correct response. Reproduced with permission from Levine (1966). © 1966 by the American Psychological Association.

this time they were not told whether they were correct or not. If subjects do have only one hypothesis left, then they should go for one attribute, say black, regardless of the shape, size or position of the letter. If they have more than one hypothesis, then they will not be consistent during these four trials without feedback. Levine found that subjects had not managed to develop a commitment to only one hypothesis at this stage, but that they tended to have about three. As there were eight possible hypotheses at the beginning, this is a reasonably good performance.

Levine's subjects must have been remembering something about the hypotheses they had rejected, because they tested fewer than the maximum number of hypotheses, even though they had not got the correct one. So suggestions that there was no memory of earlier stages (Bower & Trabasso 1964; Restle, 1962) could not be correct. It is, however, possible that hypotheses are forgotten gradually over several trials rather than on any one trial, particularly as the hypotheses are quite difficult to distinguish from one another. Hypotheses may be forgotten in some situations but not in others.

Some Limitations of Early Laboratory Studies

Levine's (1966) experiment is commonly and correctly taken to demonstrate that people can indeed form hypotheses which they test and reject. If you look at the task again, you will probably find it hard to think of anything else that subjects could do. They are being asked to use "black" as a relevant attribute when only one attribute *is* relevant, but they are not being asked to learn what "black" means, or to use the term correctly. In the experimental tasks, subjects are typically asked to guess what the experimenter is thinking. However, in real life, concepts normally require both the selection of certain features, such as stalks and petals of flowers — despite their variability in shape, size and colour — and the correct use of a name in application to somewhat novel instances, to new variations of these features. Hypothesis testing does occur in experiments and may occur in concept formation, but this is unlikely to tell the whole story.

When people form hypotheses in concept identification experiments, they do not choose the rules at random, but rather use their previous knowledge of the ways in which things are likely to go together. Heidbreder (1946) illustrated this by showing pictures to which names had to be learned. On each trial, the picture was changed but it retained one characteristic (e.g. being a face, being circular, having a particular number of items). Heidbreder showed that people were quickest at learning the concrete classes like "faces" and "buildings", were poorer at learning more abstract concepts (e.g. shapes) and worst of all when "number of things" was the feature to be abstracted. It is not easy to identify that what pictures have in common is "threeness", but it is easy to say that they are all pictures of faces, which is a much more natural way to judge pictures.

Nor do subjects choose attributes at random. Trabasso (1963) asked subjects to classify flower designs which differed on features like colour, shape, leaves and stem branchings. He found that on average only about 4 errors occurred when subjects learned a classification based on colour, whereas 19.5 errors were made when the rule was based on the angle of the leaves. That is, colour was more central for the subjects learning to classify flowers than leaf angle was. This does not mean that colour is always the most relevant attribute in deciding whether something is in a class or not. The attribute "white" is an important characteristic of milk, chalk or snow, but it occurs less readily to people who are thinking of the characteristics of sugar or baseballs (Underwood & Richardson, 1956). For some categories, colour is a dominant attribute and so acts as a major cue in a sorting task; but not so for other categories.

The line of research outlined in the preceding paragraphs concentrates on the features of objects that go together. The view implied by the studies is that all the instances of a concept share common properties and that these properties are necessary for something to belong to the category as well as sufficient to guarantee category membership. However, there is a difficulty with the idea that features are necessary and sufficient for defining a concept. Looking up the word "sheep" in a dictionary does not always help us to define it. The dictionary would list all the features of a sheep that make it a sheep. The *Concise Oxford Dictionary* defines sheep as "kinds of wild or domesticated, timid, gregarious, woolly, occasionally horned, ruminant mammal". Unfortunately, "gregarious" means "living in flocks", and "flock" is "a number of domestic animals, usually sheep, goats or geese". So, a sheep is a mammal which lives in groups like sheep do. Not surprisingly, we learn few words by looking them up in a dictionary; rather we meet them in a context that enables us to give some sense to the dictionary definition.

There are further problems with the view that features are necessary and sufficient for making decisions about category membership. One is that decades of effort by philosophers and linguists have failed to discover the defining properties that such a view would imply. The philosopher Wittgenstein (1958, pp. 31–32) identified the problem as follows:

> Consider for example the proceedings we call "games". I mean board-games, card-games, ball-games, Olympic games and so on. What is common to them all? — Don't say "There must be something common or they would not be called games", but *look* and *see* whether there is anything common to *all*. — For if you look at them you will not see something that is common to *all*, but similarities, relationships, and a whole series of them at that . . . I can think of no better expression to characterise these similarities than "family resemblances".

This idea has been taken up by many researchers. When the features of members of a category are spelled out, they do not wholly overlap, and they are rarely necessary or sufficient to determine category membership (Hampton, 1979).

Real-world objects do not fit into just one category. A sheep is a ruminant, a mammal and an animal. In the category "animal" it is joined by many creatures that share few attributes, although it is more similar to other ruminants. The tomato is not even easily classified as a fruit or a vegetable, because it is often used as a vegetable, but when the definition is made in terms of the relationship of the tomato to the tomato plant, then it is a fruit. This problem leads us into another one, which is that some members of a category are "better" examples than others. A sheep is a representative animal, a snake is not. So, while hypothesis testing and association of features are useful in some situations, they are not readily applied to how we develop real concepts.

REAL-WORLD CONCEPTS

Categories like "chair" do not contain perceptually identical instances. Chairs vary considerably in their appearance and, somewhat relatedly, in their function. Studies by Eleanor Rosch and her co-workers in the 1970s were especially responsible for shifting focus away from artificial stimuli and the view that categories could readily be defined in terms of common elements. Rosch (1978) has emphasised that natural or cultural categorisation is not arbitrary but is structured according to two principles. The first concerns the *perceived structure* in the world. If the objects in the world were made up, like many laboratory stimuli, from arbitrary combinations of attributes such as colour, size and shape, then we might end up with no basis for classification. Most natural languages do not, for example, have a name for "red, small, square objects", nor for many other combinations of attributes. The wide variety of things called "chairs" has a strong commonality of *function*. Some pairs of chairs share many perceptual features, but others very few, rather in the way that pairs of members of the same family often vary in the kind and degree of resemblances that they show. Naturally occurring assemblies of attributes have a relationship to function which is important in understanding them. When we consider these functional groupings, we can see that categorisation is not like the logical task of taking all attributes, putting them in combinations, and giving names to the combinations. Feathers, wings and beaks are frequently observed to go together but not petals, wheels and fur. We experience the world as structured by the frequency with which some perceptual and functional attributes occur together.

The second principle emphasised by Rosch is that of *cognitive economy* in categorisation. What of all the things in the world do we give a name to and what names do we most frequently use? We could develop a classification system with as many layers of categories as we choose, but the principle of cognitive economy suggests that in cultural practices a compromise is achieved between how specific and how general our categories need to be. We require cues to similarities for some purposes and we need cues to make some distinctions. Not all levels of categorisation are equally useful. When the principles of cognitive economy and the perceived structure of the world are put together, they suggest that there is one level of categorisation which is the most useful. Rosch called this the *basic level*.

Basic-level Concepts

At the basic level of categorisation are the concepts which are most commonly used and among the first to be learned. Rosch et al. (1976) asked subjects to list all the attributes they could think of for items that seemed to be at this basic level, such as chair, car and pants. They also argued for a higher or *superordinate level*, which is less specific than the basic level, and for a *subordinate level*, which is more specific. So they also asked subjects to list attributes of furniture, vehicles and clothes (superordinate), and kitchen chair, sports car and Levi's (subordinate). Each person wrote attributes for only one of the levels. If you try the task yourself, you will probably find that there are not many attributes of "furniture", that "chair" has a large number, and that "kitchen chair' has most of the attributes of chair with a few extra ones.

Subjects found it hard to produce attributes for superordinate categories. For "clothing" there were two — you wear it and it keeps you warm. For "pants" (American for the British basic category of "trousers") there were six characteristics or attributes, including being made of cloth and having two legs. The subordinate category of "Levi's" added only one more attribute to those at the basic level — they are blue. Because most of the attributes are produced for the basic level and also show up differences between categories, this is the level that is most useful, reflects the structure of the world and allows for cognitive economy.

There is more evidence that one level of categorisation is the most useful. When asked to name objects or to classify assemblies of objects, people most often adopt the basic-level terms. When you use items that are classified in the same way at the basic level you make similar movements. So sitting on different chairs involves actions that are more similar than walking on rugs or taking books out of bookcases, although both rugs and bookcases are furniture. Putting on any pair of trousers involves actions that are similar to, and quite different from putting on a jacket or a hat. Finally, items from a basic-level class are often so similar in shape they may sensibly be "averaged"; for example, two cars (basic level, "cars") are more alike in this respect than a car and a bicycle (superordinate level, "vehicles"). Overall, the notion that there is one level of category which makes most sense in ordinary life can be argued for with some conviction.

Basic-level categorisation has also been found by Berlin (1978) in studies of the folk-biological classifications of plants and animals in non-Western cultures. He concluded that at one level of categorisation of a diversity of plants or animals, the perceptual and behavioural similarities seem to "cry out" to be labelled; at a lower level of categorisation, the culture requires some further distinctions to be made for certain purposes among things having high similarity. Similarly, Newport and Bellugi (1978) confirmed the psychological salience of Rosch's three category levels in the operation of American Sign Language (ASL) used by the deaf. The English language itself gives some evidence about the existence of these levels. Subordinate category names like "kitchen chair" and "sports car" are compounds that include the basic-level concept.

It could be argued that basic-level concepts have developed in one of two ways. The common words that we learn early help to organise our experience and become more central than other category names that we learn later. The alternative is that basic perceptual and cognitive organisation of the world is primary and names follow that. Mervis and Crisafi (1982) investigated this using artificial categories. Subjects had to sort items into groups but were not given names for the groups. The responses tended to use the middle level of the possible categorisations, even though there were no names to support the distinction.

There are, of course, some words whose meanings have not developed exclusively from everyday interaction with the world, and these have definitions that do largely constrain or even determine their meaning. For example, we have the "triangles" and "squares" of geometry, "water" and "copper sulphate" of chemistry, and "velocity" and "inertia" of physics. The meanings of these terms in science are restricted, just like the strongly conventional definitions of some terms used in specialist domains such as ballet, the skilled trades, various professions and in religions. Rosch's work does not imply that a culture cannot give rise to terms which are satisfactorily defined in terms of attributes, but rather that many of our natural categories cannot readily be defined in this way.

PROTOTYPES AND FAMILY RESEMBLANCES

The work on basic-level categories is a description of what our categories are, not of how we acquire them or of how we actually use them. However, the finding that some category members are more typical than others has pointed to a way in which classification might be carried out. Orange and apple are good examples of fruit, tomato and olive are not, yet they are all in the same family. The clearest cases of category membership have been referred to as *prototypical* cases (Rosch, 1973). Prototypicality has a number of effects on the way in which people make judgements about whether items belong in a class or not. Adults are faster to respond "true" to statements like "A robin is a bird" than to statements like "A penguin is a bird". Children show even greater reaction-time discrepancies between judgements of good and poor representatives of a category, a fact which supports the earlier observations that children do not learn about fruit from pomegranates and olives (Rosch, 1973). So one way to understand the word "prototype" is to think of it as the most typical representative of a category. A robin could be said to be a prototypical bird.

These observations help to describe the structure of what we know, but they do not as yet tell us how we know it. Could we use some kind of holistic organisation of the most "central" features to give us a way of making judgements about whether items belong to a class or not? Is this what a prototype is? Is a robin a prototypical bird because it does not have extreme values on any of the dimensions on which we judge birdness? In order to answer this question, experimenters have to start to control the stimuli again, even if this produces "unnatural" categories. Look at the faces in Fig. 3.3. The upper five faces represent category 1, the lower five faces represent category 2. By studying these faces, can you decide what it is that makes a face fit into category 1 rather than category 2? Could you place new faces into the categories? If you were doing the task, would you match all the features of a new face to those already in the category, or would you try to create a pattern that was the most "central" face possible in the category and then match new faces to it? The second strategy involves the use of a prototype face, one which is not present in the display but which is a good average of all the relevant features.

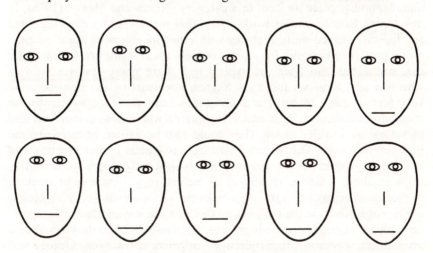

FIG. 3.3 The faces used in Reed's categorisation task. Reproduced with permission from Reed and Friedman (1973).

This was the task that Reed (1972) presented to his subjects. The faces differed on four dimensions; namely, eye separation, height of mouth, height of forehead and nose length. Subjects classified new faces and were asked how they had done it. The majority of the subjects said that they formed an abstract "image" of what a category 1 face should look like and what a category 2 face should look like, and then matched each new face to the abstractions, which we could think of as prototypes. After learning the categories, Reed's subjects were also shown faces which they had not seen before and asked to categorise them. Some of these were prototype faces which had an average value for each of the four dimensions varied in the experiment. They were easily assigned to the categories, even though they did not have features which were shown in the learning phase. Reed tested several alternative models to see which made the best predictions about the way in which classification was carried out. One was based on the frequency of particular features (a face is assigned to category A if it has features which are frequent in category A), one was based on classification by nearest neighbour (a face goes into category A if the face it is most like is in category A), and one was a prototype model which assumed that no details of individual faces were in memory but that each new face was compared to a weighted average of the dimensions of previous set of faces presented. Overall, Reed reports that subjects' classifications fitted with a model of categorisation based on prototypes, as did their subjective reports of what they felt they were doing.

A prototype can be a typical member of a class or a central representation of the features of the items already experienced. Items are more or less likely to be in a category, but just adding up features does not unambiguously place an item in a category. Rosch and Mervis (1975), in developing Rosch's earlier work, found that members of a class regarded as "typical" shared more features with other members of the class than non-typical members did. In the case of methods of transport, for example, car, truck, bus and train are typical and share many features such as wheels, roofs, windows and seats. Skates, wheelbarrow and elevator share very few of these features and properties, and are hard to identify as methods of transport. Indeed, it is arguable whether wheelbarrows and elevators are vehicles at all. They could also be garden implements and parts of buildings. This means that "car" is typical of the "methods of transport", whereas "wheelbarrow" is untypical and gives rise to boundary disputes about what really belongs in the category. One way of thinking of this is in terms of "family resemblances", which Rosch and Mervis (1975) suggested was the best way to describe the way in which items were included in a category or omitted from it. Family resemblance increases if an item shares more properties with members of its own category and decreases if the item shares more properties with members of other categories. A category may therefore involve a list of the relevant properties or features, with items which are central or prototypical having more of those properties than items which are only weakly included in the category.

All of the versions of "prototype" which we have considered allow classification in a probabilistic way, have no exhaustive set of defining features which put things into categories, have a central tendency which reflects the most typical members of a class, and a graded structure from very typical to least typical members. To that extent, the term is useful and predictions can be made in experiments. Smith and Medin (1981), however, considered that the wide range of meanings of the word "prototype" meant that the word should be avoided. Sometimes it refers to an actual object (a robin is a prototypical bird, not an average over all bird characteristics), sometimes to a central tendency or average over the exemplars, sometimes an idealised exemplar (an ideal bird), and so on. Reed's (1972) prototype was a face which had the average values on the dimensions on which all the other exemplars differed, so was both an actual face and a central tendency represented in memory. It is worth noting that the term prototype may be being used very specifically in some contexts and conclusions cannot be generalised to other meanings. In general, however, the core of the prototype view is that we do not decide that things belong to natural categories using exhaustive rules (although we can do so for things like triangles); rather, we behave as if we know what the centre of a category is and compare new items to that.

Alternatives to Prototypes

Although the development of prototype theory was in response to concerns about natural categories, some research questions have continued to involve laboratory-based studies using artificial categories, and in this context two other approaches to how categorisation is done have been developed. Both depend on similarity on particular features, and both involve complex modelling and computation. The first, exemplar theory, relates to the way in which information is stored in memory so that it can be used both for classification and for other tasks, and the second, which is based on connectionist networks, emphasises learning. We will consider them separately, before returning to problems with the general issues of features and similarity, and the question of natural categories as opposed to laboratory ones.

Exemplar Theory.   A prototype is extracted from the examples which have been experienced over time, and what is stored in memory is therefore not the actual examples themselves. This means that if we want to decide whether we have actually seen a particular item before, we have to use a different kind of memory representation from that used in classification. If people are asked to learn to carry out a laboratory classification task and then are shown more stimuli and are asked to say which of them they have seen before, there is a low correlation between classification performance and recognition performance, which supports the view that there are two different kinds of memory representation involved (Metcalfe & Fisher, 1986). However, Neumann (1977) found that if subjects were shown faces which all had extreme values on dimensions (e.g. they all had very long or very short noses), and were then shown faces which had intermediate scores on each dimension, and asked if they had seen them before, they tended to agree that they had. The average, or prototype, was recognised as familiar. Neumann also found that if the stimuli were sets of rectangles, rather than faces, subjects tended to recognise more extreme patterns than those they had previously seen, suggesting that the material being classified may have an effect on the way in which classification and recognition are carried out.

Nosofsky (1988) argued that it was not very economical to have two kinds of memory representation for these tasks and suggested that it was possible to have the same knowledge in memory for both classification (which category does this belong to?) and recognition (is this familiar?), but to have different kinds of rules for making decisions in the two tasks. He argued that all individual exemplars were stored in memory and that categorisation was based on a new item's similarity to all the exemplars experienced from one target category relative to exemplars from other categories, that is, a relative similarity in memory. So, if a subject had been learning which items fit into two categories, there would be a definite outcome to the process of classifying a new item — it is either more similar to the stored exemplars of one category or to the stored exemplars of the other. If the subject were then asked to decide whether a particular item had been seen before or not, decisions would be based on the overall familiarity of an item, that is, its total sum of similarity to all the items shown before regardless of the category they were in. So, with the same stored material in memory, different kinds of decision could produce different performances, which did not necessarily correlate.

Reed's (1972) experiment, which we discussed earlier, had provided evidence for a prototype model, and Nosofsky (1991) used Reed's face stimuli to test predictions about an exemplar model, in which classification was assumed to be based on summed similarity over all the exemplars given. After training with faces like those in Fig. 3.2, which vary in terms of eye height, eye separation, nose length and mouth height, subjects were shown two figures which had average values on each dimension, that is, they were prototype faces. These faces (which were never shown in training) were well classified, but that this was predicted on the basis of their similarity to other items in the category as well as by the fact that they were prototypes. However, two other faces, which were close to the prototypes, and should have been correctly classified into the categories, were actually hard for the subjects to separate in their classifications, and the mathematical model based on similarity within the two sets actually predicted this difficulty, which the prototype model could not do. Nosofsky also found that some faces could be recognised accurately but classified inaccurately after training or could be recognised inaccurately but classified accurately, that is, that classification and recognition were not correlated. Consider for a moment faces which are similar to lots of the other faces seen. These faces will have high overall familiarity. However, the relative difference between the summed similarity for the first category and the summed similarity for the second category is small, so it will be hard to make a consistent decision about which category they fit into. Nevertheless, in Nosofsky's study, the exemplar model with different decision rules did produce good predictions for both categorisation and recognition performance.

This exemplar theory has a great deal in common with a prototype account such as that of Reed (1972). They are both concerned with the way features are averaged in order to allow decisions to be made about whether a new item is like one known category but not like another. They differ in terms of what they assume to be represented in memory, but each predicts that the most typical members of a category are closest to the average value on most dimensions. As stated earlier, the use of "prototype" to mean a representation in memory is only one of the meanings which the word has been given in the work on categorisation. In general, however, the core of both exemplar and prototype versions of categorisation is that we do not decide that things belong to natural categories using exhaustive rules (although we can do that for things like triangles); rather, we behave as if we know what the centre of a category is and compare new items to that.

Associationism Revisited as Connectionism. Early accounts of how categories were formed included associationist accounts such as that of Hull, discussed earlier in this chapter, in which links between names of Chinese characters (the output) and the features of the stimuli (the input) were built up over time. A simplistic account of association suggests that frequency of linkage is important in building categories. Connectionist models, which we introduced in the previous chapter, are also concerned with how links are made between input and output, and have been shown to predict how humans perform on tasks such as linking a set of symptoms to a new disease name (Gluck & Bower, 1988). The view that a category results from the learning of associations between features is similar in some ways to a prototype model. Features or attributes (like "barks", "has four paws") become the input patterns to input nodes of a connectionist network. Training a network to categorise means that during learning the weights of connections to output nodes (responding "dog", for example) are modified so that a set of features ("barks", "wags tail", "has four paws") comes to activate the dog output and no other. Because all the particular exemplars are not kept in memory, these models are more like prototype models than exemplar models.

Exemplar models and network models differ in their account of what is in memory after learning and they also differ in how the learning is carried out. For a network model, learning is usually based on error, as the weights of connections to output nodes change after a categorisation is made and the system finds out whether it is correct or not. For an exemplar model, learning is based on the accumulation of exemplars which the subject discovers to be in each category. The subject is doing the same thing in each situation — classifying an item as being in one category and then finding out if that classification is correct. What differs between the models is the emphasis given to how the information is represented as categorisation develops. The models are not completely different, because Kruschke (1992) has produced a connectionist model of category learning based on exemplars. Nosofsky, Kruschke and McKinley (1992) have tested these models on their ability to learn to categorise and on their different ways of representing the category. They found that network models were better at predicting how subjects learned and transferred to classifying new patterns, but that models based on similarity, not prototypes, were better at predicting how a new pattern which was actually a prototype (i.e. has the average of all the values on all the dimensions) would be categorised. So, they argue that what is represented is based on similarity, but that learning is not just storing all the exemplars but includes error detection.

One of the advantages of the network models is that they do not only strengthen links on the basis of frequency of connections between input and output. The way in which learning takes place using the back-propagation algorithm allows features which occur in combination to have different effects on output. The origin of this comes from animal learning studies on Pavlovian conditioning (Rescorla & Wagner, 1972). An animal which receives a mild shock will produce an aversive reaction to that shock. If a light is paired with the mild shock, the light itself will eventually come to elicit the response to the shock even when the shock is not present. If a tone and a light together are paired with the shock, then does each of them have an ability to elicit the response? A simple frequency account might say yes. However, things aren't as simple as this even in animal learning. Consider the animal learning experiment in the top half of Table 3.1. If a light and tone are presented together with the shock for a number of trials and then the tone is presented by itself with *no* shock, the animal will subsequently show the shock response to the light but not the tone (condition 1). If the tone and light are presented together with the shock for a number of trials and then the tone is presented by itself *with* shock,

TABLE 3.1

Selective Learning in Animals, and in Humans Learning Categories

	Condition 1	Condition 2
Animal learning		
Training	Light + tone with shock	Light + tone with shock
	Tone with no shock	Tone with shock
Test	Light with no shock	Light with no shock
Result	Response as if to shock	Little response
Humans learning categories (Shanks, 1991)		
Training	Skin rash and dizziness linked to disease 1	Swollen glands and coughing linked to disease 2
	Skin rash not linked to disease 1	Coughing linked to disease 2
Test	Dizziness	Swollen glands
Result	Disease 1 frequent diagnosis	Disease 2 not frequent diagnosis

then the light will not subsequently elicit much shock response (condition 2). The light has actually been presented with the shock the same number of times in both cases, so mere frequency of association would predict that it should elicit the response on both occasions. Frequency is not enough to explain the results, but rather the ability of the light to tell the animal about shock differs in the two conditions. In the first condition, the light predicts shock so the response is produced; in the second condition, it doesn't and the response to shock is blocked.

This blocking isn't as complicated as it seems. If you are well acquainted with British sheep, then sheep are distinctly woolly and most other animals aren't. Woolliness and four legs occur together in many of our experiences of classifying animals as sheep. However, having four legs also occurs in many situation in which a classification of "sheep" is not correct. In other words, while having wool and four legs are properties of sheep, and having four legs is a property of every sheep, having four legs does not allow you to categorise an animal as a sheep. Woolliness, although not a perfect predictor of sheepness (shorn sheep are not woolly), is nevertheless a better predictor than having four legs. Could we actually do this kind of selection of good predictive features on an associationist or connectionist basis?

Shanks (1991) asked people to learn to categorise groups of symptoms into diseases and made some symptoms more predictive of the disease than others in exactly the same way as the animal learning features were made more predictive of shock (see the bottom part of Table 3.1). The diseases were made up specially for the experiment. Two symptoms occurred together and were related to a particular disease. Then one symptom occurred alone, and either was or was not related to the same disease. Each time subjects were presented with symptoms they had to decide which disease a patient had, and they were told if they were right or wrong. Shanks also developed a network model which set out to learn the categorisation task. He found that subjects did not link a particular symptom, like dizziness, to a particular disease based on how often it was linked to that disease in the experiment, but based on how often the disease occurred when that symptom was present. That is, it was not frequency of pairing with the disease which led to a symptom being known to be related to that disease, but predictiveness. This was the case both for the people doing the classifying, and for the network model. So, comparatively sophisticated use of differential relationships between features can be produced by a system which learns to associate input (like patterns of symptoms) to output (like the name of a disease).

Network models and exemplar models, while different in detail, suggest that when people are developing categories they are accumulating links between features and categories rather than trying to understand the world or testing hypotheses. They provide statistical models of the similarities over sets of items which can be used to decide whether a new item fits in one category or another. While the models provide excellent accounts of how some laboratory tasks are carried out on fixed sets of features in fixed categories, there are other approaches which emphasise what conceptual knowledge is for and how it might be used in the world and it is to those we now turn. We will find that they expose weakness in the approaches outlined so far and we will return to some of these models for discussion in later sections.

PROBLEMS WITH FAMILY RESEMBLANCES, TYPICALITY AND SIMILARITY

The previous section started with the work of Rosch and then considered prototype, exemplar and network models of category formation. These derive important principles from Rosch's work, the most notable of which is the view that items are not put definitely in one category or another based on rules which tell us how to categorise. Items are more or less likely to be in a category, and similarity over sets of features is what determines how likely category membership is. A particular value of similarity can be applied to allow a decision to be made about whether a new item is in a specific old category or not. Some items are more typical members of a category than others, and similarity is used both to judge how typical something is and to decide whether it is actually in the category or not. While we have been considering prototype models in comparison to exemplar and network models, these three statistically based accounts all share these properties, which are derived from Rosch. In this section, we consider three important issues in the prototypical understanding of categories. The first is the question of "family resemblances" and whether these occur because of shared properties of features being used in classification rather than because of independent features. The second takes the issue of similarity and discusses what it might mean and how we know which features are the important ones for making similarity judgements. The third issue is that of typicality, and whether the finding that there are typical members of categories tells us anything about how information is represented in memory.

Family Resemblances: Are Features Linked or Independent?

We can tell that people in one family resemble each other, even though we can't tell exactly how and they don't all share the same features, and, as we have seen, we can think of categorisation in a similar way. We have a general overall impression of how things fit into classes, rather than rules and definitions, and family resemblance theory suggests that we do this by noting the overall number of features which family members have. Medin, Wattenmaker and Hampson (1987) wondered if people could use family resemblances to sort items into categories. They carried out a series of seven experiments over a very wide range of materials including pictures of bugs and descriptions of people. The items could be varied on four dimensions, with three values for each dimension in some experiments and two values in others. In the view of family resemblances put forward by Rosch and Mervis (1975), all features and properties are treated as equally salient, so sorting items by family resemblances means taking all the features, and looking for groupings in which items share more features with others in their category than they do with items in another category. Table 3.2 shows some of the descriptions of people which were used in Medin and co-workers' experiments. There were four dimensions — conscientiousness, emotional stability, culture and agreeableness — and different words describing positive and negative values on these traits were selected from other studies which had identified groupings of personality traits. So *relaxed* and *affectionate* were used as the agreeable end of the emotional stability and agreeableness dimensions, while *careless* and *gullible* were the undesirable end of the conscientiousness and culture dimensions. The prototype of one category, Irene, has these four characteristics, while the prototype for the other category, Suzie, has opposite values for each dimension. Each of the other people in the Irene "family resemblance" group shares three dimension values with Irene and one with Suzie, while each of the other people in the Suzie "family resemblance" group shares three values with Suzie and one with Irene. The labels 0 and 1 in Table 3.2 refer to the value (positive and negative) on each dimension, and the four dimensions (conscientiousness, emotional stability, culture, agreeableness) are in order down the page for each person. If family

TABLE 3.2

Descriptions of Hypothetical People
to be Sorted into Two Categories
(See Text for Further Explanation)

Irene	Susie
(1111)	(0000)
Careless	Efficient
Relaxed	Envious
Gullible	Knowledgeable
Affectionate	Hard
Sandra	**Karen**
(1110)	(0001)
Careless	Efficient
Relaxed	Envious
Gullible	Knowledgeable
Hard	Affectionate
June	**Amanda**
(1101)	(0010)
Careless	Efficient
Relaxed	Envious
Knowledgeable	Gullible
Affectionate	Hard
Clare	**Joan**
(1011)	(0100)
Careless	Efficient
Envious	Relaxed
Gullible	Knowledgeable
Affectionate	Hard
Moira	**Anne**
(0111)	(1000)
Efficient	Careless
Relaxed	Envious
Gullible	Knowledgeable
Affectionate	Hard

resemblance theory is correct, then subjects who are given the set of descriptions and asked to sort them into two categories should produce two sets organised in this way.

You may find when you look at Table 3.2 that the names and descriptions don't really seem to cluster together into clear groups, even though they seem to have been set up to have similar values on specific dimensions. This is what Medin et al. found. Their subjects did not sort into family resemblance groupings, but tended to take one dimension and follow it (so that, for example, all the "hard" people ended up in one category), or to use some other sorting method which couldn't be clearly analysed. The lack of family resemblance sorting was found over all the types of stimuli used by Medin et al. when there were no relationships between the dimensions used. If you look at Irene and Suzie and consider the four dimensions on which they have such opposing ratings, you will notice that there are no obvious relationships between characteristics such as being envious and being knowledgeable. However, when the experiments were repeated with some of the dimensions used having relationships in normal language and experience (like being withdrawn and being soft spoken), or if the subjects were told to use a basic personality dimension which emphasised relationships between features, then one dimensional sorting was not found. When all the dimensions were related to an underlying trait of extroversion and introversion, sorting people into two groups did work on the basis of family resemblances.

Medin et al. concluded that the theme of extroversion and introversion allowed subjects to integrate the descriptors into an overall impression. They argue that the apparent use of family resemblance rules in other situations may be masking what is really happening. A core factor (like the introversion–extroversion one) may actually be causing the family resemblance features in a probabilistic way, and it is knowledge of this core which links the properties together and structures the otherwise independent properties. So, for example, a subject might decide that this person is quite extroverted, this person is very extroverted and this person is not extroverted at all, so the first two go into one category and the third into a different category, but judgement is not based on the actual similarities in the items presented. While subsequent evidence (Ahn & Medin, 1992) suggests that subjects can sort disconnected material on the basis of family resemblances, when there are more than two values on the features, they do so by first imposing a structure based on dominant dimensions and then fitting left over items in on the basis of how well they match one or other of the groups. Family resemblances in real categories may not be constructed out of a set of unrelated properties but in terms of a deeper underlying concept. Birds have the characteristics they have (hollow bones, feathers, wings, nests in trees) because they have adapted to be able to fly, and this underlies the collection of properties, giving it coherence.

Similarity and *ad hoc* Categories

If you are shown a set of schematic faces, it is relatively easy to work out what the important features are and how similar they are to each other. So, for example, a nose on a schematic face which was one inch long would be more similar to another nose which was one and a quarter inches long than it would be to a nose which was two inches long. Using such stimuli may give us an account of how they are categorised, but does it help with natural categories? If we say that plums are more like oranges than they are like lawnmowers, how do we select the features to compare them on? Are we selecting similarities which reflect categories we already know, or are we looking at all the similarities and selecting the relevant ones?

Murphy and Medin (1985) argue that the number of attributes that plums and lawnmowers have in common could be infinite. They both weigh less than 1000 kilograms, are both found on the earth, cannot hear very well, have a smell, can be dropped, take up space, and so on. You probably hadn't thought of those as being relevant attributes, so you must have some idea of what will be relevant attributes. Do these come from perception — plums and lawnmowers don't look very alike? If so, can whales be mammals, or can Yorkshire terriers and Irish wolfhounds both be dogs? Murphy and Medin argue that theories about what tends to go together are important in the natural use of coherent concepts. Concepts are represented by correlated attributes plus underlying principles that determine which correlations are noticed. Rather than making judgements about the similarity of values of different attributes when we decide whether something is in a category or not, we find a way to explain how and why things are linked together and this then works with our recognition of similarities.

Similarity may also be derived from people's goals rather than from the properties of the objects themselves. What do these things have in common: jewellery, photograph albums, manuscripts (including your just finished essay), oil paintings? They are not all paper, not all worth a lot of money, and so on. But they are all things you might take out of the house in a fire. Barsalou (1985; 1991) has found that if people are asked to provide instances of goal-directed categories of this type (things to give for birthday presents, foods to eat on a diet), then they group together objects which otherwise would be assumed to belong to different categories. The exemplars for these goal-directed categories, like those for natural categories, are seen by subjects as more and less typical, but rather than there being an average value which is seen as being very typical, the ideal value is seen as being typical (zero calories appears to be an ideal feature of foods to eat on a diet). It is context here that determines which items are selected as fitting a category. The items themselves do not constitute a category based on intrinsic similarity.

Given that we can construct *ad hoc* categories like "bad things to take when climbing a mountain", it may be that we do not use similarities when we encode new material, but when we want to solve problems in the world. To do this, we have to be able to reanalyse rather than simply use the results of our earlier information-gathering efforts. Wattenmaker (1991) argued that the set of things usually used in experimental studies of concepts were too controlled. Every value on every dimension was usually important for making decisions about whether something was in a category or not, and no features were present which were not shared with some other exemplars. This is unlike the natural situation in which there are many things which could be important, and idiosyncratic and irrelevant information is mixed with what is relevant for any particular purpose, and people are not often looking at things in order to work out which category they are in. We have to be able to remember information about examples and then extract category information from them. Wattenmaker used tasks in which subjects read descriptions of people which varied on many dimensions, and were then asked to say if they were like people they knew, without being told that they were going to categorise anything. Then they were subsequently told which one of two categories each description belonged to. Another group of subjects read the descriptions and were told about the categories, and were then asked to work out which features were important for category A and category B. The test part of the experiment came when the subjects were asked to make judgements about which features went together in which category. Surprisingly, the subjects who had not tried to categorise, but who had done something else, were actually better at answering questions about the features in the categories. This suggests that the information stored about people could be recalled and used to produce information about what made them fit into one category or another, and this was encouraged by having quite distinctive descriptions of people in the first place. Classification by post-encoding operates in restricted laboratory examples as well as in the formation of *ad hoc* categories of things which would not be useful when climbing a mountain.

Typicality: What Does it Tell Us?

In an earlier section, we pointed out that the word "prototype" was used in many different ways. Some of these uses suggest that attributes are out there in things in the world, although Rosch (1978) has pointed out that some attributes are functional (a table is something you eat on), some are relative (a piano is large relative to a stool but small relative to a building) and these attributes depend on other knowledge. Lakoff (1987a) argued that we understand some aspects of things to be properties which are relevant for categorisation because of our interactions with the environment, not because those properties are immediately perceptually obvious. Yet graded structure (some things are more typical than others) can be found in many situations and does seem to point to typicality as indicating something important about how knowledge is represented. These graded properties, which seem to be an important part of the prototype theory, and of central tendency theory in general, can, however, be found in many situations in which a central tendency account doesn't seem to make a lot of sense. So, for example, Armstrong, Gleitman and Gleitman (1983) found that subjects were quite happy to say that some odd numbers (like 3 and 7) were more typical of the category of odd numbers than other numbers (like 109 and 2003), although they knew very well that 3 was not more odd, or a better odd number, than 109.

Typicality judgements can be manipulated by asking people to make judgements about categories from other people's point of view. Could you make judgements about good films from your friend's point of view which would be different from your own? What about thinking of typical foods from the American point of view or the Chinese point of view? Different patterns of typical and non-typical items are produced by the same people when they are taking different viewpoints (Barsalou, 1987), and Barsalou argues that this means that categories do not have a fixed graded structure from typical to not-so-typical, but that this structure is produced when items are surveyed in a particular context. A very specific distinction is made here between categories and concepts. Concepts represent categories on particular occasions and contain information about the category which is category-dependent and other information which is category-independent. This means that there is core to a category which gives us expectations for interacting with that category on most occasions, but when we form a particular concept then goal-relatedness, correlations between properties and information about what is currently present in the world may all be incorporated to create a current concept. We have to conclude that the presence of prototype effects in typicality judgements need not mean that the kind of mental representation used is a prototype one. Typicality does not necessarily mean a particular kind of representation.

So, while the appeal to family resemblances, typicality and similarity made by Rosch and others gives us an improved description of how people use categories, there are problems with all of these in real-world situations. We cannot be sure how we decide which similarities are the relevant ones; in family resemblances, features may be linked and co-occur rather than be independent, and we can make typicality judgements even when we know that membership of a class is governed by a rule or when we are taking someone else's point of view. We can say that some things are more typical than others, but we may not do this by using a representation which involves a central tendency derived from all the instances we have experienced before.

CATEGORY KNOWLEDGE AND WORLD KNOWLEDGE

The early views of concept formation discussed in the first part of this chapter share a tendency to assume that concepts are clearly defined by combinations of features. The views which follow the work of Rosch reject this and argue that membership of a category is not decided by particular values on particular dimensions. However, similarity to a prototype or to exemplars which have been identified earlier is important for all of these accounts. This raises several difficulties with what it is to be similar and which dimensions of similarity are important. If selection of dimensions is not arbitrary, then how is it done? Is it simply a question of waiting for enough pairings between stimulus characteristics and response characteristics for redundant features to be dropped out, or can we actually direct our category formation?

We have already mentioned that theories are important in the use of natural concepts. This does not mean the explicit testing of hypotheses as it did in early work, but the use of more general knowledge or schematic frameworks which affect what similarity is and which features are important, based on our understanding of how features are caused, and what categories allow us to do. The argument of Murphy and Medin (1985) is concerned in part with causal relations. We ignore some of the similarities between plums and lawnmowers because our knowledge of what makes a plum a fruit concerns trees, food and what we want to do with plums. What we want to do with things may be an important early perceptual principle for classification, but it is not the basis of all conceptual structures. Nevertheless, the purposes for which we use categories may be important in understanding categorisation itself (Anderson, 1991). Similarity accounts cannot be sufficient because some features are noted and not others, some correlations between features are noted and not others, and categories are defined in terms of underlying principles, not just collections of attributes and features (Medin & Wattenmaker, 1987). Specific concepts do not arise in isolation, but are all interrelated into our general knowledge of the world.

We now give examples of three ways in which concepts are affected by information which is outside the concepts themselves. It is this property of being outside the concept which counts as theoretical or world knowledge. The first case is that of our knowledge of causation and how that can affect categorisation; the second is the use of context demands to determine how we relate concepts together to make new combinations; and the third concerns our ability to use frequency information in relation to causation to make judgements about the structure of concepts themselves.

Causation and Association

Categorisation and concept learning have in the past been regarded as higher-order types of learning which are not reducible to associative learning. The equivalence of Rescorla and Wagner's (1972) account of classical conditioning to the error rule used in simple network models has, however, suggested that categorisation is associative. This, as we have seen in discussing Shanks' work, is relevant to the issue of what makes a cue redundant in learning a category. However, there are other ways in which one might decide that a cue was redundant in learning a category, based, at least in part, on one's past learning about the world and interactions with it. For example, we may already have knowledge about cause and effect and which comes first, which affects the way in which we relate instances to a more general class. Tversky and Kahneman (1980) found that people think it is more likely that a blue-eyed mother will have a blue-eyed daughter than it is that a blue-eyed daughter will have a blue-eyed mother, presumably because causal links go from mother to daughter and not back from daughter to mother. Links from the effect back to the cause are diagnostic rather than causal. So, for example, if symptoms are related to a disease, it can be assumed that the disease causes them, rather than the other way about. However, if an associative pairing is set up in which features are linked to a response, it does not matter whether the features are causes or effect, all that matters is that the associations exist.

Waldmann and Holyoak (1992) distinguished between associative models which were causal and associative models which were diagnostic. Their subjects saw descriptions of features of fictitious people and in the causal condition they had to predict whether these features would elicit a new kind of emotional response in observers, while in the diagnostic condition they had to predict whether the features were symptoms of a new disease caused by a virus. The features were paired in predictive groupings similar to those in the network association studies of Shanks (1991) and Gluck and Bower (1988), although the subjects had to rate the features in test, not categorise new material, and there are differences with the results found by Shanks which may be based on procedural differences. However, in the diagnostic condition, subjects were exposed to descriptions of people with symptoms who did and did not have the new disease. People who were pale had the disease and people who were pale and underweight had the disease, and subjects were eventually asked to rate all the symptoms for whether they were effects of the new disease or not. In the causal condition, subjects were exposed to descriptions of people who did and did not give rise to a new emotional response in people they met. People who were pale gave rise to the emotional response in others, and people who were pale and underweight did so too, and subjects were eventually asked to rate all the physical characteristics as to whether they caused the emotional response or not.

The responses in this study indicated that the way in which a redundant feature (being underweight) was treated depended on whether it was a cause or an effect. Being underweight was ignored (or blocked as the animal learning approach would put it) when the two features were seen as causes (leading to the emotional response), but not when they were effects (symptoms of a disease). Waldman and Holyoak argued that pure associationist theory does not allow for higher-order knowledge of the direction of causality to affect how features and classification labels are linked. They suggest that their subjects learn the classification by developing causal models with links from cause to effect, and in diagnosis they know that multiple effects of a common cause do not compete. In the causal condition, the link from being underweight to being a cause of a new response was reduced not by associative blocking, but because subjects did not have any separate information about whether being underweight would lead to the emotional reaction on its own. People do not simply link input and output in these tasks; they link them in response to their knowledge of how things in the world are related.

Putting Concepts Together: Conjunctions and Disjunctions

When we put members of different categories together, do we do it according to how typical each one is within its own category? In the general class of central tendency accounts, the argument about the link between membership of a category and typicality is quite straightforward. Membership is determined by placing a criterion value on similarity so that very unsimilar things are not in the category. You are only a fish if you reach a certain value of similarity to other fish. You will be a more typical fish if your similarity is much higher than this criterion value. So, a guppy is a fish, but not a very typical one. What happens when we join our knowledge of two or more categories and make judgements about typicality and class membership? How does the prototype or central tendency view account for the outcome? A guppy is not a very typical fish, and not a very typical pet, but if you consider all the things which are both a pet and a fish, then a guppy is highly typical (Hampton, 1988). Can the guppy effect happen if concepts are combined without using information from outside the concepts themselves?

Hampton (1988) investigated the way in which subjects judged membership of two separate categories (sports and games) and rated each activity for how typical a member it was. Four weeks later, he then asked the same subjects to judge each item as a game which is also a sport, or a sport which is also a game, and to rate how typical it was. He found that subjects were likely to report that some items which they thought were a game but not a sport, or which they thought were a sport but not a game, would be judged as fitting into the category "a game which is also a sport". This is called overextension of joint class inclusion because it stretches the boundaries of what counts as a member of each class on its own. The "guppy effect" was not found, however, as the ratings for how typical a member of the joined class was could be calculated from the ratings given to its typicality in the two separate categories. Indeed, the appearance of an item as a member of the joint category could be predicted from how typical it was as a member of the two categories separately. If it was very typical in one category (game) but not in the other category (sport), the high typicality compensated to produce a quite typical member of the combined class. This suggests that membership and typicality in the new class are related, and Hampton (1988) proposed that this unitary representation of the new class is a composite of the representation for each of the constituents.

Unfortunately, the story isn't quite as simple as this in all cases of combination of concepts. What happens when a conjoined pair are an adjective and a noun so that the meaning of one is constrained by the meaning of the other? If we assume that the meaning of the noun in the pair is represented as a set of dimensions and there is a distribution of possible values for each dimension, then if 80% of apples are red then the colour dimension for apple would be heavily loaded for red (Smith & Osherson, 1987). "Red" would then not add very much to "apple" on its own, but "green" would. In addition, "red apple" would be highly typical, and "green apple" would be much less so. Medin and Shoben (1988) argued that this doesn't work because concepts are not just arbitrary collections of features but have a structure in which the dimensions are not independent. Features change together. Changing from "spoon" to "wooden spoon" changes more than just the material, it also changes size. Medin and Shoben found that metal spoons were more typical spoons than wooden spoons were, but that wooden spoons were more typical large spoons than metal spoons were. So changing the material changed typicality differently for small and large spoons. They also found that adjectives are not perceived as similar or dissimilar in isolation. For example, grey hair and white hair are judged to be quite similar, while grey hair and black hair are quite different, yet grey clouds and white clouds are different and grey clouds and black clouds are similar.

For combinations of nouns and adjectives, it is not sufficient to argue that the adjective simply changes one dimension on which the noun is evaluated. The relationship between the adjective and the noun may change values on other dimensions, and the value itself may have a different relationship to other values on the dimension for that object than it does for other objects. Murphy (1988) also showed that definitions of adjectives differed over nouns, and attributes for combined concepts were not a subset of attributes for the two separate ones. Exemplar models, which have no difficulty with wooden spoon and typicality because only the exemplars of spoons which are wooden would go into the new category, cannot deal with the way in which similarity changes for the same adjectives over different nouns. Medin and Shoben (1988) and Murphy (1988) both argue that the properties of combined categories cannot be derived just from stored prototypes or exemplars, but must involve world knowledge — that is, knowledge outside the combined categories. Grey clouds are different from white clouds because one is more likely to cause rain, whereas grey hair is similar to white hair because both are caused by ageing.

Hampton (1988) has argued for a prototype account of combination, and Medin and Shoben (1988) have argued for a world knowledge account. Chater, Lyon and Myers (1990) found that subjects did overextend concept combinations as Hampton (1988) suggested, but took a different approach to the question of why it was done. They argued that if you had to cast a part in a play which called for a man who was tall, blond, handsome and could speak with a convincing Scottish accent, you might have some difficulties in finding the appropriate actor. You might find someone short, blond and handsome with a poor Scottish accent, or tall, dark and plain with a good Scottish accent. Which would you choose? Either would be an overextension — that is, the characteristics being sought have to be stretched or overextended to accommodate either of these two cases. Chater et al. (1990) proposed that the tendency to overextend was the result of a best-fit strategy which allowed compensation and that the more attributes there were, the greater the compensation would be, and this was what they found. Best-fit matching is not independent of world knowledge. The compensation between those attributes which are not matched and those which are not fixed. If the play is performed in Scotland, then a good Scottish accent will be more important than it will be if the play is performed in Atlanta, Georgia. While a pet fish can easily be thought of by people who don't keep fish, for those who do, what is typical of pet fish will vary depending on the size of the tank available. It seems likely that in order to completely understand how concepts are combined, we will have to take theories of the world into account.

Concepts and Induction: Using Frequency Information

When we meet examples of a new class of objects, we use our old knowledge to help us get to know the new material. This knowledge may be knowledge about causation, about how central some features are likely to be because of causation, and therefore of how many times we will need to experience something before we decide it is an attribute which varies. This knowledge allows us to generalise, and is sometimes known as induction, in which instances of something induce us to offer a conclusion which cannot be fully justified because the evidence is incomplete. Thagard and Nisbett (1982) offered a thought experiment which indicates some of the ways in which our world knowledge is used to allow us to go beyond what is presented to us. They suggested:

> Imagine you are exploring a newly discovered island. You encounter three new instances of a new species of bird, called the shreeble, and all three observed shreebles are blue. What is your degree of confidence that all shreebles are blue? Compare this with your reaction to the discovery of three instances of a new metal floridium, all of which when heated burn with a blue flame. Are you more or less confident of the generalisation "All floridium burns with a blue flame" than you were of the generalisation "All shreebles are blue"? Now consider a third case. All three observed shreebles use baobab leaves as nesting material, but how confident do you feel about the generalisation "All shreebles use baobab leaves as nesting material"? (pp. 380–381)

You will probably share the intuitions of the student subjects who felt that the generalisation about the metal floridium is more certain than the assumption of uniform coloration in shreebles, and that the generalisation about their nesting materials is least secure. Professional philosophers and psychologists also agreed with this ranking of the generalisations. It isn't very difficult to justify our intuitions in terms of our partial knowledge of metals, birds and nesting materials. Thagard and Nisbett point out that our background knowledge of the variability of kinds of things is a major determinant of our confidence about generalisation from a small number of instances. We have a notion that something is a kind of thing and that instances are liable to show variability to some extent. This indicates that concepts can carry higher-order features which reflect world knowledge. Floridium is a metal we are told, and it is a property of metals that samples do not vary very much with respect to certain properties like hardness, melting temperature and colour of flame. Other features, like shape and size of the piece, do not have this non-variable property. On the other hand, birds of the same species do not all have the same colouring (male and female pheasants are very different in appearance), and nesting materials may depend on what is available in particular locations. Some of our understanding about variability may be due to our theories about cause, and about how metals have the properties they have, why birds are coloured, and so on. The thorny problem is whether the theories about cause depend on our knowledge of variability in the first place. If they do, then our accounts of concepts in terms of attributes or features and world knowledge such as causal relations may be an account which needs to be recast. How do we get to have the knowledge of causal relations which holds together our understanding of what makes things the same and different?

CONCLUSION

The study of concepts in the laboratory has often concentrated on perceptual features and, as such, has a contribution to make to theories of recognition such as those introduced in the first two chapters for words, objects and faces. It has, however, often promised to take us closer to the understanding of more complex processes in language use and thinking. Vygotsky, for example, was aiming at an understanding of the relationship between language and thought. The moves to understanding concepts as part of understanding of the causal structure of the world, to links between concepts and induction, and to considerations of how combinations of concepts alter meaning, are all engaging on this very large task. The development of the way children divide up the world in relation to language is a very important part of this developing understanding, but we have not dealt with it here because it is such a large topic. However, for both children and adults, things are more complex than simply using words correctly. Concepts, which seem to be about identification, are actually about thought itself.

SUMMARY

The task of "telling sheep from goats" was used to illustrate that using concepts may involve identification, that features (like being woolly) may be relevant in making category judgements, but may also not be defining (a sheared sheep is not woolly). In addition, it requires us to ask what the purposes are for which people might want to distinguish sheep and goats, and points us in the direction of categorisation as existing for human purposes, some of which involve prediction and causality.

We began the chapter by reviewing some early laboratory studies which involved perceptual properties of stimuli and which set up a distinction between passive associationistic links and hypothesis testing. Such approaches tended to assume that category membership could be defined by combinations of features, and this did not tap the full richness of conceptual structures. Following the work of Rosch and her colleagues, it was recognised that there is structure and non-arbitrariness in the groupings we make and give names to, and that the most commonly used levels of categorisation accord with the principle of cognitive economy, with the basic level signifying a sufficient amount of similarity between members and a sufficient differentiation between categories. Members differ in typicality and in their relationship to a prototype which is the most typical example of the category. One way in which this relationship is measured is by family resemblances.

Subsequent work has compared prototype representations in memory with exemplar representations and associationist accounts of how links between features and a category are made. These have considerable success in laboratory situations in which features are under control. However, questions have been raised about family resemblances, about similarity and about the effects of context on concept use, and these direct attention to knowledge which is outside the particular concepts used at any time. World knowledge interacts with knowledge of particulars to affect associationist links in which causal information is involved, to change similarity relations when adjectives are combined with different nouns, and to affect the ways in which combinations of concepts can be overextended to allow poor examples to be recognised as adequate ones. All of these findings suggest that the study of concepts is returning to its original goal, which is to understand how our knowledge and the words we use are related.

A good selection of papers which discuss these issues can be found in U. Neisser (Ed.) (1987), *Concepts and conceptual development* which raises developmental issues beyond the scope of the current chapter. These can also be found in F.C. Keil's (1989) *Concepts, kinds and conceptual development*. An earlier book by E.E. Smith and D.L. Medin (1981), *Categories and concepts*, reviews many of the arguments for and against prototype theories in a way which is outside the scope of this chapter.

4 Reaching for a Glass of Beer: Planning and Controlling Movements

Reaching out to pick up a glass of beer may not seem like a very difficult activity, at least in the early evening. The glass is on the table, you reach, pick it up, carry it to your mouth and drink. No-one stops to ask "How did you do that?", and you would be very surprised if they did. The ease with which we do this makes us think that there is nothing to explain and we may want to move on to activities which seem to be more difficult, and therefore more interesting. However, it is just these very simple activities that can often be the hardest to explain. In other chapters of this book, we discuss how you might read a word, like "beer", or how you would recognise the face of an acquaintance in the bar. These are also easy to do, and they don't need much explanation in ordinary life, but when we think about how we do them we realise that reading words and recognising faces are complex activities.

The study of how we make movements is important to cognition because our thought processes only have an effect on the world if they result in movement, including the movements that produce speech. However, it is not always recognised that the questions we can ask about our knowledge of movements are similar to those we can ask about other kinds of knowledge. We can ask about the nature of the movement knowledge, about how it is stored in memory, and about how we use it to plan and prepare the actions we actually produce. Questions about how we represent the meanings of words, or how we store and use visual patterns like faces, have already been raised in earlier chapters and we address this kind of question in all the chapters of this book.

In this chapter, we concentrate on movement itself, and we start with the simple example of reaching out to pick up a glass. This is an everyday example that many of us take for granted, and we will use it here as the first of several activities that give us insight into our movement plans. Later we consider other activities such as long-jumping, throwing a parcel, typing and playing the piano. Picking up a glass involves getting the hand from one place to another, and this change in position of a part of the body is central to making any kind of movement at all. If drinking beer isn't something which you do, then you could replace the word "beer" in what follows with "tea", "lemonade", "pina colada" or whatever feels appropriate to you.

REACHING AND GRASPING

When you reach for a glass, your movements seem smooth and well organised; you don't knock the glass over, and you don't take an inordinately long time to make the movement. These are aspects of your performance that we want to try to explain. Reaching is such a well-learned activity that you probably do not know how you plan and control the reach. How do you score on these three questions: Can you make the reach as well with your eyes closed as with them open? When you reach, do you keep your hand flat until you contact the glass and then curl your fingers? Would you reach in the same way for a wide glass and a narrow glass?

In order to obtain some basic information on how people reach out and pick things up, Jeannerod (1984) filmed subjects reaching for objects of different sizes and analysed the pattern of their movements and how long it took for each part of the pattern to be produced. He found that the movement could be broken down into two main phases, the *reach phase* and the *grasp phase*. The reach phase basically involves aiming the hand in the direction of the target and moving it the correct distance. The second phase of the movement, the grasp, begins during the reach, and reflects judgements about the size and shape of the object to be picked up. When subjects began to reach, their fingers were partly bent and the tips were close to the thumbs. During the first part of the movement, the fingers began to stretch and the gap between finger and thumb grew larger. After about three-quarters of the movement duration, the finger gap was reduced in order to fit the size of the target object. This grip size changed with object size, so that the fingers were quite far apart for a large object and close together for a small one, but the size of the grip had no effect on the time it took for the overall reach phase.

Jeannerod asked subjects to reach when they could see their hands and when their hands were out of sight. Being able to see the hand meant that the reach was more accurate, but this did not lead to a change in the relative timing of the two components. So, of the three questions we asked earlier, the answers are: yes, reaching with vision is more accurate than reaching without vision: yes, you do start to curl your fingers before you reach the glass; and yes, the amount you open or close your fingers does relate to the size of the glass.

Moving the Hand from Place to Place

Reaching towards a target has two main components — where to go, and how far. When subjects who are in the dark are shown a target light which is within reach but is then removed and are asked to point to where it was, they are good at pointing to the right direction, but they are less good at moving the right distance (Soechting, 1988). This does not seem to be a problem with perception of where the target was, but with the ability to relate external space to the internal coordinates needed to carry out the reach. You need to know where something is, and you also need to be able to work out where it is in relation to you, and to the hand you will be reaching with. The spatial coordinates which describe where a glass is in space need to be related to the person who is going to reach towards it. There is neurological support for the idea that the direction of movement and the amplitude of movement might be encoded separately (Schwartz & Georgopoulos, 1987), and the finding that there are cells in motor cortex of the brain which are related to direction of movement might be thought to provide comparatively simple answers to questions of how do we know how to get the hand to a glass of beer. Once the spatial location has been perceived via the visual system and translated into spatial coordinates related to the body, then there are specific neural units which control a reach in a particular direction. However, the existence of a spatial target for a hand movement is only part of the story. There is no easy one-to-one relationship between where something is in space and the path which a hand takes to get to it. If your hand is resting in your lap and you want to reach to a glass of beer sitting on a table to your right, you will reach by moving your upper arm at the shoulder joint and your lower arm at the elbow. However, if you are standing up, with your beer glass resting on a shelf, on which your elbow is also resting, the directional relationship between your hand and your beer could be the same, but the required movements round your joints would be different.

One of the great difficulties about the human motor system is that to get the hand to a location in space, there are more positions of the limbs around the joints than are actually needed. You can check this by putting your right hand in front of you at about face height, holding it still with your left hand and then raising and lowering your elbow. You can keep your hand in exactly the same place while making large changes in the angles at your wrist and shoulder. This is a small example of what is known as the degrees of freedom problem in controlling movement. There are many ways in which a movement goal can be achieved. A location in space does not specify angles at joints, the forces needed to move limbs or even which muscles to control.

Movements are made around joints, involving many groups of muscles, and so we might expect the most simple elements of movements to be curved. However, Morasso (1981) asked subjects to point to targets on a two-dimensional surface and found that the hands tended to move in straight lines. Even when people were asked to move in curved lines, it looked as if they were actually moving in straight line segments (Abend, Bizzi, & Morasso, 1982). Movements only occur when force is applied which will move the limb, and this is done by the contraction of muscles. The spatial target for a reach has to be translated into different forces round different joints and into different patterns of activation of muscle groups in such a way as to maintain a straight line path. The motor system has to deal with a very large number of joints and muscles and there is no simple set of commands from the central nervous system which relate to how arm trajectories are produced. So although we can begin to understand the organisation of hand movement as being coded in terms of geometrical coordinates (spatial coordinates of where things are in the world), we still have to work out how this can be done. The geometrical planning account is a high-level one, but it needs to be implemented in different ways in different situations, which have to be understood before we can describe how the motor system handles the execution of a movement of a limb.

We can describe a limb movement from one place to another in several different ways, only one of which involves saying there was a straight line from a starting point to a target point. We can describe how far the hand is moved, how quickly it is moved, how the velocity changes as the movement starts and stops, when acceleration is greatest, and so on. These are kinematic descriptions of movement. If you are asked to move your hand quickly to a target you will tend to produce a straight hand path, and if you plot the velocity of your hand as it moves you will find it will be a bell-shaped curve with velocity increasing until approximately the halfway point and then decreasing. If you make the movement smoothly, then the velocity will change gradually over time and your hand will accelerate and decelerate without any sudden changes. Imagine driving a car in a straight line. If you slow down smoothly, then you don't feel any jerks as acceleration changes, because the rate of change in your acceleration is low. "Jerk" isn't just an everyday term, it is also the technical term for the rate at which acceleration changes. It does not refer to changes in direction but to the way in which acceleration and deceleration change over time. Studies of how people reach to targets have described the movements in terms of displacement, velocity, acceleration and jerk, and have shown that both for reaching straight ahead and for reaching in curved paths round obstacles, hand movements are organised so that jerk is minimised (Flash & Hogan, 1985; Hogan & Flash, 1987). This is one type of answer to the question of how we control the complexities of reaching — we opt for an energy-efficient system. High jerk means that energy is wasted as the hand is speeded and slowed down, whereas minimal jerk means that energy costs are decreased.

A different way of describing movements is in terms of the forces generated at each joint and how these interact. This is a dynamic description of movement. Models of trajectory formation which emphasise the interaction of forces at joints are also concerned with energy costs, and Uno, Kawato and Suzuki (1989) have shown that minimising torque changes at the joints also produces straight line hand paths. Torque is the rotary effect of the application of a force. This kind of work is very important in robotics research — you can't just tell a robot where a target is and leave it to get there. If a robot is going to be able to reach to different places under demands from the environment, it has to be given computational procedures which will enable it to work out how to get to new targets. These procedures are inverted in that they give the target and leave the system to work out how to get there. The system then has to work out which forces to apply in which combinations in order to get a robot hand to the correct position. Spatial knowledge has to be translated into a physical account of how the movement is to be made.

Many of the movements we make are not simple reaches from one place to another. We produce curved movements in handwriting and drawing. Wann, Nimmo-Smith and Wing (1988) argue that smoothness is an important goal in writing, and that the minimisation of jerk is important in controlling smoothness. (Remember, jerk is not about changes in direction, it is about changes in rate of acceleration.) Children write more smoothly as their writing improves (Wann, 1987). Flash and Henis (1991) suggest that movements which are curved are not different from point-to-point movements in this respect. They found that if movement is being made to one target and another target appears, a point-to-point trajectory to the first target is combined with a point-to-point trajectory from the first target to the second target, and even though the second target is never reached the overall movement is a curve. This overall trajectory minimises jerk just as the point-to-point trajectories do. Morasso and Mussa-Ivaldi (1982) have suggested that the smoothness of handwriting and drawing movements may result from hidden strokes which overlap in time. These strokes are never produced, but their combination produces curves.

Accuracy in Aiming

One of the important things in being able to move your hand, finger or any other limb, to a position in space, is that you may sometimes need to be quite accurate, whereas at other times you can be fairly inaccurate. If you are using a calculator with very small keys, for example, you need to be able to put your fingers on one and only one key at a time, and very small errors in movement have to be avoided. To punch someone on the nose, you have to hit a bigger target, and small errors are not so important. How do we make our movements accurate?

One of the earliest studies of movement produced some answers to this question. It was carried out by Woodworth (1899). His subjects drew with a pencil backwards and forwards between lines on a piece of paper attached to a rotating drum. The movements were made to the beat of a metronome so that Woodworth could investigate how hand movements were made at different speeds, and the rotation of the drum meant that

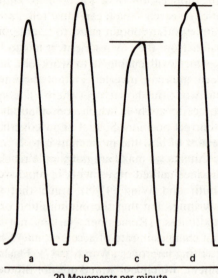

a   b   c   d

20 Movements per minute

FIG. 4.1 Tracings of different sorts of movements: (a) eyes shut, left hand;
(b) eyes shut, right hand; (c) eyes open, left hand; (d) eyes open, right hand.
Rate = 20 movements per minute. The movements with eyes shut were
supposed to be equal to each other; those with eyes open were required to
terminate on a line ruled on the paper. These are selected records, not
continuous ones. From Woodworth (1899).

any changes in the speed of the movements could be seen as changes in
the slope of the pencil marks that were produced. At slower speeds,
Woodworth found that there were two phases to movement with eyes open
— an initial one which was fast and came close to the target, and a second
phase which guided the pencil more accurately to the target (see Fig. 4.1).

Woodworth's "two-phase motor unit" can be observed if you hold your
arm straight out to one side and then move it fairly quickly so that you
touch the tip of your nose with your index finger. Unless you are quite
happy to run the risk of sticking your finger in your eye, you should notice
that there is a fast phase followed by a homing phase just before you touch
your nose. However, if the movement is very fast, this two-part movement
is not observed. When Woodworth's subjects moved back and forward
between their target lines 140 times per minute, they were much less
accurate overall, and they did not show the slower second phase. The
accuracy of their fast movements seemed to reflect only the accuracy of
the first part of the two phases, the initial impulse to move. A great deal
of subsequent research has confirmed that fast movements are generally
less accurate than slow ones and that slow ones tend to have two main
phases.

In order to start a movement, and to complete it quickly, or without being able to see what you are doing, you have to control two things. One is the amount of force you use to get the movement going, and the other is the amount of time for which the force is applied (Schmidt et al. 1979). If you want to make a long movement quickly, then you need to exert more force in the first place. If you miscalculate the amount of force, then you make a mistake. It is likely that the more force you should have exerted, the more errors occur, so fast movements (when a lot of force is required) will lead to more mistakes than slow movements.

Making movements more accurate means that they tend to be made more slowly, and Meyer et al. (1988) argued that the Schmidt et al. account did not deal with situations in which people were able to change their responses to make them more accurate, as they do with slower movements, and does not account fully for all the data which have been collected on aiming. Meyer et al. proposed a model in which the initial impulse is prone to a small amount of error, which leads to variability of the end-point of the movement. This variability round the end-point (the range of inaccuracy at the end of a movement) increases as movement distance increases and it decreases as time increases, so there is more variability for long movements and less variability if the movement is slow. Meyer et al.'s model allows subjects to make sub-movements in order to optimise their spatial accuracy, or to keep sub-movements to a minimum in order to optimise time. Woodworth's subjects used sub-movements in traces (c) and (d) in Fig. 4.1. In general, when you reach out for your glass of beer, you probably want to optimise the accuracy with which you reach the target — not too fast and not too slow. The outcome is likely to be an initial impulse and one or more sub-movements which allow you to be accurate.

Correcting an Aimed Movement

Making corrections in a reach which allow you to deal with the variability in the initial impulse can be carried out by using perceptual information about the success of the movement being made. Keele and Posner (1968) estimated how long it took people to correct the accuracy of an aiming movement during vision. They did this by turning off the lights when the movement was begun and they found that movements which took an average of 190 msec to complete were made with the same accuracy whether the lights were on or off, while movements which took 260 msec or longer were more accurate with the lights on. They concluded that it took between 190 and 260 msec to correct an aimed movement.

A much shorter time for altering a movement time based on visual feedback has been estimated by Carlton (1981), who prevented subjects from seeing their hands for most of a movement to a target, and found that there was a change in the acceleration of the hand (the first sign that a correction was being made) within about 135 msec from the hand becoming visible. The task was well learned (more than 50 repetitions of a reach) and performed very accurately, so very small corrections were in fact made, suggesting that the initial component of the movement was very precise in this case. Wallace and Newell (1983) varied the accuracy demands of movement over different movement distances, and found that short movements to wide targets were not affected by the presence or absence of vision, but movements to very small targets needed vision to be performed accurately, although they took the same length of time as longer movements to larger targets. When vision was needed, it took 200–250 msec to use it, which is the same range as that suggested by Keele and Posner (1968).

Movements made with vision may be more accurate because vision gives better information about where the target is or where the hand is, as well as giving information about any errors in direction or distance. Young and Zelaznik (1992) asked subjects to move a stylus towards a target. On some trials, the target itself began to move as the stylus was lifted from its resting position and the room light was turned off after 50 msec of movement. This amount of visual experience of the target position was enough to allow subjects to alter the end position of their movement even when the mean movement time was 165 msec. This doesn't mean that the subjects performed very accurately in these conditions, only that they could use target information to alter their action within 165 msec.

So how long will it take you to correct a reach for a glass of beer? Different experiments give different estimates of the time taken to use visual feedback depending on the combinations of movement distance, speed and practice that are used, and whether subjects know that vision will be available or not. In Carlton's task, as in many of those we have discussed, the target actually stopped the movement, so terminal velocity does not need to be controlled too finely. Instead, it is important not to make an error to the side of the target, or to move too far or not far enough. Practice reduces the amount of sideways error, so all that is needed is minor adjustment. If you reach for a glass, however, the target does not stop the movement; in fact, the glass will be knocked over unless the movement is properly controlled. The time to correct error is therefore likely to be in the range suggested by Keele and Posner (1968) and Wallace and Newell (1983), if not more.

Grasp: What Happens When You Get There?

The discussion of how we use visual information to inform us of errors in our movement planning or changes in the position of the target has raised the issue of the relationship between getting to a place and actually doing something when you get there. Punching someone on the nose is closer to many of the experimental tasks used than picking up a beer glass is, because in punching the movement is stopped by the impact (eventually), whereas in picking up a glass it is important to change the reach into a grasp and lift. As Jeannerod's observations showed, the two components of the reach and grasp develop together over time, but Jeannerod went further, and argued that the two components were controlled independently because there were two visuo-motor channels — one based on information about where things are, and the other based on information about what they are. The visual information about where the object is directs the motor system in the transport phase in which the hand is moved towards the object, and visual information about what the object is, or at least about its size, shape and orientation, direct the opening of the fingers. These two channels can be independent, but Jeannerod found that the time at which the fingers were furthest apart was also the time at which reaching movement had a low velocity, and argued that the two components were integrated in terms of the times at which grasp elements related to transport elements. In this section, we are considering whether the knowledge of what is to happen next alters the way in which reaches are produced.

If the information about how big an object is is used only to direct the grasp, while information about how far away it is affects only the reach, then object size should not affect how long it takes to move the arm to the target. Unfortunately, investigation of a wider range of object sizes has shown that movement to pick up very small targets takes longer, but that this is due to more time being spent slowing down when the target is small (Martenuik, Leavitt, Mackenzie, & Athenes, 1990), so the two kinds of information are not separate. It is of course possible that there are connections between the two visual motor components which integrate them into one overall reach, and Arbib (1985) has argued that although there are two different visuo-motor channels, there is a higher-order schema which integrates the two. Bootsma and van Wieringen (1992) think that this is not very parsimonious and just changes the question of how reach and grasp are coordinated to asking how the high-order control works. They argue that visual information about where the hand is with respect to the target changes as the hand moves towards the target, so initial direction and distance information is used only for the first part of the reach. As the hand gets closer, information about the size and shape of the object now begin to influence both the grasp and the timing of the reach.

However, purely visual information does not have the same effect in different contexts for movement – if subjects have to be more accurate, or if the object is fragile. Imagine that you are reaching out for a ceramic pot, about the same size as a beer glass, would you reach for it in the same way if you were told that it was extremely valuable? Or would this knowledge lead you to treat the object in ways which are not based solely on what it looks like? Martenuik et al. (1987) showed that when subjects reached for light bulbs which pointed towards them so that their size and shape was similar to that of a tennis ball, they had a longer deceleration phase (that is, they slowed the movement down over a longer period) than they did when they reached for a tennis ball. If the hand is travelling more slowly when it contacts the object, then the impact of the hand is decreased, so there is less chance of a delicate object breaking. On the other hand, if subjects are asked to reach and grasp an object as quickly as possible, or if they do it with their eyes closed, they reach with a greater opening of the fingers even though the object remains the same (Wallace, Weeks, & Kelso, 1988; Wing, Turton, & Fraser, 1986), and this also happens if subjects believe that the target may move before they get to it (Athenes & Wing, 1989). What people know about objects affects the way they reach for them.

The argument that the organisation of reach is affected by what one knows has been taken a stage further by Rosenbaum et al. (1990). They started with the observation that a waiter who reached for an upturned wine glass in a restaurant did so with his hand turned down, so that his thumb pointed at the table top. When he had picked it up, he turned it over and filled it with water. If he had picked up the glass with his thumb towards the ceiling, then when he turned it over he would have had to hold his hand in a very twisted position while he filled the glass. Rosenbaum et al. took this observation and carried out a series of experiments in which they asked subjects to reach out and pick up a rod which was held horizontal to the table top, and to place it upright on one of two disks. The subjects were instructed which end of the rod was to touch the disk as well as which disk was to be used. Figure 4.2 shows a diagram of the position of the rod and disks in one experiment. If you imagine picking up the rod with your right hand to place its right end on the right disk, you will probably find that you imagine picking it up overhand (i.e. with the back of your hand pointing to the ceiling), but if you imagine moving it with your right hand to stand its left end on the left disk, you will probably imagine picking it up underhand (back of your hand pointing to the table top). That is exactly what Rosenbaum et al.'s subjects did. If you try to imagine picking up the rod with the back of your hand facing up and then putting its left end on the left disk, you will find that you have to put your arm into a very awkward position. Rosenbaum et al. argued that the way in which the object was picked up depended not only on what it looked like and where it was, but on what was going to happen to it next. Their view was that the organisation of the initial grasp allowed extreme joint angles (which require more force and so are less energy-efficient) to be avoided during the next part of the

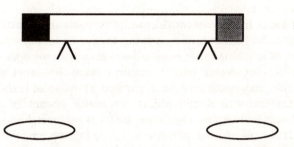

FIG. 4.2 The rod-to-disk task of Rosenbaum et al. (1990). Subjects were asked to place the rod upright (the end being specified) on one of two disks. See text for further details.

action, even if the initial position itself was sometimes not the easiest one. In planning action information about what is to be done first requires access to the information about what is to be done next and how that can be optimised by the first step in the sequence. Reach and grasp in its full complexity in the world may require more than visual knowledge of where objects are and of their shape and orientation.

Rosenbaum and Jorgensen (1992) took the idea that awkwardness at the end of a movement was avoided (or that comfort at the end of a movement was increased), and looked at a more complex task which required subjects to move a rod to one of the shelves on a tall bookcase. This also involved the rods used in the previous experiment, but this time the movements involved were much larger and they were repeated in a series going from the top shelf to the bottom or from the bottom to the top. The rod was horizontal, straight in front, and to get the right hand end to touch the front of the top shelf of the bookcase is easier if the rod is picked up overhand, while to get the same end to touch the bottom shelf it is easier to pick it up underhand. The question was, if subjects had to move the rod to each shelf in turn, when would they change from one grip to the other? They did change their grip, but they didn't change it at the same place going down the shelves as they did going up, and Rosenbaum and Jorgensen concluded that in the middle region, where the differences in awkwardness were not extreme, the grasp which had just been selected was preferred. They suggest that there is a cost to selecting a new strategy for carrying out a task and that when there is little advantage to be gained, we tend to carry on using the same method. Movements we perform now are influenced by movements we have just performed, provided they are within tolerable limits for awkwardness or for energy expenditure.

CONTROLLING SEQUENCES OF MOVEMENT

When we are acting in the world, we are continually selecting particular actions instead of others, and carrying them out in sequence. Even the simple task of reaching for an upside down glass, turning it the right way up and then pouring water into it requires many levels of planning and control. This sequence may be organised at quite a high level in the planning system, with details left to the motor system to implement in terms of forces and minimising energy costs, as we have discussed in earlier sections. If we can plan sequences of action in advance, do we also plan the movements themselves in advance? Do we create sequences of motor activity which will be simply run off in a string, or is there a continuous process of unpacking higher-order structures into more specific ones? The view that motor responses can be run off in a string is an old one. It is known as *response chaining* and is an associationist account of links between movements. The argument was that components of sequences were linked to each other in such a way that the sensations which followed one movement acted as the stimulus for the next. The time interval between one movement and the next is controlled by the time needed for the sensations from the first movement to trigger the second. This view was challenged by Lashley in 1951. He argued that there was insufficient time for sensations from one movement to trigger the next and proposed that movement sequences were organised hierarchically. A hierarchical account argues that rather than a long string of responses there are levels of output control, and that these are reflected in the temporal structure of the movement sequence. The time between adjacent movements will differ, depending on where they are in the sequence.

The Structure of Movement Sequences

Hierarchical structure in the planning of movement has been investigated using measurements of the time it takes to begin movements and the time between movements. Adding more bits to a sequence which has to be produced can increase how long it takes the sequence to be started (Inhoff, Rosenbaum, Gordon, & Campbell, 1984), and timing of the intervals between movements has also been used to suggest that hierarchies are operating. The general argument is that if responses are simply strung together (chained) so that the end of one starts the next, then there should be no consistent differences in the time taken to start different sequences of movement or between the responses themselves. Klapp and Wyatt (1976) used the task of making short (*dit*) and long (*dah*) presses on a Morse code key. They asked subjects to make one of four movement combinations of key presses (*dit–dit, dit–dah, dah–dah* or *dah–dit*) in response to one of four signal lights, and they measured the time it took to start the first key press. They found the longest reaction times when the first part of the combination was *dah* rather than *dit*, but the reaction time was shortened if the second item was the same as the first. So *dah–dah* was produced more quickly than *dah–dit*, and *dit–dit* was faster than *dit–dah*. These two findings suggest that there are two components in the pre-programming of these simple activities. To produce *dah* first takes longer because it requires a slower movement which is more complicated to program into the force impulse discussed earlier. The effect of repetitions indicates that there is another level of programming that relates to the elements in the action. If two elements are the same it takes less time to organise them, so repetition is specified at a level above force.

More evidence that sequences of movements are structured in levels comes from a study by Rosenbaum, Kenny and Derr (1983), who asked subjects to make repeated tapping patterns with different fingers. These went right-middle, left-middle, right-middle, left-middle, right-index, left-index, right-index, left-index, and instead of looking at how long it took to start a sequence, Rosenbaum et al. looked at the times that elapsed between each tap. They found the longest gap in the centre of the sequence when the pattern changed from middle to index finger, with slightly shorter gaps between the first and second pairs in each half. They argued that the sequence was broken into two between the middle and index fingers, and then into two again between the pairs of right and left taps, and that this structure was reflected when the sequence was translated into the individual finger movements that produced the taps. Rosenbaum et al. used a hierarchical structure to explain these results. In a hierarchy, the details of organisation at a lower level do not need to be known at a higher level. Depending on the levels of complexity in the output, there may be many levels in a hierarchical structure, and we will consider more levels when we look at tasks like typewriting. However, for the present, the point to note is that the pattern of times between responses suggests that they are not simply prepared in a long string.

In the kinds of tasks which we have discussed so far in this section, subjects have been told what the sequences were that they were trying to reproduce, and so structure was built into the tasks. In addition, the tasks have had a one-to-one relationship between the responses required (touch that key) and the parts of the body which made them (use that finger), so we cannot judge whether it was the actual finger movements which produced the patterns in the times, or the response elements at a more central level of organisation. Cohen, Ivry and Keele (1990) addressed these issues by training subjects to produce a learned sequence of key presses in response to visual signals and then asking if the sequence itself was independent of the effector system (the specific parts of the body) which made them. In order to look at the way learning transferred to different parts of the body, Cohen et al. varied the way in which subjects responded. They asked subjects either to respond with fingers which remained next to the response keys (like a touch-typist) or to move their whole arm back and forward using the same index finger to touch each of the keys (like a "hunt and peck" typist). The results were very clear. Asking subjects to switch from finger to arm movements or vice versa after they had practised the sequence did not affect their ability to respond on the repeated sequence, but if they had to switch to a random sequence in which lights came on in an order they had not experienced before, they became very slow in their responses. Cohen et al. (1990) argue that what is learned is spatial targets for movement responses, not motor commands specific to the effectors involved during learning. Learning the locations at which targets will appear and the locations to which responses must be made involves associations between adjacent items in the repeating set. Once the spatial sequence is known, it can be implemented by different effectors.

If association between items in a set of spatial targets controls the next movement we make, does this mean that hierarchical structure is not used in controlling output after all? The first thing to notice is that Cohen et al. (1990) are proposing a set of associations between target locations, not a chain which triggers a response on the basis of sensations from the previous response. The second point to note is that spatial ordering may only be one component of how sequences of movements are learned. Cohen et al. also showed that using repetitions within the sequence of movements so that the items occurred twice in different groupings made the task much harder. Subjects could not learn to make these responses quickly if they had to do another task at the same time, because they did not notice that items had different associative links in one context to those they had in another. Cohen et al. suggest that the whole long sequence of targets and responses has to be broken up or parsed, and a representation assigned to each of the two parts of a repeated sequence, and that this parsing of the sequence is harder to do and so does not occur if another task is involved. This kind of parsing relates to the hierarchical conclusions from the earlier studies and is found when sequences can be grouped, the groups arranged in a sequence and then the lower level of each group worked through before the next group is begun.

Keele and Jennings (1992) report a connectionist model which was required to learn Cohen et al.'s task on a purely associationistic basis and found that the sequences with repetitions were learned most poorly by the model. They argued that this was similar to what happened to humans when they had to do another task at the same time as learn to respond to the sequence. They also argued that this is because neither the model or the humans who were doing another task at the same time were able to place boundaries on the sequences, and without boundaries on sequences learning of internal structure cannot occur. The connectionist model had to be made more complex by indicating where the structure in the sequence was, and when this was done it behaved in a way which was similar to human subjects. Associationist accounts can allow for hierarchical descriptions, even though there are no explicit hierarchies in the connectionist model.

Making Sequences Flexible

We have been trying to understand some of the programming and use of memory representations that take place when we make comparatively simple movements. Although we have emphasised advance programming and the memory structure which controls sequences of movements, other factors are important in controlling our actions. If, like some neurologically impaired patients, you cannot use proprioceptive input which comes from your joints and muscles, then you will find it very difficult to perform simple sequences like crumpling a piece of paper (Jeannerod, Michel, & Prablanc, 1984). An emphasis on advance organisation does not mean that we cannot use perceptual information to change sequences of movements. If we did not, we would be like mechanical toys which continue to move their legs even when they fall over, instead of being skilled adaptive movers in the environment.

You may think that you can produce inflexible sequences of movement if you practise them enough, and you would not be alone in this. Skilled long-jumpers, for example, try to develop a run-up of a fixed number of paces, and measure distance from the board quite carefully, making the run-up as regular as they can. Yet they do not produce a fixed pattern of movement on each run-up (Lee, Lishman, & Thomson, 1982). Instead, they maintain a consistent stride pattern until they are a few strides from the board. At that point, the consistency breaks down and stride length is altered to produce an accurate position on the take-off board (see Fig. 4.3). This adjustment is based on visual information about the position of the board and involves a change in one aspect of the stride pattern, the vertical impulse of the step. The vertical impulse determines how long the flight time for the stride will be. Thus, programming does not mean that movements are run off regardless of what comes out or how relevant it is.

The long-jumper is trying to run quickly to a particular position in the environment as well as to produce thrust from that location to carry the body forward. Someone trying to hit a ball uses information from the ball itself to time the hit (Bootsma, 1989). Many other skilled acts use information from the environment to modify performance before it occurs, even though the action is well learned. There are also many cases in which the consequences of one movement are evaluated and used to alter subsequent output, that is, perceptual information is used as feedback about movement accuracy. In handwriting, for example, removing visual

(a)

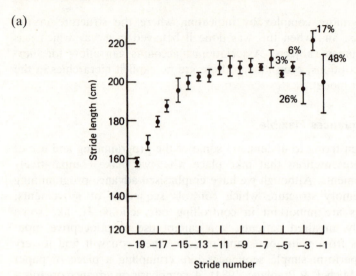

(b)

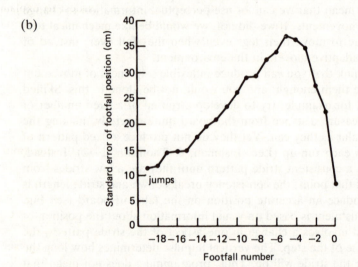

FIG. 4.3 (a) Means and standard deviations of stride lengths over six run-ups for an Olympic long-jumper. The run was over 4 m with 21 strides (first 2 strides not shown). Stride −1 is the stride onto the take-off board, stride −2 is the preceding one, etc. Numbers printed over the last strides are statistical estimates of the percentage adjustment made on the stride. (b) Standard errors of the distances of the athlete's footfalls from the take-off board. Footfall 0 is the one aimed at the board, footfall −1 the penultimate one, etc. Reproduced with permission from Lee et al. (1982). ©1982 APA.

information affects performance at two levels. First, it is much more difficult to organise the output on the space of the paper, so handwriting does not run in a straight line. Second, there are errors in the production of the number of strokes in letters like "m" and "w", and in repeated letters like "ll" (Smyth & Silvers, 1987). The first of these is similar to the use of vision in controlling strides to a board in the long-jump, as it is concerned with the organisation of action in space, while the second is probably based on visual information after the movements have been made, which enables correct judgement of the number of repeated elements in a sequence. Information about the success of our action in terms of the goals we had set is available from vision, hearing and proprioception, and such information about the success of our movements is crucial for the development of new or improved skilled actions (Jordan, 1990). Even though performance can continue in the absence of perceptual information, good performance depends on incoming information via the senses.

DEVELOPING MOVEMENT SCHEMAS

When I reach for a glass of beer, pick it up, carry it to my mouth and drink, an observer will not notice details of the movement. I will simply have lifted the glass. Yet if the glass is completely full, I will have to exert more force to lift it than if it is half empty, so the instructions to move will be different although both the intention and the description will remain the same. The ability to cope with variation within the same action develops with time and experience. We probably do not think of reaching for a glass as requiring a great deal of acquired skill, and perhaps an example used by Pew (1974) is more compelling. Pew observed post-office workers sorting packages. Each sorter stood near the source of the packages, between 5 and 10 feet away from a set of 25 mailbags. As each package appeared, it was examined and then thrown into the correct mailbag. The packages were of many different shapes and sizes, the sorter was different distances away from each of the mailbags and could be standing in slightly different positions on different occasions, yet accuracy in getting the package into the mailbag was extremely high. What interested Pew was the nature of the learned knowledge for throwing parcels, which the sorters had developed over time. It seemed implausible that they would have stored in memory instructions for every distance they had seen in the past, or every packet weight which they had felt. Pew's view, and that adopted by many others since, was that a generalised schema for movements of a particular class is developed with experience.

Before we consider the nature of these schemas for movement in more detail, we need to consider the word "schema", which is used in many contexts in psychology. In general, it refers to a knowledge structure that does not contain specific information about a particular movement or event. When Bartlett (1932, p. 201) adopted the concept of schema from its use by Head, he stated that: "'Schema' refers to an active organisation of past reactions or past experiences, which must always be supposed to be operating in any well-adapted organic response". We discuss in Chapter 9 how schemas can be used to explain the way in which past experience can be used to make sense of similar situations when they recur, but in the present context another quotation from Bartlett is more appropriate, because it is specifically directed at movement control. He wrote about making a stroke in tennis or cricket and commented that: "When I make a stroke I do not, as a matter of fact, produce something absolutely new, and I never merely repeat something old. The stroke is literally manufactured out of the living visual postural 'schemata' of the moment and their interrelationships". (p. 202).

A detailed account of generalised schemas for movement has been put forward by Schmidt (1975). In Schmidt's account, there are several stages involved in making simple movements. First, the overall situation has to be sized up and the appropriate type of action selected, and this means using the appropriate schema. Then the initial conditions such as how heavy the parcel is and how far away the mailbag is have to be assessed and translated into decisions about how to make the schema specific for that particular movement. This means calculating the specific values for parameters in the general program for these movements. "Parameters" in computer programs take particular values when a program is run, but can be different on every occasion, depending on the requirements of the situation.

One prediction from Schmidt's account is that it should be easier to generalise an action schema to new objects if practice had been allowed with a range of objects previously, and there is some evidence for this. Carson and Wiegrand (1979) asked children to practise throwing a bean bag to a target. Some children practised on one bean bag and some practised on several bean bags which were of different weights. The children who practised with the range of weights were better at throwing a bean bag of a weight they had not encountered before than were children who had practised on one bean bag only. However, Van Rossum (1990) has reported that children throwing weighted tennis balls did not show any differences when asked to generalise to new balls after practice, although there wasn't much improvement in throwing the balls during training, which suggests that the children may already have had quite well-developed ball-throwing abilities.

Schemas for controlling classes of action need to vary on more than just the amount of force exerted to deal with different weights. In picking something up, for example, sometimes the tips of the fingers and thumb are used to grasp, sometimes the palm of the hand is involved with several fingers working against it, as when you hold the handle of a hammer. When you pick up a mug by the handle, you place the thumb on top of the handle, and any number of fingers from one to four goes through the handle, depending on the size of the aperture. When you pick things up using the tip of the finger and the thumb, you can use just one finger or more than one finger. So grasping something may be an action schema, but it has to be implemented in different ways for different objects. Arbib, Iberall and Lyons (1985) have discussed the selection of the number of fingers used in picking things up in terms of the concept of a "virtual finger". They argue that for the task of picking up a cup, three virtual fingers are used — one on top of the handle, one in the handle and one left over. The five real fingers are assigned to the virtual fingers so that there is no need for a separate programme to tell the five fingers what to do in the grasp, rather all control in picking up a mug deals with three virtual fingers. The virtual fingers then have three methods in which they can be in opposition — opposition to each other, opposition to the palm, and side opposition. The "opposition space" determined by visual analysis of the object allows virtual fingers to be shaped in advance during the reach.

Arbib (1990) presented a connectionist or neural network approach to investigating the relationship between task characteristics and the selection of opposition space and virtual finger mappings. He took a set of 10 lifting tasks, each of which is done by people in a different way, and required a network model to learn how to do the tasks. Input to the network involved four units — one for length of the object, one for object width, one for the amount of force required, and one for the precision demanded in the task. Each had four hidden units and one output unit. After training by exposure to different object descriptions, generating grips and being given information about error in the grip selected, the network learned to use the palm when large forces were required and to use the tips of the fingers when the precision demands of the task increased, and to deal with different-sized objects, in ways which are similar to humans. This model indicates that information about the length and width of objects, the force needed to lift them and the precision required to deal with them, can control how a grasp is organised. The schema is flexible over a wide range of alternatives for output.

FLEXIBLE WELL-LEARNED SKILLS

Handwriting: Schemas for Spatial Patterns

What kind of schema might we have for a well-learned skill like writing a particular letter of the alphabet? When we write we make finger movements that move the pen up and down, finger movements that move the pen from side to side, and movements at the shoulder joint that move the hand across the page. Vredenbregt and Koster (1971) have shown that a mechanical model with two electric motors that drive a pen horizontally and vertically can simulate many aspects of handwriting. The diagonals and curves are the result of interactions between the forces produced by the two motors. We can think of the two sets of muscles that move the fingers as operating in a very similar way. Basically, they make vertical movements or sideways movements and the force used has to be carefully timed. Changes in the amount of force exerted vertically can lead to an increased stroke in order to produce an "l" rather than an "e", and allowing all impulses to last longer makes the writing larger (Wing, 1980).

Does the mechanical model with two electric motors relate to the way humans write and draw? Meulenbrook and Thomassen (1991) asked subjects to scribble back and forwards in a circle with the only instruction being that they had to cover the diameter of the circle on each trial. They looked at the direction of scribbles produced and found that subjects preferred horizontals, verticals and diagonals, with the verticals and horizontals being visually controlled, while the diagonals were affected most by the position in which the arm was held, (i.e. the anatomical ease with which movements could be made). They argue that there is an overall spatial framework in which writing and drawing movements are made, similar to that proposed by Vredenbregt and Koster (1971), but that, in people, this framework is implemented through a motor system which has its own constraints, some of which relate to the ease with which parts of the body can be moved in particular configurations.

On the question of exactly what is controlled in order to produce letters of different sizes, there is no easy answer, but again there may be an overall abstract spatial representation which is produced through a set of stored motor instructions which are adaptable for different circumstances. Teulings, Thomassen and van Galen (1986) looked at the consistency with which people maintained the spatial pattern on the page, the amount of force exerted in each stroke, and the time for which force was exerted when they were asked to do the same writing task over and over again. They wanted to know what remained the same when the action was repeated many times, in order to get an idea of what the most central parts of the representation were. They found that handwriting was most consistent with regard to the spatial features, and that the amount of force used could be traded off against the time for which force was used in order to keep the spatial features constant. This suggests that if you speed up your handwriting, you do not simply make each stroke more quickly. Instead, you manipulate the amount of force in relation to the time, in order to keep the spatial features of the letters as similar as possible. People with poor handwriting find it hard to control the forces required, possibly because they cannot inhibit irrelevant tremor, or neuromotor noise in the system (van Galen, Portier, Smits-Engelsman, & Schomaker, 1993).

Your individual handwriting style depends on individual spatial regularities as well as the stored procedures which you have developed for producing forces in your muscles. If you write on a blackboard you will use your whole arm, yet your handwriting style will be recognisable, which suggests that these procedures are not specific to the muscles that move your fingers (Wright, 1990). "Recognisable" need not of course mean that your handwriting is exactly the same on every occasion, and there is clearly noise as well as consistency in handwriting production. Wann and Nimmo-Smith (1990) found that the spacing between letters changed when subjects were asked to produce the same letters in small and large handwriting and that the way in which these spaces changed was not simply by multiplying the spaces for small writing to get the spaces for large writing. However, they also concluded that repetition of letters does not provide any evidence that the same temporal patterns are used consistently. What is consistent about handwriting is more likely to be spatial than temporal, and the motor system can implement this spatial representation in a variety of ways using stored schemas which can be tailored to different circumstances.

Handwriting involves the production of patterns in space, and the evidence suggests that the spatial representation in memory is dominant in producing letters. Handwriting is not just a meaningless motor activity, it is one method of producing language and so it deals with the production of words and letters. Writing is a complex cognitive and motor skill, in which the complexities of language have to be turned into a sequence of movements. The letters are best thought of as patterns for writing — not as "A", "B", and so on — and we use the term "graphemes" to describe these written units. However, a grapheme may appear in more than one form (e.g. upper- and lower-case) and so the specific allograph has to be selected. The allograph is a stored spatial pattern of stroke directions and there may be separate allographs (or forms of a grapheme) for letters written in different places in words as well as for different forms such as upper- and lower-case letters. The allograph is finally produced as a sequence of movements which leave marks on the page. In a model of handwriting put forward by van Galen (1991), it is assumed that different processing subsystems or modules pass information from one to the other, but that each level is operating at a slightly different point in real time (planning what you want to write is further ahead than the actual letter you are writing now). The four steps from words to strokes are part of a hierarchy, and there are analogies between the production of written letters and the sequence of taps which we have discussed earlier. The part of van Galen's model shown in Fig. 4.4 assumes that each processing module deals with a different unit size in the handwriting process, and that each has a working memory buffer or memory store. The size of writing is assumed to be implemented at the level in which the allograph (the stored spatial pattern of stroke directions) is the unit. The final stage involves the recruitment of the muscle groups which will actually carry out the writing. These are not part of the actual motor memory, because if

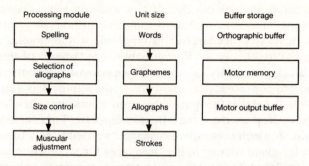

FIG. 4.4 Part of van Galen's (1991) model of handwriting showing four stages of output.

they were it would not be possible to write using the fingers, the arm, the big toe, and so on. The formation of the actual trajectory of the movements, which we have discussed earlier in the chapter in connection with getting a limb to points in space, is the very last of the stages in the production of handwriting.

Using Keyboards: Fast Movements to Many Spatial Targets

We started this chapter by looking at reaching and aiming to a target, because many of the more complicated activities we engage in involve reaching to targets. Typing and piano-playing are good examples of such complex tasks, as we have to put a finger on a key in a particular position in space in order to produce a note or a letter. The overall intention may be a very high-level one indeed (like playing a Bach fugue or writing a novel), but it has to end up as a long sequence of aiming movements. Extended sequences of movements are not run off like the music on a record; rather, they are organised according to the structure of the material which is to be typed or of a piece of music. We have suggested that structured sequences are translated into elements which will in turn be used to produce the motor output. We will now examine this approach using typing and piano-playing in turn.

Typing.   When we think of typing, we know that the typist produces a series of key presses which occur one after the other and that a good typist can do this at the rate of 500 key strokes a minute — about 100 words per minute (wpm). Typists can tell us a certain amount about what they do, but their perceptions of their performance are sometimes not borne out when tested. For example, some typists feel that they can scan quite a long way ahead on a page, and that this helps them to maintain a smooth output. However, Shaffer (1973) found that good, fast typing (100 wpm) was achieved when typists could see 8–9 letters in advance and did not improve if more letters were shown. For slower typists, preview led to good results with fewer letters, and overall it seems that typists look ahead for just as much as it takes 1 sec to type: any further look ahead adds nothing more to the skill. Shaffer also looked at the role of the material being typed and found that there was little difference between the typing speed for ordinary connected text and for nonsensical passages which contained real words in random sequences. Presenting letters in random order led to a drop of about 50% in overall speed. These results suggest that organising continuous typing requires knowledge of letter combinations in the language being typed. The responses have to be organised first at the level of letters before being turned into movements that will press the keys.

Does this mean that we know that the movements are organised in the order in which the keystrokes make the letters appear on the page? Gentner, Grudin and Conway (1980) filmed a 90 wpm typist and looked at the order in which the movements were begun. The movements are described as being like "the movement of sea grass weaving in the waves . . . all in motion at the same time" (Norman & Rumelhart, 1983, p. 47) and they did not support the view that each finger made a stroke in turn. For 21% of the keystrokes analysed, the movements did not begin in the order in which the keys were eventually struck. In these cases, the finger movements that resulted in the second of two keystrokes started before the finger movements that produced the first one. This means that the commands for future keystrokes influence the current position of the hand and finger.

On the basis of these observations, and data taken from the kinds of errors that typists make, Rumelhart and Norman (1982) produced a model for typing which they tested by running it as a computer simulation. A simulation is not intended to mean that typists are computers, but rather the degree to which the simulation behaves like a real typist is used to evaluate how similar the processes built into the model can be to the processes in the human typist. The model is called an "activation triggered schema system", and a schema is defined as an organised unit of knowledge which can have other schemas nested within it. That is, schemas are hierarchically organised, with high-level ones being "parent" schemas to others which are "child" schemas, but these in turn can act as "parents" for other still lower levels. The idea of activation used here is similar to that used in McClelland and Rumelhart's (1981) model of word recognition discussed in Chapter 2, although in the present case output units are activated.

The schema for a word to be typed activates child schemas for the keypresses that correspond to the letters in the word. These in turn act as parent schemas to excite arm, finger and hand movements. An actual movement of a particular finger in a particular direction will only occur if the schemas or knowledge units are activated sufficiently. Activation can be damped down by inhibitory links between schemas. Once a keypress has been produced, that unit is deactivated. Norman and Rumelhart argue that an orderly sequence of output is not planned in advance. Instead, several keystrokes are in competition to occur as early as possible and it is the amount of activation that leads to one appearing in the correct serial order. Advance preparation is explained by the activation of commands for future keystrokes which influence the current position of the hand and finger, but there is no organised string of letters planned before they are produced.

The kinds of mistakes people make when they type can provide evidence for models of typing. Basically, a typing error means selecting the wrong letter, the wrong hand, the wrong finger or the wrong position for a finger. Grudin (1983) has found many substitutions between hands (n→v), between fingers (a→s) and within fingers (n→b). These errors could occur because the keystrokes are in competition with each other, and this sometimes leads to the wrong movement appearing before the correct one has received enough activation. This would mean that substitution errors should be made more quickly than normal keystrokes. Omission errors are likely to occur when the same letter has recently been typed and so been deactivated. When Grudin considered the timing of substitution errors, he found that the interval before an error was not shorter than normal, as the model predicted. Instead of keystrokes being produced on a first-come, first-output basis, Grudin suggested that the overall timing of responses is regulated by a central timekeeping system using an internal clock. This means that some overall control of the output is necessary.

If there were a central timing mechanism which regulated the intervals between letters, what would happen if typing speeded up or slowed down? Would all the intervals be speeded up by a constant proportion? We have already considered this view of the invariance of timing in our discussion of handwriting and found it was not a good account of how timing changed over repetitions. Gentner (1987) asked skilled typists to type sections from a magazine at different speeds. He found that typists would normally change rate within pages, and that when asked to change rate they could do so. The relative amount of change in the intervals between key strokes was affected by the absolute rate of typing, that is, speeding up typing does not speed up all intervals by the same amount. When typing was fast, there were different time intervals between different pairs of letters and these stayed the same for repetitions of the same pair of letters, suggesting that there were peripheral constraints on timing. However, when typing was slow, these differences between pairs of letters disappeared. Gentner argues that there are both central and peripheral effects in typing performance because typists can change speeds at will, yet when they go very quickly they are compelled by the positions of their fingers to produce different intervals between different letters.

Gentner (1987) also tried to speed up and slow down the Rumelhart and Norman typing model and found that it did not perform like real typists when asked to perform slowly. This is one of several areas in which the model does not behave like real typists, although it is probably a good model of skilled typists typing quickly. There is another criticism of the model, which might be seen as more fundamental. This is that although it accounts for coarticulation — the way in which fingers get into position for later movements if they are not required by the present one — the model does not explain how a word organises its constituent letters in the first place. If order is built into the system so that the first item in a sequence is known and excitation and inhibition build up based on that sequence, then we do not know how order is really controlled. The model is specific about how schemas compete and so can be implemented on a computer, but it is not specific enough about how the word is put into the system for a full computer model to be possible (Keele, Cohen, & Ivry, 1990).

Rumelhart and Norman's model does not explain all typing performance, but what this model has done is to make it clear that explanations for our motor activity should not be completely in terms of advance planning and the development of programs for action. There are important contributions from the physical system of the body itself. What your fingers are capable of doing at any given time affects your typing, in addition to the perception of the material to be typed and the control of directed movements to keys.

Playing the Piano: Timing and Expression.   In earlier sections, we discussed timing without considering how it was done. In the study of typing, some theorists have suggested that there is no need for central timing, whereas others consider that this is the only way to explain the findings. Perhaps typing and the other tasks we have been looking at are not the most suitable activities for investigating the full extent of our timing abilities. After all, the typist is not required to do anything more than produce accurate keystrokes as quickly as possible. The targets in handwriting and typing are spatial, not temporal.

When we consider a musician, the picture is a very different one. A good pianist sight-reading a piece of music reads notes on a page and produces finger movements on a keyboard in response. However, there is more to playing than this. A competent player can play all the notes in the correct order, but an excellent player also adds expression to that order, and has to use knowledge of the type of music being played and its conventions in doing so (Sloboda, 1985). The difference is a bit like that found between a drum machine, which produces exact intervals between sounds, and a real drummer, whose intervals will be less exact, but for most of us, more interesting to listen to. Shaffer (1981) has shown that an expert pianist playing two successive performances of a Bach fugue, which he had not played for many years, structured the timing of the two performances in a very similar way. The analysis broke the music down into units with the four-bar phrase at the highest level, and the quarter bar at the lowest. The timing relations were closest at the highest level of the analysis and least similar at the lowest level, which suggests that overall there was hierarchical planning of timing for the piece of music. One very interesting finding concerned a set of errors that the pianist made in one performance. Unlike a typist's errors, these did not produce nonsense. The harmonic structure of the music was maintained and the rhythm was not disrupted.

To produce an underlying beat, the timing in music has to be controlled by a mechanism that uses a central timing mechanism, but if we can only produce the correct beat there is no expression. Playing expressively includes playing away from the beat and then returning to it. The mechanism that does this has to be responsive to timing, which is a property of the representation of the structure of the movement. So timing has to have two levels, one for a clock which produces regular intervals and one which actually produces movements to produce notes at different points in time relative to the beat. These two levels of timing control do not seem to be totally independent (Clarke, 1982). If the overall speed or tempo is changed, this affects the relative timings within sections of the music and is not independent of them, because expression of interpretation of the music involves both.

If expression is important when musicians are playing a piece of music, what do they do when they play scales? Do they simply produce notes at equal intervals? Do they have a fixed sequence of movements which they run off at different speeds but keep the intervals the same each time? MacKenzie and van Eerd (1990) asked skilled pianists to play two-octave C major scales with a metronome at different speeds. They found that there was more variability in the intervals between keypresses as the overall speed increased, which indicated that there was no overall speeding up of all movements, so even a scale is not a program for movement which can be speeded up by decreasing each component by the same proportion. They also showed that intervals between notes varied depending on the complexity of the movements to be made, so that moving the thumb to play F on the right hand on an ascending scale gave a short interval, but the interval was longer when the index finger crossed over to play G, and that, in addition, this was affected by how fast the scale was being played. This suggests biomechanical timing constraints derived from the freedom of the fingers to move into position, which are similar to those suggested in the typing model discussed earlier. While the musical structure of a piece of music may be primary, and central timing necessary, there are some constraints on timing relating to the overall tempo at which music is played, and to the biomechanical difficulties of combining finger movements.

Producing music requires many levels of representation, some of which are concerned with the knowledge of music itself, while others are auditory, spatial and motor. The pianist's knowledge of the type of music he was playing in Shaffer's study meant that he had procedures stored in memory for producing certain types of rhythmic patterns, arranging the fingering of notes and chords and planning the phasing of a sequence. These procedures allowed a representation of the structure of the music to be built up a section at a time when he was sight-reading correctly, and they also affected the section built up when a sight-reading error occurred. The abstract structural representation of a piece of music in the mind of the player is the first of a series of stages of output organisation. The later stages which specify spatial targets and represent the commands that will specify movements, and involve memory units like those discussed for typing, is derived from the first.

Although the details will be very different, we should be able to use such a framework to account for simple movements with one force impulse and little accuracy, such as banging your fist on the table to attract attention, or those as complex as producing different sequences of force impulses, of different intensity and at different times, simultaneously with the right and left hands, as a concert pianist will do. It is because there is more to moving than simply giving commands to muscles that we have included this chapter in a book on cognition, and have treated movement planning as a structured hierarchical process.

SUMMARY

In this chapter, we began with a consideration of reaching out for and grasping objects, and used this example to introduce the problem of the number of degrees of freedom which have to be controlled when the hand is moved to a new position in space, and the different types of description of movement which are possible. These descriptions can be comparatively high-order, referring to locations in space and paths between them, or they can be descriptions of the physical movement in terms of kinematics or dynamics. The spatial level of description, and of representation, not only proves useful in understanding simple aiming, but also in studies of handwriting and typing.

The accuracy of a reach can be affected by visual information which is received during it. Visual input is also important in shaping the way in which the hand opens during a reach and then closes to the appropriate size to pick up an object. Both the opening and the time taken to make the reach are also affected by what we know about the object to be picked up. In addition, the way in which we pick objects up can be altered by what we intend to do with them next.

When we put sequences of movements together, we organise them into groups and produce one group at a time, rather than producing very long strings. These structures are hierarchically organised and show up in the different patterns of timing found between items at different positions in a sequence. Even in learning sequences of keypresses, however, it is the spatial locations of the targets and their relation to one another which is acquired. Similar patterns of timing are produced even when movements are made in different ways, provided the targets are in the same spatial sequence.

In flexible, well-learned skills, we again find that stored spatial knowledge is important, whether it is knowledge of spatial patterns in hand-writing or of spatial locations in typing and piano-playing. These complex activities are structured hierarchically by the material to be produced (the text or the musical score), and translated into meaningful units which are maintained in memory before being implemented by the motor system. Some of the characteristics of these skills, however, are produced by physical constraints on the movements of the hands. Skilled motor perfor-mance can be understood in three important ways. The first considers human movement as movement of a physical system with physical con-straints which affect what is possible. The second emphasises that move-ments take place in space, and representing space is an important component of movement control. Third, the hierarchical nature of the structure of the control of movement can reflect the structure and meaning of the activity being carried out.

Some of the topics raised in this chapter, such as the need for an account of how trajectories are produced which uses descriptions of the kinematics and dynamics of movement, seem a long way from the general theme of cognition. We have included them here because, like the research pro-grammes dealing with human vision, the research programmes dealing with human movement call on the whole range of disciplines which contribute to cognitive neuroscience. Physical models of movement are important but they are only part of the story of how human knowledge is implemented in human action.

Several of the issues raised in this chapter will be found in later ones. In the next chapter, we will return to movements in considering how we do two things at once, although we move beyond movement itself to consider many other types of activity. Planning output is an important topic in Chapter 7 on the production of speech, and the issue of memory schemas is central to the discussion in Chapter 10.

There are many sources for further reading on this large topic. The text by D.A. Rosenbaum (1991), *Human motor control*, is at a relatively introductory level. A collection of papers edited by M. Jeannerod (1990), *Attention and performance XIII: Motor representation and control*, is an excellent source for more advanced further reading.

5 Tapping Your Head and Rubbing Your Stomach: Doing Two Things at Once

At a party, or sitting around with a group of friends, you might be asked to tap your head with one hand and rub your stomach with a circular motion with the other. You would probably find this quite difficult to do: people tend to tap and tap or rub and rub. It is this difficulty which makes the situation amusing. When you tap and tap instead of tapping and rubbing at the same time, one activity has captured some of the control of the other. There are many other situations in which we try to do two things at once, but we do not always find that one task captures the other. Children have been listening to pop music while writing essays for quite some time, and they tend to claim that no interference occurs, whatever their parents may say. You may find that you can talk easily to passengers while driving your car, but that you stop talking when approaching a hazard in the road. In this case, there is no capture; rather, one task is stopped entirely. If we are asked why these changes occur, most of us have answers that include paying attention, doing things automatically, or having some things in the background while others are more central. Psychologists interested in how people do things at the same time have put forward similar explanations, though usually in more complicated language.

In this chapter, we consider what the relationships between two tasks tell us about how our cognitive abilities are organised. We will not be spending the whole chapter dealing with how you tap your head and rub your stomach. Instead, we use that example to discuss some of the properties of the way in which we control our limbs, which might prevent us from doing two things at once. We then consider other constraints on what we can do, such as whether we can only make one decision at a time, or whether we have only a limited amount of attention which we can give to any task. Of course, the amount of practice and experience you have with an activity can alter your ability to do something else at the same time, and we will be discussing the effects of practice. The other tasks that we will consider include typing and talking at the same time, and reading and writing at the same time, so we do move quite a long way from tapping your head and rubbing your stomach.

SIMULTANEOUS ACTIONS WITH TWO HANDS

Can you tap your head and rub your stomach at the same time? Does it make a difference if you use your right hand to tap and the left to circle or the other way round? Why should this difficulty occur? Is there a link between the control of the hands which puts a basic limitation on our ability to do two things at once? A simpler situation, and one that has been studied in laboratories rather than at parties, is one in which people are asked to move their right and left hands rapidly to different targets. These movements are aiming movements similar to those described in Chapter 4. When a "go" signal was given to subjects in an experiment run by Kelso, Southard and Goodman (1979), they had to move both hands quickly from a position in front of the body to two targets placed to the sides. One target was further away and smaller than the other, so that it was more difficult to hit accurately. If the movements are made one at a time, it normally takes people longer to move to a small, distant target than to move to one which is close and large. However, Kelso et al. found that the two simultaneous movements reached the targets at the same time. The subjects seemed unable to make the movements independently of each other but slowed down easy movements so that they finished at the same time as difficult ones.

When we considered how movements are made (Chapter 4), we suggested that a motor program could have parameters that allowed it to be used for different movements of the same type. Schmidt et al. (1979) have suggested that when people make rapid simultaneous movements with two hands, some of the parameters applied to both hands have the same value (e.g. the movement time is the same), but other parameters have different values (different forces have to be exerted to produce movements of different extent in the same time). So there is a sense in which we can make two movements at the same time, provided we do not want the movements to be completely different. It is easier for you to control temporal elements of movements of different limbs by keeping them similar, even when movements are made over different distances. So, if you are asked to move one hand and one foot different distances at the same time, then temporal aspects of the movement (such as the point in time when the velocity is greatest) should be similar across limbs. Given that you have been asked to make movements of different sizes at the same time, this can mean that the distances you actually move are not the right length but are affected by the discrepancy between the movements required of the two limbs. Sherwood (1990) asked people to make the same and different size movements using the hands and the feet, and found that making different-sized movements did lead to error in movement length. He argued that the behaviour of the limbs is a function of the interaction of neural commands for the left and right limbs. The relationships between the hands were greater than those between the feet, or between one hand and one foot, suggesting that it is more difficult to prevent interference — or cross-talk — between commands for the right and left, when the upper limbs are being used. This would mean that the links between the hands, which often work together in manipulation of objects, may be tighter in order to allow for greater coordination between them.

Simultaneous Rhythms

If you have ever tried to become a drummer or a pianist, you will have experienced situations in which you have to try to make the two hands move at different times in order to produce interesting rhythms. Making sequences of timed rhythmical movements is very similar to tapping the head and rubbing the stomach and can be studied using very simple tapping tasks. Klapp (1979) asked people to press a key with one hand in synchrony with a light that came on at set intervals. He found that performance deteriorated if subjects also had to tap as quickly as possible with the other hand. However, if the two hands were coordinated — so that one was tapping twice as fast as the other — there was no deficit. Again, the timing of movements seems to constrain what one can do with two hands at the same time. Yet it is possible for a drummer to produce movements of the two hands that are not synchronised at regular intervals. How does this happen?

Imagine trying to tap consistently (produce a beat) with one hand and then tapping a rhythm (like a repeated melody phase) with the other. Or try to do it using the example in Fig. 5.1. You should set up the beat with one hand (try the left) and then phase in the rhythm with the other. Switch hands and try again. Try tapping the beat with the right hand and the rhythm with the left foot. Did you find some of these combinations more difficult than others?

The rhythm in Fig. 5.1 is one of three that Ibbotson and Morton (1981) asked subjects to tap. They used university students, half of whom were musicians who had been playing an instrument for at least 6 years. They asked each subject to tap the three rhythms in 12 combinations of limbs

FIG. 5.1 Rhythm and beat to be tapped simultaneously.

(all possible pairings of two feet and two hands), so each person had 36 attempts. Ibbotson and Morton found that the musicians did much better overall than the non-musicians, some of whom were unable to tap at all with their feet. In addition, the non-musicians did best when the right hand had to tap the rhythm against a beat from one of the feet or from the left hand, and combinations in which one of the feet took the rhythm and one of the hands took the beat were very difficult.

Three observations can be made from this experiment. The first point concerns the relationship between the control of the right and left hands and of the hands and feet. Differences here were only found for non-musicians and so are related to the second point, which is that musicians found the tasks easier than non-musicians did. The third point concerns a detail about how the experiment was run: Subjects were not allowed many attempts at each condition, so they could not improve with practice.

As the two hands or feet need to be closely coordinated for many activities, it does make sense for them to be dependent on each other. If we had to time each foot separately when we walk, the activity would be unnecessarily complicated. Coordination means the ability to regulate movement activity over many sets of muscles and different limbs. There is other evidence that such coordination involves dominance relationships in which one hand is more important than the other, and both hands are more important than the feet. Gunkel (1962) found that when subjects had to move one limb back and forward slowly and move another limb back and forward quickly at the same time, the rhythms were not independent. Sometimes the movements were alternated, so that when one hand was moving, the other was stationary, and vice versa. In addition, the feet were more likely to act together than the hands, and the right hand was relatively independent of the other limbs when it was used to make fast movements. Ibbotson and Morton's data agree with this. Instead of having independent control of the hands and feet, we have different degrees of linkage — or coupling — between the limbs. This makes coordination easier in ordinary tasks because normally we are trying to use the limbs together, as we do in walking, and this requires us to move the hands and feet within a common temporal framework. We can do this by specifying timing parameters which are used for more than one limb. In order to do two separate things with two limbs, we have to break some of the natural linkages.

Practice and Simultaneous Movements

Ibbotson and Morton (1981) did not allow their subjects to repeat combinations of limbs and rhythms. They argued that with practice subjects might be able to do the task but that it would not be possible to tell how they did it. One problem with practising doing two tasks at once is that it is possible to create a third task which is a combination of the first two, and then to do that one task using two limbs. The rhythm and beat patterns in Fig. 5.1 can be thought of as six events which involve tapping with one limb or tapping with two. Did you try to tap the rhythm with your foot and the beat with your right hand and find it totally impossible? Try the same combination again, but instead of trying to do both kinds of tapping separately, try this:

Count: One   Two-and   Three-and   Four

Tap: Both   Both Foot Both Foot   Both

("Both" means tap with both limbs, and "Foot" is foot only.) If you count the rhythm only and unite the two tasks in one, it should become much easier. You have created a new task that does not require you to control each limb separately.

Doing two things at once is easier if those two things can be combined into a new activity, but does this mean that musicians are better at tapping rhythms because they can produce a new "third" task more easily than non-musicians? To answer this we have to look at complex rhythmic performance, in which it is much less likely that the performer can be producing movements with one limb which are temporally linked to those produced with the other. When we look at the performance of good pianists, we discover that there are few similarities between movements made with the right hand and movements made with the left.

Piano-playing has been extensively investigated by Shaffer (1981), who attached a computer to a grand piano so that the time between the keystrokes and the intensity of every keystroke could be recorded during a performance. We have already mentioned this work in Chapter 4. In one performance, a pianist played a study by Chopin in which one hand had to play a group of three notes in the time that the other hand played four. This 3 : 4 pattern occurred twice in each bar for about 60 bars in the music. The two hands had to produce differently timed finger presses and also to move up and down the keyboard at different times. The pianist moved her hands across the keyboard at different times and she was able to produce more force in one hand independently of the other. She appeared to have independent control of her hands. However, this independence is produced within a framework for doing one task, playing one piece of music.

So, although producing different rhythms at the same time with two hands is very difficult when the two rhythms are not multiples of each other, skilled musicians are able to perform complex polyrhythms. They may do this by organising the two elements into an integrated whole so that there is no longer a dual-task situation (Deutsch, 1983). They may also do it by decoupling the strong links between the two hands so that they can perform separately timed movement sequences with the two hands, which is Shaffer's preferred explanation for the performance of the pianist described above. Studies by Jagacinski, Marchburn, Klapp and Jones (1988) have tended to show that subjects do integrate the organisation of the movements of the two hands, but this could be because they did not use subjects with high enough levels of skill.

Summers and Kennedy (1992) used subjects who all had a minimum of five years experience of playing the piano and who performed at a comparatively high level. They attempted to encourage the development of separate control by training subjects to tap with each hand separately, tapping with 300 msec between taps with the right hand and with 500 msec between taps with the left hand. When subjects were asked to put the rhythms together, musicians could do the task and non-musicians couldn't manage it at all. The non-musicians tended to tap at the same times with both hands or to tap with one hand and then the other. The musicians' performance was not captured by the strong links which normally control the timing of the two hands, and they were able to integrate these incompatible sequences into one. However, when the time at which the musicians tapped were considered, they were not found to be independent for the two hands. The faster hand taps were produced accurately and the slower taps were interleaved between them. Summers and Kennedy reported that this integrated pattern was observed even after eight days of practising tapping a 5 : 3 polyrhythm. Further work by Summers, Rosenbaum, Burns and Ford (1993) suggested that the control of the slower hand in a polyrhythm is subordinate to the control of the faster hand, that is, there is a hierarchy for controlling the hands with the faster hand at the top. They trained subjects to tap along with tones to produce a range of polyrhythms (3 : 2, 5 : 2, 4 : 3, 5 : 3 and 5 : 4) and then to continue tapping when the tones stopped. They found that the variability of fast hand responses was not affected by the polyrhythms, but that the slow hand variability was affected by which polyrhythm was required, indicating that the slow hand was subordinate. However, the musicians in this study reduced variability on the slow hand on almost all the rhythms. Summers et al. (1993) suggest that a central counting mechanism is required from which the complex counting of the skilled musician must be derived. This, they argue, is why animals cannot produce complex rhythms like those produced by human jazz percussionists — they cannot use these complex counting procedures!

DECISION AND ACTION

In the previous section, we considered some of the motor linkages that might make it difficult to do two things at the same time. However, tapping your head and rubbing your stomach, or even playing the piano or the drums, may not be the examples that come to mind when you think about doing two things at once. Most of us aren't too worried about chewing gum and walking at the same time, and we do consider, perfectly sensibly, that we can have a conversation about politics while driving home in the car. The latter activities are going on over the same section of the day; one of them seems to have a larger motor — or perceptual–motor — component than the other, which is concerned with the organisation of an argument and the production of speech. There are many things we "do" which have a considerable component that is not directly apparent in our actions. You say "Shut up, I'm thinking" to a chattering friend because you are "doing" something that does not have a very large action component. We will return to the issue of what "doing" means in a later section, but first we will consider the meaning of "at once". What are you doing when you drive and talk at the same time?

Driving and talking may go on over the same extended period, but it is possible that while you are thinking about what to say next you are not doing much driving. After all, there are many occasions when driving consists of little more than making occasional adjustments to a steering-wheel and occasional movements of one foot. If you see an obstruction ahead in the road you will have to decide what to do and produce more driving-related actions and it is likely that your contribution to the conversation would stop. Is this because you don't actually drive and talk at the same time but alternate the two? Or is it because you have a certain capacity for deciding or for doing things, which gets used up if one task is difficult?

Probing Cognitive Tasks

One way to look at this problem is to ask someone to carry out one task and then to "probe" them by asking them to respond to something else while carrying on the first task. The diagram in Fig. 5.2 shows the structure of an experiment designed by Posner and Boies (1971) to investigate this issue. Subjects had to watch a screen on which two letters were presented, with a 1 sec delay between the two. They had to press one of two keys with the index finger of the right hand if the letters were the same and the other key with the middle finger of the right hand if the letters were different, and they had to respond as quickly as possible. This first or primary task required the subjects to recognise a letter, hold it in memory, recognise another, compare them, decide if they were the same or different, and then decide which button to push and to move the correct finger. The most difficult part of the task is in the decision-making stage, although to an outsider no part of the task looks very difficult. The secondary task was to press another key with the index finger of the left hand in response to a brief auditory tone which could occur at any time.

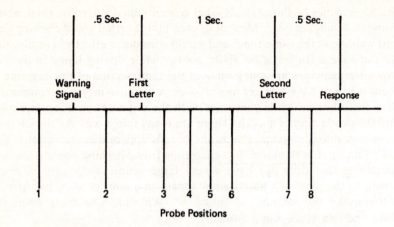

FIG. 5.2 Schematic diagram of a sequence of events in a letter-matching task used by Posner and Boies (1971), in which a series of auditory probes are placed at each of the probe positions indicated. Reproduced with permission from Posner (1973).

Posner and Boies found that the time it took subjects to respond to the auditory probe varied depending on what they were doing in the other task. If the tone was presented just before, or at the same time as, the second letter, there was an increase in the time taken to respond to the tone. This suggested that there were times when it was difficult to do two things at once and times when it was easy. If the tone appeared during an easy part of the first task, there was no increase in the time to respond to it, but if it appeared when the first task was difficult, then it was not possible to start responding to the tone until the difficulty had been dealt with, and so the reaction time was longer. The Posner and Boies study has been covered here at some length because it introduced an important method for attempting to find out what was going on and when. However, later studies have altered the method slightly and produced different results. These changes in method result from changes in the theory of how we do two things at once, and we will deal with these later in the chapter. First, however, we consider the general principles involved in the conclusion drawn by Posner and Boies.

The Psychological Refractory Period

Posner and Boies' result suggested that people could only cope with a certain amount of decision making or complexity at one time, and if something else came along to be dealt with, it had to wait. Such a proposal had been put forward by Craik (1948), who thought that there might be a limit on what people could do because there was a single "computing"

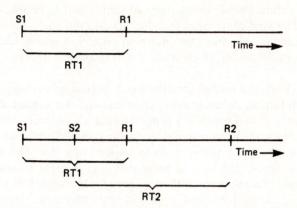

FIG. 5.3 The psychological refractory period. The reaction time (RT) to a second stimulus (S2) is increased by the interval between the second stimulus (S2) and the first response (R1).

process that dealt with incoming information one step at a time. If a second input arrived while the first was being processed, it would have to wait, so there would be an increased reaction time due to the "psychological refractory period". There have been many experiments on the refractory period, in most of which the task is to respond to one signal as quickly as possible and then to respond to a second signal. The typical finding is that if the second signal occurs before the response to the first has been made, then the reaction time to the second is lengthened by the interval between that signal and the response to the earlier one (see Fig. 5.3).

Legge and Barber (1976) have described this result as being a bit like a doctor's waiting room. If it takes 5 minutes for a consultation with the doctor, then you will emerge after 5 minutes if there is no-one before you. But if someone else goes in to see the doctor just as you arrive, then you have to add their 5 minutes to yours. You will be delayed by the length of time between your arrival and the end of the previous patient's consultation. In the same way, the response to the second signal cannot be prepared until the first one has been completed. In many experiments in the 1950s and 1960s, it was found that the delay in the second response time was not influenced by practice, that the delay occurred when one signal was visual and the other auditory, and when the two movements were made with different hands. It was concluded that there was some central decision-making channel, which was limited in that it could only make one decision at a time (Welford, 1968).

The decision that was thought to occupy the central channel was of a specific type. An increase in reaction time did not occur if a response to the first signal was being made and a new instruction required that the response should be speeded up (Vince & Welford, 1967). That is, the pattern of action already being planned simply had to be intensified, not changed. The kind of decision that did increase the second reaction time, and so limited people doing two things at once, was one which initiated a fresh pattern of action or changed the relationship between input and output.

Pashler (1991) has investigated the psychological refractory period using tasks which require different types of processing. He argues that if there is a refractory period which is a general limitation on processing information, then being about to respond to one task should affect whatever else we try to do. Pashler asked subjects to respond to a tone, and then during the reaction time to the tone he presented a set of eight letters for a very short interval of around one-fifth of a second. One letter had a little mark under it and the subject's task was to identify that letter, trying to be as accurate as possible. The letter identification task did not have to be done quickly, just accurately. The accuracy of perceiving the target on the visual task was not affected by whether or not the letters appeared during the reaction time to the tone, nor by the length of the interval between the tone itself and the presentation of the letters. So, when only one task required a very quick response and the other task involved perceptual analysis which had to be accurate, there was no refractory period and no indication that preparing a response to a tone prevented analysis of new perceptual input. If, however, the response to the perceptual task had to be made quickly, then the time to respond to it was increased if the letters appeared during the response interval to the tone. When the interval between the two presentations was short, the fast response to the first display had to be made before the fast response to the second display could be produced, just as the psychological refractory period would predict. So, the psychological refractory period does not reflect a general limitation on processing information, which means that we can do two things at once, provided "doing" one of the things does not mean choosing and making a response. However, selecting responses can impose a limitation. It is difficult to select two similar responses at the same time.

Stimulus–Response Compatibility

Although response selection affects the psychological refractory period, it does not have the same effect in all circumstances. The relationship between input and output is very important. Welford (1968) assumed that the decision or "translation" mechanism (translating from perception to action) would be used below its full capacity if there was not much translation to do. If the stimulus and response were "compatible", then little translation would be required. It will be easier for you to move a response key to the right if an arrow on a computer screen points to the right than it will if the word *elephant* appears and you have to remember a rule which says "elephant means to the right, giraffe means to the left". The arrow and the action are compatible, the word and the action are not. Greenwald and Shulman (1973) investigated compatibility in the psychological refractory period. When the first response was to move a switch in the direction of an arrow and the second was to say "one" when the word "one" was heard, there was no refractory period. Subjects were able to do these two things at exactly the same time. However, if the second task required a translation from stimulus to response (hear "A" and say "one"), then there was a longer reaction time. It was therefore not just the change of response from keypressing to talking that made the improvement in compatible conditions, but the relationships between input and output.

However, just making the relationship between input and output more direct does not necessarily get rid of refractoriness. It is much easier to move a finger which has just been touched than it is to move a finger in response to an instruction or because a light has come on (Leonard, 1959), yet Brebner (1977) found refractoriness when he used touch stimuli on the fingers of the right and left hands. Simple compatibility did not remove the "only one thing at a time" principle when the two responses involved the two hands.

In many of the earlier studies, it was thought that using different hands for the two responses was enough to show that the limitations were based on a central waiting period, not on the execution of the movements (Davis, 1956). However, we now know that moving the two hands requires very similar sorts of motor instructions and it is possible that the nature of the response systems involved causes limitations that are not due to any central waiting period. We used the Posner and Boies (1971) experiment mentioned earlier in the chapter to show that there were times when people were able to do a second task and times when they were not, just as you might expect from driving and talking. However, in Posner and Boies' task, subjects had to choose responses made by the two hands, and responding to a tone took longer if it occurred when subjects were preparing to respond to a letter-matching task. McLeod (1978) altered one aspect of the Posner and Boies task and produced quite different results. He asked his subjects to decide whether two successive letters were the same or different and to press one key for "same" and another for "different". Instead of having to use the other hand to respond to an auditory probe (which made a "bip" noise), some subjects were asked to say "bip" when they heard the tone, while others had to press a button as before. The subjects who were allowed to speak one of the two responses showed much less interference between the letter-matching and responding to the tone than did subjects who had to use their hands for both tasks, no matter when the tone was presented. The overall limitations on the ability to decide whether two letters are the same or different and to make another response at the same time was affected by separating the response systems, even though two responses had to be selected quickly.

McLeod (1978) concluded that separating response systems removed major elements of difficulty in dual-task performance. Pashler (1990) disagreed, arguing that the decrease in reaction times to the second task found when the response was vocal, rather than manual, did not reduce the time to that which would be found if the two tasks were carried out separately. This indicates that response selection is still a difficulty, even if it is less of a difficulty with two response systems. Pashler found that one of the difficulties with making two separate hand movements was that subjects sometimes moved the wrong hand, even though they knew exactly which button they wanted to hit, and they sometimes spent a little extra time deciding which hand they really meant to move. With one hand movement and one vocal response this doesn't occur. However, if subjects were told in advance which order they had to move their hands in, so that they could get the responses selected before the stimuli even appeared, then there was a much smaller effect of refractoriness. Again, the difficulty in keeping the hands separate has a large effect on our ability to select two responses within the same time interval.

Separating response systems can remove any postponement of a second movement if the first movement is a manual response to a tone and the second movement is a movement of the eyes to a visual target (Pashler, Carrier, & Hoffman, 1993). However this only happens if the eye movement is attracted by the target when it appears, not if there is a response rule to a colour to be learned. So, for example, if subjects have to move their eyes to the left when they see a green colour straight ahead, while a red colour means move the eyes to the right, then a manual response and an eye movement response do interfere. This could just mean that the second set of tasks are more difficult, or it could mean that some eye movements do not interact with the parts of the motor system involved in choosing movements of the hands. Both eye movements to targets in the world, and shadowing what someone else has said, may be tasks which happen without interfering with other actions.

The number of things we can do at one time can be limited by the relationships between our limbs, which makes it difficult to move them totally independently unless we are highly skilled. There are also limitations on the number of decisions we can make at once, but these only occur if the relationship between the input and the output is not a direct one, or if the same response systems are being used for each task. We will refer again to these issues later in the chapter, but first we will consider more fully the idea that there is a general limitation on our ability to do two things at once.

ATTENTION AND SELECTION

So far in this chapter we have ignored the term "attention", but some readers may think that what happens when we do two tasks is simply that attention has to be shared between the tasks, and there is a limit to attention. This view has been held by many psychologists, some of whom have also shared the ordinary view that sometimes we can do one thing automatically while attending to another. This view of attention is linked to our everyday experience that we can attend to, or be aware of, only a part of the potentially available information from the outside world. This is clearly a perfectly accurate account of our experience, but it may not be a good explanation for what we experience. We started by considering some of the findings when people do two things at once because we want to emphasise that we are not trying to explain what people are aware of, but what they can do. If we use attention to explain our failures to do two things at once, there is a danger that we can ignore response factors altogether, and forget that we are interested in the whole system which links our perception, our thoughts and memories and our actions, not just in perception alone.

Early and Late Selective Attention

We aren't always trying to do two things at once. When we speak of attention we are often referring to the ability to select out one thing to focus on, rather than trying to do several things. No organism can respond to all the objects and events in the world at the same time — some have to be ignored, while others are attended to. But just when does the selection of things to attend to actually happen? We have to know what is out there, in some sense, before we can attend to it. Is there a single stream of information flowing in and action flowing out, with one place at which some stimuli are selected and others are ignored? If so, at what point does this selection occur?

Research into how we select some things to attend to and ignore others has tended to concentrate on this question of when selection takes place. Early researchers argued that we can only attend to a part of what is in the world around us because there is a bottleneck somewhere in the processing system (Broadbent, 1958; Deutsch & Deutsch, 1963). Treisman and Geffen (1967), for example, asked subjects to listen to words that were played into one ear and to repeat them aloud, while at the same time other words were played into the other ear but were not to be repeated aloud. The task of repeating speech aloud as you hear it is known as "shadowing". In addition to shadowing the message that came in on one ear, subjects were asked to press a button if a particular word target appeared in either ear. The results showed that subjects could push the button when they heard targets in the message they were repeating aloud, but that they could not do so very often if the targets were in the message they were not repeating. This result was interpreted to mean that the subjects had filtered or blocked the words they were not repeating so that they were not allowed into awareness, and that this happened before the words were recognised (early selection). If you don't know what a word is, you cannot push a button in response to it. MacKay (1973), on the other hand, showed that when subjects repeated aloud ambiguous sentences like "They threw stones at the bank yesterday", and at the same time the word "river" was presented on the ear that was not being shadowed, the subjects did not remember hearing the word "river", but they remembered that the sentence was about throwing stones at the river bank, not about throwing stones at the money bank. This experiment suggested that subjects did know what the words on the unshadowed ear meant, even though they could not remember them, so MacKay argued that some selections of items which are allowed into awareness must happen after words have been recognised (late selection). More recently, investigations of early and late selection have concentrated on perceptual selectivity, so that some accounts (e.g. Treisman & Gelade, 1980) argue that selection is very early and only colour and the orientation of edges are processed before such selection in visual perception, and that spatial location is important in this early processing. Other accounts, such as that of van der Heijden (1981), have argued that objects are recognised before selection.

The early selection view of selective attention has tended to emphasise the simple physical characteristics of sensory information and, in parti-cular, spatial location. Auditory messages can be selectively shadowed (repeated aloud) if they come from different locations in space, and interference between tasks with similar outcomes is much reduced if competing targets are in different positions in space (Kahneman & Henik, 1981). So selection on the basis of spatial location does occur. However, Allport (1993) has argued that working out where things are in space is not a simple process, and doesn't always happen early in the sequence between perception and action. In our discussion of reach and grasp in Chapter 4, we referred to the distinction between processing where objects are in space and what they are. There is evidence that there are two parallel visual systems (Ungerleider & Mishkin, 1982), one important for form and object recognition and the other important for the detection of spatial relations between objects and for visual–motor links controlling movement in space. If these are parallel — that is, if information is dealt with in both systems at the same time — then it may not be necessary to think of spatial attention as coming first and the identification of what an object is as being second, because both happen together. In addition, although we tend to think in terms of a simple serial process from perception to decision to action, this may not reflect the structure of the links between input and output. We can, and do, select spatial locations to attend to, but this does not mean that other information is not processed.

The relationship between where something is and what it is has been explored using the task known as the Stroop task, which was described by Stroop in 1935. In this task, subjects are asked to name the colour of the ink in which a word is written. If the word itself is also a colour name, the subjects have great difficulty in ignoring that name and simply reporting the ink colour. Could the Stroop task be a situation in which our normal ability to select objects and events to attend to simply breaks down, because the name of the word and the colour in which it is written are found in the same location in space? Kahneman and Henik (1981) have shown that the interference between the name of the word and the name of the ink colour disappears if the colour word is in a different location from the colour which has to be named. So, the word can be ignored as long as it is not in the same spatial location as the ink colour.

Driver and Tipper (1989) have pointed out that the fact that there is no interference from the word in Kahneman and Henik's task doesn't mean that it has not been read. A lack of interference in response production does not necessarily mean that early selection has taken place. They asked subjects to concentrate on the number of red items in a display that was presented very quickly, and told them to ignore a black item on the same display. The black items were in fact digits and so could interfere with the response of naming the number of red items. (You can show this interference effect for yourself by looking at the sets of items in Table 5.1. You should be able to read out the number of items in each set in list B faster than list A — because list A is actually made up of digits and you have to make sure you don't say them.) In Driver and Tipper's experiment, the number of red things to count and the black digit were spatially separate. Driver and Tipper found no Stroop interference effect on the time taken to report the red items. However, they did find an effect on the next trial. If the black item that was ignored on one trial was different from the actual number of red items on the next trial, then the time to report the number of red items on the second trial was increased. This showed that the black items which seemed to have been ignored were actually interfering with subsequent responses. Driver and Tipper argued that stimuli which do not interfere and are not being "attended to" are processed to the same level of representation as the interfering distractors. They conclude that the identity of a distractor can be known but can be inhibited from controlling the response in a Stroop-type task. Therefore, spatial location differences make it easier for us to respond to one object rather then another, but that does not mean that we don't know what the other object is.

TABLE 5.1

Interference Between the Number of Items and the Identity of the Items Being Counted[a].

List A	List B
888	FFF
444444	GGGGGG
99999	PPPPP
6666666	HHHHHHHH
3333	KKKK

[a] You should find it more difficult to say how many items there are in each of the sets in list A than it is to say how many items there are in each set in list B.

Selection for Action

Many studies of attention and selection have asked subjects to make selections between visual inputs which are close together, or of different colours, and have looked at the kind of interference which occurs. These studies tell us something about how we can make discriminations and selections, but they may not tell us much about how we use information from the environment in everyday contexts in order to make real selections of things to attend to. Imagine you are back in the bar from the previous chapter and about to reach for your drink. Selection of the correct glass to reach for is important here because there are several glasses on the table and you only want to pick up one. So the information from one glass has to be allowed to control your action, while the information from other glasses has to be prevented from doing so. What kind of interference will there be from the other glasses? Which of the many aspects of their visual appearance will make it difficult for you to reach?

Tipper, Lortie and Bayliss (1992) argued that concentrating on the purely visual characteristics of seen objects and asking subjects to name them, made it very difficult for traditional selection experiments to give us information about selection of objects in the world. Tipper et al. asked subjects to carry out a selection task which involved action to targets rather than naming a target, in order to assess the impact of action on selection. On each trial, subjects were asked to press a button on a board if a red light next to it was illuminated, and to ignore a yellow light which would come on next to one of the other buttons. The task is shown in Figure 5.4. The time taken to make the response on each trial was measured, and it was found that the nearer the yellow distracting light was to the target the more it interfered, as previous work on spatial attention would predict.

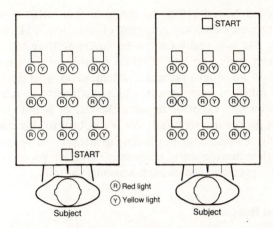

FIG. 5.4 The experimental layout in the study of Tipper et al. (1992). The subjects moved from the starting position to touch whichever one of the other squares was indicated by a red light. A yellow light appeared at another location and was to be ignored. R, red; Y, yellow. See the text for further details.

Interestingly, distracting lights in front of and behind the target light did not always have the same effect on the response time. If the subject started the movement from a position between the board and his or her body, then the front row of lights interfered more than the back row. If the subject started the movement from a position behind the board, then the back row of lights interfered more than the front row. This might be happening simply because subjects looked at the start button before they started a movement, so distractors near the start button had most effect. However, if subjects had to watch the middle light before they started to move, they still showed different interference patterns from the front and back rows depending on where the hand started from.

Tipper et al. argue that these results suggest that attention to seen objects in the world is not just visual, but is related to the actions we want to carry out. Trying to find the place where selection occurs between input and output may be a mistake. Interference may occur at the perceptual level, at the semantic level (deciding what something means) or at the action level, depending on the task. What is important is that selection relates to the inhibition of some incoming information in order to allow the task to be performed competently. When you reach for your glass, the inhibition required to prevent you reaching to other glasses will be different depending on the position of your hand before you reach.

The research carried out to distinguish between early and late selection theories is extensive, and many of the studies are very complicated. However, there is still no clear answer to whether we attend by making a selection after we know very little about the stimulus or after we know a lot. This has led Navon (1989) to conclude that either position can be stretched to accommodate any empirical observation, and that the distinction between the two really cannot be successfully tested. Perhaps the debate between early and late selection focuses on the wrong question. Maybe there is no single place for attention to operate. We have to consider the range of situations in which our ability to use information from more than one event or object either is, or is not, limited by the nature of the processing required. We will return to this question of the multiple kinds of limitations in processing later in the chapter. First, we consider another more general account of attentive processing, and look at some of the problems which such accounts can raise.

Capacity and Resources

One way to deal with the difficulty in deciding where attention operated was to reject the idea of a block in a particular part of the system, which restricts how much we can do. Kahneman (1973) suggested that instead of a particular restricted stage, there was a general limit on our ability to do mental work. This can be thought of as a limited supply of power or resources. If all the domestic ovens linked to the natural gas system in one area are turned on at the same time, the gas pressure goes down. This happens regularly at Christmas when everyone tries to cook a twenty-two pound turkey at the same time as everyone else. The gas supply is normally sufficient to meet the demand, but if the demand is increased, then either everyone's supply is decreased or there are selective changes so that high-priority users get more gas than others. Kahneman's theory of a limited amount of mental power may be compared with this. If two things have to be done at once, then performance will deteriorate on one or both when the two together go over the limit for mental power. If they don't, there is no deficit. If one task is more important, then it can be given more power or resources so that performance in that task stays high, whatever happens in the other.

Most of Kahneman's account of how we do things at once was concerned with general resources. However, he also realised that there were times when tasks used the same particular resource, that is, they interfered with each other because they used the same structures. As we have already seen, tasks that use the same kinds of response may interfere, whereas those that use different responses do not. Kahneman proposed that there would be some interference when two tasks were performed together, even if they did not share any perceptual or response mechanisms, so that even if there were no structural interference, there would be a general lowering of performance.

Another general way to describe what is limited by attention is to use the term "resources". Norman and Bobrow (1975) used the term originally in a very general way, to refer to "such things as processing effort, the varying forms of mental capacity and communication channels" (p. 45). They also included structures involved in memory processes, which we discuss in the next chapter. While processing effort is the general fuel metaphor introduced by Kahneman in 1973 and retained by Kahneman and Treisman (1984), and the communication channels might be thought of as different input and output systems (which we discuss elsewhere in this chapter), there is a sense in which any aspect of the cognitive system which can be drawn upon when it is needed is a resource for carrying out a task. This could mean that a resource limitation is a limitation in the use of any substructure of the system whatsoever. Seen like this, resources become so wide that they encourage us to look for many sources of limitation, not just a single central capacity, resource or "attention".

How can we tell whether there is a general limit to our processing capacity or not? If two tasks use less than the total capacity, they can be done at the same time; but unfortunately, the only way that we could know that they did use less than the total capacity would be to see if they could be done at the same time (Allport, 1980). Although it is possible to determine whether two tasks interfere or not, it is very difficult to test the basic notion that there is a limit to overall resources (Navon, 1984). In addition, if we have both specific and general resources, how do we tell whether one task is interfering with another because it uses general capacity or because it uses a specific resource?

One prediction made by general resource theory is that increasing the difficulty of one task should make it harder to carry out two tasks simultaneously because there is more strain on the general resource. Allport, Antonis and Reynolds (1972) asked pianists to sight-read music they had never seen before, and at the same time to shadow prose that they heard over headphones. Subjects thought that the sight-reading task was quite difficult, and shadowing someone else speaking at 150 words a minute is also difficult. Yet after a single 30 minute practice session, the subjects were able to play the piano and shadow aloud, and even to understand some of the content of the passage they were repeating. At first, there was some tendency for the rhythm of the music to appear in the subjects' speech, but this did not last. When the difficulty of the sight-reading task was altered in the second practice session, there was no change in shadowing. In this situation, difficulty did not lead to interference.

As you might expect, the subjects in Allport et al.'s study sometimes made mistakes in the sight-reading. When this happened, the performance of both tasks was interrupted. This does not necessarily mean that correcting an error requires more resources and that there is an overall limit on capacity. When an error occurs, analysis of it and choosing and implementing a response to correct it may require different processes from those already in use in the task. Checking for and correcting errors could be a specialised type of processing which both tasks have to use, so the limitation is specific to what is actually being done at the time. It may be useful to consider the circumstances in which one task interferes with another and when it does not, than to assume that an overall non-specific limitation is affecting performance.

The idea of difficulty versus similarity has been investigated by Hirst and Kalmar (1987), using simpler tasks in which more exact knowledge of exactly what people are doing in the task is available. They asked subjects to listen to two messages at the same time, one on each ear, and to make a simple response whenever they detected a particular target in either message. The two messages were lists of words which came from related categories such as body parts (hand, arm, knee, shoulder, etc.) or animals (tiger, elk, buffalo, sheep, etc.). They found that subjects had more success at detecting the word "hand" in a list of body parts they heard in one ear if they were also listening for the word "elk" in a list of animals in the other ear, than they did if they were listening for body parts (or animals) in both ears at the same time. Hirst and Kalmar suggest that the interference between similar versions of the task, when there is no change in difficulty, is evidence that a resource is used in the search for an animal name and a different resource is used in the search for a body part. The resource is whatever it is which allows us to search for body parts and which is strained if we have to search two lists at once. If we think of every category of semantic knowledge we have and then require a separate mental resource for each one, then the notion of resource becomes overextended. Hirst and Kalmar are probably being ironic when they claim separate resources for semantic categories. However, they do make an important point. If all kinds of tasks interfere when they are similar, we have to consider how such selectivity develops, given that semantic categories are not a part of the basic structure of the cognitive system but are acquired through experience.

There is some evidence that combining any two tasks leads to a decrement in performance. Bourke (1993) argued that different tasks will place different demands on a general factor, and if the *only* reason for interference is this demand, then tasks should stay in the same order of interference, regardless of the nature of the secondary task with which they are combined. He combined four tasks — tone discrimination, random letter generation, visual recognition, and screwing nuts on bolts — and found that tones interfered most with all the other tasks while the nut and bolt task interfered least, with random generation and visual recognition in the middle, in that order. This order of amount of interference was found regardless of which task was used as the secondary task. If the tasks had had specific interference effects, then this consistency in order would not have appeared. Bourke therefore argues that although specific interference is very important, there is also a decrement in performance whenever two tasks are combined, although what this general resource is, is not clear. Shallice, McLeod and Lewis (1985) have suggested that there may always be a small drop in performance (up to 10%) when any two tasks are combined, even those using different components of the cognitive system.

Disconnecting Perception and Action

If considering specific patterns of interaction and interference is sometimes more useful than notions of general limitations, then we should be able to return to the experiments of Treisman and Geffen (1967) and MacKay (1973) and consider why interference occurred in one case but not in the other. To do this we first have to analyse the tasks to see how they differ. In Treisman and Geffen's experiment, subjects had to shadow (repeat aloud) a message that they heard on one ear while another message was played to the other ear. They also had to push a button when they heard a target word, whether it came up on the shadowed ear or the non-shadowed ear. When two different streams of words are arriving in the two ears and only one stream is repeated, both inputs are closely linked to the output, but one message has to be cut off from the output system while the other is allowed access to it. The subject has to decouple one link between input and output, while retaining another. Allport (1980) argues that it is this competition for the output which makes selective shadowing so difficult, and that decoupling the speech input from vocal output also decouples that input from other outputs. In MacKay's experiment, on the other hand, no response to the words on the unshadowed ear was required, but the change in meaning was shown up in a memory test. Overall, the suggestion is that people cannot physically produce two streams of speech simultaneously, so when they are hearing two streams they have to distinguish between them and allow one to have access to speech production, and prevent the other from doing so.

McLeod and Posner (1984) have suggested that shadowing is a special activity because there is a "privileged loop" in the cognitive system between what a word sounds like and how to say it. They asked subjects to carry out a letter-matching task and to respond to a probe that appeared during it, just as Posner and Boies had done in 1971 and McLeod in 1978. As can be seen from Table 5.2, they used slightly different versions of both tasks. The first combination of letter-matching and probe tasks in Table 5.2 is the same as that used by McLeod (1977). Subjects decide whether the letters are the same or different and make a movement response. During the matching task, they hear an auditory probe (a spoken word, "up" or "down") and they respond by saying the same word. In this situation, there is no interference. In the second combination, subjects match the two letters and say either "same" or "different". The auditory

TABLE 5.2

Combinations of Letter-matching and Probe Tasks
Used by McLeod and Posner (1984)

	Matching Task	Probe Task
Combination 1	Visual input Movement output	Auditory input Vocal output
Combination 2	Visual input Vocal output	Auditory input Movement output

probe is also a word ("up" or "down") and the response is to move a switch in the appropriate direction. In this case interference between the two tasks does occur, although the input systems are different and the output systems are different. However, the link between hearing a word and saying it has been broken. Subjects hear one word ("up") and at around the same time they are about to say another word ("same"). The link between hearing one word and saying another one is so strong that having to say a different word leads to an increase in reaction time. This result extends our earlier conclusion that it is important not to use the same response system if you are trying to do two things at once. It is also important to consider the relationship between the input and the response for both tasks.

The tasks we have been considering give us some insight into how we do two things at once but they are quite far removed from ordinary experience. We can, however, think of the real-life skill of typing as being a situation in which people read words and make the appropriate movements (copy typing), or hear words and make the appropriate movements (audio typing). Do you think that a typist could read aloud while audio typing or shadow words while copy typing? In both cases, there are two verbal tasks to be carried out at the same time and a string of vocal responses is combined with a string of manual responses, so that it might seem that typists should be equally good or bad at both combinations. However, Shaffer (1975) found that typists could copy type and shadow, although there was some decrement in performance, but they could not audio type and read aloud. McLeod and Posner's results on the simple task can help us to understand the performance on the more complex ones. If in audio typing subjects hear one stream of words while they speak another, they have to disconnect the tendency to speak the words they hear, which leads to interference and increased difficulty. On the other hand, when copy typing and shadowing, the words that are heard have an easy route to speech.

AUTOMATICITY AND PRACTICE

In the experiment of Allport et al. (1972), subjects could play the piano and shadow prose at the same time, but only one subject showed no decrement in her comprehension of the passage being shadowed. This subject was the most skilled pianist in the experiment and her comprehension performance while sight-reading was as good as other people's when they only listened to the passage. The level of skill in sight-reading reflects the amount of practice the subject has had, and these two factors are an important determinant of when things can and cannot be done at the same time.

Earlier in the chapter, we discussed the ways in which practice altered movement control and allowed creation of new linkages in the motor system. Practice also affects the perceptual system and the development of links between perception and action. In our account of the refractory period, we mentioned that practice did not decrease the tendency for a second response to have to wait for the first to be finished. This was the established view put forward by Welford in 1968. However, practice in this context did not link particular stimuli to particular responses, but was practice on repeated presentation of different stimuli and responses (Hick, 1948). Links between input and output were not improved, so independence could not develop.

There are many occasions when it is very difficult for people to stop a response being produced, even when they try. Many of our language processes are so well practised that we cannot stop ourselves from using them even if we don't need to. A good example of this is the Stroop task, in which two kinds of information are present in one stimulus pattern. In a well-known version of the task, which we discussed earlier, a colour name (red) is written in coloured ink (green). The task is to name the colour of the ink. This takes longer than when the written word is not the name of a colour (Stroop, 1935). The increased time to respond suggests that it is very difficult to stop the word being read aloud so that the colour of the ink can be named. This effect can also be found when line drawings of objects have a name written inside them (Rayner & Posnansky, 1978), or when the spoken words "high" and "low" are said in either a high- or a low-pitched voice and the task is to name the pitch of the voice (Cohen & Martin, 1975). In tasks like this, one component has to be prevented from controlling output with which it has very strong links.

Schneider and Shiffrin (1977) and Shiffrin and Schneider (1977) carried out an extensive investigation of the role of practice in the development of automaticity by asking subjects to search for target letters among other letters in briefly presented displays. The targets were consonants from the first half of the alphabet and the background items were consonants from the second half. Subjects simply had to detect whether a target was present or not. Performance in this task was not very good at the beginning of practice, the subjects making many mistakes and responding quite slowly. After 1500 trials, their performance was much more accurate than it had been initially and the reaction times to find a target on any trial decreased.

At this point, the number of targets that had to be searched for at the same time did not affect the reaction time, nor did the number of non-targets that had to be searched. Subjects were able to respond to targets without having to consider all the other alternatives. In a second phase of the experiment, Schneider and Shiffrin reversed the target and the non-target items. Now, the subjects had to search for consonants from the second half of the alphabet in a background of consonants from the first half. For the first 600 trials in this phase of the experiment, performance was worse than it had been at the beginning of the experiment, and after 2100 trials it was still not as good as it had been at the end of the first phase.

This experiment created a kind of Stroop effect in which the first set of targets were identified even though they were no longer targets and the subjects could not stop this happening. Just as in the Stroop task, responses to the first set of targets had to be inhibited, or actually occurred as errors. This effect of practice only occurred if the subjects practised with the same target set in the first phase of the experiment. If the target and non-target sets were changed at every trial, the discrimination of target from background had to be different on each trial. Shiffrin, Dumais and Schneider (1981) showed that subjects could detect targets they had seen before if the background was changed, and they could detect new targets if the background remained the same. That is, what they had learned to do was to detect targets and to ignore irrelevant items.

Shiffrin and Schneider's results have been used to suggest that practice leads to a completely different kind of processing. After extensive practice, processing is said to become "automatic". This is a term we use in everyday accounts of our activities, so it has some plausibility as a description of changes with practice. Most of us can walk and chew gum at the same time because we do them "automatically". However, if two of these well-practised search tasks are combined, there are small but consistent deficits (Hoffman, Nelson, & Houek, 1983; Schneider & Fisk, 1982), just as there were in the independent tasks we discussed earlier. This could mean that we could walk more efficiently if we didn't chew gum, or it could mean that both "independent" and "automatic" refer to particular patterns of non-interference, rather than a different kind of processing.

What does it mean to say that responding to the items in a search task is automatic? Shiffrin et al. (1981) have put forward two rules for automatic processing. One is that an automatic process should not reduce the capacity for doing other tasks, and the other is that automatic processes are unstoppable, or mandatory, so that they cannot be influenced by what you intend to do. The first rule is part of general limited capacity or resource theory that we discussed earlier, and the second follows from tasks like the Stroop and practised search.

The criteria for automaticity proposed by Shiffrin et al. have been widely accepted and sometimes extended (Jonides, Naveh-Benjamin, & Palmer, 1985), but there are several problems with their use. One is that practice could build up strong relationships between patterns of input and the correct output, without the process becoming mandatory or compulsory. A copy typist is not compelled to type the letter "t" every time "t" appears, but if that typist were transferred from a QWERTY keyboard to one with a new layout, it is very likely that the old response of moving the left index finger would sometimes appear when "t" was required. The mandatory, or compulsory, nature of the processing of some information is an important topic, particularly for perception and language. Fodor (1983), for example, argues that we cannot help hearing words in a language we know as words, even if we are trying to do something else like respond to the sounds which make them up. However, the distinction between automatic and attentive processes remains difficult, and Shiffrin (1988, p. 775) acknowledges this when he writes that the "attempts to define necessary and sufficient criteria to distinguish automatic and attentive processes in complete generality, have not yet proven successful".

One difficulty is that automatic and non-automatic or controlled processing do not seem to be two completely different types of processing — rather, they lie on a continuum, and are affected both by practice and by the ways in which tasks are combined. MacLeod and Dunbar (1988) taught subjects to use colour words for arbitrary shapes which were all coloured white. After 20 trials on naming each shape, subjects could use the terms correctly, but when the shapes were then coloured, the ink colour affected the names of the shapes, but not the other way round. After practice (504 trials on naming each stimulus), the shapes began to interfere with naming of ink colour, and after a lot of practice (2520 trials with each stimulus over a total of 20 days), the shapes had a very powerful effect on the naming of the ink colour. So, automaticity is not all or nothing, but the relative amount of training on two tasks which are combined determines the nature of the interference between them.

A particular task can seem to be automatic in comparison with a second task, because it does not interfere with it, but might interfere with a third task and therefore seem to be controlled or to require attention. This view has been explored by Cohen, Dunbar and McClelland (1990), who produced a network model which learned to name colour words and to name inks and produced many Stroop-like effects, and also produced the effects shown by Dunbar and MacLeod. Cohen et al. argue that the appearance of what looks like automaticity depends on the strength of one process relative to the strengths of other competing processes. They do not view attention as limited, but rather as a source of information which can modulate or change what is going on in a processing pathway.

There are other accounts of the way change takes place with learning which suggest that the changes which do take place are more complex.

Cheng (1985) has argued that there are changes in the way people organise tasks as they learn them, which makes them simpler, but this does not mean that they are automatic. She has used a simple analogy to make this point. If you are asked to add ten twos you could do it by adding two to two, getting four, then adding two and getting six, then another two to get eight, and so on. It would take you some time to do this in your head, and you might forget how many twos you had added. Of course, if you have a little arithmetical knowledge you may know that adding ten twos is equivalent to multiplying two by ten, you have the answer to the multiplication stored in memory, so you can produce the correct answer in just one step. You will now be able to produce the correct answer very quickly, without any effort and it would seem that you have added ten twos "automatically". What has changed is not the speed with which you carry out the same operations, but the very operations themselves.

In arithmetic, we can move from a general counting procedure, or algorithm, to retrieving information from memory when we have built up a knowledge base of number facts. Logan (1988) has argued that all automatisation is like this. During early learning we use general-purpose algorithms to produce the correct response, but as we build up instances in which a particular response is made in a particular situation, we can shift to retrieving that response from memory. The more instances there are in memory, the easier and faster retrieval becomes. In an instance-based account of automaticity, automatic processing is not related to attention and capacity but to changes in the knowledge which an individual can use to carry out the task. It may still be difficult to decide whether a task is carried out automatically or not, because memory-based performance and algorithm-based performance are both available options and can compete to produce a response. Two tasks may cease to interfere because interference early in learning is interference with the algorithmic processes, and tasks which interfere with those may not interfere with memory retrieval. However, it is possible in this account that a concurrent task which did not interfere early in learning could come to interfere later, if it involved memory retrieval.

Reading and Writing at the Same Time

You may feel that your everyday assumption that you do some things automatically is being reduced from whole tasks to little parts of tasks, and that these are difficult to put together into reading, or driving a car. The tendency to break tasks down has not always been found in research in this area. In the late 1800s, two researchers at Harvard trained themselves to read stories while writing to dictation and noted how they felt the tasks were carried out (Solomons & Stein, 1896). They reported that the writing was performed without awareness, while they carried on being aware of the material they were reading. Therefore, automaticity for them was the subjective experience of lack of awareness of carrying out the task. However, subjects' awareness of one of two tasks rather than the other is not a very reliable way of establishing how tasks are being performed, as Spelke, Hirst and Neisser (1976) found when they trained two subjects to write dictated words while they read stories. They found that after 20 weeks of practice, the subjects could comprehend the stories and write the words and could even write down the name of the category to which a word belonged rather than the word itself. However, the subjects sometimes said that they thought clearly about a word before they wrote it and at other times they said that they were unaware of writing. It is for this reason that psychologists have devised many of the measures of performance that we have discussed throughout this chapter, rather than depending on what performance felt like to subjects.

Spelke et al. (1976) argued that whereas writing down a word without understanding it could be called automatic, making sense of the world is not a routine activity. Comprehension and understanding involve so much complex processing that they should never be considered to be automatic. This position was extended in a later study in which Hirst et al. (1980) also asked subjects to practise reading while writing to dictation. The dictation was not of single words but of short sentences. After extensive practice, their subjects could write the short sentences while reading aloud, they could also answer complex comprehension questions about the passage they had read while copying, and they recognised as familiar sentences that were close in meaning to the ones they had copied, so they must have understood the meaning of the copied sentences. This seemed to mean that they were doing two comprehension tasks at the same time.

It is possible to argue that subjects who can read and write at the same time are really alternating very quickly between the two tasks. In normal conversation, we can follow what is being said even if we do not hear every word because language is often redundant, and training might help subjects to exploit this redundancy more efficiently. Hirst et al. (1980) investigated this by training some subjects to read stories while they wrote dictation, but training other subjects to read encyclopaedia articles, which are much less redundant than stories. After subjects became skilled at reading and writing at the same time with one kind of reading material, they were switched to reading with the other. Hirst et al. found that subjects were just as good at reading, writing and comprehending with new material as they were with old. They concluded that their subjects were not alternating between the two tasks, and they were not doing one automatically in the sense of having no understanding of it, but rather they had restructured the task by learning new stimulus patterns and new patterns of action.

Although Hirst et al. attempted to use redundancy to show that subjects were not alternating between tasks, it is not really possible to say exactly what was going on. Subjects were tested for comprehension after they had finished reading, and there was no way in which the times at which words were presented to eye and ear could be controlled. It is possible that probing the tasks while they were being carried out would give us more information about the restructuring that is occurring, but this would break up the naturalness of the tasks. Although we may have some reservations about exactly what is going on in these tasks, the evidence suggests that new kinds of skill in reading and writing have to be explained in terms of learning to do the tasks rather that the use of processes which are effortless and "automatic".

Many of the tasks which we have discussed in earlier sections of this chapter have emphasised learning and change as important for understanding our abilities to carry out tasks at the same time. The network model of Stroop tasks produced by Cohen et al. (1990) and the evidence of interference between semantically similar tasks presented by Hirst and Kalmar (1987) argue that tasks can be carried out at the same time provided it is possible to prevent each processing system (sometimes known as a module) from picking up interfering by-products from other processing activities. Hirst and Kalmar point out that if semantic categories interfere selectively with each other, but can be learned, then at some point items which interfere because they are in the same category will be differentiated into items in a different category and therefore will no longer interfere. The skill developed would be one in which people become able to segregate features which discriminate between different inputs, and direct input to the appropriate transformation to carry out the relevant task. How segregation develops, and at which parts of complex processing operations, would be an important issue in understanding how practice affects our ability to do two things at once.

PRACTICE, KNOWLEDGE AND SKILL

The changes that occur with practice are the development of skill, and there are many kinds of skill as well as many changes with practice. Skill can be perceptual and perceptual–motor — that is, we can become better at selecting relevant information from the world, we have stronger links between patterns of input and output, and we can control the movements of our limbs in a different way. However, skill can also involve changes in memory, and in the ability to use improved memory in problem-solving tasks like playing chess. Simon and Gilmartin (1973) have calculated that an expert chess player has 50,000 units of knowledge of positions in chess, which have been developed over years of practice. These units are organisations of chess pieces rather than the individual pieces themselves and they enable experts to recognise chess positions and to produce responses without having to go through all the possible options open to them. This means that acquiring new rules that organise incoming information in a different way may be just as important as building stronger links between input and output patterns which we already know.

Is it possible that with increased practice and skill we can do as many things as we like at the same time? The answer is probably "no". Very few of us want to spend the time and effort necessary to develop independent systems for running two or more tasks, and even if we did there are some situations in which practice may not get rid of interference, because the amount of practice that has already occurred with one combination of input and output is so great that the links cannot be broken. Typists who cannot audio type and speak at the same time have spent many years building up the relationship between the sound of words and the production of them. They would probably have to spend many more years practising audio typing and speaking together before we could say whether independence was possible or not. There may be a drop in performance when any two tasks are combined; however, for a normal level of skill in two tasks, we can predict that interference will occur if the two tasks involve the same kind of operations or response processes, or if the input from one already has links to the output of another. We also know that without high levels of skill, two movements will not be independent if they have timing or rhythmic components in common or if they make use of the two hands separately. Most of us can talk and make other movements at the same time, but we cannot read a book and talk about something else at the same time and we cannot correct novel errors in one task while carrying on with another.

SUMMARY

In this chapter, we have considered some of the constraints on our abilities to do two tasks at once. Some of the most basic limitations are imposed by the motor system, which is organised so that timing patterns between the limbs are coordinated, although these patterns can be altered with practice. Making a response to a stimulus involves making a decision and there may be a delay in doing one task if another is not finished. However, this can be reduced if the stimulus and response are compatible, or if different response systems are used for the two tasks. A limit on decision making between perception and action would be a general limitation on what we can do, similar in some ways to the concept of a limited amount of attention that we can allocate to tasks. General capacity attention models have considered the question of when selection occurs in processing, but it has proved difficult to produce evidence which unequivocally favours early or late selection. Explanations for attentional limitations can also be given in terms of specific problems, particularly when well-established links between perception and action have to be broken. It is not easy to say what it means for tasks to be independent, and this is also true of the use of the term "automatic". Automaticity develops with extended practice on a task and has been thought to reflect a change in the way in which information is processed. However, it is also possible that automaticity results from changes in knowledge rather than changes in type of processing. Using memory retrieval based on memory instances of a particular link between stimulus and response or between a problem and its solution can speed up task performance and make it seem effortless. Practice and learning are the keys to successful dual-task performance in many situations.

As the term "attention" is used in many ways, books on attention do not always cover material related to doing two things at once. So, for example, A.H.C. van der Heijden's (1991) *Selective attention in vision* covers many topics in visual selection. However, *Attention: Selection, awareness and control. A tribute to Donald Broadbent*, edited by A. Baddeley and L. Weiskrantz (1993), provides a wide range of chapters covering many of the topics raised in this chapter.

6

Doing Mental Arithmetic: Holding Information and Operations for a Short Time

The experience of performing some kind of mental arithmetic is a common one, even if calculators are making it less necessary. If you want to decide whether a tube of toothpaste that costs 46 pence for 50 ml is better value than one which costs £1.05 for 125 ml, you could try to find the equivalent cost for 25 ml in each tube. Try the simpler task of adding 325 to 146 in your head. If you had a piece of paper you could set one number above the other, start at the right, add 6 to 5, write 1 in that column, carry one, add 1 to 2 to 4, write 7 in that column, and so on. If you do it in your head, you'll probably find that you break up the sum in exactly the same way and you may create an image of the numbers written as they would be set out on a piece of paper. As long as you remember the answer to each sub-component, remember where you are in the calculation, and remember the bits of the answer as you go along, the whole answer will be produced correctly. Errors can occur if the answers to parts of the problem (e.g. $6 + 5 = 11$) are not retrieved correctly, if you cannot break up the problem into the correct or most useful pieces, if you cannot keep your place in the problem, and if you cannot hold the list of digits which you have to speak to give the answer. Two of the reasons for error given above relate to knowledge held in long-term memory (how to break up sums and the knowledge that $6 + 5$ is 11), and two relate to immediate memory or working memory (keeping place and holding the list of digits).

The limitations of immediate memory are apparent in a wide variety of experiences, not just in mental arithmetic. You have just checked your shopping list of four items. While considering where the first item should be purchased, one or two of the items are forgotten and the list has to be consulted again. Someone tells you a new telephone number. You are securely repeating it to yourself and dialling the number, when someone asks who you are 'phoning, and some of the digits seem to disappear. Searching for the right word in a sentence you are constructing as you speak to a group, you forget precisely what it was you were going to say. Mental arithmetic illustrates a particular mix of the processes involved in many other activities, but it has special features of interest to us at this stage. The inputs to the task are well defined. The procedures for doing arithmetic are usually well understood and at least some of the things we do in our head probably owe much to the way in which we have been taught to do sums. The focus of the activity is to achieve a result here and now by immediate processing rather than to remember something for ever. But we cannot do any very intelligent immediate processing, like mental arithmetic, unless we have some knowledge of numbers stored away somewhere. First then, we sketch just a small fraction of the evidence and ideas that led researchers to make a distinction between a short-term memory store and a long-term memory store.

SOME BASIC PHENOMENA

Suppose you were asked to add 73,441,958 to 62,597,113 in your head; it is very doubtful that you would be able to hang on to more than about one-third of these digits, let alone start adding them up. Like the telephone example given earlier, there seems to be a basic limitation on how many items we can hold. The experience of losing information when there is rather too much to it, or when it arrives too quickly, is so common that we should not be surprised that there has been a stream of laboratory studies since the turn of the century which have investigated how many items can be held for short periods.

Immediate memory for digits, letters of the alphabet and words was investigated extensively in Wundt's laboratory at Leipzig at the end of the nineteenth century. If you were to hear a string of letters read to you just once at a rate of 2 letters per second, how many items would you recall? Wundt (1905), like many later workers, found the number of items that could be recalled in the correct order, the *span* of immediate memory, to be about 6 "single impressions". The repeated findings in a variety of studies that people could recall between 5 and 9 items, whether the items were letters, digits, or words, led Miller (1956) to argue that the span of immediate memory was, typically, 7 plus or minus 2. We need to clarify what units are implied by "7 plus or minus 2". We could say "items" again, but Miller called them "chunks". Obviously, if you can only remember 5 or 6 letters you will have difficulty with a string of 25 letters, but if they are organised into words so that you have to recall a sequence like "table, camel, paper, plate, grape", then the words become the items. If the words form short and simple sentences, then sentences might become the items. The term "chunk" acknowledges that definition of the units of information depends on what the subjects in our experiments make of the information. We will return to this interaction between our ability to hold information in immediate memory and what it means to us when we discuss expert rememberers in later sections.

Immediate memory also has an effect when subjects are asked to read or listen to word-lists of various lengths and then to recall as many of the

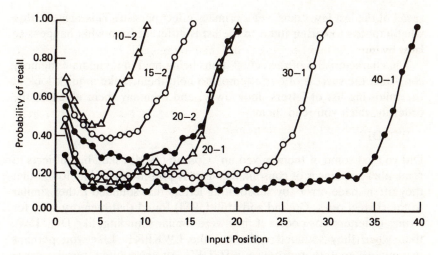

FIG. 6.1 Serial position curves for different list lengths (10, 15, 20, 30 and 40 words) and presentation times (1 or 2 sec per word). Based on Murdock (1962).

words as possible, but in any order. This style of experiment is often referred to as "list learning with free recall". The responses produced in immediate free recall are examined for their correctness, and, when correct, for the position they had in the original presentation of the list. Using groups of subjects and several different lists of words, the relationship between the probability of correctly recalling a word and its serial position — 1st, 2nd, 3rd, and so on — in the original list can be examined. Murdock (1962) carried out systematic studies of this type in which he varied list length and the rate of delivery of the words. Figure 6.1 shows his principal findings.

For all list lengths, the first few items presented are well remembered but decreasingly so with serial position. This has been called the *primacy effect*. It is as though items presented early in the list benefit from primacy in processing; they suffer less competition for time and space in immediate memory from other items. The last few items show an increasingly higher success rate with serial position. This is termed a *recency effect*. Items that have most recently entered immediate memory are most readily recalled, at least by subjects who have had a little practice at the task. For items intermediate in the presentation order, there is a low plateau of recall success, as though each item has only a small chance of being processed to sufficient depth for it to be recalled. A great deal of attention has been given to the differences in depth or kinds of processing during list learning that might account for these primacy and recency effects. Many studies have shown that delaying the moment for recall, or requiring the subject to engage in other mental activities before recall, can markedly reduce recall of the last few items, yet a primacy effect persists. This suggests that what happens to earlier items in the list is different from what happens to later ones.

The characteristics of the actual items being held in immediate memory can affect the success of our attempts to hold them. Take a quick look at the following list of letters, look away, and then say them aloud in the order in which you read them:

BTGDPC

Did you get some of them mixed up? Conrad (1964) asked his subjects to remember sequences of consonants, visually presented, and he found that they often made errors by substituting letters that sounded rather similar to the correct ones. Conrad and Hull (1964) found that memory span for strings of letters was poorer if they were similar sounding, like DCBTPV, than when they sounded different, like LWKFRT. Like you perhaps in your attempt to reproduce BTGDPC, subjects often recall several letters from the "similar sounds" condition, but fail to reproduce them in the correct order. We do better with strings of digits than with some badly chosen letter strings because digits are less confusable in how they sound.

This type of "phonemic coding" (coding by sound) of digits, letters and words, when items were output immediately to a waiting experimenter, was combined with evidence from list learning. Some phonemic or rhyming confusions appear as responses to words presented at the end of a sufficiently long list, whereas similar meaning or semantic substitutions more commonly occur for words from the beginning of the list. Primacy and recency effects indicated that more items were remembered at the beginning and end of lists, and the different error patterns found in these parts of the list suggested that in general immediate or short-term coding was phonemic, whereas long-term coding was semantic.

Phenomena and ideas such as these reinforced the distinction increasingly being made in the 1950s and 1960s between two components of memory, between some kind of short-term store and a long-term store. In addition to the laboratory studies of verbal learning in normal subjects, several studies of amnesic patients supported the distinction. Zangwill (1946) reported that amnesic patients who could not learn new material, such as making associations between arbitrarily chosen pairs of words, had no difficulty repeating series of digits or letters. Similarly, the patient H.M. studied by Milner (1970), whose amnesia resulted from an operation on the temporal lobes of the brain and the hippocampus, showed an unimpaired digit span coupled with an inability to remember what happened yesterday. There are also patients with impaired digit spans and normal long-term retention, such as patient K.F. studied by Shallice and Warrington (1970). How can we explain these findings?

MODELS OF MEMORY

The things that we can and cannot do with our memories under a variety of conditions give us clues about how our memories are organised or structured. The research on learning lists of items suggested that we have a memory system in which a short-term store acts as a holding device, a buffer store, until our long-term store of well-established memories can be accessed in some way. If the long-term store cannot be accessed quickly enough, information is lost from the short-term store. If routes to our long-term store are somehow impaired, we can repeat digits held in the short-term store but not learn them. The "information-processing models" developed from this kind of thinking were much influenced by analogies with the workings of computers.

The Computer Analogy

Computers deal with streams of input. Computers also deal with output to printers and displays as well as inputs, so we are reminded here that emphasising how we take things in may not be enough. We also need to consider how we hold output before we make use of it. A typical computer can be thought of as having three major parts: a central processor, a fast random access memory store, and various input and output devices. Each input device has its specific properties. A keypress on a keyboard generates a signal, which is encoded by circuitry into a computer symbol. The central processor may be in one of three states: (1) it may be wholly attending to the keyboard and ready to receive the next symbol; (2) it may be busy with some other task, but this task may be automatically interrupted when the keyboard signals that it is receiving information; (3) it may be busy with some other task but programmed to check the keyboard device for any activity from time to time.

The keyboard device in a computer may have its own storage space or buffer, such that a limited number of symbols can safely be held locally, even if the central processor pays it no attention and this buffer is one kind of short-term store. But the keyboard might be pressed at too high a rate for it to detect, code and store the distinctive symbols; or the central processor might fail to attend to the signals in time to avoid overflow in the keyboard buffer. Or, the central processor may be programmed to perform the minimal task of emptying the keyboard buffer of symbols from time to time, so that it never overflows, and of storing these symbols away in some part of memory — a more central form of buffer store — for later attention. In this latter case, the computer's memory, perhaps a defined amount of space for storing keyboard input, could fill up with symbols, and even overflow if they are not attended to in time. Output devices, like visual display units, robotic operators and printers, can also interact with a central processor via local or central buffers.

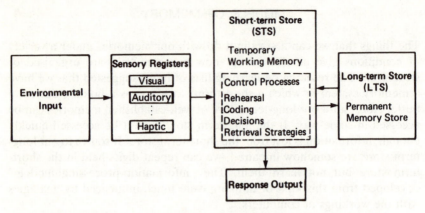

FIG. 6.2 Atkinson and Shriffin's model of memory. Reproduced with permission from Atkinson and Shiffrin (1971).

The analogy between the input, output and central processing of information by computers and the management of information by people became increasingly influential in the 1960s and 1970s. The notions that incoming information could be held in one or more buffers, that it could be part-processed in several stages and that these processes are subject to time–space constraints, were particularly attractive for research on memory.

A Three-store Model of Memory

The studies of primacy and recency, different memory codes in immediate recall and long-term recall, and neuropsychological evidence, all suggested a functional distinction between two kinds of memory. This, along with computer analogies which illustrated possible mechanisms, led to the development of models of a three-store memory system, of which the version put forward by Atkinson and Shiffrin (1968) was very influential. Their model is shown diagrammatically in Fig. 6.2.

The first kind of storage is one of a number of sensory information stores that register incoming signals, holding them for a second or two in a primitive form which is readily disrupted by further signals in the same sensory channel. The second is a short-term store (STS), the contents of which we are partially conscious, as when we hold on to a telephone number while we dial, or when we hold on to the last few words from a list read out to us. The third store is a long-term store (LTS) from which we retrieve well-established memories and in which we store well-processed new information.

In the Atkinson–Shiffrin version of STS, data received from the various sensory registers are subject to a number of control processes. *Rehearsal* is a process that requires a transformation of the (selected) incoming information into a rehearsable form such as a phonemic code for verbal material. Although maintenance rehearsal is enough for some tasks, we usually need to hold information so that something may be done with it. For one thing, we usually need to engage in further *coding* of the information by retrieving some aspects of its previous meaning to us from the LTS. The different purposes for processing information — answering a specific question, following a conversation, performing mental arithmetic, learning paired-associates in a memory experiment — are each likely to require different *search* and *retrieval strategies*. Another control process in the Atkinson–Shiffrin model is concerned with *decision making*. Decisions might include shifting the direction of a search, abandoning an item, or determining that sufficient has been retrieved for one item.

Early studies of immediate memory span had focused on the notion of the limited number of data slots or registers available for holding items. This notion is emphasised, for example, by Lindsay and Norman (1977) in their account of performing mental arithmetic tasks. Most of us experience no difficulty in multiplying two single-digit numbers like 5×9. We can assume that we retrieve the answer from LTS. But 65×9 requires a certain amount of work to be done. We can speculate that STS must at some stage hold something like the following items: 5×9, 45, 6×9, 54. Exactly how many slots this takes up is debatable, but the fact is that many of us can, with some effort, manage the task. The multiplication of two two-digit numbers, such as 89×37, is probably at or beyond the limit for most of us. That is, the number of items that have to be held in some arithmetic problems might be said to be larger than the number of slots available.

A task that has frequently been used to estimate the number of registers in STS is the digit-span task referred to earlier as part of Wundt's work. The task is used, for example, as a subtest of the major intelligence tests employed in educational and clinical diagnostic settings. The assumption had been that the immediate recall of random digit sequences is largely unaffected by the contents of LTS — at least in those who are familiar with digits. Variations among us in digit span correlate moderately well with some tasks that demand immediate mental work upon paced inputs; but the very incompleteness of the correlation is a challenge to our view of STS functioning. What else is STS doing? Beyond holding items, there are the control processes referred to in the Atkinson–Shiffrin account which might take up mental space. In the study of mental arithmetic, we can count the items that might occupy slots in STS and some partial answers may be rapidly retrieved from LTS, but the management of the whole problem, decisions about how to proceed, and the memory for "next step", are also important.

Problems for a Unitary Short-term Store

Successful as it was in capturing much of the existing data, a number of phenomena fail to fit comfortably in the framework of an Atkinson–Shiffrin type of model. One problem concerns the variety of input and output modalities that people have to manage. If we consider only the verbal medium, we can read and listen and we can speak and write. Are all these activities mediated through a single short-term store? Perhaps, like computers, different buffers are used at some stage in the operation? Murdock and Walker (1969) found that the free recall serial position curves for visually and aurally presented words differ somewhat, aural presentation giving an enhanced recency effect over visual presentation. Is this because auditory coding is the more natural medium of STS and visual codes take extra processing to become auditorily represented there? Next, errors in recall often show evidence of the input modality, visual form and auditory sound errors showing up according to the type of input in several studies. Recall modality — spoken or written — can similarly give differential results. Margrain (1967) simultaneously presented two lists of four digits, one list visually and the other aurally, and called for either spoken or written recall. Aural presentation with written recall gave the highest recall performance, whereas the "visual–spoken" input–output combination gave better performance than "visual–written". If STS is a unitary store, then how can we account for this variety of input–output coding effects?

A further challenge to the view of a unitary STS concerns the variety of tasks that we can engage in at the same time. If the recency effect in list learning is due to the activity of a unitary STS and digit span uses the same store, then if we are using the store for one of these tasks we should be unable to do another task which requires the use of the same store at the same time. Baddeley and Hitch (1977) asked subjects to listen to a sequence of unrelated words and to watch digits appear on a screen. They were asked to write down the digits one at a time, in groups of three, or in groups of six. They also had to remember the words. The effect of adding the load of holding up to three or six digits on the recall of the words can be seen in Fig. 6.3. Although a load of six digits makes recall more difficult, it does not affect the recency portion of the curve. Baddeley and Hitch (1974) had earlier shown that remembering up to six digits did not prevent subjects from comprehending sentences or doing verbal reasoning tasks, and they concluded that memory span and other aspects of immediate memory were not using the same processes. Therefore, either digit span is not a good indicator of the use of short-term memory, or else Atkinson and Shiffrin were wrong to suppose that the only route to long-term memory was via the short-term system.

De Renzi and Nichelli (1975) investigated two kinds of memory span: one was for auditorily presented digits and the other was the Corsi test of

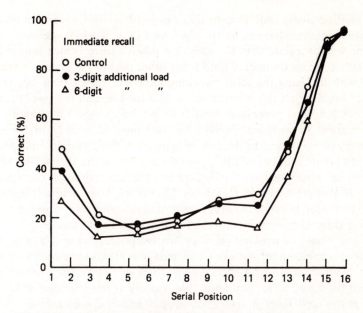

FIG. 6.3 Serial position curves with 3-digit and 6-digit additional short-term memory loads and with zero additional load ("Control"). Reproduced with permission from Baddeley and Hitch (1977).

spatial position span. In the Corsi test, the experimenter taps out a sequence of positions on a set of spatially dispersed wooden blocks and the subject has to repeat the sequence exactly. A normal span is about six blocks. De Renzi and Nichelli found one patient who had a very short digit span, about three items, and a normal spatial span, yet other patients with normal digit span could remember only two or three spatial locations. If there are short-term stores, there must be more than one; or there must be marked individual differences in the speed with which the different kinds of input are coded. Either way, the simpler conceptions of STS and its role in holding limited numbers of items are called into question.

WORKING MEMORY

There seem to be three types of problem with the concept of a single short-term memory store. These are: (1) that different inputs and outputs may use different processing routes and memory stores or data buffers; (2) that some immediate operations do not seem to occupy or to compete for the same space; and (3) that the coding of information for use in STS depends on the view that LTS takes of the information. Next, we shall recall that Atkinson and Shiffrin did not propose that STS was just a store, a space for holding items, but that it also executed control over a number of activities in immediate memory. Their idea of a "working memory" could be more appropriate than the idea of a passive store, which simply holds partially processed material until some other part of the system is ready to deal with it. Using the term "working memory" rather than "short-term store" implies that the information is held for use, and not just because it has not yet been processed enough to get into long-term memory. The information in working memory at any time is already in long-term memory in one sense. In the case of span tasks, for example remembering the telephone number 651342, you already know the digits 1–6; what is important is that they have to be kept in a particular order to carry out this task. If you are asked to remember 123456789, your span will appear to have increased because the order information is available as an economical coding from long-term memory, as well as the digits themselves.

If some uses of working memory involve processing and holding items in order, can we show that some elements of real tasks are like those which have been studied in traditional short-term memory experiments? Hitch (1978) used mental arithmetic to look closely at the relationship between operations and storage. He gave people addition problems in which a three-digit number was added to a two- or three-digit number to give a three-digit result. Some problems required a carry from one column to the next. The subjects did not have the answers to questions like "What is the sum of 347 and 52?" already in memory, so they had to deal with each column in turn, often using the units–tens–hundreds sequence which they might have learned at school. To complete the "tens" stage of the addition of 476 and 23, the subject has to retrieve 7 and 2 from temporary or working storage, retrieve the sum $(7 + 2 = 9)$ from long-term memory, and either write that bit of the result or put it back into working storage. If the answer is written down in the normal hundreds–tens–units order, then the early part of the calculation has to be held in storage until the "hundreds" column is finished. However, if subjects are asked to write the digits in reverse order, each digit is written as it is calculated. Hitch found that subjects made more errors with the "tens" and "units" when they had to hold these items until the end of the calculation than they did when they could write them down as soon as they calculated them. The partial results that are entered into working storage are forgotten quite quickly as a function of the number of intervening steps, so that errors occur. Forgetting is virtually complete after 60 sec have elapsed or after 30–40 processing steps have occurred.

Baddeley and Hitch (1974) argued that the importance of working memory was not that everything had to be held in a system that was used for digit span before it could get into long-term memory. After all, Shallice and Warrington's (1970) patient K.F. showed that it is possible for people to have a very short digit span yet manage to get access to long-term memory. Baddeley and Hitch asked subjects to remember a series of digits (e.g. 523 or 638294) while carrying out a reasoning task in which they had to judge the truth of statements like: "A is not preceded by B" in relation to "AB". They found that the time to complete the reasoning task increased when more digits had to be remembered, but the task was, nevertheless, completed. Baddeley and Hitch argued that if there was just one phonetically based store involved in holding the material for both tasks, then it should not be possible to rehearse 638294 and do the reasoning task as well. They proposed that the limited-capacity working memory consisted of a "central executive" and an "articulatory loop". The executive dealt with control processes, rather like those envisaged in the Atkinson–Shiffrin model, including a general responsibility for short-term retention. The articulatory loop was thought of as a storage device available to the executive which is especially useful for rehearsing articulatable codes, such as words or verbal reference codes for "chunks". Information could be held while another task was carried out because there were different components in the immediate memory system and these could deal with the two tasks at the same time.

Subsequent accounts of working memory have added a third subsystem, which deals with visuo-spatial material in addition to those for verbal material and the central controller or executive system, giving a three-part working memory (Baddeley, 1986). The verbal subsystem is more complex than just an articulatory loop and is thought to involve memory for phonology (what words sound like), in addition to articulation (how words are said). In the next sections, we consider the three subsystems, before returning to an overall consideration of working memory in tasks like mental arithmetic.

The Phonological and Articulatory Subsystem

The subsystem for dealing with verbal material was originally called the articulatory loop, by analogy with a loop of audio-recording tape. The loop was thought of as a self-contained system which could keep on repeating a sequence without needing any central control. In addition, the well-known finding that material which sounded similar led to confusions in recall (Conrad & Hull, 1964) could be based on confusions of articulatory coding in a rehearsal system. Baddeley, Thomson and Buchanan (1975) investigated the role of the articulatory system in memory span by asking subjects to remember short lists of words of different length. They found that the length of the word affected the number of items which the subjects could recall. This word-length effect was interpreted in terms of the difference in the length of time taken to say (i.e. articulate) short and long words. If the words are put on a short "tape loop", which holds them in a form like that used for speech, fewer of the long words will get on the loop. However, the loop is rather more complex than this suggests.

Salamé and Baddeley (1982) asked subjects to encode visually presented items for immediate recall while at the same time listening to irrelevant speech. They found that this led to interference with words being remembered, but that this was not further affected by word length. The more similar the irrelevant speech sounded to what was being remembered, the more it interfered. Salamé and Baddeley argued that the irrelevant speech was not articulated, because this would have interacted with word length, but that it did get access to a store which is especially for the phonological characteristics of speech. They therefore divided the articulatory loop into two components: a passive phonological store from which information decays, and an articulatory rehearsal process which can prevent the information being lost. So, immediate memory for verbal information involves passive storage based on what the information sounds like, and a rehearsal process which uses an internal analogue of articulation and can convert visually presented material into a phonological form.

Salamé and Baddeley (1989) have subsequently suggested that a filter which is specialised to detect the physical characteristics of speech sounds and to ignore other types of sound governs entry into the phonological store. Further research on unattended input to the phonological store has suggested that it may not simply be speech sounds which interfere with the remembered material. There is no difference in the amount of interference between unattended speech that is backwards or in a foreign language (Jones, Miles, & Page 1990), but whereas there is no interference when listening to single repeated speech sounds (H, H), there is interference when listening to four repeated speech sounds (CHJU, CHJU) (Jones, Madden, & Miles, 1992). So it seems likely that the unattended speech effect reflects more general processes which are going on in forming streams of information in memory, based on particular kinds of change in the auditory input. It may be the nature of the change which is important, rather than speech itself. It is important to realise that there are many processes involved in dealing with incoming language and producing speech (as we will see in later chapters) and there may be many language-specific stores (Monsell, 1984). These stores may not all be available for use in problem solving, mental arithmetic or other working memory tasks.

Can we identify the phonological store and articulatory rehearsal system with some of the working storage used in mental arithmetic? The argument is that the ability to rehearse is linked to the ability to articulate, and so the capacity of the rehearsal system is determined by how long words take to say. Therefore, if there is a language in which digits take a long time to say, then digit spans will be shorter than they would be in a language in which digits take a short time to say. Ellis and Hennelly (1980) looked at children who spoke both Welsh and English. They found that it takes longer to speak digits in Welsh than in English, and that bilingual children actually had shorter digit spans in Welsh than they did in English.

When the children were asked to produce irrelevant sounds to suppress articulation while they remembered the digits, the difference between the two digit spans disappeared. More interestingly, the children made more mistakes in arithmetic when they used Welsh than when they used English, even though Welsh was their first language. This suggests that they did indeed use the articulatory loop to hold digits while they calculated.

Rehearsal and Verbal Memory Span. The time taken to say words in English and Welsh is linked to the number of items which can be recalled in immediate memory. In addition, as we saw earlier, there is a word-length effect in immediate memory which means that fewer long words are recalled than short words. Baddeley's (1986) model suggests that the information held in immediate memory decays unless it is rehearsed, and that the rate at which rehearsal takes place determines the number of items which someone can recall. Rehearsal is something like the experience you get when you repeat words to yourself in order to hold on to them, although, as we will see later, it is not exactly the same as saying things aloud. If rehearsal rate is related to speech rate, then the number of items which can be recalled is linked to the amount of time it takes an individual to say those items. This relationship between speech rate and memory span has been found in a large number of studies over different languages (e.g. Naveh-Benjamin & Ayres, 1986).

Rehearsal is not the only thing which affects how many items can be remembered. Baddeley et al. (1975) asked subjects to remember sets of words but told them to count repeatedly to six as the words were presented. This counting decreased span and removed the effect of word length. It was assumed therefore to be preventing rehearsal, yet memory span performance was not completely destroyed. When articulation is suppressed in this way, there is a residual span of three or four digits or words. Some other system, not the articulatory rehearsal system, must be responsible for this. This residual span could be dealt with by the central executive, which we will discuss later, but there may also be a long-term memory contribution. Memory span is affected by how familiar the words are, that is, by their frequency in the language (Tehan & Humphreys, 1988). This suggests that long-term memory elements are indeed involved in memory span. These long-term elements are not concerned with knowledge about what words mean (their semantics), but with knowledge of what they sound like, or long-term phonological representations (Cohen & Heath, 1990; Hulme, Maugham, & Brown, 1991).

When you rehearse words which you are trying to remember, you may feel that you are "saying" the words but not making any sound. However, this does not mean that when words are rehearsed they are actually articulated. Neuropsychological data, both from patients with acquired brain lesions who have disturbances of the ability to articulate, and of children with cerebral palsy who also have such disabilities, show that normal memory span and normal effects of word length and phonological similarity are present without the ability to articulate (Baddeley & Wilson, 1985; Bishop & Robson, 1989). This suggests that it is not articulation itself which is important but an internal derivative of it. Patients who have higher-level disturbances known as apraxia of speech, whose articulatory system is not directly impaired, are unable to plan the motor sequences for speech, and they do not show word-length effects (Waters, Rochon, & Caplan, 1992). Rehearsal may not require articulation itself in the form of subvocal or actual speech, but uses the ability to specify the plans which will produce speech sounds when fed into the motor system.

In the earlier work on working memory, the idea of a rehearsal loop was based, in part, on the word-length effect. Fewer long words are remembered because fewer of them fit within the time-span of the rehearsal loop. However, rehearsal is not the only aspect of immediate memory to be affected by word length. Long words actually take longer to say when they are being recalled, and it may be this which causes memory span to become shorter. Cowan et al. (1992) have shown that words which take longer to say have a greater effect on span if they are said in the first half of a sequence than they do if they are said in the second half. Therefore, recalling a set of words with long words first followed by short words leads to poorer recall than recalling the same set of words when the short words come first. This shouldn't happen if it is the overall time to rehearse the sequence which affects span length, so perhaps the effect is due to the processes which plan and produce speech at the time of recall and not to rehearsal itself. However, as word-length effects *can* be shown when subjects recall by pointing at pictures rather than by saying words (Caplan, Rochon, & Waters, 1992), and therefore there is no effect of the time taken to actually say the words at recall, it may be that the word-length effect is due in part to rehearsal, but that this is not the complete explanation.

The relationship between rehearsal and the number of verbal items which can be recalled is not as clear as it was when it was first proposed. Our long-term knowledge of what words sound like affects how many items we can remember, and long words take longer to say when we are recalling them, which may prevent us from recalling more of them, so thinking of saying words over in our heads is an over-simple view of rehearsal. However, when subjects are actually told to rehearse, word-length effects are found for words which are hard to articulate (Martin, 1987), so explicit rehearsal *is* linked to word length. Part of the problem here may be that explicit rehearsal is only one of the many processes available to us when we remember verbal material in the short term. Explicit rehearsal may be an optional rehearsal mechanism rather than the only way in which information is maintained.

What is Short-term Phonological Memory For? While we use imme-diate memory to hold parts of calculations as we do mental arithmetic, and we can remember sequences of digits like telephone numbers, it seems unlikely that short-term memory for verbal material developed to allow us to do these things. These activities use short-term memory resources which have other primary purposes. It seems likely that they use short-term phonological representations which are needed to enable us to process, learn and remember the auditory phonological characteristics of words and to plan output when we speak. Phonological knowledge and phonological memory skills have been found to be important in the development of vocabulary, both in children learning their first language and in older children learning a second language. Gathercole and Baddeley (1990) have shown that 5-year-old children who had good phonological skills were much better at learning nonsense names like "Pimas" and "Sommel" for toy monsters than were 5-year-olds who had poorer phonological skills. Gathercole, Willis, Emslie and Baddeley (1992) have found that the ability to repeat nonwords spoken to them is a very good predictor of children's vocabulary in their first language between the ages of 4 and 6 years. Service (1992) looked at Finnish children beginning to learn English, and found that their scores on a task which involved the repetition of unfamiliar sound sequences was a good predictor of their class grades in English when they were tested 2 years later. If we think about what the phonological loop might be for, it is probably not just a tape loop to help us remember telephone numbers, but an important component in our ability to take new sounds and hold them in order to produce language learning.

Baddeley, Vallar and Wilson (1987) have also suggested, based on neuropsychological evidence, that phonological memory skills are impor-tant in sentence comprehension. Patients who have difficulties with phono-logical memory also have difficulties in understanding long or complex sentences. In these sentences, it is not always possible to work out what is being said as it is being said, and the ability to go back and check by considering the ordering of the material in phonological memory is an important part of comprehension. The short-term phonological store may have a role in checking what a sentence means when there are problems with its form (Caplan & Waters, 1990). Saffran and Martin (1990) have summed up several patterns of comprehension difficulty and their relation to short-term memory by describing the short-term phonological repre-sentation as the glue which binds together the various representations constructed when we process sentences. Defects in phonological memory are important for comprehension performance when complexity at one level of representation cannot be compensated for at another level.

Visual and Spatial Working Memory

It sometimes seems that psychologists are obsessed with words. Unless you can read it, say it, or repeat it to yourself, they are not going to be interested. Fortunately, this is not quite true and some attention has been paid to other aspects of immediate or working memory. If we return to mental arithmetic, Professor Aitken, a skilled calculator whom we will discuss in some detail later, reported using imagery during calculation (Hunter, 1977). Hayes' (1973) subjects reported that they "moved" images of symbols and that some used images even for simple operations like addition. Hayes also found that presenting a problem in an unfamiliar format made it more difficult to solve and increased computation time.

If we see words or digits we can translate them into a verbal code of some kind in order to maintain them, but we can also maintain a visual representation that will last for several seconds (Phillips & Baddeley, 1971). If you remember from our earlier discussion, Margrain (1967) presented two lists of digits at the same time, one visually and the other aurally, and found that when recall was spoken, visual items were remembered best; but that when it was written, aural presentation was remembered best. This suggests that the digits do not have to be recoded into a phonemic form, but can be held visually. Frick (1984) investigated this by presenting a set of digits visually followed by an auditory set, and asking subjects to try to visualise the first set and to rehearse the auditory one at the same time. He found an increase in span in the mixed conditions, which suggests that some of the digits presented visually were held long enough to be recalled and that they were held in a form which was separate from the phonological system.

So, we may be able to hold a visual representation which decays over time. It is also possible that purely visual information can be rehearsed (Kroll, Kellicut, & Parks, 1975), although this may be due to the construction of a different kind of code which is spatial rather than visual. The distinction between visual and spatial memory can seem a little difficult at first. In Fig. 6.4, the numbers are the same, the spatial relations are the same, but the detailed visual characteristics of the digits are quite different. It would be possible to remember the spatial arrangement (above, below, to the right, etc.) without the visual characteristics. When people report imagery associated with mental arithmetic in which digits are moved about, the important element is the spatial relationships, not the actual appearance of the digits.

Adding digits together as they are presented aloud has been found to interfere with the number of letters which can be recalled in order, but to interfere less with spatial imagery (Logie, Zucco, & Baddeley, 1990), which suggests that actually carrying out the operation of addition does not involve visuo-spatial processing. Could we, however, be using a visuo-spatial system to hold parts of the problem or to do spatial manipulations? The answer would depend on whether we could show that spatial process-ing was independent of verbal processing. This independence, discussed earlier in relation to the neurological patients of De Renzi and Nichelli

$$\begin{array}{r} 572 \\ + 469 \\ \hline \end{array} \qquad \begin{array}{r} 572 \\ + 469 \\ \hline \end{array}$$

FIG. 6.4 Arithmetic problems differing in visual characteristics but not in spatial form.

FIG. 6.5 A block-printed "F", similar to the letters used by Brooks (1967).

(1975), has been shown in a series of studies by Brooks (1967; 1968), who was concerned with the manipulation of information and not just its storage. Brooks asked subjects to imagine a block capital letter like that shown in Fig. 6.5. They were then asked to start at one corner of the letter and to evaluate each corner in turn, deciding whether it was a top or bottom corner or not. Subjects responded in different ways. One was to respond verbally by saying "yes" if the corner was on the top or bottom and "no" if it was not. A second response was to point at either a Y or an N in a spatial array of Y's and N's. The time to do the task and the errors both increased when the response was spatial pointing. In a second condition, subjects were asked to remember a sentence like "A bird in the hand is worth two in the bush" and then to evaluate each word and categorise it as either a noun or not a noun. Again the responses were saying "yes" and "no" or pointing to a spatial array of Y's and N's. With this task, time and errors both increased when the response was verbal. Brooks argued that there was interference between verbal processing and verbal responding and between spatial processing and spatial responding, but that the control processes for using spatial information were different from those involved in using verbal information.

Of course, the interference in Brooks' task might be visual rather than spatial, possibly because it is hard to hold an image when seeing new input. Here we have to remember that spatial relations are not purely visual and are more concerned with *where* things are than with *what* things are. We can have auditory information about where things are in space and visual information about where they are, but it is much more difficult to have visual information about what a tone is or auditory information about what colour an object is. Baddeley and Liebermann (1980) asked subjects to do a visually presented spatial task while carrying out a second task of detecting changes in the brightness of a patch of light (a purely visual task), and found no interference between the two tasks; but when the second task was an auditory spatial one in which subjects had to track the path of a moving sound source, then interference did occur. So two visual tasks did not interfere, but two spatial tasks did, even though one was visual and one was auditory. Spatial memory can require the same kind of processes as other spatial tasks, even when the information used is not visually presented.

Visuo-spatial and verbal tasks do not interfere with each other as much as they do with themselves. This suggests that there is a visuo-spatial short-term store which is part of an overall working memory system. In Baddeley's (1986) account of working memory, he suggests that there are indeed two slave systems which the executive component of working memory can use — one for verbal material and one for spatial material — and that both slave systems have a passive, perceptually based store in which information decays, unless it is rehearsed. The visuo-spatial system is known as the visuo-spatial scratchpad. Visuo-spatial material held there decays unless it is rehearsed by a covert (or internal) process similar to actually looking at things in the world. Therefore, in this account, when you look round an image you behave as if you are using your eyes, just as when you rehearse a sentence you behave as if you are articulating.

If people are asked to tap repeatedly round a set of four targets arranged in a square while carrying out a spatial reasoning task, their performance is impaired (Farmer, Berman, & Fletcher, 1986). Carrying out the same spatial tapping task while being presented with spatial memory items similar to those used by Corsi (which we discussed earlier in the chapter) decreases the number of spatial items in spatial memory span (Smyth & Pendleton, 1989). So, the idea that an internal analogue of moving to targets in space is used in rehearsal seems plausible. However, Smyth and Scholey (1992) have been unable to find any relationship between how fast people move their eyes or their hands between real targets and the number of spatial items they can recall in order in a spatial span task — that is, there is no link between the time taken for external production and that taken for internal rehearsal, as there is in verbal memory span. Smyth and Scholey (1994) have argued that covert shifts of spatial attention, rather than covert movements, are involved in maintaining spatial items for recall.

Investigations of visual and spatial short-term memory have run into some difficulties with the separation between visual and spatial tasks. Tasks which involve colour are assumed to be visual, not spatial, and Logie (1986) has shown that when subjects were trying to use an imagery mnemonic, they were impaired if they had to judge simultaneously whether sequentially presented squares were the same colour or not. This may mean that visual tasks can interfere with spatial tasks, but it could also mean that having to actually look in one place in order to carry out the colour judgement task makes it very difficult to mentally "look" or shift attention round the image. There has been comparatively less investigation of this subsystem than of the phonological one, and there is still a need for studies which distinguish clearly between what is being held in memory, what is being done with it, and how rehearsal and maintenance affect these.

A neuropsychological patient who has been described as having a deficit in the visuo-spatial scratchpad (Hanley, Young, & Pearson, 1991) has problems with spatial tasks and mental rotation tasks but no difficulty with verbal tasks. This suggests yet again that verbal and spatial processes can be separated, particularly as the patient reported by Vallar and Baddeley (1984) who has impaired short-term phonological memory, has no difficulty with visuo-spatial short-term memory. However, a patient reported by Farah, Hammond, Levine and Calvanio (1988), who will be discussed further in Chapter 11 on spatial processing in general, has an inability to do tasks involving shape, colour and relative size of visual items but can do spatial tasks. While these two patients do not have an exactly opposite pattern of deficits, there is clearly a difficulty in proposing one system which deals with all visual and spatial material. Farah et al. argue that mental imagery is indeed both spatial and visual because it engages both visual and spatial representations, but that these are themselves separable subsystems.

Before we leave the patient reported by Hanley et al. (1991), it is important to note that her difficulty with immediate visuo-spatial tasks was not just a laboratory problem. She also had difficulty in learning new spatial relations in the world. She could remember places and routes which she knew before her brain lesion but she could not learn new ones. This suggests that the visuo-spatial short-term memory tests used may have been showing that she could not hold new spatial material long enough to create a long-term representation of it. Short-term visuo-spatial memory has a role in learning new spatial information, and is not just an artefact of psychologists' tasks.

Hatano and Osawa (1983) have demonstrated a situation in which a visuo-spatial system may be important for mental arithmetic. They studied expert abacus users in Japan, who find they no longer need the abacus itself. These experts had very large digit spans, up to 16 items, but normal spans for words and letters, suggesting that their expertise with the abacus provides a long-term memory representation which can support manipulation within a short-term visuo-spatial system. This performance was not based on long-term recall, because the expert abacus users were not able to recognise sets of digits which they had recalled previously. Hatano, Amaiwa and Shimizu (1987) found that when abacus experts and controls were asked to do intervening tasks between the presentation of the digits and their recall, verbal tasks interfered with digit recall for the control subjects but not for the experts. However, a secondary visuo-spatial task did not have different effects on the two groups. A visuo-spatial workspace does seem to be a very good contender for the component which maintains the abacus representation in these experts, although the evidence is not conclusive.

The Executive System

In the working memory model set out by Baddeley (1986), holding information for a short time is only part of what goes on. The core of working memory is the regulation of the flow of information, the retrieval of information from long-term memory, and general-purpose storage and processing which allow operations to be applied to information held in memory. These activities have been called the *central executive subsystem* of working memory, and Baddeley (1986) has argued that the capacity of the executive system can be tapped using a task called *random generation*.

In the random generation task (Baddeley, 1966), subjects are asked to select letters at random from the 26 letters of the alphabet. This is quite a difficult task to do because there is a tendency to produce linked sequences of letters (ABC, FBI) rather than random ones. The responses become even less random if subjects are asked to do another task involving selection at the same time, and Baddeley (1986) suggested that this was because the ability to supervise selection was affected by the addition of the secondary task. Baddeley (1992) has subsequently reported that chess players who are asked to select the best move to make next when they look at a chess board with the pieces arranged from the middle of a game, find it difficult if they have to carry out random generation at the same time. This suggests that some of the complex activities engaged in playing chess and in random generation use some of the same resources.

One of the functions suggested for the central executive is that of updating information in memory. Morris and Jones (1990) used a running memory task in which they presented lists of digits to subjects one at a time and asked them to keep remembering the last four digits at any point so that they could recall them if they were asked to. As the subjects did not know when they would be asked to produce the last four digits, they had to keep updating the four digits they were holding for output. Updating of memory was found to be independent of the effects of both irrelevant speech and articulatory suppression, suggesting that the operations required to update are indeed independent of the phonological subsystem.

The central executive is similar to an overall supervisory system for dealing with tasks which require attention, which Shallice (1982) has called the Supervisory Attentional System (SAS). Shallice has argued that the schemas which control action (see Chapter 4) require little attentional control to run, but that they may sometimes come into conflict with each other. The SAS is called upon in situations which involve planning or decision making, sorting out errors, or carrying out poorly learned tasks and preventing well-learned schemas taking control when they are not required. These kinds of activities are just those which a central executive component of working memory might be called upon to do. Random generation involves the central executive in preventing the well-learned groupings (ABC, FBI) from occurring.

It has been suggested that patients who have suffered damage to the frontal lobes of the brain have an impairment of this overall attentional system (Baddeley, 1986; Shallice, 1988). Two different kinds of patients have been described by Shallice (1988) with different lesions in the frontal lobes, and with different proposed malfunctions of the supervisory system. Patients in one group find it hard to do tasks in which the response is delayed, are very easily distracted from what they are doing and find it difficult to shift hypotheses, while the patients in the other group are unable to suppress well-learned or dominant responses. The patients who are easily distracted are argued to have an impairment of the attention system and therefore control is continually taken over by incoming environmental stimuli, whereas the patients who keep repeating one action do so because the attention system cannot intervene to redirect the processing. A different pattern of dissociation between executive functions has been shown by a patient reported by Eslinger and Damasio (1985). This patient, a former accountant with high intelligence, was completely unable to make real-life decisions. He couldn't decide where to go out to for a meal and buying anything was very difficult because he had to compare all the prices and virtues of all brands. However, he could do laboratory tasks involving hypothesis testing, resistance to distraction, reasoning, and so on. It seems unlikely that a central executive system would be impaired only on making decisions about real-life events, yet distraction for this patient was only apparent in real-life situations.

Recent developments in techniques for providing images of the brain while subjects are carrying out different tasks have allowed the exploration of the activity of the frontal lobes in many situations. Studies using positron emission tomography (more familiarly known as PET scanning) have shown that many areas of the frontal lobes are involved in different attention-type tasks (Allport, 1993). The central executive may simply be a loose way of referring to a large number of possible control processes which can be used in different ways in different tasks. If it is simply a general-purpose attentional mechanism, then it is very close to the capacity models which we have dealt with in Chapter 5, and has some of the problems of those models. In particular, it becomes hard to explain anything if "executive involvement" cannot be ruled out in any experimental situation where interference between two tasks occurs. However, being able to specify the particular types of executive function and how they interact will improve our understanding of cognitive functioning. It is possible, for example, that maintaining serial order in a set of memory items may involve specific executive functions regardless of whether the information is spatial or verbal. Random generation involves access to long-term memory for the alphabet, memory for previous items selected, operations for comparing currently selected items with previous ones and for deciding on what constitutes randomness, as well as the selection and production of letters. If we find that this task interferes with another task, we need to be very specific about the components of both in order to map out executive functions.

WORKING MEMORY AT WORK

Breaking working memory down into one system which holds phono-logical material, one which holds visual and spatial material and an overall executive which controls access to long-term memory, and which is involved in the planning, scheduling and management of tasks, has allowed some explanation of the findings that people can hold information in memory while they do other things. Clearly, it is not a good idea to suggest that everything we know has gone through a unitary short-term memory system. One of the strengths of working memory is that it allows for different kinds of short-term store and allows for management of operations as well.

Several psychologists have been concerned to explore what happens when people carry out one task while holding information, which might be said to be the basic motivation for the concept of working memory in the first place. Daneman and Carpenter (1980) devised a sentence span task in which subjects had to read several sentences, decide whether each was true or not, and remember the last word of each of the sentences. Span here becomes the number of last words which can be recalled correctly. Performance on this task was found to be related to comprehension performance, and this task has been called a test of working memory span. Such a span may be related to processes involved in comprehension. Gick, Craik and Morris (1988) looked at the ability of elderly subjects and college students to do the sentence span task and found that the elderly subjects had shorter spans if the sentences were in the negative, suggesting that increasing complexity of the material to be comprehended made it harder for the elderly subjects to carry out the task. Fincher-Kiefer, Post, Greene and Voss (1988) took this task as a measure of the demands involved in processing sentences. Using subjects who knew a lot about baseball and those who knew very little about baseball, they found that if subjects were also required to remember the contents of the sentences themselves, then the span for last words was decreased for people who did not know about the content material. Again it is suggested that high levels of memory load comprehension, in this case comprehension in an expert domain, affect span performance.

Siegel and Ryan (1989) took this argument a little further and looked at whether there could be differences between different kinds of processing span, in particular between sentence span and counting span, and whether this was related to different patterns of disability in children. They found that children who were very bad at arithmetic but good at reading tended to have normal sentence spans but low spans on a counting task. This counting task required the children to count dots, remember the number, count another set, remember that number, and so on. Siegel and Ryan (1989) argued that there might be a general working memory for numerical material which could be separated from that for general verbal material. However, Hitch and McAuley (1991) showed that children who were poor at arithmetic were actually poorer at counting than other children as well as having shorter digit spans. These children therefore had deficits both of the operations to be carried out and of the short-term storage required to hold the products, so it isn't surprising that they could not do the combined task. A general-purpose arithmetic working memory deficit does not seem to give a good account of their problem.

If a working memory system is one which holds material and requires processing at the same time, and the system as a whole is determined by both the holding and the processing abilities, then any impairment in either or both should lead to poorer working memory performance. Doing mental arithmetic ($8/4 = ?$, or $16 \times 12 = ?$) has been taken by Kyllonen and Christal (1990) as one task which measures overall working memory capacity. They gave such mental arithmetic tasks to a large number of military recruits in the USA, along with tasks which required them to remember numerical values for letters and do calculations (if A = B/2, B = C−4, and C = 8, then what are A and B?) and tasks which required them to understand the orderings of sets of letters (if A precedes B, D is not preceded by C, and the first two mentioned precede the second two, what order are the letters in?). It was assumed that performance on these tasks was determined by the ability to carry out the component operations, and by the ability to carry out those operations while remembering the results from earlier parts.

Kyllonen and Christal (1990) asked whether these different tasks reflected one working memory capacity or whether the verbal reasoning task would be different from the mental arithmetic task. They found that performance on these tasks could best be described as involving a general working memory factor. That is, that the domain (arithmetic *vs* verbal reasoning) did not have separate effects on the ways individuals differed on these tasks. Kyllonen and Christal (1990) concluded that while part of working memory capacity may involve the capacity of short-term storage systems, what is more important is how the short-term store can be managed while other things are going on. They suggest that the actual capacity of short-term stores may only have a small effect on working memory, while managing the processes involved in accessing long-term memory and applying procedures to material held in short-term stores reflect more important individual differences. Craik, Morris and Gick (1990) report work with several kinds of task which supports this conception. They found that the articulatory loop component of working memory was not impaired in elderly subjects but that they were less able than younger subjects when on-going active decision making was required. Craik et al. concluded that ageing did not affect all aspects of working memory in the same way.

When we consider working memory at work, we find that the management of decision-making processes and control operations is crucially important in some tasks. However, performance on complex tasks may be limited by component processes, as Hitch and McAuley (1991) have shown. Progress in understanding how we do mental arithmetic and other working memory tasks will depend on the development of a more complete notion of what the component processes are, and how the activities which we have called "management" can be separated into specific aspects of control.

EXPERT IMMEDIATE MEMORY

At the beginning of this chapter, we pointed out that in order to do mental arithmetic at all, we have to have knowledge in long-term memory as well as in immediate memory. Multiplication is very difficult if you have not learned that $7 \times 8 = 56$ and $8 \times 9 = 72$, and so on. You also have to know how to break up calculations in order to execute one part at a time. If you were asked to multiply 123 by 456, you would know how to break it up into components and the answers for all the sub-calculations, but you would require too many slots to hold the parts of the problem. However, when Hunter (1962; 1978) asked Professor A.C. Aitken to multiply 123 by 456, Aitken was silent for 2 sec and then produced the answer, 56,088, giving the digits in their natural left-to-right order starting from 5. Hunter (1978, p. 341) quotes Professor Aitken:

> I do this in two moves: I see at once that 123 times 45 is 5535 and that 123 times 6 is 738; I hardly have to think. Then 55,350 plus 738 gives 56,088. Even at the moment of registering 56,088, I have checked it by dividing by 8; so 7011 and this by 9,779. I recognise 779 as 41 by 19; and 41 by 3 is 123, 19 by 24 is 456.

Professor Aitken, as you will gather, is rather special in his ability to perform mental arithmetic. He is one of a small group of virtuoso mental calculators who have been studied by psychologists. Aitken enjoyed numbers, he liked to think about numbers and calculations for their own sake, and over time he developed a very large store of knowledge about numerical equivalents (e.g. $123 \times 45 = 5535$) which most of us do not have. In addition, he had a store of methods for dividing problems up into sections which make calculations easier. For a calculation like the one given above, there is very little strain on immediate or short-term memory. This is not because his immediate memory is larger, but because there is still a comparatively small number of steps.

Mrs Shakuntala Devi, who is cited in the *Guinness Book of Records* for correctly multiplying 7,686,369,774,870 by 2465,099,745,779, has performed mental arithmetic feats since she was 5, when she could extract cube roots in her head. Very few studies of such special abilities relate to the building blocks of immediate memory which we are considering in this chapter, but Jensen (1990) reports that when Mrs Devi was asked to hold a series of digits in memory and then to decide whether a particular digit was in the list, the time it took her to make the decision did not increase as the size of the set of digits increased. For control subjects, the time to match a digit with a sequence held in memory does increase as the set gets larger and each of the digits in their serial order is compared to the target. Mrs Devi does not represent incoming numbers in a short-term serial form. Rather, each number is codable in many different ways. For example, 720 is immediately seen to be 6 factorial, a four-digit number may be seen as the sum of the cubes of two other numbers, and so on. Mrs Devi is not strictly a mnemonist — that is, she does not set out to remember large strings of numbers — but she can remember long strings as the multiplication of two 13 digit numbers indicates. Her number knowledge supports what seem to be amazing feats of immediate memory.

Can we take an ordinary person and change his or her ability to remember large numbers? This was the question that Ericsson, Chase and Faloon (1980) asked when they asked one person to spend 200 hours spread out over 18 months remembering lists of digits. By the end of the 18 months, this subject, S.F., could listen to a list of 81 digits read to him at one digit per second and repeat them back perfectly. To do this, he had developed a series of strategies for coding groups of digits into one unit. One of these strategies developed from the subject's interest in running. He had a wide knowledge of times for running different distances at different standards, so when he heard 3492 he could recode is as "3 min 49.2 sec, close to the world record for the mile".

This strategy used by S.F. involves a specific kind of knowledge in long-term memory; it does not improve span performance in other tasks. Memory for a list of letters, for instance, stayed at six even though the span for digits was very large. In addition, these are not really immediate memory span tasks, as the experts are able to remember lists of digits which they have learned on previous sessions. Training of this form does not improve immediate memory by adding more slots, but by altering how information is put into long-term memory and retrieved from it. Kliegel, Smith, Heckhausen and Baltes (1987) argued that teaching subjects a memory encoding strategy or mnemonic, giving them a retrieval strategy to help organise recall, and then giving them a large amount of training, should be enough to increase anyone's memory for digits. They used two systems — one involving dates of historical events and one involving concrete nouns — and found that subjects who had never used the systems before could learn to do so over a number of months. They could recall up to 90 items with the first system and 80 with the second. Again, the increase was based on being able to encode digits into long-term memory and then to retrieve then when required. Immediate memory for verbal material in general was not affected. Maintenance rehearsal of the original input items can play little part in such a skill, but the encoding strategies may be only very advanced versions of procedures available to all of us when we notice meaningful groupings within seemingly meaningless material.

OVERVIEW OF WORKING MEMORY

We have come a long way from the simpler views of the use of a short-term store for the immediate recall of strings of letters and digits and for recalling lists of words. While the Atkinson–Shiffrin model provided a focal summary of earlier views, they also emphasised the expression "working memory" and gave attention to control processes. Baddeley and others developed a view of working memory with its central executive and the specialised subsystems, the phonological loop and the visuo-spatial system. The picture of immediate processing has become quite compli-cated in recent times, but it should be admitted that several writers over the years (e.g. James, 1890; Broadbent, 1958; Miller, Galanter, & Pribram, 1960) had speculated that we have such special systems for particular purposes.

Certainly our initial attempt to account for our difficulties in performing mental arithmetic in terms of a simple view of a limited-capacity immediate memory store comes to grief. When S.F. recalls 81 digits that he has just heard, he cannot be recalling 81 articulated items from a short-term articulatory store; he has performed a great deal of on-line processing, reduction coding and storage as the digits arrived. Similarly, Professor Aitken's speedy recognition of the deep properties of many numbers and his speedy retrieval or development of memory-efficient procedures show ways in which our system can, admittedly with much effort and practice, learn to cope with extraordinary loads and tasks. Of course, even Professor Aitken met calculations that were outside his capacity and, like the rest of us, he reached for a pen and paper or for a calculator. The overall point is that whether the task is a nominally simple one like a memory span task or whether it is evidently more complex like mental arithmetic or, as we shall see in later chapters, listening and speaking, our working memory involves a very complex set of processes handling a variety of inputs, selecting, retrieving, storing, planning and preparing outputs, probably using a number of subsystems adapted for special purposes.

When we think about the way our immediate memory is limited, we have to recognise that people had these limitations before they started to do mental arithmetic. However, they have always needed to extract order and structure from events that occurred over time. This may be one reason why working memory is partly parasitic on speech systems. If we were able to take everything we perceive and put it straight into memory, that is if we had virtually infinite capacity to hold new information as it arrived, we would have all the sounds produced by a lecturer "taped" in long-term memory. But we would not understand the lecture until we had run the tape and we would not be able to find items in memory which were actually there in the lecture. Without processing incoming information, we would have a lot of memories and no knowledge. We need to be able to respond to events as they happen, yet to take in enough information to make sense of the world. Limitations on our input systems reflect a trade-off between these requirements.

SUMMARY

In this chapter, we have focused on the immediate processing of inputs to the cognitive system. This is important both when the inputs arrive too quickly and when the operations we wish to perform on the inputs strain our capacity to hold on to all the bits we need successfully to complete the task. Doing mental arithmetic comes close to illustrating these problems.

We began by describing a few phenomena and sketching some ideas from early studies of memory. We know that most people can remember between 5 and 9 items, whether they are letters, digits or words. Confusions in recall can occur because words sound similar, suggesting that the sound of words is important in this kind of memory. The Atkinson–Shiffrin model marked a phase of consolidation of what many researchers thought about the memory system. Short-term and long-term memory were sharply distinguished and it was argued that there was a single short-term store through which items had to pass to reach long-term memory. However, problems arose with this model when it was found that it was possible to hold items in immediate memory while carrying out tasks which should have involved the storage they used; that it was possible to maintain visuo-spatial information separately from verbal information; that neuropsychological patients had separate impairments of verbal and spatial memory;

and that it was possible to have little immediate memory but good long-term memory. Immediate memory, conceived as "working memory", came to be seen as a current processing activity, as an interaction of the analysis of perceptual inputs, long-term knowledge, preparation for output, and overall task management. Baddeley's working memory model made some of these activities explicit in sub-components of a system with two short-term memory stores, one phonological and one visuo-spatial, each with a rehearsal mechanism to prevent decay, both under the control of a central executive.

Rather than study the sub-components of working memory, it is also possible to investigate the capacity of immediate memory during active processing in comprehension and mental arithmetic. The ability to hold and process information does not seem to be different in mental arithmetic from that found in verbal reasoning. Management of information in memory while carrying out operations on it reflects individual differences which are not the same as those found for the simple memory span, so holding material by rehearsal is not the only important part of working memory. This is why we have chosen mental arithmetic rather than digit span to represent the activities supported by immediate memory.

Some individuals are able to remember extremely long sets of numbers which are presented to them. This is not because they have bigger short-term stores than most people, as their extended capacity is only found for numbers, not for other verbal material. These experts have extensive number knowledge in long-term memory which enables them to encode strings of digits by recognising the deep properties of many numbers. People who have perfectly normal memories for digits can be trained to remember very long sets by developing encoding strategies and organising recall appropriately.

Our story is necessarily incomplete. Memory and its role in immediate processing lie at the core of every activity in which we engage, and later chapters take up some of the issues raised here. A.D. Baddeley (1986), *Working memory*, gives an account of one important model in the field, and G. Vallar, and T. Shallice (1990), *Neuropsychological impairments of short-term memory*, is a rich source for both data and debate from the neuropsychological perspective.

7 Answering the Question: Planning and Producing Speech

Imagine the scenario of being in an interview for a job: your first full-time job and one that you want very much. Not surprisingly, the interviewers keep asking you questions and you, as interviewee, attempt to provide intelligent and informed answers which reflect something of what you truly think and, perhaps, something of what you believe the interviewers hope you think. For our purposes, what matters in this scenario is that there are things which you very much want to say. We are interested, that is, in the cognitive processes involved in translating thoughts into speech. The real-world activity of speaking is both the example we use to illustrate the problems and the topic of the chapter as well.

Speech production is not an easy skill to study in the laboratory, and the psychologist who wishes to investigate speaking has to exploit rather devious and perhaps indirect sources of evidence. Chief among these are the distribution of hesitations in spontaneous speech, the occasional involuntary slips of the tongue to which all speakers are prone, and the patterns of language disorder that can occur following brain injury. We shall use these sources of evidence to follow a thought through its translation into language to its external realisation as a sound wave, and shall discuss in some detail the model of speech production developed by Gary Dell.

PLANNING UNITS AND PLANNING LEVELS

After lunch, the interview starts. Fifteen minutes into the interview and everything is going swimmingly: the questions are gentle and the atmosphere is relaxed and friendly, you feel as though this would be a nice place to work. Suddenly along comes one of those questions that you had dreaded: "Why do you think you would be good at this job?" You begin to regret that second glass of wine as you strive to put together a coherent answer without appearing glib or complacent. In Table 7.1, we have invented a transcript of the reply you might give: it is a nervous response and it is not meant to be ideal, far from it, but we hope it has some semblance of realism and we shall use it to illustrate various points about speech production later in the chapter.

TABLE 7.1

A Simulated Transcript of Spontaneous Speech

Why would I be good at the job? Er, well . . . I think there are lots of reasons . . . er . . . like . . . well it's difficult to know quite what to say. I think I am very highly motivated so I would work hard and from what I know of teachers that seems important, particularly in their first year when so much is having to be planned almost from scratch. And then . . . well . . . I think that . . . well I know teacher training involved teaching practice . . . but erm before that my previous experience in voluntary work where I was in charge of small groups of children will be helpful . . . I'm not too naive about how difficult young children can be. And then, well . . . it's a bit embarrassing blowing one's own trumpet but . . . erm . . . I think that I do get on very well with children which is absolutely vital isn't it? I like their energy, seeing the way they grow and change and being part of all that.

Oh!, and of course, obviously, there's the training I've had so far . . . I mean I realise that one never stops learning but the work I did during my degree taught me a lot not just about teaching but about how to work on my own, how to plan my time that kind of thing . . . which, certainly from the teachers I've talked to, seems important. [A long pause, as you search for more to say, the interviewer just looks at you and you feel compelled to go on.]

On the other hand, it's not just a matter of my qualities and experience is it? I mean . . . it's . . . well, it's also a matter of what I feel about the job and I think that it's a marvellous job: interesting, challenging and rewarding. I'm not terribly worried about the money [laughs nervously] which is just as well . . . I also feel I have got lots of ideas for lessons and activities . . . though of course I'm sure that people here already do lots of interesting things . . . I want to encourage the children to learn for themselves because that's so important.

Ermm . . . I suppose that, on balance, the *main* things are my motivation, my experience and, well, I also like to think I've got my fair share of common sense which should help keep me on an even keel . . . a sense of proportion . . . of humour . . . I think I have those and they should help shouldn't they?

The Sound of Silence

When we produce short monologues, such as a response in an interview, it is clear that we are not talking all of the time: there are silences. These pauses, short though they often seem to the participants, occupy more time than one might think. For example, when Goldman-Eisler (1968) asked subjects to give impromptu talks on selected topics, the amount of time occupied by pauses ranged from 35 to 67% (where a pause is defined as a silence longer than 250 msec or more). Interviews were rather more fluent, with the amount of utterance time taken up by pauses varying from 4 to 54%. So it is quite possible for spontaneous speech to contain between one-third and one-half silence.

Why is speech so full of silence? It is likely that the amount and patterns of silence within speech are multiply-determined, that is, there is no one factor which can account for everything (O'Connell & Kowal, 1983). Pauses may be a factor influencing when speakers exchange turns in conversations and they may be coordinated with aspects of non-verbal communication such as nods of the head (Beattie, 1983). They can also be used by speakers for rhetorical purposes, such as pausing before a particularly dramatic utterance, which occurs in an extreme form as the ritually prolonged pause before announcing a competition winner. They may be a fleeting difficulty in finding the exact word that you want to express your thought. Pauses may also reflect a moment of discomfort before announcing something the speaker knows will be mutually embarrassing. On other occasions, a pause may be an attempt to downplay one's enthusiasm for a suggestion made by the other speaker. One can go on thinking of similar situations where pausing might be strongly affected by social circumstances. The patterning of one's speech and intonation in general is a part of the speaker's communicative ability that is, to some degree, under intentional control and so purely cognitive explanations are unlikely to be sufficient (Levelt, 1989). There may also be physical factors confusing the pattern of pausing such as speech rate, how much air one expels with each word, and so on. However, given these cautions, do pauses also tell us anything about the cognitive processes underlying speech production? In this section, we shall look at three cognitive factors that seem to account for some aspects of pausing: the conceptual difficulty of what is being said, the syntactic structure of an utterance, and phonological factors (that is, factors to do with with the sound forms being produced).

It is conceivable that some pauses in speech occur because speakers are planning what to say next. That is, speakers may sometimes finish saying one thing before they have planned and prepared the next. If speech follows a pattern of plan–execute–plan–execute, and if at least some hesitations are indicative of planning in progress, then pauses in speech should not occur at random, but should be more likely to occur at the beginnings of planning units. However, such an effect may only really become apparent when the processes of planning are under some form of pressure. Greene and Cappella (1986) took monologues from people who had been asked to argue in favour of a proposal to introduce a particular new law on drugs. All of the monologues that they used were at least 45 sec long. They found that when speakers switched from one major goal in their argument to another (a so-called "move"), there was a substantial decrease in the fluency of speech at the transition point. When Greene and Cappella repeated the study but provided the speakers with a structure around which to organise their argument, the tendency for dysfluency at these move boundaries disappeared. This is consistent with the idea that where the cognitive demands of planning are sufficiently onerous, there is an increase in the number of pauses in speech and, in this particular study, the idea that pausing might be used for rhetorical purposes does not explain the differences between the two conditions. In general, it appears that the greater the conceptual difficulty of what is being spoken about, the greater the amount of pausing (Good & Butterworth, 1980).

Studies of the distribution of pauses in spontaneous speech have also found that pauses tend to cluster at the boundaries between one sentence and the next (Ford & Holmes, 1978; Goldman-Eisler, 1968), thereby implying the sentence as one unit of planning. But pause analysis has also revealed another smaller grammatical unit — the *clause*. There are various forms of clause, but basically it is a group of words centred grammatically on a verb. Suppose one were to say, "I would work hard which everyone tells me is so important because everything is planned almost from scratch". That is all one sentence, but it contains three main verbs (*work, tell* and *plan*) and thus three clauses:

1. I would work hard
2. which everyone tells me is so important
3. because everything is planned almost from scratch

Work on pause distributions shows that pauses within sentences tend to cluster at clause boundaries (Butterworth, 1980; Garrett, 1982). In the above example, the speaker would tend to pause (or say "um" or "er") before or after "which" or "because". We say "after" as well as "before" because another way to signal that a pause does not imply the end of a conversational turn is to say the first conjoining word of the next clause before pausing. The speaker might thus say, "I would work hard which . . . erm . . . everyone". Ford (1982) looked at the distributions of pauses in spontaneous speech. As with previous work, she found that pauses tended to coincide with clause boundaries, but she also found that pauses did not differ in duration according to the complexity of the clause structure. Goldman-Eisler (1968) had previously found that structural complexity had little impact on pauses. From this evidence, Levelt (1989) concludes that although the clause is a planning unit, pauses at the end of a clause reflect semantic processes rather than ones to do with sentence structure (so-called "syntactic processes"). Such a conclusion fits with the idea that syntactic processes are relatively automatic and so make fewer demands on more central processes than do semantic processes. The contention that syntactic processes are automatic is a theme to which we will return in Chapter 8.

Slips of the Tongue and the Clause as a Planning Unit

A second line of evidence that suggests the clause is an important planning unit when producing speech comes from analyses of involuntary and unintentional speech errors or "slips of the tongue". Imagine that a speaker intends to say "we'll be able to afford a house in the country" but instead says "we'll be able to afford a country in the house". The speaker is mildly embarrassed by the slip but a nearby psycholinguist smiles ruefully, takes out a little pocket book and writes the error down. Later, after amassing quite a large collection of errors, the psycholinguist sits down to examine them. It soon becomes clear that they can be divided into several categories and that the resulting types have rather different properties, that is, slips of the tongue are not random but demonstrate regularities and these regularities can be informative about the cognitive processes leading to the production of speech.

Garrett (1975; 1976) collected and reported just such an analysis of a corpus of around 3400 slips of the tongue. Ninety-seven of these were word exchanges like the example given above or like the following (where "I:" denotes what the speaker intended to say and "E:" denotes what they actually said):

I: I've got to go home and give my back a hot bath.
E: I've got to go home and give my bath a hot back.

I: She'll have my guts for garters.
E: She'll have my garters for guts.

I: One spoon of sugar.
E: One sugar of spoon.

Garrett observed that all of the word exchanges in his collection involved two words from within the same sentence, and that 85% came from within the same clause. Another type of exchange error found to respect clause boundaries was the morpheme exchange error. Examples of this type of error are:

I: She slants her writing.
E: She writes her slanting (Garrett, 1982).

I: The hills are snowy.
E: The snows are hilly.

I: The prongs of a fork.
E: The forks of a prong

In these errors, the "root morphemes" of the words (*slant, write, hill, snow, prong* and *fork*) have become detached from the "inflectional morphemes" to which they should be attached (*-ing, -ed,* and *-s*). The roots exchange positions, while the inflections remain "stranded" in their original, intended positions. On examining the grammatical distributions of these errors, Garrett (1975) found that 42 of his 46 (91%) morpheme exchanges involved two words from the same clause. Again the significance of the clause as a planning unit is apparent.

Elsewhere in this book we have encountered the idea of units which represent the sounds, letters or words that we know, and many models of speech production assume that we have a store of units which represent knowledge about the forms of words that we can say (Dell, 1986; Garrett, 1982). Word exchanges suggest that when we are speaking, several of these units are active at the same time; if they were not, it would be hard to see how such exchanges could occur. This simultaneous activation of different forms is a kind of parallelism in speech planning and it helps ensure fluency within clauses. However, Garrett's observation that the majority of word exchanges occur within clauses suggests that word forms beyond the current clause receive little if any activation. As a consequence, one would expect some of the pausing between clauses to be due to a build-up of activation in the word forms needed for the upcoming clause.

Most studies of slips of the tongue have looked at naturally occurring errors where there was a reasonably clear discrepancy between what the speaker intended and what he or she actually said. However, there are also errors where what we say does not match what we are supposed to say according to the prescriptive grammars of English. A common example of this is the failure to make the subject and verb of a sentence agree in number. An example of such an error, with the disagreeing items in italics, is:

1. The *demo tape* from the popular rock singers *were* listened to carefully.

Bock and Cutting (1992) induced such errors by giving subjects the beginnings of a statement, such as "The demo tape from the popular rock singers", and asking them to repeat it back together with a plausible continuation (as in the example above). Bock and Cutting found that the probability of such errors varied according to the characteristics of the sentence opening provided. For example, take the imaginary errors in sentences (2) and (3) below.

2. The consultants for the growing firm was very highly paid.
3. The consultants who advised the firm was very highly paid.

In both cases there is the same basic error: the subject (consultants) and main verb (was) disagree in number. Such errors are made more likely by the presence of a singular form (firm) intervening between the subject and its corresponding verb. Crucially, Bock and Cutting also found that errors such as that in sentence (2) were more likely than errors such as that in sentence (3). The crucial structure difference between sentences (2) and (3) is that in (2) the intervening singular "firm" is part of a phrase whereas in (3) it is part of a subordinate clause. Why should this matter? According to Bock and Cutting, it matters because early on in speech production the contents of different clauses are separated from one another (see Fig. 7.1). As the unit of planning is the clause, in sentence (2) the phrase containing "firm" belongs to the same planning unit as the main verb "was" (see Fig. 7.1a). On the other hand, in sentence (3) the singular form "firm" is part of a subordinate clause which is planned separately from the main clause (see Fig. 7.1b). The separation of the two clauses in the planning of sentence (3) means that the singular "firm" is less likely to cause an agreement error. Thus the findings of Bock and Cutting support the idea that in the early stages of speech production, utterances are planned in clause-sized units.

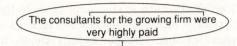

The consultants for the growing firm were very highly paid

(a) Agreeing elements separated by intervening phrase

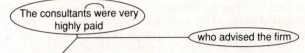

The consultants who advised the firm were very highly paid

(b) Agreeing elements separated by intervening relative clause

FIG. 7.1 Agreement between elements in a sentence where functionally separate processing units are in different ellipses. Lines within ellipses connect elements supposed to agree. Based on Bock and Cutting (1992).

Various sources of evidence suggest that speech is planned in units about the size of a clause: patterns of pauses, the distribution of speech errors, and experimental work on the difficulty in making the subject and verb of a sentence agree. However, as Levelt (1989) points out, saying something is a planning unit in speech is not the same as saying it is the only such unit, as we shall see in later sections.

FINDING THE RIGHT WORD

Part of planning what you are going to say involves selecting the appropriate words and wording to express your intentions. In most speech situations, there is a potentially huge number of ways of conveying your message. Cognitive theories of speech production are not so much concerned with why you choose a particular phrase as with how the relevant knowledge is organised and how you are able to access the desired wording. When one considers how individual words are selected, there are a number of sources of evidence and we shall consider two of them: tip-of-the-tongue states and speech errors.

Tip-of-the-tongue (TOT) States

We have discussed hesitations at the onset of idea units and hesitations at the onset of sentences or clauses. The pattern of hesitations has been informative about how speech is planned. There is, however, one other notable location and cause of pauses that we must mention. We have all probably experienced that awful moment when you suddenly cannot recall the precise word you want to use — you can remember plenty about its meaning but its exact form escapes you. This is known as a tip-of-the-tongue

(TOT) state and we shall return to it several times in the course of this chapter. William James — brother of the novelist Henry James — captured the tantalising agony of this state particularly vividly in the following famous passage (James, 1890, p. 251):

> Suppose we try to recall a forgotten name. The state of our consciousness is peculiar. There is a gap therein; but no mere gap. It is a gap that is intensely active. A sort of wraith of the name is in it, beckoning us in a given direction, making us at moments tingle with the sense of our closeness, and then letting us sink back without the longed for term. If wrong names are proposed to us, this singularly definite gap acts immediately so as to negate them. They do not fit its mould . . . The rhythm of a lost word may be there without a sound to clothe it; or the evanescent sense of something which is the initial vowel or consonant may mock us fitfully, without growing more distinct.

From a psychological perspective, TOT states are valuable for the way they help us appreciate the distinction between a concept and the verbal label (word or phrase) used to denote it. A speaker in a TOT state knows full well the concept that is to be communicated but cannot recall its label. The victim can give a paraphrase or definition of the sought-for word, and can bring to mind related words, but knows them to be incorrect. Brown and McNeill (1966) managed to induce TOT states in subjects by reading them definitions of uncommon words and asking them to supply the word. The signs of a TOT state, they say, were unmistakable. The subject "would appear to be in a mild torment, something like the brink of a sneeze, and if he found the word his relief was considerable". The subjects could often offer words similar either in meaning or sound to the target. Thus, the definition, "A navigational instrument used in measuring angular distances, especially the altitude of the sun, moon and stars at sea", for which the correct response is "*sextant,*" induced the similar-meaning attempts *astrolabe, compass, dividers* and *protractor*, and the similar-sound attempts *secant, sextet* and *sexton*. Subjects were sometimes so close to the target as to be able to say how many syllables it had, or what letter or sound it began with. This latter information was presumably the basis upon which the similar-sound attempts were constructed.

A TOT state clearly reflects some form of memory failure — the failure to retrieve the word that matches a concept. But what is the nature of the memory store which lets the speaker down, albeit only temporarily, since the elusive word usually comes to mind eventually? Psychologists usually refer to the memory store for words as "the mental lexicon". There are reasons, however, for believing that the mind may contain more than one word store, for example separate stores for the production and recognition of spoken and written words (see Allport, 1983; Morton, 1979), so we will be cautious here and refer to the store from which words are retrieved in speaking, and whose failure causes TOT states, as the *speech output lexicon*.

When in a TOT state, you can usually retrieve some information about the target word. In particular, people are often able to retrieve one or more of the following pieces of information: the number of syllables in the word, the stress pattern, the initial letters or sounds of the word (Brown & McNeill, 1966; Cohen & Faulkner, 1986). Other aspects of the sound of the word, such as the number of sounds in it, are rarely reported and do not seem as accessible as those aspects mentioned previously.

When in a TOT state, it feels as though one has accessed the word's meaning perfectly adequately — one can often give definitions or related words, for example — what seems to be missing is the complete sound form. This subjective impression is supported by a study by Jones and Langford (1987). In line with previous experimental work, they gave subjects some definitions of rare words or items as for *sextant* in the above example. On some occasions, these definitions induce TOT states. Immediately after these definitions, Jones and Langford gave people a word which was related to the target word either in meaning, such as *compass*, or in sound, such as *sextet*. This word was known as a blocker. By doing this, Jones and Langford found that the chances of a TOT state being induced was increased only if the blocker was related in sound to the target. They concluded that this supported the idea that semantic access had been achieved, hence meaning-related blockers did not interfere, but that the phonological trace had not been fully recovered and sound-related forms would get in the way of further specification of the sound form of the target. The idea of full activation of meanings but only partial activation of phonological representations has been developed into a model that accounts for various characteristics of TOT states (Burke, MacKay, Worthley, & Wade, 1991), and we will return to discuss this model in more detail later in the chapter.

More on Slips of the Tongue

We have already seen that slips of the tongue can tell us something about how speech is planned and that TOT states can tell us something about how information on words is organised and accessed. The characteristics of other forms of speech error are a further source of evidence about the selection and storage of words. Word substitutions occur when the speaker intends to say one word but actually produces another. Some examples of substitutions are given below:

I: You'll find the ice-cream in the fridge.
E: You'll find the ice-cream in the oven.

I: Can you wiggle your ankles?
E: Can you wiggle your elbows?

In both of these word substitutions, the intended word and the erroneous word are related in meaning; the intended concept seems to activate the wrong word in the speech output lexicon. In other word substitutions, the intended word and the error seem to be unrelated in meaning (even when the context of the utterance is taken into account):

I: Trains full of commuters.
E: Trains full of computers.

Here the overlap in sound between the two words seems to have led to the misselection. The intended word and the error word in substitutions are nearly always from the same syntactic class — that is, nouns substitute for nouns, verbs for verbs, and so on

While purely meaning-based and purely sound-based word substitutions do occur, many word substitutions seem to be a mix of the two, that is, both similarity in meaning and in sound have contributed to the error. Some of this overlap could occur by chance, but it is not clear whether it can all be attributed to chance. In an attempt to answer this, Martin, Weisberg and Saffran (1989) moved away from naturally occurring errors and used an experimental technique devised by Levelt (1983) for inducing word substitutions. They gave subjects arrays of pictures on a grid and asked them to describe the layout as they were speaking to someone who could not see the grid (see Fig. 7.2 for an example of a grid). When asked to do this quickly, people occasionally make substitution errors. Martin et al. found that when the picture names were related in either meaning or sound alone, errors did occur. However, errors were even more likely to occur if the picture names were related on both dimensions. For example, there were more speech errors on the pair *pigeon–penguin* (same number of syllables and same initial sound) than on the pair *pigeon–swan*.

Word blends are another error that seem to occur in retrieval of forms from the speech output lexicon. Here there are two words in the speaker's lexicon which could be used equally well to communicate a particular idea. What emerges is a blend of the two. Note that for some blends the similarity in meaning may be obvious even without reference to the context, whereas for others some information about the context is necessary for one to appreciate the similarity. The two blending words are nearly always of the same syntactic class. In the following examples, the two blended words are shown in brackets after the error.

You can't swip   (swap + switch)
It's blowing a gizzard   (gale + blizzard)
Just the poo of us   (pair + two)
I'm not that dick   (daft + thick)

To date we have seen that there are a number of regularities in word substitutions and word blends: the words are nearly always of the same

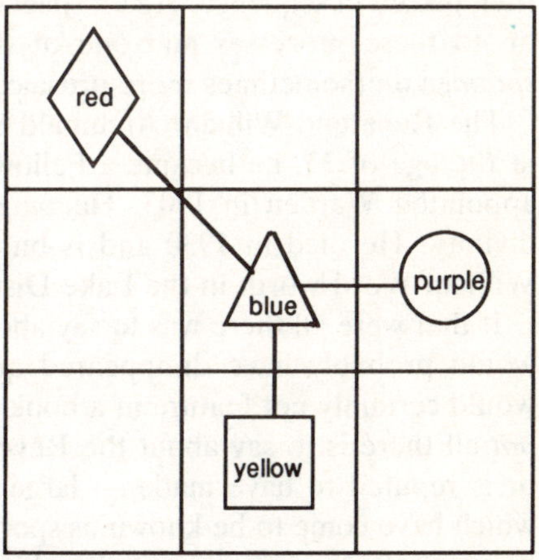

FIG. 7.2 An example of a test pattern from Martin et al. (1989). Subjects were required to name objects and their colour following the path given by the lines. For example: "red diamond–blue triangle–purple circle–blue triangle–yellow square". Reproduced with permission.

syntactic class; there is usually a similarity in meaning and/or sound. As with TOT states, it is assumed that these patterns are providing information about the underlying processes — in this case, about retrieval of word forms from the lexicon. In a later section, we will consider a model that attempts to explain how the various constraints operate in word selection.

Finally, there are characteristics of slips of the tongue which provide information about how words are stored in the speech output lexicon. The slips in question are those involving the exchange of two root morphemes. The fact that, for example, *hill* can exchange with *snow* in the error "The snows are hilly", leaving the *-s* and *-y* stranded, has been taken to imply that root morphemes and some of the "bound morphemes" (*-s* and *-y* in this case) that can be tacked on to them may be stored separately in the lexicon (Henderson, 1985). Slips like the following, in which incorrect bound morphemes have been attached to roots, carry the same implication:

I: He understood it
E: He understanded it

I: most heavily
E: heaviestly

I: . . . made him so popular
E: . . . maked him so popular

THE SOUND LEVEL

In the previous section, we discussed some sources of evidence about how word forms are retrieved from the speech output lexicon. In this section, we are more concerned with evidence about how the sounds of words are then placed in sequence. Again speech errors prove to be a useful window on to these processes and one of the most useful errors of all is the *spoonerism* (sometimes more prosaically called a sound exchange).

The Reverend William Archibald Spooner was born in 1844. In 1867, at the age of 23, he became a Fellow of New College, Oxford, and was appointed Warden in 1903. He taught ancient history, philosophy and divinity. He died in 1930 and is buried with his wife close to the poet William Wordsworth in the Lake District village of Grasmere.

If that were all there was to say about the Reverend Spooner, his name would probably have disappeared quietly into history by now, and he would certainly not feature in a book on cognitive psychology. But that is *not* all there is to say about the Reverend Spooner, because he made — or is reputed to have made — large numbers of speech errors of a sort which have come to be known as spoonerisms. He is said, for example, to have rebuked a student by telling him, "You have hissed all my mystery lectures" (I: ". . . missed all my history lectures"), and informed another that, "I saw you fight a liar in the back quad; in fact you have tasted the whole worm" (I: ". . . light a fire . . . wasted the whole term").

The truth is probably that very few of the errors attributed to Spooner were actually made by him, and that the majority were invented by the Oxford wags of the time (Potter, 1980). Spooner was a shy man, and not at all proud of his reputation as an errorsmith, but the name has stuck, and "spoonerism" is now the term widely employed to refer to slips of the tongue which involve the exchange (reversal) of two phonemes. Examples taken from the Appendix to Fromkin (1973) include:

I: left hemisphere
E: *h*eft *l*emisphere

I: heap of rubbish
E: *r*eap of *h*ubbish

I: bed bugs
E: b*u*d b*e*gs

I: You better stop for gas
E: You *g*etter stop for *b*as

The properties and characteristics of genuine spoonerisms have been closely studied (Cutler, 1982; Fromkin, 1973; 1980). The picture that emerges is that both consonant and vowels can exchange, but consonants only exchange with consonants (as in the first two of the preceding examples) and vowels only exchange with vowels (the third example). Reversing sounds come from so-called "content" or "open-class" words (nouns, verbs and adjectives) rather than from "function" or "closed-class" words (*through, from, to, then*). The exchanging sounds tend to be similar in form, so that, other things being equal, a "p" will be more likely to exchange with "b" than with "s". The sounds also tend to come from similar positions within their respective words and syllables. The exchanging sounds in a spoonerism also often have the same repeated sound adjacent to them; so, for example, in the exchange "left hemisphere– *h*eft *l*emisphere", the exchanging *l* and *h* are both adjacent to the vowel "e". Dell (1984) has shown that this effect of similarity stretches beyond just the immediately adjacent phonemes. Spoonerisms do not cross sentence boundaries, and Garrett (1975; 1976) found that 93% of them occurred within a clause. Although this list of characteristics is certainly not an exhaustive one, it again provides a number of constraints on theories of how the sequences of sound that make up the speech stream are constructed.

It appears, then, that speech planning in roughly clause-sized units extends from higher conceptual and syntactic levels right down to the level at which the individual phonemes of words are activated and readied for articulation. Spoonerisms show that words being planned are not spelled out as phoneme sequences one at a time. In the last of the four examples above, the word *gas* must already have been retrieved as a phoneme string from the speech output lexicon at the time the speaker wished to say *better*, otherwise the "g" of gas would not have been available to exchange with and replace the "b" of better. In Lashley's (1951) words, spoonerisms are "indications that prior to the internal or overt enunciation of the sentence, an aggregate of word units is partially activated or readied".

If an "aggregate of words" is to be partially activated as phoneme strings the sound level must be equipped with the necessary storage capacity to hold them ready for articulation. Following Morton (1970), Ellis (1979) argued that this storage capacity might be what subjects draw upon when they are asked to repeat random sequences of letters, digits or words in psychological experiments on "short-term memory". Others have argued that such short-term storage involves memory stores more closely linked to the perception and comprehension of speech (see Chapter 8).

ARTICULATION

We cannot leave our speaker quite there, with everything planned and readied but nothing yet spoken (or only errors anyway). Sounds must be articulated: they must be realised by moving the lips, the tongue and teeth in a coordinated manner while air is expired and the vocal chords vibrated so as to produce that perturbation of the air that we call speech.

One theory of how this is achieved is that given a particular sound or sound sequence, there is a set of spatial locations which the articulators (the lips, tongue, etc.) must achieve in order to produce them (MacNeilage, 1970). The task for the motor system is to compute the movements necessary to reach the next target position from the present one. The computation will depend on the current position of the articulators, so that, for example, the movements to produce a "t" will be different following an "a" than an "s".

This theory, however, soon ran into problems when Folkins and Abbs (1975) showed that if movement of the lower lip is suddenly impeded during a lip closure, the upper lip compensates rapidly with greater than normal lowering (lip closure usually occurs when producing sounds such as a "p" or "b"). In effect, this means that the target location for an articulator has been altered because of a change in the degree of freedom allowed the other articulators, yet the same sound is still produced. Similarly, it is possible to produce intelligible speech while holding a pipe between your teeth or while maintaining a fixed smile for a photographer: we produce similar sounds to when our articulators have complete freedom, but the sounds are produced using different movements.

A revised theory which tries to counter this criticism makes use of something called "coordinative structures". According to this idea, a set of muscles can be set to serve different functions. For example, many of the muscles involved in speech are also involved in eating and "normal" breathing (that is, when one is not speaking). The muscle movements within each of these functions is a subset of all the muscles' possible movements. The patterns of movement will vary according to the context: the pattern of respiration is very different when talking from when not talking (Lenneberg, 1967). In a coordinative structure there is a separation of the task to be performed, say closing of the lips in producing a "b" sound, and the means by which it is realised. This separation captures the fact that a "b" will require lip closure but that this can be achieved with or without jaw movement (depending on which diabolical restriction is being imposed by the research phonetician). Consequently, at one level of the structure there is some kind of general specification of the articulatory task which ignores the precise positions of the articulators (sometimes called a context-free mechanism), while lower down the structure there is a system which takes account of this task, the current positions of the articulators, and any gross resistances to movements. Clearly, this lower-level system is extremely complicated. The basic problem for such a system is that it is trying to produce a solution but it is constrained in how it can do so. These constraints are sometimes obvious and inflexible (the tip of the tongue cannot be in two places at once), while in others they are more like ideals (for example, "t" may be more or less clearly articulated depending on exactly where the tongue tip makes contact with the inside of the mouth). Satisfying these multiple constraints would seem to require an awful lot of cognitive effort, yet articulation certainly does not feel so demanding. However, connectionist networks, which were introduced in Chapter 2 and which we shall encounter again in the next section, seem particularly good at satisfying multiple constraints and so are good candidates for providing a way of describing how this lower-level system works.

We have already discussed evidence supporting the idea that speech is preplanned at the higher levels, but there is also evidence that preplanning extends right down to the articulatory level where it is revealed in the phenomenon of co-articulation. Try saying the word "stick" and freeze your movement as you say the "t". Now try it again for "stoop". You should find that your lips are in rather different positions in anticipation of the vowel. In fact, you can detect some difference as early as the "s". Co-articulation of this sort can extend across word boundaries. Try saying the following phrases rapidly: "Bring it?" versus "Bring who?" If you film lip movements of such phrases, you can see that towards the end of "Bring" in "Bring who?", the lips are already beginning to be pushed out to form a rounded shape for the "u" vowel of "who". Again this planning would not be possible if aggregates of words were not planned as groups. It also fits with the hierarchical nature of planning in coordinative structures, because while one element of the speech plan is being realised by the muscles, elements later in the plan will be making demands on the same network so that the specifications overlap to some degree.

A MODEL OF WORD RETRIEVAL IN SPEECH PRODUCTION

In this section, we will look at a model of word retrieval developed by Dell (1986; Dell and O'Seaghda, 1992). Other models, such as that of Garrett (1982), provide more detail on aspects of speech production such as the syntactic processes and we consider this model in a later section. However, Dell's model does attempt to explain in detail many of the characteristics of speech production that we have described so far in this chapter, including several of the regularities observed in various kinds of speech error. We will present the model in slightly simplified form, omitting those elements of it which are not central to explaining those speech error regularities with which we are concerned. The model has been implemented on a computer, which means that one can actually run the model to see if it produces errors and whether the errors produced are similar to those which people produce (clearly, if they are not, it suggests the model is wrong).

Dell's model has much in common with models described elsewhere in this book (see, for example, Chapter 2 on word recognition and naming). In the same spirit as these models, it consists of simple units, which can have activations, and links between these units for transmitting activation.

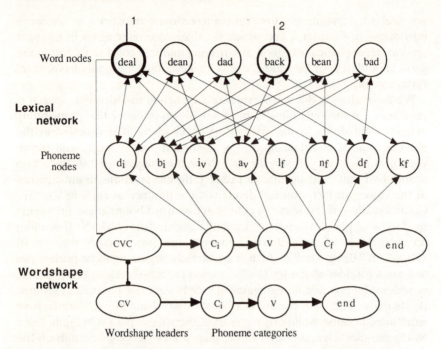

FIG. 7.3 Dell's spreading activation model of speech production showing part of the network. Here the phrase being spoken is "deal back" with "deal" being the current word. All connections within the lexical network are excitatory. In the wordshape network, inhibitory links are indicated by ●———●. Adapted from Dell (1988).

In this particular model, most of the links are excitatory — that is, activation passed from one node to another node can only serve to increase the activation of the other node. The basic structure of Dell's model is shown in Fig. 7.3. Most of Dell's work has focused on the access of the word and sound forms. For example, in Fig. 7.3, the word node for *deal* is shown. This word node then links to the constituent phonemes via bidirectional excitatory links — that is, links where activation can flow down from the word node to the phoneme nodes and vice versa. The word node is also linked to syllable nodes in the wordshape network. In turn, the syllable nodes are linked to nodes for the onset and rime: the onset of a syllable being the initial consonant or consonant cluster, the rime being the vowel sound and any final consonant(s). Finally, in this model, onset and rime nodes are linked to phonemes, with these phoneme nodes being marked for syllabic position. This means, for example, that the two "d's" in *dread* are represented by different nodes (d_i and d_f). Linkages continue in a similar way down to distinctive features (characteristics which are used to distinguish sounds from one another). These nodes and connections make up the lexical network.

Alongside the spread of activation through the lexical network, there is also a spread of activation through a network that provides a structure for the utterance (known as the tactic frames; Dell, 1986). The structure includes a sequence of syntactic slots, such as noun, verb, adverb, etc. Items from the lexical network are inserted into these slots to achieve the correct sequencing of words and sounds. To achieve this, a set of insertion rules operate; they select the most activated lexical node that is compatible with the slot's specifications. There is a wordshape network that specifies the structure of words and syllables and the type of sound which can fit into particular parts of the structure (Dell, 1988).

Assuming that a particular semantic representation is active, it passes on activation to all words that match some of its characteristics. For example, if one wished to say *dog*, then a large number of word nodes, such as *wolf, fox, hound, cat, Fido*, would receive some activation. Normally, however, the node for *dog* would achieve the highest activation. When ready to speak the word, a jolt of activation is given to the selected word node. It would then be inserted into the most active slot in the syntactic frame provided it met the criteria of the rule — that is, it is of the correct syntactic class. Activation spreads down the network and the most active elements are selected and inserted into the appropriate slots. Note that all the time activation is spreading down to a node, it is immediately sending activation back up to any nodes to which it is connected. For example, as the constituent sounds of *dog* receive activation, they will return activation up to other word nodes such as *log, dot, hog*, and so on. The amount of activation such neighbouring nodes receive will be a function of their similarity to the target. Once selected, the activation levels of nodes are reduced to their starting level to prevent them being selected over and over again.

For any model of speech production to be an adequate one, it is crucial that it is capable of making errors. Dell (1988) proposes that there are three major sources of error in his model. First, there is interference from nodes other than the intended one, nodes which receive activation as "spill out" from activation of the target. As we have already seen with the example of *dog*, this happens because of the pattern of connections and the interactive nature of the network. Second, words that have just been spoken or are to be spoken immediately after the current word, will be active to some extent (as should be evident from some of the evidence on planning units discussed above). When we are speaking quickly, the potential for confusion should be greater. Third, there is activation from other cognitive and perceptual processes which may not be linked directly to the speech plan. For example, you may be talking about dogs but you still notice other events around you. A fourth source of error, explicitly not used by Dell in his model but used in other models of a similar sort, is the idea of small random fluctuations in activation levels (Stemberger,

1982). The rationale for these fluctuations is that some kind of random variation is present in many physical systems. All these sources of error combine to produce the occasional erroneous output from the model. There is not room here to explain all of the error characteristics that the model can mimic, so we shall simply consider some of them in some detail to give a feel for how the model accounts for them and some of their characteristics.

Word Substitutions

Earlier in this chapter we described word substitutions where the two words were related in terms of meaning, sound or both. The easiest way to see how substitutions occur in Dell's model is to consider how a sound-based word substitution such as saying *computer* for *commuter* could arise. Suppose that the target word node *commuter* initially receives a lot of activation from the semantic and syntactic levels. This activation will spread to a particular word structure in the word shape network (one that specifies three syllables) and, via a set of syllable nodes, to the constituent phonemes. As these lower-level nodes rise in activation, so they will pass activation back up to any other connected nodes. So, for example, any word node beginning "com" (such as *competitor*) will be receiving activation from the relevant phonemic nodes. Nodes receiving appreciable amounts of activation from other levels are known as neighbours of the target node. Now in terms of sound, *computer* is just about as similar to *commuter* as one can get and, on some occasions, due to extraneous activation or random fluctuation in starting levels of activation and shared syntactic class (see below), *computer* will receive more activation than the target, *commuter*, and so it will be substituted for it in the utterance. A similar account can work for meaning-based word substitutions. The model also suggests that if a competing word is similar in both meaning and sound to the target, then, other things being equal, it is more likely to replace it than competing words which overlap only in terms of meaning or sound. This is in line with the findings of Martin et al. (1989) as well as similar findings with naturally occurring word substitutions (Dell & Reich, 1981).

When looking at corpora of real speech errors, semantic and/or sound similarity does not appear to be sufficient for a substitution to occur. For example, although one might have a noun and an adjective which are very close in terms of their sounds, such as *rudder* and *ruddy*, it is very unlikely that they would form a target–error pair because, as noted in a previous section, word substitutions nearly always involve words from the same syntactic class. According to Dell's model, the reason for this is that in the frame constructed at the syntactic level, there is a specification of the syntactic class of the current target word. If this specification is "noun", then when the insertion rule selects an item from the activated word nodes to be slotted into the frame, the rule specifies that the selected item must be from the required syntactic class (Dell, 1986).

The above account suggests that all substitutions occur for the same reason — that is, the target and error words share a substantial number of nodes at another level in the network. Doesn't this predict that the closer a neighbour is to the target the more likely it is to substitute for it? And, if so, why don't we all make the same speech errors? Well, in reality things are not quite so simple. For example, Dell's model — in line with many other cognitive models — proposes that the frequency with which a word is spoken has an effect on the resting activation level of the corresponding word node. For rarer words at least, frequencies will vary substantially between people. The recency with which a word was used may also be important, as it is in TOT states, and again this will vary between individuals. Also, the communicative contexts in which a particular word is selected will vary considerably, so that the nature of the interference will also vary. Consequently, similarity is not the sole influence on the particular form of a real speech error, but it does provide constraints on the general characteristics.

Spoonerisms

Spoonerisms, such as "*r*eap of *h*ubbish", arise in the following way in Dell's model. In spoonerisms, and word exchanges for that matter, the right components have been selected for production, what goes wrong is the sequencing. Mackay (1981; 1987), in a model very similar to Dell's, draws a useful distinction between *priming activation* and *execution activation*. Priming activation is preparatory activation that is given to all nodes that form part of the planning unit, whereas execution activation is that jolt of activation that ultimately leads to the words being spoken. In a spoonerism, all the right phonemes receive some priming activation, but when executed a later phoneme receives more activation than the target and so is selected by the insertion rules for insertion into the target's slot. In the present example, the "r" of "rubbish" is the offending item. Having been selected in this way, Dell assumes that the activation for that phoneme node is then set to zero. Consequently, having made the anticipatory error of saying "*r*eap", the phoneme node for "r" is at or near zero activation, whereas the node for "h" is still available and is selected by mistake.

A number of points need to be made about this account. First, how come that on some occasions we make anticipation errors, such as "*r*eap of rubbish", and on others we make perseveration errors, such as "heap of *h*ubbish", rather than always making exchange errors? Without going into too much detail, Dell assumes that this variation is due to the activation of phonemes rebounding after initially being set to zero or a phoneme remaining active because of the variability that is inherent in the system. In Dell's model, both of these factors are less likely to have an effect at rapid speech rates. Consequently, this model makes the prediction that when speaking rapidly, exchanges should become more common relative to anticipations and perseverations. This novel prediction was tested experimentally and confirmed by Dell (1986). Second, studies of spoonerisms have shown that the exchanging phonemes nearly always come from the same position in the word or syllable (so errors like "*vong drile*" for "long drive" don't occur; MacKay, 1972). Dell's model is able to account for this because the insertion rules will only select a phoneme provided it fits the category required — that is, if the slot is at the onset of a syllable, the phoneme must be flagged as in the onset version of that phoneme (as in r_o and h_o for *rubbish* and *heap*).

Dell has shown that his model can account for a large number of the known characteristics of spoonerisms as well as making predictions about new characteristics which have subsequently been supported by experimentations. Although the model is not without problems, particularly over access on the basis of semantics and of sound (Levelt et al., 1991), its successes are encouraging. It is also worth noting that Dell's model is not simply a pencil and paper account, where a skeptic might say, "That all sounds very well but I bet it wouldn't really behave like that". Dell has a response to this, which is that his model has been implemented on a computer and it does make errors — though not all of the time — and these errors fit many of the characteristics of human speech errors. This advantage of implementing a model on a computer and seeing if it really does work as intended is a considerable one.

Modelling Tip-of-the-tongue States

In a model similar in spirit though differing in details to that of Dell (1986), Burke et al. (1991) have developed another account of tip-of-the-tongue states. Again this model makes use of MacKay's distinction between priming and execution activation. Tip-of-the-tongue states occur because of a deficit in the transmission of activation to the phonological level (Cohen & Faulkner, 1986) — that is, although the semantic nodes are appropriately activated for some reason, the phonological ones are not. This idea can explain a number of characteristics of TOT states. For example, Burke et al. propose that the strength of links carrying activation from semantic to phonological nodes is related to the amount of use — so the more frequently a word is used, the stronger the links. Consequently, a TOT state should be more likely on low-frequency words. This was confirmed by Burke et al. using an experimental procedure for inducing TOTS similar to that described earlier in this chapter.

Burke et al. deal with a number of other characteristics of TOT states within the framework of an activation model (see Fig. 7.4 for a representation of the model). For example, people in a TOT state often

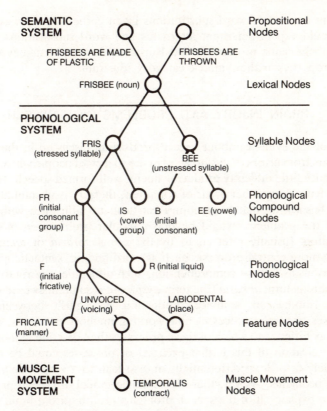

FIG. 7.4 A simplified version of Burke and co-workers' (1991) model of speech production showing hierarchical access of phonological information. Reproduced with permission.

say that they are constantly finding that a particular word, which is not the target, comes to mind even when they do not want it to (Reason & Lucas, 1984). Burke et al. call these "persistent alternates" and give the example of someone in a TOT state seeking the target *chastity* but finding that the persistent alternate *charity* comes to mind. These two words share some aspects of meaning, so that the node for *charity* does receive some top-down activation from this level. Activation then spreads to the component nodes in the phonological system. However, because of the weak transmission along the links from *chastity*, its components do not receive as much activation as those of *charity*, nor is there reinforcing feedback from these phonological nodes to the *chastity* node. Consequently, the node for *charity* becomes much more active. Not only this, but because the processes beyond the semantic specification of the word are automatic, the person cannot prevent *charity* from continuously coming to mind unbidden. You may have noticed that this account has much in common with the account of word substitutions given earlier. As a consequence, one would expect persistent alternates and word substitutions to share some of the same properties, and Burke et al. show that they do share such properties as the syntactic category constraint.

BRAIN INJURY AND PROBLEMS WITH SPEECH

Much of the evidence about speech production discussed in this chapter has come from errors or dysfluencies in the speech of people who otherwise experience little difficulty producing fluent, well-formed speech. However, in line with many other areas of cognition, there is a substantial body of research showing that brain injury can lead to difficulties with speech. Where the problems extend beyond muscular problems in moving the articulators (usually referred to by the terms *apraxia* or *anarthria*) to include more central processes such as word finding, syntactic processing and various aspects of comprehension, such difficulties are referred to by the umbrella term *aphasia* (the term *dysphasia* is sometimes used instead).

Most models of sentence production distinguish between lexical processes, syntactic processes and working memory processes, although they may differ as to which of these processes they describe in most detail. The implication of this is that each set of processes could be damaged separately or at least differentially and so lead to a very wide variety of speech problems. As yet, there is no single model of speech production that can explain all of the speech problems resulting from brain damage. However, we will consider briefly a general framework that is helpful for interpreting a number of speech difficulties. This framework, unlike Dell's, considers more than word retrieval and is based on the work of Garrett (1975; 1982).

In this model, speech production begins with a conceptual plan which represents the speaker's communicative intention. This plan is then used to set in motion both the processes of word retrieval and to assign syntactic roles to the retrieved words. At this early stage, word forms are selected according to meaning. The syntactic roles are thematic and specify things such as the agent of an action. Taken together, these processes result in a linguistic representation which contains abstract lexical forms and syntactic information such as main verb, agent of an action, etc. These two sets of information are integrated and the resulting representation is called the *functional level representation*. In the functional level representation, for example, a particular lexical item is tagged as being the main verb. However, this representation does not contain details of the sound form of the lexical items, nor does it contain details about the precise syntactic form of the sentence, such as whether it is to be passive or active. Consequently, the next stage, guided by the information in the functional level representation, involves retrieving the sound form of the individual lexical items and creating a detailed planning frame for the sentence. The planning frame is a fairly complex affair and specifies the position of function words (*of, the*) and inflectional affixes (*-ing, -es*) as well as the prosodic form of the sentence (this refers to things like the pitch and stress patterns within an utterance). The sound forms of the individual lexical items are then slotted into this planning frame. The result is a representation which specifies the order of the words, their sound forms, and the sound pattern of the utterance. The *positional level representation* roughly corresponds to what we earlier called the sound level. This representation is transformed into a *phonetic level representation* and, finally, *articulation*. Though these last two stages represent far from trivial problems, the model is less concerned with them than the earlier stages of sentence production.

Garrett's model proposes that utterances are produced via a number of stages with processing operating in what is known as a "top-down" manner (loosely, this can be thought of as processing that proceeds from more central processes, such as reasoning, down to more peripheral processes, such as articulation, where the processing at a higher level determines processing at the next level down without any feedback from that lower level). While the model has been used to account for a number of characteristics of speech errors and hesitations (Garrett, 1982), it has also been used as a framework for explaining characteristics of aphasia (Bradley, Garrett, & Zurif, 1980). Chapter 6 looked at short-term memory difficulties and in the following sections we will look briefly at some examples of the impairments to syntactic and word-finding processes.

Syntactic Deficits

Syntax refers to those processes which take a conceptual input and create a structure for the sentence. Most models of speech production assume that as the final form of a sentence is constructed, there is a distinction between processes that specify the structure of the sentence, which consists of slots, and processes responsible for retrieving sound forms from the lexicon and inserted into the appropriate slots (see both Dell's and Garrett's models described above). In Garrett's model, some items are selected by syntactic processes rather than semantic ones. These items are closed-class items and include grammatical morphemes such as articles (*the, a, an*), and inflections (*-ed, s, -es*). Items selected primarily by semantic processes are open-class items (nouns, verbs, adverbs, etc.) and are inserted into the frame which already specifies the closed-class items.

Patients who have suffered damage to the syntactic processes alone should know the message they would like to communicate, should be able to retrieve the appropriate content words, and should be able to articulate them fluently and without error. They should have difficulty, however, in assembling the syntactic framework for the utterance. Saffran, Schwartz and Marin (1980) describe such a patient. When shown a picture of a woman putting clothes into a washing machine, this patient said, "The lady . . . the lady launders the . . . the lady puts the washes . . . wash on . . . puts on the wash with the laundry". All the necessary content words are here in these efforts but the syntactic structure is inadequate. The implication is that the early stages of syntactic processing where the structure of the sentence is constructed are not functioning properly.

Garrett's model proposes that closed- and open-class items are processed separately. This claim is consistent with evidence from aphasia where production of closed- and open-class lexical items is differentially impaired. That is, the distinction made by linguists between closed- and open-class items is also discernible in cognitive processing. Caramazza and Hillis (1989) describe a patient, M.L., whose sentence comprehension is good and who can repeat single words equally well whether they are closed- or open-class. However, on a number of tasks where M.L. had to produce sentences, she omitted closed-class items on a very high percentage of occasions. For example, in self-initiated speech during therapy she often omitted pronouns and articles ("[. . .] heard [. . .] radio . . . [. . .] more [. . .] . . . [. . .] coming tonight . . . more snow"). On more constrained tasks where she had to repeat back 10-word sentences or describe a picture, she again made proportionately many more omissions of closed-class items. For example, when describing a complex picture of someone stealing cookies, she said, "Mother washing sink . . . water flowing floor . . . running water . . . dishes slopping . . . cookie jar . . . stealing cookies . . . toppling stool". In this extract, there are virtually no free-standing closed-class items. Caramazza and Hillis (1989) argue that this pattern of problem is consistent with Garrett's proposal that some lexical items are primarily specified by syntactic processes and that this patient's deficit is in the construction of a positional level representation.

Word-finding Difficulties

Many people in everyday life have the experience of being unable to remember a particular word and sometimes this difficulty can become intense and frustrating as in TOT states. However, the difficulty is considerably worse in a number of people suffering from aphasia and such difficulties are described by the term *anomia*. Indeed, although we described M.L. as having a syntactic deficit, ultimately her problem could have been in retrieving particular words albeit ones specified by syntactic processes. Usually, when talking about anomia, however, we are talking about people who have difficulties retrieving open-class items on the basis of semantics.

In Garrett's model, this means difficulties in accessing lexical forms at the functional level. Furthermore, the separation of retrieval of open-class lexical forms from the processes that create syntactic structures means that impairment of the lexical retrieval processes should result in problems in accessing content words, but this impairment need not affect the person's ability to construct sentence frameworks. Allport and Funnell (1981, p. 405) describe a patient who had difficulties retrieving open-class words. For example, when asked to describe a picture of a kitchen scene, he produced the following attempt (where the words in square brackets are Allport and Funnell's attempts to guess what he was trying to say):

> Well, it's a . . . [kitchen], it's a place, and it's a girl and a boy, and they've got obviously something which is made . . . some . . . [biscuits], some . . . made . . . Well . . . [the stool] it's just beginning to . . . [fall] go and be rather unpleasant . . . And . . . this is the . . . [mother?] the woman, and she is [pouring?] putting some . . . [water] stuff . . .

One might object that this pattern does not necessarily show a deficit in retrieving the form of words on the basis of meaning; after all, might not someone who could access meaning-based forms but not sound-based ones produce the same kind of speech? That this patient's underlying deficit is indeed in semantically based access was indicated by his performance on other sorts of task. If he was shown a picture of an object and two written object names, the patient could select the correct name provided that the two names were not close semantic associates. For example, he would have no difficulty selecting *nail* to match to a picture of a nail if the second "distractor" name was *bird*. But if the "distractor" was *screw*, he would have great difficulty. It was not that he did not know the difference between a nail and a screw, because he could use the two objects appropriately, taking a hammer to the one and a screwdriver to the other. In Allport's (1983, p. 77) words, "it appears that his disability must be located in the processes that translate between the word-forms and their underlying conceptual representations".

A similar difficulty in precise specification of words according to their meaning arises in something called *deep dysphasia*. Deep dysphasia is a rare form of aphasia, the key features of which are that patients are very poor at repeating simple nonwords and sometimes produce semantic errors when asked to repeat real words, a pattern analogous to a form of acquired dyslexia known as *deep dyslexia*. Martin and Saffran (1992) describe a patient, N.C., who had just this pattern of difficulties. For example, when asked to repeat the word *gravity*, N.C. responded with the semantically related word *science*, while on a nonword repetition task he repeated only 10% correctly. In spontaneous speech, N.C. produced large numbers of formal paraphasias (akin to malapropisms, where the intended word and the produced word are similar in sound but not in meaning) and neologisms (where the target is a real word but the person produces a non-word, e.g. saying *kooter* when *octopus* was intended). N.C. also had a number of difficulties with speech comprehension, so that he performed poorly on a task where he was required to match a spoken word to one of four pictures. Despite this, when given a test based solely on pictures to evaluate his understanding of the functions of objects, N.C. scored highly compared with non-brain damaged subjects of the same age. Consequently, like the patient seen by Allport and Funnell, the semantic difficulties N.C. had in comprehending and producing speech seem not to be due to damage to a central semantic system.

Many models of word retrieval propose that accessing words in the lexicon involves activation of the appropriate information, and we saw this kind of explanation earlier when discussing Dell's model. Most models also include the idea of decay — that is, unless an item is continually receiving activation, its activation tends to subside to some resting level. Martin and Saffran (1992) use the concepts of activation and decay in order to explain some of the errors in deep dysphasia. They propose that N.C.'s difficulties are due to the brain damage having resulted in more rapid decay of activation at nodes in the lexical network. This accelerated decay means that there is an increased probability that other words in the lexicon related to the target (either phonologically or semantically or both) are selected by mistake. Hence in both spontaneous speech and word repetition tasks, N.C. sometimes produces related words. When asked to repeat a nonword, the lack of a lexical node to support activation of the target phonemes combined with the rapid decay rate, means that by the time N.C. attempts to select the required phonemes, activation in the network is too weak to favour the target nodes. These explanations, couched in terms of decay in activation, are similar to accounts that attribute deficits in nonword repetition to short-term memory problems (Trojano, Stanzioni, & Grossi, 1992).

SUMMARY

The focus of this chapter has been the processes underlying the production of speech. We began by considering pauses and hesitations in speech. It is likely that pauses have multiple causes, but one contributing factor seems to be the size of the planning unit in spontaneous speech. Both the patterns of silences in speech and regularities in slips of the tongue suggest that the sentence and the clause are planning units when producing utterances. For example, misordering errors almost always involve two elements from within the same sentence and usually from within the same clause.

Producing any utterance requires us to access words, hopefully the desired and appropriate ones. Usually the processes involved work smoothly, but occasionally things go wrong, and when they do the characteristics of the difficulties can shed light on the underlying processes. Two examples of such difficulties are tip-of-the-tongue states and slips of the tongue. Tip-of-the-tongue states occur when we feel we know the word we want to say but simply cannot retrieve its exact sound form. Milder TOT states can be responsible for some of the shorter pauses that occur within clauses, but most of the studies have been of more extreme states where the speaker struggles for some time to find the right word. Such studies of TOT states suggest that the phonological information in words is differentially accessible so that, for example, when in a TOT state, people often know the number of syllables in the desired word without knowing such things as whether or not it contains a consonant cluster. Likewise, slips of the tongue demonstrate regularities which suggest that they are not simply random occurrences and which tell us something about the underlying processes.

Having planned an utterance and retrieved the appropriate words, the constituent sounds have to be produced in the right order and pronounced in a way that is comprehensible. The way in which the later phonological and articulatory processes proceed are again illuminated by studies of errors. Other phenomena, such as the adjustment of articulatory movements to the surrounding context, show how even these later processes are sensitive to items later in the planned utterance.

Having looked at some of the processes intervening between the intention to speak and the act of speaking, we went on to look at a more detailed model of how words may be retrieved. We looked at how the models of Dell (1986) and Burke et al. (1991) attempt to account for a wide range of characteristics of speech errors, such as word substitution errors, spoonerisms and TOT states. Dell's model is far from a complete explanation of speech production, but it does show how a computer model of a cognitive process can both reproduce some of the characteristic findings in an area and make new predictions prompting investigators to look for evidence that is or is not consistent with those predictions. Finally, we looked at how a more general model of speech production (Garrett, 1976) can be used to interpret the impact that brain damage can have on our ability to speak, and how processes such as word finding and syntactic processing can be selectively impaired.

The end of speech production is the beginning of speech perception and comprehension, which we consider in more detail in the next chapter. However, like language as a whole, it is hard to isolate speech production as a topic because it relates to so many other areas, such as memory. Consequently, the contents of many of the other chapters in this book are relevant to issues considered here and as theories of speech production develop they will need to take note of such information as well as contributions from many other areas of psychology.

The literature on speech production tends to be rather technical. Readers who wish to pursue it are recommended to start with a general text such as Ellis and Beattie's (1986) *Psychology of language and* communication. Moving on to more detailed discussions, readers can be caught in a quagmire of linguistic terminology; to help with this, readers might like to consult an introductory linguistic text such as Fromkin and Rodman's (1988) *Introduction to language*, which is both readable and relevant to issues covered in this chapter and Chapters 2 and 8. For those who develop an interest in the area of speech production, *Speaking: From intention to articulation* by Levelt (1989) is the definitive text which covers all the topics considered in this chapter and many others besides.

8 Listening to a Lecture: Perceiving, Understanding or Ignoring a Spoken Message

You are sitting in the back row of a lecture theatre listening to a lecture. The lecturer is not using a microphone and around you there is the usual rustle of papers, coughing, the occasional clatter of a dropped pen, nearby a whispered discussion of last night's party and, perish the thought, even a stifled yawn or two. Despite this background noise, you are able to hear what the lecturer says and, hopefully, you are able to understand much of the content of the lecture. As in this scenario, much of our processing of speech occurs in less than ideal circumstances, yet frequently we manage to understand with little conscious effort. The central question for a cognitive psychologist is how we are able to process speech in such a way that ultimately we can understand and act upon the incoming information.

Language in one form or another recurs as a topic of investigation over and over again in cognitive psychology. Most of us are fortunate enough to be able to hear, and being able to perceive and understand speech is a key part of our everyday life. We shall begin by considering the early stages of perceiving speech and the possible role of context in these processes. We shall then consider how the syntax of the incoming utterances is analysed and remembered and explore ideas about how the meanings of words and sentences might be extracted. This leads us on to the question of how background knowledge is brought to bear when interpreting even simple utterances. The next section is concerned with how some understanding of the nature of conversation itself enables us to make sense of such everyday aspects of speech as irony and humour. Finally, we consider what happens to the speech signal when it is actively ignored.

SEGMENTING THE SPEECH SIGNAL

It is instructive when thinking about speech perception to contrast the situation faced by a listener with that faced by a reader (see Chapter 2). If you cut out a printed word from a book or magazine, the word continues to be perfectly recognisable. The same is not true of spoken words. Lieberman (1963) recorded speakers saying phrases like "A stitch in time saves nine" or "Neither a borrower nor a lender be". The phrases were all perfectly intelligible when played in their entirety. However, words spliced out of these phrases and presented in isolation with no supporting context were much less easy to make out. The word "nine" was correctly identified only 50% of the time, "borrower" 45% of the time, and "lender" a mere 10%.

These results support the claim that listeners utilise the contexts in which words occur to assist in their recognition, and there is no shortage of experimental evidence to support this claim. Miller, Heise and Lichten (1951) presented listeners with either single words or sentences embedded in a background of hissing "white" noise, and found that words in sentence contexts were identified much better than words in isolation. Marslen-Wilson and Tyler (1980) asked subjects to listen out for target words in three types of two-sentence "passage". The first type was normal, coherent prose; the second was "anomalous" prose which was grammatical but nonsensical; and the third was "scrambled" prose which was both ungrammatical and nonsensical. Examples of the three types, in which the target word *lead* is italicised, are:

1. Normal prose:
   The church was broken into last week. Some thieves stole most of the *lead* off the roof.
2. Anomalous but grammatically correct prose:
   The power was located in great water. No buns puzzle some in the *lead* off the text.
3. Scrambled prose:
   It was great power water the located. Some the no puzzle buns in *lead* text the off.

Although the subjects' task was simply to press a button as quickly as possible when they heard the target word *lead*, reaction times were nevertheless faster in the normal prose condition (305 msec) than in either the anomalous (373 msec) or the scrambled (364 msec) prose conditions. The difference between the last two conditions was not, in fact, statistically significant, which suggests that the facilitating effects of normal context are mostly due to its coherence of meaning rather than its simple grammaticality. The later the target word occurred in the normal passages, the greater was its advantage over targets in comparable positions in anomalous or scrambled passages. This shows that the beneficial effects of context increase as more information becomes available to guide the predictive processes.

In many ways, the early stages of speech perception are even more tricky than already outlined. For example, knowing where one word ends and another begins seems effortless in our everyday listening. However, it is not so easy to see how we manage this when one looks at speech as a physical signal. The most obvious cue, silence, is far from being an infallible guide to where words begin and end, because often there can be as long a silence within a word as between words. For example, when two consonants such as "b" and "d" are adjacent, as in *abduct*, there can be quite a long period of silence. However, most theories of language processing assume that we are able to discriminate word boundaries so that we can derive the appropriate syntactic structure and meanings for utterances.

One set of cues to where word boundaries fall comes from the rhythmic aspects of speech (Cutler & Butterfield, 1992). In English, there is a distinction between strong and weak syllables. For example, the word *baker* has a strong first syllable and a weak second one. Strong syllables are stressed and usually contain full vowels, whereas weak syllables are unstressed and the vowel sound is usually reduced. In English, when a vowel is reduced it is often pronounced as something known as "schwa". Schwa sounds something like "uh" and is present in a number of the words in the following list [strong syllables are in capitals and weaker, less stressed syllable(s) are in lower case]: MALlet, BUTler, MEDicine, deMAND, BASket, corrUPtion, WAGon, BRACElet. Cutler and Carter (1987) took a sample of British English from conversations and looked at the distribution of strong and weak syllables around word boundaries. They found that if one ignored grammatical words such as *the, and, of*, which are usually realised as weak syllables, 90% of the words began with a strong syllable. Given this distribution of strong and weak syllables, Cutler and Butterfield argue that it would make sense if the processes of speech perception exploited this property when trying to identify word boundaries

Cutler and Butterfield (1992) cite a range of evidence which suggests that people do make use of the strength of a syllable as a cue to word boundaries. The most systematic evidence comes from an experiment where they asked people to listen to passages of speech played very quietly. If people misperceived what was said and this misperception involved a confusion about a word boundary, then a boundary would be more likely to be *inserted* before a strong syllable, and *deleted* before a weak one. This is exactly what they found. For example, the sentence "Achieve her ways instead" was heard by one subject as "A cheaper way to stay", where a boundary is inserted before a strong syllable ("aCHIEVE" becomes "a CHEAP") and deleted before a weak one ("CHIEVE her" becomes "CHEAPer").

In everyday speech, the stimulus quality is often poor, so that if errors are to be avoided in the early stages of speech perception, useful information contained within the speech signal must be exploited. Such useful information will include anything that approaches a constancy across speech situations, such as the patterns of stress on syllables. However, cues to word boundaries, such as stress, are language-specific and some may even be accent-specific. For instance, just when you think you have a reasonable grasp of a foreign language, it can be a sobering experience to hear it spoken by a native speaker talking at their usual pace — all of a sudden, the word boundaries seem to get lost and your well-practised vocabulary becomes next to useless. Here other cues may become important, so that identifying one or two words in the speech stream provides context that may be used to help identify other items.

Models of Auditory Word Recognition

What kinds of processes allow listeners to receive the incoming speech signal and from it access various syntactic and semantic properties of what was said? A number of models of spoken word recognition have been developed that attempt to explain the processes that allow this linking between different types of information. One that pays particular attention to the fact that heard words are spread out over time is the cohort model (Marslen-Wilson & Welsh, 1978; Marslen-Wilson, 1987).

In the same way that the face recognition model introduced in Chapter 1 proposes that we have a "face recognition unit" for each person we know, the cohort model proposes that each word in a listener's vocabulary is represented by a different unit or node (see also the models of word recognition discussed in Chapter 2 and of word retrieval in Chapter 7). Heard words are strung out in time with speech sounds impinging sequentially upon the auditory system. According to the cohort model, the early parts of the sound of a word activate the recognition units of all words known by the listener that begin in the same way. This set is known as the "word initial cohort". The degree of activation of members of the cohort is related to the frequency with which the hearer has encountered them: more frequent words becoming more active. As more sound comes in, words that are incompatible with the new input decline in activation. Eventually, one word is left that is much more highly activated than the others, as it is the only one consistent with the whole of the incoming sound sequence. Suppose, for example, that you have just heard the initial part of a word beginning "tre". From this opening, the speaker could be in the process of saying a large number of English words (*trek, trellis, treasure, treble*, etc.). If the next sound was an "m", then most of the earlier cohort lose activation, leaving only candidates such as *tremolo, tremor, tremulous* and *tremble* (as well as variants such as *tremolos, tremors*, etc.). If the next section of sound is consistent with a "b", then the word *tremble* will have by far the most activated recognition unit.

Despite the evidence described earlier about the difficulty of identifying words extracted from their context, it is also true that, in general, we have no difficulty in understanding words in unusual contexts: if a lecturer took it into his or her head to say "He ate the radiator" (which means it is almost certainly a lecture on psycholinguistics), then chances are you would still be able to recognise the word *radiator* even if that recognition was slowed down (Marslen-Wilson, 1987). This observation has led Marslen-Wilson to propose that context has no effect on the make-up of the cohort: context does not exclude words as "not being allowed" in the cohort. Where context does have an impact is on the time it takes to integrate the word being processed with an existing higher-level representation of the meaning of what was previously said, so that context can still affect overall processing speed without affecting the size of the cohort *per se*.

All of these processes occur in real time, so that in the 300–400 msec (thousandths of a second) that it takes to say a single word, all these complex access and selection procedures take place. This seems to stretch credibility, but then we have already seen at several points in this book how shaky our introspections about cognitive processes can be. There is good experimental evidence for the rapidity of these access and selection processes. Marslen-Wilson (1980) describes an experiment where subjects were asked to listen to a passage and press a button as soon as they heard a particular target word. The average duration of the target words was 370 msec, yet the average time to press the button indicating recognition was only 275 msec after the start of the word. That is, the button had normally been pressed when the word was only three-quarters finished, and if we bear in mind that it takes time to execute a button push, then we realise that the target words were being identified after only about half their length.

You may have noticed a difficulty with the cohort model as outlined. For example, if you are listening to the lecturer and he or she makes a small slip of the tongue and says, for example, *plank* instead of *blank*, it is quite likely that you will not detect such a mispronunciation; more often than not you are likely to recognise the word as intended (Cole, 1973). The problem for the model is that the incoming physical signal corresponds to *plank* and so the word initial cohort triggered contains all the words beginning with "p" and only those words. This being so, how does the word *blank ever* become part of the cohort at all and why don't we detect every mispronunciation? To deal with this problem, Marslen-Wilson suggests that access to the word recognition units is not based on a signal that has been segmented into phonemes (that is, split into sounds such as "p" and "b"), but on a signal which is not segmented at all. The activation of words in the cohort is not all-or-nothing, but depends on the degree of match with the physical signal; so, for example, words beginning with "b" do receive *some* activation when the incoming signal is from a "p", as there is great overlap between the physical signals for "p" and "b". This solution also fits with a number of recent linguistic theories which have cast doubt on the usefulness of the idea of a phoneme (Kaye, 1989).

Visual Aspects of Listening

Next time you have the opportunity, try this simple experiment. Switch your television on to a news or similar programme where there is someone talking straight to the camera. Have the volume set quite low. Now turn on your radio and tune in between stations so that it produces a hissing noise. Turn the radio's volume up until it begins to be difficult to make out the words being spoken by the television announcer. Now observe the effects on the intelligibility of the speech of either looking at the face of the person who is talking or closing your eyes. If you have got the set-up right, you should find that the speech is much easier to discern against the hissing noise coming from the radio, and seems much clearer, when you have your eyes open and are looking at the speaker than if you have your eyes closed. In the lecture scenario with which we opened this chapter, you might find that amidst the inevitable background noise in the lecture hall, you can make out what the lecturer is saying rather better if you can see his or her face and lip movements than if you cannot. These examples draw attention to the finding that visual information from the speaker's lips and face seems to aid the perception and recognition of words in the sound wave (Dodd & Campbell, 1986).

Cotton (1935) provided an early demonstration of this phenomenon. He sat a speaker in a soundproof booth and relayed his speech via loudspeakers to listeners seated outside. The speech was made harder to understand by removing high frequencies and adding a buzzing noise. When the light inside the booth was switched on, so that the listeners could see the speaker's face through a window, the listeners could follow the speech, but with the light off and the speaker no longer visible, the speech was unintelligible. Cotton interpreted this finding as indicating that "there is an important element of visual hearing in all normal individuals".

If the speech wave provides a noisy signal, and if the movements of the speaker's lips and face provide useful supplementary information regarding the words being spoken, then it would seem useful to combine the two sources of input when engaged in everyday, face-to-face interaction. Evidence provided by McGurk and MacDonald (1976) suggests that this combining occurs very early on in the processing of the two signals. They made a videotape of someone simply saying "ba-ba-ba. . ." over and over again. They then replaced the sound channel with the synchronised voice of someone saying "ga-ga-ga. . .". The face and lips were thus indicating one syllable ("ba-ba") and the voice another ("ga-ga"). If you closed your eyes, you heard "ga-ga" clearly enough, but if you opened them and looked at the face your heard neither "ga-ga", nor "ba-ba", but "da-da". Presented with two conflicting signals, one visual and the other auditory, the perceptual system resolves upon a compromise — in this case "d", which is intermediate between "b" and "g". This striking illusion shows that visual and auditory information combine at a point before any conscious percept is formed, and demonstrates also that what we consciously perceive is the end-product, not the starting point, of extensive processing.

PROCESSING SENTENCE STRUCTURE

Explaining how we recognise heard words is an important and difficult task for cognitive psychology, but words themselves participate in higher-level, rule-governed linguistic units we call sentences. There are intermediates too. A sentence like "John ate his tea then he switched on the television" can be divided into two clauses (the division coming after "tea") and a larger number of phrases.

We have seen that you do not wait until all of a word has been spoken before you start to process and identify it. So it is with sentences — listeners do not wait until a speaker has finished a sentence before beginning to process and comprehend it. The context experiments discussed earlier illustrate this, since they show that listeners will use the meaning of the initial portion of a sentence to help them identify words later in the sentence. Another illustration of our efforts to make sense of sentences continuously as we hear (or read) them is provided by sentences like the following:

4. The man pushed through the door fell.
5. I told the girl the cat scratched Bill would help her.
6. The old dog the footsteps of the young.

In these sentences, there is a strong tendency to construe the early portion in a way which the later portion shows to be incorrect. They are known in the literature, for obvious reasons, as "garden-path" sentences. In sentence (6), for example, the tendency is to interpret *dog* as a noun qualified by the adjective *old*, whereas the end of the sentence makes it apparent that *dog* should have been interpreted as a verb. This would not happen if the interpretation of a sentence was deferred until it had been heard or read in its entirety, but because we try to process the sentences as we perceive them word by word, we are "led down the garden path".

It may have struck many of you that in real life we may hear the kinds of garden-path sentence referred to above and do not experience them as misleading. In spoken language, however, there are strong cues to sentence structure in the prosody of speech (things such as its rhythm, patterns of stress, pausing, and so on). There is evidence that when garden-path sentences are spoken with a disambiguating intonation, listeners usually interpret them correctly and with little conscious difficulty, though this is not the same as showing that there is no extra processing required for such sentences.

Sentence Structure and Sentence Meaning

Consider a simple sentence like "The cat chased the mouse". It is unlikely you have any difficulty understanding that sentence and forming a mental picture of what is going on. But what are the elements of the sentence from which you derive its meaning? There are the key words *cat, chase,* and *mouse,* which tell you who the participants are and what activity is going on. You learn who is chasing whom, however, not from the words themselves, but from their arrangements in the sentence. This is readily demonstrated by the fact that we can retain all the same words but arrange them in a different order and change the meaning of the sentence, as in "The mouse chased the cat". This illustrates one of the prime reasons that explaining how sentence structure — or syntax — is processed is a key task if we want to understand how language is produced and understood: syntax allows us to say and to interpret unusual things. Note that only certain arrangements are easily interpreted: "Chased mouse the cat the" is not a sentence in English and is difficult to understand with much confidence (though if someone with a weak grasp of English came up to you and said it, you could have a guess at what was meant — of which more later).

The rules that determine which strings of words are legal sentences, and which enable us to use the information provided by the arrangements of words in sentences, are called the syntax of the language. To understand a sentence we must make use of both the meanings of the individual words and their syntactic arrangement. To describe the syntax of a sentence it is necessary first to assign each word to one of a small set of grammatical categories. In the above example, *cat* and *mouse* are nouns, *chased* is a verb and *the* is a determiner. Other categories include adjectives (e.g. *fierce, timorous*) which "qualify" nouns, adverbs (e.g. *hurriedly, yesterday*) which qualify verbs, pronouns like *we, her* or *it*, and prepositions like *above* or *until*.

The next step is to group the words together in a description which captures the overall syntactic structure of the sentence. In our cat-and-mouse example, this would involve identifying *The cat* as a noun phrase with *cat* as the subject of the sentence, and *chased the mouse* as a verb phrase containing the verb *chase* (in the past tense) and another noun phrase, *the mouse*, where *mouse* is the grammatical object of the sentence. We can represent this structure diagrammatically as in Fig. 8.1.

In psychological theories of language processing, the cognitive component that is given the job of describing a sentence's syntactic structure in this manner is referred to as the *parser* (to "parse" a sentence is to assign a structural, syntactic description to it). If the human parser is to keep up with the speech being heard, then it must constantly be making the best guess from the information it already has as to the structure that should be assigned to the words in the sentence. When it makes a mistake, as in garden-path sentences, it must be able to go back and parse the sentence differently. Modern theories assume that the parser uses a set of strategies in its attempts to describe sentence structure (Pullman, 1987). So-called function words like *a, the, to, at, because, or* and *when* play an important

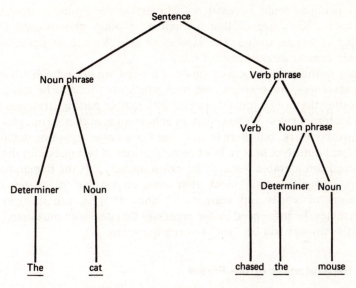

FIG. 8.1 Syntactic structure of a sentence.

part in such strategies (note that function words correspond closely to closed-class items introduced in Chapter 7). For example, the determiners *a/an* and *the* usually signal the beginning of a new noun phrase, while auxiliaries such as *is, was, were* and *have* signal the beginnings of verb phrases. Words like *which, because* and *since* often mark the onsets of new clauses, and so on.

Kelly (1992) suggests that there are a range of cues in how words are pronounced that can help the listener assign words to a particular grammatical category, such as verb, which can in turn aid the parsing process. For example, as we have already seen when discussing segmentation of the speech signal, multisyllabic words in English are usually stressed on the first syllable. However, there is an important qualification to this. Compare the following two sentences:

7. The record finally stopped playing
8. To record a track press the red button

In sentence (7), the word *record* is functioning as a noun and is stressed on the first syllable (REcord), whereas in sentence (8) it is functioning as a verb and is stressed on the second syllable (reCORD). This tendency is a strong one: nouns are nearly always stressed on the first syllable, whereas verbs are more likely to be stressed on the second syllable (Kelly & Bock, 1988). Where a sentence begins something like "The town permits . . .", the stress pattern may help listeners decide whether *permits* is a noun (PERmits for parking) or a verb (perMITS parking in this area), and so stress patterns could be used to help derive the syntactic structure of utterances. Kelly argues that a number of other phonological characteristics of words, such as the number of syllables and its duration, also provide cues to its grammatical role.

Cues to the grammatical category of a word are not infallible. Garden-path sentences, for example, are ones which are prone to be mis-parsed, suggesting that we do indeed operate with fallible parsing strategies rather than foolproof rules. We have hinted at how some of these strategies might conceivably work, but there is no current consensus regarding details. We shall limit ourselves here to brief considerations of two questions that have attracted considerable research attention; namely, "Is the human parser a separate cognitive component from those responsible for processing the meanings of words and sentences?" and "If it is, can its operations nevertheless be influenced by the processes that deal with meanings?" Our tentative answer will be "yes" to both questions.

The Separateness of the Parser

There is no *a priori* reason why sentence structure should be processed separately from word and sentence meaning. Computer programs have been built which do not make this assumption and run with some success (e.g. Schank, 1975). Nevertheless, there are reasons for thinking that the human parser might operate independently from meaning. One line of evidence comes from a particular disorder of language processing that can arise as a result of brain injury.

In one type of language difficulty arising from brain damage, commonly known as Broca's aphasia, the person appears to lose the capacity to process sentence structure while retaining the capacity to identify word meanings and formulate hypotheses as to sentence meanings. Caramazza and Zurif (1976) asked their patients to match sentences to a choice of two pictures. Some of the sentences were of the type: "The apple that the boy is eating is red". Suppose you could understand the "content words" — akin to open-class items — *apple, boy, eat* and *red*, but could not make use of word order or of the function words *the, that* and *is*. Despite your difficulty, you would probably arrive at the correct interpretation because other interpretations (e.g. an apple was eating a red boy) are less plausible. Caramazza and Zurif found that the Broca's aphasics interpreted over 90% of these sentences correctly.

Another class of sentences used by Caramazza and Zurif (1976), however, depended on syntax for their correct interpretation. These were sentences like: "The cow that the monkey is scaring is yellow". Armed only with the meanings of *cow, monkey, scaring* and *yellow* and without any syntactic skill, you would be at a loss to know whether the sentence was about a yellow monkey scaring a cow, a yellow monkey being scared by a cow, etc. Caramazza and Zurif found their Broca's aphasics to be quite unable to select correctly between pictures depicting such alternatives, though both people without a language disorder and aphasics suffering from other sorts of language difficulty performed well on the same task. The behaviour of the Broca's aphasics is consistent with the hypothesis that they have an impairment of syntactic parsing mechanisms. It is hard to see how a selective impairment of syntactic parsing could occur unless the parser were a discrete cognitive component, separate from the processes which handle meanings with the latter remaining intact in Broca's aphasics.

Despite impairments to syntactic processing, aphasics can often still understand large chunks of text or speech fairly well. Caplan and Evans (1990) compared 16 people who had some form of aphasia with 16 other people matched on age and level of education. Caplan and Evans constructed sentences of increasing syntactic complexity: the simplest were active sentences (such as "The elephant hit the monkey"), and the most complex were known as subject–object relative sentences (such as "The elephant hit the monkey that hugged the rabbit"). Previous research had shown that when tested on their comprehension of these individual spoken sentences, people without an aphasia performed almost perfectly irrespective of differences in complexity (Caplan, 1987). However, the aphasics in Caplan and Evans' study had real difficulty understanding all but the simplest sentences and their difficulty increased with increasing syntactic complexity. After the sentence comprehension task, aphasics were asked to listen to four short stories. Following each story, they were asked a few questions aimed at tapping how well they understood the story. Each story had two versions: one a syntactically simple version and the other syntactically complex. On the basis of the results from the sentence comprehension task, the obvious expectation would be that aphasics would have more difficulty with the syntactically complex version of the story, whereas the non-aphasic controls should not be much affected by the different levels of syntactic complexity. However, this is not what Caplan and Evans found: while those with aphasia did understand less of the stories than those without aphasia, their understanding was not affected by the complexity of the sentences. That is, the aphasics were no worse on the syntactically complex version than on the syntactically simple one. This set of findings is at least compatible with the idea that understanding a discourse such as a story requires more than syntactic processing, and that these additional processes are separable from syntactic comprehension and can compensate for a syntactic deficit in some circumstances. This is not to say that the two tasks do not share some processes in common — such as some aspects of working memory (see Chapter 6).

Higher-level Influences on the Parser

Our second question was directed at whether the parser, even if a distinct component, might nevertheless be influenced by other linguistic processes in normal processing, that is, do the various processes interact with one another? How might one set about answering this question? Psycholinguists who have addressed themselves to the issue of interaction have asked whether the meanings of words in a sentence or more general background information can influence the ease with which people parse a sentence. Before addressing this question directly, however, we need to consider in a little more detail an example of a parsing strategy.

We have already introduced the idea of parsing strategies and one such strategy is *minimal attachment* (Frazier, 1978; 1987). Minimal attachment means that the parser attempts to keep the number of nodes in the hierarchy as few as possible, which means that as each word is encountered, it is attached to the syntactic structure being constructed in a way that requires the fewest possible additional nodes (see Fig. 8.1). Consider the following sentence:

9. The girl hit the ball with the racket.

Readers of this sentence have little trouble with it. The phrase *with the racket* is what is known as a prepositional phrase and in this sentence it is attached directly to the verb phrase (see Fig. 8.2a). This accords with the minimal attachment strategy because, in dealing with a phrase, only one extra node is created (besides those needed for the individual words themselves). It also provides the correct interpretation of the sentence because clearly *racket* belongs with the verb *hit*. To sum up, sentence (9) is easy to process because the structure preferred by the minimal attachment strategy and the structure that leads to the correct interpretation of the sentence are one and the same.

Consider the following sentence:

10. The girl hit the ball with the spot.

The correct interpretation of sentence (10) requires that the prepositional phrase *with the spot* is not attached directly to the verb. Instead, *with the spot* needs to be bracketed with the noun *ball*. To achieve this the phrase structure shown in Fig. 8.2b needs to be derived.

Comparing the two phrase structures for sentences (9) and (10) (see Figs 8.2a and 8.2b, respectively), one can seen that the structure for (10) contains one more node in its hierarchy. However, if minimal attachment is a strategy that is automatically applied, parsing of *with the spot* in sentence (10) would result in a structure akin to that in Fig. 8.2a. The problem with this is that it does not provide a sensible interpretation of the phrase *with the spot* and so an alternative structure, such as that in Fig.

(a)

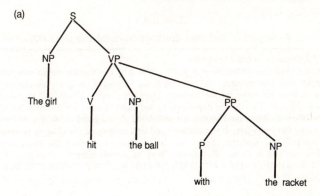

(b)

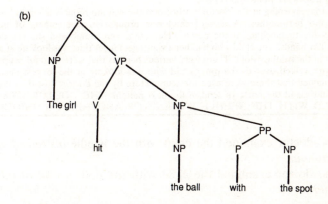

FIG. 8.2 Parsing trees for similar sentences. Tree (b) violates the minimal attachment strategy. S = subject, P = preposition, V = verb, NP = noun phrase, PP = prepositional phrase, VP = verb phrase.

8.2b, needs to be computed. Consequently, for sentence (10), application of minimal attachment provides a syntactic structure that does not give a sensible interpretation and so it needs to be corrected (or the conflict with an alternative formulation resolved), something that should result in extra processing time. Rayner, Carlson and Frazier (1983) looked at the reading times of sentences such as (9) and (10), that is sentences that did or did not violate the minimal attachment strategy, and found that those violating minimal attachment did take longer to read.

Findings like those of Rayner et al. suggest that parsing strategies are applied automatically even when they are inappropriate. However, a recurring question is whether or not such strategies may be overridden in some contexts, that is, are the parser and the strategies that it uses sometimes sensitive to information from other cognitive processes? To examine this idea, Britt, Perfetti, Garrod and Rayner (1992) looked at whether or not the strategy of minimal attachment might not be applied in some cases. They considered two types of sentence:

TABLE 8.1

Examples of Different Contexts from Britt et al. (1992)

Example of a sentence in biasing context
It was Saturday morning at the neurologist's office and the waiting room was empty except for one child and her mother. A little girl was brought in complaining of numbness presumably due to pinching of the nerves. Her arms were numb and she couldn't hold anything in her hands. The doctor explained to the child and her mother that an acupuncture technique is often used in examining nerve problems. It is a good technique he explained but it involves using long needles. If the doctor used this technique the diagnosis would be more complete and reliable. But the child was nervous and upset since the child hated needles and would never touch them. The doctor had to decide which technique to use. THE DOCTOR EXAMINED THE CHILD WITH THE NEEDLE INSTEAD OF ANOTHER TECHNIQUE.

Example of a sentence in neutral context
It was Saturday morning at the doctor's office and the waiting room was empty except for one child and her mother. A second child was brought in complaining of numbness presumably due to pinching of the nerves. Her arms were numb and she couldn't hold anything in her hands. The child who had been waiting a longer time was looking at a display in a cabinet in the waiting room. There were various needles that were used for acupuncture. The little girl walked over to the other child who was looking at the longest needle. The mother explained that these were used for acupuncture by the doctor. Just then the doctor came out and asked the nurse to send in the next patient. THE DOCTOR EXAMINED THE CHILD WITH THE NEEDLE INSTEAD OF ANOTHER TECHNIQUE.

---

11. The doctor examined the child with the needle *instead of another technique*.

12. The doctor examined the child with the doll *instead of the other child*.

The words in italics are the critical regions of difference between the two sentences. As expected, when asked to read these sentences in isolation, minimal attachment was automatically applied and people took longer to read the critical region in sentence (12) than the corresponding region in sentence (11). However, if subjects were asked to read the same sentences embedded in a passage which gave lots of background context to the events described, Britt et al. found no differences in times to read the critical regions in sentences (11) and (12). It is also important to note that the effect of context occurred as the sentences were being read, that is, it affected the moment-to-moment decisions of the syntactic parser. Two examples of the kind of context used by Britt et al. are shown in Table 8.1.

The findings of Britt et al. (1992) support the idea that sometimes parsing strategies are not applied automatically and so the parser is affected by information from other cognitive processes. However, in the same series of experiments, they report some forms of parsing preference which are *not* overridden by context. For example, comparing sentences of the type in (13) and (14) they found that even with a biasing context, the critical region (in italics) was *always* read more slowly in sentences such as (14) than in sentences such as (13):

13. The woman rushed to the hospital *without taking her laundry*.
14. The woman rushed to the hospital *had given birth safely*.

Although there is always the possibility that the biasing contexts used were not sufficiently strong, the general implication of these findings is that while some aspects of syntactic processing may be autonomous, others can be influenced by context in which one reads or hears sentences. The task then becomes one of identifying which processes fall into which category and developing theories of why they do so.

In the experiments described above, context was taken to mean information about the general situation to which the sentences of interest were related. The experiments were also done with written material. However, earlier in this chapter, we pointed out that speech contains cues to sentence structure which may prevent the listener being "led down the garden path". The tendency to employ strategies such as minimal attachment when listening to speech may be influenced by prosodic cues. Marslen-Wilson et al. (1992) asked people to listen to sentences (which had been recorded being spoken at conversational rate) such as:

15. The workers considered that the last offer from the management was an insult.
16. The workers considered the last offer from the management was an insult.
17. The workers considered the last offer from the management of the factory.

During each sentence, just after the word *management*, the speech stopped and the word WAS was presented visually to subjects and they had to name it as quickly as possible. Marslen-Wilson et al. reasoned that in sentence (15), minimal attachment would not occur at all because of the presence of the complementiser *that*. However, if minimal attachment is a default strategy which is unaffected by the prosody of the sentence, then it would be applied automatically to sentence (16) and lead to an incorrect parsing which would, in turn, slow naming of the visual probe. On the other hand, if minimal attachment can be stopped by inappropriate prosody, then subjects would not mis-parse sentence (16) in the first place, and so there would be no difference in response times to sentences (15) and (16). In sentence (17), the sentence is correctly parsed using minimal attachment but the visual probe WAS allows only non-minimal attachment, so there is a conflict between the preceding prosody and the visual probe, and therefore responses to this sentence should definitely be slower than to sentence (15). When they ran the experiment, Marslen-Wilson et al. found no differences in response times in sentences such as (15) and (16), whereas responses to sentences such as (17) were slower. They conclude that, in processing speech, prosody can prevent structural ambiguities slowing our understanding, and they speculate that such cues are even more important in everyday conversations than in the kind of isolated sentences they used in their experiment.

RETENTION AND LOSS OF SURFACE STRUCTURE

In Chapter 7, we noted several lines of evidence that point to the importance of the grammatical clause as a unit of sentence formulation. A significant proportion of hesitations, for example, occur between one clause and the next, and certain categories of slip of the tongue occur within but rarely between clauses. If speakers package conceptual messages into clause-sized units, then it would seem likely that listeners will also employ those units in their attempts to reconstruct the speaker's message within their own minds.

This possibility was tested in an experiment by Caplan (1972). His design is best illustrated by an example. Subjects heard sentences which could be like either (18) or (19):

18. Now that artists are working in OIL / prints are rare.
19. Now that artists are working fewer hours / OIL prints are rare.

In these sentences, "/" marks the position of the clause boundary. The reader will note that the endings of the two sentences are the same, but their construction is such that the word OIL occurs at the end of the first clause in (18) but at the beginning of the second clause in (19). It is, however, the fourth from last word in both sentences.

After hearing a sentence, the subjects in Caplan's (1972) experiment were presented with a "probe" word. Their task was to decide as quickly as possible whether or not the probe word had occurred in the preceding sentence. For sentences (18) and (19), the probe word would be OIL, the word which occurs the same distance from the end in both sentences but which is in the first clause of (18) but the second clause of (19). Caplan found that "yes' responses were significantly faster for probe words in the second clause than for probe words in the first clause.

Jarvella (1970; 1971) had subjects listen to lengthy passages of text. Occasionally, the text was interrupted and the subjects asked to write down, word for word, as much as they could of the passage immediately preceding the interruption. The interruption was always timed to come after a sequence of three clauses. In one condition of the experiment, the first two clauses formed one sentence and the third clause another. For example:

The document had also blamed him for having failed to disprove the charges.
Taylor was later fired by the President.

In the other condition of the experiment, the first clause stood alone as a sentence with the second and third clauses combining into another sentence. For example:

> The tone of the document was threatening. Having failed to disprove the charges, Taylor was later fired by the President.

It will be noted that the second clause ("having failed to disprove the charges') is the same in both conditions. However, a sentence boundary stands between this clause and the point of interruption in the first condition but not the second. Jarvella found 54% correct recall of the crucial second clause where it was part of the most recent sentence, but only 24% correct recall when a sentence boundary had intervened. The presence of the third clause seems to have caused some loss of the verbatim form of the second clause, even when the two are combined in the most recently heard sentence. This supports Caplan's (1972) claim that clause boundaries are important in sentence comprehension.

A range of other research has shown that immediate verbatim recall of sentences can be good, certainly much greater than the seven or so items so often associated with the recall of word-lists (Potter & Lombardi, 1990). An obvious explanation of this finding is that there is some kind of verbatim record in a short-term memory store, but Potter and Lombardi suggest an alternative explanation which they call the *regeneration hypothesis*. Here the recalled sentence is regenerated from a conceptual representation of the sentence together with selection of activated lexical nodes. At recall, the person uses the conceptual representation to select lexical nodes, and any node that is already active, such as the ones present in the original sentence, stands a greater chance of being selected. Potter and Lombardi argue that for the sentences they used, this combination is such that usually only one syntactic structure, the original one, could be constructed.

As a direct test of the regeneration hypothesis, Lombardi and Potter (1992) asked subjects to read a sentence, engage in a subsequent distractor task, and then try to recall the sentence word for word. In the distractor task, subjects had to read a sequence of five verbs followed by a single verb and then decide whether the single verb had been in the list of five. The key thing was that among the verbs in the distractor task, was a verb that was very similar in meaning to the main verb of the original sentence. For example, suppose that the original sentence was the following:

20. The rich widow is going to give a million dollars to the university.

Following this, one might be given the list of five distractor items: *fight, explain, donate, carry, purchase*. The verb *donate* is very similar in meaning to *give* in this context and, from their previous research, Lombardi and Potter expected that on some occasions *donate* would intrude from the distractor list and be incorporated into the recalled form of the sentence. They propose this because *donate* fits the conceptual representation as well as *give* does, and so sometimes subjects will use the word *donate* by mistake. In this situation, *donate* can also be fitted into the syntactic structure of the original sentence. However, consider the following sentence which initially seems very similar to (20):

21. The rich widow is going to give the university a million dollars.

Again this would be followed by presentation of the distractor list: *fight, explain, donate, carry, purchase*. However, here the key thing is that while *donate* still seems to fit conceptually, it does not allow the same kind of syntactic structure as *give*. For example, while a subject given sentence (20) could recall it as:

The rich widow is going to donate a million dollars to the university.

which preserves the original syntactic structure, a subject given sentence (21) who remembered the original syntax but thought the verb was *donate* could only recall it as:

The rich widow is going to donate the university a million dollars.

which is ungrammatical and would suggest that something was being remembered incorrectly. If, on the other hand, subjects did not recall the syntax but regenerated it on the basis of particular lexical items, then subjects given sentence (21) should occasionally recall it as something like:

The rich widow is going to donate a million dollars to the university.

where the syntax has been dictated by the particular verb selected. Lombardi and Potter found that not only did intrusions such as *donate* for *give* occur, but they were not prevented by an incompatible syntax, and that the syntactic structure accommodated the intruding verb on 90% of occasions. They conclude that syntax is not remembered but is regenerated according to the verb that is selected at recall and usually this leads to the same syntactic structure, so that it looks as though there was verbatim recall of the sentence structure.

This explanation is less easily applied to occasional instances of long-term recall of the exact wording of an utterance. For example, Keenan, MacWhinney and Mayhew (1977) found that people could sometimes recall the exact wording of remarks made in conversations, particularly when these were instances of humour or personal remarks. Despite these exceptions, it is likely that after a short interval or an intervening sentence, the surface form of an utterance usually becomes lost as the products of comprehension are woven into the developing representation of the meaning of the utterance as a whole.

THE MEANINGS OF WORDS

It may have struck you as odd that so far the models of word recognition that we have discussed have had little to say about meaning. Yet if you are listening to a lecture, the main point of the exercise is that you are striving to understand what is being said, and understanding — whatever it is — seems intimately connected to the idea of meaning. Things are not that simple, of course, and there has been considerable dispute over what "meaning" is and if it makes sense to think of meanings as residing in people's heads, let alone whether we can study how meanings are represented and processed. Even if we leave these complex debates aside, it is still fairly easy to see some difficulties. For one thing, although you can identify what words the lecturer is speaking and feel that you understand them, you can still find it hard to say how or what the representations of their meanings might be like. Johnson-Laird (1983) quotes St. Augustine on this problem: "What, then, is time? If no-one asks me I know what it is. If I wish to explain it to him who asks, I do not know". Introspection seems a poor basis for theorising about what meanings are — something which somehow seems rather more bizarre than being unable to introspect about other cognitive processes such as how we recognise faces. It is also fair to say that many other areas of cognitive psychology have been concerned with issues to do with meaning. For example, in Chapter 3, we talk about how concepts are represented and that seems to be central to ideas of meaning and understanding. Likewise, the theories of semantic memory discussed in Chapter 10 are also intimately concerned with how we understand. Such overlap should not be surprising as understanding and producing language is necessarily dependent on memory, and the deeper one delves into the processing of language, the harder it is to see what is uniquely linguistic about much of the knowledge that may be accessed (Allport, 1985).

The full interpretation of utterances involves the meaning of individual words (an area sometimes known as "lexical semantics"). Consider the following pairs of sentences:

22a. My only car is a big saloon.
  b. My only car is a small hatchback.
23a. My house is spacious.
  b. My house is roomy.

Assuming that they are uttered by the same speaker and immediately after one another, a relationship holds between these sentences: (22a) and (22b) seem incompatible, whereas (23a) and (23b) are nearly synonymous. These relationships seem to depend upon word meanings or the senses of words and not upon how the words are pronounced or on the sentences' syntax.

To the extent that language is a means of accessing concepts, theories of how word meanings are represented obviously overlap with the theories of how concepts are represented that were introduced in Chapter 3. It is not surprising then that one type of theory about how word meanings are represented is as a set of semantic features. For example, the meaning of *bird* might consist of the features "has a beak", "has feathers", "has legs", "can fly", and so on. For word meanings, the idea is that when a word is encountered in a sentence, it is replaced by a semantic representation which consists of its features. In Chapter 3, we encountered Wittgenstein's (1958) vivid example of how it is impossible to come up with a list of features that are common to all instances of the word *game*, that is, there is no necessary and sufficient set of features that define *game*. In theories of word meaning, the idea of feature lists has been retained but not in the form of necessary and sufficient features. Instead, more recent accounts propose that while some features might be defining, the majority are merely characteristic. So, for example, "can fly" is not a defining feature of the meaning of *bird*, but it is characteristic of most birds (Smith, Shoben, & Rips, 1974). On this kind of view, features are probabilistic, so that different features are weighted differently with some being more important than others when determining whether or not something is an instance of a concept (or is appropriately described by a particular word).

As accounts of word meanings, feature models provide good accounts of traditional topics in semantics such as explaining why two terms are synonymous. On a features model of word meaning, the relationship between sentences (23a) and (23b) can be explained by looking at the features of the words *spacious* and *roomy*: the two are very similar and so the overall meanings of the two sentences are the same despite containing different words. Likewise, feature models provide accounts of why words such as *bank* — and many, many others in English — can sometimes produce ambiguity by proposing that such words trigger more than one set of features, leading to alternative interpretations of sentences such as "The bank was on fire". Ambiguity is resolved or avoided by words elsewhere in an utterance constraining which set of features is selected for the final interpretation of that utterance.

While having some plausibility as psychological models of word meanings, feature models encounter a number of difficulties. First, while they may provide reasonable accounts of concrete words (e.g. *bird*, *table*, *throw*), it is hard to see how more abstract words (e.g. *hope*, *really*, *attempt*, *achieve*) are decomposed into sets of features (Garnham, 1985). Second, lists of features can appear just that — lists — without there being anything in the list which reflects important relationships between the features (Armstrong et al., 1983). For example, the meaning of *bird* is likely to incorporate the features "lays eggs" and "builds nests", but a list would not reflect that there is a relation between these features, which seems an important aspect of our understanding of the general concept. Third, there have been a number of failed attempts to uncover effects on processing time predicted by traditional feature models. Most of these tests have focused on the idea that, according to feature theories, when words are processed for meaning they are decomposed into their constituent features. As the representations of some words are more complex than others, greater complexity should result in longer processing time, because the decomposition process should take longer. For example, consider the word *man*. Its features may be "adult", "human", "male", whereas for the word *adult* the representation should be less complex, as it is does not have the additional features "human" or "male". However, a number of studies looking for effects of complexity on processing time have failed to find an increase in processing time with increasing complexity (Johnson-Laird, 1983).

An alternative to feature-style models is that word meanings are represented by procedural semantics (Johnson-Laird, 1983; Miller & Johnson-Laird, 1976). As the term itself implies, in procedural semantics word meanings correspond to procedures, akin to computer programs, which are triggered when a particular word is encountered. For example, if the word *sister-in-law* is encountered, the procedures encapsulate the knowledge that a sister-in-law is *either* one's brother's wife *or* one's spouse's sister (Garnham, 1985). As a further example, the verb *push* would trigger a set of conditions that specify what kind of action is specified by that verb. Garnham points out that a crucial difference from feature models is provided by components of the procedures such as *or*. In feature lists, the usual assumption is that features are simply listed and connected by *and*. Clearly, the use of other forms of relationships such as *or, if . . . then* make it far easier to express some concepts. A second aspect of procedural semantics is that the meaning of a word need not be specified simply in terms of other words, so other forms of representation such as mathematical ones may be used.

BACKGROUND KNOWLEDGE AND INTERPRETING UTTERANCES

There you are in the lecture: your perceptual and word recognition processes are working smoothly, parsing seems effortless, your auditory–verbal store is up and running, and the meanings of the words being spoken by the lecturer seem to make sense. This is an impressive array of processes, but even with all this cognitive equipment purring away, it does not explain the extent of the listener's understanding of much of the lecture. One of the main reasons for this, we will argue, is that the listener uses background knowledge of the world and cues linking different contributions to conversation to make inferences from what is said. In particular, we need to know more than the senses of individual words; we also need to know to what the words refer. In other circumstances, the need to make inferences about various aspects of the incoming sentences is required to fully understand the incoming speech. For example, consider the importance of inferences in grasping the full import of the following:

24. Martin got a lift with Dennis to the pub because his car was in the garage.
25. You could tell the goalkeeper was annoyed with himself as he picked the ball out of the net.
26. She hastily moved the car when she saw a traffic warden approaching.

Even when these utterances are removed from the contexts in which they were originally spoken, you can use your knowledge of the world, including knowledge of cultural practices and laws, to help construct an interpretation of them. In sentence (24), you would probably infer that there was a car being repaired and that it belonged to Martin, which relies on knowledge of getting lifts, cars, the nature of garages and their interrelationships. In utterance (25), one can use knowledge of sport to conclude that there has probably been a goal, that the keeper feels he was partly to blame, and so on. In utterance (26), one can use one's knowledge of the parking laws to conclude that the driver was probably illegally parked and so on. All of this background knowledge leads to richer interpretations of the utterances.

Mental Models

One approach to explaining how we comprehend language that emphasises the importance of reference is the mental models approach (Johnson-Laird, 1983, see also Chapter 12). The basic idea is that we understand the world by constructing internal working models of it. Such models are necessarily simplifications of the world, so that they do not, for example, encode every last feature of a scene. In understanding language, the listener constructs an internal model derived from what the speaker is saying: the structure and content of the model changing as new information comes in. The model makes use of information about syntactic structure, the senses of individual words, and inferences based on general knowledge.

The model develops from what are known as propositional representations, which were developed in studies of logic. Propositions consist of relations and arguments. For example, the sentence "The cat chased the sparrows" would by represented by the proposition CHASE (CAT, SPARROWS), where *chase* is the relation and *cat* and *sparrow* are the arguments. A more complex example from Kintsch (1988) is the representation of the sentence "Lucy persuaded Mary to bake a cake" as the proposition PERSUADE (LUCY, MARY (BAKE (MARY, CAKE)). One thing to note about propositions is that they retain information about syntactic structure in the ordering of the arguments, so one can recover the information that it was Lucy who was persuading Mary. The propositions also trigger the meanings of the individual words. Propositions are a powerful means of expressing information, so much so that some cognitivists such as Pylyshyn (1973) believe that they are the fundamental means through which information is represented in our minds.

From a mental models point of view, propositional representations do not provide a sufficient account of how we understand language because they do not contain information about referents; for example, they do not contain information about which cat was chasing which sparrows, and so on. As Johnson-Laird (1983, p. 407) remarks: "The significance of an utterance goes beyond meaning because it depends on recovering referents and some minimal idea of the speaker's intentions". In order to obtain information about referents, Johnson-Laird argues that we make inferences based on the propositional representations and these inferences become part of our mental model of an utterance. Consider the following sentence:

27. The girl sat down beside the road exhausted.

Parsing and individual word meanings allow the reader or listener to understand what is meant. However, as it stands, it is just an abstracted sentence, it is not embedded in a context that would give it a richer significance. Had it been part of a novel, then in all probability you would have known to whom "the girl" referred, why she was exhausted, where the road was, etc., giving a much richer grasp of the full significance of the statement. However, this richer interpretation does require use of background knowledge to make the appropriate inferences. To take another example, when pronouns like "they" are encountered, more than some definition-like representation needs to be incorporated into the model; inferences also add into the model a representation of the people, events, etc., to which "they" refers. Inferences then seem a key process in language understanding and we shall consider evidence of this in more detail in the following section.

Making Inferences

If background knowledge provides essential flesh on the bones of individual word meanings, it is equally clear that for such knowledge to be brought to bear, some basic understanding of the context is important. In a classic experiment, Bransford and Johnson (1973) showed how descriptions of even everyday activities can be incomprehensible unless some context is provided. Try and interpret the following:

The procedure is actually quite simple. First you arrange things into different groups. Of course, one pile may be sufficient depending on how much there is to do. If you have to go somewhere else due to lack of facilities that is the next step, otherwise you are pretty well set. It is important not to do things. That is, it is better to do too few things than too many. In the short run this may not seem easy but complications can easily arise. A mistake can be expensive as well. At first the whole procedure will seem complicated. Soon, however, it will become just another facet of life. It is difficult to foresee any end to the necessity for this task in the immediate future but then one can never tell. After the procedure is completed one arranges the materials into different groups again. Then they can be put into their appropriate places. Eventually they will be used once more and the whole cycle will then have to be repeated. However, that is part of life. (Bransford & Johnson, 1972, p.400)

This seems an obtuse and difficult passage and when asked to read it presented as above, people found it both difficult to understand and difficult to remember. However, if before they read it, the passage was given the title "Washing clothes", people found it both easier to understand and to remember ideas from it: the title provided a context in which the appropriate background knowledge could be brought to bear and so aided comprehension. In turn, this comprehension facilitated later recall of the passage perhaps because a more integrated entry was encoded into memory (see Chapter 10). The way in which we draw on background knowledge must involve memory and highlights how interwoven language understanding and memory processes become. It is also reasonable to speculate that this kind of phenomenon may not be limited to language: certain social and cultural activities may be very hard to interpret and remember unless one is provided with a context that allows background knowledge to be brought to bear.

Our ability to make such inferences seems necessary if communication is to be reasonably efficient. For example, in the washing clothes scenario above, once given the title we can infer that *things* and *piles* in the first couple of sentences both refer to clothes, but without it communication seems to fail. Garnham (1981) found that the sentence pair:

The fish attacked the swimmer. The shark swam rapidly through the water.

was read more quickly than:

The fish avoided the swimmer. The shark swam rapidly through the water.

The inference linking the two sentences is more easily made in the first of these pairs based on our knowledge of the world and therefore the likelihood of a shark being the referent of *fish*. Without inferring what the referents might be for terms such as *things* and even more specific ones such as *fish*, communication would be laborious to say the least. As a further example of this, consider the following description of a set of events:

> When it got late, the road became icy. I yawned then shook myself to try and concentrate. Suddenly, the truck ahead swerved out of control and I saw a car being rammed on to the embankment.

This is an imaginary description but, we hope, not an incomprehensible one. Notice, however, the number of assumptions that you as the listener could reasonably make. You probably assumed that the road became icy because it got colder, which often happens in the evening. This in turn implies that it had been wet during the day. It *might* have got icy for other reasons. For example, it could have been snowing and the compacted snow was becoming more like ice. A pipe might have burst nearby or a tanker might have been leaking. However, you were not puzzled about *why* it was icy because you assumed, without conscious thought, that the most likely explanation would be to do with wet roads and lower temperatures. Here are some other inferences that you probably made: that "I" was the driver; that the truck skidded on the ice; that the truck hit another car; that the other car had been on the road. The speaker has to assume that listeners' make these kind of inferences all the time; if they did not, communication would be unbearably laborious.

It may have struck you that it is difficult to see where inferencing might end, and if inferences are incorporated into mental models, as suggested by Johnson-Laird, such models would become extraordinarily large and complex. For example, in the above example, one might continue to make inferences such as: "trucks skid on ice because ice is slippy" (plausible), or "trucks skid on ice because ice makes brakes fail" (less plausible), or "trucks skid on ice because truck drivers drive too fast" etc. Some theorists attempt to get round this problem by suggesting a distinction between necessary and elaborative inferences (Garnham, 1989). Although this distinction is primarily applied to texts, it has clear relevance to spoken language. Necessary inferences enable the person to understand the incoming language as coherent so, for example, information given in an earlier exchange can be seen as necessary for understanding the current contribution:

> A: They found his fingerprints on the weapon.
> B: So it was his fault all along then!

For the speakers in this conversation to maintain some coherence, they must be able to infer to whom they are referring and that they are both referring to the same person. Elaborative inferences are not usually produced but can be made if they are demanded within the context. Frequently these may be triggered by questions ("I wonder why he did it?"). What this also allows is the possibility that sometimes, when inferences are not necessary at all, we rely solely on propositional representations and do not construct mental models whereas when inferences are necessary a mental model is constructed (Garnham, 1987).

The issue of what counts as "necessary" now becomes a thorny one and is likely to be a product of the specific circumstances in which a listener finds him or herself. Noordman and Vonk (1992) have also argued that whether one makes elaborative inferences or not depends upon the degree of cognitive effort involved. For example, they claim that when one is an expert in an area, elaborative inferences are made habitually because they require very little extra cognitive effort.

There are principles guiding conversation that enable us to distinguish between what we are and what we are not assumed to know already within a conversation, which, in turn, are guides to what are and what are not necessary inferences. Clark and Haviland (1977) propose that speakers and listeners distinguish between assumed knowledge and new knowledge by sharing in something called the "given-new contract". According to this contract, speakers should make given information identifiable to the listener. For example, in the sentence "THE CRASH was caused by a brake failure", the most common interpretation is that the listener already knows something about a crash but that the information about the cause of the crash is new. Taylor and Taylor (1990) claim that given information can be distinguished from new information by the following tendencies: given information is more likely to occur early in sentences; given information receives weaker stress; given information is signalled by use of the definite article; a pronoun can often be substituted for the given information; the given information tends to be what the sentence is "about", whereas the new information is commentary on it. Although this list is not exhaustive, it gives some of idea of the variety of devices the speaker and listener share for signalling what is and what is not assumed.

Given the central importance of inferences, it should not be surprising that we can make them automatically. Bransford, Barclay and Franks (1972) showed this when they presented people with one or other of the following passages:

> John was trying to fix the bird house. He was *pounding* the nail when his father came out to watch him and to help him do the work.

> John was trying to fix the bird house. He was *looking* for the nail when his father came out to watch him and to help him do the work.

Later, subjects were asked to say whether the following sentence had occurred previously:

> John was using the *hammer* to fix the bird house when his father came out to watch him and to help him do the work.

Subjects who had seen the verb *pounding* were much more likely to mistake the test sentence for one they had encountered earlier. It would seem that the context and a specific verb combine to create an inference about the likely instrument that John used. Again such inferences highlight how interdependent theories of language and memory become.

Apart from experiments showing how important inferences and world knowledge are in language comprehension, the centrality of these processes has also been demonstrated in computer models of memory (Schank, 1982) and of language comprehension (Winograd, 1972). As in the Bransford et al. study, in real life we occasionally make inferences that can lead to "mistakes": we have all been guilty of assuming too much on the basis of what someone has said. Of course, in real life such mistakes are generally a cost worth paying, because inferences are invaluable if communication is to be bearable.

In this section, we have considered how appropriate background knowledge can be invoked by context, how this then allows us to make inferences, which in turn help us to develop a richer idea of the speaker's intentions, and how the given-new contract provides people with ways of focusing on what is and what is not assumed to be known. However, understanding what a speaker says requires some idea of the principles governing the social activity in which one is engaged. Although this can be considered to be a form of "background knowledge" about a social practice, it is particularly specific to social interactions and so we consider these principles in a section of their own.

UNDERSTANDING SPEECH IN CONVERSATION

Conversation as a Cooperative Activity

Suppose that at the end of the lecture you walk out with a friend and you start to chat about what you might do that evening. No doubt all of the processes we have described so far would be necessary for the conversation to be satisfactory. However, it is also true that conversation itself is an activity that is governed by principles not captured by any of the processes mentioned to date. For example, we needs ways of ensuring that we take turns in contributing rather than constantly talking at once. We also need ways of deciding how much or how little we need to say on a particular topic or what will constitute a relevant response (Grice, 1975). To date, the means of achieving these ends have often been characterised by a set of principles, that is, statements describing a set of guidelines that people usually follow during conversation. One of the most influential statements of these principles is Grice's (1975) Cooperative Principle. Grice argued that conversations are not strings of disconnected remarks and so must involve some degree of mutual cooperation. He specified that for such cooperation, speakers must make contributions as required at particular points in the conversation and according to the purpose or direction of the conversation (Grice, 1975, p. 45). This may seem a very general guideline, but Grice proposed more specific guidelines — known as *maxims* — which, he argued, all needed to be followed if conversations were to satisfy the goals of the participants (see Levinson, 1983, for a thorough account). While these principles seem to explain social practices, there is an argument that they must also be internalised, that is, people must "know" (albeit not consciously) these principles if they are to understand and to contribute effectively to conversations.

The contention that people possess knowledge of what is allowable in conversations is supported by evidence that people can lose this knowledge and so become unable to appreciate all the richness of conversation. Rehak, Kaplan and Gardner (1992) looked at a group of people who had suffered strokes which had led to damage in the right hemisphere. They presented these patients with tape-recordings of scripted conversations. At the end of the conversation, the patients were asked to: rate how unusual the conversation was; interpret the intention of the person who spoke last; explain what effect the final statement was likely to have on the other person in the conversation; and to choose a continuation for the conversation from a set of three options offered (see Table 8.2). In some conversations, the participants' contributions followed the cooperative principle throughout and none of the Gricean maxims were violated (see Table 8.2a for an example). The patient's judgements of these "ordinary" conversations were no different from judgements made by a group of people of similar age and background who had not suffered brain damage. In some of the other conversations that the participants heard, the final statement violated a Gricean maxim in an extreme way. For example, in Table 8.2b, Sam's final contribution to the conversation is tangential and so violates the maxim of relevance (which states that speakers should make their contributions relevant to the aims of the conversation). When these deviant conversations were played to people who had suffered right hemisphere damage, they were less likely than the controls to judge such conversations as abnormal, they were less likely to select the most plausible interpretation of the final statement (that the speaker wanted to change the subject), and they were less likely to interpret the last remark as causing some offence to the other participant in the conversation.

Rehak et al. suggest that the right hemisphere damaged patients have a reduced ability to appreciate the intentions of speakers and the appropriateness of contributions in conversations. Consequently, it is argued that their mental models of conversations are impoverished compared with those developed by people without such brain damage (though it should be noted that there is no evidence that all people who suffer right hemisphere damage experience these difficulties). As yet, there has been

Table 8.2

Materials Showing Endings that Do (a) and Do Not (b) Obey Gricean Maxims (from Rehak et al., 1992)

Scene Beth and Dan meet coming out of the subway one morning.

Beth: Dan, guess what happened yesterday. My boss told me I'm being promoted to supervisor down at the plant. Not only that, but **he gave me some other good news that was also a real surprise.**

Dan: I'm really glad for you Beth! Getting a promotion is a terrific feeling. I'm sure you're really going to do well in your new position.

Beth: Thanks Dan, it's nice of you to say that. I'm really excited about it, though I'm a little scared too, I guess. But **it's the other thing my boss told me about that really makes me happy**.

Dan: *Maybe you could tell me more about this other news that he gave you yesterday.*

(a) Ending obeys Gricean maxim.

Scene: Judy sees Sam in the hospital waiting room.

Judy: Sam, the most awful thing has happened. My mother fell on patch of ice in front of her house and may have broken her hip. The doctor called me at the office and told me to come right over. **I'm especially worried because of what my mother found out last week.**

Sam: Oh Judy, I'm sorry to hear that. You must be very worried about her. Have you been here long?

Judy: I've been waiting around for nearly an hour, and there's no word on her condition. **This whole thing wouldn't be so bad if it weren't for what the doctor told her a couple of days ago.**

Sam: There is a big path of ice near the building where I live. It's a nice building, though and I really enjoy living there.

(b) Ending violates maxim of relevance.

relatively little work on how such principles can be incorporated into cognitive models of language use and language comprehension.

Speech Acts

When we take part in conversations or listen to lectures, the speech that we hear does not simply result in rich mental models of the speaker's intended meanings; speech actually helps change the state of the world, meaning that our circumstances and actions can be changed by that speech. Returning to the lecture theatre, the lecturer might do more than simply describe findings, theories or academic debates. For example, he or she might say: "Hand in your first piece of coursework by the fourth week of term". This is not a description, it is a form of directive, an attempt to get the listener to do something. Take another example. In your conversation on the way out of the lecture, your friend says "I *promise* you, I'll be there for 8 o'clock". This is more than a statement, it is a commitment to act in a particular way and the fact that your friend has expressed it as a promise may well lead you to act in a different way than if they had said "I'll probably be there at 8 o'clock".

Prison sentences, marriages, promises, resignations, redundancies, divorces, promotions, contracts and many other things can all be achieved through speaking and such utterances are referred to as speech acts (Searle, 1969). Sometimes the form of the speech act is made explicit in the verb that is used: "I tell you that we are lost"; "I congratulate you on your exam success"; "I guarantee that it's a genuine ming vase". However, more often the verb which makes the act clear is omitted: "We are lost"; "Well done in the exams"; "This is a real ming vase".

Many of our speech acts are not as direct as those quoted above (Austin, 1962; Searle, 1969). For example, imagine the situation where, on a freezing cold day, you return home from the lecture, walk into a warm living room and plonk yourself down on the settee only to hear someone say "You've forgotten again". Now this utterance is a statement and it has a literal meaning, but the speaker's intention might not have been to make a statement about the reliability of your memory so much as to make a request to shut the door. This gap between literal and indirect interpretations can be exploited: we have all been victims of, and I dare say perpetrators of, witticisms [sic] such as this:

Speaker A: Can you pass me the salt?
Speaker B: Yes.

Much of our speech is indirect, yet we often manage to interpret the intentions of the speaker correctly: if we did not, then there would be no point in couching requests in the form of statements — the door would never be shut — or expecting people to find responses based on literal interpretations amusing.

As with Grice's conversational maxims, there is some evidence that the ability to distinguish these different types of interpretations is internalised. In particular, damage to the right hemisphere of the brain can lead to some impairment of a person's ability to appreciate the appropriateness of speech acts, especially where these are indirect. Foldi (1987) showed a group of right hemisphere damaged patients slides of an interaction between two people. The slides were accompanied by a tape of a conversation between the pair. In some of these conversations, one speaker was issuing a direct command to the other ("Put away your toys"), while in others the command was phrased as a question, that is, it was an indirect speech act ("Is it possible for you to put away your toys?"). In the crucial conditions, the second speaker responded to the indirect act either by interpreting it appropriately ("I'll put them in the cupboard") or inappropriately, that is taking the literal meaning ("Yes, I have two free arms"). Foldi found that when such scenarios were presented to non-brain-damaged controls, the appropriate response was seen as far more acceptable than the literal interpretation. However, for the right hemisphere patients, the reverse was found: they thought the literal interpretation was more acceptable. For patients with left hemisphere damage, there was no difference.

It may be that some of the "difficulties" experienced by adults with right hemisphere damage mirror some of the characteristics of young children's speech production and comprehension: the tendency to produce apparently tangential remarks, the difficulty in deciding why a child is using a particular phrase (Ryan, 1974), and the inability of the child to understand some plays on words. The implication is that many of these aspects of language use are learned: they may be more or less perfectly acquired and they may be selectively damaged if they are located in neurologically well-defined areas. It remains to be seen how young children's acquisition of speech acts and conversational maxims varies and how such variation compares with deficits that might emerge in adulthood.

IGNORING SPEECH

Our conversations often take place against the background noise of other conversations: in cafes, restaurants, pubs, shops, and so on. And it is not unknown for people in the audience at a lecture to exchange remarks in whispered conversation while the lecturer is talking. How is it that you are able to shut out that nearby conversation about last night's party while listening in rapture to the lecture — at least until, all of sudden, you hear your own name mentioned followed by suppressed chuckles? In this chapter, we have assumed that the listener is attempting to make sense of the utterances that he or she is hearing. We have discussed the wealth of cognitive processes devoted to processing speech and making some sense of it, yet, in the scenarios just described, we seem able to ignore some aspects of incoming speech. One strong line of argument is that many speech recognition processes, especially word recognition and parsing, are automatic — we cannot prevent them happening, so that even when we feel that we are ignoring some input it is actually being processed to some degree (Fodor, 1983). If this is so, what happens when we try to focus on one speaker's utterances when others are talking at the same time? How come the products of these automatic processes do not constantly interrupt?

Research on how people cope with two rival speech signals has tended to be pigeonholed as "selective attention" rather than "speech processing". In Chapter 5, we looked briefly at aspects of people's performance on a task in which they are required to monitor two incoming speech signals and respond to them in some way. There we were concerned with possible limitations on people's capacity to do two things at once; here we approach the same literature from a different position, that of trying to discover what happens to speech which is actively ignored.

Cherry (1953) inaugurated research into how people cope with two competing speech signals. He called it the "cocktail party phenomenon" after the way one can attend to the conversation of a nearby group of people at a party and ignore that of your own group. Cherry's (1953) subjects wore headphones, with one message being presented to the left ear and another to the right. The subjects' task was to "shadow" (repeat continuously) one of the messages but ignore the other (the so-called "dichotic listening task").

This is relatively easy to do if the two signals are perceptually different, are in two different voices or languages, or are presented at two different locations. It is also fairly easy if the signals are conceptually different passages on different topics. It becomes very difficult, however, if perceptual and conceptual cues are removed. Cherry and Taylor (1954) constructed two passages from strings of clichés (e.g. "I am happy to be here today to talk to the man in the street. Gentlemen, the time has come to stop beating about the bush . . ."). When the two passages were presented at the same location in the same voice, subjects found it almost impossible to shadow one and ignore the other because all of the cues which might normally enable a listener to keep the two signals apart had been removed.

It would seem that attention can act at a peripheral, perceptual level or at a central, conceptual level to select one signal or message and ignore another. In most normal situations, the rival signals will be coming from two different speakers with two different voices in two different locations. We might expect that under such circumstances one signal can be blocked out completely while the other is attended to. That is certainly what it feels like: Cherry's (1953) subjects claimed to be utterly unaware of the content of the neglected message, often failing to notice when it switched from normal English either to German or to English played backwards, and showing virtually no recall of the content of the ignored message at the end of the experiment.

There is now a considerable body of evidence showing that although speakers may have little or no *conscious* awareness of the unattended message, something of its meaning can be shown to have been registered. Lackner and Garrett (1972), for example, had subjects attend to, and then paraphrase or interpret, sentences presented to one ear while ignoring sentences presented to the other ear. Some of the sentences they had to interpret were ambiguous. For instance, in the sentence "The spy put out the torch as our signal to attack", "put out" could be taken to mean either "switched off" or "made visible". Although subjects, as usual, claimed to have been largely unaware of the content of the ignored sentences, they nevertheless interpreted "put out" more often in the first sense when the accompanying, ignored sentence contained the word "extinguished", and more often in the second sense when the accompanying sentence contained the word "displayed". The significance of this finding is that this sort of biasing of the interpretation given to the attended message could only occur if the unattended (ignored) message was processed for its meaning, even if that meaning never entered consciousness.

How do we relate these findings on the meanings of the words of which listeners are unaware to the research on recognising and understanding speech which we discussed earlier in the chapter? According to the theory outlined earlier, a word is recognised according to the level of activity in its recognition unit relative to that of other word recognition units. So, if you are following one message, a set of units will be activated as a sentence progresses and words will be recognised quickly if they fit the context. If at least some of the words that are *not* being attended to also activate their recognition units, then the effects which we have described would result.

We can take Lackner and Garrett's (1972) result as an example. Here a word that is clearly heard has more than one meaning, so several units and several meanings could be activated. However, the unattended word adds to the activation of one of those meanings, so that comes to be the dominant one.

Work on the fate of the unattended signal has been limited to word and meaning recognition. We do not know whether listeners can process the sentence structure of an unattended speech signal, or whether syntactic analysis is confined to the attended channel. Studies of simultaneous comprehension reported in Chapter 5 suggest that some high-level analysis is possible after extended practice, but for normal perception it seems likely that the complexities of the analysis required make it impossible to perceive two streams of speech at the same time. Context and coherence guide the resolution of ambiguity and lead to selection of one input from other possible ones.

SUMMARY

Speech perception often occurs in unfavourable circumstances. To be able to process it efficiently, we need to make use of as many cues as possible within the signal that can help identify the structures in utterances. Segmenting the incoming stream into separate words allows activation of stored representations of those words. Two key factors in the final activation level of units are the frequency of an item and the context in which it is heard. A further cue to the content of the speech signal is, perhaps surprisingly, not an auditory one at all, but arises from the visual information provided by a speaker's lip and face movements.

To appreciate the meaning of an utterance frequently requires some kind of structural description of it, and this is provided by a set of processes that make up the parser. The parser makes use of various strategies for constructing a sentence structure, though these are not foolproof as occasionally we mis-parse sentences (as in "garden-path" sentences). The parser seems able to operate as an independent subsystem, but its operations do seem to be influenced by the results of interpretations of word and sentence meanings. These influences may be restricted and may only override some parsing strategies.

Understanding a sentence also requires some idea of the meanings of individual words. A number of models of how such meanings may be represented have been proposed, such as feature models (see also Chapter 3) and procedural semantics. The parsing of utterances and the processing of word meanings seem to be effortless processes, and there is evidence that even an ignored signal does receive some processing for meaning. This evidence fits with the view that some language processes are triggered automatically by an incoming signal.

Particular word meanings combine with our general knowledge of the world in ways that allow us to construct rich interpretations of what people say. These interpretations go beyond what was literally said and include inferences about what the speaker intended. While they occasionally lead to errors, in general such inferences mean that communication is more efficient and less time-consuming than it would be otherwise.

Much of our speech comprehension does not take place in a purely passive way; often it takes place within conversations and has an effect upon how we act. For this to be so, we need knowledge of what kinds of principles guide conversation as an activity and in this chapter we have reviewed some evidence that knowledge of these principles can be selectively impaired by brain damage.

Garnham (1985), *Psycholinguistics: Central topics*, remains a good introduction to many of the issues discussed in this chapter, as does the first half of Stevenson (1993), *Language, thought and representation*.

9 Witnessing an Accident: Encoding, Storing and Retrieving Memories

WITNESSING AN ACCIDENT

You are walking home along the road that leads to your house. Suddenly, a white car swerves out of a side street and, without slowing down, cuts across the oncoming traffic. There is a squeal of brakes and a red car that was travelling along your road has to swing away. It skids and crashes into a lamp-post. The white car accelerates off. The driver of the red car climbs out, swearing, and comes over to you. "Did you see that?" he shouts, "I was only doing 30 miles an hour and that stupid woman just cut out without looking". A policeman appears. You agree that you did see what happened. The policeman asks you about the white car. Did you get its number? What was its make? How fast did it come out of the side street? Did it stop at the Stop sign? Could you describe the driver? How many people were in the car? How fast was the red car going? Did the white car try to avoid the red car? You answer the questions as best you can. The policeman draws up a statement that you sign and you continue home, rather shaken, and thinking over the few seconds of the incident. You expect to be called as a witness if the driver of the white car is charged. What will you say?

As you think about the crash, you find that you have a series of vivid mental images of the events. You can see again the white car swinging out and the red car swerving. You can see the white car with two occupants racing away. You remember the look on the face of the driver of the red car as he climbed out. However, there are lots of things that you cannot remember, and some of these seem odd to you. You can "see" the white car, but you cannot "see" it clearly enough to read any of the letters on its number plate. You think that it was a woman driving, that is what you told the policeman, but you are not really sure. The driver of the red car was sure, and he ought to know. You feel it probably was a woman. You know that there is a common view that women are worse drivers than men, but also that women are more cautious than men. Would a woman have driven out so recklessly? Or was it especially reckless? Did the white car slow down at the junction? Was its view obscured by another car? You saw the whole thing, but you find that you cannot really remember. The policeman was very tolerant with the way you couldn't give all the details that he hoped for, but you feel a fool for not being able to answer questions such as the make of the car. You wonder what sort of witness you will appear to be if you are faced by a good lawyer who will highlight the gaps and uncertainties in your evidence. At least you feel that you are certain of some things. You can vividly remember the sight of the two people in the car as it drove away.

We will use the example that we have just given to illustrate some of the processes underlying memory. We should emphasise, at this point, that we have chosen an example of witnessing an accident to illustrate general memory processes. We will not be attempting, in this chapter, to review the very considerable research upon eyewitness testimony. An excellent recent review of memory and eyewitness testimony will be found in Fruzzetti, Toland, Teller and Loftus (1992). Nevertheless, we will mention some important research on eyewitness testimony during the chapter.

We will begin by making the common distinction between encoding, storage and retrieval. Encoding refers to whatever changes take place within the cognitive system to allow subsequent recall or recognition to be possible. Some trace or record of the event remains as a result of encoding. It will be seen that encoding is a consequence of the cognitive activities that are taking place at the time, and the way in which any new information is processed will make a crucial difference to its likelihood of being recalled at some subsequent time. For recall to take place at that time, it is necessary for whatever change or modification has to take place within the system to be retained without being deleted or modified to the extent that it cannot provide the necessary information for retrieval. This is the storage stage. Finally, at some point, the information that has been stored may be used to construct a new piece of cognitive activity that we would call an act of remembering. It might be the conscious re-experiencing of the original events in the richness that is possible for autobiographical recall and in dreams, or it might be merely the awareness that we had encountered the information earlier. So, taking our example of witnessing an accident, you might be able to "see" the white car and the two people in it as it drove away. You might not, however, similarly be able to recall the face of the driver. However, if shown a photograph of the driver among other "suspects", you might recognise having seen them before.

ENCODING

The Importance of the Processing Task

The activity that goes on when we comprehend whatever we are seeing, hearing or reading determines what is encoded. Active, ongoing processing triggers related information that is stored in long-term memory and makes it available to aid the current activity of making sense of the particular situation we are in. All the time our cognitive systems are actively working towards fulfilling whatever current task we have been set, or have set ourselves. This may be merely the comprehension of what we are hearing or seeing, but in other circumstances it may be more specific and more or less demanding.

How does this apply to our witnessing example? In that example, the demands are very low, the task is merely to walk home without accident, and this task, with its well-practised components (walking, avoiding other pedestrians, etc.), makes few cognitive demands. Indeed, it is very likely that we will be doing other things at the same time. We may be thinking over events that have happened to us, we may be daydreaming, but whatever we are doing, not much processing of the world around us will be necessary. In other situations we may have a far more complicated task to carry out. Crossing a busy road requires far more analysis of the world around us.

How do the processing tasks influence our encoding into memory? The answer appears to be that they are very important. The experiments that we will shortly describe show that what is encoded seems to be a by-product of the processing that has taken place. If the processing has required the careful analysis of some item or event, then a richer code recording that analysis will be laid down in the memories. On the other hand, if the current tasks determining the activity in the cognitive workspace are such that very little analysis is required, then the resulting record that is encoded will be sketchy. What is more, what is encoded will be not just a record of the specific processing, but will include other details from the current cognitive activity. It will record details relating to the time, the place, the emotional state we are in, and so on.

Poor Memories of Familiar Objects

What evidence do we have to claim that the type of task is so important to encoding? One source of evidence is that we often have very poor memories for highly familiar things that we see and use every day. Nickerson and Adams (1979), for example, tested the memory that American adults have for a US "penny". Only one person (a coin collector) in the 20 they tested could recall all the eight main features of the penny (the writing, the direction the head faces, etc.) and locate them in their correct places. On average, people can correctly recall and locate only three of the eight features. Nor was this poor memory merely the result of testing by requiring the subjects to draw the coins. When Nickerson and Adams asked their subjects in a later experiment to pick out the correct drawing of the coin from among 14 incorrect drawings, only

15 of their 36 subjects selected the accurate drawing as the one they thought most likely to be correct. In a study of 100 first-year British undergraduates, one of the authors (Morris, 1988) found even poorer recognition of the correct appearance of a 10 pence piece. Only 15% of those tested were able to select the correct design from among 12 alternatives. Not only were the details of the coin not recalled correctly, but 48% of the subjects selected alternatives in which the Queen's head was facing in the wrong direction (see also Richardson, 1993).

Why are people so bad at recognising or describing something that they use every day and may have known all their lives? The most likely answer is that they do not need to attend to the details of the coins when they are using them. Highly skilled perceptual tasks develop so that only those features relevant to making the necessary decisions are processed. Normally, we select coins from among change made up of quite distinctive sets of coins and there is no need to process them for the details of their wording. We need only distinguish the coins by shape, colour and size. If the tasks do not demand a careful processing, the memory that is laid down at encoding will also be crude.

Evidence for the poor memory of objects used every day is not restricted to memory for coins. In the days when British telephones had the alphabet as well as the ten digits on the dial, Morton (1967) found that none of his 50 subjects could correctly recall the locations of all of the numbers and digits on the dial. When telephoning, the letters and numbers are available in front of the person and there is no need to process exactly where they are placed. It would be possible to learn these placings in a matter of minutes if that was a task set for a subject in a psychology experiment, but in everyday life it is the task set by the demands of the world which determines what is processed, and what is processed determines what subsequently will be remembered.

The experiments of Nickerson and Adams (1979), Morris (1988) and Morton (1967) demonstrate that to memorise something it is necessary to do more than just encounter it, however frequently that encounter may occur. The very important conclusion to be drawn from these experiments is that good memory is not just a function of the number of times we have seen or heard the item to be remembered. In a similar way, Bekerian and Baddeley (1980) showed that a saturation advertising campaign to acquaint listeners with a new set of wavelengths for radio broadcasts led to an almost complete lack of precise learning of the new wavelengths. Craik and Watkins (1973) illustrated that the simple repetition of words over and over again does not lead to any appreciable increase in their ease of recall. They had their subjects learn lists of 12 words, with one group of subjects being required to repeat out loud the last four words in the list for 20 sec before recalling the list. On that immediate test, the subjects could remember those four words well, but at a test a few minutes later, the subjects who had spent the extra time repeating the last four words were no better at recalling those words than were the subjects who had a mere 3 sec to learn each word.

Craik and Lockhart (1972) argued that there are two types of rehearsal. One, which they termed *maintenance rehearsal*, merely retains the information without carrying out any more elaboration or enriching of the encoding. This might happen if the items were held in the phenonic loop of working memory. Such rehearsal, Craik and Lockhart hypothesised, would not lead to good long-term retention, as found by Craik and Watkins (1973). However, cognitive activity that explored the meaning of the items being retained, sought related associations, and so on, was termed *elaborative rehearsal*, and they predicted that better encoding would occur.

Where memory is tested by requiring recall, Craik and Lockhart's prediction has been supported. As in Craik and Watkins' (1973) study, frequent repetition does not, of itself, improve recall. Glenberg, Smith and Green (1977), for example, tested subjects upon their recall of words they had been repeating as a filler task in an experiment ostensibly involving the retention of numbers. Even with a difference of nine times in the repetitions, there was virtually no difference in recall. However, some improvement in recognition of the words — in this case, an increase in the probability of recognition from 0.65 to 0.74 — has tended to be observed. Nevertheless, in general, it has been found that the strategy of just repeating what one wants to learn, with no other attempt to analyse the meaning, leads to especially poor encoding (cf. Morris, 1979).

How does this research apply to our witnessing example? In that example, we imagined that you were walking home; a familiar task with little to demand attention to your surroundings. All the time, every day, cars will be passing. There is no reason why your cognitive system should process the fact beyond ascertaining that the cars were not about to do something dangerous, such as mount the sidewalk and threaten to mow you down. Until something special occurred, there was no demand on your system to do elaborate processing, and the result will have been that, although you will have been aware of the white car before it swung into the main road, the details of it that you will have encoded will be few and sparse.

Factors Leading to Good Encoding

What then will lead to good encoding? To answer this question, we must consider the problems faced by any system which has to record large amounts of information to be used in the future under conditions that at the time of encoding are not clearly known. The efficiency of encoding is inextricably linked to the information available at the time when retrieval is required. The appropriate information must be selected from that which is stored, and to allow for this a sufficiently specific record must be laid down at encoding. Most of us keep books or files of some sort, and these give an idea of the problems of encoding and retrieval that have been faced during the evolution of the cognitive system.

Suppose that you are looking for a book on a single shelf. If the shelf is reasonably small, it does not take too long to look at every book, seeing if it is the one required. Equally, we may need to have available little information about the book to be able to find it. Knowing that it has a blue cover will be enough if it is your only book with such a cover. However, as we acquire larger libraries, we find that the serial searching through every book becomes extremely inefficient. What is more, we need to know more about the book that we are searching for before we can locate it. Now we have many blue books, and need to know the title or the author. In a large library, a serial search through the stock would be ridiculously inefficient. It becomes necessary to examine each book as it is purchased by the library and to make a record of special distinctive features of the book. Libraries classify books according to their subjects, their titles and their authors. It would, in theory, be possible to classify them in other ways also. Their colour, size and date of publication might be other ways of specifying each book. When the book is required, it is quite easy to find it so long as one knows the appropriate piece of information on which the book was classified when it was placed in the library. Notice two things here. First, one needs to know the right information — knowing the size and colour is no help unless they were used to code the book when it was first shelved. Second, the ease of access (retrieval) depends on the work done when the book was entered (encoded) into the library. Suppose that you went to a library to look for a book knowing only its colour and date of publication; another time you go knowing the name of the author; another time knowing the book's size and subtitle. In most real libraries, only your second visit would be successful. However, it would be possible for a very keen, efficient library to provide records of all its books on the basis of colour, size, etc. By themselves these would not, perhaps, specify just one book; but, taken together, these records could allow you to locate the book you sought. The point of this example is that the more details that are encoded when a new book (or memory) enters the system, the more likely it is that at some time in the future, with only selective and scrappy information, you will be able to locate the book (or memory) again. What is more, the more distinctively the information you possess identifies one and only one book (or memory), the more easily that item will be distinguished from the rest, and retrieved.

This example suggests that encoding into the human memory system will be most efficient when what is laid down is a record with much richness and elaboration that is as distinct as possible from other memory entries. Such a memory trace has more opportunities to be retrieved because of the many facets of its encoding, and is less likely to be competing with alternative memories that might be located with the same retrieval information.

Elaboration of Encoding

What evidence is there that the more details that are processed, the better will be the subsequent recall? Several research programmes have accumulated considerable evidence to support the view that more elaborate and distinctive encoding leads to better recall. Craik and Tulving (1975), for example, had subjects judge whether nouns would fit within sentences that they had already been given. The sentences themselves were varied to be either short and simple, such as "she cooked the . . .", or complex, such as "the small lady angrily picked up the red . . .". The words that the subjects were shown either did or did not fit into the sentences. Craik and Tulving found that (when the words did fit the sentence) recall of the words, when subsequently tested, was far better when complex sentences had been used. This effect was especially strong, with twice the recall with complex sentences, when the sentences themselves were provided as cues to the recall. By processing the word in a context of an elaborate and complex sentence, the subjects had produced an elaborate and distinctive memory trace that could be easily located, especially when the sentence itself was available as a recall cue.

Notice how in Craik and Tulving's experiment the ease of recalling the same items was strongly influenced by the particular encoding task. Johnson-Laird, Gibbs and de Mowbray (1978) illustrated how it is the processing that is carried out upon an item to be remembered, not just the nature of the item itself, which determines the likelihood of future recall. They showed their subjects a series of names of things that could be classified as liquid or solid and consumable or non-consumable; words such as *milk, cheese, petrol* and *coal*. The subjects' task was to indicate which items met a given specification. For one group of subjects it was consumable liquids, for another consumable solids, so that for each of the possible combinations of the properties a different group classified the same word-list. Subsequently, the subjects were asked to recall the list of items. Johnson-Laird et al. found that about 50% of those items were recalled which, in a particular subject's list, possessed *both* of the properties on which the list was being classified, whereas about 21% of those items with just *one* property were recalled. Of those with *neither* of the properties, only about 11% were recalled. One important point to note here is that the same words were being tested with each group, but that the probability of a given word being recalled varied from 0.5 to 0.11

depending on whether both or neither of the properties of the word matched the classification given to the classifying group of subjects. Where neither property was possessed by the item, then, when the subjects searched their memories for their knowledge of the terms to be classified, they were able to stop their processing when it had been ascertained that one of the two properties was not possessed by the item. If both were possessed, then further processing was necessary to determine that both were indeed true for the item. So, for example, if the subjects' task was to identify non-consumable solids, they could stop processing *milk* as soon as they had identified *either* that it was a liquid *or* that it was consumable. On the other hand, for *coal*, they would have to identify not only that it was a solid but also that it was not normally eaten.

Hanley and Morris (1987) extended Johnson-Laird and co-workers' study by investigating whether it is the overall number of processing decisions made by subjects that determines recall, or whether, as McClelland, Rawles and Sinclair (1981) had proposed, what is important is the number of *positive* decisions (e.g. that *coal* is a solid), with negative decisions (e.g. that *coal* is not consumable) making little contribution to recallability. Hanley and Morris found that the number of positive decisions were the main contributors to later recall.

Levels of Processing

Can we go further in specifying how different processing tasks will influence encoding, and develop a theory of what leads to good encoding? Craik and Lockhart (1972) emphasised that what is encoded is a by-product of the ongoing perceptual processes. They therefore tried to predict the amount that would be remembered on the basis of their theory of the nature of the perceptual processing that might be activated by different tasks. They initially proposed that a given item might be processed to different *levels* within the processing system, and that the level would determine the ease with which the item would be recognised or recalled subsequently because of the resulting elaboration of encoding of the particular entry in memory that had occurred. They suggested that superficial levels of encoding would involve just the physical appearance of the word, but deeper levels would progressively involve the sound and the meaning of the item.

By how much can variations in processing task change the amount subsequently remembered? A good example is provided by Craik and Tulving (1975), who showed that the probability of later recognising a noun such as *table* as having been previously presented, varied from about 0.85 to less than 0.20 depending on whether the subject's task was to decide if the word fitted a given sentence (e.g. "He sat down to eat at the . . ."), or to decide if it was shown in capital letters. These sorts of differences remained even when the subjects knew that a test of their memory would follow the experiment, suggesting that it was the task itself rather than the subjects' wish to learn that determined the quality of the encoding. Research on mnemonics (e.g. Morris, 1979) shows how people can dramatically alter the amount that they remember by adopting appropriate strategies. This is brought about by the individuals, in effect, setting themselves a task that will lead to good encoding.

While the levels of processing framework did, rightly, place the processing activity that was undertaken as a central aspect in the determining of what will be remembered, there were many weaknesses in the specific theoretical proposals that were highlighted subsequently (see Baddeley, 1990, for a recent review). There were dangers, as in much psychological research, of circular arguments. Depth of processing was deduced from the level of recall observed, but then this deduced "depth" was given as an explanation of the amount recalled. Clearly, independent evidence for the manipulation of the processing was required, even though the task demands did plausibly suggest what processing would take place. While Parkin (1979) did provide independent evidence of the nature of processing that had occurred, this did not become a standard procedure.

Other criticisms were even more telling for the detailed levels of processing theory. The idea of a stage-by-stage perceptual processing mechanism that begins with analysing physical features and moves on to a "deeper" semantic level was inconsistent with the newer theories of the perception of meaningful words, in which top-down processes play a part from a very early stage.

It also was shown that it can be misleading to think of "good" and "poor" encoding independently of the conditions under which retrieval takes place. Morris, Bransford and Franks (1977) followed the normal levels of processing design by requiring their subjects to answer semantic or rhyme questions of a list of words. However, they tested memory in two ways. A standard, recognition test involving selecting old words from among new words showed the conventional superiority for those in the semantic condition. But when asked to select words that *rhymed* with the words in the original list, more were selected that rhymed with those in the "rhyme" condition. Morris et al. (1977) referred to *transfer appropriate processing*. They argued that different encoding tasks will lead to the selective storage of different properties of items. Good or poor recall will depend upon the task being undertaken at retrieval. A rhyme task at retrieval is more appropriate to a rhyme than to a semantic encoding activity, so better performance will follow the rhyme encoding. We will return to the interdependence of encoding and retrieval later, in the section on retrieval.

The Influence of Expertise on New Encoding

So far, we have dealt only with things like coins or common words with which everyone is familiar. However, as we will discuss in Chapter 10, new encoding depends on the existing knowledge (e.g. in schemas) that is activated by the current situation. Surely people differ in the knowledge they possess? How will this influence what they encode? For example, in our witnessing example, we assumed that you did not remember the make of the car. Perhaps we were unfair. Perhaps you are very knowledgeable about cars and think that you would have remembered what type it was. You would be assuming that experts on some topic, in this case makes of cars, will be more likely to remember new information on their favourite topic than will novices. Is this true? Perhaps experts might have poorer memories? They will have many similar instances encoded in memory if they spend their time dealing with one specialist type of information. Perhaps this will make it *harder* for an expert to learn and remember a new piece of information about their special topic. How will experts and novices differ?

The best known examples of experts showing far superior memory to novices come from chess. Chess masters shown a 5-sec glimpse from the midgame of a chess match, can reproduce 20 or more of the positions of the pieces on the board. Novices can manage to correctly position only 4 or 5 pieces. If, however, the pieces are arranged randomly, rather than in a realistic position from an actual game, the superiority of the chess masters disappears and they can perform no better than the novices. What is more, the experts describe the experience of trying to reconstruct a random arrangement as disturbing. The relationships of the pieces and their positioning breaks the well-established rules that were so much a part of the chess master's life (Chase & Simon, 1973; De Groot 1966).

How do chess masters achieve their superior memory of the board? With the real position from the game, they can draw upon two sources of their expertise to help them encode and remember the arrangement. First, they may recognise the position as one from a particular type of game. Simon and Gilmartin (1973) and Chase and Simon (1973) followed up de Groot's research and studied the recall of chess positions by experts and novices. They concluded that chess masters have memories of up to 50,000 chess positions from games, which they can bring to aid the classification of a given board. Therefore, for the chess master in this case, what is encoded is not the individual positioning on the board, but the memory that the board represents, for example, "move 16 in the Sicilian Defence". Second, even if the expert does not recognise the actual position from the game, the way that the expert perceives the board differs from the novice. To the novice they are simply pieces on the board. To the expert they represent attacks, threats, defences, and common arrangements such as the king, rook and pawn pattern that follows castling. The expert sees the board from a real game as an integrated battleground with far fewer independent units than are seen by the novice.

Other Encoding Benefits from Expertise. What evidence is there for expertise leading to better recall in other circumstances? What will be the reasons for such better memory? In recent years, there have been several demonstrations of better recall by experts in several areas of expertise. However, the reasons for the better memory will vary from situation to situation. For example, Spilich, Vesonder, Chiesi and Voss (1979) showed that knowledge of baseball predicted the recall of stories describing episodes from a baseball match. In this case, the terms used are quite technical and the experts probably benefit from being able to comprehend what is happening, whereas novices may get lost in a collection of poorly understood terms.

In other situations, the better performance of the expert may have a different basis. Morris, Gruneberg, Sykes and Merrick (1981) looked at the recall of soccer scores that were broadcast during the experiment. They found that there was a very close relationship between the number of these new scores that any subject could recall and that subject's knowledge about soccer measured by a questionnaire. Soccer "experts" could not predict

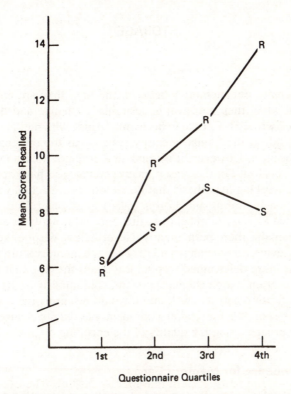

FIG. 9.1 Recall of real (R) and simulated (S) soccer scores as a function of the level of knowledge about soccer measured by questionnaire.

the scores in advance any better than novices, but they acquired them much more easily. Morris et al. argued that this was probably because the experts processed the implications of the results and produced a much richer encoding. In a subsequent study, Morris, Tweedy and Gruneberg (1985) showed that the soccer experts had better memory than novices for real scores but not for simulated scores, even though the simulated scores were composed so as to be indistinguishable in form from the real scores. The experts had, however, been informed that they were simulated.

As Fig. 9.1 shows, for the quarter of the subjects who knew least about soccer, the recall of the real and simulated scores was identical. However, as soccer knowledge increased, so did the superiority of recall of the real results over the ones that had been simulated. This suggests that the experts do not automatically process better anything that seems like a soccer result. Rather, they must know that the result has real implications before their expertise comes into play. So people who have specialist knowledge do not always use it. They need to have that knowledge activated before it will improve their encoding.

STORAGE

Decay

What happens to our memories between the time they are encoded and the moment when their retrieval is desirable? "Change and decay in all around I see" wrote H. F. Lyte in his hymn "Abide with me", and it would certainly be odd if the human memory system was the only exception to this generalisation. However, it is impossible to prove that a memory has been irrevocably lost. For this reason, many psychologists have been tempted to adopt the working hypothesis that no memories are actually lost during the storage stage. Loftus and Loftus (1980) questioned 75 psychologists and found that 84% of them believed that once information is entered into memory it remains there permanently. Nevertheless, despite the problems in providing evidence of change and decay in the memory store that would convince the more determined sceptic, it remains the case that the human body with its brain is a biochemical system, continuously in the process of decay, modification and renewal, and it would be surprising if the aspects of the brain responsible for retaining our memories did not change and decay over time, perhaps losing the quality of the encoding originally laid down.

Possible Evidence for Memory Decay

Is the loss of information from memory simply a matter of it decaying? It is easy to find evidence that seems to fit neatly with this assumption. In one of the first experimental studies of memory, Ebbinghaus (1885) tested how long it would take him to relearn lists of nonsense syllables after delays of from 20 min to 1 month. Nonsense syllables are syllables composed of a consonant, a vowel, then another consonant, which do not form a meaningful word (e.g. *haf, fet*). Ebbinghaus found that the "savings" in the time to relearn was quite considerable after 20 min, but declined with a curve suggesting exponential loss of the information over time (see Fig. 9.2a).

This decline in the amount that can be remembered, as time passes, is demonstrated in many different situations. The graph in Fig. 9.2b shows the relationship between the number of words recognised and the length of the delay in testing summarised by Woodworth (1938). Evidence for the loss of information over time is not restricted to artificial material such as nonsense syllables. Boreas (1930) found a similar information loss for memory of poems, and more recently Squire and Slater (1975) showed that people's ability to remember the names of television programmes or of racehorses who won famous races declines steadily over time. Linton (1982), who kept a record of two "salient events" for each day for 6 years, similarly found a steady decline in her ability to recall the events across time.

In almost every psychological study where new information has been acquired under the sort of conditions that are easily carried out in the laboratory (i.e. one or only a few encounters with the new information, which is itself relatively neutral in its evoking of emotions), it has been found that recall and recognition decline with passing time. However, it would be wrong to conclude that all forgetting follows a simple decay curve. At least two types of knowledge have been shown to be far more resistant to forgetting than the standard laboratory study would imply. One of these are the vivid, autobiographical memories sometimes known as *flash bulb memories*. In Chapter 10, we discuss how such memories of personally important, often surprising, emotional events appear to be far more resistant to forgetting than do more mundane autobiographical memories. The second example is that of memory for information that has been used frequently over a period of time. An early demonstration was by Bahrick, Bahrick and Wittlinger (1975), who showed that, even over a period of 30 years, there was no evidence for a decline in the recognition of school friends who appeared in old school photographs. Bahrick (1984) contrasted this with the decline by university lecturers in recognition of the faces and names of their students (see Fig. 9.3). Bahrick (1984) similarly found that although there was an initial forgetting of Spanish learned at school and college by his American subjects over the first 3 years, this decline then stabilised and there was no further evidence of forgetting for the next 20+ years.

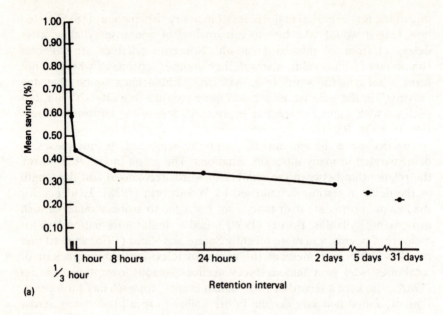

(a)

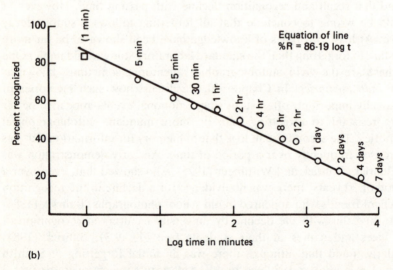

(b)

FIG. 9.2 (a) Decline in the time saved when relearning a list of nonsense syllables, as a function of the delay before testing (Ebbinghaus, 1885). (b) Decline in recognition over time (Woodworth, 1938).

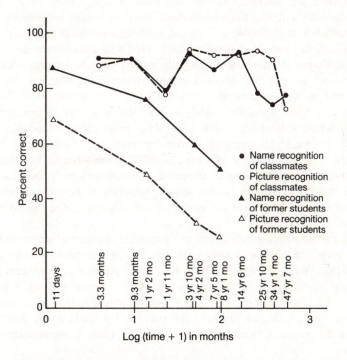

FIG. 9.3 Comparison of retention of former classmates and former students. Reproduced with permission from Bahrick (1984a).

These demonstrations would, in themselves, disprove a theory which explained all forgetting on the basis of a decay in the memory trace. Nevertheless, these examples of what Bahrick (1984a) termed "permastore" may involve a different mechanism underlying the retention of the information. There are, however, other reasons for an inability to recall than the decay of a memory trace.

Retrieval Problems as an Alternative Explanation to Decay

Is the usual observation of poorer memory after a longer time interval convincing evidence of the decay of the memory trace? It is not, because it is possible to propose plausible alternative accounts of what is happening. One possibility that deserves consideration is that the memory may not decay with time but it may be changed when new information is encoded. We will consider this possibility shortly. Second, the same retrieval cues may be adequate to cue retrieval after a short delay, but may be inadequate after a long delay if many more similar entries have been made in memory in the meantime. The memory trace need not have changed, but if it must be discriminated on the later occasion from many more similar memory entries, then its retrieval may no longer be possible. By analogy, with a single bookshelf we can retrieve a book on the basis of its colour alone. If 10 more shelves are then filled with an assortment of new books (analogous to new memories), then there may be several books of the same colour and our original means of retrieving the one that we wanted will no longer succeed.

There is a third possibility. This is, that the way that we interpret a given situation will change with time. Our schemas are modified and updated, as we have changed in our interests and knowledge. Consequently, even though the obvious, external conditions at the time of attempting retrieval may appear the same, the way they are processed and the cues that our cognitive system actually supplies to the memory system may have changed and may no longer adequately match the stored entry in memory.

All of the accounts given above are plausible reasons why the amount that we recall declines with time, whether or not the memory trace does itself decay. What is more, there has been considerable research to show that these types of influences do play a major part in what is remembered. Consequently, although it remains plausible that our memories may decay with time, we show in the rest of this section that there are enough other reasons to explain why we forget, even if our memories do not decay.

Are Stored Memories Modified by New Entries?   The idea that subsequent learning may modify the memory trace of an earlier memory was suggested by Webb (1917) and especially championed by Melton and Irwin (1940) and Barnes and Underwood (1959). Melton and Irwin (1940) showed that the more lists of nonsense syllables their subjects learned, the harder they found the relearning of their first list. For Melton and Irwin, the important thing was that when the original list was relearned, the number of mistakes that the subjects made by giving, incorrectly, nonsense syllables that they had learned in the intervening lists also *declined* as more intervening lists were learned. Melton and Irwin argued that if the poorer relearning of the original list was to be explained by subjects retrieving syllables from the intervening list and having problems in telling whether or not they came from the original list, then the number of such intrusions should *increase* as more intervening lists were learned. This, as we have just said, was not so. Melton and Irwin therefore attributed the forgetting to *unlearning* of the original list during the learning of the new lists.

Barnes and Underwood (1959) gave their subjects the opportunity to recall two responses learned to each of eight nonsense syllable stimuli.

They found that as their subjects had more trials on the second pairing, their ability to recall the first pairing that they had learned declined. Again, this was attributed to the unlearning of the association of the nonsense syllable stimulus and the adjective response as a result of a new adjective being learned as a response to the original stimulus.

Despite the evidence of the studies by Melton and Irwin and by Barnes and Underwood, the case for unlearning was not especially convincing. The argument was that unlearning must occur because there was no evidence of the other major explanation of forgetting then current, the competition of other learned responses. Many psychologists were not convinced that forgetting was best conceptualised in this simple way, and since there were alternative explanations of Melton and Irwin's and Barnes and Underwood's findings (cf. Baddeley, 1976), it was not necessary to accept their conclusion. For example, as the second list in the Barnes and Underwood (1959) study is better and better learned, it may become harder to retrieve the first list because the second list is always found first, automatically terminating the memory search. In other words, allowing for retrieval as Barnes and Underwood did does not mean that retrieval will be possible, even though the entry remains in store.

The Misinformation Effect

The idea of changes in the memory where information has been stored was again raised by Elizabeth Loftus and her associates. Loftus and Palmer (1974) demonstrated that the evidence given by subjects who saw a film of a traffic accident could be distorted by the inclusion of questions about the accident which added further "information" to the subjects. When asked how fast the cars were going when they *smashed* into each other, not only did subjects give higher estimates of the speed than if asked how fast they were going when they *contacted* each other, but they were twice as likely to agree (wrongly) when questioned later that they had seen broken glass. The idea of the cars smashing into one another not only distorted the speed estimate, but also changed the recall of other events. Loftus, Miller and Burns (1978) followed up the distorting effects of questions by showing a series of photographs which together as a sequence depicted a traffic accident. Before the accident, a car was seen beside either a Stop or a Yield (Give Way) sign. In questions to the subjects, one group were asked about the car at the road sign. However, for them, the sign mentioned in the question was *different* from that actually seen. Loftus et al. found that in a subsequent test when the subjects had to choose between the actual picture shown and one with the sign mentioned in the question, 80% erroneously chose the one referred to in the question. In subsequent experiments, Loftus and her associates went on to demonstrate that the biasing effect of the questions was *not* the result of their subjects giving the results which they guessed the experimenters were seeking. Subjects were offered payments of up to $25 for correct answers, but went on making the same errors.

Loftus (1981) varied the time at which the misleading information was given to the subjects, and found that it was most effective the longer the interval since the original exposure to the event and the shorter the time before recall was required. Loftus (1983) also found that the biasing questions were most effective if the misleading information was not the central theme of the questions but slipped in as an assumption within a complex question. So, for example, the reference to the loan sign in the question "Was the woman who was sitting at the desk with the loan sign biting her fingers?" led more subjects to report having seen a loan sign than did the more direct and simpler leading question of "Was the loan sign knocked off the desk by the robber?"

Loftus and Loftus (1980) argue that the memories of the original event were actually *changed* by the misleading questions, which became incorporated into the memory entry. Like Barnes and Underwood (1959), Loftus (1979) tried to see if her subjects still had memories of the correct details. Perhaps, for example, the confident assumption of the alternative details made in the misleading questions had led them to doubt what they could recall? In this new experiment, a key character was seen reading a green book. Misleading information given subsequently implied that the book was yellow and, interestingly, the first guesses at the book colour tended to be a compromise colour combining the original with the one suggested in the misleading question. Loftus then asked her subjects to make a second guess at the possible book colour. This second guess, however, turned out to be no better than chance guessing might have been.

There is no doubt that Loftus's findings have important implications for predictions of what will be recalled by eyewitnesses. There have now been many demonstrations that misleading post-event information can alter eyewitnesses' memory report (e.g. Belli, 1989; Chandler, 1989). However, the *alteration hypothesis* proposed by Loftus and her colleagues has been challenged by several other alternative theories. The *co-existence hypothesis* maintains that the original information is still available, unmodified, within the memory system, but that it is inaccessible in the normal research design used by Loftus and her colleagues.

There is a fundamental problem, however, which Loftus and Loftus (1980) themselves acknowledge. This is showing that the memory entry has been changed. Could it be that what is recalled by the subjects is a construction from both the original and the misleading information? Or that although the new, misleading information is all that can be recalled (in the situations examined by Loftus), there may still be ways in which the old memory, so far unfound in memory, but there nevertheless, may be retrieved in the appropriate circumstances? Bekerian and Bowers (1983) were able to show that the original memory was still available and that the problem in the Loftus experiments was that the conditions at recall led to the retrieval of the misleading information. They replicated the Loftus experiment with the Stop and Yield signs, but then changed the testing procedure. Loftus had tested by randomly ordering her test pictures. Bekerian and Bowers argued that this did not give the greatest opportunity for memory of the original to be cued. They tested recognition of the pictures from the story in the order they had originally been shown, so that the representation of the story would help retrieve what had been stored. In this condition, they found that the Loftus effect of misleading information did not occur, and the subjects were able to select the correct picture which they had seen when the story was originally shown.

One alternative account of the misinformation effect suggested by Johnson and Lindsay (1986, cited in Fruzzetti et al., 1992) is that both memories exist but the misleading information is misattributed to the original event. A more critical position is proposed by McCloskey and Zaragoza (1985). They argued that the memories are not modified by the misleading information. Rather, the effect comes from subjects who do not notice the original critical information; they may accept the new information as true. Others may assume that the misleading information must be correct because it was provided by the experimenter. While these factors may contribute to the misinformation effect, studies designed to circumvent these possible flaws in the standard procedure have still found misinformation effects (e.g. Lindsay, 1990; Tversky & Tuchin, 1989). Fruzzetti et al. (1992) review this still disputed issue.

As yet, there is little convincing evidence that what is stored in our memories is actually changed by new events, rather than being added to or supplemented by further entries. Even so, there would be attractions in a memory system that was able to replace out-of-date information with a more appropriate substitute. There would be less storage capacity required, and no possibility of recalling the old rather than the new items. Such a memory system would be especially useful in storing our intentions to do things (see Chapter 4).

To return to the example with which we began the chapter, Loftus's research suggests that your accuracy as a witness may have been reduced by the comment you heard from the angry driver or the assumptions that the policeman made during his questioning. Perhaps you did not really see a woman driving, but were influenced by the way the angry driver assumed that it was a woman driver? You would probably doubt this since you can retrieve an image of the woman in the driving seat. Would you be right?

RETRIEVAL

The most efficient encoding and storage system is worthless unless the stored information can be retrieved when it is needed. As emphasised in the section on encoding, it is the information that is stored at encoding that must be used to discriminate one memory from another. To retrieve the information, however, appropriate cues must be actively being processed in the cognitive system.

Retrieval as an Automatic, Continuous Process

When does retrieval take place? It is tempting to think of retrieval as an occasional, deliberate process, because in everyday life we only occasionally make a deliberate effort to search for something we have stored. However, if we consider what memory is *for*, we recognise that it is for making sense of what is *currently* happening to us and for predicting what is *likely to happen* in the future. Since we continuously need to understand what are the implications of our present experiences, we need to probe memory constantly for suitable information to help us make sense of what is going on. If we can retrieve high-level schemes that organise and clarify what is going on, if we recall similar situations and their implications, we can be much more efficient at coping with the world. Consequently, memory systems are necessary for the continuous process of comprehending the sensory input (see Chapter 10), and we should expect the memory system to make available automatically any suitable information that resembles the current active processing going on in the cognitive system. One way to conceptualise retrieval processes is as a continuous matching of what is currently active in the processing system with the stored memories. If the active elements that are being processed match sufficiently a stored entry in memory, then that memory becomes potentially available for recall. It is only potentially available because other memories may also be activated and the system is able to select one or none of them. Also, the current plan being processed in the cognitive system may be one which, because of its capacity demands or for some other reason, does not allow the activated memory to be actually read out from memory.

Matching and Mismatching with Current Cognitive Activity

Suppose that, while on holiday, you return to a place which reminds you of happy memories of an earlier holiday. You may not retrieve such memories if you have too many of them stored with this single context as the retrieval code. Nor will such memories recur if, at that moment, a car comes dangerously round the bend and you have to occupy yourself with more important actions of steering to safety. At any particular moment there are three possibilities for the matching of the processes active in the cognitive system with those previously stored in memory. One is that no entry in memory will match sufficiently for it to be made available; the second is that one entry will be activated with sufficient strength and to a degree that sets its activation clearly above other partially activated memories; the third is that several entries in memory are all activated but none to a sufficiently greater extent than the others to make it clearly discriminable from its competitors. Nothing would be recalled in the first condition, in the second condition the memory entry would normally be read off into the working memory, and in the third condition no item would be sufficiently clearly appropriate to be read off. It is worth pausing over this third condition. As will become clear shortly, the evidence on retrieval and retrieval problems suggests that when competing memories are activated, then none of them will be recalled unless one is far more strongly activated than the others. Nevertheless, this assumes certain properties of the retrieval system which might well be otherwise. It assumes that the system does not or cannot make a random choice between the competing memories and that there are limitations of the number of memories that can be read out at one time. Perhaps neither of these is surprising. A random choice between competing memories would frequently lead to an inappropriate choice with considerable harm to the accuracy of the resulting construction composed in the workspace. There are advantages in a conservative strategy in the retrieval of information, since it would often be impossible to construct a suitable interpretation of the situation if memories from very different past situations were introduced into the working memory.

Interference Explanations for Forgetting

From the 1930s to the 1960s, much of the study of memory was based on the investigation of how the learning of similar material interfered with recall. A good illustration of interference is the experiment by McGeoch and MacDonald (1931). They first taught their subjects a list of 10 adjectives, until the list could be recalled through once without an error. Then, in the next 10 min, the subjects either rested or learned a new list. The new lists were constructed to vary the similarity between them and the original list. For example, one list consisted of three-digit numbers, another of unrelated adjectives, and another of synonyms of the words in the first list. When they were retested on the first list, the amount that the subjects could recall decreased as the items learned in the intervening period increased in similarity to the original adjective list. On the first trial after the intervening period, subjects who had rested could recall, on average, 45% of the adjectives in their correct positions; those who had

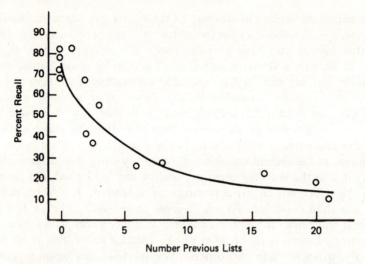

FIG. 9.4 Decline in the amount remembered from a list of nonsense syllables after 24 hours, as a function of the number of similar lists learned previously (Underwood, 1957).

learned the digit list could recall 37%; those who had just been learning unrelated adjectives could remember only 22%; and those who had learned a synonym list could recall only 12.5%. The explanation would seem to be that, for these different groups, the entries in memory differed in their distinctiveness. For those subjects who had rested, there were no competing entries in memory. For those who learned the lists of numbers, there were entries of those numbers which were coded as having been memorised in the experiment, but the memory entries for the numbers were sufficiently distinctive from the entries for the adjectives for them to be discriminated and be quite well recalled. However, the entry for the synonyms must have been very similar both in the record of the time and context of the learning and the nature of the words themselves. Consequently, it was very difficult for the subjects to recall the correct words.

McGeoch and MacDonald's experiment illustrates the problem for retrieval created by the entry in memory of similar items to those to be remembered at a time after the learning of the items to be remembered. The interference of these items with recall is known as *retroactive interference*. Items learned before those to be recalled can also cause retrieval problems and such interference is called *proactive interference*. Underwood (1957), for example, showed that the more lists a subject had previously learned, the less could be recalled of a new list when it was tested 24 hours later (see Fig. 9.4).

Underwood's (1957) demonstration that the more similar the information that had been learned earlier the poorer the recall after a delay, could have serious implications for students — perhaps the more one learns the quicker one forgets? Fortunately, Underwood's findings seem to be restricted to the repetition learning of very similar and essentially meaningless material where there is little benefit from the experience in terms of developing a richer knowledge base. With more realistic material, the expert appears to be no more likely to forget than the novice. So, for example, Morris (1988) found that while those knowledgeable about soccer could recall newly encountered scores more easily than subjects less knowledgeable, there was no difference in the rate of forgetting over several days, even when the experiment was designed to minimise the rehearsal of the scores by the experts. Traditionally, the explanation of interference effects involved a combination of the unlearning of the memory and problems in discriminating between competing learned memories. In recent years, there has been a greater recognition of the need for appropriate retrieval cues at recall.

Context-, State- and Mood-dependent Recall

In our sketch of the retrieval process, we pointed out that retrieval depends on the currently active information in the cognitive system activating entries in memory. Obviously, the closer the current processing is to the original conditions under which learning took place, the better should be the retrieval of the information. Support for this conclusion comes from research on context-, state- and mood-dependent learning. The general finding of this research is that the closer the recall situation resembles the learning situation, the better the recall.

Godden and Baddeley (1975) illustrated the influence of the context of learning on recall when they had divers learn and recall lists of words either under water or on land. Recall was tested in either the same context (above or below water) or in the reverse condition to that in which learning took place, i.e. divers who had learned the lists above water were tested under water and vice versa. Recall of the words in the same context as when learning had taken place was 47% better than when the context was switched. Of course, the contexts above and below water are very different.

Merely changing from one room to another does not alter the context so dramatically. Nevertheless, powerful effects of context have been reported where both the room and the way in which the material to be learned was presented were made markedly different (e.g. Greenspoon & Ranyard, 1957). Smith (1988) reviews research in which the contextual cues from the environment have been changed, and concludes that, although differences are not always found (Fernandez & Glenberg, 1985), environmental context does usually influence recall. It is not necessary for the physical context to be reinstated if the subjects can imagine it (e.g. Smith, 1979).

There are many anecdotes about drunks who forget what they have done when they sober up, only to recall again when drunk once more. Research upon the influence of drugs such as alcohol and marijuana, which influence the state experienced by the subjects, has supported these stories. In general, with alcohol and many other drugs, recall is better if the state in which learning took place is re-created at the recall stage. Material learnt while under the influence of alcohol tends to be best recalled when similarly inebriated (Davies & Thompson, 1988; Eich, 1980; 1989).

We have considered examples involving quite gross changes in the context of learning and recall, or the influence of drugs. What about less dramatic changes? Even differences in our moods can influence what we recall. Bower (1983) manipulated the moods of his subjects either by hypnosis or other techniques such as the reading of statements designed to induce happiness or sadness. He found that recall was as much as halved if the mood state was switched between learning and recall. In work with manic-depressive patients, Teasdale (1983) has shown similar dependencies of memories on the mood state at the time of encoding. One implication of this research is that an aspect of depression is the self-sustaining nature of the state. Once someone is depressed, they will find it easier to recall depressing memories than happy ones, and this will deepen the depression.

There are a number of problems concerning context effects that are discussed in Davies and Thompson (1988) and Smith (1994). These include failures to replicate on occasions, despite a preponderance of positive findings. There are questions concerning how to develop a more refined theoretical account of context, since the term covers such a wide range of possible influences on memory. One popular distinction has been between intrinsic and extrinsic context (Geiselman & Bjork, 1980). Intrinsic context is an incidental part of the stimulus itself, such as the voice in which the words are spoken, while extrinsic context is not part of the stimulus. Geiselman and Bjork (1980) and Baddeley (1982) suggested that this distinction could help to explain a common finding that context manipulations influence recall but not recognition (e.g. Godden & Baddeley, 1980). Smith (in press), however, concludes that intrinsic and extrinsic cues function in the same way. Smith (1988) favours the *overshadowing* and *outshining* explanations for the recall/recognition difference. Overshadowing occurs when more salient cues are encoded when learning takes place, so that the context cues may be ignored and consequently unavailable to one for recall. Outshining refers to differences between cues at recall. In a situation in which there are plentiful cues available, particular cues may have little influence — just as a dim light may be overwhelmed by several other bright lights. Recognition tests, where the items themselves are represented, provide more retrieval cues than recall tests. Therefore, it is in the latter that any influence of context as a cue is likely to be observed.

Encoding Specificity

The results of the experiments on context, state and mood dependency are examples of the *encoding specificity principle* (Tulving & Thomson, 1973; Tulving, 1983). The principle asserts that retrieval depends on the compatibility of the stored information and the retrieval information. Recall requires appropriate retrieval information — information that is suitable for the particular memory trace that has been stored at the time of encoding.

It is not just the context in which information is encoded that can vary and so influence the conditions required for retrieval. The ways in which words and concepts are interpreted when they are encoded will determine what makes an appropriate retrieval cue. This is illustrated in an experiment by Barclay et al. (1974), who manipulated the properties of objects that were emphasised by the sentences in which they were mentioned. Two example sentences are: "The student spilled the ink" and "The student picked up the ink". The first sentence is likely to remind the reader that ink is messy when spilled, the second that it is kept in a bottle. Barclay et al. read 10 such sentences to two groups of subjects, one group having sentences emphasising other properties. Then both groups were given a list of 20 cues to recall: 10 were relevant to the properties emphasised to one group, 10 to the other group. For example, the list included the cues "something in a bottle" and "something messy", the former being appropriate to the group who had the sentence about picking up the ink, the latter to those who heard about the ink being spilled. Subjects wrote down the noun of which they were reminded by the cues. On average, 47% of the target words were recalled to the appropriate cues and only 16% to the inappropriate cues. At encoding, only some aspects of the objects were considered and interpreted when the sentences were comprehended. At the recall stage, only the processing of information related to those aspects encountered during comprehension made the subsequent retrieval possible.

GAPS and Synergistic Ecphory

Tulving (1983) developed his earlier encoding specificity principle into what he termed the General Abstract Processing System (GAPS). In the learning stage, the "cognitive environment" within the individual is combined with the encoding of the observed event to produce a memory trace or engram. Later, some retrieval cue from the internal or external environment will interact with this memory trace. This process of interaction

Tulving calls *ecphory*. The result is ecphoric information that, if it is sufficient, will lead to a response or a recollective experience of the original event. One important aspect of the theory is that the memory trace and the retrieval cues interact and can supplement one another, so that a weak memory trace may still be cued by rich retrieval input. Furthermore, the encoding and cueing are for specific events. This was well illustrated in an experiment by Tulving and Thomson (1973). They showed that it is possible for recognition of the original items shown in an experiment to be poorer than their cued recall. The to-be-remembered (TBR) words were initially paired with weak associates (e.g. COLD with *ground*). The associates would have led to a particular encoding of COLD, as in the study of Barclay et al (1974). Later, the subjects generated associates of words which were actually strong associates of the TBR words (e.g. *hot* for COLD). Of course, the subjects usually generated the TBR words plus some others. When asked to indicate which of these words were in the original list, recognition was quite poor, and much worse than recall when the original weak associates were given as cues. The explanation in the GAPS model is that the meaning of COLD generated to the strong associate *hot* would be likely to be different from that originally encoded. The ecphoric information would not be sufficient for recognition, since it would not combine to recreate the original. However, this would occur for the combination of the original memory trace and the weak associate retrieval cue.

Retrieving Increases the Likelihood of Future Recall

It is known from everyday experience, especially among people who have little opportunity for fresh, interesting experiences, such as the infirm elderly, that the same stories repeatedly come to mind and are retold. Does retrieving an item from memory have an effect on the memory itself? The act of retrieval is in itself a processing event and the result will be to alter the ease with which the item can be recalled again. Retrieving something from memory increases the likelihood that it will be remembered again in the future. This has been shown in research on the learning of lists of words, where the act of testing recall of the list can be as effective as showing the list again (Cooper & Monk, 1976). As we describe in the section entitled Memory Improvement, Landauer and Bjork (1978) have used the retrieval practice effect to develop a mnemonic strategy for improving learning.

It is likely that at least two processes lead to the strengthening of memories when they are recalled. One has already been suggested. In effect, a new entry in memory is made when the old memory is recalled, since the system will make a new record of the use to which the memory is put. The other factor relates to the old memory itself. After a memory has been activated, it is likely that the amount of input necessary to reactivate the memory in the future is lowered (Brown, 1968; Rundus, 1973). In the future, less specific information will be required before the memory is made available. This concept of a lowering of the threshold for activation is a common one for cognitive models (see, for example, the models of face and word processing in Chapters 1 and 2). The lowering of the threshold may be especially marked immediately after retrieval and may decline with time.

Memory Blocked by Other Recalled Items

The result of making a memory easier to activate can be interesting and leads to some apparently odd memory phenomena. Being reminded of part of what you have been asked to remember can make remembering the rest harder! Brown (1968) asked two groups of subjects to recall the names of the states that make up the USA. He provided one group with the names of 25 of the states. These subjects were actually *poorer* at recalling the names of the remaining 25 states than those subjects who had to try to recall all 50 states. Reading the names of the 25 states activated those states' entries in the memories of the subjects and made them more likely to be re-activated when the subjects searched their memories for the names of the States of the Union. The result was that competing names kept being recalled by the subjects and in turn this recall strengthened the memory and made it even more likely in the future that the competing names kept being recalled instead of the name of the states as yet unrecalled.

Have you experienced this phenomenon of an unwanted response repeatedly coming to mind when trying to remember something such as a name of a friend or a place, or the exact word in a crossword? Reason and Lucas (1984) had subjects keep diaries of occasions when they had such memory blocks, and they found that the persistent recalling of an unwanted word (which Reason and Lucas called a "blocker") happened on over 50% of occasions where a tip-of-the-tongue (TOT) state was eventually resolved. The proportion may be much higher in unresolved TOT states.

In such situations where a word feels on the tip of one's tongue but cannot be retrieved, the common advice is to wait a while and it will come. The sense of this can be seen, since waiting allows the threshold of the competing response to increase, while a new attempt at recall in the future will be in a context of rather different current activities in the cognitive system, so that another set of features will be activated in memory and the blocker may no longer be the one which is most highly activated.

RECONSTRUCTING AND INTERPRETING

The Function of Memory

Because memory logically involves encoding, storage and retrieval, and because it is easy to illustrate such processes with examples of the storage of real objects, such as books, there is a temptation to think that memory is analogous to the storing of objects. A book is put on a shelf, kept there, and later the same book is taken down and used again. It is important to remember that this analogy when pushed this far may be inappropriate for memory. Encoding must take place, but that encoding is merely some change within the system which could in the future be "read out" again. The use of magnetic tape for the recording of video- or audio-cassettes is a good example of storage where the result of the encoding, the magnetic changes made on the tape, is clearly different from the original input, but from which, given the right system, the original can be retrieved again when required.

We should not expect encoding to be such that the readout will exactly resemble the original experience, although it may do. The memory system is involved in making sense of the world, in predicting the future and in supplying components to aid in the planning of future actions. Exact readout may not be the best aim of such a system; what will be best will be some compromise between ease of access and usefulness. What is encoded may be the *interpreted* meaning of the input rather than the *exact* form of words (or whatever) in which the input was received (see also Chapter 10).

Just as encoding is rarely a copying of the original input, so retrieval is unlikely to be merely the simple readout of what has been stored in memory. Again, it is worth remembering what the memory system is principally for: it is to provide minute-by-minute information to help interpretation and prediction; it is not a video- or tape-recorder. Our memories have not evolved specifically to cope with the reproduction with great accuracy of large amounts of past experience, but rather to provide quick answers to implicit questions such as "What does this mean?" and "What will happen now?". Consequently, when we use our memories to try to give a detailed account of a whole series of events or of a story, what can be retrieved from memory rarely provides enough information by itself. As in the witnessing example with which we began, our memories of events are often a collection of stills and highlights. This may be because little more was encoded, or it may reflect the inappropriate nature of the retrieval cues available.

Memory in Non-literate Societies

It is sometimes assumed that people in literate societies have lost much of their powers of memory, and that in non-literate societies, where there are no written records to rely on and no books or computers, people make far more use of their memories and are more accurate in their recall. In particular, it is often assumed that in such cultures there is accurate, word-perfect recall of such important oral traditions as the genealogy of the king or the words of epic songs or folk tales. Hunter (1979; 1985) has studied the literature on such oral traditions and concludes that what he calls "lengthy verbatim recall' is not a feature of the performance of those who retain the verbal traditions. The wording of stories and genealogies change with telling. What are valued are other aspects of the performance: the poetry, the singing, the placing of the king as a descendant of all the important and often mythical characters in the tradition. Where no opportunity to compare a performance with a verbatim record has existed, not surprisingly, the skill of exact recall has not been valued. It is in literate cultures where the accurate learning of religious and artistic works has been valued that lengthy verbatim recall has been achieved. The perform-ance of the transmitters of oral tradition in non-literate societies is structured by the demands of the situation. Our own recall is also structured by a mixture of the memories we can recall, the higher-level plan into which we would expect the recall to fit, and our other knowledge that we bring to the situation. Recall, at least as it is written or spoken, is very much a process of reconstruction.

Role of Expertise During Retrieval

When Bartlett (1932) presented his Cambridge undergraduates with an Indian folk tale ("The war of the ghosts"), they found it difficult to understand. Bartlett observed that the recall attempts by his subjects reflected an "effort after meaning". The stories reflected an attempt to make sense of what could be remembered, often at the expense of the insertion of details that were not in the original. Some of these errors may reflect mistakes in encoding, but many can be interpreted, as Bartlett did, as evidence for memory being a reconstructive process. Bartlett wrote of the influence of schemas, the "active organisation of past reactions, or of past experiences", which he believed directed the reconstruction. To him:

> Remembering is not the re-excitation of innumerable fixed, lifeless and fragmentary traces. It is an imaginative reconstruction, or construction, built out of the relation of our attitude towards a whole mass of organised past reactions or experience, and to a little outstanding detail which commonly appears in image or in language form. (Bartlett, 1932, p. 213)

It is not always easy to tell whether the influence of past experience and prior knowledge is upon the initial encoding or the retrieval of the information, and it is quite likely to be upon both. The prior knowledge will help in the initial interpretation of the new experience and will also

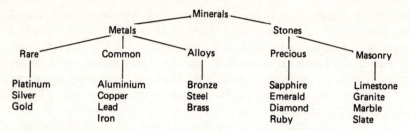

FIG. 9.5 The hierarchy for "minerals" from the list of Bower et al. (1969).

provide a framework to guide retrieval. It helps to ensure the matching of encoding and retrieval conditions, which we have identified as of such importance in effective recall. So, for example, when Bower, Clark, Lesgold and Winzenz (1969) gave their subjects hierarchical lists to learn such as that in Fig. 9.5, they found that these could be learned more than four times as quickly than when the words were randomly placed in the layout. Here the structure probably helped the subjects at encoding by emphasising related properties of the words, and aided recall by supplying a suitable framework within which recall could be attempted.

Anderson and Pichert (1978) were able to show the influence of prior knowledge upon the recall stage in the following way. They had their subjects read a story about two boys who stayed at home instead of going to school. Prior to reading the story, the subjects were instructed to read it from the perspective of either a burglar or a housebuyer. The story contained 72 ideas: some, such as the mentioning of the leaky roof, being important to a housebuyer but not to a burglar; others, such as reference to a collection of rare coins, being interesting to a burglar but not a buyer. Both groups of subjects recalled what they could of the story and were tested again after a short delay. On this second test, they were asked either to recall from the same or other perspective they had used when reading. The switch in perspective led to the subjects now recalling more, while those who used the same perspective recalled slightly less. Changing perspective changed the retrieval conditions and gave a different framework to recall.

Confidence and Accuracy During Recall

In our original example, we suggested that you would be confident that there were two people in the car because you could recall a mental image of them as they drove away. Could you be wrong? Just because something is retrieved from memory when we try to remember it does not mean that what we recall is accurate. Mental images are especially convincing, since they seem to be a snapshot from the past. For particularly emotional moments in our lives we can often remember a lot of details, with mental images of the scene. We describe research on these "flashbulb" memories in Chapter 10.

Bartlett (1932) had commented that mental images give a confidence that is unjustified. Morris (1992) examined the accuracy and confidence related to mental images of scenes from video films. He found that questions about the film were far more accurately answered when subjects reported having a mental image of the scene. However, subjects were significantly more confident of answers which were actually wrong but to which they had images than they were to answers which were *correct* but *not* accompanied by images.

The relationship between confidence and accuracy has been one of the concerns of researchers studying eyewitness testimony. Jurors and judges give more credence to eyewitness evidence than is confidently asserted (e.g. Lindsay, Wells, & O'Connor, 1989), and Cutter, Penrod and Stuve (1988) found witness confidence to be the only significant predictor in a laboratory study of jury decision making. However, a large number of studies have shown high correlations between witness confidence and accuracy (Bothwell, Öffenbacher, & Brigham, 1987), so that witnesses who express certainty are quite likely to be less accurate than those admitting that they may be mistaken.

MEMORY IMPROVEMENT

Improving Encoding

What can be done to improve retrieval of information from memory? Many mnemonic techniques exist which will help make the most of encoding (see, e.g. Higbee, 1988; Morris 1979). These seek to encourage elaborate, distinctive, integrated memories and provide good cues for retrieval.

For meaningful material, they emphasise active questioning, the linking to existing knowledge, and retrieval practice. For meaningless links, for example between names and telephone numbers, more complex mnemonic techniques are required. Higbee (1988) reviews both approaches and describes the traditional mnemonic techniques, often based upon mental images that link items together, which have been shown to be highly successful methods of improving recall if sufficient effort is expended to find suitable images for encoding (see, e.g. Morris & Stevens, 1974; Morris & Greer, 1984). Gruneberg (1992) has applied these techniques very successfully to commercially available language-learning courses. He uses the link word technique, where words from the foreign language are converted to imageable words from the learner's own language and an image formed linking this word with the meaning of the foreign word.

Similar mnemonics have been shown to be successful for the learning of people's names (Morris, Jones, & Hampson, 1978).

While powerful mnemonics have been demonstrated to considerably improve recall under appropriate conditions, their application has been limited by the effort required at encoding. Alternative approaches have been advocated by Herrmann and his associates (e.g. Herrmann & Palmisano, 1992). They argue for a much more flexible approach to memory improvement. These include the fuller use of external memory aids such as notes and diaries (Herrmann & Petro, 1991; Intons-Peterson & Newsome, 1992), and the optimising of "non-memory" factors such as physical and emotional states and environmental conditions.

Improving Retrieval

The techniques already mentioned are applicable only if one is aware at the encoding stage that a special effort to learn should be made. However, for example, there was little that could have been done to improve encoding during the witnessing example that we have used.

The object of retrieval techniques must be to re-create the type of processing that occurred when the event was originally encoded. One initial problem is that if an attempt at retrieval fails, memory search may be abandoned. Searching memory is a complex activity, and more than one line of search may be followed at a time. Evidence suggesting that retrieval will be unlikely can lead to a search being abandoned. If you are asked to recall Charles Dickens' telephone number, you will quickly recall enough about Dickens, telephones and your other knowledge about telephone numbers (the fact that you do not even remember those of some of your friends) for you to rapidly classify the question as unanswerable, if not silly. If I ask you what you were doing on Monday afternoon in the third week of October 2 years ago, you will probably refuse to try once you have recalled what the words mean and constructed what is implied. Lindsay and Norman (1977), however, claim that if you can be persuaded to try, you will probably go through a problem-solving routine of gradually reconstructing the context of 2 years ago using what you can remember. One problem is that you may remember what you *think* are details from the day, but what if they are memories from another day, recalled because you are so determined to recall something that your criteria for acceptance are lowered? Read and Bruce (1982) had people try over a long period of time to recall the names of classmates from their school days. The result was a steady and dramatic increase in the number of false names offered.

Hypnosis. Every so often there is a report in the press of a hypnotist enabling a witness to remember something they were unable to recall without aid. There is no doubt that during hypnosis several useful aids to retrieval will occur. Individuals may be more relaxed and genuinely able to attempt recall, they will try for some time, and it has long been known that reminiscence — the recalling of information not recallable on earlier attempts — is common even after many recall attempts. Perhaps most importantly, the hypnotist will attempt to reconstruct the events, in so far as they are known, in the imagination of the subject. All this probably provides the source of the anecdotes on hypnotism, since some recall will take place under hypnosis that did not occur earlier. Nevertheless, from the many studies of hypnosis as a means of improving the accuracy of eyewitnesses, there is no evidence that it reliably improves the accuracy of recall (Orne, Soskis, Dinges, & Orne, 1984). It does seem to increase the number of false items "remembered", which is, of course, particularly dangerous in witnessing, where there is often no external check on accuracy.

Reconstructing Context. If the context in which the events to be remembered took place is known, it is possible to improve recall by, for example, supplying photographs of the scene (Smith, 1979). Alternatively, witnesses can be carefully led through a reconstruction of the events in their imagination. Malpass and Devine (1981) arranged what appeared to their subjects to be an act of vandalism and then interviewed them 5 months later. One group were reminded of the events with a detailed interview which explored their feelings, memories for the room, and immediate reactions. When these subjects tried to identify the vandal, they were more accurate than controls subjects who had not received the preceding reconstruction of the events. It is important, however, that these efforts prior to recall should reconstruct the appropriate conditions. Loftus, Manber and Keating (1983) showed their subjects a highly stressful film of a fire in a hospital. Some subjects were reminded of events early in the film, prior to the fire, and shown slides of the hospital as it appeared then. These subjects had poorer recall, and Loftus et al. speculated that this might be because the emotions associated with the non-stressful early part of the film were not appropriate to the stressful part on which the questions were based.

Morris and Morris (1985) argued that the best recall would be obtained if the ordering of questions best matched the structure of information as it had been entered in memory and if what was initially tested by the questions could serve as good retrieval cues for the later recall. They used the same set of questions to test recall of short video sequences that had been taken from TV police thrillers. The questions were ordered (1) randomly, (2) in the order of the time sequence of the film, (3) beginning with the main characters, or (4) beginning with the main event (a car chase). Using the time sequence or beginning with the main characters turned out to lead to the more accurate recall.

Geiselman and his colleagues (e.g. Geiselman, 1988) have developed a technique that they term the "cognitive interview" to maximise accurate recall by eyewitnesses. The procedure incorporates four principles discussed earlier in this chapter. There is an effort to mentally reinstate the encoding context before recall of the event begins. Witnesses are encouraged to recall everything they can with no attempt to select for apparent relevance or to speed up the proceedings. The witnesses attempt to recall from different perspectives in addition to their own, e.g. from that of the driver of another car involved in a witnessed accident. Also, different orders of recall are attempted, for example reverse order or from the thing that most impressed the witness. The cognitive interview has proved to be very successful. For example, Geiselman (1988) found that it elicited 35% more correct information than standard interviews carried out by professional police officers, while the amount of incorrect information given was less for the cognitive interview than for the standard police interview.

SUMMARY

Let us return to our original example and apply what has been discussed subsequently in the chapter. We have argued that what is encoded into memory depends on the processing demands at the time. For a simple task like walking home you need do little processing of the surrounding world, and it is not surprising that what you remembered from the early stages of the accident was vague and sketchy. We have suggested that what can be recalled depends on the extent to which the current processes in the cognitive system match those which took place when the memory was encoded. Your memory of the scene will depend on how well you can re-create the situation for yourself. We have also pointed out several ways in which your memory may be distorted. The comments of the policeman or the other driver, or later your friends, lawyers, and so on, in so far as they seem to imply knowledge of what took place, may be entered in memory and subsequently retrieved to distort what you recall. You felt confident that at least the part of your memories that were supported by mental images were accurate, yet, although it is the case that such memories are likely to be more accurate than others, they tend to give a misleading sense of confidence. Finally, we pointed out that our memory systems have evolved to supply information in answer to specific situations where we need to know what is happening and what will take place next. They have not evolved to act as video-recorders, storing away exactly what we perceive. We should neither expect our memories to supply exact photographic recall nor feel ashamed that they do not. Rather, we should be impressed that we have evolved a system that can so quickly and readily supply information to prevent the world seeming like the world which William James assumed greeted the newborn infant — a booming, buzzing confusion.

References to further reading on memory will be found at the end of Chapter 10.

10 Celebrating a Birthday: Memory of Your Past, in the Present and for the Future

INTRODUCTION

We have many different sorts of memories. The most familiar is our ability to almost live again moments from our past. We can see again scenes from our past, and these *autobiographical* memories are, perhaps, what we typically think of as a memory. However, our cognitive systems have not evolved just to allow us to tell stories about the past. Our memories play a part in almost everything that we do. They are vital to making sense of the present and we use them to plan for the future. This is why we have referred to the past, present and future in the title of this chapter. But let us take a more specific example to see the different types of remembering that enter into our lives.

It will soon be your aunt's birthday. You have decided, as usual, to send her a card, but you are also going to bake her a special cake and take it to her when you visit her on her birthday. Therefore, you have to organise some parts of the celebration in advance. You must buy the card and post it in reasonable time (but not too early), bake the cake, arrange your trip, and make sure that you don't commit yourself to doing something else on that day. All of these require you to remember to do things at the appropriate time. Eventually, you are on your way to visit your aunt. Travelling to her neighbourhood you recognise familiar scenes that you have not recalled since your last visit. Walking to her house you have a vivid recollection of walking along the same path years ago on your first visit. Your aunt welcomes you in and you follow the same routine that you remember from other visits on her birthday.

In more subtle ways, too, the context and the flow of the conversation will have modified what you can remember from the past and what you will remember in the future. You will not be aware of all — indeed of many — of the ways in which the visit will have modified your memory system. Imagine, for example, that on the way home you decide to buy some flowers. You are unlikely to realise that your choice of carnations was influenced by seeing them earlier in your aunt's garden. Such influences upon our memories where we have no conscious recollection of the event that led to our memories being modified are known as implicit memories.

Celebrating your aunt's birthday is an example of a comparatively everyday kind of activity which will enable us to show how different types of memory support such everyday activities and experiences. In this chapter, we will discuss research and theorising on these types of memory, using the birthday as an example. Psychologists have focused on different aspects of memory, and these we will introduce to you over the next few pages. It is, however, worth pointing out at the beginning that the terms prospective, autobiographical, semantic, explicit and implicit memory, and others that we use, are best thought of as indicating the sorts of uses to which the memory system is being put rather than, necessarily, naming independent components of the memory system. There are debates about the independence or otherwise of each of these. We will discuss these debates at the appropriate points later in the chapter. Our object is not to claim that the memory system should be subdivided. It may turn out that the same basic processes underlie all these different aspects of memory. However, as you will see, what goes on during prospective, autobiographical and the other types of remembering are sufficiently different to have led psychologists to see them as separate fields worthy of research interest in their own right. Our aim is to give you an introduction to these research areas.

PROSPECTIVE MEMORY

When you were planning to send your aunt a card, you were intending to do something in the future and at a fairly circumscribed time. To do this, you have to form an intention, remember that intention when the time arrives, and carry out the action. Prospective memory is a term used for this kind of memory and it is, perhaps, the one that we notice most when it fails us! We can make a distinction here between prospective memory and habitual actions. When you make a mug of tea, there is a sense in which you intend to put a teabag in the mug, but putting the bag in is part of a habitual action sequence, not something which you have to set out to remember to do at a particular time or in a particular context. Slips of habitual action can occur in very familiar sequences and they often take the form of "strong but wrong" habit intrusions, where an even more familiar action is carried out while our thinking is distracted elsewhere (Reason, 1990). Action slips, such as putting instant coffee into a cup twice, or walking to the table without having added the water, do not involve forming intentions to carry out the various stages of the action, nor are the stages consciously monitored. On the other hand, the form of memory that we are referring to as prospective does involve such monitoring. We are having to change the habits that normally guide our day-to-day life and modify them by the insertion of the prospective memory.

Suppose, for example, that you decided to buy your aunt's card on your way home from college or work. You have to change the normal, habitual routine that you follow when going home to remember to go to the card shop. In many cases, we may fail to interrupt our regular routine. Prospective memories often involve arrangements with other people (e.g. visiting your aunt on her birthday). Forgetting to go to your aunt's would be extremely embarrassing; she would be hurt and so would you. Perhaps because of this or because prospective memory is involved in forwarding the plans that we make to meet our goals and objects for the future, failures in prospective memory are among the most common complaints about memory inadequacies (see, e.g. Reason & Mysielska, 1982).

Intending to visit your aunt next week is a very long-term piece of planning, whereas checking the baking of the cake in half an hour is a comparatively short-term one. In between is intending to go out and buy the card. Most studies of prospective memory have tended to refer to the half-hour check in cooking as short term and the "some time today" as long term. In prospective memory, there are also different demands in relation to time. Some actions must be performed at a particular time (posting the card 2 days before the birthday, ringing your brother at the only time he's going to be at home), whereas other elements are related to events which make them appropriate, like telling your sister about your aunt's birthday when you bump into her, or buying a card when you pass the card shop. Ellis (1988) has distinguished between what she calls *pulses* and *steps*, where pulses are intentions with a short "window of opportunity" for the intention to be fulfilled. They are essentially time-based, whereas steps are less time-dependent. Ellis found that when subjects kept a diary of prospective memories, pulses were rated as involving memories of more personal importance, were more likely to be remembered prior to the time and often involved the use of more memory aids. Therefore, some prospective memories are time-based and others are event-based.

Doing things at particular times requires the ability to monitor time itself. If the cake that you are baking for your aunt needs checking after 30 min you might set a timer to remind you. However, most people, most of the time, rely on checking a watch or clock to see when 30 min have passed. But you do not want to sit watching the clock and waiting for the time to pass. You can normally rely upon your short-term prospective memory to remind you to check the time. How do you know when to do so? How often do you look at the clock? How does the skill of monitoring time develop?

Ceci and Bronfenbrenner (1985) were interested in the way that 10-year-olds monitored time while cooking cupcakes which required 30 min in the oven. When the cooking took place in the children's own homes, the children looked several times at the clock that was provided during the first 5 min but then made few checks during the next 15 min, before frequently checking the clock during the last 5 min. This U-shaped pattern of checking was similar to the one found by Harris and Wilkins (1982) when they asked adults to hold up cards at predetermined times during the watching of a movie.

Why should the pattern of several checks at the beginning, few in the middle, and several at the end of the cooking appear? Harris and Wilkins (1982) suggest that during the first few minutes, an internal timing mechanism was being calibrated by the initial checks on the clock. This was then set up for a "wait" period until near the time when the response was required. Then a much shorter "wait" period was set up requiring a check as the end approached, and maybe another short period, and so on. Harris and Wilkins called this the test–wait–test–exit mechanism, which is basically a feedback loop which checks the time, sets the wait, checks the time, sets another wait, and so on.

How might one test whether children do operate such a test–wait–test–exit mechanism? Ceci, Baker and Bronfenbrenner (1988) had the idea of changing the speed with which the clock was running. They hypothesised that if the clock ran fast or slow, then the same U function should occur, but adjusted to the time as shown by the clock. They repeated their cake cooking experiment, but arranged for the clock that the children could see to run 10 or 33% too fast or too slow. As they had predicted, the same pattern of glancing at the clock occurred, with the children looking at it frequently for the first few minutes, rarely for the middle few minutes, and then repeatedly as the time for taking the cakes out of the oven approached, as shown by the clock. Therefore, the children had calibrated their test–wait–test–exit feedback mechanism to the clock. But how far can you mislead someone in this situation? Suppose that, while cooking the cake for your aunt's birthday, something had gone wrong with the clock. We have our own internal ways of estimating the passing of time, and if they are too inconsistent with an external clock, then we may doubt the accuracy of that external clock. Ceci et al. (1988) seemed to have reached this point when they used clocks that ran 50% too fast or too slow. Under these conditions, the U-shaped relationship in looking at the clock disappeared and the children kept glancing at the clock. It appears that the discrepancy between their own estimation about how time should be passing and that of the clock disturbed their normal procedure of employing a test–wait–test–exit mechanism.

We have been looking at studies that have examined time-based, short-term prospective memory. What about prospective remembering that needs to take place when an event occurs rather than after the passage of some specified time? Also, do people differ in their ability to remember to do things? It has sometimes been found that elderly people perform less well on some memory tasks. Will elderly people be poorer at prospective memory? Epstein and McDaniel (1990) devised a task that allowed them to examine both these questions. To the subjects in their experiment (who were either elderly or younger people), the object of the experiment appeared to be a short-term memory task. The subjects were given lists of words to recall back to the experimenter as accurately as possible. However, they were also asked to undertake a second task. In the event-based condition the subjects had to report if they heard a particular target word in the lists that they were being given to remember. In the time-based condition, the subjects had to carry out a specified action every 10 min. Epstein and McDaniel found that the younger and elderly individuals did not differ in their ability at the event-based task, but that the elderly were markedly poorer at the time-based task, and this was reflected in them much less frequently monitoring the clock provided as the critical time approached.

How can prospective memory be investigated so that the tasks are sufficiently like those encountered in real life, while at the same time having sufficient control over the conditions in the study that it is possible to begin to answer questions about what determines the accuracy of the memories and when they occur? So far, we have looked at research on short-term prospective memory. Longer periods between forming the intention to do something in the future and the actual time when the action must take place raises severe practical problems in designing research. If an experiment seems unrealistic to the subjects, will they tackle their remembering in the same way as they do in ordinary life? If you cannot observe or control the conditions under which they actually remember, how are you to discover what leads to the recall? These two problems often conflict. There have been studies where the experimenter has asked the subjects to telephone or mail a postcard at a specific time (e.g. Maylor, 1990; Meacham & Leiman, 1975). Such studies are realistic in that people do need to telephone others or send letters, but they have little control over the circumstances that lead to recall. People taking part in such experiments may resort to memory aids such as writing notes to themselves or leaving the postcard in a prominent place. If they adopt these strategies just for the experiment, then the results will be unrealistic. On the other hand, it would be wrong to try to rule out the use of such memory aids entirely from prospective memory research. Many people cope with remembering to do things in the future by using diaries, notes written on their hands, etc. (see, e.g. Intons-Peterson & Fournier, 1986.) How are such strategies integrated with our use of prospective memory? There is evidence that they may change with age (e.g. Beal, 1988) and a full account of prospective memory will certainly need to take them into account.

An interesting attempt to retain the natural conditions of prospective memory but to bring it under laboratory control was made by Kvavilashvili (1987). During what appeared to be the main study, she asked subjects to remember a message for another experiment and to remind her to pass it on at the end of the experiment. She was then able to ask the question: Is remembering the message itself and remembering to remind her to pass it on related, or are they separate memories? They did appear to be unrelated, suggesting that the prospective memory task of remembering to remind her and the retrospective memory task of remembering the content of the message involved different memory systems. She also asked the subjects to report on the frequency with which the need to remind her had popped into their minds while carrying out the other task. She found such perseverations to be more frequent for the subjects with the better prospective memory performance. James (1990) also found that such perseverations increased as the time for performing a prospective memory action approached. Clearly, there is some mechanism that makes the prospective memory available at around the correct time, and which may operate early to give the perseverations reported by Kvavilashvili and James.

Is this system for prospective memory different from that for other (retrospective) memory tasks? If we return to our example, is your remembering to buy your aunt a card or to bake her the cake the result of the same memory system as the one that leads to your memories of her always offering you a drink, or of your vivid memory of your first visit to her? One way of tackling such a question is to see whether the same people are either good or poor at prospective and retrospective memory tasks. If the tasks use the same underlying mechanisms, then we would expect someone with a good prospective memory to also have a good memory for events from their past. They do not necessarily have good memories for remembering to do things. The two types of memory appear to be unrelated. For example, Maylor (1990) found no correlation between performance on prospective and retrospective tasks (see Morris, 1992, for a review of this issue). Perhaps prospective memory requires different mechanisms to retrospective memory? Most retrospective memory seems to be describable by the principles of encoding specificity and synergistic ecphory that we discussed in Chapter 9 (see Tulving, 1983). However, prospective memory often involves recall in a situation that is very different from the one in which the intention to carry out an action was made. Taking our example, the conditions at the time when you decided to bake a cake for your aunt's birthday are likely to have little in common with those at the time when you have to remember to buy the ingredients and actually make the cake. Of course, this lack of overlap may account for many of the problems in prospective recall, but they also suggest that different mechanisms may need to have been developed.

The study of prospective memory is still in its infancy. A good review of the types of prospective memory tasks will be found in Kvavilashvili (1992), while Morris (1992) gives a more general review of prospective memory theorising and research. It is now time, however, for us to turn from considering how prospective memory is involved in planning your visit to your aunt's to considering the memories of previous visits that are recreated as you approach her door. These are autobiographical memories and such memories have been the subject of considerable research in recent years.

AUTOBIOGRAPHICAL MEMORY

As you walk up your aunt's path, you feel again the way that you had on your first visit to her house. You remember the steps up to the door and even the flowers that you were carrying as a present. Why should you remember such details now, years later? Why are such memories so rich in imagery and full of apparently irrelevant details? Are those details really as accurate as they seem? You see yourself, in your memory, carrying chrysanthemums, but does this mean that you can be really confident that it was chrysanthemums you brought?

Vivid memories, such as that of visiting your aunt, are the most dramatic aspect of autobiographical memory. If asked what was meant by "remembering", it would be such examples that would come to most people's minds. Perhaps, therefore, it is not surprising that one of the earliest studies of memory was carried out by Sir Francis Galton (1883), who used cue words to trigger the recall of personal recollections from his life. For almost 100 years this technique was forgotten, but it was revived and extended in the 1970s by Crovitz and Schiffman (1974) in what became a widely used technique, subjects being asked to remember personal experiences to cue words. Robinson (1976), for example, found that it takes much longer to recall memories to the names of emotions (e.g. anger, sadness) than to the names of objects.

If we use this cueing technique to interrogate our autobiographical memories, what sorts of memories will we retrieve? Will they be just of recent events or of special experiences, or will they take us right back to our early childhood? Such recall does, in fact, have quite a regular pattern. Rubin (1982), for example, showed that more recent events are more likely to be remembered and that the likelihood of an event being recalled declines with time in a power function. However, there are two other factors that modify this basic pattern. Rubin, Wetzler and Nebes (1986) found similar patterns of recall for 50-year-old and 70-year-old subjects — there was a preponderance of recent memories, but also a peak of memories from adolescence and early adulthood. Also, something strange happens to influence recall from early childhood. People have very few memories from their first one or two years of life, and this is known as "childhood amnesia". Why should there be these two special times in life?

Why do many autobiographical memories come from the adolescent and early adult years? At least part of the answer lies in the many new aspects of life that are opening up for the individual. Fromholt and Larsen (1991) noted that events which are conventional landmarks in life — such as marriages, births and deaths, or the start of new careers — form 20–30% of the recall from these periods. In ordinary, everyday life, there may be little that is new, distinctive and demanding of intensive processing. On the other hand, when we are in novel situations, we have to develop new schema for understanding and predicting what is happening. Perhaps this is why, in novel situations, the formation of future autobiographical memories seems to be common. For example, Pillemer, Goldsmith, Panter and White (1988) found that a high proportion of memories from college days come from the very first day at the college.

Childhood amnesia is surprising because many 2-year-old children have excellent memories. Why should it be that a 2-year-old who can remember from week to week much about their lives will, many years later, be able to remember little or nothing from these early years? There are several possibilities. One is that the conceptual schema with which children interpret the world changes as they grow older, so that the memories that are laid down in their early years are not triggered again by the quite different cognitive processing in adult life. Perhaps memory systems develop at different rates, so that young children may have a general event memory system but not an autobiographical system (Nelson, 1988). One of the big changes in the first few years of life is the development of language. Does this play a part in childhood amnesia? Schactel (1947) argued that the development of language leads to experience being encoded in a different way and that this is the reason that earlier memories are not cued. On the other hand, Fivush and Hudson (1990) were able to find little evidence for young children's event memories being organised differently from those of adults. The basis of childhood amnesia still remains to be properly understood.

Our discussion of memories from early adulthood suggested that novel situations may lead to detailed memories. Is this so? Why do we have memories of unexpected and dramatic events? An early study of such "flashbulb" memories, which are rich in apparently irrelevant details — such as who one was with and where one was standing when a particular event occurred — was carried out by Colegrove (1899). Of the 179 people he asked to recount how they had heard of the death of Abraham Lincoln 30 years earlier, 127 were able to give details of what they were doing and who they were with when they heard the dramatic news. Brown and Kulik (1977) carried out a fuller study when they explored memories for 10 important events, such as the assassination of President Kennedy. As Colegrove had found, details that were irrelevant to the basic memory of the main event were often recalled, and it appeared that the respondents had often retained in memory a very brief moment of time associated with the emotional event. Brown and Kulik speculated that there was a biological advantage in retaining the details of a salient, novel event so that the key features could be abstracted from it and later instances.

In our example of your autobiographical memory of taking flowers to your aunt, we suggested that you remembered carrying chrysanthemums but, as we said then, how can you be sure? As Morris (1992) discusses, the experiencing of a mental image of a past event gives people considerable confidence that their memory is accurate. However, Morris showed that confidence could often be misplaced and that people gave more confident ratings of being correct to answers that were accompanied by mental images than they did to *correct* answers for which they had no accompanying image. Are flashbulb memories any more accurate than other memories? Neisser (1982) suggested that, despite the vivid details apparently re-experienced with such memories, the actual memories could be incorrect. He gave a personal example of remembering listening to a baseball game when hearing of the bombing of Pearl Harbor. However, baseball is not played at that time of year, so his memory must have been an error. However, Thompson and Cowan (1986) discovered that a football game was being broadcast between teams that shared the names of famous baseball sides and was taking place at a famous baseball ground when the news of Pearl Harbor was broadcast. Perhaps, therefore, Neisser's error was not so great!

But how can one check on the reliability of autobiographical memories? One technique used recently has been to collect reports of memories for surprising events (the *Challenger* space shuttle explosion, earthquakes, etc.) very soon after they have occurred and study their modifications several months later. McCloskey, Wibel and Cohen (1988) recorded memories of the *Challenger* disaster a few days after it occurred, and again 9 months later. Some strong theories of flashbulb memory have suggested that there is a special mechanism which is immune to forgetting when such emotional events are involved. McCloskey et al. found that although there were recall accuracies of 89% and greater after the 9 month delay, recall did not appear to be perfect. They therefore argued that some forgetting had taken place.

What should we conclude from McCloskey and co-workers' study? Perhaps, that flashbulb memories are not perfect. On the other hand, isn't it impressive that such accurate, detailed recall could take place almost a year later? Also, was it reasonable to assume that everyone who saw the disaster would be similarly affected and be expected to have a flashbulb memory? To what extent will the degree of involvement of an individual in an event influence future flashbulb memories?

There were some hints in earlier studies of autobiographical memory that the personal importance and personal involvement of the individual was important in the laying down of the memory. For example, Rubin and Kozin (1984) asked their subjects to rate the characteristics of the three most vivid memories that they could recall. The highest rated properties of the events were their personal importance and their unexpectedness, both properties that would be related to the degree of involvement of the individual.

How might one look at the importance of the degree of involvement of the individual? One way would be to compare the flashbulb memories of people who had been deeply affected by an event with those who were less concerned. Bohannon (1988) did just this for flashbulb memories of the space shuttle disaster. Subjects were classified on the basis of how upset they had been, how they had heard about the disaster, and their retelling of their personal experience. Bohannon found more detailed and confident recall after 8 months by those who were more upset and who had rehearsed their accounts more often. But can you go further than this and look at degree of personal involvement itself? By taking advantage of the San Francisco earthquake, Neisser, Winograd and Weldon (1991) were able to compare memories of those caught up in the earthquake with those who had only heard about the disaster. Those personally involved retained their memory with little loss, whereas people who had heard about the quake on the other side of the USA lost much in accuracy.

You may have noticed how many of these studies of autobiographical memory rely either upon the recall of major, national events or depend entirely upon the report of the individual, with no opportunity of checking its accuracy. National events are, inherently, unpredictable and rare. They may also not be a good sample of all possible autobiographical memory. What can be done about the problem of verifying what people report? How far can their recall be trusted for accuracy? Don't people sometimes confidently report things that did not, in fact, happen? There are accounts of patients who, following frontal lobe damage, provide vivid accounts of what they claim to be autobiographical experiences but which turn out to be confabulations (see, e.g. Baddeley & Wilson, 1986). Of course, most of those who take part in autobiographical memory experiments have not suffered frontal lobe damage! Nevertheless, there is a need for verification of autobiographical recall.

How might such reliable data be collected? One way would be to keep detailed diaries of events that could later be probed for the accuracy of their recall. Some individuals have dutifully compiled diaries recording events from their own lives for considerable periods so that they can be used for memory experiments. Wagenaar (1988b), for example, kept a diary for a period of 6 years, recording events in terms of *who, what, where* and *when* the events took place. Using these questions as cues, he subsequently found that the *what* cues were most effective and that the *when* cues were, by themselves, of little use in prompting recall. The *when* cues were much more effective when combined with one of the other types of cue. It was thus possible to explore the type of cues that activate autobiographical memories, as well as being confident in the accuracy, or not, of the memory itself.

How appropriate are studies like these based on the recall of individuals? Surely psychologists who test their own memories are not a good representation of ordinary people? Is it, in any case, a good idea to rely upon what individuals regard themselves as an important event? How might one circumvent these problems? Brewer (1988) collected data from a wider group with no selection of the items by the subjects themselves. His subjects carried an electric beeper which produced a beep approximately every 2 hours, but on a random basis. When the beeper went off, the subjects filled in their response cards and gave a short description of their current activity. Brewer used data collected in this way in a variety of tests of subsequent memory. In one study, subjects rated their recognition of their written record after intervals of up to 140 days. Using this data, Brewer was able to examine a number of the features of the original events as factors determining the later recall. For example, he found that memory for actions was superior to memory for thoughts. Memorable events were rated high on pleasantness and emotionality and less frequent events were better remembered than frequent ones. What other properties of cues to recall might be effective? Brewer provided descriptions based on *time, location, time and location, thought* and *action* Again, Brewer found that *action* cues were very effective and, like Wagenaar, cues based on the time that the memory occurred were poor. In other words, our memory systems do not appear to be organised on the basis of the way in which we record time, but rather upon the actions, activities, emotions and importance of the events themselves.

Let us now return to our original example of your aunt's birthday. Most of your memories will be autobiographical ones, at least that is how it will seem. The conscious experience of vivid memories of the past can sometimes seem to be all that there is to remembering. In the history of the study of memory, the idea that remembering is the experiencing of a mental image goes back at least to the writings of Aristotle (see Morris, 1994). There is, however, much more to remembering than autobiographical memories, and implicit as well as explicit memory has interested psychologists in recent years. Further information on autobiographical memory can be found in Conway (1990). We will consider next memories with little or no conscious content.

IMPLICIT AND EXPLICIT MEMORY

There is much that you will have learned on your visits to your aunt that will have affected you, but of which you will not be consciously aware. We have already given the example of your choice of flowers on the way home being influenced by the ones you have seen in your aunt's garden. However, much of your thinking and talking in the following days may have been modified as a result of whatever you saw or heard when you visited your aunt.

Why should we be consciously aware of the situations in which learning takes place? Very simple organisms have their behaviour modified through learning, so why should we assume that the conscious aspects of remembering are the only ones? Consider some of the skills that you possess. Can you remember when you learned to use the words that you are reading now, or to walk, or to throw a ball? It is very easy to slip into thinking that the vivid memories of autobiographical events are the only type of memory that there is. For many years, most of the laboratory studies of memory were directed towards the recall of events of which the subjects were consciously aware (Morris, 1994; Morris and Gruneberg, 1994).

On the one hand, therefore, we have memories that involve events that we can consciously recall; on the other, there have been changes in our behaviour, such as the choice of flowers following the visit to your aunt, that involve no conscious awareness of the key event. Memories of which we have a conscious awareness are called *explicit* memories, while those that are not so linked to conscious awareness are called *implicit* memories.

The earliest demonstrations of implicit memory came from research with amnesic patients. Milner (1966) studied a patient, H.M., who was severely amnesic following the surgical removal of his hippocampus and surrounding brain structure. Milner found that H.M. could learn new motor skills, despite having no memory for virtually all new experiences. Warrington and Weiskrantz (1970) examined implicit memory using, among other techniques, what is known as the *stem completion task*. The task involves showing subjects the first three letters of a word and asking them to complete the word. Normally, there is more than one way in which the stems can be completed. Normal individuals are strongly influenced in their choice of the word that they give by words beginning with the first three letters that they have recently encountered. Warrington and Weiskrantz were able to show that their amnesic patients showed the same degree of this *priming*, even though they were far poorer at recognising that they had seen the words earlier.

Perhaps, you might suspect, amnesic patients still have some explicit memories. Even more convincing, therefore, is the study by Schacter, Tulving and Wang (1981) involving Korsakoff amnesic patients. They asked their patients to choose answers from a set of alternatives to trivia questions. When the patients were incorrect, as they often were, they were shown the correct response. Later, the patients often selected the correct answer when the question was asked again, but, while they were now likely to be correct, they consistently were unable to say why this was the case.

These demonstrations of implicit memory come from the study of patients with brain damage. Surely, if implicit memory is important, it can be demonstrated in the remembering of normal individuals? That is exactly the sort of question which led Tulving, Schacter and Stark (1982) to seek for evidence of implicit memory that was distinct from explicit memory in the performance of normal individuals. Their task was to have subjects complete word fragments (e.g. the subject might be given T- I- and be required to fill in the missing spaces to make a meaningful word). However, some time prior to this fragment completion task, the subjects were shown a list of words and then tested on their ability to recognise these words from among a set of the old words and new distractors. Presenting the word list influenced the fragment completion task. The words primed the fragment completions so that subjects tended to complete the fragments with words that had been shown in the earlier list. However, the important point that Tulving et al. were able to demonstrate was that the influence these words had upon priming seemed to be independent of the ability of the subjects to actually recall the words that caused the priming. They were able to show this independence in two ways. They looked at the accuracy of word recognition and fragment completion performance over a period of 9 days. Fragment completion performance did not decline over this time period, but the accuracy of word recognition decreased considerably. Thus, the two processes seemed to be different. Furthermore, it was possible to look at the fragment completion priming for those words which subjects had been shown originally, but which they failed to identify as old words. Tulving et al. found that the priming was just as strong for these words as for words that had been correctly recognised. This would be very surprising if both fragment completion and word recognition were used in the same processes.

Another strong demonstration of the different ways in which earlier experience could modify such performance was given by Jacoby (1983). His subjects studied what he defined as "to-be-remembered" words under one of three different conditions. The first of these conditions was a *no context* condition, in which the to-be-remembered word was simply proceeded by a set of ×s. So, if for example the to-be-remembered word was COLD, the presentation would involve ×××–COLD. A second condition was a *correct context* condition, in which the to-be-remembered word was preceded by an antonym (e.g. *hot*–COLD). In both of these conditions, the subjects read the to-be-remembered word aloud. In the third, *generate* condition, the antonym alone was given, so that, for example, if a subject was given *hot* he or she would normally produce the word COLD.

Following encountering sets of words in one of these three different conditions, different groups of subjects were tested in one of two ways. One group here given the conventional recognition test of explicit memory, in which the to-be-remembered words were mixed with new words. As in Tulving and co-workers' study, the old and new words had to be identified. Jacoby found that in this test performance was best in the generate condition, next best in the context condition and poorest in the no context condition. Other subjects, however, carried out a perceptual identification task. In this task, the old words and new words were shown very briefly in a tachistoscope and had to be identified. Now, the levels of performance were reversed. The highest level of identification was for words that had been in the no context condition, with the context condition coming next and the generate condition being the poorest. The important point here was that the subjects who had taken part in the perceptual identification task were unaware that their performance had been affected by their earlier study of the words. In fact, not only had it been so influenced, but that influence was in the opposite direction to the explicit recognition memory test.

More recently, programmes of research by Gardiner and his colleagues and Nelson and his associates have accumulated demonstrations of dissociations between what appeared to be parallel but independent memory processes. Gardiner's technique (e.g. Gardiner & Java, 1993; Gardiner, 1988) is based upon a conventional test of recognition such as that used by Tulving et al. (1982) and Jacoby (1983). However, in addition to identifying those words which are old and which are new, the subjects specify for each item whether they have a conscious recollection of seeing the item in the earlier part of the experiment or whether they feel that they know the item is familiar but with no recollective experience. Then, the probability of a correct response is analysed separately for these "remember" and "know" items. Gardiner and his collaborators have demonstrated several dissociations. For example, in one study, the initial task undertaken by the subjects manipulated the level of processing by requiring semantic or acoustic processing. Semantic processing can be encouraged by asking for decisions about the meaning of the words, while acoustic processing is directed by asking about rhyming words. Gardiner showed that there was better recognition following semantic processing as measured by the "remember" responses, but no difference for the "know" responses. Gardiner found several other ways of influencing the "remember" responses without affecting the "know" responses. For example, intentional learning instructions and the manipulation of word frequency both affect "remember" responses, with intentional learning and low word frequency leading to better performance. However, in neither case is recall as measured by the "know" responses differentially affected (Gardiner & Java, 1993).

On the other hand, Gardiner was able to show that in some circumstances other tests lead to big differences in the "know" responses but no difference in the "remember" responses. So, for example, Gardiner

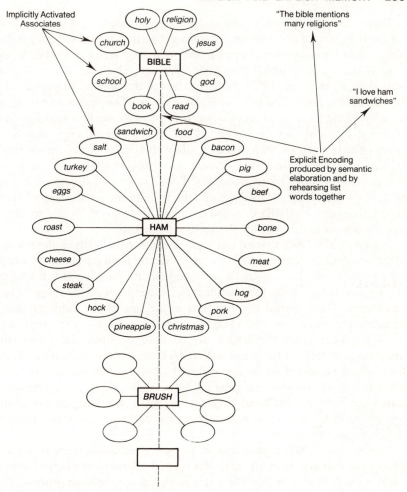

Implicitly Activated Associates

holy · religion

church · jesus

BIBLE

school · god

book · read

sandwich · food

salt · bacon

turkey · pig

eggs · beef

roast · HAM · bone

cheese · meat

steak · hog

hock · pork

pineapple · christmas

BRUSH

"The bible mentions many religions"

"I love ham sandwiches"

Explicit Encoding produced by semantic elaboration and by rehearsing list words together

FIG. 10.1 Associates implicitly activated by "Bible" (a small set) and "Ham" (a large set) (Nelson, 1994).

(1992) had subjects observe a very rapidly presented list of words and then tested recognition either with visual or auditory presentation. "Remember" responses were unaffected by this change in testing, but there was a big detrimental effect for the "know" responses. In a study requiring the lexical decision that the presented letter strings were or were not meaningful words, Gardiner and Java (1990) found that, for the "remember" responses, there was better recognition for words than non-words, but the reverse occurred for the "know" responses. All of these studies support the view that different forms of memory processing and perhaps quite different memory systems underlie conscious remembering and the sense of knowing with no conscious recall.

There are other approaches to studying implicit memory. One is to look for the influence of the structure of semantic memory upon memory tasks. Nelson and his co-workers have carried out a long series of studies based around the variable which they called *set size*. (Nelson, 1994; Nelson, Schreiber, & McEvoy, 1992). Set size refers to the number of pre-existing associates that are linked to a particular stimulus. They measured such set sizes by asking large numbers of subjects to generate the first associate that occurred to them and then counted the number of different words so generated. In most of their research, they compared words with a small set size generating 8 or fewer different associates with those of a large set size generating 16 or more associates. For example, as illustrated in Fig. 10.1, they found that BIBLE generates 8 different associates, whereas HAM generates 18. BIBLE would be a candidate word for the small set size conditions and HAM for the large set size lists.

Nelson et al. (1992) carried out many experiments in which the set size of the words to be remembered (the *target* set size) and the set of the words used to cue recall (*cue* set size) were manipulated. They found that smaller cue set size led to about 15% better recall under a very wide range of test conditions. These included: variations in the age of the subjects; using associatively related words, category names, pictures, word stems and word fragment cues; the length of the time to study the items, the immediacy or delay of the recall test; and whether or not the subjects knew they would be tested on recall. Figure 10.2 shows the results for recall when target set size was manipulated. Once again, there was a consistent difference between small and large set size which was independent of the processing task, the rate of presentation, the concreteness of the items or the expectation of a test.

Nelson et al. (1992) argued that the set size effect arises from an implicit processing that automatically activates related information when a familiar word is read. This is an important step in the comprehension process. The conditions under which Nelson et al. failed to find a set size effect were those in which the critical items were presented along with associated words, either as paired associates or in sentences. They argued that the activation of an associate means that the other associates of the studied word, although initially activated, are rapidly inhibited by the strongly activated link (see Chapter 2 for a discussion of connectionist models which incorporate such inhibition). Nelson (1994) reviews the studies of his research team and describes in more detail their model, which they call PIER — processing of implicit and explicit representations.

Theoretical Explanations of Implicit Memory

How can we explain these differences between implicit and explicit memory? Are there really quite different systems, or is there essentially

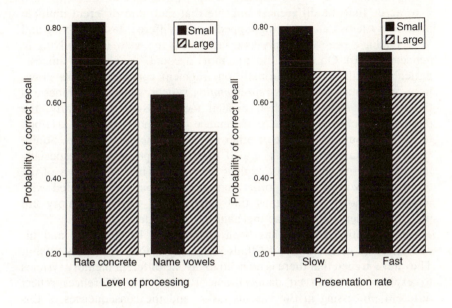

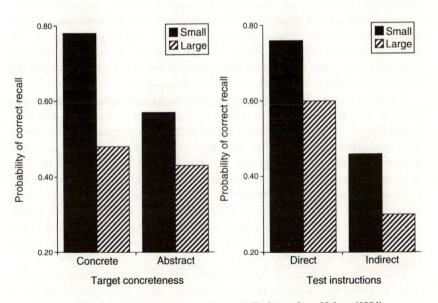

FIG. 10.2 The effect of set size upon recall. Redrawn from Nelson (1994).

just one system that processes in different ways? There are two main competing explanations for the implicit memory phenomenon. One approach is to argue that the differences indicate that there are different multiple memory systems that are being tapped by the different tasks. Tulving and Schacter have been especially associated with this view (e.g. Tulving & Schacter, 1990). On this multiple memory account, the ability of amnesic patients to still perform normally on fragment completion tasks draws upon some intact *perceptual representation system*, while their amnesia is the result of damage to their explicit memory system. Similarly, the dissociations observed in the performance of normal subjects is ascribed to the contributions of these or other co-existing memory systems. Squire (1992) goes further and has argued that the hippocampus is especially important in the encoding of explicit memories, while other parts of the brain are involved in the other memory phenomena associated with implicit memory. This means that implicit and explicit memory are physically independent in the mechanisms that underlie them.

An alternative account has been championed by Roediger and his colleagues (e.g. Roediger, 1990; Roediger, Weldon, & Challis, 1989). They have argued that there is no need to invoke different memory systems to explain the observed dissociations. Rather, the differences reflect different processing in the various tasks, and the consequences of this processing. They base their explanation on two main assumptions. The first is that test performance depends upon the match between the encoding and the test conditions — that is, *transfer appropriate processing*. The second assumption is that cognitive operations are essentially of two types — data-driven processes and conceptually driven processes. Data-driven processes are "bottom-up" and depend to a large extent on the physical and perceptual features of the stimulus; conceptually driven processes are "top-down" and draw mainly on the existing knowledge stored within the system and emphasise meaning.

Roediger argues that explicit tests tend to be conceptually driven and implicit tests data-driven. Therefore, fragment completion tasks are seen primarily as being data-driven, whereas recall is conceptually driven. The dissociations between implicit and explicit memory tasks is, then, explained in terms of changes in the type of processing and the transfer appropriateness of the processing. So, on this view, fragment completion is heavily dependent on perceptual processes. Priming of fragments is reduced if the words are heard or conveyed as the names of pictures, rather than being shown visually as words, when the perceptual processing of the word will be most appropriate to the later test on completing the fragment (e.g. Roediger & Blaxton, 1987).

This processing account has the attraction of parsimony, avoiding the need to postulate multiple memory systems. However, it has been criticised on several counts. Nelson (1994) argues that it shares the danger of circularity of which the levels of processing approach was accused (see Chapter 9). There need to be measures of the degree of transfer and the extent to which a process is data-driven or conceptually driven which are independent of memory performance. Further problems have arisen as differences between implicit tests have been demonstrated. Both word fragment completion and perceptual identification are supposed to be data-driven tests, but Witherspoon and Moscovitch (1989) found that the processes underlying perceptual identification and fragment completion for the same words were statistically independent, and Weldon (1991) has shown that the meaning of the word that is encoded affects word fragment completion priming but not perceptual identification.

Perhaps the two approaches are less incompatible than has been maintained by their proponents. At the functional level at which cognitive psychologists operate, the distinction between different hypothetical processes and different hypothetical systems is not always clear. Furthermore, quite highly specified models would be required to distinguish between processes and systems, how different systems use similar or different processes, and so on. Much clarification of the theoretical accounts can be expected in the future.

Nevertheless, the research on implicit memory has highlighted some of the many ways in which experience modifies future cognition, over and above the explicit memory tasks that were the focus of research and theorising during the 1970s and 1980s.

SCHEMAS AND SCRIPTS

When you visited your aunt, you knew a great deal about things which you take for granted, but which you must have learned at one time, and which would puzzle a visitor from outer space, or even from another culture. You knew the rules about driving your car, the conventions about parking, where to buy flowers, and so on. In everyday life, we are continually making use of knowledge that we have acquired and can now use in a systematic way to help guide our actions or make sense of our current experiences. Such knowledge has often been assumed to be organised in special memory packages known as *schemas* or *scripts*.

Although the idea of schemas guiding perception was argued strongly by Bartlett (1932), it was when cognitive scientists began to try to program computers to understand language that the concept of schemas became popular. When faced with the problem of programming a computer to understand a short story, it soon became apparent that the computer needed to be equipped with a vast array of expectations of what was likely to happen in a given situation. Several cognitive scientists began to develop models of the representation and use of this knowledge about the workings of the world. Minsky (1975) wrote of *frames*, Schank (1982) and Schank and Abelson (1977) of *scripts*, and others more generally of *schemas*.

The common set of ideas underlying these theories are that they assume that there are organised structures of knowledge in memory. These are derived from past experience, and can be retrieved to guide comprehension and recall. These schemas provide the framework for the interpretation of the new experience. They specify what to look for in the input, and they indicate what is likely to happen next, which allows inferences to be drawn.

One of the best known examples is the script for "eating in a restaurant" developed by Schank and Abelson (1977). By equipping their computer program SAM with expectations about the routine of going to a restaurant, they were able to produce a program that could interpret simple stories about restaurants and answer simple questions. The following is an example from the script scene for ordering in the restaurant:

Ordering
Customer picks up menu
Customer looks at menu
Customer decides on food
Customer signals waitress
Waitress comes to table
etc.

One advantage of such script knowledge is that it allows the person or computer to fill in gaps left by the storyteller. So, if there is no mention of the customer deciding on her food, or of the waitress coming to the table, but the story picks up the script further on, it can be inferred that these steps have taken place.

Bower, Black and Turner (1979) explored the psychological basis of such scripts, and found that most people give similar accounts of activities such as going to a restaurant. They went on to study how these expectations of what will happen in a familiar situation will influence subsequent memory of stories based on the script.

What sort of errors would you expect in the recall of a story based closely on a script for a familiar event such as going to a restaurant, a lecture or a doctor? As you might have guessed, either when recalling, or when being tested on recognition of sentences from the stories, by far the most common error was to import statements that were implied in the general script. So, for example, people might mention paying the bill in the restaurant or going into the doctor's surgery, even though neither was specifically mentioned in the original story. Perhaps the subject had deduced these steps in the script when comprehending the story. Alteratively, when using the script to guide retrieval, the subject may have been unable to discriminate whether or not the statement had been in the story. Bower et al. also found that there was a strong tendency for events that they had deliberately moved from their normal place in the scripts either to be forgotten or to be shifted back to their normal position.

How do scripts influence us? One way is in helping to specify what should happen next. Often, what interests us are situations where the normal expectations are *not* fulfilled. What, asked Bower et al., would this do to our memory of the story? To find out, they introduced non-script actions into the stories. For example, the normal running of the restaurant script might be disrupted by the wrong food being brought or the dishes being dropped.

A story that is purely based on a script with nothing unusual happening is a very boring story; in fact, Brewer and Lichenstein (1981) found that people rate such passages as barely being stories at all! The only point in telling a story is to acquaint the listener with something they do not already know, to go *beyond* the knowledge that is represented in their scripts. Bower et al. investigated the effect of two types of deviations from conventional scripts. One was merely to introduce irrelevant statements with no essential place in the causal flow of the events (e.g. describing the waitress's hair); the other has to break the smooth flow by introducing an obstacle (e.g. you cannot read the menu because it is in French), an error (e.g. you are brought snails when you ordered soup) or a distraction which temporarily suspends the running of the script (e.g. the waitress spills soup over you). Bower et al. found that obstacles, errors or distractions were especially well remembered by their subjects, who, on average, remembered 58% of such interruptions, compared with 38% of the script actions. Irrelevancies were the poorest recalled (32%). Therefore, one role of the script was to specify what was interesting by helping to identify when normal expectations were not immediately fulfilled. We look for what is new in any story. It is the interruptions in a scheme that make the story worth telling, and it is these that are most attended to and recalled.

Many different schemas will be activated during our waking moments. The culture shock experienced by someone moving to a different society reflects the lack of suitable schemas, and the activation of their old, inappropriate schemas. The use of a schema when reading a book is just one example of schemas in action.

SCHANK'S MODEL OF DYNAMIC MEMORY

How are scripts retrieved from memory? How do they develop through our experience? How are they modified to meet our needs? Is there just one type of script, or should we think of a more complex structure to the knowledge that we use when we process a new experience?

Schank (1982) became dissatisfied with the limitations of the script concept. He suspected that many of the past experiences that aid our understanding do not seem to be of the frequently experienced, highly predictable type. For example, people have expectations about what will happen in many situations that they have never experienced, such as earthquakes and breaking off diplomatic relations. Can they have scripts available in memory for these events? Then there are the sorts of mistakes that people make when they confuse memories of going, say, to a doctor and a dentist. In the original formulation of the script concept there should be a separate one for dentists and for doctors. How could such errors come about? Schank argued that such errors would occur only if the memories shared some higher-level properties, but this led to many problems with generalised scripts. The whole point of a script is that it gives you specific expectations for a given situation. If you did not have separate dentist and doctor scripts, you would have problems over what to expect from each. For example, in Britain, you have to pay dentists but not doctors. Your doctor would be surprised if you lay down on his couch with your mouth open, and your dentist would think it odd if you sat in an ordinary chair waiting to be asked what was wrong with you. It would, therefore, be difficult to make up a script that applied to both doctors and dentists.

Schank tackled these problems by examining instances where our memories are stimulated and one event reminds us of another. For example, someone told Schank of an occasion when, while waiting in a long queue at a post office, they noticed that the person ahead had been waiting to buy just one stamp. This reminded Schank of people who only buy a dollar or two of petrol at a petrol station. Clearly, there was something about both occasions which transcended the scripts being run and which led to the one event reminding Schank of the other.

By analysing many examples of reminding, Schank was led to the view that memory is dynamic and failure-driven. It is when something goes wrong in our predictions that we must modify our memories so that they will be more likely to cope in the future. Schank suggested that we store the details of the scene in which a failure occurred. With further failures the memory will be modified and elaborated to make prediction more accurate.

At any one time, Schank argues, more than one level of memory structure will be activated. In the lower levels there will be *scenes*, which are general structures that describe how and when a particular set of actions take place. When going to a doctor's, for example, there will be reception scenes, waiting-room scenes and surgery scenes. Scenes organise specific memories. These represent a kind of *snapshot* of one's surroundings at a given time (Schank, 1982, p. 96).

Scenes then, according to Schank, are organised into what he calls "memory organisation packets" (MOPs). These consist of a set of scenes directed towards the achievement of a goal. Each MOP has one major scene whose goal is the essence or purpose of the events organised by the MOP. Finding the appropriate MOP in memory enables one to predict which scene will come next.

Schank suggests that MOPs are themselves organised by meta-MOPs into higher-level structures, representing, for example, trips. The meta MOP "mM-TRIP" can deal, for example, with the stages in a visit by activating MOPs such as M-AIRPLANE, M-HOTEL, M-MEETING. Beyond MOPs there are other structures dealing with more abstract information, which are called, "thematic organisation points" (TOPs). These allow us to be reminded of abstract principles that are independent of a particular context. So, for example, when a city council gives way to a big businessman, we may bring to mind the effect of the appeasement of Hitler over Munich. The principles we abstract are sufficiently similar, even though the actual events have no other features in common. It would be inconceivable that we should remember the potentially useful knowledge about appeasement if there wasn't some high-level process abstracting and retaining it.

MEMORY REPRESENTATION

We have argued that comprehension is heavily dependent on memories of past experience which make available knowledge about what to expect and what to look for in a given situation. Such information, in the form of schemas, can guide the construction of the representation of what has occurred. At a more detailed level, shared objects and events, and causal and motivational links, all contribute to the construction of a mental representation of a story. What form does this representation take? What type of information is normally retained in our memories after, for example, your visit to your aunt? How is the information interconnected and related to our other memories? Almost anything that we experience *can* be stored in our memories. We can recall, for example, how things looked, smelt, tasted, or the exact words of songs and quotations. Memory is very flexible. As is argued in Chapter 9, what is stored in memory is a product of the processes of making sense of the undertaking at the time.

In some situations, it is valuable to remember exactly the words in which a message was conveyed. On such occasions, the detailed wording may be remembered (e.g. Kintsch & Bates, 1977; Wanner 1968). However, when we listen to a conversation or read a story, we are not usually concerned with the exact words used, but rather with the message that the speaker or author is trying to convey. The words are a means of transmitting the message, but the same message could usually be sent in another way. You could use different words, or, if both you and your listener spoke another language, it would be possible to say the same thing in that language. It is the *meaning* of the message that is important, not the particular way in which it is conveyed. The meaning of a message is often described by philosophers in terms of *propositions*. Propositions are the fundamental elements of meaning, which are either true or false and which are independent of the way the message is transmitted. The same propositions underlie my saying "I love you" in English, "Je t'aime" in French, or "t'amo" in Italian. It is the propositions that need to be identified to build into a representation. The result is that, when trying to recall a conversation, such as that with your aunt, we normally find that we have forgotten the exact wording, except for the telling or unusual phrase which especially attracted our attention beyond our processing of it for the message it conveyed.

When Whipple (1912, p. 267) summarised early German research on the recall of prose passages, he described it as:

> . . . a progressive abbreviation of the anecdotes; the story becomes less definite and more general in phrasing; each report deviates to two or three points from the preceding; the errors are confusions, substitutions, alterations of temporal and spatial setting; names and dates suffer particularly.

Later, Bartlett (1932) emphasised the "effort after meaning" reflected in the recall by his subjects when they tried to reproduce either a story from another culture, or to pass on the disjointed attempt at recall made by another subject. Bartlett noted how the style and details of the original were lost. Gomulicki (1956) found that it was hard for subjects to distinguish attempts at recall, from précis written with the passage available at the time. All this suggests that what is normally stored in memory after reading a story is the essential meaning of the text but not the details.

So, people are usually quite good at recognising if the meaning of sentences they are shown are different from those they saw earlier, but they are not normally good at spotting if the structure of the sentence itself is different; if, for example, it has switched from active to passive (Mary kissed John; John was kissed by Mary) (e.g. Sachs, 1967).

NETWORK MODELS OF MEMORY

We have a rough outline of what will be stored in memory after your visit to your aunt. It will be in terms of episodes constructed from the basic events of your day The encoding will be modified by the particular schema you possess.

Can we go beyond these generalisations and try to produce a more detailed model of the sort of information that is stored in memory? Several psychologists have tried to devise such models. One recent approach has been via connectionist models (discussed in Chapter 2). An older approach has been to try to represent the associations between the various elements of the new knowledge in a network. The most elaborate of these models has been developed by John Anderson and refined and applied over many years (Anderson & Bower, 1973; Anderson, 1976; 1983).

Underlying these network models is the assumption that what we experience (e.g. read or hear) is analysed for its underlying propositional contents. Then a record of this contents is built up by linking together related propositions. The end result is an integrated representation of an episode which has lost the details of the original wording of the story but still contains the fundamental message.

Network models assume that what is heard, seen or read is analysed for its propositions. A proposition is the smallest unit of knowledge that can be sensibly considered true or false. They involve a *relationship* (such as giving, hitting, being beautiful) and *arguments* to which the relations apply. Relations usually correspond to the verbs and adjectives in the story, and the arguments correspond to the nouns. Relations like *hit* will always have three arguments, since there must be someone doing the hitting, someone or something being hit, and something being used for the hitting. The sentence "I visited my aunt" would be interpreted as one proposition, with *visited* as the relation and myself and my aunt as the appropriate arguments.

Longer sentences or passages can be broken down into propositions. Take the sentence "The girl broke the window on the porch". This consists of two propositions: (1) The girl broke the window, and (2) The window is on the porch. Figure 10.3 represents propositions (1) and (2) in the system used by Anderson (1985). The representations in Fig. 10.3 are for the two separate propositions, but, of course, it is the same window that is referred to. Hence, someone reading the sentence "The girl broke the window on the porch" would combine the two representations as in Fig. 10.4 via the entry for *window*.

Suppose that a person reads or listens to the following sentences:

1. The girl broke the window on the porch.
2. The girl who lives next door broke the window on the porch.
3. The girl who lives next door broke the large window.

These sentences are made up of four simple propositions: (i) "The girl broke the window", (ii) "The window is on the porch"; (iii) "The girl lives next door"; (iv) "The window is large". No sentence contains all these propositions, but to understand what was being said, we can assume that the listener will attempt to construct a representation integrating all the propositions. They can do that in a way that would be written:

4. The girl who lives next door broke the large window on the porch.

This can be represented in the propositional network by Fig. 10.5.

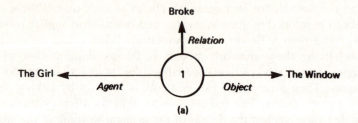

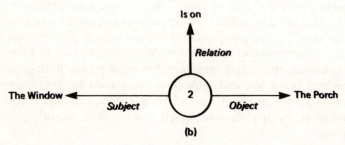

FIG. 10.3 Propositional network representations of the sentences "The girl broke the window" and "The window is on the porch".

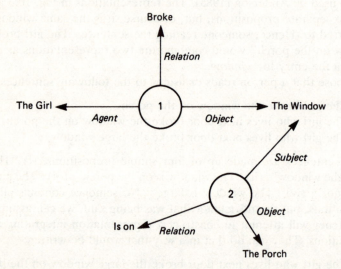

FIG. 10.4 The combination of the two propositions in Fig. 10.3 into a single network.

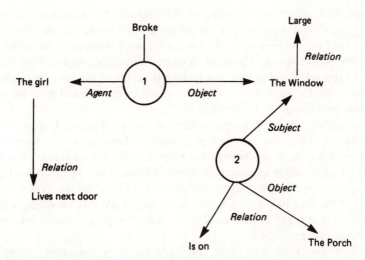

FIG. 10.5 Representation of the sentence "The girl who lives next door broke the large window on the porch".

Several things can be noted about this representation of the episode. First, it contains the essence of what occurred but does not record the way in which the information was derived. Second, the same structure could have been formed in many different ways, through listening to any of a large set of possible combinations of the sentences. Afterwards, however, *which* sentences occurred cannot be deduced from the representation.

The example just given illustrates the development of a semantic network in memory. What uses might it have? One might be to retrieve information when answering questions. For example, when a question is read, it could be composed into a new network which matches one stored already in memory. This could then make available that stored information and any additional, connected information in memory (e.g. Anderson & Bower, 1973).

SUMMARY

In this chapter, we have tried to show how many aspects of memory may be involved in as ordinary an activity as visiting your aunt on her birthday. These are all those aspects of memory associated with planning your actions. These prospective memories will, as we have shown, be important in preparing for your visit to your aunt.

When actually travelling to or when you are with your aunt, you may re-experience images from your past. These autobiographical memories are often retained from important and unexpected events in our lives. To many people, it is the re-experiencing of these images from the past, often with their associated memories of the emotions that we felt at the time, which constitute what seems to be the core of memory. However, we pointed out that the past shapes our present in many ways. Studies of implicit memory have been revealing in that, even though we may have no conscious recall of some past experience, how we respond in the present may be shaped by our past exposure to events.

Our ability to comprehend, interpret and plan depend upon our past experience. One way in which psychologists have seen this experience as organised has been in schemas that help us to predict what normally occurs in a given, familiar situation. Schemas influence our recall as well as our interpretation of our current circumstances. Finally, we have discussed one view of the way in which what we have been currently encoding might be stored in the form of networks that retain the propositional information we have just processed.

When you visit your aunt, multiple memory resources, prospective memory, schemas and other stored information will be available to guide your cognitions. The consequences of your visit will be both explicit memory, but also implicit learning that will carry over to modify your interpretations of future visits to your aunt, or any similar activities.

Chapters by experts on most of the aspects of memory discussed above will be found in either M. Gruneberg and P. Morris (Eds) (1992), *Aspects of memory, Vol. 1: The practical aspects* or P. Morris and M. Gruneberg (Eds) (1994), *Theoretical aspects of memory*. A. J. Parkin (1993), *Memory: Phenomena, experiment and theory*, provides a recent review of memory research by a single author. A. Baddeley (1990), *Human memory: Theory and practice*, gives a wide-ranging review of memory research from the perspective of one of its leading figures. M. Conway (1990), *Autobiographical memory: An introduction*, provides a very good review of research on autobiographical memory.

11 Arriving in a New City: Acquiring and Using Spatial Knowledge

Imagine you are visiting a strange town or city for the first time. You are met at the airport or the railway station by a friend who drives you through unknown streets until you have no idea where you are. You don't know how to get back to where you started from and you don't even know if you are north, south, east or west from that point. You know that you went past a large church and some civic buildings, you noticed a demolition area, a couple of fruit-market stalls, and two men having a fight in the street. You also had a conversation with your friend. Later, when you realise that you have to go out and find your way about, you start to panic. It's easy to get lost and you could be late for important appointments if you take a wrong turn, find yourself outside the wrong building, or catch the wrong bus.

After you've lived in the same town for a few months, you can drive or walk confidently from your home to your friend's home, to the office, to the theatre. You don't know everything about the city, but you have a rough idea of the direction of places with which you aren't acquainted: You know many ways to get from place to place and you can invent new routes if familiar ones are obstructed. The new knowledge you have obtained is related to the spatial characteristics of the environment and it is this spatial knowledge which concerns us in this chapter. We spend a part of this chapter dealing with the development of large-scale spatial knowledge and then relate that to more theoretical questions about how we store and use spatial information in general.

ROUTES AND MAPS

Imagine again that you are on your first visit to a new town. Your friend tells you how to get from the house where you are staying to the bus station. If you were visiting Lancaster, for example, the instructions for how to get from Dale Street to the bus station would be something like this:

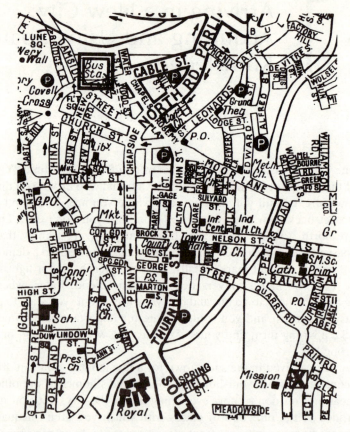

FIG. 11.1 Part of the map of Lancaster. "X" (lower right-hand corner) represents the starting point for the walk to the bus station (upper left-hand corner). Reproduced with the permission of Geographia Ltd.

When you leave the house, turn right and walk along the road. The road swings to the left at the Moorlands pub and you follow it. Keep going straight downhill. When the road levels out there is a right turn. Don't take that one. After that turn there is the back of the town hall. Pass that and then turn right at the main road. Walk along that road, past the edge of a square with a statue of Queen Victoria, and then downhill. At the bottom of the hill, the main road swings to the right. You don't go that way, but at that point you turn left. The bus station should be in sight. It is to the right, after the left turn.

This set of instructions contains a list of commands which link up various sights and even feelings. There is some emphasis on landmarks — pub and town hall, for example — and there are instructions to change direction, to keep going straight, and extra information such as the road goes downhill. Basically, your friend has given you a route to follow.

Of course, your friend could just give you a map and let you work it out from there. Look at the map in Fig. 11.1 This is a representation of part of Lancaster and it contains road, landmarks and directions to travel, some of which are in the form of verbal labels like names, whereas others have a more direct relationship to the town. This map may be more difficult to use while walking than a list of actions would be, but it allows you to go back along a route, it allows you to use one of several routes to get to the bus station, and to construct a new route if an old one goes wrong.

When we look at the knowledge of the environment which we build up with experience, we find that sometimes we use route information, which we can think of in terms of links between conditions and actions, and sometimes our knowledge has more of the characteristics of a map. These include *reversibility* — knowing how to get from A to B implies knowing how to get from B to A; *transitivity* — knowing how to go from A to B and from B to C allows you to go from A to C; and *flexibility* — the ability to take more than one route from A to B. The three kinds of operations that can be performed on real maps can also be performed on our internal representations of the environment (Pick & Lockman, 1981), and it is because we can take detours, reverse journeys and put components of journeys together that the name "cognitive map" has so often been applied to our knowledge of the space in which we live.

Because maps are a way of representing the real environment on paper, it is easy to use them as analogies for our mental representations, but we have to be quite careful about the analogy. On a printed map, like that in Fig. 11.1, there are several ways in which things are represented. The label "Town Hall" has only an arbitrary relationship to the object it stands for, and the label doesn't have any qualities resembling those of the building itself. On the other hand, some information on a map does have a similarity to what is being represented. For example, one can tell that the town hall is closer to the police station than it is to the bus station and this is true both for the map and for the world it represents. There are also omissions from most maps. In the map in Fig. 11.1, for example, there are no contours and no information is given about the three-dimensional structure of the surface.

DEVELOPING A REPRESENTATION OF THE ENVIRONMENT

When you move to a new town or to a new university campus, you have many sources of information available to you. Some will come from instructions, some from maps, and some from moving around in the environment. We will look at the way we use external maps in a later section, but first we consider the overall changes in knowledge of the environment that occur with experience.

At the beginning of the chapter, we presented a list of instructions and a map and compared them as ways of understanding the environment. The most general change in our spatial knowledge with experience is probably from a sequential route-based type of representation to a more flexible one like the survey map. Siegel and White (1975) argued that routes are important units within an overall cognitive map, and that development of the general structure or schema for a route starts with the knowledge of landmarks, with little about the spatial relations between them. This then changes to a sequential ordering of landmarks and an overall grasp of the layout of the route. With several routes through an area we can eventually combine them into one map.

There has been some dispute over this suggested order of development, both over the movement from landmarks to routes and the movement from routes to maps. Appleyard (1976) found that people who had lived in a city for less than a year drew sketch maps which showed routes, whereas those who had been there longer emphasised boundaries of areas and landmarks, so had a more integrated approach. Devlin (1976) also found that routes were very important in the early stages, with the landmarks more important later. However, it is not always clear what the function of a landmark is in a map. Evans, Marrero and Butler (1981) found that adults who had lived in a town for a year produced more interconnecting links and pathways between landmarks, but that the landmarks themselves were the same as those used by people who had been in the town for a short time. That is, the landmarks, which originally function as places on a route, become positioned in a space that can be crossed by many routes, and so become a major part of the organisational framework for the map of the town.

Asking people to draw sketch maps can lead to problems and may be influenced by drawing skill (Bryant, 1984), and has been criticised as a method of finding out about environmental knowledge. However, Blades (1990) has shown that when subjects are asked to draw the same route twice, 1 week apart, there is a high correlation between the detail and accuracy of their maps. The maps vary depending on how familiar the subjects are with the route, but they do give reliable information about the subject's route knowledge. Rovine and Weisman (1989) found that the ability to go from one place to another after one guided trip round a new town was very strongly related to sketch map accuracy.

Studies of whether routes are the key developmental units within a representation have tended not to use a map-drawing approach. Some have used artificial presentation of a route in order to investigate the way in which subjects create a coherent unit. Jenkins, Wald and Pittenger (1978) showed subjects slides that simulated a walk across an unfamiliar campus. Afterwards, the subjects were shown another set of slides and asked to judge whether they had occurred in the original sequence or not.

It was found that subjects could recognise slides which they had seen and could reject slides which did not belong to the route at all. However, they tended to recognise slides which did in fact belong to the route, but which they had not actually been shown in the first series. Jenkins et al. suggest that subjects are developing a general representation of the route itself, which is not a memory of the individual slides. There are some similarities between this and work on comprehension of sentences, discussed in more detail in Chapter 9. Bransford and Franks (1971), for example, found that subjects recognised sentences that fitted with the meaning of a series of sentences they had read previously, even though this meant they sometimes "recognised" sentences they hadn't actually seen.

However, having to actively navigate a route and being passively transported through it, may lead to different kinds of environmental learning. Gale, Golledge, Pellegrino and Doherty (1990) took a group of 9- to 12-year-olds and walked through an unfamiliar town with half of them and showed the other half a video of such a walk. After repeated trials in which the walking group had to choose which way to go and the video group simply watched, both groups were able to recognise slides of road junctions as being from the route, but, as might be expected, the video group was quite poor at actually navigating the route.

When we travel in a new environment we do not use only one route, and it is likely that some routes will intersect so that one landmark could be on two routes. If routes are the basic unit of representation, then that landmark will exist separately in two schemas and the relationship between the two routes will not be developed until after the routes themselves are established. It is, of course, also possible that the developing schemas are based on a more complex unit that connects the routes from the beginning. Moar and Carleton (1982) investigated this using the presentation of slides of two different but intersecting routes through an unfamiliar area. Subjects later judged distances and directions between pairs of places within routes and between routes, and there were no differences in accuracy between these judgements, which suggest that the routes were not being maintained separately. However, with a few presentations of the routes, subjects made more errors when they judged the distance and direction between two slides which were presented in the direction opposite to that of travel along the route. That is, they knew how far it was from A to B, but they didn't also know how far it was from B to A. The early presentations of a route seem to be chained together in one direction and do not yet have map-like reversibility. Even if routes are not basic separate elements of a map, they are different from maps in important respects.

To investigate the role of experience in the development of cognitive maps, we can ask people to use their knowledge in a laboratory situation, by drawing maps for example, or we can try to present new artificial routes to them in order to control their activity within the areas they are learning about. We can also take people out into the environment and ask them to do things that will expose their knowledge. Kirasic, Allen and Siegel (1984) asked university students to make judgements about the direction and distance to well-known places from an experimental room. Students who were in their first year on campus were less accurate in their judgement when the room had no windows, but there was no difference between them and second- and third-year students when they had extra cues available to them through a window. This does not mean that there is no functional difference between the knowledge of a first-year student and that of second- and third-year students, but rather that the "realistic" situation provides enough cues to enable them to carry out this particular task. The experienced students had a more stable cognitive map, in that the relations between the distances and directions they gave were more accurate, and they can also be said to be more flexible in that they could use the information in a wider range of situations. "Realistic" tests of spatial knowledge may not allow such differences to appear.

MAPS, PICTURES AND IMAGES

We can set out to learn the spatial relationships between places printed on a piece of paper, we can listen to information about the relationship between places, and we can walk or drive around and develop spatial knowledge by navigation. Although we do not use the information derived from printed maps in the same way as we use that from navigation, it is easy to think that we must have something corresponding to a physical map in our minds. That is, we can imagine that using spatial knowledge means finding the current mental map, putting it on a mental "map table" and then "looking" at it. When you are asked "How many windows are there in the front of your house?", you can answer the question even though you may never have counted the windows. You may feel that you imagine the front of the house and then count the windows, so you feel you are using a mental picture which you "look at" in your mind.

This commonsense description of the mind's eye is one account of how we cognitively represent spatial knowledge. It can be attacked because it suggests that we have an extremely large number of stored mental pictures which are somehow unprocessed and so cannot be organised in memory. How, then, do we know how to find the relevant one? In addition, the evidence about error in mental pictures or maps suggests that when we forget information it is an organised feature or group of features that disappears, not a random fragment as would happen if you tore a piece off a paper map. So it is unlikely that we simply "photograph" information about the environment and then bring it out to make decisions about later.

But if we don't have a large store of mental pictures, which include maps, how do we represent spatial knowledge?

The answers to this question are very complicated, and are usually discussed in the context of mental images, rather than mental maps. However, they are just as relevant here. There are two major alternatives. The first suggests that mental images are like percepts, not pictures; that is, they are interpreted knowledge, not undigested snapshots. Therefore, the information is coherent and organised in memory because it is the result of a great deal of processing. This view, put forward by Kosslyn and Pomerantz (1979), also suggests that images, including spatial representations of the world, are analogous to the things they represent. Some aspects of survey maps maintain distance and direction between represented places which are like the distances and directions found in the world; that is, we can call them analogue representations. On the other hand, the word *church* retains nothing about the actual nature of a church, just as the word *left* only gives a spatial instruction if you speak English. Our general knowledge may be a mixture of analogue and non-analogue codes, but according to this view of images, spatial knowledge is analogue.

The opposing view, argued by Pylyshyn (1973; 1981), is that all knowledge is represented in the same way. The end-product of all perceptual processing, whether reading the words on a map or learning the spatial relations, is a non-specific, abstract representation. It is rather hard to understand what this is if we try to think of it as being non-verbal and non-visual, but it can be thought of as the underlying meaning of a scene or map. Images or pictures stand in place of an aspect of the world. The abstract representations (called "propositions") tell us what things are and how they are related (see Fig.11.2). Propositional models of how space is represented suggest that what is important is not the experience of images of stored spatial knowledge, but rather what happens when we use that knowledge.

Kosslyn (1980; 1981) has put forward a theory of imagery and spatial knowledge which allows for both propositional and analogue information to be stored in memory. He argues that the knowledge we have in long-term memory is used to generate a surface representation which is active while we carry out a task. It is this active representation that gives us the experience of having things in "the mind's eye", but it is the underlying long-term knowledge that is developed with experience. It is not clear which of these two components is actually the cognitive map. Obviously, if we use the map analogy too strictly, we can have difficulty with the idea that the permanently stored knowledge is different from the information we use to solve the problem, because a paper map has both roles. It is probably most useful to think of the long-term knowledge as the overall map of the environment, with the active representation containing the information necessary to solve particular problems.

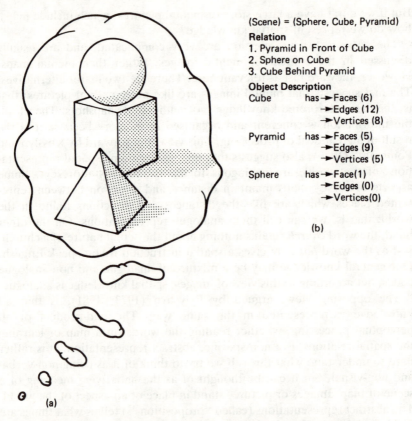

(Scene) = (Sphere, Cube, Pyramid)

Relation
1. Pyramid in Front of Cube
2. Sphere on Cube
3. Cube Behind Pyramid

Object Description

Cube   has → Faces (6)
                    → Edges (12)
                    → Vertices (8)

Pyramid   has → Faces (5)
                    → Edges (9)
                    → Vertices (5)

Sphere   has → Face(1)
                    → Edges (0)
                    → Vertices(0)

(b)

(a)

FIG. 11.2 (a) A simple pictorial representation. In some models, this surface image is constructed from an underlying abstract representation (e.g. Kosslyn & Schwartz, 1981). (b) An abstract description (grossly oversimplified). Reproduced with permission from Morris and Hampson (1983).

In Kosslyn's account, the long-term storage of spatial information could be propositional or analogue. When the information is to be retrieved, searches could be made in both forms, but if the propositional system does not provide the answer, then the analogue system will. So, for example, when you are asked "How many windows are there in the front of your house?", you could remember that the answer is "five" because you have counted them before, or you could create a spatial representation from the knowledge you have of your house and count the windows.

Kosslyn and Schwartz (1981) have investigated the active and long-term components of spatial knowledge in two ways. One of these considers the data or information which is in a representation and the other considers the structures that hold the representation. For the active representation of spatial information, Kosslyn and Schwartz propose that the "visual" type space in which images are held while being used is limited in both size and shape. If you are asked to imagine an object and then mentally walk towards it, it seems to get larger and eventually overflows so that bits disappear. It is not possible to be very close and still have all the information available in the image space. In addition, the resolution — or the amount of detail in an image — is greatest at the centre and least at the edges (Finke & Kosslyn, 1980). If you are using environmental spatial information to walk through a route in your head, you will not be able to image all the surrounding areas in equal detail, even though you have such detail stored in your long-term memory for the area.

The content and format of the active spatial representation seem most relevant to issues involving spatial knowledge. If the representations are an analogue of the object in some way (like a drawing of a duck on a wax tablet) rather than a list of propositions (a list of a duck's visual characteristics), then answering questions about spatial knowledge should be affected by factors such as size and distance in the image, and this does appear to be the case (Kosslyn, 1973). Indeed, the literature on imagery suggests that images may be quite like pictures in that they have size (Kosslyn, 1976), shape (Shepard & Chipman, 1970) and colour (Finke & Schmidt, 1977), as well as distance.

Further evidence about the nature of the format of the active spatial representation comes from experiments on "mental rotation". In these studies, subjects are asked to judge whether two two-dimensional pictures of three-dimensional objects are actually pictures of the same object which has been rotated to a new position, or whether one is different from the other (see Fig. 11.3). To do the task, subjects have to change the orientation of one picture and then match the two (Metzler & Shepard, 1974). The time to make the judgement was longer if the object had to be turned further, which implies that the object was mentally rotated and that greater rotation took a longer time, just as it would if a real object was rotated. There have been criticisms of the conclusions of this study because the subjects could be rearranging only a small part of the image, not rotating all of it, or they could have arrived at the answer by a method that did not involve an image, but be mimicking what they know about the time it takes to turn real objects (Anderson, 1978).

One interesting question which theories of shape perception in images has posed concerns whether images can be ambiguous, just like pictures can be. The duck–rabbit drawing in Fig. 11.4 is just such an ambiguous figure, and Chambers and Reisberg (1985) found that once subjects had perceived one version they could not find the other interpretation in their remembered image, suggesting that constructing an image meant interpreting it as something, not just "looking" at it. However, there is evidence that new interpretations of an image are possible, as Finke, Pinker and Farah (1989) showed when they asked subjects to imagine one element,

Rotate in picture plane for "SAME"

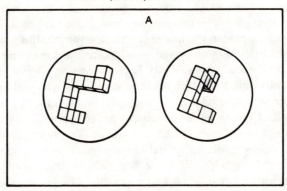

All rotations lead to "DIFFERENT"

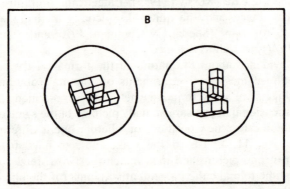

FIG. 11.3 Two-dimensional drawings of three-dimensional stimuli used in a mental rotation task. Subjects have to decide whether the two drawings are of the same object or different objects. Based on Metzler and Shepard (1974).

do something to it, add another element and say what they had created. So, for example, if you imagine a "D", then imagine its shape rotated anti-clockwise 90°, then add a "J" to the middle of the straight line on the "D", what do you get? Finke et al.'s subjects often thought that the result was like an open umbrella, suggesting that new information could be discovered from images. Following this, both Peterson, Kihlstrom, Rose and Glisky (1992) and Chambers and Reisberg (1992) have also found that reversals can occur in mental images of the duck–rabbit figure, although subjects do need to have a large number of hints before they can do this.

FIG. 11.4 The duck–rabbit figure.
People who see a rabbit on first
presentation have difficulty seeing a
duck, and vice versa.

Is Imagery Like Perception?

Imagine that you are standing in a square which you know well, with your back to a building in the middle of one side of the square. Can you name or describe the buildings which go round the square starting on your right? Now imagine you are standing on the opposite side of the square. Can you do the same thing, starting on the left? You should find that you name the same buildings in the reverse order — that is, that you can take up different positions in your environmental image, just as you can in the world. Bisiach and Luzzatti (1979) gave this task to patients who had suffered damage to the right parietal lobe of the brain, and who showed the pattern of behaviour known as "visual neglect" — that is, they paid no attention to things in the left half of their visual field, even though there was no damage to the visual system itself. These patients described the square they were asked to imagine themselves in, but they left out the left side. When asked to imagine themselves at the other end of the square and repeat the task, they again left out the left side. But this time the buildings they left out were the very ones they had reported the first time. The patients seemed to be neglecting the left side of the image just as they neglected the left side of real space. Could this mean that using images and using perceptual input is really very similar?

One of the difficulties with the claim that imagery involves perceptual systems is that some imagery effects can be altered by what experimenters think is going to happen (Intons-Peterson & White, 1981). A second and perhaps more interesting problem is that congenitally blind subjects can show effects which are very similar to those shown by sighted people in tests involving rotating, inspecting and scanning images. Kosslyn (1975) asked subjects to imagine a medium-sized object next to an elephant (so the object was relatively small) and to imagine the same object next to a fly (so that the object was relatively large). He found that subjects took longer to inspect the parts of small-scale images than of large-scale images, presumably because the differences were easier to "see" on the large-scale ones. However, Kerr (1983) asked blind subjects to imagine objects next to a car or a paper clip and found that they, too, took longer to find details on a small-scale object.

One way of approaching the question of whether images use the perceptual system has been suggested by Farah (1988). She argues that patients like those reported by Bisiach and Luzzatti (1979) cannot have been affected by what the experimenter wanted, or even by what they themselves expected, because they did not acknowledge that they had a problem with the left side of space, even in the real world. In addition, there is evidence from neuropsychology that visual areas of the brain are involved in imagery. Cerebral blood flow in visual areas of the cortex increases when subjects answer colour questions, but not when they answer semantic ones (Goldenberg et al., 1987), and patients who become colour-blind following brain damage also lose colour in images (Humphreys & Riddoch, 1990). A patient who was blind in the left visual field following removal of the right occipital lobe of the cortex (the visual area of the brain), also had a reduction in the size of her visual image, but only in the horizontal direction, not vertically (Farah, Soso, & Dashieff, 1992), although she had no difficulty in reporting both sides of images. Farah (1988) argues that imagery is not visual in the sense of using information acquired through vision, but rather that it is visual in the sense that it uses some of the same neural structures for representation which vision uses. It is the way in which these representation structures in the brain work which constrains what happens when subjects use images.

Among the patients described above, some have deficits which are purely visual, like colour, whereas others have deficits which are spatial, although the initial sensory information involved in acquiring the spatial information is probably visual, and these are reflected in different locations for their brain lesions. Problems involving colour and form tend to have occipital involvement, while those involving localisation tend to have parietal involvement (Stein, 1991). If we think about knowledge of large-scale space, it is clear that much of our knowledge is spatial, rather than purely visual. Farah et al. (1988) have reported a patient who had difficulties on imagery tasks involving colour, shape and judging the sizes of similar objects, but who performed normally on imagery tasks involving mental rotation, mental scanning and spatial locations. Knowing about form and colour may involve purely visual information, but knowing about space, while dependent on visual information for sighted subjects, may not require visual input. Blind subjects, whose spatial knowledge is acquired by touch, sound and the consequences of their own motion (and so cannot be tested about the size of animals' body parts for anything other than domestic animals) may nevertheless use spatial knowledge in the same way as the sighted.

Imagining Three Dimensions

Much of the literature on imagery assumes that images are a bit like two-dimensional pictures. If we consider real-life space, however, and ask about how we might have images or models of three dimensions, it all becomes a bit more complex. A three-dimensional image which you can rotate in front of you is still thought of as something seen from outside and imagined from outside. But the three-dimensional environment is all around. Franklin and Tversky (1990) wondered what happened when people read descriptions of three-dimensional scenes. Did they have a position within them? Did they orient themselves in one particular way? Here is an example of the kind of material they used, with some of the detail omitted for simplicity:

> You are at the opera. At the moment you are standing next to the railing of a wide elegant balcony overlooking the first floor. Directly behind you, at your eye level, is an ornate lamp which is attached to the balcony wall. Straight ahead of you, mounted on a nearby wall beyond the balcony, you see a large bronze plaque dedicated to the architect who designed the theatre. Sitting on a shelf directly to your right is a beautiful bouquet of flowers. Looking up, you see that a large loudspeaker is mounted to the theatre's ceiling directly above you. Leaning over the balcony's railing you see that a marble sculpture stands on the floor directly below you . . ."
> (Franklin & Tversky, 1990, p. 65)

Having read this passage and tried to remember what was where, you may be able to think of yourself in a three-dimensional space, but would you know where every object was equally well? Franklin and Tversky found that subjects were fastest to locate objects above or below, then slower for objects in front, followed by those to the back, with left and right slowest of all. This suggests that not all mental directions are the same and that subjects don't mentally rotate from a front facing position. Subjects did report that they felt they were mentally turning when doing the task, but even when Franklin and Tversky instructed them to mentally rotate before responding, they still responded fastest for up and down, next fast for front, slower for back, and slowest for right and left. Therefore, even when subjects were trying to mentally turn, they still took less time for back judgement (which would require longer turns) than for left and right.

Franklin and Tversky (1990) argued that mental coordinates are fastest for up and down because that is a very salient axis in the world. It is specified by gravity, which produces real asymmetries between up and down. Right and left do not have such asymmetries and so decisions about them are harder. So what happens if people do the imaging themselves in a scene, but imagine themselves lying down? (Lying down on the opera balcony may not seem any more odd to most subjects than going to the opera at all.) In general, the task becomes harder to do, but overall subjects become better at deciding what is to their front or back, next for head/feet and still slowest for right/left. In both upright and lying down positions, a decision about what is to the left and right is slowest to make.

Franklin and Tversky argue that when we are moving through the real world, the direction of our head is clearly different from that of our feet because gravity provides a framework for body space, what we have in front can be seen and touched, what is behind us cannot be seen and cannot easily be touched. However, right and left is bilaterally symmetrical, and there is no obvious way to decide which is which. Their data suggest that mental models of space around us are organised in just the same way and they argue that the analogue, continuous aspects of imagery which are related to perception, simply do not predict these data. Rather, it is the conception of space, not the perception of it, which produces the finding that different spatial locations are differentially accessible in a mental model of an environment.

Another way to think of the conception of space as Franklin and Tversky present it, is to think of the spatial world in which we act as being different in some ways from the perceptual information we have about objects. Kosslyn (1991), in a revision of his earlier accounts of how imagery is related to perception, considers the distinction between knowing where and knowing what, which we introduced in Chapter 4. This distinction is based on two different cortical systems for dealing with visual input (Ungerleider & Mishkin, 1982). Kosslyn suggests that images dealing with spatial relations involving knowledge from the "where" system, also include information for action just as visual knowledge does. In the situation used by Franklin and Tversky, the images include information for action, which is based on spatial knowledge within a three-dimensional world.

ARE COGNITIVE MAPS LIKE SURVEY MAPS?

When we draw maps of the world, we can choose to emphasise some aspects of the surface and ignore others. For example, in the London Underground map, stations are often marked in straight lines and equidistant (see Fig. 11.5). However, if you take the High Barnet branch of the Northern Line from Camden Town, you do not actually travel straight north, and Kentish Town and Tufnell Park are actually closer together than Archway and Highgate, although the distances are shown to be the same. Of course, the traveller needs to know how many stops there are to travel rather than the absolute distance, and the map would be very hard to follow if all the lines wriggled about as they actually do underground. This kind of map is called a "network map" and is very useful when specific information is needed. In a "survey map", on the other hand, the distance and direction between two points are accurate — a distance which is twice a particular distance on the map is also twice that distance on the ground, for example. Using our real maps as analogies again, we can ask whether

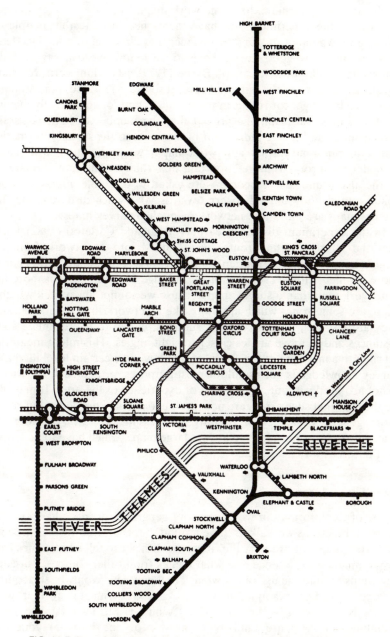

FIG. 11.5 Part of the map of the London Underground. The Northern Line is in solid black. This is a network map in which distances and directions are not an accurate reflection of the actual spatial arrangement of the underground lines.

the geometry of our mental representation is the same as that of the world itself, or more schematic, like a network map.

Many of the experiments we have mentioned indicate that people do become very good at judging the distance and direction of one place from another, but how good do we have to be before we can say that the knowledge is like a survey map? Byrne (1979) asked long-term residents of a town to estimate the length of several routes. He found that estimates tended to be longer for routes in town centres and for routes with changes of direction. As a result, he argued that the number of landmarks and turns contributed to the judgement of distance, so the stored information was similar in some ways to a network map in which the number of places, or nodes, on a route is more important than their overall spatial relations. Byrne also found that if people were asked to draw the angles at which roads joined, they tended to err towards 90°, which also suggests that mental maps are more like network maps than survey maps.

In the experiment discussed earlier, Moar and Carleton (1982) found that the interconnecting routes were linked into a network from the beginning. With more experience the network is expanded and becomes more detailed. However, it is difficult to judge whether a map is more like a network map than a survey map because we cannot always tell whether there are some zones which are more like a network than others, because they are less well known. Byrne's subjects tended to overestimate some distances and to move angles closer to right angles. This might mean that all cognitive maps are of this form, or that beyond a certain level increased survey knowledge is not useful for most purposes, or that such knowledge is not acquired without a great deal of experience of the area. It may also be the case that such errors are not specific to spatial knowledge but reflect more general principles of cognitive processing. We will consider this question after we have looked at very large maps, which have to be known in a different way.

Very Large Maps

Some of the information we have about geographical space has not been learned directly as we walk or drive around, but is derived from instruction and from maps. In ordinary life, it can be difficult to tell what comes from environmental experience and what comes from other sources, but some questions require the use of knowledge that could have only been acquired in one way. For example, if you are asked "Which is further west, Reno, Nevada or Los Angeles?" or "Which is further west, Bristol or Edinburgh?", you are unlikely to answer on the basis of your own experience of the land surface of the USA or the UK, but you can answer. If you are becoming suspicious of the kinds of questions asked in psychology books, you would be right to be so in this case. Many people will answer that Los Angeles is further west than Reno, or that Bristol is further west than Edinburgh. Both answers are wrong. In Britain, people seem to answer the question by using the information that Edinburgh is near the east coast of Scotland and that Bristol is near the west coast of England; they reckon that Scotland is due north of England, so Edinburgh is further east than Bristol. In the USA, people tend to reason that California is further west than Nevada, Los Angeles is in California, while Reno is in Nevada, so Los Angeles is further west than Reno (Stevens & Coupe, 1978).

When we try to remember the positions of places we use heuristics or strategies which make the task easier (Tversky, 1981). For example, up and down on a land area are taken to correspond to north and south, while right and left of the area may be aligned to be east and west. That is, in the absence of any other reference points that allow us to judge the alignment of a land mass such as Great Britain, we tend to square it up with the reference frame of the map itself by rotating its axis so that it matches the north–south line. This explains why Bristol is thought to be west of Edinburgh (Moar, 1979). A second general heuristic for solving geographical problems is to use a part–whole strategy within a hierarchical framework of countries, states and cities, as Stevens and Coupe (1978) found with California and Nevada. It is not necessary to know the relationships between every place in Nevada and every place in California when the single piece of information that California is west of Nevada allows you to be right most of the time. A similar strategy is used within countries, so the Canadian and US border is straightened and all points in Canada are thought to be to the north of all points in the USA.

Knowledge about the relative positions of Reno and Los Angeles or Bristol and Edinburgh, is derived from general information about the relationships between states or east and west coastlines. It does not involve fine-grain knowledge of the spatial relations between the two places, but functions as category knowledge with a hierarchical structure. Spatial relations may preserve some of the characteristics of the environment, like distances or angles, but may also generally involve category knowledge as well, and so may be understandable in some of the same ways as other sorts of knowledge.

If we think about episodes or events which we have experienced, we are able to report some information about what happened, where it happened and when it happened. Some of these may be exact, some may be approximations and reconstructions, as we have seen in previous chapters. Tversky (1981) argued that errors such as realignment and straightening of edges which occur when people make judgements about large areas, are not errors specific to mental maps. She considers that these errors are perceptual errors that occur in many situations when input is regularised and simplified to make it easier to deal with, and that maps may be stored in memory in an inaccurate form. However, the general heuristics are also used in inference when there are gaps in knowledge, and error can arise from such inferences. The spatial knowledge of countries, which is derived from instruction and from actual maps, can be organised hierarchically, can be regularised to provide a stable frame of reference, or can contain genuine spatial information. However, this knowledge may not be the same kind of knowledge structure as that developed for more local surroundings derived from experience of moving around.

Huttenlocher, Hedges and Duncan (1991) took the idea that these errors are not specific to maps and moved from errors based on perception to errors based on the structure of concepts. They suggested that each sort of knowledge of an event may be affected by general category values (tomatoes tend to be red and roofs tend to be on top of buildings), as well as by specific fine-grained information, which may or may not be correct (the shade of the tomato, the height of the roof). If people are asked to say where things are, they may make errors, and these can be attributed to biases, such as the bias to make angles into right angles as in Byrne (1979), or to work in a hierarchical structure as in Stevens and Coupe (1978), or the bias towards putting things close to landmarks, which was reported by Nelson and Chaiklin (1980). Huttenlocher et al. looked at the errors people made in their reports of where things were by simply asking them to look at a dot in a circle and then to remember where it was, and to put it in on a blank circle. They found that their subjects' responses indicated that they tended to divide a circle up into four quadrants, and misplaced dots towards the centres of those quadrants, so they were tending to use average angles and distances over the quadrants, rather than actual ones. This tendency to use a prototypic value (see Chapter 4 for more detail on prototypes) was greater if there was an interfering task between presentation and recall of the dot, indicating that when the actual spatial location was less well known, there was a larger contribution from the prototype. Bias in spatial judgements does not mean that people have a built-in tendency to get things wrong. Rather, the errors people make when they straighten edges, make junctions more like right angles, put things closer to landmarks, and remember average rather than specific positions, are indications of the way in which knowledge of spatial information is dealt with. Like the formation of concepts, the regularising of spatial information reduces the need to maintain all the features of an environment which might possibly be relevant and allows approximate solutions to problems for which precise location is unnecessary.

USING REAL MAPS AND COGNITIVE MAPS

When people make judgements about distances within their mental maps, they may be doing something quite similar to the way in which they judge actual distances. Baum and Jonides (1979) investigated this by asking students to estimate the distance between familiar locations on their university campus — from the library to the student union building, for example. However, the interesting part of the experiment is not the accuracy with which they made the judgements, but the time it took to make them. Baum and Jonides found that it took students longer to answer the question when the actual distance was longer; in fact, they found that the time taken to answer the question was linearly related to the distance between places.

Why does it take longer to estimate the length of a longer route? Baum and Jonides suggested that subjects used a mental measuring tape and that it took longer to "unroll the tape" for longer distances, just as it would if the measurement were being carried out in the real world instead of in the head, just as it takes longer to scan a larger mental image. But the remembered length of a route is affected by more than just its actual length. There is evidence that when adults and children are asked to judge the distance between two objects, they tend to report that the distance is longer when a barrier is put between the objects (Kosslyn, Pick, & Fariello, 1974) — that is, the way people judge a real distance can be affected by items within that distance. Thorndyke (1981) argued that using cognitive maps is similar to using actual ones, and that errors in distance judgement and the effects of distance and number of places might be based on the use of the representation, rather than the representation itself. He asked subjects to learn fictitious maps of roads linking several towns and cities and then asked them to estimate distances, by road, between pairs of cities. Both the distance between the two targets and the number of intervening places were varied. The results showed that distance estimates increased both with the number of intervening places and the actual distance on the map. Thorndyke thought that these errors were not part of the memorised map but occurred at retrieval when distance judgements were made, so he asked another group of subjects to judge the distances between pairs of cities while looking at actual maps, without memorising them. He found that yet again both the actual distance and the number of places between two points affected the distance judgements, although these effects were smaller than those in the memory condition. Estimating distances as being longer because there are more places between the two points is not necessarily based on errors in the map or representation itself, but in the way it is used.

If visual imagery and visual perception share underlying mechanisms, then imagining carrying an object may include many kinds of imagery, just as actually carrying an object gives information about weight, colour, size, how it feels when you lift it, and so on. Intons-Peterson and Roskos-Ewoldsen (1989) asked subjects to imagine themselves carrying a balloon, a ball (weighing 3 lb) and a cannonball (weighing 30 lb), each of 3 in diameter, around a campus which they had learned about on a schematic map. They found that the length of time subjects took to make each trip depended on the distance they had to imagine travelling (implying that they did move through an image), that subjects took most time when they carried a cannonball, and that the trips took longer if the subjects imagined the map than they did if they looked at it, unless pictures of the landmarks were put on the real map. However, the imagined map and the real map showed different relationships between the cannonball, the ball and the balloon. For the real map, the cannonball had quite a large effect on time, but the ball and balloon did not differ from each other, or from just walking without carrying anything, although they did differ from each other for the imagined map. Intons-Peterson and Roskos-Ewoldsen suggested that using a real schematic map and an imagined map was not the same. When using the imagined map extra detail about the landmarks seemed to be available, which made trips longer overall, and which was not accessed when an ordinary schematic map was used. In addition, with an imagined map the small weight difference between a ball and a balloon did make a difference, while with the real map it did not, again suggesting that real and imagined maps do not have the same effects.

When we are learning a new environment, it is not easy to disentangle the contribution of navigation and map learning. Thorndyke and Hayes-Roth (1982) took a group of people who worked in a complex building who had never seen a map of it, and compared them with people who had no experience of walking about in the building but had seen a map of it. They found that map-learning subjects were better at estimating straight-line distances than route distances, whereas those who had walked around were better at route estimation. With greater experience of using the building, straight-line distance judgements became as accurate as those made by people who learned maps, and the route estimates improved even more. Walking around in an environment provides an accurate representation of the segments of routes, which can be added together to give an overall distance, but it also leads to a map-like representation of straight-line distances.

Subjects who had learned a map in this study were good at putting locations on paper in relation to other locations, but poorer at judging the direction of one place from another, whereas subjects who had experience of walking around judged direction more accurately than location. This suggests that making a judgement of the direction of one place from another required map-learning subjects to take a different perspective than the one they had used previously. For subjects with experience of the building, judging direction is more like seeing along a straight line of sight through transparent buildings than looking down on a map from above. This contrasts with the study of Keenan and Moore (1979), in which subjects were told to image two objects with one concealed within the other (e.g. a harp is inside the torch held up by the Statue of Liberty), or to image scenes in which both objects were visible (a harp is sitting on top of the torch of the Statue of Liberty). When one object was imaged inside the other, fewer details of the scenes were reported, suggesting that when the scenes were imaged, the harp was not present when it was in the torch and so was not recalled later. The images did not seem to contain all the pieces, because some covered others and were not transparent. That is, the image was like a real scene in which some objects were hidden. Active knowledge of an environment produces a representation which is unlike a visual scene viewed from one position. Instructions to visualise an unknown scene, on the other hand, produces imagery which is unlike that found with real places.

The ability to take a perspective through buildings was also found by Sholl (1987), who asked student subjects to imagine standing in one place in a well-known campus location and then to point in the direction of well-known buildings. She found that they were equally fast to respond to buildings which could actually be seen from that location and to buildings which could not, although places in front were responded to more quickly than places behind. Even when carrying out an imagery task, people who know an area well know the direction of buildings which they cannot have in a visual image. The "cognitive map" involves knowledge which is within, rather than above, the world which is represented.

One of the differences between maps and the environment in which we move is that memory for the information learned from maps seems to be linked to the orientation at which it was learned. On the other hand, if you get your information about a layout from walking through it, you tend to have more flexibility and are not limited to one orientation. Presson, Delange and Hazelrigg (1989) looked at the difference between learning a layout as if it were a map and learning a layout as if it were a path through the environment. They made displays on the floor and told half the subjects that the display was a map, and half that it was a path, and they showed another group of subjects a small-scale map of the array. The displays had four segments, and two open ends, and examples are shown in Fig. 11.6. Subjects looked at the layout on the floor from one particular orientation, were blindfolded and led in a meandering path to one end of the layout, told which end they were on and which direction they were facing, and then they were asked to point to other positions. For both map and path instructions, subjects who saw the layout on the floor were not influenced by the orientation in which they had originally seen the array — they could point equally well whether they were facing the same way as they were when they studied the array, or facing the opposite way. For the small map, however, very good performance was found if the orientation in study and test were the same, but there was poor performance if they were different.

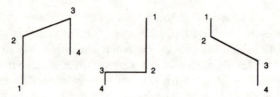

FIG. 11.6 Examples of the maps and paths used by Presson et al. (1989). See text for further details.

Presson et al. went on to investigate just when a small version would be treated in an orientation-specific way, and when it would be treated without a specific orientation. When 2 ft arrays were used, they were treated as if from the same orientation all the time; 12 ft arrays showed no orientation effect, and 8ft arrays were in the middle. They suggested that one form of spatial representation was picture-like, and seen from one direction, while another form of spatial information is related to the maintenance of the stable perceptual world through which we move. Think about how you use a map. You tend to hold it in one way and if you are travelling along, you may have to rotate your map in order to try to find the correct direction to go, because the task of doing that rotation in the head is very difficult. If you are standing in the kitchen of your home, it probably doesn't matter whether you face the door or the cooker, you can point to other locations with considerable accuracy. Recalling this kind of information is more flexible than map knowledge, and the information is specified in terms of the environment, and relations within it, rather than in terms of something to be seen from the outside. Thus, we should not expect all kinds of spatial representation to have the same effects, and we should be careful when we generalise from knowledge of a map to knowledge of the environment in which we move.

HOW IS SPATIAL MEMORY ORGANISED?

When we walk around in the world, we pass buildings and other objects and we can relate them together in space and in time. We may also find that buildings with similar uses tend to occur together — as in the banking areas of some cities, for example, or groups of large stores in a shopping area. Hirtle and Mascolo (1986) found that when subjects learned maps with place names on them, they tended to move a recreational building which was close to a city building cluster further away, suggesting that this kind of category knowledge did affect memory for where objects were.

Given that buildings and other environmental objects do consistently occur together in space, do we represent them as related on that basis? So, for example, if we think of the church on Wested Street, will we find it easy to recognise the post office which is next to it? When we considered semantic relations in earlier chapters, we showed that presenting one word makes recognition of a related word faster; for example, we can recognise *fork* more quickly if we have just recognised *knife* (Meyer & Schvaneveldt, 1971). This is known as semantic priming, and semantic relatedness determines the amount of increase in the speed and accuracy of recognition of the second item. Semantic priming does not just apply to words. Guenther, Klatzky and Putnam (1980) have shown that recognising a picture of a fork makes it easier to recognise a picture of a spoon, and that a picture of a fork also primes recognition of the word *spoon*. These priming relations have been important in helping us understand the structure of semantic memory. Can we find a similar indication of the structure of spatial memory? Is knowledge of space stored in a structure that resembles space itself, so that accessing one piece of spatial information makes it easier to access other pieces of spatial information which are close to it in the real world?

McNamara, Ratcliff and McKoon (1984) gave subjects a simple map to learn and then tested their recognition for place names on the map. They found that recognition was faster when a town name came after the name of a nearby town on the same road. This spatial priming effect suggested that memory for maps was indeed organised spatially. However, Clayton and Chattin (1989) found that spatial priming did not occur when the names of places which the subjects had learned before the experiment were used (like parts of a university campus). Spatial priming only happened if subjects had to make a judgement about where the places actually were. Recognising the name of one place did not automatically make it faster to recognise the names of places which were closer to it, which suggests that recognition does not use spatial information. Clayton and Habibi (1991) took this a little bit further and argued that when people look at a map with lots of names on it, and they study the map a section at a time, then objects close together in space will be studied together in time, and spatial priming, which reveals these groupings (McNamara, Hardy & Hirtle, 1989), might be based on the temporal groupings of the way they were studied. In a real environment, like a campus, there may also be links between places which are both spatial and temporal, but recognition of the names of buildings has occurred in many other contexts too, so does not lead to priming effects.

Clayton and Habibi (1991) presented displays on a computer screen in which dots were paired with town names, but only one was ever presented at a time. This meant that items could be presented close together in time (one after another), close together in space, or both. The results did show spatial priming, but only when items were presented close together in *both* space and time. If items were spatially close but far apart in time, priming did not occur. Therefore, Clayton and Habibi concluded that for map learning tasks, associations based on temporal links are at least as important in constructing spatial representations as spatial links are, and perhaps even more so.

McNamara, Halpin and Hardy (1992) also found that priming occurred only when items were neighbours in space and time, but that the time to make judgements of the distance between items was affected by time of presentation if the items were close together, but not when they were far apart. This suggests that the relationship between spatial priming and distance judgements reflects different aspects of the way in which spatial knowledge is represented. Some elements of spatial judgements are hierarchical and propositional (California is west of Nevada), others could involve distance in analogical form (how far apart places are on a map), while others may involve time and frequency with which places have been linked together. Spatial knowledge is represented in very complex ways, not just in terms of spatial relations like those in the world.

SUMMARY

In this chapter, we have taken questions about our mental representations of the layout of the world we live in and used them to address issues which concern spatial knowledge in general. We began with an account of how knowledge of an area is developed and then introduced the topic of mental images. Images involve spatial information as well as information based on the purely perceptual characteristics of objects in the world such as form, colour and weight. Neuropsychological evidence also indicates that spatial knowledge and purely visual information can be separated, although visual imagery may use neural representations which are also used for visual perception. In spatial imagery, there is a contribution from preparation for action, which means that all locations in imagined space are not equally available. Relating this spatial knowledge to map-based knowledge is complex, and our use of maps and our spatial representations have some similarities and some important differences. One difference is that map knowledge may be orientation-specific, whereas three-dimensional spatial knowledge is not. If we ask about the structure of spatial knowledge and probe it with priming tasks, we reach the conclusion that it may involve propositional, categorical and analogue information as well as being affected by time and frequency of association.

The issues involved in understanding our abilities to know about and use our environment are very complex. In developing a computer model which had some characteristics of the human learner of a city environment, Gopal, Klatzky and Smith (1989) reviewed issues in the imagery debate, in the hierarchical structuring of knowledge, in the use of strategies and biases, and then placed them within a memory framework in which working memory involved both perceptual input and activated information from long-term memory, and long-term memory itself was structured as a network. All of this was necessary to produce a model which simulated the early stages of route learning. Understanding the acquisition and use of spatial knowledge is not a separate part of cognitive psychology — it involves all aspects of cognition.

We have covered a wide range of material on visual and spatial cognition in this chapter. Further reading on the environmental aspects of spatial cognition can be found in T. Garling and G. W. Evans (Eds) (1991), *Environment, cognition and action: An integrated approach*. Introductions to the imagery literature can be found in two edited volumes: R. H. Logie and M. Denis (1991), *Mental images in human cognition*; P. J. Hampson, D. F. Marks and J. T. E. Richardson (1990), *Imagery: Current developments*.

12 Investigating a Murder: Making Inferences and Solving Problems

Sherlock Holmes has examined the scene with great care. He turns to the police detectives, who admit that they have found no clues, and says:

> There has been murder done, and the murderer was a man. He was more than six feet high, was in the prime of life, had small feet for his height, wore coarse, square-toed boots and smoked a Trichinopoly cigar. He came here with his victim in a four-wheeled cab, which was drawn by a horse with three old shoes and one new one on his off fore-leg. In all probability the murderer had a florid face, and the fingernails of his right hand were remarkably long. These are only a few indications, but they may assist you. (*A Study in Scarlet*)

How did Holmes reach these conclusions? Some you can probably guess. Marks observed on the ground — perhaps in the soft surface of a driveway or depressions in a thick carpet — gave the basis for some inferences. Cigar ash or the smell in the room may have led to another. But the man's height, his "florid face", the state of his fingernails, and other details seem rather distant from what might reasonably have been observed. Unfairly perhaps, the reader of Sherlock Holmes' stories does not know all the clues that are available to the great man. In many other detective stories, the readers have shared the clues with the fictional detective, but only later are they told about how the crucial inferences are drawn.

Inferential processes have been introduced in other chapters. In Chapter 10, it was pointed out that comprehension is not merely a matter of looking up the meanings of words in some mental lexicon, but of constructing scenarios within which the sentences have some emergent and connected meaning, sometimes creating a tentative schema, referencing some familiar scripts and plans, inferring causality, making attributions, and so on. The real or fictional detective is said to work by careful observation and deduction. "Elementary, my dear Watson" said Holmes to his companion as he began to recount the links between observations and successful inferences, but most of us are just as impressed as Watson by Holmes' constructions and reconstructions of the evidence.

This chapter is about the role of inferences and their management on those occasions when we have to think a little harder, when we attempt to reason and when we attempt to solve problems. We start by considering what it means to make logical inferences. Can Holmes, or a real detective, be regarded as an expert in deduction? What is the role of logic in human reasoning? Then we turn to consider what other skills might be required to solve problems which have greater variety than those found in the study of logical reasoning. To what extent are there general skills in thinking and reasoning and to what extent do knowledge and experience play a part? To anticipate, our thinking skills depend very much upon all the processes that we have described in earlier chapters.

DEDUCTION

Categorical Reasoning

We make inferences when we move from what we already know to be the case to something which follows from it. Deductive inferences are particular kinds of inference studied by logicians and their rules have sometimes been claimed to define "laws of thought". In the light of these rules, many studies have been conducted in which people are given statements and asked to say whether something follows. For example, in the following argument, does the third statement follow from the first two statements when these are assumed to be true?

Some detectives are fictional characters	(Premise 1)
Some fictional characters are famous	(Premise 2)
Therefore some detectives are famous	(Conclusion)

This is an example of the *categorical syllogism* first studied in depth by the Greek philosopher Aristotle some 2300 years ago. The first two statements are referred to as the *premises* and the logician's concern is to determine whether or not the conclusion necessarily follows from the premises, whether it may be deduced from the premises. From this perspective, the above argument is not valid, although many of us would regard it to be so. Even though we might believe all three statements to be true and well-related to each other, it can be shown that the third statement does not necessarily follow from the premises. Indeed, no conclusion is logically necessary. It is logically possible that "No detectives are famous" or that "All detectives are famous". Remember that we are not discussing the truth of the supposed conclusion given all the things we know, but simply how it relates to the premises.

Logicians extract the *forms* of the valid arguments. In classical logic, four kinds of statement may take the part of a premise or a conclusion. Using symbols like A, B and C to represent sets of things, these are: "All As are Bs"; "Some As are Bs"; "No As are Bs"; and, "Some As are not Bs".

These may be combined, with A and B in one premise, B and C in another, and A and C in the third line, to produce the forms of all possible syllogisms, only some of which are valid.

The syllogism has been used by psychologists for some decades now in the study of human reasoning. By and large, people are not very good at detecting logically valid and invalid arguments among the forms. You may already have found yourself struggling, with the examples just given, to distinguish the logician's notion of the valid form of an argument and such things as the real-world truth of the statements, or your beliefs about them, and the general plausibility of an argument. There are other features which create difficulties for us and lead to wrong answers and long solution times. Some errors have been ascribed to the "atmosphere effect" first proposed by Woodworth and Sells (1935). This refers to the tendency of subjects to assert a particular ("some") conclusion rather than a universal ("all") conclusion when at least one premise is particular; and to include a negative ("no", "not") in the conclusion when at least one premise contains a negative. Terms like "some" and "no" are said to set the atmosphere for a style of conclusion. These tendencies, which do have some partial validity, seem to lead subjects to state some logically unjustified conclusions. Another possible source of error is the "illicit conversion" of premises. The premise "All *A*s are *B*s" could mean, but does not necessarily mean, that "All *B*s are *A*s". The premise "Some *A*s are *B*s" is even more rife with possible meanings for overlapping set memberships when one recognises that "some" for a classical logician means "at least one and possibly all".

More recently, Johnson-Laird (1983) has studied the "figural effect". To understand this, consider what conclusions might follow from the following pairs of premises:

1. Some *A*s are *B*s   2. All *B*s are *A*s
   All *B*s are *C*s   No *C*s are *B*s

The first turns out to be very easy and the second very difficult. Ignoring the all's, some's and none's — those aspects which may generate atmosphere — the *figure* of a syllogism refers to the spatial arrangement of *A*, *B* and *C* in the premises. In (1), most subjects readily favour conclusions of the form *A-C*, correctly eliminating the middle term, *B*, and making a connection between *A* and *C*. The valid conclusion in this case is "Some *A*s are *C*s". For the premises in (2), many subjects favour conclusions of the form *C-A*, drawing the invalid conclusion "Some *C*s are not *A*s" rather than the valid conclusion "Some *A*s are not *C*s". The middle term, *B*, is not easy to "eliminate" in this figure: it certainly is an awkward one.

Subjects in these studies do not use knowledge of the formal rules of the syllogism. These are quite difficult to learn and it took professional logicians some time to develop them. Johnson-Laird (1983, Ch. 5) accounts for the difficulties in the following way. The subjects must gain mental representations of the premises as acts of comprehension, and they must integrate these and examine the implications. Let us suppose that we employ some kind of mental "tokens" like D for "Detective", C for "fictional Character" and F for "Famous" to help represent the meaning of the premises "Some Ds are Cs" and "Some Cs are F". In comprehending these premises and combining them, we might sequentially construct the following:

Premise 1	Premise 2	An Integrated Model
$D = C$	$C = F$	$D = C$
$D = C$	$C = F$	$D = C = F$
$(D)\,(C)$	$(C)\,(F)$	$C = F$
		$(D)\,(C)\,(F)$

The displays represent interpretations of the premises. In Premise 1, for example, the arbitrary number of tokens joined by the "equals" signs show that at least some Ds are Cs, and the unattached tokens in brackets show that some Ds may not be Cs and some Cs may not be Ds. Premise 2 has the same form in Cs and Fs. We can envisage that as its interpretation proceeds, it rapidly attaches to Premise 1 to form the integrated model.

Now suppose that we were asked to say whether or not it follows that "some detectives are famous"; we would "read off" the answer from the integrated model and say "Yes", and we would be incorrect. Recall that the logical question is: Does the conclusion *necessarily* follow from the premises? In fact, the above premises can give rise to a number of different integrated models and to respond to the logical question we must test whether *any* model could exist which represents the premises and yet give a counter-example to the offered conclusion. The crucial counter-example is:

$$D = C$$
$$C = F$$
$$(D)\,(C)\,(F)$$

which while being consistent with both of the premises shows that there is no logical necessity for any detective to be famous.

Johnson-Laird and Bara (1982, cited in Johnson-Laird, 1983) showed that the numbers of incorrect responses produced were strongly related to the numbers of alternative models that would need to be constructed to test the necessity of any proposed conclusion. For example, the premises "No Bs are As" and "All Bs are Cs" requires three models. None of their 20 subjects found the valid conclusion "Some Cs are not As". The mental model of the first premise is likely to be generated in a form which is not well-suited to integration with the information supplied by the second premise, and the struggle to shuffle the symbols around increases the difficulty of considering all possible integrated models. We shall need to refer to these ideas again, but first let us look at the use of other logical problems in the study of reasoning.

The Case of If and Then

The little words like *if/then*, *and*, *not* and *or*, which link parts of sentences together in very different ways, can also be understood as logical connections between ideas. Many psychologists have proposed that there are separate logical rules for understanding these connectives (Braine, 1978; Rips 1988; Sperber & Wilson, 1986). Rips (1983) suggested that deductive reasoning consisted of the application of "mental reasoning rules" to the premises and conclusions of an argument, and compared the steps taken in mental reasoning to the explicit proofs found in elementary logic.

The abstract argument:

if p then q
p
therefore q

is very easy to understand, and if someone gives you the problem:

If she has an essay to write then she will study late in the library
She has an essay to write

you can probably conclude that she will study late in the library. However, if the second premise was:

She will not study late in the library

you might find it harder to conclude that she does not have an essay to write. The second argument is of the form:

if p then q
not p
therefore not q.

In terms of rules in logic, the rule to apply to get from p to q in the first example above is known as *modus ponens*, and that used to get from *not q* to *not p* is known as *modus tollens*. Modus ponens is so straightforward that most natural logic theories of reasoning include it as a rule, although they do not include modus tollens, which people often get wrong.

The understanding of how people reason with *if/then* has been extensively investigated, often using a task known as the "selection task", which was devised by Wason (1966). Two forms of the task are illustrated below. You should attempt them before reading on and record your answers.

Selection Task 1

Consider the following four cards:

| A | D | 4 | 7 |

Each card has a letter on one side and a number on the other side.
You are given the following rule about these cards:

If the card has an A on one side then there is a 4 on the other side

Your task is to say which of the cards you need to turn over (i.e. select) in order to find out whether the rule is true or false.

Selection Task 2

Consider the following four cards:

| Beer | Coke | 25 | 16 |

Each card has the name of a drink on one side and a number on the other, and each of the cards represents a person of a certain age drinking in a bar. The rule states:

If someone is drinking beer then that person must be over 21

Again, the task is to say which cards must be turned over to decide whether the rule is true or false.

You should note here that there are two meanings of the term "rule" which can become confused. One is the logical rule or rule of reasoning, which may or may not be involved when people do deductions of many kinds. The second is the specific task rule used in any version of the selection task. In the selection task, the task rule might be characterised as "If p then q", where in Task 1 p stands for "there is an A on one side" and q stands for "there is a 4 on the other side". Applications of reasoning rules might then produce answers to the problem. Over a series of experiments using university students, most subjects said that either the p and q cards (A and 4) or the p card (A) alone must be turned over to find out whether the rule is true or false (Johnson-Laird & Wason, 1977, p. 145; Evans, 1982). These responses are incorrect, or at least incomplete.

In Task 2, most subjects realised that they should turn over the *Beer* and the *16* cards (Griggs & Cox, 1982). It does not matter what age someone is who drinks coke and it does not matter what someone drinks if they are over 21, but a 16-year-old should not be drinking beer in a bar. In addition, in Britain a person must be over 18 to drink beer. So we should check the age of the person drinking beer and what the 16-year-old is drinking. It is quite unnecessary to check the other two cards. This real-world reasoning corresponds to the requirements of the logical form for which the correct answer is to turn over the *p* and not-*q* cards, and most people get it right.

If we carefully apply the Beer–Age argument to Task 1 with *A, 4, D* and *7*, we can see that the correct answer is that the *A* (*p*) and 7 (*not-q*) cards should be chosen. There is little doubt for subjects that the *A* card should be chosen: if there is not a *4* on the other side, then the rule is clearly violated. It is quite unnecessary to inspect the other side of the card bearing the *4* because the rule does not say that only cards having an *A* on one side have a *4* on the other side. It is, however, essential to inspect the other side of the *7* card because if it shows an *A*, then the rule is violated. (This inference is at the core of the selection task, if *not-q* then *not-p*, the rule in propositional logic we mentioned earlier, which is known as modus tollens.) Very few subjects want to inspect the *D* card: any number, including *4*, could be on the other side without impinging upon the rule. A small number of subjects show what has been termed "partial insight": they select cards *A, 4* and *7* (the *p, q* and *not-q* items), but they fail to eliminate the *q* card which, whatever was on the other side, could not violate the rule.

Many variants of this task have been studied in an attempt to pin down its difficulty. Johnson-Laird, Legrenzi and Legrenzi (1972) employed a British postal rule about the higher and lower values of postage stamps that are required for sending sealed and unsealed envelopes. The task rule was: "If a letter is sealed, then it has a 5d stamp on it". Unsealed envelopes were allowed to carry a 4d stamp. Subjects were to imagine that they were postal workers sorting letters and the task was to determine if the task rule had been violated. Twenty-two subjects out of 24 performed this task correctly, choosing to inspect sealed letters (*p*) and envelopes bearing 4d stamps (*not-q*), but only 7 of them solved the abstract form of the task. Later studies by Reich and Ruth (1982) and Cheng and Holyoak (1985) found that both British and American subjects did better on this task if they were old enough to remember the postal rule, i.e. if they had actual experience of the rule in the task. Given a realistic content, the problem is solved more readily so long as the task rule has been sufficiently experienced by the subjects and is not merely one clothed arbitrarily in concrete terms.

It is possible to learn something about these tasks. Berry (1983) found that a few sentences of explanation of the correct reasoning in a particular concrete but unexperienced case, followed by further experience and verbalisation of their reasoning by the subjects, was highly effective in improving performance and this improvement transferred to an abstract version of the task that most subjects had failed earlier. That is, subjects can be persuaded to adopt the strictly logical interpretation of the task even if it is not their usual approach, at least in the immediate context of the experiences and training that Berry provided. Cheng, Holyoak, Nisbett and Oliver (1986), however, showed that extensive direct training in propositional logic, including extended discussion of the modus tollens case — so critical for selection of the *not-q* card in Wason's task — did not improve subjects' performances on the selection task itself. Training in logic does not always help us to reason using logical rules.

Pragmatic Reasoning Schemas

If the selection task is successfully completed when it contains sufficiently experienced real-life rules, why is it not solved in the abstract version? After all, if people know enough to get the answer in a large variety of situations, they might be thought to have some knowledge of how the logical rule works. Yet when we have realistic rules we can understand the problem. Why do we not abstract the essential logical structure from these experiences and come to employ its generality of application?

Cheng and her colleagues (Cheng & Holyoak, 1985; Cheng et al., 1986) argued that people do develop abstract rules for reasoning from their experiences but at a pragmatic level rather than at a logical or syntactic level. Consider the rule "If a passenger wishes to enter the country, then he or she must have had an inoculation against cholera" along with the choices "entering", "not entering", "inoculated" and "not inoculated". Subjects were as successful with this task as with the Beer–Age task, yet subjects were much less likely to have had direct experience of the operation of immigration rules than of those about drinking. From this result, Cheng et al. claimed that subjects were cued to use a "permission schema" — a set of rules or conditions that permit beer drinking or immigration — rather than to use the rules of propositional logic. The rules of the permission schema may be expressed as follows:

1. If action *A* is taken, precondition *P* must be satisfied.
2. If action *A* is not taken, precondition *P* need not be satisfied.
3. If precondition *P* is satisfied, action *A* can be taken.
4. If precondition *P* is not satisfied, action *A* must not be taken.

These rules can be used to check as to whether or not a permission contract has been violated: rules 1 and 4 containing "must" and "must not" provide the essential checks. The rules are abstract in the sense that many specific items might be used in place of "action *A*" and "precondition *P*", but note that important semantic variations reside in the use of "must be", need not be", "can be" and "must not be".

Cheng et al. also considered rules like "If one works for the armed forces, then one must vote in the elections" and gave subjects the choices "armed forces", "not armed forces", "vote" and "not vote". Although this rule has the same superficial form as those above, it expresses an "obligation" rather than a "permission". Subjects were again as successful with this as with more familiar contractual obligations, such as "If any miner gets lung cancer, then the company will pay the miner a sickness pension".

Thus Cheng et al. suggested that people come to possess abstract knowledge structures expressed as pragmatic reasoning schemas. The schemas for permission and obligation are differentially cued by semantic aspects of a particular rule and performances on both familiar and less familiar rules are similarly facilitated. We should note, however, that the effect of familiarity cannot be ruled out altogether. Pollard and Evans (1987) invited subjects to act as secret police checking a regulation about identity cards for which the rule was "if there is a B on a card, then there is a number over 18 on it". Only limited facilitation occurred in this situation, even though subjects appear to be cued to use a permission schema. (The similarity of the rule to the Beer–Age rule should be evident to the reader if not to the subjects of this experiment.) The use of a schema may depend upon some minimally realistic content and perhaps also requires the use of "must" in the statement of the rule.

The way people interpret a conditional statement is not wholly dependent on easily acceptable reasoning schemas which everyone uses in the same context. For example, if there is a rule:

If you tidy your room then you may go out to play

with a parent as the agent who prefers tidy rooms and a child as the actor who prefers going out to play, and subjects are instructed to take the child's perspective and see if the parent keeps the rule or to take the parent's perspective and see if the child keeps the rule, then different cards are turned over. When it was important to see if the parent broke the rule, then the *p* and *not-q* cards were turned over, but where it was important to see if the child broke the rule, then the *not-p* and *q* cards were turned over (Manketelow & Over, 1991). Similar differences depending on the point of view taken by the subject have been found with other scenarios, including consumers who want to see that a commercial promise is honestly applied versus managers who want to see if the same promise is carefully applied so that the firm doesn't lose out (Politzer & Nguyen-Xuan, 1992). Reasoning with conditionals in the selection task when there is realistic content produces different results depending on how the content is construed. The strictly logical interpretation of these *if/then* rules, in line with the selection task, neglects some of the pragmatic elements of language in the declaration of social contracts.

Finally, consider the role of "necessity" and "sufficiency" in the operation of "causal" rules. The essence of *if/then* as employed in the selection task is that while *p* is *sufficient* for *q*, it is not necessary because other things can cause *q*. Morris, Cheng and Nisbett (1991, reported in Smith, Langston, & Nisbett, 1992) showed that subjects can readily understand that some causes are both necessary and sufficient as in the rule "a 100°C temperature causes water to boil"; that some causes are necessary but not sufficient as when a virus is said to cause a viral infection; and that some causes are neither necessary nor sufficient as when smoking is said to cause lung cancer. A strong argument for the existence of schemas for this kind of reasoning came especially from subjects' success with unfamiliar rules. For example, given the hypothesis that "Temperature above 1500°C causes the element floridium to turn into a gas", over 70% of the subjects correctly determined that all four "cards" — temperature above 1500°C, temperature below 1500°C, floridium in gaseous form, floridium in liquid form — should be checked to see if the hypothesis has been overturned.

Overall, people are not very good at tasks defined in terms of logical operations, at least when abstract forms are used. The emergence of work on other kinds of formal structures, such as the pragmatic schemas discussed above, offers a new perspective on how real-world reasoning might proceed, and suggests that other understandings of the relationships within the premises given are more important in human reasoning than the logical meaning of *if/then*.

THE ROLE OF LOGIC

When people reason, they don't produce answers which fit with formal logic. One problem is that formal logic allows, and indeed requires, an infinite number of valid conclusions which people don't make. For example, people do not bother to repeat in a conclusion something which is actually stated in the premise. So if you are asked what follows from the premise:

The black cat is on the roof and the grey cat is in the garden

You would probably not conclude that:

The black cat is on the roof

Although this is a perfectly correct conclusion, and follows from the conjunction signalled by "and", it has less semantic information than the first premise. Johnson-Laird (1983) has argued that people who are not trained in logic understand deduction to mean three things: (1) the semantic information is maintained; (2) the conclusion is simpler than the premises; and (3) the conclusion should be new, not a repetition of the premises. Therefore, a psychological theory of deductive reasoning cannot be a purely logical theory of how these connections work, because people tend to declare that nothing follows from premises if they can't do these three things, and a purely logical theory will allow conclusions to follow even when they are not new. Indeed, people have difficulty in understanding the very notion that "correctness" in terms of the structure of an argument can lead to conclusions which they don't believe, and they are likely to accept conclusions which they do believe (Oakhill & Johnson-Laird, 1985).

In addition, some people interpret connectives differently from others, and individuals are not consistent, even with abstract content. Evans and Newstead (1980) found that most people interpret disjunctives as inclusives (*A or B* is understood as *A or B or both*), but a sizeable minority favoured the exclusive interpretation (*A or B but not both*). With a neutral content *if/then* problem, the interpretation is sometimes as a conditional (if *A*, then *B*) and sometimes as a biconditional (if *A*, then *B*, AND if *B*, then *A*), and individuals are not consistent as to which one they use (Staudenmayer & Bourne, 1978; Wason & Johnson-Laird, 1972). We have been considering above situations in which people are affected by the way an argument is laid out, the atmosphere effect, and their failure to understand modus tollens in abstract cases. Does this mean that people do not use logical rules when they reason?

Logical Rules

Rips (1983) accepted several of the human limitations in reasoning discussed in the last section when he studied performances on a range of propositional reasoning tasks as a function of the availability of natural deduction rules, the use of suppositions and a limited working memory capacity. Consider the following argument (Rips, 1983, p. 39):

If there is not both an *M* and a *P* on the blackboard, then there is an *R*
Therefore, if there is no *M*, then there is an *R*
Is this argument valid?

Subjects tackled a series of such problems which varied in the mix of logical rules required for their correct solution. Rips developed a mathematical model which attempted to account for the times subjects took to achieve correct and incorrect solutions. The model assumed that subjects had available the deductive rules, such as "*not* (p *or* q) = *not* p *and not* q", which were required for a particular problem, but that they would not always retrieve them or apply them correctly. The difficulty of the problems corresponded to the number of component rules that had to be retrieved, which might be interpreted as showing the limits of working memory rather than simple ignorance of logical operations. Braine (1978) has similarly delineated what he terms a "natural logic of reasoning" — a form of propositional logic — which subjects can be shown to operate without specific training. Braine, Reiser and Rumain (1984) showed that variation in the rated difficulty of reasoning tasks — tasks similar to those used by Rips — was strongly predicted by an index constructed from the lengths of the original problems and the number of steps required for their solution.

What kind of behaviour would allow us to say that people had a rule for a general form of an argument? Smith et al. (1992) point out that subjects in a number of experiments perform very well with *if p then q/p/ therefore q*. They are correct with familiar and unfamiliar materials; they even succeed with abstract items; and, they may often explain their reasoning in terms of the general form of the rule. In one study in which subjects made errors with modus ponens (Byrne, 1989), this was only achieved by changing what subjects took the initial premise to be. Smith et al. identify the major issues as those of how abstractly we represent problems and whether or not we process explicitly represented rules. They suggest that the criteria identified here, along with others, can form the basis of a judgement about whether or not people use abstract rules in reasoning.

Modus tollens — the logical rule that may be required for successful performance of the selection task — fails to be a rule of reasoning by the criteria put forward by Smith et al. Performance is poor for less familiar items and for abstract items, and subjects rather rarely give evidence in protocols that they have used the rule or that they know the rule.

If there is a modus ponens rule in natural logic, but no modus tollens rule, then to work though the deduction:

if *p* then *q*
not *p*
therefore not *p*

human reasoners have to take the first premise, hypothesise *p*, and so get *q* by modus ponens. They then have both *q* and *not-q* (from the second premise), so they know that the outcome of the hypothesised *p* is a contradiction. They then know that if hypothesising something leads to a contradiction, the initial hypothesis must be false, so they can conclude "therefore, not *p*". A complex procedure, and one which people get wrong. We could operate a formal system of logical rules, but difficulties arise because of our cognitive limitations when faced with the longer problem statements and a larger number of steps.

Mental Models

More recently, Johnson-Laird's "mental models" approach has been developing as a counter to those who seek to ascribe our reasoning powers to the operation of logical rules. We discussed the mental models approach earlier in the chapter. The emphasis of the mental models approach is on the meaning of the statements in an argument, but not purely on the pragmatics, as it is in pragmatic reasoning schemas. We can think of comprehension as a process which lays bare a logical form, at which point rules are used to produce conclusions, or we can think of a fuller account of meaning which involves a consideration of the meaning of the connectives in propositions, and the meaning of the propositions themselves, and uses these meanings to generate conclusions. Johnson-Laird, Byrne and Schaeken (1992) have proposed that propositional reasoning — the kind that depends upon use of *if*, *or*, *and* and *not* — is a semantic process based upon the operations of mental models rather than upon purely syntactic operations.

Johnson-Laird et al. (1992) use the meanings of propositions in a natural way in order to produce the kinds of conclusions normally produced by people not trained in logic. This approach allows a distinction to be made between comprehending the premises and actually reasoning with the models. For example, people often find it hard to reason with negation. Johnson-Laird et al. argue that there are two reasons for this; one is that negation affects comprehension, and the other is that negation affects reasoning. The statement "it is not the case that there is no black cat on the sofa" is hard to understand, and it takes longer to understand than the logically equivalent statement "the black cat is on the sofa". This is a problem about the meaning of the statement itself, not about reasoning with negatives. Once the premises have been understood and represented as mental models, then reasoning with them depends on the number of mental models you have. So a negation like:

It is not the case that there is a cat or there is a dog.

is hard to understand, but because it actually needs only one mental model:

no cat   no dog

reasoning with that model is quite easy. Using "and" instead of "or" changes things, although there is only one negation as before:

It is not the case that there is both a cat and a dog.

This statement needs three different models to represent its full meaning:

no cat   dog
cat   no dog
no cat   no dog

so reasoning becomes harder as conclusions have to be checked against all three models. Negation is harder to comprehend, but that does not mean that subsequent reasoning will be more difficult. What makes reasoning more difficult is the number of mental models which have to be considered, or searched for, in order to produce a conclusion. In general, Johnson-Laird et al. (1992) show a close relationship between problem difficulty and the number of models that must be constructed for successful solution.

Belief Bias. We mentioned earlier that in reasoning tasks, people tend to accept conclusions in which they believe, even if the argument doesn't follow. This could be because they focus on the conclusion, and only really bother with reasoning if the conclusion is hard to accept, or it could be that people do not really understand the idea that something "must follow", or be logically necessary. Newstead, Pollard, Evans and Allen (1992a) investigated these two accounts of belief bias and came to the conclusion that mental models provided a better account than either of these two views. They suggested that in multiple-model tasks, subjects looked for alternative mental models when they came to an unbelievable conclusion — that is, one of the things which triggers the search for alternative models is a conclusion which seems to follow, but is hard to believe. Oakhill, Johnson-Laird and Garnham (1989) gave subjects syllogistic reasoning problems of the "some As are Bs, no Bs are Cs type", for which several mental models were possible and also found that subjects tended to produce an erroneous conclusion when one of the models produced a believable, but incorrect, answer. This account doesn't work when there is only one possible model for a problem and belief bias still occurs. Oakhill et al. (1989) argued that when this happens, subjects must reject their own correct conclusion (often replacing it with the conclusion that nothing follows) when they don't believe it. Rather than only engaging reasoning processes if the conclusion seems unreasonable, people may decide *after* they have reasoned that the answer cannot be correct (Newstead & Evans, 1993). If people can reason correctly and then fail to accept the result, then we have to include the decision-making process in our understanding of reasoning.

Rules and Representations

Natural logics, pragmatic schemas and mental models are three of the most important types of accounts of how people reason. They all lay different emphasis on the relationship between initial comprehension and subsequent reasoning processes. Two argue for general processes (natural logic and mental models) and two for semantic processes (mental models and pragmatic reasoning schemas). The core psychological issue concerns the extent to which some current inference is made by reference to a representation of the problem that is more general or more abstract than the problem itself. Some of the natural logic rules, such as that for modus ponens, fit the criteria which Smith et al. (1992) put forward for the existence of a rule, and the notion of pragmatic rules or schemas which allow correct answers to a task involving modus tollens is supported in respect of at least some of the criteria for a rule system. For example, subjects are often surprisingly good at reasoning about wholly novel (i.e. invented) causal rules. The mental models debate concerns the extent to which these rules operate by virtue of their form or syntax, or whether we reason about them by modelling possible states of affairs.

Shafir and Tversky (1992) suggest that the problems with the selection task which we have discussed at so much length are connected to problems in other domains, including decision making. They suggest that people have difficulty engaging in hypothesis testing about what would happen if they turned the cards over and it is because they do not engage that they fail to solve the task correctly. Pragmatic schemas work in some content domains, but that does not mean that we should stop trying to understand why the abstract case is failed. If people do not engage with a reasoning task, then it may be inappropriate to ask whether they have rules or not. We might conclude that a great deal remains to be explained in human deductive reasoning, but it is not readily done in terms of logic, at least not logic alone.

PROBLEM SOLVING

At this point, we can take another look at some of Sherlock Holmes' deductions. In *A Study in Scarlet*, he said that the murderer was a tall man. Later he explains that 9 out of 10 tall men have a large stride, and the murderer's footprints showed that he had a large stride, which made it likely that he was tall. This was confirmed by the finding that a message had been written 6 feet from the floor because a man will tend to write on a wall at eye level. What Holmes is doing here is not deduction at all. If he were, he would argue like this:

Some tall men have large strides
The murderer has a large stride
Therefore the murderer is tall

This argument is not a valid one, and neither is the argument:

Some men write on walls at eye level
The murderer wrote on the wall 6 feet up
Therefore the murderer's eyes are 6 feet from the ground

What Sherlock Holmes is actually doing is much closer to the problems of medical diagnosis to be discussed in the next chapter. He is making probabilistic statements, basing plausible hypotheses on them, and making further inferences.

In another incident, when he meets Dr Watson, he immediately "perceives" that the doctor has returned from Afghanistan (where British troops were involved in a war at the time). Later he explains that the doctor is browned by the tropical sun and holds his arm stiffly, so he must have been wounded. Afghanistan is the only place in which a British officer could get both brown and wounded, therefore Watson had been in Afghanistan. Put like that, it is clear that Holmes was imaginative and lucky rather than logical. Wounds, he assumed occurred in wars, but they can occur in other ways, and suntans can be acquired in other places. Holmes' main achievements are observation and the application of knowledge to generate plausible accounts rather than the possession of any formal deductive powers. He recognised signs which other detectives ignored, so that problems were seen quite differently; he interpreted what he saw against a wide background of knowledge and he did not get trapped into ruts as the fictional Scotland Yard detectives did. He can better be characterised as a skilled problem solver rather than as a logician.

Getting Stuck

Inspector Lestrade from Scotland Yard makes assumptions which prevent him from solving problems. His thoughts are blocked or misdirected. Investigations of factors which block or misdirect our thinking were a feature of many early studies of thinking. Maier (1930; 1931) showed subjects to a room in which two strings were hanging from the ceiling. The task was to tie the two strings together, but, holding onto one of the strings, a subject could not reach the other. The essence of the solution is to tie an object of sufficient weight onto one of the strings so that it can be caused to swing back and forth like a pendulum. Then holding onto the second string, the swinging string can be caught when it approaches. We can envisage subjects holding onto one string, reaching in vain towards the other string and looking puzzled. In one experiment, Maier offered hints to those failing to solve the problem. First, he brushed past one of the strings setting it in motion. To those who still failed to solve the problem, he handed a pair of pliers, saying: "With the aid of this and no other object there is another way of solving the problem". For some subjects, a pair of pliers remained an item which is used to grip things and not to act as a weighty object; that is, their thinking was blocked by seeing pliers in a particular way. Those who solved the problem following the first hint tended to do so rapidly and often without any awareness of what had caused the redirection in their thinking.

Among the several studies which followed Maier's work, Birch and Rabinowitz (1951) varied the subjects' previous experiences with the objects that might be used to weight the pendulum. All subjects were asked to complete an electrical circuit, one group using a switch and another group using a device called a relay. Both the switch and the relay were present when subjects were asked to attempt Maier's two-string task. Of course, many subjects required the redirective hint, the experimenter's "accidental" brush past one of the strings to set it in motion. All subjects eventually succeeded in the task, but all those who had fitted the relay to the electrical circuit used the switch as the pendulum weight, whereas most of those who had earlier fitted the switch to the circuit used the relay as the weight. This suggested that the recent use of an item in its normal role had made its other properties (e.g. weight) less available, whereas the unused item was freer to take on alternative functions. Duncker (1945) had termed this phenomenon *functional fixedness*, the "inhibition in discovering an appropriate use of an object owing to the subject's previous use of the object in a function dissimilar to that required by the present situation".

Functional fixedness, and mental blocks generally, are clearly an aspect of prior experience that we bring to a new task. It is an example of what Wertheimer (1945) termed *reproductive* thinking (as opposed to *productive* thinking), he gave examples from the learning of mathematics in which pupils are liable to pick up specific routines, perhaps a particular formula, which may not readily transfer to new representations of the problem. These and other classic Gestalt studies of thinking tended to emphasise the negative effects of past experience, whether this is the experience of a particular function of something (e.g. pliers) distributed over several years, or a concentrated recent experience, perhaps of success with a procedure, which creates a dysfunctional mental set with respect to new problems. Of course, it can also be demonstrated that our mental habits — the fixedness and the mental sets — can be overcome in the right conditions. Maier (1945) showed that subjects who could be led to solve one unusual problem were more likely to be successful at another when sufficient features were shared between them. Cofer (1951) showed that a prior verbal learning task in which words like *rope, swing* and *pendulum* were to be memorised facilitated correct solutions to the Maier two-string problem relative to the performance of control subjects who learned other words. Maier also, you may recall, found that "hints" were able to shift the direction for many of his subjects.

In most cases, when students learn to categorise geometry problems as requiring a certain sort of approach, they will be helping themselves to find the solution. However, for some problems, we are alerted to the need for a change of approach by our self-evident failure to solve them, and for these it would be well to have techniques which help us overcome the blocks and avoid the familiar channels in which our thinking runs. Similarly, when modern detectives set out to investigate crimes, they use a very wide range of routine activities such as questioning witnesses and searching the scene of the crime for evidence. In many cases, the routine methods and habitual ways of thinking will lead to a solution. In some cases, habitual ways of thinking — perhaps assumptions about the sort of person most likely or unlikely to have committed the crime or which witness is to be believed — may inhibit solution. Clearly we cannot restrict thinking and problem solving to any set of rules, whether logical or not. We have to create a model of problem solving which will encompass a wide range of approaches, abilities and skills. We turn now to consider a particular characterisation of problem-solving processes that has dominated recent accounts.

Problem Solving as a Search Process

One of the greatest difficulties facing the detective is to define what can be called the *problem space*, the range of possibilities — potential actors and action sequences — that might have led to the crime and which might now form the basis for enquiry, search, inference and successful solution. Whereas the Gestalt psychologists discussed thinking and problem solving in such general terms as "restructuring" the problem, "redirection" and "insight", those developing the *information-processing* approach in the 1950s and 1960s emphasised the need to make explicit the detailed mental operations and sequences of operations by which the subject solved problems. The terminology of Ernst and Newell (1969) has been widely adopted both for human problem solving and for problem solving by computer. To introduce the terminology, consider the following problem:

> Three detectives have captured three desperate criminals in the wilds and are taking them on foot through field and forest. Each criminal has his legs chained together to restrict his speed of movement. The detectives hold the keys to the leg-irons and the essential food supplies. The six men come to a river which they must cross. A rowing boat is available which will only take two men at a time. Two men can cross in the boat but one must row it back so that others can get across. The problem is that if at any time there are more criminals than detectives on a river bank they will overpower their guard(s), recover the keys to their leg-irons, take the food supplies, and escape with all speed. How is the crossing managed?

Table 12.1 gives a solution to the problem and illustrates the components of the problem space. The *initial state* of the problem is expressed by the diagram at State 1 in which all the detectives (*DDD*) and criminals (*CCC*) are on the left bank of the river along with the boat. The *goal state* is that state achieved when all the detectives and criminals are on the right bank of the river and is shown as State 12. The *operators* are the set of permissible state-transforming operations. For example, from State 1 the boat could carry the following alternative sets of passengers: *DD, CC, DC,*

TABLE 12.1

Solution to the "Detectives and Criminals" Problem

		Moves	
State	Left Bank	River Operation	Right Bank
1	DDD		
	CCC		
2	DDD	CC	
	C	→	CC
3	DDD	C	
	CC	←	C
4	DDD	CC	
		→	CCC
5	DDD	C	
	C	←	CC
6	D	DD	DD
	C	→	CC
7	DD	CD	D
	CC	←	C
8		DD	DDD
	CC	→	C
9		C	DDD
	CCC	←	
10		CC	DDD
	C	→	CC
11		C	DDD
	CC	←	C
12		CC	DDD
		→	CCC

D or C. However, some of these "boating operations" or journeys are not allowed to follow from State 1. Only journeys by CC, DC and C are permitted by the rules which say that the criminals must not outnumber the detectives on either river bank. The three permissible journeys transform State 1 into three different problem states. If the first journey is undertaken by CC, then there is only one useful next move — in which a C returns with the boat — if we are not to return to State 1. If the first journey is undertaken by CD, then only the return of D is permitted within the rules. If C alone makes the first trip across the river, then there is only one possible operation and that is for C to return as he came, thus recreating State 1. We can explore all permissible operations, moving from state to state, and looking ahead we can evaluate whether the move might be useful. The initial state, the goal state and the set of operations or operators define the *problem space*. In fact, the alternative paths through the problem space for this problem are extremely limited. There are some minor variants of the solution to this problem at the beginning of the sequence and towards the end. Nevertheless, this apparently simple problem allows us to illustrate some features of the information-processing approach.

First, we could attempt to solve this problem by trying all permissible moves from each problem state legitimately achieved. This would define the complete *search space* for the problem. A procedure which guarantees solution, as this one would for the "Detectives and Criminals" problem, is referred to as an *algorithm* or an algorithmic procedure. It is extremely unlikely that you found yourself using this approach when you attempted the problem. If you are like many of the subjects who have tried the equivalent "Cannibals and Missionaries" problem, then you will have got a bit stuck in State 6, being somewhat reluctant to take two men back across the river, or even being blind to the possibility of this move. This, along with much other evidence, suggests that human search through the problem space is directed by *heuristic* principles — that is, by general-purpose principles which tend to help us out, rather than algorithms which will definitely give the solution.

In the present context, it is suggested that we use the principle of attempting to increase the number of men who have crossed the river at each stage. It is as though we evaluate the possible moves in terms of which one takes us nearest to the goal state. Judging whether a move will take us nearer to the goal is helpful in many problems and, indeed, knowing when a state is similar to the goal state is something which changes as we become more expert at problems of a particular type (Anderson, 1990). It seems to be this difference reduction principle which prevents us from going backwards in solving a problem, because that means the position is less similar to the goal than the present one.

Another heuristic principle is "subgoal setting". You may have guessed that the problem is solved by taking all the criminals across first and that if this subgoal state can be achieved, then the goal state proper might be more obviously in sight. Or you may have anticipated by working backwards that if State 9 can be reached, then the goal state is certainly achievable. Anderson and Kushmerick, referred to in Anderson (1993), used another laboratory problem called the "Tower of Hanoi" (see Fig. 12.1), and found that the time it took to make a move was correlated with the number of subgoals which had to be set up before the move was made.

Taken together, difference reduction and the formation of subgoals are part of problem solving by means–ends analysis. The problem solver looks for the biggest difference between a goal and current states and tries to reduce it. This involves making a subgoal to reduce that difference. Heuristic principles can now be described more specifically as devices for reducing the size of the "search tree" to be examined to a manageable number of branches which, hopefully, lead quickly to the goal state. The heuristic, path-reducing principles of means–ends analysis and of develop-

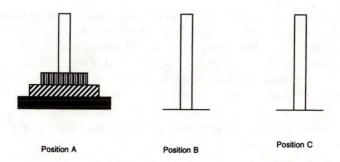

Position A   Position B   Position C

FIG. 12.1. The Tower of Hanoi problem (simplified version). Can you move the three discs from the pole in position A to the pole in position C, moving one disc at a time and never putting a larger disc on top of a smaller one? Could you do it with four, five or more discs?

ing a hierarchy of subgoals were successfully implemented in a computer program called the "General Problem Solver" (Ernst & Newell, 1969), which solved a variant of the missionaries and cannibals problem, some problems in mathematics and a number of other tasks. The program was regarded as successful, because it avoided the exhaustive search of all possibilities and demonstrated the value of general heuristic principles even for fully determinate problems.

Some problems, like those given in laboratory studies, are well defined, but the task of the detective is not well defined in this way. However, if we broaden what we normally mean by "problem", it is possible to show that problem solving is a fairly normal activity:

> I want to hand in my essay. What's the difference between what I want and what I have? I haven't printed it yet. What would change that? My printer. My printer won't work. What would make it work? More paper. What has more paper? The office. But the office is closed . . . and so on.

These kinds of everyday tasks may not even appear to us like problem solving because we usually think of problems as situations in which the solution is hard to find, but this kind of analysis of an everyday task uses means–ends analysis. In many kinds of academic contexts, problem solving is more explicit, but it may not show both difference reduction and subgoaling in an obvious form. For example, in Jeffries, Polson, Razran and Atwood's (1977) account of river-crossing problems, subgoaling was not evident in some cases, so difference reduction meant that successive steps just brought the problem solver closer to a solution. Getting closer and closer is like climbing a hill, and for some problems hill climbing is a reasonable account of what subjects seem to do.

In most of these tasks, there are fairly clear limits to what is relevant and what is not; the problem is well-defined. Small everyday tasks like getting your essay printed may also have comparatively small spaces to search through. If we have no specialised knowledge which enables us to solve problems based on specific experience, then these "weak" or general-purpose methods are very useful. However, for many specialised problem-solving situations, like the situation of a detective on a murder enquiry, there isn't an easily defined problem space. Experience has to guide the selection of heuristics and the formulation of the problem itself. We will return to questions of expertise and experience later, but first we consider the experience of insight which allows a solution to appear.

Insight in Problem Solving

If you are trying to get your essay printed so that you can hand it in, you may not experience a moment when the answer, or part of the answer suddenly becomes available. You probably wouldn't leap out of your bath and rush over to the computer centre shouting "eureka". However, there are many situations in which problem solution involves a subjective experience in which we feel that insight into the problem has been gained. Duncker's studies on functional fixedness, which we discussed earlier, often seemed to involve a moment of enlightenment, and "aha!" experience, which had something to do with a shift in the way in which the problem was represented. Maier's (1931) study also involves a change in the representation of the problem and a feeling of insight when this occurs. Explaining and understanding this insight has not been easy, and it is sometimes linked with creativity. Boden (1990) suggests that even scientific discovery, such as Kekule's discovery of the ring structure of the benzene molecule, can be explained in terms of a range of heuristics within normal problem solving.

Kaplan and Simon (1990) looked at the question of how the "aha!" experience occurs. They used a problem called the "mutilated checkerboard", which is shown in Fig. 12.2. The task is to use 31 dominoes to cover the 62 squares remaining when two opposite corner squares are taken from a checkerboard, or to prove that such a covering is simply not possible. Each domino covers two adjacent squares. You may want to stop for a moment and try to work out how to cover the board with 31 dominoes, each of which covers two adjacent squares either horizontally or vertically.

Given that there are 62 squares and 31 dominoes, it does look as if it should be possible to cover all the squares. Kaplan and Simon report a graduate student in chemical engineering who spent 18 hours and filled 61 pages of a lab notebook with notes, but did not solve the problem. A computer program which proved the problem to be impossible by exhaustively trying all ways of covering the squares required 758,148 placements of dominoes to do so. To solve this problem (i.e. to prove that the mutilated checkerboard can't be covered) requires a different way of representing the problem, a new problem space.

A covering is impossible. If you look again at the mutilated checkerboard in Fig. 12.2 and consider the two squares which were removed, you

FIG. 12.2 The mutilated
checkerboard problem. Can this
board be covered by 31 dominoes,
each of which covers two adjacent
squares either horizontally or
vertically?

will see that they were both white. Given that two squares of the same
colour have been removed, it is not possible to make up 31 pairs of
adjacent black and white squares. Once 30 dominoes have been used,
there will always be two squares of the same colour left over, and these
cannot be adjacent. Kaplan and Simon argued that the problem is only
solved when the alternation of black and white squares is seen as crucial.
They gave different versions of the problem to subjects and gave them
hints which enabled solution to occur within 30 minutes. They found that
making the pair structure of the board more salient affected solution time
and that hints which directed subjects to attend to the colour or other
features of the pairs were most successful in precipitating a successful
search for a new problem space, often accompanied with an "aha!"
experience. With the problem represented in terms of pairs of different
squares, finding the solution became comparatively easy.

   What happens when we, or our hypothetical detectives, get stuck in
trying to solve a problem? At some point, we have to decide that trying
to find the solution with the present representation is not going to succeed
and then search for a new representation instead. To search effectively for
a solution we need to know how to search for a new representation or
problem space, and then how that representation affects the search for
a solution. However, we don't very often meet problems which are
completely new in all aspects. Even in the toy problems of the laboratory,
our past experience can be useful in helping us to get out of blockages.
Gick and McGarry (1992) found that earlier experiences of failure to solve
mutilated checkerboard-type problems helped subjects when they transferred to subsequent problems. In addition, we may have ways of
representing problems which are different when we have met many such
problems before. Expertise and experience can affect both problem
representation and problem solution.

LEARNING AND EXPERTISE

Our detective is a kind of expert and Sherlock Holmes succeeds because he is more expert than other detectives. In what ways do experts differ from intelligent novices? Undoubtedly, they differ in the amount of practice and experience, but what is the nature of the difference? How are the effects of practice and experience expressed in the expert? One kind of expert that has been much studied in recent years is the master chess player, whom we have already met in Chapter 10.

The first difference between a master and a novice chess player is that the former encodes chess positions faster. Shown a chess position for only 5 sec, masters reproduced it with 91% accuracy, whereas novices were only 41% correct (de Groot, 1966). Masters and novices, however, were similarly poor at reproducing random arrangements of chess pieces (Chase & Simon, 1973). It was clear from the way in which the subjects placed pieces on the board when reproducing a real board position, and from the frequency of their head movements when copying a position from one board to another, that the masters and novices differed markedly in the size of the "chunks" — groups of chess pieces in relationship — that are represented in their respective knowledge bases.

These studies give us warning that playing chess well is likely to require rather more than a "search all possibilities" strategy. Indeed, de Groot (1965) and Newell and Simon (1972) found that masters tend not to perform much of a search at all; masters and novices did not differ in the number of possible moves they considered, nor how far they looked ahead. Rather, we might suppose that the expert is faster to encode and to evaluate, what for him would be stereotypical positions and moves, leaving more time for exploration of one or two novel points in the board position. In contrast, many of the early computer programs for chess focused on search and look-ahead methods for determining next moves. While they came to out-perform many human players, limits of advance towards grandmaster standards were reached. Currently, advances are being made in machine chess, not by extending their ability to search the problem space to greater depths, but by giving them knowledge of chess positions and of the "rules of thumb", or special chess-specific heuristics, for selecting a limited range of possible moves to be explored. Most importantly, the chess expert may envision a future state of the board which he would like to achieve and he or she will explore whether it is achievable. It is rather difficult to specify the rules for this kind of subgoal setting, which rests so heavily on the understanding of the game. Thus while earlier studies of thinking and problem solving focused upon the general processes, studies of chess expertise have led us to place great importance upon specific knowledge structures, the representation of that knowledge, and knowledge about that knowledge.

Similarly, studies of novices and experts solving physics problems have led to a shift away from explanations of problem solving in terms of processes, or generally applicable procedures, to knowledge-based explanations. The subjects in the study by Chi, Feltovich and Glaser (1981) were asked to categorise some problems in mechanics. Novices typically saw the problems as being about inclined planes, springs, pulleys and friction, the terms in which the problems were expressed. When they tackled the problems, they generated equations that matched the data present in the problem statement. The experts, however, tended to categorise the problems as calling upon principles of mechanics, such as the conservation of energy principle or Newton's force law. Their solutions formed an integrated argument about the problem, whereas many solutions offered by the novices clearly had the style of shuffling equations around to solve for unknowns. The novices' approach is rather as one might write for a simple, data-driven computer program: match elements of the data presented with algebraic rules held in memory, setting up equations to be solved as though it were simply a mathematical "jigsaw" problem. The method works but the conceptual level implied may not facilitate subsequent learning in physics. Further, following McDermott and Larkin (1978), the representations available to novices and experts differ in line with their different styles of categorisation and solution. The experts can have four stages or levels of representation: (1) the literal elements of the problem; (2) a spatial arrangement of the original objects (e.g. ball on inclined plane); (3) an idealised representation which gives a place to the necessary physical concepts such as centre of gravity or forces; and (4) the mathematical equations which abstract the relations from (3). Novices may lack stages (2) and (3).

Holyoak and Spellman (1993) characterise the expert in three ways, all of which are related to more abstract knowledge structures such as rules and schemas, which can make details more relevant for an expert than for a novice. First, analogical reasoning between examples means that schemas are extracted, then schematic knowledge leads to more expert transfer even when content domains seem to be superficially different and, finally, expertise in turn allows new analogues of past experiences to be processed more efficiently. The detective as expert is most naively seen as someone who collects evidence for analysis from which logical deductions are made. No doubt there is some truth in this account. A more likely account is that because of past experience of similar situations, the detective has a package of procedures which may be relevant. Just as the chess expert will have much use for well-remembered games and will envision possible positions for testing, so the experienced detective will also have a large number of scripts and plans from previous investigations which he can check against the possible scenarios for the current crime. In this sense, the skills of chess masters, physicists and detectives are strongly embedded in their respective knowledge bases. Within this knowledge context the detective will notice discrepancies, and seek further evidence. Studies of mental logic and information processing do not give wholly adequate accounts of how we think and reason about things, because we have to combine the processes with the knowledge structures that are evidently required for expertise.

Using Analogies

The account of expertise given above emphasises how generalised knowledge structures based on past experiences guide and direct the way we approach problems. We can also recognise that a current problem is like one seen before, even if only in some way, and that may or may not be useful to us. The use of analogy is very important in understanding how we apply our knowledge to new situations. It requires either that we remember specific examples from the past, or that we get general principles from examples and apply those. Agatha Christie's Miss Marple has a nasty habit of finding the new curate very like the girl who used to work in the grocer's shop and then predicting an outcome for the curate based on very different things which happened to the girl. The exact nature of the similarity isn't obvious to the reader, and is usually at a level involving ethical behaviour within a structure of social relations, so that physical similarities are not involved. Miss Marple has a large store of knowledge about people, she notices similarities which other people do not notice, and they are structural, not surface similarities. She does not simply make generalisations about curates or shop assistants. Like all of us, Miss Marple must make some generalisations about shop assistants in order to interact with them in shops, but she also remembers individual, or exemplar, information. In Chapter 3 we discussed issues of whether we learn in terms of exemplars or generalised prototypes, and showed that it wasn't always easy to decide just what made things similar and what made them different. Many of the issues in thinking about learning and problem solving are very similar to those in concept formation.

Gentner and Gentner (1983) discuss the way in which novice physicists may use the flow of water from reservoirs and through pipes, or the movement of crowds of people through restricted pathways, as analogues for reasoning about electrical flow in circuits of various designs. In teaching about heat flow, it is possible to use the analogy of how water flows under pressure. In such an analogy, the relationship is not between intrinsically similar objects (heat flowing along a metal bar from a cup of coffee to a cube of ice, does not have many surface similarities to water flowing along a pipe from the bottom of a large container into a small one). Rather, the similarity is between structural relations in the two problems. Gentner (1989) has distinguished between "mere-appearance" matches, in which two things share physical similarities; literal similarity, in which much of the appearance and the properties of two things are shared; and analogy, in which only relational properties are shared. She notes that in some cases an underlying rule may be used so that two problems in physics are not solved in the same way because they have relational similarities, but because they are based on the same rule. These similarities overlap to some extent, but novices often get stuck with mere similarity in which two problems have similar surface appearance, although this does not help with solution.

To use an analogy you have first to notice some similarity, which involves access to the source problem; then you have to map the relationships between elements in the source problem to those in the target problem and evaluate the match. There may be situations in which having noticed the similarity, the problem solver or learner simply transfers as much as possible from the source to the new problem, because the new problem is in a domain about which little is known. In other cases, both domains will be familiar and the mapping involves matching the relationships rather than conveying new knowledge. These are very extreme cases. In most cases, there is a mixture of knowledge and lack of knowledge in both domains, and we may need some general principles to help us make analogies. The pragmatic reasoning schemas which we discussed earlier in this chapter are "general principle" accounts of how we solve problems involving permission schemas. Gick and Holyoak (1983) suggested that when people are given two examples of a type of problem, they extract a schema based on the similarity or dissimilarity of these two examples and that this enhances analogical transfer, so similar problems are performed more easily in future. Such a schema is concerned with the goal of the problem solver and with pragmatic issues about how to proceed, and the difference between surface and structural similarities is basically a difference in how relevant a property is to attaining a successful solution, that is, to the goal of the problem solver (Holyoak, 1985).

Holyoak and Koh (1987) found that both of these kinds of similarity affected spontaneous recognition that a past problem was relevant to a new problem, but when a hint was given to use the first problem to solve the second, only structural similarity was helpful in actually producing a solution. Consider this problem:

A doctor has a patient who has a malignant tumour in his stomach. The tumour cannot be operated on, but has to be treated or the patient will die. There is a kind of ray which can be used to destroy the tumour, but if it is used at full intensity then the healthy tissue it passes through before it reaches the tumour will be destroyed as well as the tumour. Full intensity is needed to destroy the tumour. At low intensities the healthy tissue will not be destroyed, but neither will the tumour. What can the doctor do?

One way to solve this problem is to think of directing weak rays at the tumour from different directions. If you have already solved a problem in which a general who wanted to capture a fortress could not mount a full attack from any one direction because all the roads had been mined and only small groups of soldiers could get through on each road, then you would have been able to work out that the general should send in troops from all directions in small parties which would re-group to attack the fortress. This is structurally similar to the ray problem and could help you to the solution. The pragmatic account requires that you would have to recognise the relevance of one problem to the other and that what is relevant has to be known in some way before the processes of analogy can operate.

In some studies of analogies, it has been quite difficult to induce people to make analogies without hints. This is not surprising given that the analogies required may be between topics as different as generals attacking fortresses and treating a tumour with rays (Holyoak & Koh, 1987), that is, they are across domains of knowledge. So the difficulty in these analogies lies in transferring the structure from the earlier domain to the new domain, and people need to be told that the tasks may be similar in some way, so that they hunt for the relationship. Hints suggest that one problem is relevant to another. Ross (1989) has suggested that analogies across domains and within domains are different, and that novices learning to do a new kind of problem, do not remember the earlier problem structure very well, do not have an abstract principle and so have a poor understanding of the underlying structure. In such a case, only the superficial properties can be recalled. Of course, in learning a set of problems within a domain, it is likely that similar surface properties will reflect similar structures, so the remindings of previous problems can be helpful. Remember that Chi et al. (1981) found that novice physicists recognised problems about pulleys and friction as being similar, and this could be useful in early learning. Surface similarities are useful within particular domains of learning.

In general, for novices, noticing a relationship does seem to be related to surface similarities. Ross (1984) looked at subjects learning to use a computer text editor and found that if they learned to carry out two ways to move words in two different literary contexts and then were tested on material which was similar to one of the contexts, they tended to use the procedure they had learned in that context the first time. However, Ross (1987) went on to show that surface similarity did not help problem solution if the principles involved in the problem were distinctive, so that previous learning of the principle itself could be invoked. Noticing similarities between superficial features was more common than noticing structural correspondences but led to fewer correct solutions.

Gick and McGarry (1992) have suggested that too much attention is paid to the similarities in the source and target problems in research on analogies, and not enough to the similarity between failures to solve the problems, which may eventually lead to success. They used the mutilated checkerboard problem which we discussed earlier and invented different versions of it which made the pair structure clearer (e.g. replacing black and white squares with men and women, having two men leave, and then asking if the remainder can make up opposite sex pairs for dancing). They found that surface similarity did not facilitate transfer, but that early failures to solve the first problem (before hints were given), which were similar to failures in the second problem, did lead to transfer. They argue that surface similarity may only be effective if the problem elements manipulated are likely to be incorporated into subjects' representations of the problem. The similarity between solution failures, on the other hand, had its main effect on what subjects noticed in the second problem which reminded them of the first, and this may be because some solution failures actually become part of a subject's representation of the problem. "I've had this difficulty with a problem before" can be important in providing access to past representations.

Analogical reasoning and the processes of access and mapping between domains require the interrelation of many cognitive systems involved in perception, long-term memory, concept formation, inference, short-term maintenance while search goes on, language comprehension, and so on. Although we have concentrated on specific "toy" problem-solving tasks, we can see that Sherlock Holmes is a clever observer and a good guesser; he builds a scenario within which the critical events might have taken place, and this in turn leads him selectively to seek other clues which by inference ought to exist if the scenario is on the right lines. His knowledge of life and the ways of criminals supply many fragments to the picture he builds up as he surveys the scene. The real detective as an expert of a particular kind has many ready-made frameworks for action and thinking; but the experienced professional also has a store of cautionary tales about when standard scenarios have been misleading and when standard practices have failed. To account for the thinking and reasoning of experts and to prescribe how more effectively we might gain our chosen expertise continues to be a major challenge for research.

SUMMARY

Many studies of thinking and reasoning have adopted some well-defined forms for deductive inference developed by logicians, which have often been assumed to provide standards for human inference. By these standards, our reasoning is sometimes found to be defective. This is especially the case when the structure of an argument is expressed in abstract terms. If a realistic content and context is given to an argument form, we tend to perform much better; but even here we can be led to make errors. Perceptual and linguistic factors and the limitations of immediate memory have been invoked to account for many of the errors which people make, and the question of whether or not we use logical rules when we reason can be obscured by some of these issues.

It is possible that we have simple logical rules for reasoning of the sort: if *p* then *q*/ *p* therefore *q*, but there is debate over what makes a logical rule a plausible one for human beings to use. When we reason with *if* and *then*, we may use general pragmatic schemas in some problems in which permissions and prohibitions are important. These schemas cannot explain all our performance on *if/then* reasoning, but do suggest that pragmatics rather than logical forms are important. Other accounts argue that rather than using rules we create mental models of states of affairs and reason using those. Errors appear when we do not create the correct number of mental models, or are unable to produce answers which are compatible with all the models created. In addition, people may make mistakes because they do not engage fully with problems when they think that an answer cannot be produced.

The wider range of tasks used in studies of problem solving show that many other skills are required for their successful solution. In novel tasks, it may sometimes be necessary to overcome the routine ways of thinking provided by our experience, which may be prompted by the appearances of the task. Some problems require us to trace a path from a current state of knowledge to a "goal state". In well-defined problems, we seek a route through a "search space". Our skills lie in the use of heuristic principles which sometimes allow us to avoid exploring every one of a large number of search paths. In less well-defined problems, our skills may reside in the ability to give some preliminary definition to the space that the problem occupies. How we go about solving problems, especially the less well-defined ones, refers to skills beyond those of routine deductive inference. Experts will have a store of general structures from their experience which can often readily take on the special features of the current problem and be "run" to produce answers. It is not expertise in problem solving itself, but expertise in the domain within which the problems are solved and in the relation between this problem and previous ones, which is important.

Analogies have been part of the study of problem solving for a long time. They may require hints to make them usable, and they will be affected by the expertise of the problem solver. Similarity of surface detail may be important early in learning within a domain, but it can be counterproductive, leading to perceived similarities which are not helpful in problem solution. Overall, analogical reasoning in problem solving requires many interrelated cognitive processes, which have been addressed in many sections of this book.

There are many books about thinking and problem solving. *Thinking, problem solving and cognition* by R.E. Mayer (1992, 2nd edn), an introductory text, is particularly interesting because it brings together accounts of concept identification, schemas, the structure of semantic memory and cognitive development, along with the usual topics. More difficult and specialised books include *Similarity and analogical reasoning*, edited by S. Vosniadou and A. Ortony (1989), which brings together many different views on concepts and analogies, and P.N. Johnson-Laird and R. M. J. Byrne's (1991), *Deduction*, which presents the mental models case in full.

13 Diagnosing an Illness: Uncertainty and Risk in Making Decisions

I experience abdominal, stomach and chest pains and a slight headache. I reflect upon the rather heavy meal I ate earlier this evening, the intense conversation and the second bottle of wine we ordered. I take an indigestion tablet, but decide against taking an aspirin. The next day I feel fine. So it was simply indigestion. But then again, I recall that I have had this experience on several occasions over the past few months. I think that it has been happening more frequently recently. I recall friends or acquaintances who have had duodenal ulcers, bouts of sickness, mild food poisoning, stomach cancer, and pains in the chest that preceded a heart attack. Perhaps I had better visit the doctor? Wait . . . I had a heavy meal, the tablet worked and so I was suffering from simple indigestion. But then I don't know what the other things feel like. Visiting the doctor is a bit of a nuisance and it would be embarrassing if she found nothing wrong with me. I will eat more slowly in future. I will visit the doctor next time. But I could be dying or need an operation and the problem might get worse if I leave it. But it would be very embarrassing just to be told to eat more slowly, to sit straight and to try to relax when I am eating. No, must have been simple indigestion: the tablet worked and . . . but I wonder how often the tablet would apparently relieve the symptoms of the more serious conditions?

My doctor has more information than I do about the relationship of symptoms to diseases, but she too has problems in decision making. She has some models of diseases and the way in which they express themselves. She knows a lot about how often this causes that, how often it causes something else, and some cautionary tales of misdiagnosis from her own and others' experience. But even she does not know everything and further investigations — X-rays, blood tests, calling in a consultant — all cost time and money, and may bring in their own risks.

All decisions involve an interplay between information, costs and risk. There are many personal decisions, such as purchasing a house, selecting a partner, taking out insurance, backing a horse, and crossing a busy road. Organisations also make decisions. A manufacturer steps up production and employs more sales staff in expectation of higher demand; a nation makes a military gesture and risks war; and a government raises interest rates and levels of taxation hoping to contain inflation. The organisations have information about what happened in the past and about the current state of affairs. They also lack information about many things, so they have to devise ways of making judgements which take into account what they know and the anticipated costs and benefits. Many decisions are difficult and we may agonise over them, but clearly not all decisions are like this; some decisions are straightforward, and can be made quickly without apparent effort. Much of the decision-making research focuses on decisions which do require conscious effort and which are frequently difficult, but bear in mind that in our everyday lives decisions are not always so demanding.

One way to start studying how we make decisions is to look at situations in which people know about the risks and benefits and then see if they make decisions in a systematic way. After all, if there are a lot of complex factors in decision making, ignorance or forgetting would play a part. We need to start somewhere and there are some common situations in which decisions are made within a comparatively restricted setting. Gambling is one such setting. Much real gambling, however, such as betting on horses, is complicated by the fact that the punters often have information which they believe allows them to beat the bookmaker.

The earliest studies of decision making looked at the purest instances of gambling, using coin tosses, dice throws, roulette-like spinning wheels, lotteries and similar well-defined events, in order to see how people behave when the chances and the gains and losses are objectively defined. The objective definitions used usually arise from work in probability theory and cognitive psychologists have taken that work as the starting point because, by providing clear and precise descriptions of some situations, probability theory allows one to identify optimal choices. This optimal choice can then be seen as the best or the most rational choice and so acts as a model of rational behaviour. Precise descriptions of probabilities were first described for simple gambles involving random events, and so in the early part of this chapter we look at how people behave in such situations. As so many theories of decision making define what is rational using some form of probability theory, in places we will need to describe some fairly simple calculations. However, we should offer a warning at this stage, which is that probability theory is often just that, theory, and there are frequently substantial disputes between statisticians about what constitutes the "correct" description of a situation. Consequently, not only does the concept of what is rational depend on whether one accepts probabilities as the only criteria, but it can also depend upon which kind of probability theory one supports. After looking at simple situations with clearly defined probabilities, we discuss a number of phenomena which point to some properties of cognition in the face of uncertainty, including material which presents problems for the simpler theories, that people behave like some well-tuned probability theorist. We conclude by looking at some alternative possible bases for rational decision making. We cannot yet expect, however, to gain anything like a complete understanding of the issues in decision making, a topic which remains one of the greatest challenges in the study of higher cognitive processes.

SIMPLE GAMBLES AND THE EXPECTED UTILITY PRINCIPLE

By looking at a subset of situations where the objective probabilities of events occurring are known, one can determine how people's decisions do or do not conform to the predicted pattern. If there are deviations, then these have to be explained by a new or altered version of the theory. As we will see, early theories in the area owed much to existing theories in probability theory and economics. In this early work on rational decision making, decisions were often characterised as choices between risky actions, which were marked by two features: the probabilities associated with each of the possible outcomes and the monetary values — gains or losses — associated with these possible outcomes.

Expected Value

Consider a simple gamble where you stake 10p on the toss of a coin: if it comes down heads you gain 10p, but if it comes down tails you lose your 10p stake. If we can assume that the coin is unbiased and that it is tossed in a fair manner, then we can say that it is just as likely to come down heads as it is to come down tails. As the two outcomes — heads and tails — are equally likely, the probability of getting one of them (say, heads) is one in two, or a half. Let us symbolise this statement as $P\{\text{Head}\} = 0.5$ and $P\{\text{Tail}\} = 0.5$. If you know how likely one outcome is, and what it is worth to you, and how likely the other outcome is and what it is worth, then you can calculate the overall benefit or value of the gamble. To do this, you take all the possible outcomes (such as "Head" and "Tail"), and for each outcome you multiply its probability by its value and then add the totals together over all outcomes. For the simple gamble suggested above, the expected value, $E\{V\}$, of the gamble is

$$E\{V\} = P\{\text{Head}\}\cdot(+10p) + P\{\text{Tail}\}\cdot(-10p)$$
$$= 0.5 \times 10p + 0.5 \times (-10p) = 0p$$

where P is the probability of the event. The calculation shows the obvious result, that with half a chance of winning 10p and half a chance of losing 10p, the expected outcome is zero gain or loss. Of course, this outcome refers to "in the long run" — for any single toss of the coin you would either lose 10p or gain 10p. Although coin-tossing games such as "pitch and toss" were quite a popular form of gambling up to the beginning of this century, it is doubtful if many students will be gripped by this experience nowadays. However, the belief that we are now too sophisticated either to enjoy such games or to make the simple "mistake" of believing that we can win on such gambles may be a little premature. For example, Coton (1992) describes how in 1983 a leading bookmaking firm offered a price on the outcome of the toss of a coin for a cricket match. Each of the outcomes was priced at 20-21 (that is, stake £21 to win £20), which is of course worse than the true probability which is 50:50 (that is, stake £21 to win £21, which in betting parlance is known as an evens chance). As advertisements are costly and bookmakers are not renowned for throwing away their money, it does suggest that punters are not always guided by probabilities.

Of course, most real-life gambles are more complex than simple coin tossing and so we need to develop this rather trivial example. One scenario that has been used frequently in the literature on decision making is that of participating in a lottery (Kahneman & Tversky, 1979; Schneider & Lopes, 1986). Imagine that you are asked to decide which of the two lotteries shown below you would choose to enter. You are allowed to take one ticket selected randomly from the 100 tickets issued in just one of the gambles. To encourage you to play, you do not have to pay for your ticket; you cannot lose anything in making a choice. The outcomes (e.g. "Win 10p") are printed on the tickets inside their sealed envelopes. Which gamble would you choose?

Situation A
Gamble 1: "Win £10" on 60 tickets; "Win £20" on 40 tickets
or
Gamble 2: "Win £50" on 20 tickets; "Win £5" on 80 tickets

Now also make choices between gambles in each of the following two further situations based on Allais (1953):

Situation B
Gamble 3: "Win £1000" on all 100 tickets
or
Gamble 4: "Win £5000" on 10 tickets; "Win £1000" on 89 tickets; "Win Nothing" on 1 ticket

Situation C
Gamble 5: "Win £1000" on 11 tickets; "Win Nothing" on 89 tickets
or
Gamble 6: "Win £5000" on 10 tickets; "Win Nothing" on 90 tickets

Now, in general, the expected value of a gamble is

$$E\{V\} = P_1V_1 + P_2V_2 + \ldots$$

where the probability (P) and monetary value (V) for each outcome (1,2, . . .) are multiplied and summed over the possible outcomes. If the expected value is positive, then the gamble is favourable (for the gambler); if zero, then it is a fair gamble; if negative, then it is an unfavourable gamble.

The expected values for the gambles in Situation A are calculated as follows:

Gamble 1: $E\{V_1\} = 0.6 \times £10 + 0.4 \times £20 = £14$
Gamble 2: $E\{V_2\} = 0.2 \times £50 + 0.8 \times £5 = £16$

Note that the probabilities of 0.6 and 0.4, which multiply £10 and £20 respectively, correspond to the relative frequencies of 60/100 and 40/100.

Now unlike real lotteries which commonly have a negative expected value for the participants, the calculations show that both lotteries are favourable. Gamble 2 has the greater expected value by a small margin and would by this principle be the rational choice to make. You should by now be able to calculate the expected values for the choices in the second and third situations for yourself. Did you make the "rational" choices between Gambles 3 and 4 and between Gambles 5 and 6? We will return to discuss these cases later in the chapter.

Expected Value as a Normative Principle

Along with the calculation for expected value, a further assumption is proposed which is that given the choice of two actions (in this case gambles), people will choose the one with the highest expect value — something which is referred to as the *expected value rule*.

Combining the expected value rule with the expected value calculation provides a *normative* principle for making risk-laden decisions; that is, for decisions made under uncertainty and carrying risks of various gains and losses, the highest expected value calculation indicates the rational or ideal choice among the actions considered. If a real-life decision between alternative courses of action can be expressed in the form of choices between gambles with given probabilities and costs, then, it has been argued, the expected value calculation indicates the best possible decision. Clearly, then, if people's thought processes mirror these kinds of statistical calculations, we should be able to predict the kinds of decisions they make at least for choices where the calculation of expected value is clear.

Consider, for example, that my doctor has been very thoughtful about my complaint — my experience of indigestion in recent months — and that she is able to declare the data displayed below. The costs and benefits are expressed in arbitrary units, though they could be thought of as corresponding to costs and savings of money:

| | True States of Health | | |
Actions	Not Ill (P = 0.90)	Moderately Ill (P = 0.09)	Seriously Ill (P = 0.01)
Do nothing	+100	−100	−1000
Give pills	− 10	+100	− 500
Refer to specialist	−200	−100	+1000

Assume that she has been able to perform a decision analysis. From what I have said and from her examination of me, she has worked out the chances of my truly being in various states of health and also the gains and losses to be achieved for me in each true state of health for each of the possible medical decisions ("Actions"). She has taken into account that if some wrong action is chosen initially, then things might get worse and incur greater discomfort and costs later in my treatment, whereas correct identification of a serious illness and speedy referral to a specialist has high positive value for me.

If the expected values are worked out for each of the possible actions ("gambles") and a decision is made to adopt the action that gives maximum expected gain (or minimum expected loss) then "Do nothing" is the selected action in this case.

Questions have been raised by studies adopting this approach to decision making. One is whether decision makers, and especially experienced or successful ones, do use the expected value principle. If they do not, then might they be trained to do so? Another is whether, when the probabilities and costs are well identified — as in the simpler gambles illustrated above — people in general conform to this principle. Another is whether even experienced gamblers learn to optimise their winnings by using the principle (or indeed any other principle). A large number of studies have demonstrated that the probabilities and the monetary values do indeed have a strong influence on our choices in simple gambles, but not always wholly in accordance with the expected value decision rule. The sections that follow point to ways in which people depart from the rule and from other indications of normative behaviour in psychologically interesting ways, ways that prompt us to think more deeply about how we go about making decisions. Therefore, although the expected value principle may seem a little simplistic, it has had the important effect of prompting psychologists and others interested in decision making to test and develop new ideas.

SUBJECTIVE EVALUATION OF GAINS AND LOSSES

We do not always maintain a clear perspective when dealing with random events. Also, we have already seen that the expected value principle is unlikely to provide a good description of how people arrive at decisions in gambles. Perhaps an important additional factor is that our subjective evaluation of money does not correspond to the public scale of money. As early as 1738, Bernoulli proposed that money had a diminishing marginal value so that, for example, it seems reasonable to suppose that the personal value of gaining £250,000 may not be so great when you already have £1,000,000 than when you only have £10,000, or even just £100. More money is usually regarded as better by a gambler, but how much more is required to count as a substantial improvement is more difficult to specify. The personal scaling of the objective cash values in terms of the usefulness of money to a particular person leads to the notion of subjective value or utility, and in turn to a modified decision rule based upon maximising subjective expected utility (Bernoulli, 1738/1967). One deficiency of this view was that it could only really deal with a series of decisions rather than single choices. However, developments by von Neumann and Morgenstern (1947) and Savage (1954) led to modern utility theory, which allowed the principle to be adapted to single choices as well as incorporating the idea of *subjective utility* (Slovic, Lichtenstein, & Fischhoff, 1990).

There have been attempts to establish both subjective probabilities and utility functions for individuals. For example, Davidson, Suppes and Siegel (1957) invited subjects to choose among a large variety of gambles in order to discover the subjects' scaling of money. The question was: Could the subjects' scaling of utility for money be determined so that the "maximise expected utility" rule would fit their observed choices among gambles. In fact, many of the subjects could be regarded as showing reasonable adherence to the rule when their personal valuations of money were determined. Several studies have demonstrated that the laboratory gambling behaviour of *some* subjects can be made to fit the "maximise expected utility" rule when monetary values are suitably scaled. For these subjects, the utility of various amounts of money gained or lost varies in an orderly way, such that a simple mathematical function expresses their personal scale of the value of money. In general, however, it has been apparent since the work of Edwards (1954) that people do not typically follow the "maximise expected utility rule" even when the rule is explained to them (Lichtenstein, Slovic, & Zinc, 1969).

There have been some important critiques of utility theory which have undermined it as a comprehensive theory of human decision making. For example, several pages back you were invited to choose between some lottery-style gambles and also to perform the calculations prescribed by the expected value rule. The expected values for the gambles in Situation B are:

Gamble 3: $E\{V_3\} = 1.0 \times £1000 = £1000$
Gamble 4: $E\{V_4\} = 0.10 \times £5000 + 0.89 \times £1000 + 0.01 \times £0 = £1390$

Here Gamble 4 has the greater expected value, but many people — and perhaps you — chose Gamble 3 (Allais, 1953). Many of us would argue that we strongly prefer the certainty of a £1000 gain in Gamble 3 to the higher "expectation" from Gamble 4, but one marred by the admittedly very small chance of coming away with nothing. This kind of phenomenon is often referred to as *risk aversion*. The expected values for the gambles in Situation C are:

Gamble 5: $E\{V_5\} = 0.11 \times £1000 + 0.89 \times £0 = £110$
Gamble 6: $E\{V_6\} = 0.10 \times £5000 + 0.90 \times £0 = £500$

Gamble 6 clearly has the greater expected value and most people choose it. Here we seem to be prepared to exchange a slightly higher risk of achieving nothing — a probability of 0.89 compared with one of 0.90 — for the opportunity to achieve a much higher sum when we do win.

The comparison of Situation B with Situation C, however, produces a paradox which has been the source of much debate over the years since Allais first employed the examples cited here (see, e.g. Wright, 1984, ch. 3). The paradox lies in the fact that both situations can be described as offering identical choices if we are prepared to ignore the lottery tickets that are common to each pair of gambles. Specifically, in Situation B, 89 tickets in each gamble have "Win £1000" on them, leaving the following difference between the gambles:

Gamble 3:   "Win £1000" on 1 ticket; "Win £1000" on a further 10 tickets
Gamble 4:   "Win nothing" on 1 ticket; "Win £5000" on 10 tickets

Similarly, in Situation C, 89 tickets in each gamble have "Win Nothing" on them, leaving exactly the same pattern of gambles as those shown for Situation 2 above on the remaining 11 tickets. Hence, it can be argued that if Gamble 3 is preferred to Gamble 4, then Gamble 5 should be preferred to Gamble 6; the common parts — the essential 11 tickets — from each pair of gambles might reasonably have been expected to determine the choices made. However, people don't behave in this way, and so if utility theory is to account for both preferences it ends up with contradictory assertions.

A further difficulty for utility theory comes from the observation that people may not always think through the consequences of different decision paths. This can lead to violations of something known as the *sure thing principle* (Savage, 1954). The sure thing principle seems the epitome of common sense: it asserts that given two options A and B, if we prefer A to B whatever the circumstances, then we should prefer A to B even if we do not know what the circumstances are. For example, suppose you have agreed to bet on the toss of a coin where if it lands heads you win £200 but if it lands tails you lose £100 (clearly a favourable bet!). The coin is tossed and you are told the outcome. You are then offered the same bet again. In this case, the majority of people accept the second gamble whether or not they lost on the first gamble (Tversky & Shafir, 1992). However, if people are not told the outcome, they are less likely to bet on the second gamble. Shafir and Tversky (1992) show the same phenomenon operates for a range of problems and argue that it is an example of quasi-magical thinking: people sometimes behave in a way which suggests that their behaviour can affect the outcome of something that has already happened (even though people would reject holding such a belief).

Even in the restricted worlds of the laboratory or the gambling casino where probabilities and possible gains and losses are known, decision making is somehow more complicated than expected utility theory would suggest. There is no doubt that probabilities and monetary values, subjectively scaled or not, markedly influence our choices among gambles, but it is doubtful that we find it natural to acknowledge the consequences of the detailed calculations specified by the model. Long ago, Simon (1955) had warned us that real decision behaviour was likely to deviate from the norms indicated by the economists' model: our perceptual and conceptual systems respond to selected features of the task and its context; and our limited computational or information-processing capacities create what he termed a "bounded rationality". When explaining the idea of expected utility, it was taken for granted that people attempt to "maximise" the utility. Simon argues that it is better to see the decision maker as someone who seeks a satisfactory level of return, which may or may not correspond to the maximum available return. These critiques have prompted increasing attention to the mental operations underlying real decision making and a move away from the idea of expected utility towards more complex models.

OTHER DECISION PRINCIPLES

We have considered the maximise expected value rule at some length because it has long dominated the literature on decision making and has guided so many of the empirical studies. Are there alternative bases for rational decision making?

We should first note that millions of people gamble on horses, lotteries, football pools, the turn of a wheel at a casino and the spinning of three wheels of symbols in the one-arm bandit. The expected value for the gambler of all these activities is surely negative, since the organisers of these activities rarely go out of business, they maintain staff to run the place and take our money, they presumably pay some taxes and make a profit. Similarly, insurance, viewed as a gamble, has negative expected value for those who buy it, since the insurance companies plan to make a profit out of their business. Overall, people are bound to pay out more than, on average, they get back. Yet somehow it is regarded as rational to insure our houses, cars and valuables, among other things. Some of the mismatches between the rule — maximising expected value — and what some people choose to do may be resolved by correcting their probabilities and utilities. In other cases, the mismatch can be lessened by placing a value on the gambling activity itself or by understanding behaviour in terms of avoiding risk. In yet other cases, it may be necessary to adopt a quite different conception of decision making.

I insure my valuables, my holiday, and so on, because I wish to avoid the worst losses. Some people may elect to "gamble" on these things. I do not care for gambling on repeated coin tosses, but I would not be averse to a lottery with major prizes at low stake but also very poor odds. What is your style of risk taking? Some people are regular gamblers. They may focus upon the maximum gain possible as in a lottery — a sort of negative "regret". This is not to say that we shall be able to "rationalise" all those behaviours which appear to disobey the expected utility rule, but alternative conceptions and alternative procedures might come rather closer to explaining how real choices and risky decisions are made.

In his "portfolio theory" of risk, Coombs (1969; 1975) offered a new conception of the old problems of choosing among gambles. While we do give some recognition to the probabilities, the utilities and the expected values of gambles, these things only partially determine our choices. The perceived "riskiness" of gambles varies and we operate a preferred level of risk. For example, if we are prepared to gamble at all, some of us might prefer a very small chance of winning a very high gain, say £250,000 in a repeated gamble at £1 a time; others might prefer to chance £100 on a 2–to-1 on favourite now and again. Strong preferences can exist among gambles having equal expected value. Higher or lower levels of expected value can be traded for less or more risk around an individual's most preferred or ideal kind of gamble. The notion of "risk" remains undefined, but Coombs' data show that subjects do indeed exhibit strong personal preferences for what amount to different styles of gamble.

Prospect Theory

One of the most important alternative conceptualisations of decision making is prospect theory (Kahneman & Tversky, 1979). A key distinction in the theory is that between risk aversion and risk seeking. Earlier we argued that people are generally averse to taking risks when as an alternative there is a sufficiently positive and certain outcome to be had, and that this "certainty effect" was consistent with expected utility theory. As a further example of risk aversion, imagine that you are given the following choice of lotteries:

1. 90 out of 100 tickets win £3000; 10 out of 100 tickets win £0, *or*
2. 45 out of 100 tickets win £6000; 55 out of 100 tickets win £0

Which would you choose? Most people opt for Lottery 1, which is consistent with the idea of risk aversion (86% in Kahneman & Tversky, 1979). However, when it comes to losses, it appears that we tend to be risk seeking. For example, suppose that you are given the following, rather less pleasant, choice of lotteries:

3. 90 out of 100 tickets lose £3000; 10 out of 100 tickets lose £0, *or*
4. 45 out of 100 tickets lose £6000; 55 out of 100 tickets lose £0

In this case, most people opt for Lottery 4 rather than Lottery 3 (92% in Kahneman & Tversky, 1979). That is, rather than settle for a very high probability of a smaller loss, people choose a riskier option although the overall outcome is the same in both cases. Kahneman and Tversky called the switch from risk aversion to risk seeking the *reflection effect*, and the actual switch over point is often referred to as the *aspiration level* (March, 1988; Payne, Laughhunn, & Crum, 1980).

In addition to the key idea of a reference point, prospect theory also proposes two key stages in decision making. The first stage is an editing stage, where the prospects available are altered in a way that simplifies their mental representations and so simplifies the choice to be made between them. The second stage is an evaluation of the edited prospects followed by choice of the prospect with the most favourable subjective outcome. During editing, there is a coding operation where each outcome is described relative to the aspiration level, so that whether or not a choice is coded as a gain or loss depends on its relation to this point.

The coding of a choice as gain or loss is not independent of the context in which the decision is made. In particular, the way in which a decision is presented seems to have a marked effect on which option people tend to prefer. This effect of presentation is known as the *framing effect* and has, in turn, led to editing being referred to as framing (Tversky & Kahneman, 1981). As an example of the effect, consider the following scenarios from Tversky and Kahneman's work:

Imagine that the US is preparing for the outbreak of an unusual Asian disease, which is expected to kill 600 people. Two alternative programs to combat the disease have been proposed. Assume that the exact scientific estimate of the programs are as follows:

If Program A is adopted, 200 people will be saved.
If Program B is adopted there is 0.33 probability that 600 people will be saved and a 0.67 probability that no people will be saved.
Which program do you favour?

Presented like this, most people (72%) favoured adopting Program A, which is a risk-averse choice (because the preferred outcome is certain). However, when essentially the same choice was framed as follows:

Imagine that the US is preparing for the outbreak of an unusual Asian disease, which is expected to kill 600 people. Two alternative programs to combat the disease have been proposed. Assume that the exact scientific estimate of the programs are as follows:

If Program C is adopted, 400 people will die.
If Program D is adopted there is 0.33 probability that nobody will die and a 0.67 probability that 600 people will die.
Which program do you favour?

In this case, preference was reversed and 78% preferred Program D, which is the risk-seeking option. In prospect theory, this framing effect occurs because the evaluation of the first version of the problem is coded in terms of gain — "lives saved" — while the second version of the problem is cast in terms of loss — "people dying".

Consider again my decision whether or not to visit the doctor about the discomfort that I have recently suffered. I do not know whether or not I have a continuing state of illness, but there are risks and costs associated with my decision. According to prospect theory, a key guiding factor in my decision will be whether I frame the choice primarily in terms of loss (serious illness) or gain (continued good health). A number of studies have shown that framing effects do influence real-world style decisions in this way. For example, Meyerowitz and Chaiken (1987) looked at the effect of different wording in pamphlets designed to encourage women to examine their breasts regularly. Specifically, they predicted from prospect theory that such pamphlets would be more effective if they phrased arguments in terms of possible negative consequences rather than phrasing arguments in terms of the positive consequences of self-examination. All pamphlets gave the same basic facts on breast cancer and how to examine one's breasts. However, there were three variations of the pamphlet: in the first, no arguments for self-examination were presented; in the second, arguments were couched in terms of gain; and in the third, the same arguments were couched in terms of loss. For example, one of the arguments used by Meyerowitz and Chaiken was as follows (the wording in parentheses is the gain version and that in the square brackets is the loss version):

Research shows that women who (do) [not do] breast self examination have (an increased) [a decreased] chance of finding a tumor in the early, more treatable stage of the disease.

Immediately afterwards, those women who had read the loss version expressed more positive attitudes towards breast self-examination and this was maintained 4 months later. There was also some evidence that the loss version had led to more breast self-examination behaviour than had the gain version. Meyerowitz and Chaiken ruled out the possibility that these differences were due to differences in memory for the different versions of the pamphlet or to differences in the amount of fear aroused by them.

One problem for prospect theory is that framing effects are not as consistent as the theory would predict, particularly when referring to loss (Schneider, 1992). For example, wider factors such as perceived desirability within the culture can remove both the standard preference for risk aversion with positive framing and risk seeking with negative framing. Some theorists have proposed that one needs to introduce another reference point, the *survival reference point*, which becomes particularly salient when total loss is considered (Lopes, 1987; March & Shapiro, 1987). One's risk-taking behaviour varies according to which of the reference points — aspiration level or survival — is focused upon, and that this focus changes according to the history of outcomes of previous decisions (March & Shapiro, 1992).

Even within negatively framed problems, changing the precise surface wording of a problem had a marked impact on the proportion of people choosing the riskier option (Wagenaar, Keren, & Lichtenstein, 1988). For example, Wagenaar et al. altered a problem so that subjects in one version were asked to make choices as if they were a public health officer and in another as though they were a member of the population at risk. When doing the latter version, people tended to be more risk averse in their choices. Therefore, it would seem that factors such as the group referred to do affect choices, yet prospect theory has difficulty coping with such effects, as it does not really have any explanation of how during the editing stage of a decision there can be an effect of such factors.

Regret Theory

Prospect theory has had some notable successes but, as we have just highlighted, it does also have shortcomings as an explanation of human decision making. A style of theory that has attempted to deal with individual differences in decision making is one that involves comparing possible outcomes in terms of the degree of regret or rejoicing (Bell, 1982; Loomes & Sugden, 1982). Regret and rejoicing are not treated as absolutes but as resulting from comparisons of different possible outcomes. If I find it attractive to minimise my maximum regret, I may visit the doctor so as to avoid the worst possible outcome even when that outcome has a very small probability — the potential regret for not doing so is simply too great to risk. Many of us have probably used such a strategy consciously when making real-life decisions. Imagine that time when something that you really wanted was offered at a bargain price — though still expensive — in a sale: how would you feel if you went home without it? What about that horse with the same name as your best friend — it might be a 25/1 outsider, but what if it won and you hadn't put a pound or two on it? What about that offer of a job which is exactly what you want to do but which takes you away from an area and a lifestyle you enjoy — would you always regret it if you turned it down? Now whatever one decided in these cases, one is clearly employing a form of decision making which has some semblance of rationality but one which is not easily expressed as a combination of probabilities and outcomes.

Josephs, Larrick, Steele and Nisbett (1992) proposed a version of regret theory which assumed that the expectation of feedback on outcomes and maintenance of a good self-image were key factors when taking a decision. The idea has received some empirical support with, for example, people with lower self-esteem being more likely to take decisions that reduce the likelihood of experiencing regret (Josephs et al., 1992; Larrick, 1993).

The details of recent developments in regret theory and supporting evidence begin to take us away from cognitive psychology, but the theory does highlight how our conceptualisation of decision making may need to integrate a wide range of ideas from work in probability theory to notions such as self-protection. Overall, there are several possibilities for "rationalising" decision making using a number of principles. This is not to suggest, however, that all decision making can readily be characterised as a rational process. It is clear that no single rational procedure appears to be natural or untutored; and we must recall Simon's warning about our cognitive limitations in handling information. We now turn to consider several robust psychological mechanisms that further illuminate our capacities and limitations in judgement of uncertain situations.

PROBABILITY JUDGEMENTS

Many of the decisions that we make cannot be based on objective probabilities as, more often than not, such information is not available. Therefore, a crucial part of some decision making is deriving a subjective probability which may be expressed numerically or linguistically. For example, suppose we return to my various aches and pains. According to utility theory, I could outline my pay-off matrix as follows:

	True State of Health	
Actions	Ill (P = 0.01)	Not Ill P = 0.99
Visit	1000	−100
Not Visit	−1000	100

The probabilities arise from *my* judgement of the chances. I do not have a long run of experiences of making exactly this kind of decision and of learning the consequences; nor can I examine the features of the situation so clearly that I can determine the probabilities in any objective way. In fact, the subjectively determined probabilities given above can only express my relative confidence in the true state of my health. There are also subjective evaluations of the costs and benefits, i.e. utilities. The resulting numbers which would be needed to calculate the expected utility are simply relative values in arbitrary units.

Over a number of years, Tversky and Kahneman have explored some of the principles by which we make the difficult task of assessing probabilities rather easier (Kahneman & Tversky, 1972; 1982a; 1982b; Tversky and Kahneman, 1974; 1983). This research is in the same spirit as Simon's ideas concerning bounded rationality: our cognitive limitations force us to simplify decision making. Sometimes, as we shall see, this leads to errors.

Representativeness

Researchers in decision making frequently make the distinction between algorithms and heuristics (see also Chapter 12). Broadly speaking, algorithms are well-specified procedures which guarantee finding a solution to a problem if a solution exists. Heuristics are less well-specified and are frequently described as rules of thumb: procedures which frequently find the correct solution but are by no means guaranteed to do so. It has been claimed for some time that when making judgements about the probabilities of events or outcomes, people frequently do not make them in accordance with statistical theory (Tversky & Kahneman, 1973). Instead, it is claimed, they make use of heuristics — "cognitive short-cuts" — to make probabilistic judgements.

Consider the following question taken from the work of Kahneman and Tversky (1982a):

1. Tossing a coin six times, which of the following sequences is the more likely to occur:

   (a) HHHTTT; (b) HTHTHT; or (c) HTTHTH?

Typically, people regard the three sequences of coins as having different chances of occurring, sequences (a) and (b) being thought to be less likely than (c); yet the chances of observing such sequences are, in fact, equal. To many people, the sequence HHHTTT seems somehow special compared with one like HTTHTH — to us the former does not seem to reflect the key property of randomness, that is, HTTHTH seems more *representative* of our intuitive notion of randomness. However, arguments from theory — or trials with coins, an experiment which the theory would claim to represent — show that the sequences are equally likely and that our notion of what random sequences look like is rather shaky. As in the gambler's fallacy, we expect small samples too frequently to echo the features of the longer run sequences: some random outcomes — as in the sets of digits shown earlier — appear "more random" than others.

Consider another example from Kahneman and Tversky (1973) which illustrates the operation of the representativeness heuristic. Imagine that there is a group of 100 people and you are told that 70 of them are lawyers and 30 of them are engineers. A person is picked from the group at random and you are asked to estimate the chances of that person being an engineer. Most people correctly estimate the chance as being 30%. You are now told that a second person has been selected at random from the group, but this time you are given the following short, biographical sketch of that person:

> 2a. Dick is a 30 year old man. He is married with no children. A man of high ability and high motivation, he promises to be quite successful in his field. He is well liked by his colleagues.

You are now asked to estimate the chances of this person being an engineer. Overall, people estimated that the probability of Dick being an engineer was around 50%. In this case, the biographical and personal information is fairly neutral and one might not expect it to help people decide whether Dick is a lawyer or an engineer. However, the knowledge of the 70:30 mix in the group should have affected the judgements. That is, if the person could have come from either group, then it is more probable that he came from the larger one. People seem to be ignoring the initial proportions of lawyers and engineers (the so-called "base rates").

Tversky and Kahneman also used sketches that seemed to fit with stereotypes of engineers or lawyers, such as the following:

> 2b. Joe is a 45 year old man. He is married with four children. He is generally conservative, careful, and ambitious. He shows no interest in politics and social issues and spends most of his time on his many hobbies, which include home carpentry, sailing and mathematical puzzles.

Here the lack of impact of base rates was even more marked and even with knowledge of the base rate of 30% engineers, people estimated the chances of Joe being an engineer at over 90%. According to a statistical theory known as *Bayes' Theorem*, if one is to derive an accurate probability estimate in these cases, it is essential to take such base-rate information into account and not just rely on the representativeness of the description. People, however, seem to be guided by images of what lawyers and engineers are like and how representative an individual is of a group. In a later section, we will return to the argument about base rates and consider it in more detail but, for now, the data from Tversky and Kahneman illustrate what a powerful influence information that seems relevant to "representativeness" can have when assessing probabilities and how it can lead to incorrect estimates.

Consider a final example from Kahneman and Tversky (1982a), illustrating the effects of representativeness:

3. Linda is 31 years old, single, outspoken and very bright. She majored in philosophy. As a student, she was deeply concerned with issues of discrimination and social justice, and participated in anti-nuclear demonstrations.

Which of the following statements about Linda is more probable?

A. Linda is a bank teller;

B. Linda is a bank teller who is active in the feminist movement.

Some 86% of statistically naive undergraduates chose Statement B as more probable. Even among statistically sophisticated psychology graduate students, 50% endorsed that answer. Further, when the above two statements were embedded in a list of eight comparable statements about Linda, over 80% of both groups endorsed Statement B. It seems as though Statement B is somehow more representative of the "kind of person" Linda seems to be.

Statement B is less probable by the following argument. Represent the statement by:

A. Linda is X;

B. Linda is both X and Y.

The chances of Linda being both X and Y cannot be greater than her chances of being X. Note that Statement A does not exclude the possibility that Linda is both X and Y, but it does also allow other possibilities such as Linda is both X and Z but not Y, etc. At best, the characteristics X and Y can be perfectly associated (that is, every time X occurs then so does Y), which would mean that both statements would be equally probable. A conditional probability such as B cannot be greater than an associated simple probability such as A.

When given the statement, "the probability of a conjunction of both X and Y cannot exceed the probability of X or of the probability of Y", 83% of statistically naive students accepted it. However, only 43% accepted the equivalent argument in relation to the statements above, that is:

Statement A is more probable than B because the probability that Linda is *both* a bank teller and an active feminist must be smaller than the probability that she is a bank teller.

Many of these people were failing to apply a rule which they correctly endorsed when presented in its abstract form. It is possible that Statement B is more representative of Linda; it conforms more with our expectations. People seem to be asking themselves: Is B more like Linda than A? This is not exactly what is asked, but it does seem to be what is evoked.

Representativeness is a heuristic that can be used to guide probability judgements. In everyday life where exact probabilities may rarely be known or where rough approximations may be sufficient, such a heuristic may be a sensible strategy. However, as the above examples demonstrate, it can clearly lead people to make erroneous judgements and these too may have their costs.

Availability

Representativeness is one heuristic which can bias our judgements about how probable something is relative to the answers provided by probability theory. Another mechanism we may employ is illustrated by responses to the following question:

4. The frequency of appearance of letters in the English language was studied. A typical text was selected, and the relative frequency with which various letters of the alphabet appeared in first and third positions in words was recorded. Words of less than three letters were excluded from the count. Consider the letter R. Is R more likely to appear in
— the first position?
— the third position?

By now you may have become alerted to the fact that our answers to these selected questions are often wrong. Many subjects say that R is more likely to appear in the first position than in the third. In fact, the letter R appears in the third position more frequently than in the first position. For example, you might note that in the question itself, the letter R comes third in eight words and first in only two words. In response to such questions, we may find ourselves attempting to retrieve words which begin with the letter R and those which have R in third position. After a little effort, we find it easier to retrieve the former than the latter and use "ease of access" as a guide to how many words have a letter in that position. For reasons that probably derive from the way we store words, words beginning with R are more available. The extent to which we can use our store of knowledge and experience when we are faced with a problem is limited by the restrictions on our ability to recall. The features of the situation, the specific stimuli involved and retrieval strategies we may employ will all affect the success of memory retrieval (see Chapter 10). Rather than search through every single item in memory, we retrieve a small subset of items which are easily found and use those. That is, we use an availability heuristic in judging the relative frequency of events in our experience.

Judging the relative frequency of words beginning with various letters of the alphabet may seem somewhat distant from risk judgement in general. However, Slovic, Fischhoff and Lichtenstein (1980) have shown how the availability heuristic may operate to influence our perceptions of everyday events. In their study of the judged frequency of causes of death, there was a general tendency for subjects to overestimate the frequency of the rarer causes such as botulism, floods, measles and tornadoes, and to underestimate the frequency of the more common causes such as strokes, various cancers and diabetes. Coombs and Slovic (1979) studied the relation between these perceptions of risk and the relative frequency of reported deaths in newspapers. Not surprisingly, it was found that the newspapers frequently featured homicides, accidents and some natural disasters and markedly under-represented strokes, various cancers and diabetes. The interesting finding was that to a large extent people's judgements of risk corresponded to the frequency of deaths reported in the newspapers, even when allowance was made for the extent to which both people and newspapers reflect some knowledge of the objective risks.

Perhaps we are better able to make these judgements when we experience events for ourselves or when the events are our professional concern? Fischhoff, Slovic and Lichtenstein (1978) asked three groups of college students to estimate the relative frequency of major deficiencies that might cause a car to fail to start. One group was provided with a diagram of a "fault tree" showing details of the major groups of causes of "car won't start" shown in brief form below:

1. Battery charge insufficient, e.g. faulty ground connection: paint, corrosion, dirt, loose connections.
2. Starting system defective, e.g. switches defective: ignition switch, starter relay, neutral start switch, solenoid.
3. Fuel system defective, e.g. insufficient fuel: car out of gas, clogged fuel line, leak.
4. Ignition system defective, e.g. coil faulty: cap cracked, electrodes corroded, improper point gap.
5. Other engine problems, e.g. poor compression: leaking head gasket, cracked cylinder head, valve burnt.
6. Mischievous acts or vandalism, e.g. theft or breakage of vital part, siphoning of gas, disruption of wiring.
7. All other problems.

All headings were fully elaborated with possibilities except the last category. Subjects were asked to examine the diagram carefully and to estimate how often in 100 trips which are delayed due to a "starting failure", those delays are caused by each of the seven factors and to make

TABLE 13.1

Attribution of Starting Failures for Pruned and Unpruned Fault Trees by College Students and Experts: Proportions of Failures Assigned to Causes[a]

Group	n	Causes 1, 3, 5	Causes 2, 4, 6	Other
College students				
Full tree	93	0.53	0.39	0.08
Pruned 1	29	0.86	—	0.14
Pruned 2	26	—	0.78	0.23
Experts				
Full tree	13	0.56	0.38	0.06
Pruned 1	16	0.79	—	0.21

[a] Adapted and rounded from Fischhoff et al. (1978).

sure that the responses summed to 100. Two other groups were given "pruned trees" — fault trees in which a selection of only three of the major groups of causes plus the residual "all other problems" category was presented. If subjects were sensitive to the missing causes, then the increased use of the "all other problems" category should reflect the proportions that would otherwise have been assigned elsewhere. The responses of the three college student groups are compared in the upper part of Table 13.1.

Fischhoff et al. took the first group's result as typical of what happens when all causes are mentioned. They argued that if the subjects in the "Pruned 1" group had been sensitive to the omitted causes, they might have been expected to assign 47% (proportions 0.39 + 0.08 in Table 13.1) of causes to the "other" category. Similarly, the "Pruned 2" group might have been expected to assign 61% (0.53 + 0.08) of causes to "other". In fact, although the use of "other" increased between two and three times in response to the omitted causes, it should have increased between six and eight times. Professional automobile mechanics ("experts" in Table 13.1) shown the restricted list of causes similarly overestimated the prevalence of those causes when compared with the judgements made by fellow experts who used the full list. For both college students and experts, what was out of sight — not immediately available — was, in effect, out of mind. By contrast, the immediate availability of events featured in the media can create exaggerated perceptions of risk. Football attendance drops after a fire in a football stadium and recent aircraft accidents make people more apprehensive about flying. Advertisers, politicians and insurance companies no doubt benefit from this phenomenon.

Another sign of the bias towards available information is seen by adding together the results for the "Pruned 1" and "Pruned 2" groups. If one does this, it would seem that the probability of causes 1–6 (0.86 + 0.78) is greater than 1, yet probabilities can only range between 0 and 1, thus a basic rule of probability is broken. This phenomenon is not rare in human judgements. Formal systems like a probability theory employ a strong notion of consistency. In school geometry, for example, if two lines are defined to be parallel at the outset, then we would rightly be surprised if later in some proof or derivation they were found not to be parallel. In real probability judgements, however, a subject can apparently tolerate inconsistency, or at least not perceive it immediately.

People do not seem to use the three rules of probability theory when they make judgements. Instead, they use cognitive short-cuts which are based on the way memory works. If an event or sequence of events is regarded as typical or representative it is thought to be more probable, and if events are easily retrieved in memory they are thought to be more probable. So, if I am deciding whether to visit the doctor about my pain which may or may not be indigestion, my judgement will be affected by information which does not actually alter the probability that I have indigestion. If a colleague at work has recently been diagnosed as suffering from a duodenal ulcer, and I have just heard that my neighbour's father has stomach cancer, then I will be more inclined to judge that I should visit the doctor. However, those two events, although available to me, do not change the probability that I have a serious illness.

Of course, I do not have much access to tables of statistics which tell me how probable it is that I have a serious illness. It is possible that I use a heuristic like availability because I do not have anything else, and it is possible that in many everyday situations they are adequate guides to decision making. However, what happens if I am given the objective probabilities? Do I use them correctly once I have got them?

Base Rates and Updating Information

The availability and representativeness heuristics might well be employed for judgements when we are not aware of the objective frequencies of events in the world. When this information is available, it has to be integrated with additional evidence from our current experiences. Earlier, the experiment by Kahneman and Tversky on representativeness, in which people were asked to make judgements about the probability of an individual selected from a group being a lawyer or an engineer, showed that the integration, or updating, is not very easy to do. In particular, people in that study seemed not to take sufficient account of base rate information.

Phillips and Edwards (1966) showed that subjects who were asked to revise an initial judgement of probability given some new information, failed to revise the probability estimate sufficiently. That is, they kept closer to their own original estimate than was justified given the importance of the new information. So, when subjects were given prior information in Kahneman and Tversky's "engineers–lawyers" experiment, they ignored it, and when in Phillips and Edwards' study they were using their own estimates of prior probability, they did not give enough value to new information. Some of these differences may be due to the experimental situation. There may be no reason for subjects to pay any attention to the unexperienced and seemingly arbitrary information that there are 70 lawyers and 30 engineers in the group in Kahneman and Tversky's study. Where base rates that have been experienced are challenged by new data presented in an experiment, as in Phillips and Edwards' study, subjects may be unlikely to make instant adjustments. As Navon (1978) has pointed out, typically the new data we experience may not be wholly independent of prior knowledge and so would not deserve the degree of updating assumed for truly novel and uncorrelated data. The conservatism in adjusting to new data may result from the cautionary "drag" of the many connections that have been made among the old data. As Bar-Hillel (1980) remarks, people may well ignore base rate information because they see it as essentially irrelevant to the decision that they are making. In certain circumstances, people can be sensitive to relevant factors such as sample size — that is, when given different options, they will be more confident in judgements based on larger samples (Kunda & Nisbett, 1986a; 1986b). However, this sensitivity can lead people to aggregate information so as to create a larger sample without really considering whether or not the data being aggregated are comparable. Schaller (1992) showed this in a study in which people were asked to judge the abilities of fictitious racquet ball players based on their previous records in various leagues. Where the players' records were sparse, people tended to aggregate performance across leagues without paying sufficient attention to the different standards of the leagues. Certainly, the issue of how information is integrated when making decisions is no simple matter.

A study focusing on this issue in an applied setting was conducted by Eddy (1982), who reviewed the problems of uncertain reasoning among physicians in the diagnosis of breast cancer. Women present themselves to a physician complaining of a "lump", an unusual mass of tissue. Following a general examination, the physician may have recourse to a mammogram, an X-ray examination, in which cancer cells may be seen to absorb the X-rays differently from non-malignant cells. The physician may further call for a biopsy, surgical removal of some or all of the tissue in the mass for microscopic examination. The latter procedure can be regarded as reliably definitive but, of course, it can also be disfiguring to various degrees, depending upon the amount of tissue removed. Even a minor scar, along with the cost to personal or public resources and the nuisance and danger of an operation, can be serious in a case where life turns out not to be at risk. Further, if the mammogram has any validity as a diagnostic stage, then in some cases surgery should be avoidable even though there is some residual risk of incorrect diagnosis. Or, if surgery is to be employed in all cases, then the mammogram is redundant.

Eddy asked physicians to consider the following data. From general examination of a particular case, a physician estimates that the probability of the lump being cancerous is small, approximately 0.01 or 1%

TABLE 13.2

Probabilities of Positive and Negative Mammography Reports given that Cancer is or is not Present[a]

X-ray result	Cancer (ca)	No cancer (nc)
Positive (+)	0.8	0.1
Negative (−)	0.2	0.9
Total	1.0	1.0

[a]Adapted (rounded) from Eddy (1982, p. 253); base data taken from Snyder (1966).

(probabilities of events are expressed as values between 0 and 1 inclusive, where 0 corresponds to the event not happening and 1 to the event always happening). The physician orders a mammogram and the radiologist's report comes back saying "Positive: cancer suspected". What now should the estimate be of the chances of cancer? A simple answer would be to say that this estimate should be very high, to reflect what the radiologist reported. However, we have to ask how the original estimate (probability of 0.01) has changed, given that the mammograph result is not always correct. The probabilities of positive (+) and negative (−) mammography reports when cancer is present (ca) and when cancer is not present (nc) are shown in Table 13.2. In particular, the data include values for the conditional probabilities $P\{+ \mid ca\}$ $P\{ + \mid nc\}$. But these show the retrospective accuracy of a positive outcome to the test when the true nature of the cells in the tissue is known. What we need to find is the probabilities of cancer given the mammography reports — that is, the predictive accuracy of the test. We especially require a value for $P\{ca \mid +\}$.

The relation between the two kinds of data is given by Bayes' theorem, which calculates the probability that an hypothesis is true (this patient has cancer) given that a piece of evidence exists (the mammogram is positive). The theorem works for any hypothesis and any piece of evidence, but for this particular situation we can write the equation as:

$$P\{ ca \mid +\} = \frac{P\{+ \mid ca\} \cdot P\{ca\}}{P\{+ \mid ca\} \cdot P\{ca\} + P\{+ \mid nc\} \cdot P\{nc\}}$$

To review: we are trying to find the revised probability for the hypothesis that the patient has cancer given that: (a) the physician originally thought that she probably did not have cancer ($P\{ca\} = 0.01$); (b) the test gets it right 80% of the time when there is a cancer ($P\{+ \mid ca\} = 0.8$); and (c) that the test gets it wrong 10% of the time when there is no cancer ($P\{+ \mid nc\} = 0.1$). The remaining expression stands for the prior probability of not having cancer ($P\{nc\}$), which is equal to $1 - P\{ca\}$ or 0.99. So we fill in the values as follows:

$$P\{ca \mid +\} = \frac{(0.8)(0.01)}{(0.8)(0.01) + (0.1)(0.99)} = 0.075$$

The revised estimate is that there is now a 7 to 8% chance of cancer. Many of the physicians studied by Eddy put the figure nearer to 0.8 (80%). They probably confused the accuracy of the test when cancer is known to be present with the predictive accuracy of the test. Because it is not very likely that the patient has cancer in the first place, the test result increases the probability by rather less than our intuitions would suggest, despite the accuracy of the test. (Test the operation of the formula for yourself, e.g. by calculating what the result would be if the test was 95%, or even 100%, accurate when cancer is known to be present.) Remember that the test gives positive signs 10% of the time that cancer is not present and that the probability of no cancer present prior to the test is 99% ($P\{nc\} = 0.99$). Table 13.3 gives the full set of calculations for the case considered by Eddy using Bayes' theorem. The outcomes of the X-ray test cause the probability of cancer present to swing between 0.075 (+) and 0.002 (−). While the second value more-or-less matches one's intuitions about the negative outcome of a test, the first value is certainly different from many people's judgement or guess given a positive outcome.

Eddy's review of decision making in medicine points to frequent misinterpretation of probability data in the medical literature. If we do not find it easy to make well-judged use of probabilities when these are supplied, it is not surprising that the expected value decision rule, which depends so strongly upon the probability values employed, is not good at describing our decision-making behaviour even in simple gambles. However, several problems are left out of this analysis. First, our discussion of Eddy's review has left out any mention of costs. While we know that physicians may sometimes estimate probabilities wrongly, they may nevertheless make sensible decisions in practice using some kind of compound of probability and costs. We should also recognise that base rate data supplied in an experiment — such as $P\{ca\} = 0.01$ — may not be as effective as data acquired by personal experience. So long as the physicians are not found to be referring every patient for an operation

TABLE 13.3

The Probabilities of Cancer or No Cancer Present Given that the X-ray Report is Positive or Negative and that $P\{ca\} = 0.01$[a]

Clinical Outcome	X-ray Positive (+)	X-ray Negative (−)
Cancer (ca)	0.075	0.002
No cancer (nc)	0.925	0.998
Total	1.000	1.000

[a]Computed from Table 13.2 using Bayes' theorem.

regardless of the outcome of preliminary tests, there is the possibility that their decisions have some rational basis. To date there is no clear basis for adopting this more optimistic view; but we ought perhaps to suspend judgement until more work has been done on alternative bases for decisions.

Overconfidence

A number of studies have shown that people are often more confident in their judgement than they should be given the facts (Fischoff, Slovic, & Lichtenstein, 1977; Lichtenstein, Fischhoff, & Phillips, 1982). For example, in a typical study, subjects are given questions which contain alternative answers, such as "Which is longer, the Suez canal or the Panama canal?", they make their selection and then express their confidence in that choice (in terms of an estimate of the probability that they are correct). When subjects' performance is analysed, the most common finding is that their confidence is greater than the proportion of responses correct. Overconfidence seems to persist when subjects are expert in an area (Wagenaar & Keren, 1986). Perhaps the most intriguing example of overconfidence is in our ability to predict our own actions and those of our peers (Dunning, Griffin, Milojkovic, & Ross, 1990; Vallone, Griffin, Lin, & Ross, 1990). Overconfidence seems resistant to manipulations such as offering monetary rewards for accurate assessments or being warned about the phenomenon in advance (Fischoff, 1982). However, overconfidence is not universal, and some studies have shown that when asked to answer very easy questions and rate their confidence, then people tend to be underconfident (Lichtenstein et al., 1982).

In accounting for both overconfidence and underconfidence, Griffin and Tversky (1992) distinguish between the strength and weight of evidence considered when making a decision. Strength refers to the extremeness of the evidence. For example, when selecting a horse to back in a race, strong evidence might be that it has won its last three races. Weight refers to the credibility or predictive validity of the evidence. For example, what was the standard of the races that the horse won and were they comparable to the current race? Griffin and Tversky use other examples such as a job reference. Here one can distinguish between strength as reflected in the tone of the letter (warm recommendation) and the weight of the evidence as reflected in the credibility of the source (How well did they know the applicant? Do the referees have any particular vested interests in this applicant getting the job?).

Having drawn up a distinction between strength and weight, Griffin and Tversky argue that people typically place too much reliance on the strength of evidence and not enough on its weight: initially, we focus on the strength of the evidence and only subsequently make an (insufficient) adjustment for its weight. This is an example of a general heuristic which is called *anchoring and adjustment* (Slovic & Lichtenstein, 1971; Tversky & Kahneman, 1974). Where the strength of evidence is high and the weight of the evidence is low, this account predicts overconfidence will occur. That is, where one receives a very enthusiastic reference from someone who knows the applicant only slightly, one tends to be overconfident that the reference predicts that the person will succeed at the job. On the other hand, underconfidence will occur when a moderate reference comes from a highly knowledgeable referee who knows the candidate well.

Griffin and Tversky tested this prediction more systematically using, perhaps not surprisingly, a scenario involving coins. Cunningly, however, it was not a case of coin tossing but one of coin spinning. Subjects were told that when spinning a coin, imperfections on its rim lead to a systematic bias in which side lands face up. The bias is, of course, not all-or-none, but let us suppose it tends to land with one side face up on 60% of occasions. The problem for the subjects was that they were not told which way the bias goes — that is, it might have been a bias to heads or a bias to tails. Subjects were then given tables of "spin outcomes" and asked to estimate the probability that the coin used had a bias of 60% (such an estimate is taken to be a measure of confidence). Strength was reflected in the proportion of the spins that were heads (stronger evidence being higher proportions) and weight was reflected in the number of spins from which the data were derived (greater weight being a larger number of spins). An example of the kind of table presented to students is given below:

Number of Heads	Number of Tails	Sample Size
2	1	3
3	0	3
3	2	5
4	1	5
5	0	5
9	8	17
10	7	17
11	6	17

Now, using Bayes theorem, which we introduced earlier, one can derive a probability of a particular pattern for a particular sample size being evidence for a 3:2 bias for heads. What Griffin and Tversky found was that where strength was high and weight was low, subjects' confidence was greater than the calculated probability. For example, given the pattern 3:0, subjects' median confidence level was 85%, whereas the statistical probability by Bayes' theorem is only 0.77. However, when strength was low and weight was high, subjects tended to be underconfident. For example, given the pattern 10:7, the statistical probability is again 0.77, but the median confidence rating was 59.5%. In this case, subjects' estimates are not being sufficiently qualified by the change in the weight of the evidence. This demonstrates one of the beauties of the strength–weight account, which is that it can account for underconfidence as well as overconfidence. As an extreme contrast, given the ratio of 2:1, the median confidence rating was 63% when the probability was 0.6, a very slight overconfidence. However, with a sample size of 33 and a 19:14 split, median confidence was only 60%, yet the probability is 0.88. Both patterns can be explained by the idea that subjects focus too much on strength and do not adjust this initial judgement sufficiently in the light of the weight of the evidence. We should offer one caution at this point about Griffin and Tversky's account, which is that their reliance on Bayesian statistics to produce the "correct" answer is not something with which all statisticians would agree (Gigerenzer, Hoffrage, & Kleinbolting, 1991; von Mises, 1957).

Clearly, in many real-life tasks, it is not easy to tease apart strength and weight, but Griffin and Tversky argue that these factors remain relevant and may have a vital role in everyday beliefs. Returning to the scenario with which we opened this chapter, we may place considerable reliance on the strength of a symptom so that we are more certain we are ill and so more likely to consult a doctor when pain is sudden and severe than when it is long-lasting but mild. Here the strength of the evidence may be too dominant and its weight (the validity of our medical opinion) neglected.

OTHER CONCEPTIONS OF DECISION MAKING

So far, we have pointed to possible defects in our appreciation of probabilities and our failure to use the formal reasoning procedures underlying probability theory. In addition, the expected value decision rule, which had so dominated the research on decision making, is not easy to apply to situations beyond the simple gambles. We do not usually have enough data on probabilities and the utilities of outcomes for many real decisions; and when data are supplied, we do not often seem to use the rule.

Now, critics of the line of studies initiated by Tversky and Kahneman have offered us a number of cautionary notes. First, it should be said that the examples used to illustrate the biases and heuristics were selected from a large number of such tasks. Not all of the tasks which appeared to have the same formal properties reliably show the phenomena claimed (e.g. Jungerman, 1983). Second, variations in wording or in the context supplied for the tasks sometimes have a marked effect on the strength of an alleged bias in judgement (see the above section on framing effects and Bar-Hillel, 1983). Third, it can sometimes be argued that the subjects of these experiments perceive the tasks differently from that intended by the experimenter and hold to different goals in performing the tasks (e.g. Jungerman, 1983; Phillips, 1983).

More generally, a number of wider questions have been raised about whether it is sensible for us to believe that rationality in all decision making resides in some small number of principles which may be applied to a wide variety of decisions. In part, the debate echoes the one discussed in Chapter 12 in relation to the role of logic and other abstract or formal prescriptions for thinking and problem solving. We may sometimes agree that there are some well-defined situations for which the formal rules are "best" in a well-understood sense. For example, given enough data on probabilities and utilities along with an agreement that maximising expected gain is our aim, there is no doubt what rules should be used. But different tasks in life may deserve different formulations of the rules and different statements of goals. The controversy is not about whether probability theory or decision theory are "true", but about when or how they are sensibly mapped onto our knowledge of events in the world. If this is the case, then how we come selectively to apply the rules — how we are cued to adopt particular approaches — is a major issue for psychological study. In summary, if some formal way of thinking can be shown to be useful, the questions are: When might it usefully be applied? What is its domain of reference? How do we come to learn and apply the rule selectively?

Without, however, taking the extremely optimistic view that all human judgements and decisions are, if did we but know it, entirely "best" and "rational", we should nevertheless allow that most of life's decisions have multiple attributes. When we are choosing a job, a car or a house, the probabilities and costs are not well identified. We have to work at such choices, seeking out information, exploring many dimensions of the options open to us, and perhaps reflecting upon the alternative futures likely to be experienced. Hence, a recent trend in decision research has been to regard decision making as more akin to the process of solving a difficult problem, the moment at which a formula or rule may be applied being only a small part of the process. As we gather information and views about the alternatives, the structure of our knowledge may well shift dramatically, as when we achieve a new understanding in learning something. Also, we cannot usually delay these decisions for too long. Job opportunities come and go, an old car is no longer safe, and desirable houses may be sold to others. A sufficient solution, knowing what we know and being unable to wait for more information, is what we must typically accept.

Similarly, the process of medical diagnosis, at least in the more difficult cases, is badly described if it is characterised as a simple matter of gathering evidence and making a decision. Rather, preliminary symptoms lead to some preliminary hypotheses. More evidence is sought in line with those hypotheses, further guesses are made, old evidence may be re-evaluated, and so on. What may appear to be an untidy process continues until a decision can be made with sufficient certainty, having regard to the, by then, elaborated structure of knowledge, including the risks and the costs where these can be evaluated.

SUMMARY

Decision making has long been studied as a choice among gambles for which the probabilities of the various outcomes and the associated gains and losses are known. Rules based upon expected utility theory which have been applied to such data are not wholly successful in modelling human decision-making behaviour, whether in laboratory studies of simple gambles or in more complex real decisions. In general, the research leaves one pessimistic about the descriptive status of expected utility theory in either its objective or subjective guises; but the extensive range of phenomena exposed in these studies raises a number of issues. For one, the probabilities we employ do not always correspond to the objective or publicly acknowledged values. Perhaps we do not reliably register the relative frequencies of events in the environment? Evidence is accumulating that we not only deviate from what probability theory and expected utility theory would specify as ideal behaviour, but that we employ some short-cut heuristic principles and we exhibit some systematic biases. These heuristics and biases are sometimes interpretable as due to the way in which our memories work. Immediately available information naturally influences our thinking more readily than hard-to-retrieve information. We have strong notions from experience about the representativeness of sample events from variable domains. We do not seem to integrate base information with new information efficiently.

Against these doubts about the rationality of human decision making, there are also doubts about the assumptions in some of this research. We do not commonly face the purest random devices, like coin tosses, in nature. Few of our decisions can be informed by clear probabilities and costs for simple options. We must treat with caution the view that the phenomena of availability and representativeness bias our judgements in some decision-making tasks; these heuristics must reflect the way our memories are organised so as to be sufficiently useful for many of the tasks we face. One cannot always assume that there is perfect agreement among statisticians about which is the appropriate way of using probability theory. Decision making is also often concerned with complex sequences of information gathering and hypothesis testing — as in medical diagnosis — and to characterise only the moment of final decision by a rule may be to oversimplify matters and to overlook the problem-solving nature of reaching a decision. Taking decisions and taking risks seems to be an important activity not only for getting through life, but for defining ourselves psychologically (Douglas & Wildavsky, 1982). As Lopes (1987) points out, to understand risky choices fully will require going beyond the boundaries of cognition to consider such things as cultural expectations and roles.

Further reading about the continuing attempts to find the proper place of probabilities and utilities in human decision making can be found in G. Wright (1984), *Behavioural decision theory: An introduction*. A detailed review is also provided by P. Slovic, S. Lichtenstein and B. Fischoff (1990). A broad collection of papers, including several cited in this chapter, is provided by D. Kahneman, P. Slovic, and A. Tversky (Eds) (1982), *Judgement under uncertainty: Heuristics and biases*. The *Paradoxes of gambling behaviour* (1988,a) by W. A. Wagenaar compares the explanatory powers of the heuristics and biases approach with that of expected utility theory using studies of public lotteries and casino games. The review of *Medical thinking* by S. Schwartz and T. Griffin (1986) takes on board a variety of perspectives on decision making and the psychological mechanisms that may influence medical judgements.

References

Abend, W., Bizzi, E., & Morasso, P. (1982). Human arm trajectory formation. *Brain, 105*, 331–348.

Ahn, W. K., & Medin, D. L. (1992). A two-stage model of category construction. *Cognitive Science, 16*, 81–121.

Aitchison, J. (1987). *Words in the mind: An introduction to the mental lexicon.* Oxford: Blackwell.

Allais, M. (1953). Le comportement de l'homme rationel devant le risque: Critique des postulats et axiomes de l'ecole americaine. *Econometrica, 21*, 503–546.

Allport, D. A. (1980). Attention and performance. In G. Claxton (Ed.), *Cognitive psychology: New directions.* London: Routledge and Kegan Paul.

Allport, D. A. (1983). Language and cognition. In R. Harris (Ed.), *Approaches to language.* Oxford: Pergamon Press.

Allport, D. A. (1985). Distributed memory, modular subsystems and dysphasia. In S. Newman and R. Epstein (Eds), *Dysphasia.* Edinburgh: Churchill Livingstone.

Allport, D. A. (1993). Attention and control: Have we been asking the wrong questions? In D. E. Meyer and S. Kornblum (Eds), *Attention and performance XIV: A silver jubilee.* Cambridge, MA: MIT Press.

Allport, D. A., & Funnell, E. (1981). Components of the mental lexicon. *Philosophical Transactions of the Royal Society, London, B295*, 397–410.

Allport, D. A., Antonis, B., & Reynolds, P. (1972). On the division of attention: A disproof of the single channel hypothesis. *Quarterly Journal of Experimental Psychology, 24*, 225–235.

Anderson, J. R. (1976). *Language, memory and thought.* Hillsdale, NJ: Lawrence Erlbaum Associates Inc.

Anderson, J. R. (1978). Arguments concerning representations for mental imagery. *Psychological Review, 85*, 249–277.

Anderson, J. R. (1983). *The architecture of cognition.* Cambridge, MA: Harvard University Press.

Anderson, J. R. (1985). *Cognitive psychology and its implications*, 2nd edn. New York: W. H. Freeman.

Anderson, J. R. (1990). *The adaptive character of thought.* Hillsdale, NJ: Lawrence Erlbaum Associates Inc.

Anderson, J. R. (1991). The adaptive nature of human categorisation. *Psychological Review, 98*, 409–429.

Anderson, J. R. (1993). Problem solving and learning. *American Psychologist, 48*, 35–44.

Anderson, J. R., & Bower, G. H. (1973). *Human associative memory.* Washington, DC: Hemisphere.

Anderson, R. C., & Pichert, J. W. (1978). Recall of previously unrecallable information following a shift in perspective. *Journal of Verbal Learning and Memory.*

Appleyard, D. A. (1976). *Planning a pluralistic city.* Cambridge, MA: MIT Press.

Arbib, M. A. (1985). Schemas for the temporal organization of behaviour. *Human Neurobiology, 4*, 63–72.

Arbib, M. A. (1990). Programs, schemas and neural networks for control of hand movements: Beyond the RS framework. In M. Jeannerod (Ed.), *Attention and performance XIII: Motor representation and control*. Hillsdale, NJ: Lawrence Erlbaum Associates Inc.

Arbib, M. A., Iberall, T., & Lyons, D. (1985). Coordinated control programs for movements of the hand. In A. W. Goodman & I. Darian-Smith (Eds), *Hand function and the neocortex*. New York: Springer-Verlag.

Armstrong, S. L., Gleitman, L. R., & Gleitman, H. (1983). On what some concepts might not be. *Cognition, 13*, 263–308.

Athenes, S., & Wing, A. M. (1989). Knowledge directed coordination in reaching for objects in the environment. In S. A. Wallace (Ed.), *Perspectives on the coordination of movement*, pp. 285–301. Amsterdam: North-Holland.

Atkinson, R. C., & Shiffrin, R. M. (1968). Human memory: A proposed system and its control processes. In K. W. Spence & J. T. Spence (Eds), *The psychology of learning and motivation: Advances in research and theory*, Vol. 2. New York: Academic Press.

Atkinson, R. C., & Shriffrin, R. M. (1971). The control of short-term memory. *Scientific American, 225*, 82–90.

Austin, J. L. (1962). *How to do things with words*. Cambridge, MA: Harvard University Press.

Baddeley, A. D. (1966). The capacity for generating information by randomisation. *Quarterly Journal of Experimental Psychology. 18*, 119–129.

Baddeley, A. D. (1976). *The psychology of memory*. New York: Basic Books.

Baddeley, A. D. (1979). Working memory and reading. In P. A. Kolers, M. E. Wrolstad, and H. Bouma (Eds), *Processing of visible language*. New York: Plenum Press.

Baddeley, A. D. (1982). Domains of recollection. *Psychological Review, 89*, 708–729.

Baddeley, A. D. (1986). *Working memory*. Oxford, Oxford University Press.

Baddeley, A. D. (1990). *Human memory: Theory and practice*. Hove: Lawrence Erlbaum Associates Ltd.

Baddeley, A. D. (1992). Is working memory working? *Quarterly Journal of Experimental Psychology, 44A*, 1–32.

Baddeley, A. D., & Hitch, G. J. (1974). Working memory. In G. H. Bower (Ed.), *The psychology of learning and motivation*, Vol. 2. New York: Academic Press.

Baddeley, A. D., & Hitch, G. (1977). Recency re-examined. In S. Dornic (Ed.), *Attention and performance VI*. London: Academic Press.

Baddeley, A. D., & Liebermann, K. (1980). Spatial working memory. In R. Nickerson (Ed.), *Attention and performance VIII*. Hillsdale, NJ: Lawrence Erlbaum Associates Inc.

Baddeley, A. D., & Wiezkrantz, L. (1993). *Attention: Selection, awareness and control. A tribute to Donald Broadbent*. Oxford: Clarendon Press.

Baddeley, A. D. & Wilson, B. (1985). Phonological coding and short-term memory in patients without speech. *Journal of Memory and Language, 24*, 490–502.

Baddeley, A. D., & Wilson, B. (1986). Amnesia, autobiographical memory and confabulation. In D. Rubin (Ed.), *Autobiographical memory*. New York: Cambridge University Press.

Baddeley, A. D., Thomson, N., & Buchanan, M. (1975). Word length and the structure of short-term memory. *Journal of Verbal Learning and Verbal Behaviour, 14*, 575–589.

Baddeley, A. D., Vallar, G., & Wilson B. (1987). Comprehension and the articulatory loop: Some neuropsychological evidence. In M. Coltheart (Ed.), *Attention and performance XII*. Hove: Lawrence Erlbaum Associates Ltd.

Bahrick, H. P. (1984a). Semantic memory content in permastore: Fifty years of memory for Spanish learned at school. *Journal of Experimental Psychology: General, 113*, 1–29.

Bahrick, H. P. (1984b). Memory for people. In J. E. Harris & P. E. Morris (Eds), *Everyday memory, actions and absentmindedness*. London: Academic Press.

Bahrick, H. P., Bahrick, P. O., & Wittlinger, R. P. (1975). Fifty years of memory for names and faces: A cross-sectional approach. *Journal of Experimental Psychology: General, 104,* 54–75.

Baluch, B., & Besner, D. (1991). Visual word recognition: Evidence for strategic control of lexical and nonlexical routines in oral reading. *Journal of Experimental Psychology: Learning, Memory, and Cognition, 17,* 644–652.

Barclay, J. R., Bransford, J. D., Franks, J. J., McCarrell, N. S., & Nitsch, K. (1974). Comprehension and semantic flexibility. *Journal of Verbal Learning and Verbal Behavior, 13,* 471–481.

Bar-Hillel, M. (1980). The base rate fallacy in probability judgments. *Acta Psychologica, 44,* 211–233.

Bar-Hillel, M. (1983). The base rate fallacy. In R.W. Scholz (Ed.), *Decision making under uncertainty.* Amsterdam: Elsevier.

Barnes, J. M., & Underwood, B. J. (1959). "Fate" of first-list associations in transfer theory. *Journal of Experimental Psychology, 58,* 97–105.

Barsalou, L. W. (1985). Ideals, central tendency, and frequency of instantiation as determinants of graded structure in categories. *Journal of Experimental Psychology: Learning, Memory and Cognition, 11,* 629–654.

Barsalou, L. W. (1987). The instability of graded structure: Implications for the nature of concepts. In U. Neisser (Ed.), *Concepts and conceptual development.* Cambridge: Cambridge University Press.

Barsalou, L. W. (1991). Deriving categories to achieve goals. *Psychology of Learning and Motivation, 27,* 1–64.

Bartlett, F. C. (1932). *Remembering.* Cambridge: Cambridge University Press.

Baum, D. R., & Jonides, J. J. (1979). Cognitive maps: Analysis of comparative judgements of distance. *Memory and Cognition, 7,* 462–468.

Beal, C. R. (1988). The development of prospective memory skills. In M. M. Gruneberg, P. E. Morris, & R.N. Sykes (Eds), *Practical aspects of memory: Current research and issues,* Vol. 1. Chichester: John Wiley.

Beattie, G. (1983). *Talk: An analysis of speech and non-verbal behaviour in conversation.* Milton Keynes: Open University Press.

Bekerian, D. A., & Baddeley, A. D. (1980). Saturation advertising and the repetition effect. *Journal of Verbal Learning and Verbal Behavior, 19,* 17–25.

Bekerian, D. A., & Bowers, J. M. (1983). Eyewitness testimony: Were we misled? *Journal of Experimental Psychology: Learning and Cognition, 9,* 139–145.

Bell, D. (1982). Regret in decision making under uncertainty. *Operations Research, 30,* 961–981.

Belli, R. F. (1989). Influences of misleading post-event information: Misinformation interference and acceptance. *Journal of Experimental Psychology. General, 118,* 72–85.

Berlin, B. (1978). Ethnobiological classification. In E. Rosch & B. B. Lloyd (Eds), *Cognition and categorization.* Hillsdale, NJ: Lawrence Erlbaum Associates Inc.

Bernoulli, D. (1738/1967). *Exposition of a new theory on the measurement of risk.* Farnborough: Gregg Press.

Berry, D. C. (1983). Metacognitive experience and transfer of logical reasoning. *Quarterly Journal of Experimental Psychology, 35A,* 39–49.

Besner, D., Twilley, L., McCann, R. S., & Seergobin, K. (1990). On the association between connectionism and data: Are a few words necessary? *Psychological Review, 97,* 432–446.

Bigsby, P. (1988). The visual processor module and normal adult readers. *British Journal of Psychology, 79,* 455–469.

Bigsby, P. (1990). Abstract letter identities and developmental dyslexia. *British Journal of Psychology, 81,* 227–263.

Birch, H. G., & Rabinowitz, H. S. (1951). The negative effect of previous experience on productive thinking. *Journal of Experimental Psychology, 41,* 121–125.

Bishop, D. V. M., & Robson, J. (1989). Unimpaired short-term memory and rhyme judgement in congenitally speechless individuals: Implications for the notion of "articulatory coding". *Quarterly Journal of Experimental Psychology, 41A*, 123–140.

Bisiach, E., & Luzzatti, C. (1978). Unilateral neglect of representational space. *Cortex, 14*, 129–133.

Blades, M. (1990). The reliability of data collected from sketch maps. *Journal of Environmental Psychology, 10*, 327–339.

Bock, K & Cutting, J. C. (1992). Regulating mental energy: Performance units in language production. *Journal of Memory and Language, 31*, 99–127.

Boden, M. (1990). *The Creative Mind*. London: Weidenfeld and Nicholson.

Bohannon, J. N. (1988). Flashbulb memories for the Space Shuttle disaster: A tale of two theories. *Cognition, 29*, 174–196.

Bootsma, R. J. (1989). Accuracy of perceptual processes subserving different perception-action systems. *Quarterly Journal of Experimental Psychology, 41A*, 489–500.

Bootsma, R. J. & van Wieringen, P. C. (1992). Spatio-temporal organisation of natural prehension. Special Issue: Sequencing and timing of human movement. *Human Movement Science, 11*, 205–215.

Boreas, T. (1930). Experimental studies of memory 2: The rate of forgetting. *Praktilea Academy, Athens, 5*, 382–396. Quoted by R. S. Woodworth & H. Schlosberg (1954). *Experimental Psychology*. New York: Holt, Rinehart and Winston.

Bothwell, R. K., Öffenbacher, K. A., & Brigham, J. C. (1987). Correlation of eyewitness accuracy and confidence: Optimality hypothesis revisited. *Journal of Applied Psychology, 72*, 691–695.

Bourke, P. (1993). *A general factor in dual task decrement*. Unpublished PhD thesis, University of Cambridge.

Bower, G. H. (1983). Affect and cognition. *Philosophical Transactions of the Royal Society of London*, B302, 387–402.

Bower, G. H., & Trabasso, T. R. (1964). Concept identification. In R. C. Atkinson (Ed.), *Studies in mathematical psychology*. Stanford, CA: Stanford University Press.

Bower, G. H., Clark, M. C., Lesgold, A. M., & Winzenz, D. (1969). Hierarchical retrieval schemes in recall of categorized word lists. *Journal of Verbal Learning and Verbal Behavior, 8*, 323–343.

Bower, G. H., Black, J. B., & Turner, T. J. (1979). Scripts in memory for text. *Cognitive Psychology, 11*, 177–220.

Bradley, D. C., Garrett, M. F., & Zurif, E.B. (1980). Syntactic deficits in Broca's aphasia. In D. Caplan (Ed.)., *Biological Studies of mental processes*. Cambridge, MA: MIT Press.

Braine, M. D. S. (1978). On the relation between the natural logic of reasoning and standard logic. *Psychological Review, 85*, 1–21.

Braine, M. D. S., Reiser, B. J., & Rumain, B. (1984). *Some empirical justification for a theory of natural propositional logic*. The Psychology of Learning and Motivation, Vol. 18. San Diego, CA: Academic Press.

Bransford, J. D. & Franks, J. J. (1971). The abstraction of linguistic ideas. *Cognitive Psychology, 2*, 331–350.

Bransford, J. D., & Johnson, M. K. (1972). Contextual prerequisites for understanding: Some investigations of comprehension and recall. *Journal of Verbal Learning and Verbal Behavior, 11*, 717–726.

Bransford, J. D., & Johnson, M. K. (1973). Considerations of some problems of comprehension. In W. G. Chase (Ed.), *Visual information processing*. New York: Academic Press.

Bransford, J. D., Barclay, J. R., & Franks, J. J. (1972). Sentence memory: A constructive versus interpretive approach. *Cognitive Psychology, 3*, 193–209.

Brebner, J. (1977). The search for exceptions to the psychological refractory period. In S. Dornic (Ed.), *Attention and Performance VI*. Hillsdale, NJ: Lawrence Erlbaum Associates Inc.

Brewer, W. F. (1988). Qualitative analysis of the recalls of randomly sampled autobiographical events. In M. M. Gruneberg, P. E. Morris, & R. N. Sykes (Eds), *Practical aspects of memory: Current research and issues*, Vol. 1. Chichester: John Wiley.

Brewer, W. F., & Lichtenstein, E. H. (1981). Event schemas, story schemas, and story grammars. In J. Long & A. Baddeley (Eds), *Attention and performance IX*. Hillsdale, NJ: Lawrence Erlbaum Associates Inc.

Britt, M. A., Perfetti, C. A., Garrod, S., & Rayner, K. (1992). Parsing effects in discourse: Context effects and their limits. *Journal of Memory and Language, 31*, 293–314.

Broadbent, D. E. (1958). *Perception and communication*. Oxford: Pergamon Press.

Brooks, L. R. (1967). The suppression of visualization by reading. *Quarterly Journal of Experimental Psychology, 19*, 289–299.

Brooks, L. R. (1968). Spatial and verbal components of the act of recall. *Canadian Journal of Psychology, 22*, 349–368.

Brown, G. D. (1987). Resolving inconsistency: A computational model of word naming. *Journal of Memory and Language, 26*, 1–23.

Brown, J. (1968). Reciprocal facilitation and impairment of face recall. *Psychonomic Science, 10*, 41–42.

Brown, R., & Kulik, J. (1977). Flashbulb memories. *Cognition, 5*, 73–99.

Brown, R., & McNeill, D. (1966). The "tip of the tongue" phenomenon. *Journal of Verbal Learning and Verbal Behavior, 5*, 325–337.

Bruce, V. (1983). Recognising faces. *Philosophical Transactions of the Royal Society of London*, 423–436.

Bruce, V., & Green, P. R. (1990). *Visual perception: Physiology, psychology and ecology*, 2nd edn. Hove: Lawrence Erlbaum Associates Ltd.

Bruce, V., & Valentine, T. (1985). What's up? The Margaret Thatcher Illusion revisited. *Perception, 14*, 515–516.

Bruce, V., & Valentine, T. (1986). Semantic priming of familiar faces. *Quarterly Journal of Experimental Psychology, 38A*, 125–150.

Bruce, V., & Young, A. (1986). Understanding face recognition. *British Journal of Psychology, 77*, 305–327.

Bruner, J. S., Goodnow, J. J., & Austin, G. A. (1956). *A study of thinking*. New York: John Wiley.

Bryant, K. J. (1984). Methodological convergence as an issue within environmental cognition. *Journal of Environmental Psychology, 4*, 43–60.

Bub, D., Cancelliere, A., & Kertesz, A. (1985). Whole-word and analytic translation of spelling to sound in a nonsemantic reader. In K. E. Patterson, J. C. Marshall, & M. Coltheart (Eds), *Surface dyslexia: Neuropsychological and cognitive studies of phonological reading*. Hove: Lawrence Erlbaum Associates Ltd.

Burke, D. M., MacKay, D. G., Worthley, J. S., & Wade, E. (1991). On the tip of the tongue: What causes word finding failures in young and older adults? *Journal of Memory and Language, 30*, 542–579.

Burton, A. M., & Bruce, V. (1992). I recognise your face but I can't remember your name: A simple explanation? *British Journal of Psychology, 83*, 45–60.

Burton, A. M., Bruce, V., & Johnston, R. A. (1990). Understanding face recognition with an interactive activation model. *British Journal of Psychology, 81*, 361–380.

Butterworth, B. (1980). Evidence from pauses. In B. Butterworth (Ed.), *Language Production* Vol. 1. London: Academic Press.

Byrne, R. (1979). Memory for urban geography. *Quarterly Journal of Experimental Psychology, 31*, 147–154.

Byrne, R. M. J. (1989). Suppressing valid inferences with conditionals. *Cognition, 31*, 61–83.

Campbell, R., Landis, T., & Regard, M. (1986). Face recognition and lip reading: A neurological dissociation. *Brain, 109*, 509–521.

Caplan, D. (1972). Clause boundaries and recognition latencies for words in sentences. *Perception and Psychophysics, 12*, 73–76.

Caplan, D. (1987). Discrimination of normal and aphasic subjects on a test of syntactic comprehension. *Neuropsychologia, 25*, 173–184.

Caplan, D., & Evans, K. L. (1990). The effects of syntactic structure on discourse comprehension in patients with parsing impairments. *Brain and Language, 39*, 206–234.

Caplan, D., & Waters, G. S. (1990). Short-term memory and language comprehension: A critical review. In G. Vallar & T. Shallice (Eds), *Neuropsychological impairments of S.T.M.* Cambridge: Cambridge University Press.

Caplan, D., Rochon, E., & Waters, G. S. (1992). Articulatory and phonological determinants of word-length effects in span tasks. *Quarterly Journal of Experimental Psychology: Human Experimental Psychology, 45*, 177–192.

Caramazza, A., & Hillis, A. E. (1989). The disruption of sentence production: Some dissociations. *Brain and Language, 36*, 625–650.

Caramazza, A., & Zurif, E. B. (1976). Dissociation of algorithmic and heuristic processes in language comprehension: Evidence from aphasia. *Brain and Language, 3*, 572–582.

Carlton, L. G. (1981). Processing visual feedback information for movement control. *Journal of Experimental Psychology: Human Perception and Performance, 7*, 1019–1030.

Carson, L. M., & Wiegrand, R. L. (1979). Motor schema formation and retention in young children: A test of Schmidt's schema theory. *Journal of Motor Behavior, 11*, 247–251.

Ceci, S. J., Baker, J. G., & Bronfenbrenner, U. (1988). Prospective remembering, temporal calibration and context. In M. M. Gruneberg, P. E. Morris, & R. N. Sykes (Eds), *Practical aspects of memory: Current research and issues*, Vol. 1. Chichester: John Wiley.

Ceci, S. J., & Bronfenbrenner, U. (1985). Don't forget to take the cup cakes out of the oven: Prospective memory, strategic time monitoring and context. *Child Development, 56*, 152–164.

Chambers, D., & Reisberg, D. (1985). Can mental images be ambiguous. *Journal of Experimental Psychology: Human Perception and Performance, 11*, 317–328.

Chambers, D., & Reisberg, D. (1992). What an image depicts depends on what an image means. *Cognitive Psychology, 24*, 145–174.

Chandler, C. C. (1989). Specific retroactive interference in modified recognition tests: Evidence for an unknown cause of interference. *Journal of Experimental Psychology: Learning, Memory and Cognition, 15*, 256–265.

Chase, W. G., & Simon, H. A. (1973). Perception in chess. *Cognitive Psychology, 4*, 55–81.

Chater, N., Lyon, K., & Myers, T. (1990). Why are conjunctive categories overextended? *Journal of Experimental Psychology: Learning, Memory and Cognition, 16*, 497–508.

Cheng, P. N. (1985). Restructuring versus automaticity: Alternative accounts of skill acquisition. *Psychological Review, 94*, 414–423.

Cheng, P. N. & Holyoak, K. J., (1985). Pragmatic reasoning schemes. *Cognitive Psychology 17*, 391–416.

Cheng, P. N., Holyoak, K. J., Nisbett, R. E., & Oliver, L. M. (1986). Pragmatic versus syntactic approaches to training deductive reasoning. *Cognitive Psychology, 18*, 293–328.

Cherry, E. C. (1953). Some experiments on the recognition of speech with one and two ears. *Journal of the Acoustical Society of America, 25*, 975–979.

Cherry, E. C., & Taylor, W. K. (1954). Some further experiments upon the recognition of speech with one, and with two ears. *Journal of the Acoustical Society of America, 26*, 554–559.

Chi, M. T. H., Feltovich, P. J., & Glaser, R. (1981). Categorisation and representation of physics problems by experts and novices. *Cognitive Science, 5*, 121–152.

Clark, H. H., & Haviland, S. E. (1977). Comprehension and the given-new contract. In R. O. Feedle (Ed.), *Discourse production and comprehension*. Norwood, NJ: Ablex.

Clarke, E. F. (1982). Timing in the performance of Erik Satie's "Vexations". *Acta Psychologica, 50*, 1–19.

Clayton, K., & Chattin, D. (1989). Spatial and semantic priming effects in tests of spatial knowledge. *Journal of Experimental Psychology: Learning, Memory and Cognition, 15*, 495–506.

Clayton, K., & Habibi, A. (1991). Contribution of temporal contiguity to the spatial priming effect. *Journal of Experimental Psychology: Learning, Memory and Cognition, 17*, 263–271.

Clowes, M. B. (1971). On seeing things. *Artificial Intelligence, 2*, 79–112.

Cofer, C. N. (1951). Verbal behaviour in relation to reasoning and values. In H. Guetzkow (Ed.), *Group leadership and men*. Pittsburgh, PA: Carnegie Press.

Cohen, A., Ivry, R. I., & Keele, S. W. (1990). Attention and structure in sequence learning. *Journal of Experimental Psychology: Learning, Memory and Cognition, 16*, 17–30.

Cohen, G. (1983). *The psychology of cognition*, 2nd edn. London: Academic Press.

Cohen, G. & Faulkner, D. (1986). Memory for proper names: Age differences in retrieval. *British Journal of Developmental Psychology, 4*, 187–197.

Cohen, G., & Martin, M. (1975). Hemisphere differences in an auditory Stroop test. *Perception and Psychophysics, 17*, 79–83.

Cohen, J. D., Dunbar, K., & McClelland, J. L. (1990). On the control of automatic processes: A parallel distributed processing account of the Stroop effect. *Psychological Review, 97*, 332–361.

Cohen, R. L., & Heath, M. (1990). The development of serial short-term memory and the articulatory loop hypothesis. *Intelligence, 14*, 151–171.

Cole, R. A. (1973). Listening for mispronunciations: A measure of what we hear during speech. *Psychophysics, 13*, 153–156.

Colegrove, F. W. (1899). Individual memories. *American Journal of Psychology, 10*, 228–255.

Coltheart, M. (1981). Disorders of reading and their implications for models of normal reading. *Visible Language, 15*, 245–286.

Coltheart, M., Patterson, K. E., & Marshall, J. C. (Eds) (1980). *Deep dyslexia*. London: Routledge and Kegan Paul.

Coltheart, V., Avons, S. E., Masterson, J., & Laxon, V.J. (1991). The role of assembled phonology in reading comprehension. *Memory and Cognition, 19*, 387–400.

Conrad, R. (1964). Acoustic confusions in immediate memory. *British Journal of Psychology, 55*, 77–84.

Conrad, R., & Hull, A. J. (1964). Information, acoustic confusion and memory span. *British Journal of Psychology, 55*, 429–432.

Conway, M. (1990). *Autobiographical memory: An introduction*. Buckingham: Open University Press.

Coombs, B., & Slovic, P. (1979). Causes of death: Biased newspaper coverage and biased judgments. *Journalism Quarterly, 56*, 837–843.

Coombs, C. H. (1969). Portfolio theory: A theory of risky decision making. *La Decision*. Paris: Centre de la Recherche Scientifique.

Coombs, C. H. (1975). Portfolio theory and the measurement of risk. In M. F. Kaplan & S. Schwartz (Eds), *Human judgement and decision processes*. New York: Academic Press.

Cooper, A. J. R., & Monk, A. (1976). Learning for recall and learning for recognition. In J. Brown (Ed.), *Recall and Recognition*. Chichester: John Wiley.

Coslett, H. B. (1991). Read but not write "idea". Evidence for a third reading mechanism. *Brain and Language, 40*, 425–443.

Coton, M. (1992). *Value betting*. Oswestry: Aesculus Press.

Cotton, J. (1935). Normal "visual hearing". *Science, 82*, 592–593.

Cowan, N., Day, L., Saults, J. S., Keller, T. A., Johnson, T., & Flores, I. (1992). The role of verbal output time in the effects of word length on immediate memory. *Journal of Memory and Language, 31*, 1–17.

Craik, F. I. M. (1986). A functional account of age differences in memory. In F. Klix & H. Hagendorf (Eds), *Human memory and cognitive capabilities*. Amsterdam: North-Holland.

Craik, F. I. M., & Lockhart, R. S. (1972). Levels of processing: A framework for memory research. *Journal of Verbal Learning and Verbal Behavior, 11*, 671–684.

Craik, F. I. M., & Tulving, E. (1975). Depth of processing and the retention of words in episodic memory. *Journal of Experimental Psychology: General, 104*, 268–294.

Craik, F. I. M., & Watkins, J. J. (1973). The role of rehearsal in short-term memory. *Journal of Verbal Learning and Verbal Behavior, 12*, 599–607.

Craik, K. J. W. (1948). Theory of the human operator in control systems. II: Man as an element in a control system. *British Journal of Psychology, 38*, 142–148.

Crovitz, H. F., & Schiffman, H. (1974). Frequency of episodic memories as a function of their age. *Bulletin of the Psychonomic Society, 4*, 517–518.

Cutler, A. (1982). *Slips of the tongue*. The Hague: Mouton.

Cutler, A., & Butterfield, S. (1992). Rhythmic cues to speech segmentation. Evidence from juncture misperception. *Journal of Memory and Language, 31*, 218–236.

Cutler, A., & Carter, D. M. (1987). The predominance of strong initial syllables in the English vocabulary. *Computer Speech and Language, 2*, 133–142.

Cutter, B. L., Penrod, S. D., & Stuve, T. E. (1988). Juror decision making in eyewitness identification cases. *Law and Human Behaviour, 12*, 41–55.

Daneman, M. & Carpenter, P. A. (1980). Individual differences in working memory and reading. *Journal of Verbal Learning and Verbal Behavior, 19*, 450–466.

Davidson, D., Suppes, P., & Siegel, S. (1957). *Decision-making: An Experimental approach*, Stanford, CA: Stanford University Press.

Davies, G., & Thompson, D. (Eds) (1988). *Memory in context: Context in memory*. New York: John Wiley.

Davis, R. (1956). The limits of the "psychological refractory period". *Quarterly Journal of Experimental Psychology, 9*, 119–129.

Dell, G. S. (1984). Representation of serial order in speech: Evidence from the repeated phoneme effect in speech errors. *Journal of Experimental Psychology: Learning, Memory, and Cognition, 10*, 222–233.

Dell, G. S. (1986). A spreading-activation theory of retrieval in sentence production. *Psychological Review, 93*, 283–321.

Dell, G. S. (1988). The retrieval of phonological forms in production: Tests of predictions from a connectionist model. *Journal of Memory and Language, 27*, 124–142.

Dell, G. S. & O'Seaghda, P. G. (1992). Stages of lexical access in language production. *Cognition, 42*, 287–314.

Dell, G. S., & Reich, P. A. (1981). Stages in sentence production: An analysis of speech error data. *Journal of Verbal Learning and Verbal Behavior, 20*, 611–629.

De Renzi, E., & Nichelli, P. (1975). Verbal and non-verbal short-term memory impairment following hemispheric damage. *Cortex, 11*, 341–354.

Deutsch, D. (1983). The generation of 2 isochronous sequences in parallel. *Perception and Psychophysics, 34*, 331–337.

Deutsch, J. A., & Deutsch, D. (1963). Attention: Some theoretical considerations. *Psychological Review, 70*, 80–90.

Devlin, A. S. (1976). The small town cognitive map: Adjusting to a new environment. In G. T. Moore & R. G. Golledge (Eds), *Environmental knowing*. Strowdsberg, PA: Dowden, Hutchinson and Ross.

Dodd, B., & Campbell, R. (1986). *Hearing by eye: The psychology of lip reading*. Hove: Lawrence Erlbaum Associates Ltd.

Dodge, R. (1900). Visual perception during eye movement. *Psychological Review, 7*, 454–465.

Douglas, M. & Wildavsky, A. (1982). *Risk and Culture*. Berkeley, CA: University of California Press.

Driver, J. & Tipper, S. P. (1989). On the nonselectivity of "selective seeing": Contrasts between interference and priming in selective attention. *Journal of Experimental Psychology: Human Perception and Performance, 15*, 304–314.

Duncker, K. (1945). On problem solving. *Psychological Monographs, 58*, (Whole No. 270).
Dunning, D., Griffin, D. W., Milojkovic, J., & Ross, L. (1990). The overconfidence effect in social prediction. *Journal of Personality and Social Psychology, 58*, 568–581.
Ebbinghaus, H. (1885). *Über das Gedachtris*. Leipzig: Dunker. Translated by H. Ruyer & C. E. Bussenius (1913). *Memory*. New York: Teachers College Press.
Eddy, D. M. (1982). Probabilistic reasoning in clinical medicine: Problems and opportunities. In D. Kahneman, P. Slovic, & A. Tversky (Eds), *Judgement under uncertainty: Heuristics and biases*. Cambridge: Cambridge University Press.
Edwards, W. (1954). The theory of decision making. *Psychological Bulletin, 51*, 380–417.
Edwards, W. (1955). The prediction of decisions among bets. *Journal of Experimental Psychology, 51*, 201–214.
Eich, J. E. (1980). The cue-dependent nature of state-dependent retrieval. *Memory and Cognition, 8*, 157–173.
Eich, J. E. (1989). Theoretical issues in state-dependent memory. In H. L. Roediger & F.I.M. Craik (Eds), *Varieties of memory and consciousness: Essays in honor of Endel Tulving*. Hillsdale, NJ: Lawrence Erlbaum Associates Inc.
Ellis, A. W. (1979). Speech production and short-term memory. In J. Morton & J. C. Marshall (Eds), *Psycholinguistics series*, Vol. 2. London: Elek/Cambridge, MA: MIT Press.
Ellis, A. W. (1984). *Reading, writing and dyslexia: A cognitive analysis*. Hove: Lawrence Erlbaum Associates Ltd.
Ellis, A. W. (1993). *Reading, writing and dyslexia, 2nd edn*. Hove: Lawrence Erlbaum Associates Ltd.
Ellis, A. W. & Beattie, G. (1986). *The psychology of language and communication*. London: Weidenfeld and Nicolson.
Ellis, H. D. (1975). Recognising faces. *British Journal of Psychology, 66*, 409–426.
Ellis, H. D., Shepherd, J. W., & Davies, G. M. (1979). Identification of familiar and unfamiliar faces from internal and external features: Some implications for theories of face recognition. *Perception, 8*, 431–439.
Ellis, J. A. (1988). Memory for future intentions: Investigating pulses and steps. In M. M. Gruneberg, P. E. Morris, & R. N. Sykes (Eds), *Practical aspects of memory: Current research and issues*, Vol. 1. Chichester: Wiley.
Ellis, N. C., & Hennelly, R. A. (1980). A bilingual word-length effect: Implications for intelligence testing and the relative ease of mental calculations in Welsh and English. *British Journal of Psychology, 71*, 43–52.
Epstein, G. O., & McDaniel, M. A. (1990). Normal aging and prospective memory. *Journal of Experimental Psychology: Learning, Memory and Cognition, 16*, 717–726.
Ericsson, K. A., Chase, W. G., & Faloon, S. (1980). Acquisition of a memory skill. *Science, 208*, 1181–1182.
Ernst, G. W., & Newell, A. (1969). *GPS: A case study in generality and problem solving*. New York: Academic Press.
Eslinger, P. J., & Damasio, A. R. (1985). Severe disturbance of higher cognition after bilateral frontal lobe ablation — Patient EVR. *Neurology, 35*, 1731–1741.
Evans, G. W., Marrero, D. G., & Butler, P. A. (1981). Environmental learning and cognitive mapping. *Environmental Behaviour 13*, 83–104.
Evans, J. St. B. T. (1982). *The psychology of deductive reasoning*. London: Routledge and Kegan Paul.
Evans, J. St. B. T. (1989). *Bias in human reasoning: Causes and consequences*. Hove: Lawrence Erlbaum Associates Ltd.
Evans, J. St. B. T., & Newstead, S. E. (1980). A study of disjunctive reasoning. *Psychological Research, 41*, 373–388.
Evett, L. J., & Humphreys, G. W. (1981). The use of abstract graphemic information in lexical access. *Quarterly Journal of Experimental Psychology, 33A*, 325–350.

Farah, M. J. (1988). Is visual-imagery really visual — overlooked evidence from neuro-psychology. *Psychological Review, 95*, 307–317.

Farah, M. J., Hammond, K. M., Levine, D. N., & Calvanio, R. (1988). Visual and spatial mental imagery: Dissociable systems of representation. *Cognitive Psychology, 20*, 439–462.

Farah, M. J., Soso, M. J., & Dashieff, R. M. (1992). Visual angle of the mind's eye before and after unilateral occipital lobectomy. *Journal of Experimental Psychology: Human Perception and Performance, 18*, 241–246.

Farmer, E. W., Berman, J. V. F., & Fletcher, Y. L. (1986). Evidence for a visuo-spatial scratch pad in working memory. *Quarterly Journal of Experimental Psychology, 38A*, 675–688.

Fernandez, A., & Glenberg, A. M. (1985). Changing environmental context does not reliably affect memory. *Memory and Cognition, 13*, 333–345.

Fincher-Kiefer, R., Post, T. A., Greene, T. R., & Voss, J. F. (1988). On the role of prior knowledge and task demands in the processing of text. *Journal of Memory and Language, 27*. 416–428.

Finke, R. A., & Kosslyn, S. M. (1980). Mental imagery circuitry in the peripheral visual field. *Journal of Experimental Psychology: Human Perception and Performance, 6*, 126–139.

Finke, R. A., & Schmidt, M. J. (1977). Orientation-specific color after-effects following imagination. *Journal of Experimental Psychology: Human Perception and Performance, 3*, 599–606.

Finke, R. A., Pinker, S., & Farah, M. J. (1989). Reinterpreting visual-patterns in mental imagery. *Cognitive Science, 13*, 51–78.

Fischhoff, B. (1982). Debiasing. In D. Kahneman, P. Slovic, & A. Tversky (Eds), *Judgement under uncertainty: Heuristics and biases*. New York: Cambridge University Press.

Fischhoff, B., Slovic, P., & Lichtenstein, S. (1977). Knowing with certainty: The appropriateness of extreme confidence. *Journal of Experimental Psychology: Human Perception and Performance, 3*, 552–564.

Fischhoff, B., Slovic, P., & Lichtenstein, S. (1978). Fault trees: Sensitivity of estimated failure probabilities to problem representation. *Journal of Experimental Psychology: Human Perception and Performance, 4*, 330–334.

Fivush, R., & Hudson, J.A. (1990). *Knowing and remembering in young children*. New York: Cambridge University Press.

Flash, T., & Henis, E. (1991). Arm trajectory modifications during reaching towards visual targets. *Journal of Cognitive Neuroscience, 3*, 220–230.

Flash, T., & Hogan, N. (1985). The coordination of arm movements: An experimentally confirmed mathematical model. *Journal of Neuroscience, 5*, 1688–1703.

Fodor, J. A. (1983). *The modularity of mind*. Cambridge, MA: MIT Press.

Foldi, N. S. (1987). Appreciation of pragmatic interpretations of indirect commands: Comparison of right and left hemisphere brain-damaged patients. *Brain and Language, 31*, 88–108.

Folkins, J. W., & Abbs, J. H. (1975). Lip and jaw motor control during speech responses to resistive loading of the jaw. *Journal of Speech and Hearing Research, 18*, 207–220.

Ford, M. (1982). Sentence planning units: Implications for the speaker's representation of meaningful relations underlying sentences. In J. Bresnan (Ed.), *The mental representation of grammatical relations*. Cambridge, MA: MIT Press.

Ford, M., & Holmes, V. (1978). Planning units and syntax in sentence production. *Cognition, 6*, 35–53.

Franklin, N., & Tversky, B. (1990). Searching imagined environments. *Journal of Experimental Psychology: General, 119*, 63–76.

Frazier, L. (1978). On comprehending sentences: Syntactic parsing strategies. Unpublished doctoral dissertation. University of Connecticut.

Frazier, L. (1987). Sentence processing: A tutorial review. In M. Coltheart (Ed.), *Attention and Performance XII: The psychology of reading*. Hillsdale, NJ: Lawrence Erlbaum Associates Inc.

Frick, R. W. (1984). Using both an auditory and a visual short-term store to increase digit span. *Memory and Cognition, 12*, 507–514.

Frisby, J. P. (1979). *Seeing: Mind, brain and illusion*. Oxford: Oxford University Press.

Fromholt, R., & Larsen, S. F. (1991). Autobiographical memory in normal aging and primary degenerative dementia (dementia of Alzheimer's type). *Journal of Gerontology, 46*, 85–91.

Fromkin, V. A. (Ed.) (1973). *Speech errors as linguistic evidence*. The Hague: Mouton.

Fromkin, V. A. (Ed.) (1980). *Errors in linguistic performance: Slips of the tongue, ear, pen and hand*. New York: Academic Press.

Fromkin, V., & Rodman, R. (1988). *Introduction to language, 4th edn*. New York: Rinehart.

Fruzzetti, A. E., Toland, K., Teller, S. A., & Loftus, E. F. (1992). Memory and eyewitness testimony. In M. M. Gruneberg & P. E. Morris (Eds), *Aspects of Memory, Vol. 1: The Practical Aspects*, 2nd edn. London: Routledge.

Funnell, E. (1983). Phonological processes in reading: New evidence from acquired dyslexia. *British Journal of Psychology, 74*, 159–180.

Gale, N., Golledge, R. G., Pellegrino, J. W., & Doherty, S. (1990). The acquisition and integration of route knowledge in an unfamiliar neighborhood. *Journal of Environmental Psychology, 10*, 3–25.

Galton, F. (1883). *Inquiries into human faculty and its development*. London: Macmillan.

Gardiner, J. M. (1988). Functional aspects of recollective experience. *Memory and Cognition, 16*, 309–313.

Gardiner, J. M. (1992). *Consciousness and memory*. Paper presented to the Annual Conference of the British Psychological Society, Scarborough.

Gardiner, J. M., & Java, R. I. (1990). Recollective experience in word and nonword recognition. *Memory and Cognition, 18*, 23–30.

Gardiner, J. M., & Java, R. I. (1993). Recognising and remembering. In A. F. Collins, S. E. Gathercole, M. A. Conway, & P. E. Morris (Eds), *Theories of memory*. Hove: Lawrence Erlbaum Associates Ltd.

Garling, T., & Evans, G. W. (Eds) (1991). *Environment, cognition and action: An integrated approach*. Oxford: Oxford University Press.

Garnham, A. (1981). Mental models as representations of text. *Memory and cognition, 9*, 560–565.

Garnham, A. (1985). *Psycholinguistics: Central topics*. London: Methuen.

Garnham, A. (1987). *Mental models as representations of discourse and text*. Chichester: Ellis Horwood.

Garnham, A. (1989). Inference in language understanding: What, when, why and how. In R. Dietrich & C. F. Graumann (Eds), *Language processing and social "context"*. Amsterdam: North-Holland.

Garrett, M. F. (1975). The analysis of sentence production. In G. H. Bower (Ed.), *The psychology of learning and motivation, Vol. 9*. New York: Academic Press.

Garrett, M. F. (1976). Syntactic processes in sentence production. In R. Wales & E. J. Walker (Eds), *New Approaches to language mechanisms*. Amsterdam: North-Holland.

Garrett, M. F. (1982). Production of speech: Observations from normal and pathological language use. In A. W. Ellis (Ed.), *Normality and pathology in cognitive functions*. London: Academic Press.

Gathercole, S. E., & Baddeley, A. D. (1990). The role of phonological memory in vocabulary acquisition — a study of young children learning new names. *British Journal of Psychology, 81*, 439–454.

Gathercole, S. E., Willis, C., Emslie, H., & Baddeley, A. D. (1992). Phonological memory and vocabulary development during the early school years: A longditudinal study. *Developmental Psychology, 28*, 887–898.

Geiselman, E. (1988). Improving eyewitness memory through mental reinstatement of context. In G. M. Davies & D. M. Thomson (Eds), *Memory in context: Context in memory*. New York: John Wiley.

Geiselman, R. E., & Bjork, R. A. (1980). Primary versus secondary rehearsal in imagined voices: Differential effects on recognition. *Cognitive Psychology, 12,* 188–205.

Gentner, D. (1989). The mechanism of analogical learning. In S. Vosniadou & A. Ortony (Eds), *Similarity and analogical reasoning.* Cambridge: Cambridge University Press.

Gentner, D., & Gentner, D. R. (1983). Flowing waters or teeming crowds. In D. Gentner & A. L. Stevens (Eds), *Mental models.* Hillsdale, NJ: Lawrence Erlbaum Associates Inc.

Gentner, D. R. (1987). Timing of skilled motor performance: Tests of the proportional duration model. *Psychological Review, 94,* 255–276.

Gentner, D. R., Grudin, J., & Conway, E. (1980). *Finger movements in transcription typing.* Technical Report 8001. La Jolla, CA: University of California at San Diego, Center for Human Information Processing.

Georgeson, M., & Shackleton, T. (1989). What's the use of Fourier filters? A new theory of edge computation in vision. Paper presented to the *Experimental Psychology Society,* Swansea, April.

Gibson, J. J. (1950). *The perception of the visual world.* Boston, MA: Houghton Mifflin.

Gibson, J. J. (1966). *The senses considered as perceptual systems.* Boston, MA: Houghton Mifflin.

Gibson, J. J. (1979). *The ecological approach to visual perception.* Boston, MA: Houghton Mifflin.

Gick, M. L., & Holyoak, K. J. (1983). Schema induction and analogical transfer. *Cognitive Psychology, 15,* 1–38.

Gick, M. L., & McGarry, S. J. (1992). Learning from mistakes: Inducing analogous solution failures to a source problem produces later success in analogical transfer. *Journal of Experimental Psychology: Human Learning and Memory, 18,* 623–639.

Gick, M. L., Craik, F. I. M., & Morris, R. G. (1988). Task complexity and age-differences in working memory. *Memory and Cognition, 16.* 353–361.

Gigerenzer, G., Hoffrage, U., & Kleinbolting, H. (1991). Probabilistic mental models: A Brunswikian theory of confidence. *Psychological Review, 98,* 537–557.

Glenberg, A. M., Smith, S. M., & Green, C. (1977). Type 1 rehearsal: Maintenance and more. *Journal of Verbal Learning and Verbal Behaviour, 16,* 339–352.

Gluck, M. A., & Bower, G. H. (1988). From conditioning to category learning: An adaptive network model. *Journal of Experimental Psychology: General, 117,* 227–247.

Glushko, R. J. (1979). The organization and activation of orthographic knowledge in reading aloud. *Journal of Experimental Psychology: Human Perception and Performance, 5,* 674–691.

Godden, D. R., & Baddeley, A. D. (1975). Context dependent memory in two natural environments: On land and underwater. *British Journal of Psychology, 66,* 325–332.

Godden, D., & Baddeley, A. D. (1980). When does context influence recognition memory? *British Journal of Psychology, 71,* 99–104.

Goldenberg, G., Podreka, I., Suess, E., Steiner, M., Deecke, L., & Willmes, K. (1987). Regional cerebral blood flow patterns in verbal and visuospatial imagery tasks — results of single photon-emission computer-tomography (Spect). *Journal of Clinical and Experimental Neuropsychology, 9,* 284.

Goldman-Eisler, F. (1968). *Psycholinguistics: Experiments in spontaneous speech.* London: Academic Press.

Gomulicki, B. R. (1956). Recall as an abstractive process. *Acta Psychologica, 12,* 77–94.

Good, D. A., & Butterworth, B. (1980). Hesitancy as a conversational resource: Some methodological implications. In H. W. Dechert and M. Raupach (Eds), *Temporal variables in speech.* The Hague: Mouton.

Gopal, S., Klatzky, R. L., & Smith, T. R. (1989). Navigator: A psychologically based model of environmental learning through navigation. *Journal of Environmental Psychology, 9,* 309–332.

Greene, J. O., & Cappella, J. N. (1986). Cognition and talk: The relationship of semantic units to temporal patterns of fluency in spontaneous speech. *Language and Speech, 29*, 141–157.

Greenspoon, J., & Ranyard, R. (1957). Stimulus conditions and retroactive inhibition. *Journal of Experimental Psychology, 53*, 55–59.

Greenwald, A. G., & Shulman, H. G. (1973). On doing two things at once. II: Elimination of the psychological refractory period. *Journal of Experimental Psychology, 101*, 70–76.

Grice, H. P. (1975). Logic and conversation. In P. Cole and J. Morgan (Eds), *Syntax and semantics 9: Pragmatics*. New York: Academic Press.

Griffin, D., & Tversky, A. (1992). The weighing of evidence and the determinants of confidence. *Cognitive Psychology, 24*, 411–435.

Griggs, R. A., & Cox, J. R. (1982). The elusive thematic materials effect in Wason's selection task. *British Journal of Psychology, 73*, 407–420.

Groot, A. D. de (1965). *Thought and choice in chess*. The Hague: Mouton.

Groot, A. D. de (1966). Perception and memory versus thought: Some old ideas and recent findings. In B. Kleinmuntz (Ed.), *Problem solving: Research, method and theory*. New York: John Wiley.

Grudin, J. T. (1983). Error patterns in novice and skilled transcription typing. In W. E. Cooper (Ed.), *Cognitive aspects of skilled typewriting*. New York: Springer-Verlag.

Gruneberg, M. M. (1992). The practical application of memory aids: Knowing how, knowing when and knowing when not. In M. M. Gruneberg & P. E. Morris (Eds), *Aspects of memory, Vol. 1: The Practical Aspects,* 2nd edn. London: Routledge.

Gruneberg, M. M., & Morris, P. E. (Eds.) (1992). *Aspects of memory, Vol. 1: The practical aspects*, 2nd edn. London: Routledge.

Guenther, R. K., Klatsky, R. L., & Putnam, W. (1980). Commonalities and differences in semantic decisions about pictures and words. *Journal of Verbal Learning and Verbal Behavior, 19*, 54–74.

Gunkel, M. (1962). Über relative Koordination bei willkurlichen menschlichen Glieder-bewegungen. *Pflügers Archiv für gesamte Physiologie, 275*, 472–477.

Guzman, A. (1968). Decomposition of a visual scene into three-dimensional bodies. *AFIPS Proceedings of the Fall Joint Computer Conference, 33*, 291–304.

Hampson, P. J., Marks, D. F., & Richardson, J. T. E. (Eds) (1990). *Imagery: Current developments*. London: Routledge.

Hampton, J. A. (1979). Polymorphous concepts in semantic memory. *Journal of Verbal Learning and Verbal Behavior, 18*, 441–461.

Hampton, J. A. (1988). Disjunction of natural concepts. *Memory and Cognition, 16*, 579–591.

Hampton, J. A. (1988b). Overextension of conjunctive concepts: Evidence for a unitary model of concept typicality and class inclusion. *Journal of Experimental Psychology: Learning, Memory and Cognition, 14*, 12–32.

Hanley, J. R., & Morris, P. E. (1987). The effects of amount of processing on recall and recognition. *Quarterly Journal of Experimental Psychology, 39A*, 431–450.

Hanley, J. R., Young, A. W., & Pearson, N. A. (1991). Impairment of the visuo-spatial scratch pad. *Quarterly Journal of Experimental Psychology, 43A*, 101–125.

Harris, J. E., & Wilkins, A. J. (1982). Remembering to do things: A theoretical framework and illustrative experiment. *Human Learning, 1*, 123–136.

Hatano, G., & Osawa, K. (1983). Digit memory of grand experts in abacus-derived mental calculation. *Cognition, 15*, 95–110.

Hatano, G., Amaiwa, S., & Shimizu, K. (1987). Formation of a mental abacus for computation and its use as a memory device for digits: A developmental study. *Developmental Psychology, 23*, 832–838.

Hay, D. C., & Young, A. W. (1982). The human face. In A. W. Ellis (Ed.), *Normality and pathology in cognitive functions*. London: Academic Press.

Hayes, J. R. (1973). On the function of visual imagery in elementary mathematics. In W. G. Chase (Ed.), *Visual information processing*. New York: Academic Press.

Heidbreder, E. (1946). The attainment of concepts. *Journal of General Psychology*, 35, 173–189.

Henderson, L. (1982a). *Orthography, accuracy and confidence: Optimality hypothesis revisited. Journal of Applied Psychology*, 72, 691–695.

Henderson, L. (1982b). *Orthography and word recognition in reading*. London: Academic Press.

Henderson, L. (1985). The psychology of morphemes. In A. W. Ellis (Ed.), *Progress in the psychology of language*, Vol. 1. Hove: Lawrence Erlbaum Associates Ltd.

Herrmann, D. J., & Palmisano, M. (1992). The facilitation of memory performance. In M. Gruneberg & P. E. Morris (Eds), *Aspects of memory, Vol. 1: The practical aspects*, 2nd edn. London: Routledge.

Herrmann, D. J., & Petro, S. (1991). Commercial memory aids. *Applied Cognitive Psychology*, 4, 439–450.

Hick, W. E. (1948). The discontinuous functioning of the human operator in pursuit tasks. *Quarterly Journal of Experimental Psychology*, 1, 36–51.

Higbee, K. L. (1988). *Your memory*, 2nd edn. New York: Prentice-Hall.

Hinton, G. E., McClelland, J. L., & Rumelhart, D. E. (1986). Distributed representations. In D. E. Rumelhart and J. L. McClelland (Eds), *Parallel distributed processing: Explorations in microcognition: Volume 1*. Cambridge, MA: MIT Press.

Hirst, W., & Kalmar, D. (1987). Characterising attentional resources. *Journal of Experimental Psychology: General*, 116, 68–81.

Hirst, W., Spelke, E. S., Reaves, C. C., Caharack, G., & Neisser, U. (1980). Dividing attention without alternation or automaticity. *Journal of Experimental Psychology: General*, 109, 98–117.

Hirtle, S. C., & Mascolo, M. F. (1986). Effect of semantic clustering on the memory of spatial locations. *Journal of Experimental Psychology: Learning, Memory and Cognition*, 12, 182–189.

Hitch, G. J. (1978). The role of short-term working memory in mental arithmetic. *Cognitive Psychology*, 10, 302–323.

Hitch, G. J., & McAuley, E. (1991). Working memory in children with specific arithmetical learning difficulties. *British Journal of Psychology*, 82, 375–386.

Hoffman, J. E., Nelson, B., & Houek, M. R. (1983). The role of attentional resources in automatic detection. *Cognitive Psychology*, 15, 379–410.

Hogan, N., & Flash, T. (1987). Moving gracefully: Quantitative theories of motor coordination. *Trends in Neurosciences*, 10, 170–174.

Holt, E. B. (1903). Eye-movement and central anaesthesia. 1: The problem of anaesthesia during eye-movement. *Psychological Review Monographs*, 4, 3–45.

Holyoak, K. J. (1985). The pragmatics of analogical transfer. *Psychology of Learning and Motivation*, 19, 59–87.

Holyoak, K.J., & Koh, K. (1987). Surface and structural similarity in analogical transfer. *Memory and Cognition*, 15, 332–340.

Holyoak, K. J., & Spellman, B. A. (1993). Thinking. *Annual Review of Psychology*, 44, 265–315.

Huey, E. B. (1908). *The psychology and pedagogy of reading* (reprinted 1968). Cambridge, MA: MIT Press.

Hull, C. L. (1920). Quantitative aspects of the evolution of concepts. *Psychological Monographs*, 28, (Whole No.123).

Hulme, C., Maughan, S., & Brown, G. D. A. (1991). Memory for words and non-words: Evidence for a long-term memory contribution to short-term memory tasks. *Journal of Memory and Language*, 30, 685–701.

Humphreys, G. W., & Bruce, V. (1989). *Visual cognition: Computational, experimental and neuropsychological perspectives*. Hove: Lawrence Erlbaum Associates Ltd.

Humphreys, G. W., & Riddoch, M. J. (1990). Visual and attentional processes in Balint's syndrome. *Perception, 19*, 268–269.

Humphreys, G. W., Evett, L. J., & Quinlan, P. T. (1990). Orthographic processing in visual word identification. *Cognitive Psychology, 22*, 517–560.

Hunter, I. M. L. (1962). An exceptional talent for calculative thinking. *British Journal of Psychology, 53*, 243–258.

Hunter, I. M. L. (1977). An exceptional memory. *British Journal of Psychology, 68*, 155–164.

Hunter, I. M. L. (1978). The role of memory in expert mental calculations. In M. M. Gruneberg, P. E. Morris, & R. N. Sykes (Eds), *Practical aspects of memory*. London: Academic Press.

Hunter, I. M. L. (1979). Memory in everyday life. In M. M. Gruneberg & P. E. Morris (Eds), *Applied problems in memory*. London: Academic Press.

Hunter, I. M. L. (1985). Lengthy verbatim recall: The role of text. In A. W. Ellis (Ed.), *Progress in the psychology of language*, Vol. 1. Hove: Lawrence Erlbaum Associates Ltd.

Huttenlocher, J., Hedges, L. V., & Duncan, S. (1991). Categories and particulars — prototype effects in estimating spatial location. *Psychological Review, 98*, 352–376.

Ibbotson, N. R., & Morton, J. (1981). Rhythm and dominance. *Cognition, 9*, 125–138.

Inhoff, A. W., Pollatsek, A., Posner, M. I., & Rayner, K. (1989). Covert attention and eye movements during reading. *Quarterly Journal of Experimental Psychology, 41A*, 63–89.

Intons-Peterson, M. J., & Fournier, J. (1986). External and internal memory aids: When and how do we use them? *Journal of Experimental Psychology, 115*, 276–280.

Intons-Peterson, M. J., & Newsome, G. L. (1992). External memory aids: Effects and effectiveness. In D. Herrmann, H. Weingarner, A. Searleman, & C. McEvoy (Eds), *Memory improvement: Implications for memory theory*. New York: Springer-Verlag.

Intons-Peterson, M. J., & Roskos-Ewoldsen, B. B. (1989). Sensory–perceptual qualities of images. *Journal of Experimental Psychology: Learning, Memory and Cognition, 15*, 188–199.

Intons-Peterson, M. J., & White, A. R. (1981). Experimenter naivete and imaginal judgments. *Journal of Experimental Psychology: Human Perception and Performance, 7*, 833–843.

Ittelson, W. H. (1952). *The Ames demonstrations in perception*. New York: Hafner.

Jacobs, R. A., Jordan, M. I., & Barto, A. G. (1991). Task decomposition through competition in a modular connectionist architecture — the what and where vision tasks. *Cognitive Science, 15*, 219–250.

Jacoby, L. L. (1983). Remembering the data: Analysing the interactive processes in reading. *Journal of Verbal Learning and Verbal Behavior, 22*, 485–508.

Jagacinski, R. J., Marchburn, E., Klapp, S. T., & Jones, M. R. (1988). Tests of parallel versus integrated structure in polyrhythmic tapping. *Journal of Motor Behavior, 20*, 416–442.

James, I. (1990). *Prospective memory in the real world*. Unpublished PhD thesis, Lancaster University.

James, W. (1890). *The principles of psychology*. New York: Holt.

Jarvella, R. J. (1970). Effects of syntax on running memory span for connected discourse. *Psychonomic Sequence, 19*, 235–236.

Jarvella, R. J. (1971). Syntactic processing of connected speech. *Journal of Verbal Learning and Verbal Behavior, 10*, 409–416.

Jeannerod, M. (1984). The timing of natural prehension movements. *Journal of Motor Behaviour, 16*, 235–254.

Jeannerod, M. (Ed.) (1990). *Attention and performance XIII: Motor representation and control*. Hillsdale, NJ: Lawrence Erlbaum Associates Inc.

Jeannerod, M., Michel, F., & Prablanc, C. (1984). The control of hand movements in a case of hemianaesthesia following a parietal lesion. *Brain, 107*, 899–920.

Jeffries, R., Polson, P. G., Razran, L., & Atwood, M. E. (1977). A process model for missionaries — cannibals and other river crossing problems. *Cognitive Psychology, 9*, 412–440.

Jenkins, J. J., Wald, J., & Pittenger, J. B. (1978). Apprehending pictorial events: An instance of psychological cohesion. In C. W. Savage (Ed.), *Minnesota studies in the philosophy of science*, Vol. 9. Minneapolis: University of Minnesota Press.

Jensen, A. R. (1990). Speed of information processing in a calculating prodigy. *Intelligence, 14*, 259–274.

Johnson-Laird, P. N. (1983). *Mental models*. Cambridge: Cambridge University Press.

Johnson-Laird, P. N., & Byrne, R. M. J., (1991). *Deduction*. Hillsdale, NJ: Lawrence Erlbaum Associates Inc.

Johnson-Laird, P. N., & Wason, P. C. (Eds.) (1977). *Thinking: Readings in cognitive science*. Cambridge: Cambridge University Press.

Johnson-Laird, P. N., Legrenzi, P., & Legrenzi, S. L. (1972). Reasoning and a sense of reality. *British Journal of Psychology, 63*, 395–400.

Johnson-Laird, P. N., Gibbs, G., & de Mowbray, J. (1978). Meaning, amount of processing and memory for words. *Memory and Cognition, 6*, 372–375.

Johnson-Laird, P. N., Schaeken, W., & Byrne, R. M. J. (1992). Propositional reasoning by model. *Psychological Review, 99*, 418–439.

Jones, D. T., Miles, C., & Page, J. (1990). Disruption of proof reading by irrelevant speech: Effects of attention, arousal, or memory? *Applied Cognitive Psychology, 4*, 89–108.

Jones, D. T., Madden, C., & Miles, C. (1992). Privileged access by irrelevant speech to short-term memory: The role of changing state. *Quarterly Journal of Psychology, 44A*, 645–669.

Jones, G. V., & Langford, S. (1987). Phonological blocking in the tip of the tongue state. *Cognition, 26*, 115–122.

Jonides, J., Naveh-Benjamin, M., & Palmer, J. (1985). Assessing automaticity. *Acta Psychologica, 60*, 157–171.

Jordan, M.I. (1990). Motor learning and the degrees of freedom problem. In M. Jeannerod (Ed.), *Attention and performance XIII: Motor representation and control*. Hillsdale, NJ: Lawrence Erlbaum Associates Inc.

Josephs, R. A., Larrick, R. P., Steele, C. M., & Nisbett, R. E. (1992). Protecting the self from the negative consequences of risky decisions. *Journal of Personality and Social Psychology, 62*, 26–37.

Julesz, B. I. (1964). Binocular depth perception without familiarity cues. *Science, 15*, 355–362.

Julesz, B. (1971). *Foundations of cyclopean perception*. Chicago, IL: University of Chicago Press.

Jungerman, H. (1983). Two camps of rationality. In R. W. Scholz (Ed.), *Decision making under uncertainty*. Amsterdam: Elsevier.

Kahneman, D. (1973). *Attention and effort*. Englewood Cliffs, NJ: Prentice-Hall.

Kahneman, D., & Henik, A. (1981). Perceptual organisation and attention. In M. Kubovy & J. R. Pomerantz (Eds), *Perceptual organisation*. Hillsdale, NJ: Lawrence Erlbaum Associates Inc.

Kahneman, D., & Treisman, A.M. (1984). Changing views of attention and automaticity. In R. Parasuraman & D. R. Davies (Eds), *Varieties of attention*. New York: Academic Press.

Kahneman, D., & Tversky, A. (1972). Subjective probability: A judgement of representativeness. *Cognitive Psychology, 3*, 430–454.

Kahneman, D., & Tversky, A. (1973). On the psychology of prediction. *Psychological Review, 80*, 237–251.

Kahneman, D., & Tversky, A. (1979). Prospect theory: An analysis of decision under risk. *Econometrica, 47*, 263–291.

Kahneman, D., & Tversky, A. (1982a). Subjective probability: A judgement of representativeness. In D. Kahneman, P. Slovic, & A. Tversky (Eds), *Judgement under uncertainty: Heuristics and biases*. Cambridge: Cambridge University Press.

Kahneman, D., & Tversky, A. (1982b). Variants of uncertainty. In D. Kahneman, P. Slovic, & A. Tversky (Eds), *Judgement under uncertainty: Heuristics and biases*. Cambridge: Cambridge University Press.

Kahneman, D., Slovic, P., & Tversky, A. (Eds) (1982). *Judgement under uncertainty: Heuristics and biases*. Cambridge: Cambridge University Press.

Kaplan, C.A., & Simon, H. A. (1990). In search of insight. *Cognitive Psychology, 22,* 374–419.

Kaye, J. (1989). *Phonology: A cognitive view*. Hove: Lawrence Erlbaum Associates Ltd.

Keele, S. W., & Jennings, P. J. (1992). Attention in the representation of sequence: Experiment and theory. *Human Movement Science, 11,* 125–140.

Keele, S. W., & Posner, M. I. (1968). Processing visual feedback in rapid movements. *Journal of Experimental Psychology, 77,* 155–158.

Keele, S. W., Cohen, A., & Ivry, R. I. (1990). Motor programs: Concepts and issues. In M. Jeannerod (Ed.), *Attention and performance XIII: Motor representation and control*. Hillsdale, NJ: Lawrence Erlbaum Associates Inc.

Keenan, J., MacWhinney, B., & Mayhew, D. (1977). Pragmatics in memory: A study of natural conversation. *Journal of Verbal Learning and Verbal Behavior, 16,* 549–560.

Keenan, J. M., & Moore, R. E. (1979). Memory for images of concealed objects: A re-examination of Neisser and Kern. *Journal of Experimental Psychology: Human Learning and Memory, 5,* 374–385.

Keil, F. C. (1989). *Concepts, kinds and conceptual development*. Cambridge, MA: MIT Press.

Kelly, M. H. (1992). Using sound to solve syntatic problems: The role of phonology in grammatical category assignments. *Psychological Review, 99,* 349–364.

Kelly, M. H., & Bock, J. K. (1988). Stress in time. *Journal of Experimental Psychology: Human Perception and Performance, 14,* 389–403.

Kelso, J. A. S., Southard, D. L., & Goodman, D. (1979). On the coordination of two handed movements. *Journal of Experimental Psychology: Human Perception and Performance, 5,* 229–238.

Kerr, N. H. (1983). The role of vision in visual-imagery experiments: Evidence from the congenitally blind. *Journal of Experimental Psychology: General, 112,* 265–277.

Kintsch, W. (1974). *The representation of meaning in memory*. Hillsdale, NJ: Lawrence Erlbaum Associates Inc.

Kintsch, W. (1988). The role of knowledge in discourse comprehension: A construction–integration model. *Psychological Review, 95,* 163–182.

Kintsch, W., & Bates, E. (1977). Recognition memory for statements from a classroom lecture. *Journal of Experimental Psychology: Human Learning and Memory, 3,* 150–159.

Kirasic, K. C., Allen, G. L., & Siegel, A. W. (1984). Expression of configurational knowledge of large scale environments. *Environment and Behaviour, 16,* 687–712.

Klapp, S. T. (1979). Doing two things at once: The role of temporal compatibility. *Memory and Cognition, 5,* 375–381.

Klapp, S. T., & Wyatt, E. P. (1976). Motor programming within a sequence of responses. *Journal of Motor Behaviour, 8,* 19–26.

Kliegel, R., Smith, J., Heckhausen, J., & Baltes, P. B. (1987). Mnemonic training for the acquisition of skilled digit memory. *Cognition and Instruction, 4,* 203–223.

Kohonen, T. (1984). *Self-organization and associative memory*. Berlin: Springer Verlag.

Kosslyn, S. M. (1973). Scanning visual images: Some structural implications. *Perception and Psychophysics, 14,* 90–94.

Kosslyn, S. M. (1975). Information representation in visual images. *Cognitive Psychology, 7,* 341–370.

Kosslyn, S. M. (1976). Can imagery be distinguished from other forms of internal representation? Evidence from studies of retrieval time. *Memory and Cognition, 4,* 291–297.

Kosslyn, S. M. (1980). *Image and mind*. Cambridge, MA: Harvard University Press.

Kosslyn, S. M. (1981). The medium and the message in mental imagery: A theory. *Psychological Review, 88,* 46–66.

Kosslyn, S. M. (1991). A cognitive neuroscience of visual cognition: Further developments. In R. H. Logie & M. Denis (Eds), *Mental images in human cognition*, pp. 351–381. Amsterdam: North Holland.

Kosslyn, S. M., & Pomerantz, J. R. (1979). Imagery, propositions and the form of internal representations. *Cognitive Psychology, 9*, 52–76.

Kosslyn, S. M., & Schwartz, S. P. (1981). Empirical constraints on theories of visual mental imagery. In J. Long & A. Baddeley (Eds), *Attention and performance IX*. Hillsdale, NJ: Lawrence Erlbaum Associates Inc.

Kosslyn, S. M., Pick, H., & Fariello, G. (1974). Cognitive maps in children and men. *Child Development, 45*, 707–716.

Kosslyn, S. M., Van-Kleeck, M. H., & Kirby, K. N. (1990). A neurologically plausible model of individual differences in visual mental imagery. In P. J. Hampson, D. F. Marks, & J. T. E. Richardson (Eds), *Imagery: Current developments*, pp. 39–77. London: Routledge.

Kroll, N. E. A., Kellicut, M. H., & Parks, T. E. (1975). Rehearsal of visual and auditory stimuli while shadowing. *Journal of Experimental Psychology: Human Learning and Memory, 4*, 215–222.

Kruschke, J. K. (1992). ALCOVE: An exemplar-based connectionist model of category learning. *Psychological Review, 99*, 22–44.

Kunda, Z., & Nisbett, R. E. (1986a). The psychometrics of everyday life. *Cognitive Psychology, 18*, 195–224.

Kunda, Z., & Nisbett, R. E. (1986b). Prediction and the partial understanding of the law of large numbers. *Cognitive Psychology, 22*, 339–354.

Kvavilashvili, L. (1987). Remembering: Intention as a distinct form of memory. *British Journal of Psychology, 78*. 507–518

Kvavilashvili, L. (1992). Remembering intentions: A critical review of existing experimental paradigms. *Applied Cognitive Psychology, 6*, 507–524.

Kyllonen, P. C., & Christal, R. E. (1990). Reasoning ability is (little more than) working memory capacity?! *Intelligence, 14*, 389–433.

Lackner, J. R., & Garrett, M. F. (1972). Resolving ambiguity: Effects of biasing context in the unattended ear. *Cognition, 1*, 359–372.

Lakoff, G. (1987). Cognitive models and prototype theory. In U. Neisser (Ed.), *Concepts and conceptual development: The ecological and intellectual bases of categories*. Cambridge: Cambridge University Press.

Landauer, T. K., & Bjork, R. A. (1978). Optimum rehearsal patterns and name learning. In M. M. Gruneberg, P. E. Morris, & R. N. Sykes, (Eds), *Practical aspects of memory*. London: Academic Press

Larrick, R. P. (1993). Motivational factors in decision theories: The role of self-protection. *Psychological Bulletin, 113*, 440–450.

Lashley, K. S. (1951). The problem of serial order in behaviour. In L.A. Jeffress (Ed.), *Cerebral mechanisms in behaviour*. New York: John Wiley.

Latour, P.L. (1962). Visual threshold during eye movements. *Vision Research, 2*, 261–262.

Lee, D. N., Lishman, J. R., & Thomson, J. A. (1982). Regulation of gait in long jumping. *Journal of Experimental Psychology: Human Perception and Performance, 8*, 448–459.

Legge, D., & Barber, P. (1976). *Information and skill*. London: Methuen.

Lenneberg, E. H. (1967). *Biological foundations of language*. New York: John Wiley.

Leonard, J. A. (1959). Tactual choice reactions. *Quarterly Journal of Experimental Psychology, 11*, 76–83.

Levelt, W. J. M. (1983). Monitoring and self-repair in speech. *Cognition, 14*, 41–104.

Levelt, W. J. M. (1989). *Speaking: From intention to articulation*. Cambridge, MA: MIT Press.

Levelt, W. J. M., Schriefers, H., Vorberg, D., Myers, A. D., Pechman, T., & Havinga, J. (1991). The time course of lexical access in speech production: A study of picture naming. *Psychological Review, 98*, 122–142.

Levine, M. (1966). Hypothesis behaviour by humans during discrimination learning. *Journal of Experimental Psychology, 71*, 331–338.

Levinson, S. (1983). *Pragmatics*. Cambridge: Cambridge University Press.

Lichtenstein, E. H., & Brewer, W. F. (1980). Memory for goal-directed events. *Cognitive Psychology, 12*, 412–445.

Lichtenstein, S., Slovic, P., & Zinc, D. (1969). Effect of instruction in expected value on optimality of gambling decisions. *Journal of Experimental Psychology, 79*, 236–240.

Lichtenstein, S., Fischhoff, B., & Phillips, L. D. (1982). Calibration of probabilities. In D. Kahneman, P. Slovic, & A. Tversky (Eds), *Judgment under uncertainty: Heuristics and biases*. New York: Cambridge University Press.

Lieberman, P. (1963). Some effects of semantic and grammatical context on the production and perception of speech. *Language and Speech, 6*, 172–187.

Lindsay, D. S. (1990). Misleading suggestions can impair eyewitness's ability to remember event details. *Journal of Experimental Psychology: Learning, Memory and Cognition, 16*, 1077–1083.

Lindsay, P. H., & Norman, D. A. (1977). *Human information processing*, 2nd edn. New York: Academic Press.

Lindsay, R. C., Wells, G. L., & O'Connor, F. J. (1989). Mock-juror belief of accurate and inaccurate eyewitnesses: A replication and extension. *Law and Human Behaviour, 13*, 333–339.

Linton, M. (1982). Transformations of memory in everyday life. In: U. Neisser (Ed.), *Memory observed*. San Francisco, CA: W.H. Freeman.

Loftus, E. F. (1979). *Eyewitness testimony*. Cambridge, MA: Harvard University Press.

Loftus, E. F. (1981). Mentalmorphosis: Alterations in memory produced by the mental bonding of new information to old. In J. Long & A. Baddeley (Eds), *Attention and performance IX* Hillsdale, NJ: Lawrence Erlbaum Associates Inc.

Loftus, E. F. (1983). Misfortunes of memory. *Philosophical Transactions of the Royal Society of London, B302*, 413–421.

Loftus, E. F., & Loftus, G. R. (1980). On the permanence of stored information in the human brain. *American Psychologist, 35*, 409–420.

Loftus, E. F., & Palmer, J. C. (1974). Reconstruction of automobile destruction: An example of the interaction between language and memory. *Journal of Verbal Learning and Verbal Behavior, 13*, 585–589.

Loftus, E. F., Miller, D.G., & Burns, H. J., (1978). Semantic integration of verbal information into a visual memory. *Journal of Experimental Psychology: Human Learning and Memory, 4*, 19–31.

Loftus, E. F., Manber, M., & Keating, J. P. (1983). Recollection of naturalistic events: Context enhancement versus negative cueing. *Human Learning, 2*, 83–92.

Logan, G. D., (1988). Towards an instance theory of automatization. *Psychological Review, 95*, 492–527.

Logie, R. H. (1986). Visuo-spatial processing in working memory. *Quarterly Journal of Experimental Psychology, 38A*, 229–248.

Logie, R. H., & Denis, M. (Eds) (1991). *Mental images in human cognition*. Amsterdam: North Holland.

Logie, R. H., Zucco, G. M., & Baddeley, A. D. (1990). Interference with visual short-term memory. *Acta Psychologica, 75*, 55–74.

Lombardi, L., & Potter, M.C. (1992). The regeneration of syntax in short-term memory. *Journal of Memory and Language, 31*, 713–733.

Loomes, G., & Sugden, R. (1982). Regret theory: An alternative theory of rational choice under uncertainty. *Economic Journal, 92*, 805–824.

Loomis, J. M. (1990). A model of character recognition and legibility. *Journal of Experimental Psychology: Human Perception and Performance, 16*, 106–120.

Lopes, L. L. (1987). Between hope and fear. In L. Berkowitz (Ed.), *Advances in experimental social psychology*, Vol. 20, pp. 255–295. New York: Academic Press.

Lytton, W. W., & Brust, J. C. M. (1989). Direct dyslexia: Preserved oral reading of real words in Wernicke's aphasia. *Brain, 112*, 583–594.

McClelland, A. G. R., Rawles, R. E., & Sinclair, F. E. (1981). The effects of search criteria and retrieval cue availability on memory for words. *Memory and Cognition, 9*, 164–168.

McClelland, J. L., & Rumelhart, D. E. (1981). An interactive activation model of context effects in letter perception. Part 1: An account of basic findings. *Psychological Review, 88*, 375–407.

McCloskey, M., & Zaragoza, M. (1985). Misleading post-event information and memory events: Arguments and evidence against memory hypothesis. *Journal of Experimental Psychology, 114*, 1–16.

McCloskey, M., Wibel, C. G., & Cohen, N. J. (1988). Is there a special flashbulb-memory mechanism? *Journal of Experimental Psychology: General, 117*, 171–181.

McConkie, G. W. (1983). Eye movements and perception during reading. In K. Rayner (Ed.), *Eye movements in reading: Perceptual and language processes.* New York: Academic Press.

McDermott, J., & Larkin, J. H. (1978). Re-representing textbook physics problems. In *Proceedings of the 2nd National Conference, Canadian Society for Computational Studies of Intelligence.* Toronto: University of Toronto Press.

McGeoch, J. A., & MacDonald, W. T. (1931). Meaningful relation and retroactive inhibition. *American Journal of Psychology, 43*, 579–588.

McGurk, H., & MacDonald, J. (1976). Hearing lips and seeing voices. *Nature, 264*, 746–748.

McLeod, P. D. (1977). A dual-task response modality effect: support for multiprocessor models of attention. *Quarterly Journal of Experimental Psychology, 29*, 651–667.

McLeod, P. (1978). Does probe RT measure control processing demand? *Quarterly Journal of Experimental Psychology, 30*, 83–89.

McLeod, P., & Posner, M. I. (1984). Privileged loops from percept to act. In H. Bouma & D. G. Bouwhuis (Eds), *Attention and performance X.* Hillsdale, NJ: Lawrence Erlbaum Associates Inc.

McNamara, T. P., Ratcliff, R., & McKoon, G. (1984). The mental representation of knowledge acquired from maps. *Journal of Experimental Psychology: Learning, Memory and Cognition, 10*, 723–732.

McNamara, T. P., Hardy, J. K., & Hirtle, S. C. (1989). Subjective hierarchies in spatial memory. *Journal of Experimental Psychology: Learning, Memory and Cognition, 15*, 211–227.

McNamara, T. P., Halpin, J. A., & Hardy, J. K. (1992). Spatial and temporal contributions to the structure of spatial memory. *Journal of Experimental Psychology: Learning, Memory and Cognition, 18*, 555–564.

McWeeny, K. H., Young, A. W., Hay, D. C., & Ellis, A. W. (1987). Putting names to faces. *British Journal of Psychology, 78*, 148–150.

MacKay, D. G. (1972). The structure of words and syllables: Evidence from errors in speech. *Cognitive Psychology, 3*, 210–227.

MacKay, D. G. (1973). Aspects of the theory of comprehension, memory and attention. *Quarterly Journal of Experimental Psychology, 25*, 22–40.

MacKay, D. G. (1981). The problem of rehearsal or mental practice. *Journal of Motor Behavior, 13*, 274–285.

MacKay, D. G. (1987). *The organization of perception and action: A theory for language and other cognitive skills.* New York: Springer Verlag.

MacKenzie, C. L., & Van Eerd, D. L. (1990). Rhythmic precision in the performance of piano scales: Motor psychophysics and motor programming. In M. Jeannerod (Ed.), *Attention and performance XIII: Motor representation and control.* Hillsdale, NJ: Lawrence Erlbaum Associates Inc.

MacLeod, C. M., & Dunbar, K. (1988). Training and Stroop-like interference: Evidence for a continuum of automaticity. *Journal of Experimental Psychology: Learning, Memory and Cognition, 14*, 126–135.

MacNeilage, P. F. (1970). Motor control of serial ordering of speech. *Psychological Review*, 77, 182–196.

Maier, N. R. F. (1930). Reasoning in humans. I: On direction. *Journal of Comparative Psychology*, 10, 115–143.

Maier, N. R. F. (1931). Reasoning in humans. II: The solution of a problem and its appearance in consciousness. *Journal of Comparative Psychology*, 12, 181–194.

Maier, N. R. F. (1945). Reasoning in humans. III: The mechanisms of equivalent stimuli and of reasoning. *Journal of Experimental Psychology*, 35, 349–360.

Malpass, R. S., & Devine, P. G. (1981). Guided memory in eyewitness identification. *Journal of Applied Psychology*, 66, 343–350.

Manktelow, K. I., & Over, D. E. (1991). Social roles and utilities in reasoning with deontic conditionals. *Cognition*, 39, 85–105.

March, J. G. (1988). Variable risk preferences and adaptive aspirations. *Journal of Economic Behaviour and Organization*, 9, 5–24.

March, J. G., & Shapiro, Z. (1987). Managerial perspectives on risk and risk taking. *Management Science*, 33, 1404–1418.

March, J. G., & Shapiro, Z. (1992). Variable risk preferences and the focus of attention. *Psychological Review*, 99, 172–183.

Margrain, S. A. (1967). Short-term memory as a function of input modality. *Quarterly Journal of Experimental Psychology*, 25, 368–377.

Marr, D. (1982). *Vision: A computational investigation into the human representation and processing of visual information*. San Francisco CA: W.H. Freeman.

Marr, D., & Hildreth, E. (1980). Theory of edge detection. *Proceedings of the Royal Society of London*, B207, 187–216.

Marr, D., & Nishihara, H. K. (1978). Representation and recognition of the spatial organisation of three-dimensional shapes. *Proceedings of the Royal Society of London*, B200, 269–294.

Marr, D., & Poggio, T. (1976). Cooperative computation of stereo disparity. *Science*, 194, 283–287.

Marshall, J. C., & Newcombe, F. (1973). Patterns of paralexia: A psycholinguistic approach. *Journal of Psycholinguistic Research*, 2, 175–199.

Marslen-Wilson, W. D. (1980). Speech understanding as a psychological process. In J. C. Simon (Ed.), *Spoken language generation and understanding*. Dortrecht: Reidel.

Marslen-Wilson, W. D. (1987). Functional parallelism in spoken word recognition. *Cognition*, 25, 71–102.

Marslen-Wilson, W. D., & Tyler, L. K. (1980). The temporal structure of spoken language understanding. *Cognition*, 8, 1–71.

Marslen-Wilson, W. D., & Welsh, A. (1978). Processing interactions and lexical access during word recognition in continuous speech. *Cognitive Psychology*, 10, 29–63.

Marslen-Wilson, W. D., Tyler, L. K., Warren, P., Grenier, P., & Lee, C. S. (1992) Prosodic effects in minimal attachment. *Quarterly Journal of Experimental Psychology*, 45A, 73–87.

Martenuik, R. G., MacKenzie, C. L., Jeannerod, M., Athenes, S., & Douglas, C. (1987). Constraints on human arm movement trajectories. *Canadian Journal of Psychology*, 41, 365–373.

Martenuik, R. G., Leavitt, J. L., Mackenzie, C. L., & Athenes, S. (1990). Functional relationships between grasp and transport components in a prehension task. *Human Movement Science*, 9, 149–176.

Martin, N., & Saffran, E. M. (1992). A computational account of deep dysphasia: Evidence from a single case study. *Brain and Language*, 43, 240–274.

Martin, N., Weisberg, R. W., & Saffran, E. M. (1989). Variables influencing the occurrence of naming errors: Implications for models of lexical retrieval. *Journal of Memory and Language*, 28, 462–485.

Martin, R. (1987). The role of short-term memory in sentence processing. *Brain and Language, 32*, 159–192.

Massaro, D. W. (1988). Some criticisms of connectionist models of human performance. *Journal of Memory and Language, 27*, 213–234.

Mayer, R. E. (1992). *Thinking, problem solving and cognition, 2nd Edn.* New York: W. H. Freeman.

Maylor, E. A. (1990). Age and prospective memory. *Quarterly Journal of Experimental Psychology, 42A*, 471–493.

Meacham, J. A., & Leiman, B. (1975). Remembering to perform future actions. In: U. Neisser (Ed.), *Memory observed: Remembering in natural contexts.* San Francisco, CA: W. H. Freeman.

Medin, D. L., & Shoben, E. J. (1988). Context and structure in conceptual combination. *Cognitive Psychology, 20*, 158–190.

Medin, D. L., & Wattenmaker, W. D. (1987). Category cohesiveness, theories, and cognitive archeology. In U. Neisser (Ed.), *Concepts and conceptual development: The ecological and intellectual bases of categories.* Cambridge: Cambridge University Press.

Medin, D. L., Wattenmaker, W. D., & Hampson, S. E. (1987). Family resemblance, conceptual cohesiveness, and category construction. *Cognitive Psychology, 19*, 242–279.

Melton, A. W., & Irwin, J. M. (1940). The influence of degree of interpolated learning on retroactive inhibition and the overt transfer of specific responses. *American Journal of Psychology, 53*, 173–203.

Mervis, C.B., & Crisafi, K.A. (1982). Order of acquisition of subordinate-, basic- and superordinate-level categories. *Child Development, 53*, 258–266.

Metcalfe, J., & Fisher, R. P. (1986). The relation between recognition memory and classification. *Memory and Cognition 14*, 164–173.

Metzler, J. & Shepard, R. N. (1974). Transformational studies of the internal representation of three-dimensional objects. In R. L. Solso (Ed.). *Theories of cognitive psychology: The Loyola symposium.* Hillsdale, NJ: Lawrence Erlbaum Associates Inc.

Meulenbroek, R. G., & Thomassen, A. J. (1991). Stroke direction preferences in drawing and handwriting. *Human Movement Science, 10*, 247–270.

Meyer, D. E., Abrams, R. A., Kornblum, S., Wright, C. E., & Smith, J. E. K. (1988). Optimality in human motor performance: Ideal control of rapid aimed movements. *Psychological Review, 95*, 340–370.

Meyer, D. E., & Schvaneveldt, R.W. (1971). Facilitation in recognising pairs of words: Evidence of a dependence between retrieval operations. *Journal of Experimental Psychology, 90*, 227–234.

Meyerowitz, B. E., & Chaiken, S. (1987). The effect of message framing on breast self-examination attitudes, intentions and behaviour. *Journal of Personality and Social Psychology, 52*, 500–510.

Miller, G. A. (1956). The magic number seven, plus or minus two: Some limits on our capacity for processing information. *Psychological Review, 63*, 81–97.

Miller, G. A., & Johnson-Laird, P. N. (1976). *Language and perception.* Cambridge: Cambridge University Press.

Miller, G. A., Heise, G. A., & Lichten, W. (1951). The intelligibility of speech as a function of the context of the test materials. *Journal of Experimental Psychology, 41*, 329–335.

Miller, G. A., Galanter, E., & Pribram, K. H. (1960). *Plans and the structure of behavior.* New York: Holt, Rinehart and Winston.

Milner, B. (1966). Amnesia following operation on the temporal lobes. In C. W. M. Whitty & O. L. Zangwill (Eds), *Amnesia.* London: Butterworths.

Milner, B. (1970). Memory and the medial temporal regions of the brain. In K. H. Pribram & D. E. Broadbent (Eds), *Biology of memory.* New York: Academic Press.

Minsky, M. (1975). A framework for representing knowledge. In P. H. Winston (Ed.), The psychology of computer vision. New York: McGraw-Hill.

Moar, I. (1979). *The internal geometry of cognitive maps*. Unpublished doctoral dissertation, Cambridge University.

Moar, I., & Carleton, L. R. (1982). Memory for routes. *Quarterly Journal of Experimental Psychology, 34*, 381–394.

Monsell, S. (1984). Components of working memory underlying verbal skills: A "distributed capacities" view. In H. Bouma & D. G. Bouwhuis (Eds), *Attention and Performance X*. London: Lawrence Erlbaum Associates Ltd.

Monsell, S., Patterson, K. E., Graham, A., Hughes, C., & Milroy, R. (1992). Lexical and sublexical translation of spelling to sound: Strategic anticipation of lexical status. *Journal of Experimental Psychology: Learning, Memory and Cognition, 18*, 452–467.

Moore, G. T. (1991). Life-span developmental issues in environmental assessment, cognition, and action: Applications to environmental policy, planning, and design. In T. Garling & G. W. Evans (Eds), *Environment, cognition and action: An integrated approach*, pp. 309–331. Oxford: Oxford University Press.

Morasso, P. (1981). Spatial control of arm movements. *Experimental Brain Research, 42*, 223–237.

Morasso, P., & Mussa-Ivaldi, F. A. (1982). Trajectory formation and handwriting: A computational model. *Biological Cybernetics, 45*, 131–142.

Morris, C. D., Bransford, J. D., & Franks, J. J. (1977). Levels of processing versus transfer appropriate processing. *Journal of Verbal Learning and Verbal Behavior, 16*, 519–533.

Morris, N. and Jones, D. T. (1990). Memory updating in working memory: The role of the central executive. *British Journal of Psychology, 81*, 111–121.

Morris, P. E. (1979). Strategies for learning and recall. In M. M. Gruneberg & P.E. Morris (Eds), *Applied problems in memory*. London: Academic Press.

Morris, P. E. (1988). Expertise and everyday memory. In M.M. Gruneberg, P.E. Morris, & R. N. Sykes (Eds), *Practical aspects of memory: Current research and issues*, Vol. 1. Chichester: John Wiley.

Morris, P. E. (1992). Cognition and consciousness. *The Psychologist, 5*, 3–8.

Morris, P. E. (1994). Theories of memory: An historical perspective. In P. E. Morris & M. Gruneberg (Eds), *Theoretical aspects of memory*. 2nd edn. London: Routledge.

Morris, P. E., & Greer, P. J. (1984). The effectiveness of the phonetic mnemonic system. *Human Learning, 3*, 137–142.

Morris, P. E., & Gruneberg, M. (1994). The major aspects of memory. In P.E. Morris & M. Gruneberg (Eds), *Theoretical aspects of memory*, 2nd edn. London: Routledge.

Morris, P.E., & Hampson, P. J. (1983). *Imagery and consciousness*. London: Academic Press.

Morris, P. E., & Stevens, R. (1974). Linking images and free recall. *Journal of Verbal Learning and Verbal Behavior, 13*, 310–315.

Morris, P. E., Jones, S., & Hampson, P. J. (1978). An imagery mnemonic for the learning of people's names. *British Journal of Psychology, 69*, 335–336.

Morris, P. E., Gruneberg, M. M., Sykes, R. N., & Merrick, A. (1981). Football knowledge and the acquisition of new results. *British Journal of Psychology, 72*, 479–483.

Morris, P. E., Tweedy, M., & Gruneberg, M. M. (1985). Interest, knowledge and the memorizing of soccer scores. *British Journal of Psychology, 76*, 417–425.

Morris, V., & Morris, P. E. (1985). The influence of question order on eyewitness accuracy. *British Journal of Psychology, 76*, 365–371.

Morton, J. (1967). A singular lack of incidental learning. *Nature, 215*, 203–204.

Morton, J. (1970). A functional model for memory. In D. A. Norman (Ed.), *Models of human memory* New York: Academic Press.

Morton, J. (1979). Word recognition. In J. Morton & J.C. Marshall (Eds), *Psycholinguistics series*, Vol. 2. London: Elek Science/Cambridge, MA: MIT Press.

Murdock, B. B., Jr (1962). The serial position effect in free recall. *Journal of Experimental Psychology, 64*, 482–488.

Murdock, B. B. Jr, & Walker, K. D. (1969). Modality effects in free recall. *Journal of Verbal Learning and Verbal Behavior, 8*, 665–676.

Murphy, G. L. (1988). Comprehending complex concepts. *Cognitive Science, 12*, 529–562.

Murphy, G. L., & Medin, D. L. (1985). The role of theories in conceptual coherence. *Psychological Review, 92*, 289–316.

Naveh-Benjamin, M., & Ayres, T. J. (1986). Digit span, reading rate, and linguistic relativity. *Quarterly Journal of Experimental Psychology, 38A*, 739–751.

Navon, D. (1978). The importance of being conservative: Some reflections on human Bayesian behaviour. *British Journal of Mathematical and Statistical Psychology, 31*, 33–48.

Navon, D. (1984). Resources: A theoretical soup stone? *Psychological Review, 91*, 216–234.

Navon, D. (1989). The locus of attentional selection: Is it early, late or neither? *European Journal of Cognitive Psychology, 1*, 47–68.

Neisser, U. (1982). *Memory observed*. San Francisco CA: W. H. Freeman.

Neisser, U. (1987). *Concepts and conceptual development: Ecological and intellectual factors in categorisation*. Cambridge: Cambridge University Press.

Neisser, U., Winograd, E., & Weldon, M. S. (1991). Remembering the earthquake: "What I experienced" versus "How I heard the news". Paper presented to the *32nd Annual Meeting of the Psychomanic Society*, San Francisco, CA.

Nelson, D. L. (1988). How what we know interferes with that we remember. In: M. M. Gruneberg, P. E. Morris & R. N. Sykes (Eds), *Practical aspects of memory: Current research and issues*, Vol. 1. New York: John Wiley

Nelson, D. L. (1994). Implicit memory. In P.E. Morris & M. Gruneberg (Eds), *Theoretical aspects of memory*, 2nd edn. London: Routledge.

Nelson, D. L., Schreiber, T. A., & McEvoy, C. L. (1992). Processing implicit and explicit representations. *Psychological Review, 99*, 322–348.

Nelson, T.O., & Chaiklin, S. (1980). Immediate memory for spatial location. *Journal of Experimental Psychology: Human Learning and Memory, 6*, 529–545.

Neumann, P. G. (1977). Visual prototype formation with discontinuous representation of dimensions of variability. *Memory and Cognition, 5*, 187–197.

Newell, A., & Simon, H. A. (1972). *Human problem solving*. Englewood Cliffs, NJ: Prentice-Hall.

Newell, A., Shaw, J. C., & Simon, H. A. (1958). Elements of a theory of human problem solving. *Psychological Reveiw, 65*, 151–166.

Newport, E. L., & Bellugi, U. (1978). Linguistic expression of category levels in a visual–gestural language: A flower is a flower is a flower. In E. Rosch & B. B. Lloyd (Eds), *Cognition and categorization*. Hillsdale, NJ: Lawrence Erlbaum Associates Inc.

Newstead, S. E., Pollard, P., Evans, J. St. B. T., & Allen, J. L. (1992). The source of belief bias effects in syllogistic reasoning. *Cognition, 45*, 257–284.

Newstead, S. E., & Evans, J. St. B. T. (1993). Mental models as an explanation of belief bias in syllogistic reasoning. *Cognition, 46*, 93–97.

Nickerson, R. S., & Adams, M. J. (1979). Long-term memory for a common object. *Cognitive Psychology, 11*, 287–307.

Noordman, L. G. M., & Vonk, W. (1992). Readers' knowledge and the control of inferences in reading. *Language and Cognitive Processes, 7*, 373–391.

Norman, D. A., & Bobrow, D.G. (1975). On data-limited and resource-limited processes. *Cognitive Psychology, 7*, 44–64.

Norman, D. A., & Rumelhart, D. E. (1983). Studies of typing from the LNR Research Group. In W.E. Cooper (Ed.), *Cognitive aspects of skilled typewriting*. New York: Springer-Verlag.

Nosofsky, R. M. (1988). Exemplar-based accounts of relations between classification, recognition, and typicality. *Journal of Experimental Psychology: Learning, Memory and Cognition, 14*, 700–708.

Nosofsky, R. M. (1991). Tests of an exemplar model for relating perceptual classification and recognition memory. *Journal of Experimental Psychology: Human Perception and Performance, 17*, 3–27.

Nosofsky, R. M., Kruschke, J. K., & McKinley, S. C. (1992). Combining exemplar-based category representations and connectionist learning rules. *Journal of Experimental Psychology: Learning, Memory and Cognition, 18*, 211–233.

Oakhill, J. V., & Johnson-Laird, P.N. (1985). The effects of belief on the spontaneous production of syllogistic conclusions. *Quarterly Journal of Experimental Psychology, 37A*, 553–569.

Oakhill, J., Johnson-Laird, P. N., & Garnham, A. (1989). Believability and syllogistic reasoning. *Cognition, 31*, 117–140.

O'Connell, D., & Kowal, S. (1983). Pausology. In W. A. Sedelow and S. Y. Sedelow (Eds), *Computers in language research: Part 1, Formalization in literary and discourse analysis.* Berlin: Mouton.

Oden, G. C. (1979). A fuzzy logic model of letter identification. *Journal of Experimental Psychology: Human Perception and Performance, 5*, 336–352.

O'Regan, J. K., & Jacobs, A. M. (1992). Optimal viewing position effect in word recognition: A challenge to current theory. *Journal of Experimental Psychology: Human Perception and Performance, 18*, 185–197.

Orne, M. T., Soskis, D. A., Dinges, & Orne, E. C. (1984). Hypnotically induced testimony. In G. L. Wells & E. F. Loftus (Eds), *Eyewitness testimony: Psychological perspectives.* New York: Cambridge University Press.

Paivio, A. (1971). *Imagery and verbal processes.* New York: Holt, Rinehart, and Winston.

Palmer, S. E. (1975). The effects of contextual scenes on the identification of objects. *Memory and Cognition, 3*, 519–526.

Parkin, A. J. (1979). Specifying levels of processing. *Quarterly Journal of Experimental Psychology, 31*, 175–195.

Parkin, A. J. (1993). *Memory: Phenoma, experiment and theory.* Oxford: Blackwell.

Pashler, H. (1990). Do response modality effects support multiprocessor models of divided attention? *Journal of Experimental Psychology: Human Perception and Performance, 16*, 826–842.

Pashler, H. (1991). Shifting visual attention and selecting motor responses: Distinct attentional mechanisms. *Journal of Experimental Psychology: Human Perception and Performance, 17*, 1023–1040.

Pashler, H., Carrier, M., & Hoffman, J. (1993). Saccadic eye movements and dual task interference. *Quarterly Journal of Experimental Psychology, 46A*, 51–82.

Patterson, K. E., Marshall, J. C., & Coltheart, M. (Eds) (1985). *Surface dyslexia: Neuropsychological and cognitive analyses of phonological reading.* London: Lawrence Erlbaum Associates Ltd.

Patterson, K. E., Seidenberg, M. S., & McClelland, J. L. (1989). Connections and disconnections: Acquired dyslexia in a computational model of reading processes. In R. G. Morris (Ed.), *Parallel distributed processing: Implication for pyschology and neurobiology.* Oxford: Oxford University Press.

Payne, J. W., Laughhunn, D. J., & Crum, P. (1980). Translation of gambles and aspiration level effects in risky choice behavior. *Management Science, 27*, 953–958.

Pearson, D. E., & Robinson, J. A. (1985). Visual communications at a very low data rate. *Proceedings of the IEEE, 73*, 795–812.

Pearson, D. E., Hanna, E., & Martinez, K. (1986). Computer-generated cartoons. In: *Proceedings of the Rank Prize Funds Symposium on Images and Understanding*, London, October. Cambridge: Cambridge University Press.

Perrett, D. I., Smith, P. A. J., Potter, D. D., Mistlin, A. J., Head, A. S., Milner, A. D., & Jeeves, M.A. (1984). Neurones responsive to faces in the temporal cortex: Studies in functional organization, sensitivity to identity and relation to perception. *Human Neurobiology, 3*, 197–208.

Perrett, D. I., Mistlin, A. J., Potter, D. D., Smith, P. A. J., Head, A. S., Chitty, A. J., Broennimann, R., Milner, A. D., & Jeeves, M. A. (1986). Functional organisation of visual neurones processing face identity. In H. D. Ellis, M.A. Jeeves, F. Newcombe, & A. Young (Eds), *Aspects of face processing*. Dordrecht: Martinus Niijhoff.

Peterson, M. A., Kihlstrom, J. F., Rose, P. M., & Glisky, M. L. (1992). Mental images can be ambiguous: Reconstruals and reference-frame reversals. *Memory and Cognition, 20.* 107–123.

Pew, R. W. (1974). Human perceptual-motor performance. In B. H. Kantowitz (Ed.), *Human information processing: Tutorials in performance and cognition*. Hillsdale, NJ: Lawrence Erlbaum Associates Inc.

Phillips, L. D. (1983). A theoretical perspective on heuristics and biases in probabilistic thinking. In P. Humphreys, O. Svenson, & A. Vari (Eds), *Analysing and aiding decision processes*. Amsterdam: North-Holland.

Phillips, L., & Edwards, W. (1966). Conservatism in a simple probability task. *Journal of Experimental Psychology, 72*, 346–354.

Phillips, W. A., & Baddeley, A. D. (1971). Reaction time and short-term visual memory. *Psychonomic Science, 22*, 73–74.

Pick, H. L., & Lockman, J. J. (1981). From frames of reference to spatial representations. In L. S. Liben, A. H. Patterson, & N. Newcombe (Eds), *Spatial representation and behavior across the life span*. New York: Academic Press.

Pillemer, D. B., Goldsmith, L. R., Panter, A. T., & White, S. H. (1988). Very long term memories of the first year in college. *Journal of Experimental Psychology: Learning, Memory and Cognition, 14*, 709–715.

Pillsbury, W. B. (1897). A study in apperception. *American Journal of Psychology, 8*, 315–393.

Politzer, G., & Nguyen-Xuan, A. (1992). Reasoning about conditional promises and warnings: Darwinian algorithms, mental models, relevance judgements or pragmatic schemas? *Quarterly Journal of Experimental Psychology, 44A*, 401–421.

Pollard, P. & Evans, J.St. B. T. (1987). Content and context effects in reasoning. *American Journal of Psychology, 100*, 41–60.

Pollatsek, A., & Rayner, K. (1989). Eye movements and lexical access in reading. In D. A. Balota, G. B. Flores d'Arcais, and K. Rayner (Eds), *Comprehension processes in reading*. Hillsdale, NJ: Lawrence Erlbaum Associates Inc.

Pollatsek, A., Bolozky, S., Well, A. D., & Rayner, K. (1981). Asymmetries in the perceptual span for Israeli readers. *Brain and Language, 14*, 174–180.

Posner, M. I. (1973). *Cognition: An introduction*. Glenview, IL: Scott Foresman and Co.

Posner, M. I., & Boies, S. J. (1971). Components of attention. *Psychological Review, 78*, 391–408.

Posner, M. I., & Mitchell, R. F. (1967). Chronometric analysis of classification. *Psychological Review, 74*, 392–409.

Potter, J. M. (1980). What was the matter with Dr. Spooner? In V. A. Fromkin (Ed.), *Errors in linguistic performance: Slips of the tongue, ear, pen and hand*. New York: Academic Press.

Potter, M. C., & Lombardi, L. (1990). Regeneration in the short-term recall of sentences. *Journal of Memory and Language, 29*, 633–654.

Presson, C. C., Delange, N., & Hazelrigg, M. D. (1989). Orientation specificity in spatial memory: What makes a path different from a map of the path. *Journal of Experimental Psychology: Learning, Memory and Cognition, 15*, 887–897.

Pullman, S. G. (1987). Computational models of parsing. In A. W. Ellis (Ed.), *Progress in the psychology of language*, Vol. 3. London: Lawrence Erlbaum Associates Ltd.

Pylyshyn, Z. W. (1973). What the mind's eye tells the mind's brain: A critique of mental imagery. *Psychological Bulletin, 80*, 1–24.

Pylyshyn, Z. W. (1981). The imagery debate: Analogue media versus tacit knowledge. *Psychological Review, 86*, 16–45.

Pylyshyn, Z. W. (1984). *Computation and cognition: Toward a foundation for cognitive science*. Cambridge, MA: MIT Press.

Quinlan, P. (1991). *Connectionism and psychology*. Hemel Hempstead: Harvester Wheatsheaf.

Rayner, K. (1979). Eye guidance in reading: Fixation locations in words. *Perception, 8*, 21–30.

Rayner, K., & Morris, R. K. (1992). Eye movement control in reading: Evidence against semantic preprocessing. *Journal of Experimental Psychology: Human Perception and Performance, 18*, 163–172.

Rayner, K., & Posnansky, C. (1978). Stages of processing in word identification. *Journal of Experimental Psychology: General, 107*, 64–80.

Rayner, K., Well, A. D., & Pollatsek, A. (1980). Asymmetry of the effective visual field in reading. *Perception and Psychophysics, 27*, 537–544.

Rayner, K., Carlson, M., & Frazier, L. (1983). The interaction of syntax and semantics during sentence processing: Eye movements in the analysis of semantically biased sentences. *Journal of Verbal Learning and Verbal Behavior, 22*, 358–374.

Read, J. D., & Bruce, D. (1982). Longitudinal tracking of difficult memory retrievals. *Cognitive Psychology, 14*, 280–300.

Reason, J. T. (1990). *Human error*. Cambridge: Cambridge University Press.

Reason, J. T., & Lucas, D. (1984). Using cognitive diaries to investigate naturally occurring memory blocks. In J. E. Harris & P. E. Morris (Eds), *Everyday memory, actions and absentmindedness*. London: Academic Press.

Reason, J. T., & Mysielska, K. (1982). *Absent minded? The psychology of mental lapses and everyday errors*, Englewood Cliffs, NJ: Prentice-Hall.

Reed, S. K. (1972). Pattern recognition and categorization. *Cognitive Psychology, 3*, 382–407.

Reed, S. K., & Friedman, M. P. (1973). Perceptual *vs* conceptual categorisation. *Memory and Cognition, 1*, 157–163.

Rehak, A., Kaplan, J. A., & Gardner, H. (1992). Sensitivity to conversational deviance in right hemisphere damaged patients. *Brain and Language, 42*, 203–217.

Reich, S. S., & Ruth, P. (1982). Wason's selection task: Verification, falsification and matching. *British Journal of Psychology, 73*, 395–405.

Reicher, G. M. (1969). Perceptual recognition as a function of meaningfulness of stimulus material. *Journal of Experimental Psychology, 81*, 274–280.

Rescorla, R. A., & Wagner, A. R. (1972). A theory of Pavlovian conditioning: variations in the effectiveness of reinforcement and nonreinforcement. In A. H. Black & W. F. Prokasy (Eds), *Classical conditioning II: Current theory and research*. New York: Appleton-Century-Crofts.

Restle, F. (1962). The selection of strategies in cue learning. *Psychological Review, 69*, 329–343.

Richardson, J. (1993). The curious case of coins: Remembering the appearance of familiar objects. *The Psychologist, 6*, 360–366.

Riddoch, M. J., & Humphreys, G. W. (1987). A case of integrative visual agnosia. *Brain, 110*, 1431–1462.

Rips, L. J. (1983). Cognitive processes in propositional reasoning. *Psychological Review, 90*, 38–71.

Rips, L. J. (1988). Deduction. In R. J. Sternberg & E. E. Smith (Eds), *The psychology of human thought*. Cambridge: Cambridge University Press.

Robinson, J. A. (1976). Sampling autobiographical memory. *Cognitive Psychology, 8*, 578–595.

Roediger, H. L. (1990). Implicit memory: Retention without remembering. *American Psychologist, 45*, 1043–1056.

Roediger, H. L., & Blaxton, T. A. (1987). Retrieval modes produce dissociations in memory for surface information. In D. Garfein & P. R. Hoffman (Eds), *Memory and cognitive processes: The Ebbinghaus centennial conference*. Hillsdale, NJ: Lawrence Erlbaum Associates Inc.

Roediger, H. L., Weldon, M. S., & Challis, B. H. (1989). Explaining dissociations between implicit and explicit measures of retention: A processing account. In H. L. Roediger & F. I. M. Craik (Eds), *Varieties of memory and consciousness: Essays in honor of Endel Tulving*. Hillsdale, NJ: Lawrence Erlbaum Associates Inc.

Rosch, E. (1973). Natural categories. *Cognitive Psychology, 4,* 328–350.

Rosch, E. (1978). Principles of categorization. In E. Rosch & B. B. Lloyd (Eds), *Cognition and categorization.* Hillsdale, NJ: Lawrence Erlbaum Associates Inc.

Rosch, E., & Mervis, C. B. (1975). Family resemblances: Studies in the internal structure of categories. *Cognitive Psychology, 7,* 573–605.

Rosch, E., Mervis, C. B., Gray, W., Johnson, D., & Boyes-Braem, P. (1976). Basic objects in natural categories. *Cognitive Psychology, 8,* 382–439.

Rosenbaum, D. A. (1991). *Human motor control.* New York: Academic Press.

Rosenbaum, D. A., & Jorgensen, M. J. (1992). Planning macroscopic aspects of manual control. *Human Movement Science, 11,* 61–70.

Rosenbaum, D. A., Kenny, S. B., & Derr, M. A. (1983). Hierarchical control of rapid movement sequences. *Journal of Experimental Psychology: Human Perception and Performance, 9,* 86–102.

Rosenbaum, D. A., Marchak, F., Barnes, H. J., Vaughan, J., Slotta, J. D., & Jorgensen, M. J. (1990). Constraints for action selection: overhand versus underhand grips. In M. Jeannerod (Ed.), *Attention and performance XIII: Motor representation and control.* Hillsdale, NJ: Lawrence Erlbaum Associates Inc.

Ross, B. H. (1984). Remindings and their effects in learning a cognitive skill. *Cognitive Psychology, 16,* 371–416.

Ross, B. H. (1987). This is like that: The use of earlier problems and the separation of similarity effects. *Journal of Experimental Psychology: Learning, Memory and Cognition, 13,* 629–639.

Ross, B. H. (1989). Remindings in learning and instruction. In S. Vosniadou & A. Ortony (Eds), *Similarity and analogical reasoning.* Cambridge; Cambridge University Press.

Rovine, M. J., & Weisman, G. D. (1989). Sketch-map variables as predictors of way-finding performance. *Journal of Environmental Psychology, 9,* 217–232.

Rubin, D. C. (1982). On the retention function for autobiographical memory. *Journal of Verbal Learning and Verbal Behavior, 21,* 21–38.

Rubin, D. C., & Kozin, M. (1984). Vivid memories. *Cognition, 16,* 81–95.

Rubin, D. C., Wetzler, S. E., & Nebes, R. D. (1986). Autobiographical across the lifespan. In D. C. Rubin (Ed.), *Autobiographical memory.* Cambridge: Cambridge University Press.

Rumelhart, D. E. (1989). The architecture of the mind: A connectionist approach. In M. I. Posner (Ed.), *Issues in cognitive science.* Cambridge, MA: MIT Press.

Rumelhart, D. E., & McClelland, J. L. (1982). An interactive activation model of context effects in letter perception. Part 2: The contextual enhancement effect and some tests and extensions of the model. *Psychological Review, 89,* 60–94.

Rumelhart, D. E., & McClelland, J. L. (1986). PDP models and general issues in cognitive science. In D. E. Rumelhart and J. L. McClelland (Eds), *Parallel distributed processing: Explorations in microcognition. Volume 1: Foundations.* Cambridge, MA: MIT Press.

Rumelhart, D. E., & Norman, D. A. (1982). Simulating a skilled typist: A study of skilled perceptual motor performance. *Cognitive Science, 6,* 1–36.

Rumelhart, D. E., Hinton, G. E., & Williams, R. J. (1986). Learning internal representations by error propogation. In D. E. Rumelhart and J. L. McClelland (Eds), *Parallel distributed processing: Explorations in microcognition. Volume 1: Foundations.* Cambridge, MA: MIT Press.

Rundus, D. (1973). Negative effects of using list items as recall cues. *Journal of Verbal Learning and Verbal Behavior, 12,* 43–50.

Ryan, J. (1974). Early language development: Towards a communicational analysis. In M. P. M. Richards (Ed.), *The integration of the child into a social world.* Cambridge: Cambridge University Press.

Sachs, J. S. (1967). Recognition memory for syntactic and semantic aspects of connected discourse. *Perception and Psychophysics, 2,* 437–442.

Saffran, E. M., & Martin, N. (1990). Short-term memory impairment and sentence processing: A case study. In G. Vallar & T. Shallice (Eds) *Neuropsychology impairments of short-term memory.* Cambridge: Cambridge University Press.

Saffran, E. M., Schwartz, M. F., & Marin, O. S. M. (1980). The word order problem in agrammatism. II. Production. *Brain and Language, 10*, 249–262.

Salamé, P., & Baddeley, A. D. (1982). Disruption of short-term memory by unattended speech: Implications for the structure of working memory. *Journal of Verbal Learning and Verbal Behavior, 21*, 150–164.

Salamé, P., & Baddeley, A. D. (1989). Effects of background music on phonological short-term memory. *Quarterly Journal of Experimental Psychology, 41A*, 107–122.

Savage, L. J. (1954). *The foundations of statistics*. New York: John Wiley.

Schactel, E. (1947). On memory and childhood amnesia. *Psychiatry, 10*, 1–26.

Schaller, M. (1992). Sample size, aggregation, and statistical reasoning in social inference. *Journal of Experimental Social Psychology, 28*, 65–85.

Schank, R. C. (1975). *Conceptual information processing*. Amsterdam: North-Holland.

Schank, R. C. (1982). *Dynamic memory*. Cambridge: Cambridge University Press.

Schank, R. C., & Abelson, R. (1977). *Scripts, plans, goals and understanding*. Hillsdale, NJ: Lawrence Erlbaum Associates Inc.

Schmidt, R. A. (1975). A schema theory of discrete motor skill learning. *Psychological Review, 82*, 225–260.

Schmidt, R. A., Zelaznik, H. N., Hawkins, B., Frank, J. S., & Quinn, J. T. Jr. (1979). Motor output variability: A theory for the accuracy of rapid motor acts. *Psychological Review, 86*, 415–451.

Schneider, S. L. (1992). Framing and conflict: Aspiration level contingency, the status quo, and current theories of risky choice. *Journal of Experimental Psychology: Learning, Memory and Cognition, 18*, 1040–1057.

Schneider, S. L., & Lopes, L. L. (1986). Reflection in preferences under risk: Who and when may suggest why. *Journal of Experimental Psychology: Human Perception and Performance, 12*, 535–548.

Schneider, W., & Fisk, A. D. (1982). Concurrent automatic and controlled visual research: Can processing occur without resource cost? *Journal of Experimental Psychology: Learning, Memory and Cognition, 8*, 261–279.

Schneider, W., & Shiffrin, R. M. (1977). Controlled and automatic information processing. 1: Detection, search and attention. *Psychological Review, 84*, 1–66.

Schwartz, A. B., & Georgopoulos, A. B. (1987). Relations between the amplitude of 2–dimensional arm movements and single cell discharge in primate motor cortex. *Society for Neuroscience Abstracts, 13*, 244.

Schwartz, M. F., Saffran, E. M.,, & Marin, O. S. M. (1980). Fractionating the reading process in dementia: Evidence for word-specific print-to-sound associations. In M. Coltheart, K. E. Patterson, & J. C. Marshall (Eds), *Deep dyslexia*. London: Routledge and Kegan Paul.

Schwartz, S., & Griffin, T. (1986). *Medical thinking: The psychology of medical judgement and decision making*. London: Springer-Verlag.

Searle, J. (1969). *Speech acts: An essay in the philosophy of language*. Cambridge: Cambridge University Press.

Seidenberg, M. S. (1985). The time course of phonological activation in two writing systems. *Cognition, 19*, 1–30.

Seidenberg, M. S., & McClelland, J. L. (1989). A distributed, developmental model of word recognition and naming. *Psychological Review, 96*, 523–568.

Service, E. (1992). Phonology, working memory, and foreign-language learning. *Quarterly Journal of Experimental Psychology: Human Experimental Psychology, 45. 1*, 21–50.

Seymour, P. H. K. (1973). A model for reading, naming and comparison. *British Journal of Psychology, 64*, 35–49.

Shaffer, L. H. (1973). Latency mechanisms in transcription. In S. Kornblum (Ed.), *Attention and Performance IV*. New York: Academic Press.

Sergent, J. (1984). An investigation into component and configurational processes underlying face perception. *British Journal of Psychology, 75*, 221–242.

Shaffer, L. H. (1975). Multiple attention in continuous verbal tasks. In P. M. A. Rabbitt & S. Dornic (Eds), *Attention and performance V.* New York: Academic Press.

Shaffer, L. H. (1981). Performances of Chopin, Bach and Bartok: Studies in motor programming. *Cognitive Psychology, 13*, 327–376.

Shafir, E., & Tversky, T. (1992). Thinking through uncertainty: Nonconsequential reasoning and choice. *Cognitive Psychology, 24*, 449–474.

Shallice, T. (1982). Specific impairments of planning. *Philosophical Transactions of the Royal Society, London B 298*, 199–209.

Shallice, T. (1988). *From neuropsychology to mental structure.* Cambridge: Cambridge University Press.

Shallice, T., & Warrington, E. K. (1970). Independent functioning of verbal memory stores: A neuropsychological study. *Quarterly Journal of Experimental Psychology, 22*, 261–273.

Shallice, T., McLeod, P., & Lewis, K. (1985). Isolating cognitive modules with the dual task paradigm: Are speech perception and production separate processes? *Quarterly Journal of Experimental Psychology, 37A*, 507–532.

Shanks, D. R. (1991). Categorization by a connectionist network. *Journal of Experimental Psychology: Learning, Memory and Cognition, 17*, 433–443.

Shepard, R. N., & Chipman, S. (1970). Second-order isomorphism of internal representations: Shapes of states. *Cognitive Psychology, 1*, 1–17.

Shepherd, J., Davies, G., & Ellis, H. D. (1981). Studies of cue saliency. In G. Davies, H. Ellis, & J. Shepherd (Eds), *Perceiving and remembering faces.* London: Academic Press.

Sherrington, C. S. (1906/1947). *Integrative action of the nervous system.* New Haven, CT: Yale University Press.

Sherwood, D. E. (1990). Practice and assimilation effects in a multilimb aiming task. *Journal of Motor Behavior, 22*, 267–291.

Shiffrin, R. M. (1988). Attention. In R. C. Atkinson, R. J. Herrnstein, G. Lindzey, & R. D. Luce (Eds), *Stevens' handbook of experimental psychology, Vol. 2: Learning and cognition.* New York: John Wiley.

Shiffrin, R. M., & Schneider, W. (1977). Controlled and automatic human information processing. II. Perceptual learning, automatic attending, and a general theory. *Psychological Review, 84*, 127–190.

Shiffrin, R. M., Dumais, S. T., & Schneider, W. (1981). Characteristics of automatism. In J. Long & A. Baddeley (Eds), *Attention and Performance IX.* Hillsdale, NJ: Lawrence Erlbaum Associates Inc.

Sholl, M. J. (1987). Cognitive maps as orienting schemata. *Journal of Experimental Psychology: Learning, Memory and Cognition, 13*, 615–628.

Siegel, A. W., & White, S. H. (1975). The development of spatial representations of large scale environments. In H. W. Reese (Ed.), *Advances in child development and behavior, Vol. 10.* New York: Academic Press.

Siegel, L. S., & Ryan, E. B. (1989). The development of working memory in normally achieving and subtypes of learning disabled children. *Child Development, 60*, 973–980.

Simon, H. A. (1955). A behavioural model of rational choice. *Quarterly Journal of Economics, 69*, 99–118.

Simon, H. A., & Gilmartin, K. (1973). Simulation of memory for chess positions. *Cognitive Psychology, 5*, 29–46.

Slobada, J. A. (1985). Expressive skill in 2 pianists: Metrical communication in real and simulated performances. *Canadian Journal of Psychology, 39*, 273–293.

Slovic, P., & Lichtenstein, S. (1971). Comparison of Bayesian and regression approaches to the study of information processing in judgment. *Organizational Behavior and Human Performance, 6*, 649–744.

Slovic, P., & Tversky, A. (1974). Who accepts Savage's axiom? *Behavioral Science, 19,* 368–373.

Slovic, P., Fischoff, B., & Lichtenstein, S. (1980). Facts *vs* fears: Understanding perceived risk. In R. Schwing & W. A. Albers Jr (Eds), *Societal risk assessment: How safe is safe enough?* New York: Plenum Press.

Slovic, P., Lichtenstein, S., & Fischhoff, B. (1990). Decision making. In M. I. Posner (Ed.), *Foundations of cognitive science.* Cambridge, MA: MIT Press.

Smith, E. E., & Medin, D. L. (1981). *Categories and concepts.* Cambridge, MA: Harvard University Press.

Smith, E. E., & Osherson, D. N. (1987). Compositionality and typicality. In S. Schifter & S. Steele (Eds), *The 2nd Arizona Colloquium on Cognitive Science.* Tuscon, AZ: University of Tuscon Press.

Smith, E. E., Shoben, E. J., & Rips, L. J. (1974). Structure and process in semantic memory: A featural model for semantic decisions. *Psychological Review, 81,* 214–241.

Smith, E. E., Langston, C., & Nisbett, R. E. (1992). The case for rules in reasoning. *Cognitive Science, 16,* 1–40.

Smith, S. M. (1979). Remembering in and out of context. *Journal of Experimental Psychology: Human Learning and Memory, 5,* 466–471.

Smith, S. M. (1988). Environmental context-dependent memory. In G. M. Davies & D. M. Thomson (Eds), *Memory in context: Context in memory,* New York: John Wiley.

Smith, S. M. (1994). Theoretical principles of context-dependent memory. In P. E. Morris & M. Gruneberg (Eds), *Theoretical aspects of memory.* 2nd edn. London: Routledge.

Smyth, M. M., & Pendleton, L. R. (1989). Working memory for movements. *Quarterly Journal of Experimental Psychology, 41A,* 235–250.

Smyth, M. M., & Scholey, K. A. (1992). Determining spatial memory span: The role of movement time and articulation rate. *Quarterly Journal of Experimental Psychology, 45A,* 479–501.

Smyth, M. M., & Scholey, K. A. (1994). Interference in immediate spatial memory. *Memory and Cognition, 22,* 1–13.

Smyth, M. M., & Silvers, G. (1987). Functions of vision in the control of handwriting. *Acta Psychologica, 65,* 47–64.

Soechting, J. F. (1988). Elements of coordinated arm movements in three dimensional space. In S. A. Wallace (Ed.), *Perspectives on the coordination of movement.* New York: North-Holland.

Solomons, L., & Stein, G. (1896). Normal motor automatism. *Psychological Review, 3,* 492–512.

Spelke, E., Hirst, W., & Neisser, U. (1976). Skills of divided attention. *Cognition, 4,* 215–230.

Sperber, D., & Wilson, D. (1986). *Relevance: Communication and cognition.* Oxford: Blackwell.

Spilich, G. J., Vesonder, G. T., Chiesi, H. L., & Voss, J. F. (1979). Text processing of domain-related information for individuals with high and low domain knowledge. *Journal of Verbal Learning and Verbal Behavior, 18,* 275–290.

Squire, L. R. (1992). Memory and the hippocampus: A synthesis from findings with rats, monkeys and humans. *Psychological Review, 99,* 195–231.

Squire, L. R., & Slater, P. C. (1975). Forgetting in very long term memory as assessed by an improved questionnaire technique. *Journal of Experimental Psychology: Human Learning and Memory, 104,* 50–54.

Stanhope, N., & Parkin, A. J. (1987). Further explorations of the consistency effect in word and non-word pronunciation. *Memory and Cognition, 15,* 169–179.

Staudenmayer, H., & Bourne, L. E. (1978). The nature of denied propositions in the conditional reasoning task: Interpretation and learning. In R. Revlin & R. E. Mayer (Eds), *Human reasoning.* New York: John Wiley.

Stein, J. F. (1991). Space and the parietal association areas. In J. Paillard (Ed.), *Brain and space.* Oxford: Oxford University Press.

Stemberger, J. P. (1982). *The lexicon in a model of language production.* Unpublished doctoral dissertation, University of California, San Diego.

Stevens, A., & Coupe, P. (1978). Distortions in judged spatial relations. *Cognitive Psychology, 10,* 422–437.

Stevenson, R. J. (1993). *Language, thought and representation,* Chichester: John Wiley.

Stroop, J. R. (1935). Studies of interference in spatial verbal reactions. *Journal of Experimental Psychology, 18,* 643–662.

Summers, J. J., & Kennedy, T. M. (1992). Strategies in the production of a 5:3 polyrhythm. *Human Movement Science, 11,* 101–112.

Summers, J. J., Rosenbaum, D. A., Burns, B. D., & Ford, S. K. (1993). Production of polyrhythms. *Journal of Experimental Psychology: Human Perception and Performance, 19,* 416–428.

Taraban, R., & McClelland, J. L. (1987). Conspiracy effects in word pronunciation. *Journal of Memory and Language, 26,* 608–631.

Taylor, I., & Taylor, M. M. (1990). *Psycholinguistics: Learning and using language.* Englewood Cliffs, NJ: Prentice-Hall.

Teasdale, J. D. (1983). Affect and accessibility. *Philosophical Transactions of the Royal Society of London, B302,* 403–412.

Tehan, G., & Humphreys, M. S. (1988). Articulatory loop explanations of memory span and pronunciation rate correspondences: A cautionary note. *Bulletin of the Psychonomic Society, 26,* 293–296.

Teulings, H. L., Thomassen, A. J. W. M., & Van Galen, G. P. (1986). Invariants in handwriting: The information contained in a motor program. In H. S. R. Kao, G. P. van Galen, & R. Housain (Eds), *Graphonomics: Contemporary research in handwriting.* Amsterdam: North-Holland.

Thagard, P., & Nisbett, R. E. (1982). Variability and confirmation. *Philosophical Studies, 42,* 379–394.

Thompson, C. P., & Cowan, T. (1986). Flashbulb memories: A nicer interpretation of a Neisser recollection. *Cognition, 22,* 199–200.

Thorndyke, P. W. (1981). Distance estimation from cognitive maps. *Cognitive Psychology, 13,* 526–550.

Thorndyke, P. W., & Hayes-Roth, B. (1982). Differences in spatial knowledge acquired from maps and navigation. *Cognitive Psychology, 14,* 560–589.

Tipper, S. P., Lortie, C., & Bayliss, G. C. (1992). Selective reaching: Evidence for action-centered attention. *Journal of Experimental Psychology: Human Perception and Performance, 18,* 891–905.

Trabasso, T. R. (1963). Stimulus emphasis and all-or-none learning in concept identification. *Journal of Experimental Psychology, 65,* 398–406.

Treisman, A. M., & Geffen, G. (1967). Selective attention: Perception or response? *Quarterly Journal of Experimental Psychology, 19,* 1–17.

Treisman, A. M., & Gelade, G. (1980). Feature-integration theory of attention. *Cognitive Psychology, 12,* 97–136.

Trojano, L., Stanzioni, M., & Grossi, D. (1992). Short-term memory and verbal learning with auditory phonological coding defect: A neuropsychological case-study. *Brain and Cognition, 18,* 12–33.

Tulving, E. (1983). *Elements of episodic memory,* Oxford: Oxford University Press.

Tulving, E., & Schacter, D. H. (1990). Priming and human memory systems. *Science, 247,* 301–396.

Tulving, E., & Thomson, D. M. (1973). Encoding specificity and retrieval processes in episodic memory. *Psychological Review, 80*, 352–373.

Tulving, E., Schacter, D. L., & Stark, H. A. (1982). Priming effects in word completion are independent of recognition memory. *Journal of Experimental Psychology: Learning, Memory and Cognition, 8*, 336–342.

Tversky, A., & Kahneman, D. (1973). Availability: A heuristic for judging frequency and probability. *Cognitive Psychology, 4*, 207–232.

Tversky, A., & Kahneman, D. (1974). Judgement under uncertainty: Heuristics and biases. *Science, 185*, 1124–1131.

Tversky, A., & Kahneman, D. (1981). The framing of decisions and the psychology of choice. *Science, 211*, 453–458.

Tversky, A., & Kahneman, D. (1983). Extensional versus intuitive reasoning: The conjunction fallacy in probability judgment. *Psychological Review*, 293–315.

Tversky, A, & Shafir, E. (1992). The disjunction effect in choice under uncertainty. *Psychological Science, 3*, 305–309.

Tversky, B. (1981). Distortions in memory for maps. *Cognitive Psychology, 13*, 407–433.

Tversky, B., & Kahneman, D. (1980). Causal schemas in judgments under uncertainty. In M. Fishbein (Ed.), *Progress in social psychology*. Hillsdale, NJ: Lawrence Erlbaum Associates Inc.

Tversky, B., & Tuchin, M. (1989). A reconciliation of the evidence on eyewitness testimony: Comments on McCloskey and Zaragoza. *Journal of Experimental Psychology: General, 118*, 86–91.

Underwood, B. J. (1957). Interference and forgetting. *Psychological Review, 64*, 49–60.

Underwood, B. J., & Richardson, J. (1956). Some verbal materials for the study of concept formation. *Psychological Bulletin, 53*, 84–95.

Ungerleider, L. G., & Mishkin, M. (1982). Two cortical visual systems. In D. J. Ingle, M. A. Goodale, & R. J. W. Mansfield (Eds), *Analysis of visual behavior*. Cambridge, MA: MIT Press.

Uno, Y., Kawato, M., & Suzuki, R. (1989). Formation and control of optional trajectory in human multijoint arm movement. *Biological Cybernetics, 61*, 89–101.

Valentine, T. (1991). A unified account of the effect of distinctiveness, inversion and race in face recognition. *Quarterly Journal of Psychology, 43A*, 161–204.

Valentine, T., & Endo, M. (1992). Towards an exemplar model of face processing: The effects of race and distinctiveness, *Quarterly Journal of Psychology, 44A*, 671–703.

Valentine, T., & Ferrara, A. (1991). Typicality in categorization, recognition and identification: Evidence from face recognition. *British Journal of Psychology, 82*, 87–102.

Vallar, G., & Baddeley, A. D. (1984). Fractionation of working memory: Neuropsychological evidence for a phonological short-term store. *Journal of Verbal Learning and Verbal Behavior, 23*, 151–161.

Vallar, G., & Shallice, T. (Eds) (1990). *Neuropsychological impairments of short-term memory*. Cambridge: Cambridge University Press.

Vallone, R. P., Griffin, D. W., Lin, S., & Ross, L. (1990). The overconfident prediction of future actions and outcomes by self and others. *Journal of Personality and Social Psychology, 58*, 582–592.

Van der Heijden, A. H. C. (1981). *Short term visual information forgetting*. London: Routledge and Kegan Paul.

Van der Heijden, A. H. C. (1991). *Selective attention in vision*. London: Routledge.

Van Galen, G. P. (1991). Handwriting: Issues for a psychomotor theory. *Human Movement Science, 10*, 165–191.

Van Galen, G. P., Portier, S. J., Smits-Engelsman, B. C. M., & Schomaker, L. R. B. (1993). Neuromotor noise and poor handwriting in children. *Acta Psychologica, 82*, 161–178.

Van Orden, G. C. (1987). A ROWS is a ROSE: Spelling, sound and reading. *Memory and Cognition*, *15*, 181–198.

Van Orden, G. C., Johnston, J. C., & Hale, B. L. (1988). Word identification in reading proceeds from spelling to sound to meaning. *Journal of Experimental Psychology: Learning, Memory, and Cognition*, *14*, 371–385.

Van Orden, G. C., Pennington, B. F., & Stone, G. O. (1990). Word identification and the promise of subsymbolic psycholinguistics. *Psychological Review*, *97*, 488–522.

Van Rossum, J. H. A. (1990). Schmidt's schema theory: The empirical base of the variability of practice hypothesis. *Human Movement Science*, *9*, 387–436.

Vince, M. A., & Welford, A. T. (1967). Time taken to change the speed of a response. *Nature*, *213*, 532–533.

Von Mises, R. (1957). *Probability, statistics, and truth*. New York: Dover.

von Neumann, J., & Morgenstern, O. (1947). *Theory of games and economic behaviour*. Princeton, NJ: Princeton University Press.

Vosniadou, S. & Ortony, A. (1989). *Similarity and analogical reasoning*. Cambridge: Cambridge University Press.

Vredenbregt, J., & Koster, W. G. (1971). Analysis and synthesis of handwriting. *Philips Technical Review*, *32*, 73–78.

Vygotsky, L. S. (1934/1962). *Thought and language* (translated and edited by E. Hanfmann & G. Vakar). Cambridge, MA: MIT Press.

Wagenaar, W. A. (1988a). *Paradoxes of gambling behaviour*. Hove: Lawrence Erlbaum Associates Ltd.

Wagenaar, W. A. (1988b). People and places in my memory: A study on cue specificity and retrieval from autobiographical memory. In M. M. Gruneberg, P. E. Morris, & R. N. Sykes (Eds), *Practical aspects of memory: Current research and issues*, Vol. 1. Chichester: John Wiley.

Wagenaar, W. A., & Keren, G. (1986). Does the expert know? The reliability of predictions and confidence ratings of experts. In E. Hollnagel, G. Maneini, & D. Woods (Eds), *Intelligent decision support in process environments*. Berlin: Springer-Verlag.

Wagenaar, W. A., Keren, G., & Lichtenstein, S. (1988). Islanders and hostages: Deep and surface structures of decision making problems. *Acta Psychologica*, *67*, 175–189.

Waldmann, M. R., & Holyoak, K. J. (1992). Predictive and diagnostic learning within causal models: Asymmetries in cue competition. *Journal of Experimental Psychology: General*, *121*, 222–236.

Wallace, S. A., & Newell, K. M. (1983). Visual control of discrete aiming movements. *Quarterly Journal of Experimental Psychology*, *35*, 311–321.

Wallace, S. A., Weeks, D. L., & Kelso, J. A. S. (1988). Temporal constraints in the control of prehensile movement. *Journal of Motor Behavior*, *20*, 151–171.

Waltz, D. L. (1975). Generating semantic descriptions from scenes with shadows. In P. H. Winston (Ed.), *The psychology of computer vision*. New York: McGraw-Hill.

Wann, J. P. (1987). Trends in the refinement and optimization of fine-motor trajectories: Observations from an analysis of the handwriting of primary school children. *Journal of Motor Behavior*, *19*, 13–37.

Wann, J. P., & Nimmo Smith, I. (1990). Evidence against the relative invariance of timing in handwriting. *Quarterly Journal of Experimental Psychology*, *42A*, 105–119.

Wann, J. P., Nimmo Smith, I., & Wing, A. M. (1988). Relation between velocity and curvature in movement: Equivalence and divergence between a power law and a minimum jerk model. *Journal of Experimental Psychology: Human Perception and Performance*, *14*, 622–637.

Wanner, H. E. (1968). *On remembering, forgetting and understanding sentences: A study of the deep structure hypothesis*. Unpublished doctoral dissertation, Harvard University.

Warren, C., & Morton, J. (1982). The effects of priming on picture recognition. *British Journal of Psychology*, *73*, 117–130.

Warrington, E. K., & Weiskrantz, L. (1970). Amnesic syndrome: Consolidation or retrieval? *Nature, 228*, 628–630.

Wason, P. C. (1966). Reasoning. In B. Foss (Ed.), *New horizons in psychology*, Vol. I. Harmondsworth: Penguin.

Wason, P. C., & Johnson-Laird, P. N. (1972). *The psychology of reasoning: Structure and context*. Harmondsworth: Penguin.

Waters, G. S., Rochon, E., & Caplan, D. (1992). The role of high-level planning in rehearsal: Evidence from patients with apraxia of speech. *Journal of Memory and Language, 31*, 54–73.

Watt, R. J. (1988). *Visual processing: Computerised, psychological, psychophysical and cognitive research*. Hove: Lawrence Erlbaum Associates Ltd.

Wattenmaker, W. D. (1991). Learning modes, feature correlations and memory-based categorization. *Journal of Experimental Psychology: Learning, Memory and Cognition, 17*, 908–923.

Webb, L. W. (1917). Transfer of training and retroaction: A comparative study. *Psychological Monographs, 24* (Whole no. 104).

Weldon, M. S. (1991). Mechanisms underlying priming on perceptual tests. *Journal of Experimental Psychology: Learning, Memory and Cognition, 15*, 269–280.

Welford, A. T. (1968). *Fundamentals of skill*. London: Methuen.

Wertheimer, M. (1945). *Productive thinking*. New York: Harper and Row.

Wheeler, D. D. (1970). Processes in word recognition. *Cognitive Psychology, 1*, 59–85.

Whipple, G. M. (1912). Psychology of testimony and report. *Psychological Bulletin, 9*, 264–269.

Wing, A. M. (1980). The height of handwriting. *Acta Psychologica, 46*, 141–151.

Wing, A. M., Turton, A., & Fraser, C. (1986). Grasp size and accuracy of approach in reaching. *Journal of Motor Behavior, 18*, 245–260.

Winograd, T. (1972). *Understanding natural language*. New York: Academic Press.

Witherspoon, D., & Moscovitch, M. (1989). Stochastic independence between two implicit memory tasks. *Journal of Experimental Psychology: Learning, Memory and Cognition, 15*, 22–30.

Wittgenstein, I. (1958). *Philosophical investigations* (2nd edn translated by G. E. M. Anscombe). Oxford: Blackwell.

Woodworth, R. S. (1899). The accuracy of voluntary movement. *Psychological Review, Monograph Supplement, 3*.

Woodworth, R. S. (1938). *Experimental Psychology*. New York: Holt, Rinehart & Winston.

Woodworth, R. S., & Sells, S. B. (1935). An atmosphere effect in formal syllogistic reasoning. *Journal of Experimental Psychology, 18*, 451–460.

Wright, C. E. (1990). Generalized motor programs: Reexamining claims of effect on independance in writing. In M. Jeannerod (Ed.) *Attention and performance XIII: Motor represention and control*. Hillsdale, NJ: Lawrence Erlbaum Associates Inc.

Wright, G. (1984). *Behavioural decision theory: An introduction*. Harmondsworth, Penguin.

Wundt, W. (1905). *Grundriss der Psychologie*. Leipzig: Engelmann.

Young, A. W., Hay, D. C., & Ellis, A. W. (1985). The faces that launched a thousand slips: Everyday difficulties and errors in recognising people. *British Journal of Experimental Psychology, 38A*, 297–318.

Young, R. P., & Zelaznik, H. N. (1992). The visual control of aimed hand movements to stationary and moving targets. *Acta Psychologica, 79*, 59–78.

Zangwill, O. L. (1946). Some qualitative observations on verbal memory in cases of cerebral lesion. *British Journal of Psychology, 37*, 8–19.

Author Index

Subject Index